GW01368319

MEGALITHIC MOURNE

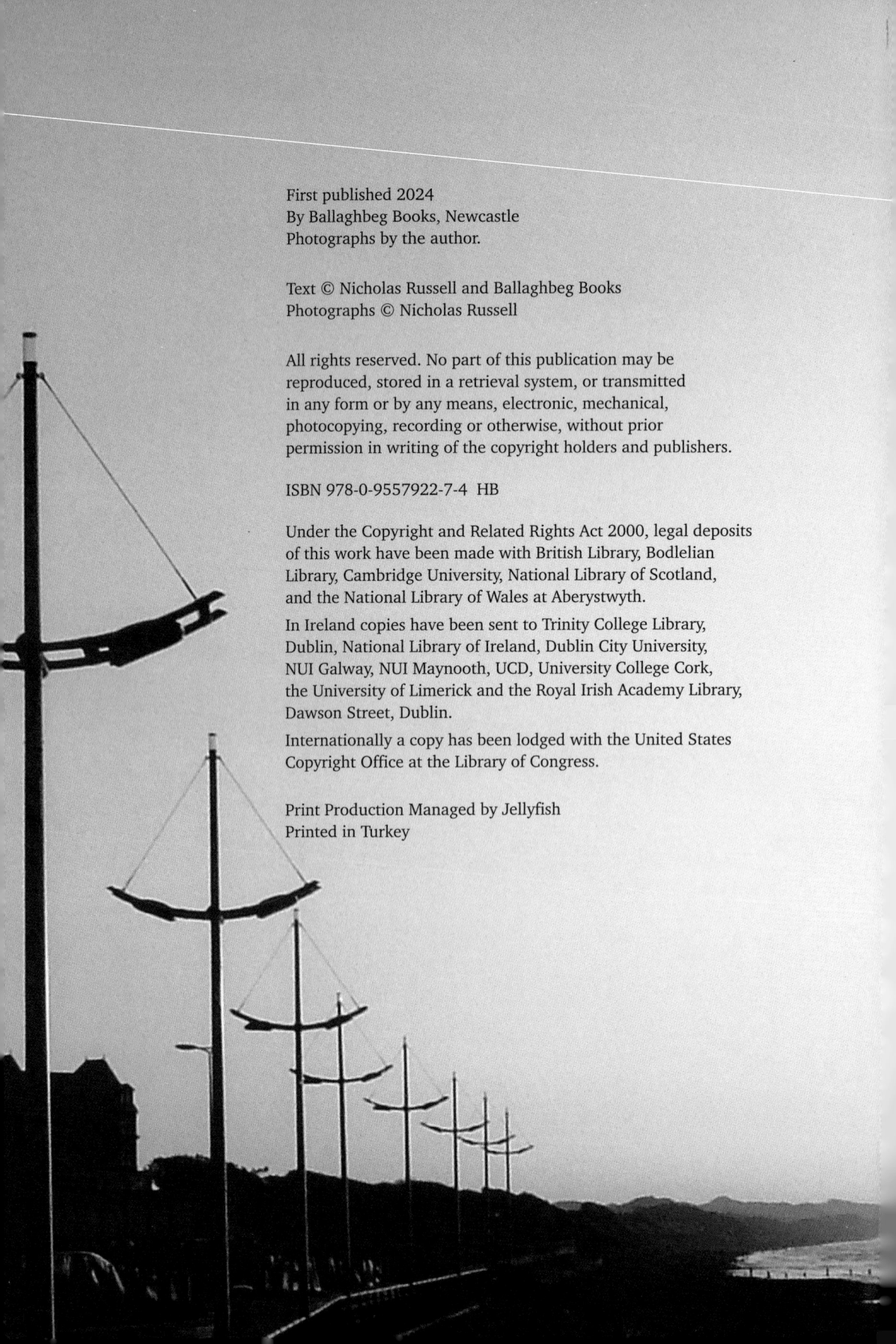

First published 2024
By Ballaghbeg Books, Newcastle
Photographs by the author.

Text © Nicholas Russell and Ballaghbeg Books
Photographs © Nicholas Russell

All rights reserved. No part of this publication may be reproduced, stored in a retrieval system, or transmitted in any form or by any means, electronic, mechanical, photocopying, recording or otherwise, without prior permission in writing of the copyright holders and publishers.

ISBN 978-0-9557922-7-4 HB

Under the Copyright and Related Rights Act 2000, legal deposits of this work have been made with British Library, Bodlelian Library, Cambridge University, National Library of Scotland, and the National Library of Wales at Aberystwyth.

In Ireland copies have been sent to Trinity College Library, Dublin, National Library of Ireland, Dublin City University, NUI Galway, NUI Maynooth, UCD, University College Cork, the University of Limerick and the Royal Irish Academy Library, Dawson Street, Dublin.

Internationally a copy has been lodged with the United States Copyright Office at the Library of Congress.

Print Production Managed by Jellyfish
Printed in Turkey

Contents

Sun Stones	1
Face Stones	15
Sculptural Treasures of Mourne	71
Male Stones	119
Female Stones	227
Womb Stones	275
Begetting Stones	299
Fellatio Stones	317
Some more Place-names and Megaliths	343
The Red Hand of Ulster	365
St Patrick drives out the 'Snakes'	373
Appendix	388

This page (ii & iii): Promenade near Slieve Donard Hotel
Page iv: Sphagnum Moss
Page v: Pot of Legawherry from Luke's Mountain
Page vi: The Movement of the Sun

Dedicated to those who love Mourne and to a dear friend who told me long ago to disregard the critics and keep writing.

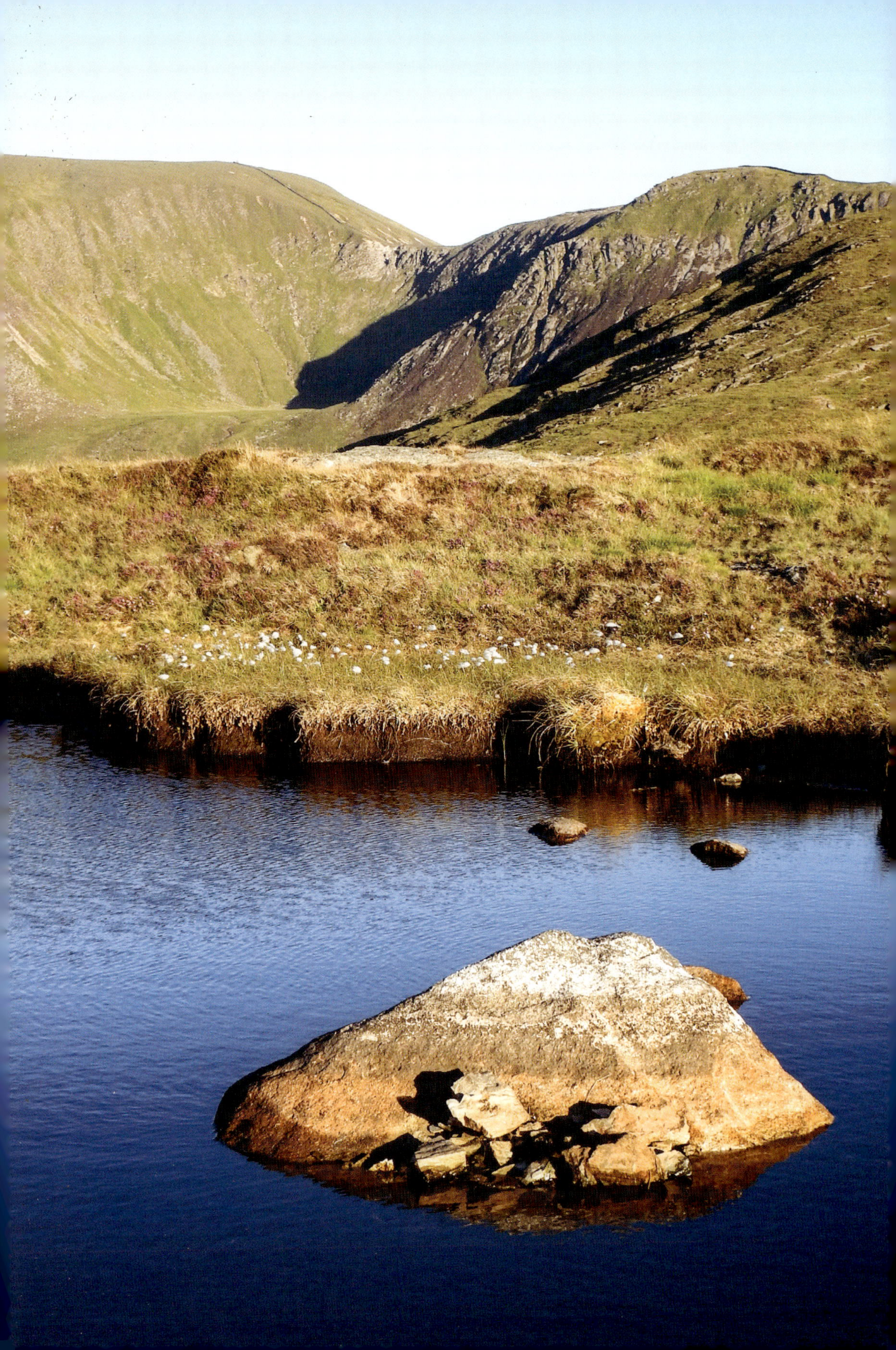

THE MOVEMENTS OF THE SUN

The major events of the Solar Year as seen from Newcastle.

The Central Point is the position of the observer; the lines indicate the directions in which sunrise and sunset can be seen at different dates.

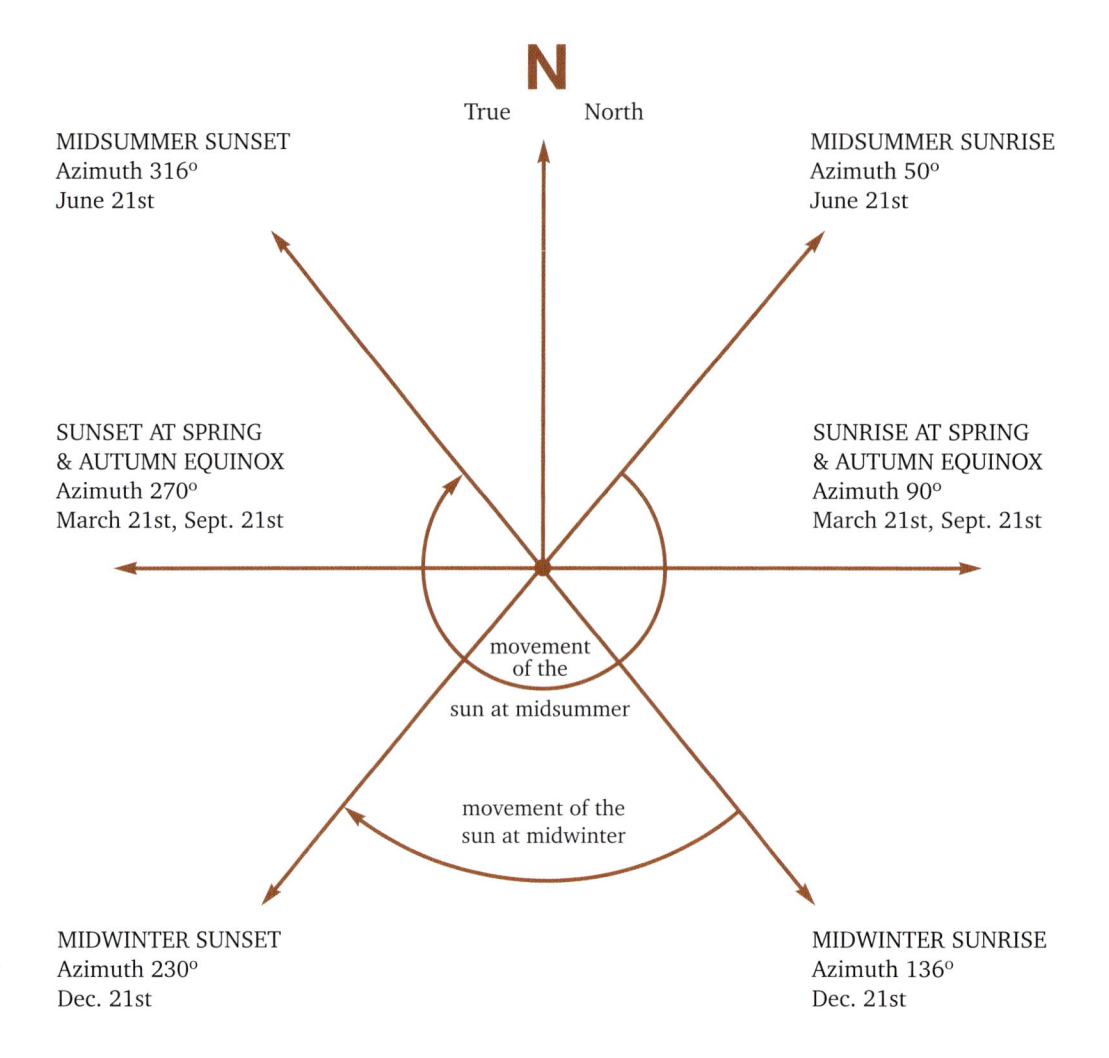

N
True North

MIDSUMMER SUNSET
Azimuth 316°
June 21st

MIDSUMMER SUNRISE
Azimuth 50°
June 21st

SUNSET AT SPRING
& AUTUMN EQUINOX
Azimuth 270°
March 21st, Sept. 21st

SUNRISE AT SPRING
& AUTUMN EQUINOX
Azimuth 90°
March 21st, Sept. 21st

movement of the sun at midsummer

movement of the sun at midwinter

MIDWINTER SUNSET
Azimuth 230°
Dec. 21st

MIDWINTER SUNRISE
Azimuth 136°
Dec. 21st

Azimuth is a direction measured in degrees clockwise from True North (e.g. east = azimuth 90°; south = azimuth 180°; west = azimuth 270°). Degrees given here are 'uncorrected' i.e. they are for magnetic north as you would see on your compass.

Azimuths are approximate and assume a horizon level with the observer. The dates of the equinoxes and solstices (midsummer and midwinter) can vary by a day or two.

SUN STONES

Mar, dálta na gréine seo do-chímíd, éirigheann sí gach lá ar ar son d'órdughadh Dé; acht ní flaitheas di, choidhche, ná ní buan dá gléineacht; acht lucht a hadhartha is dona a raghaid i ndubh-phiantaibh.
'For the sun which we see, by God's command, rises daily for our sakes, but it will never reign nor will its radiance endure, but all who worship it will come to a bad end in wretched punishment as well.'
(60: St Patrick's Confession)

Dia Dhuit 'God with you'

It was the Smuggler's Seat on Leganabruchan that first opened the door to the existence of 'sun stones' and after that to the wealth of megaliths across Mourne. The discovery was quite inadvertent. The initial inspiration had come from a remark by Professor E. Estyn Evans
> 'One of the most interesting of the many reputed smugglers' caves in the Mournes lies immediately under the sharp southern peak of Millstone Mountain which is known locally as 'The Nab'. (p.173, *Mourne Country*).

From the back, the Nab stone on Leganabruchan gave every appearance of a monk with his cowl up and so it had the Irish name of **An Áb**, 'the Abbot'. Some misinterpreted the name and, thinking in English, believed the name implied the capture of smugglers by the Excise men. The Nab is a great phallic sun stone perched on a steep cliff edge. Measuring at least 2.5 metres high and a good metre across the side and front, this is a formidable megalith. The large spear edge down the seaward corner is really a pointer to winter solstice dawn. The smuggler's cave, however, was the object of the search and it wasn't an easy search either.

It was while tramping back and forth along the front of the mountain that the look-out seat was found. The location is superb. To the north-east you have the sweep of St John's Point and Dundrum Bay. To the south you can see to Glasdrumman. The little stone seat made a wonderful vantage point and at half a metre in height it was a comfortable resting place as well. The significance of the stone became apparent at leaving. The top surface has a distinctive light coloured infusion line. On intuition this line was checked with a compass and the instinct proved correct. The line on the stone pointed out to sea directly to winter solstice sunrise. It was a most auspicious discovery and the start of many. The seat would have proved most useful to smugglers on look-out but had probably been placed in situ thousands of years beforehand by our earliest inhabitants, the fertility loving sun worshippers, the *Fir Builg*, 'Men of the Womb'. The seat had two other attributes that enhanced its fertility credentials. It is first of all a 'two tone stone' in that it is comprised of part granite and part shale. It is a union of opposites and is a metaphor for the union of male and female. Secondly, if you get the chance to examine this little beauty then note the little upright shale point at the southern end that is almost five centimetres. Doubtlessly it was intended to evoke a little phallus. The presence of little horns at the top or end of great megaliths is an interesting detail to watch out for.

In speaking of sun stones, the diagram of the movements of the sun at the start of the chapter may prove of some use to walkers wishing to identify megaliths whose placements have been influenced by first light of solstice. The mountains along the coast provide a clear view of the horizon out to sea. Further inland, where no direct view is possible, it becomes necessary to make estimates where the sun will rise. It is helpful to remember that if you have found the spot for winter solstice sunrise, then a straight line behind you will point to summer solstice sunset. Likewise for summer solstice sunrise, a line behind you would point to winter solstice sunset. The absence of a level horizon plays havoc with sun sight lines yet it is amazing how accurately the sharp points on great megaliths are unerringly directed to where solstice sun appears or disappears. Considering that our ancient forebearers did not have compasses, the conclusion is that they slept out on the mountains to ensure getting a perfect fix on the sun's location at dawn. It is also quite likely that the climate at Mourne some millennia ago was warmer, drier and sunnier.

The smuggler's cave, when finally found, proved to be seventy metres higher than the smuggler's seat. For those who wish to visit the cave where the signal fires were once lit the GPS coordinates are:
    N. 54° 10. 844'
    W. 005° 53. 596'   Elevation 396m.
The cave is near the very top of Leganabruchan. Don't miss the dog-leg flue hole, carved into the rock and on into the cave, on the left side of the entrance. This mini chimney helped give a 'draw' to the signal fire when lit.

An Áb, 'the Abbot', is a great sun stone and is to be found on the east slope of Leganabruchan at GPS:
N. 54° 10. 802'
W. 005° 53. 517'   Elevation 307m.
The distinctive 'pie slice' edge on the front of the stone is the pointer to winter solstice sunrise. The monk's 'cowl' from which the stone got its Irish name can only be seen on the top at the other side

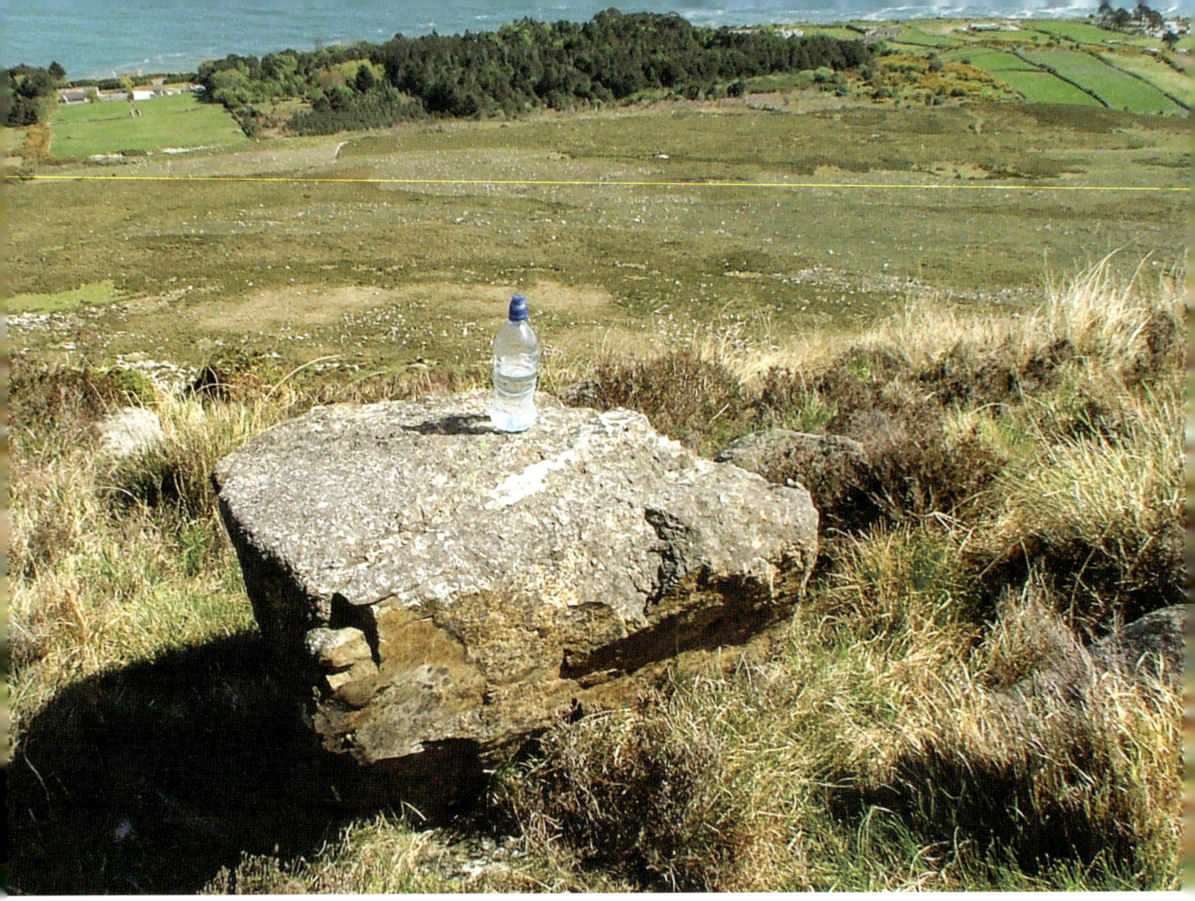

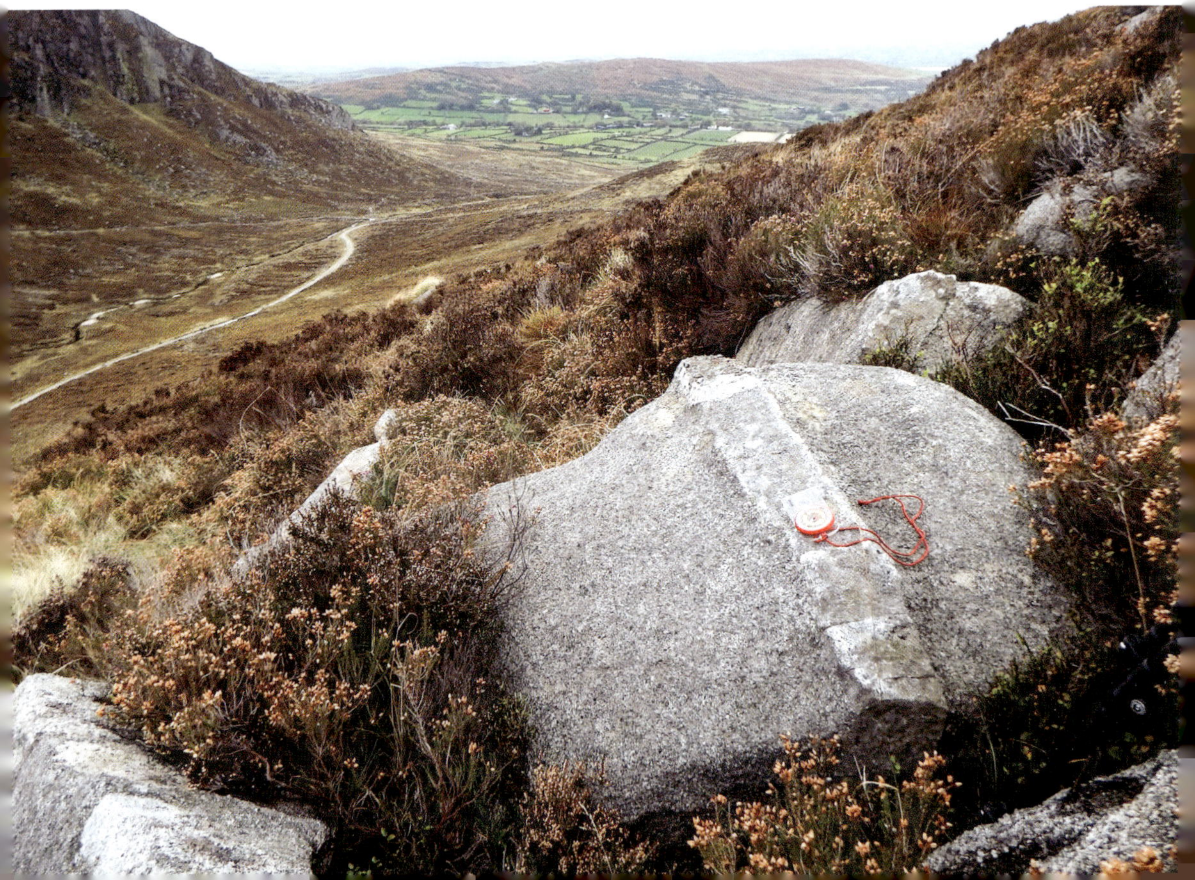

Top opposite: You could say this was the stone that started it all. The fusion line across the top of the 'Smuggler's Seat' aligns neatly to winter solstice sunrise at 136° uncorrected. Its GPS is:

                        N. 54° 10. 882'
                        W. 005° 53. 542'   Elevation 326m.

Lower opposite: There are many other stones besides the Smuggler's Seat that use infused lines to point to solstice. I named this boulder, found on the north-west flank of Slievenaglogh, 'The Sunset Strip' as the raised and infused band down the middle points neatly to summer solstice sunset. The GPS is:

                        N. 54° 11. 761'
                        W. 005° 58. 597'   Elevation 433m.

The infusion band is a good 10cm wide.

Mirror Stones

There are many variations on the idea of 'sun stones' such as the cavities, recesses or openings that are intended to be illuminated at solstice dawn. The ultimate expression of this idea is the great world heritage passage grave of Newgrange where the sun reaches right back into the heart of the tomb at winter solstice dawn. The name of Newgrange is only a mnemonic of the Irish *Nua-Grian*, 'new sun'. This understanding of the hill of Newgrange as a sun monument has profound implications for the irregular shape of the mound (exactly depicting the flattened bottom of the rising sun as it is about to 'detach' from the horizon), the use of grey levelled kerbstones (representing the horizon out at sea), the understanding of the K1 stone at the entrance (a stylised map of Mourne) and particularly for the facing of the monument with quartz which enjoys the Irish name *Cloch Gréine*, 'stone of the sun'.* In this work megaliths that enjoy the entrance or penetration of the sun at solstice appear under 'womb stones'.

Mirror stones may be described as large flat faced stones so placed as to receive the first light of solstice. There is no certainty as to why the ancients used stones such as these so frequently but it wouldn't be a surprise if it was connected to the high regard for precious winter sun in millennia past. It is almost as if the large flat surface wished to absorb every possible shred of the all important light. Finding a block of granite with a large flat surface is not as easy as one might imagine and the sourcing, relocating and placement of such stones must have taken much time and effort.

---

* See Newgrange and Mourne, pages 361-391, *Prehistoric Mourne*, 2015

Hammered out of the rock surface at the top of Millstone mountain is a profile of the Mourne Mountains as seen from around Murlough or Dundrum. This beautiful piece of rock art is probably thousands of years old and has to be the earliest depiction of the Mournes sweeping down to the Sea. The five prominent expanding crescents on the left represent the growing light of a rising winter solstice sun. The artist was facing in that direction when he created his design. The oval photo shows the artwork in relation to Newcastle harbour. The GPS for this depiction of the rising sun is:

N. 54° 11. 283'
W. 005° 53. 860'   Elevation 450m.

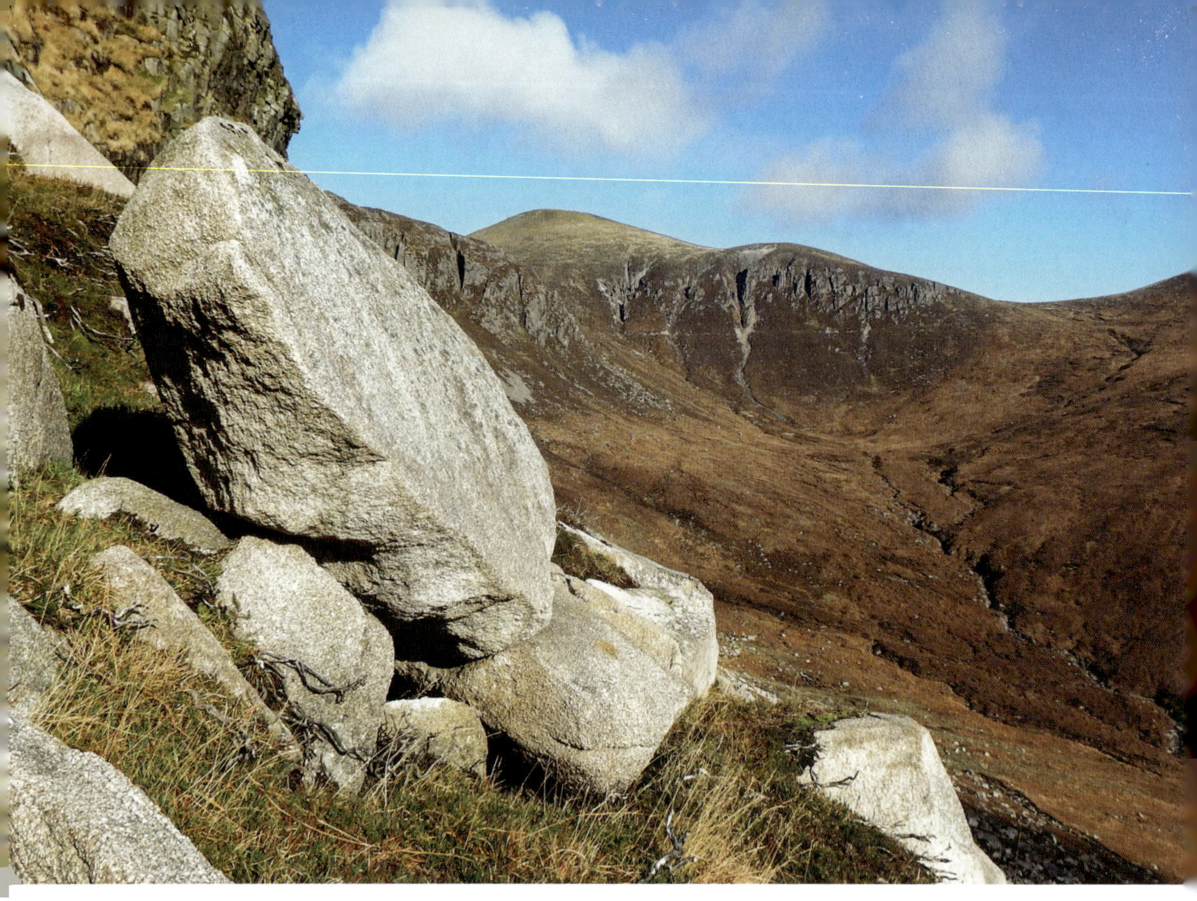

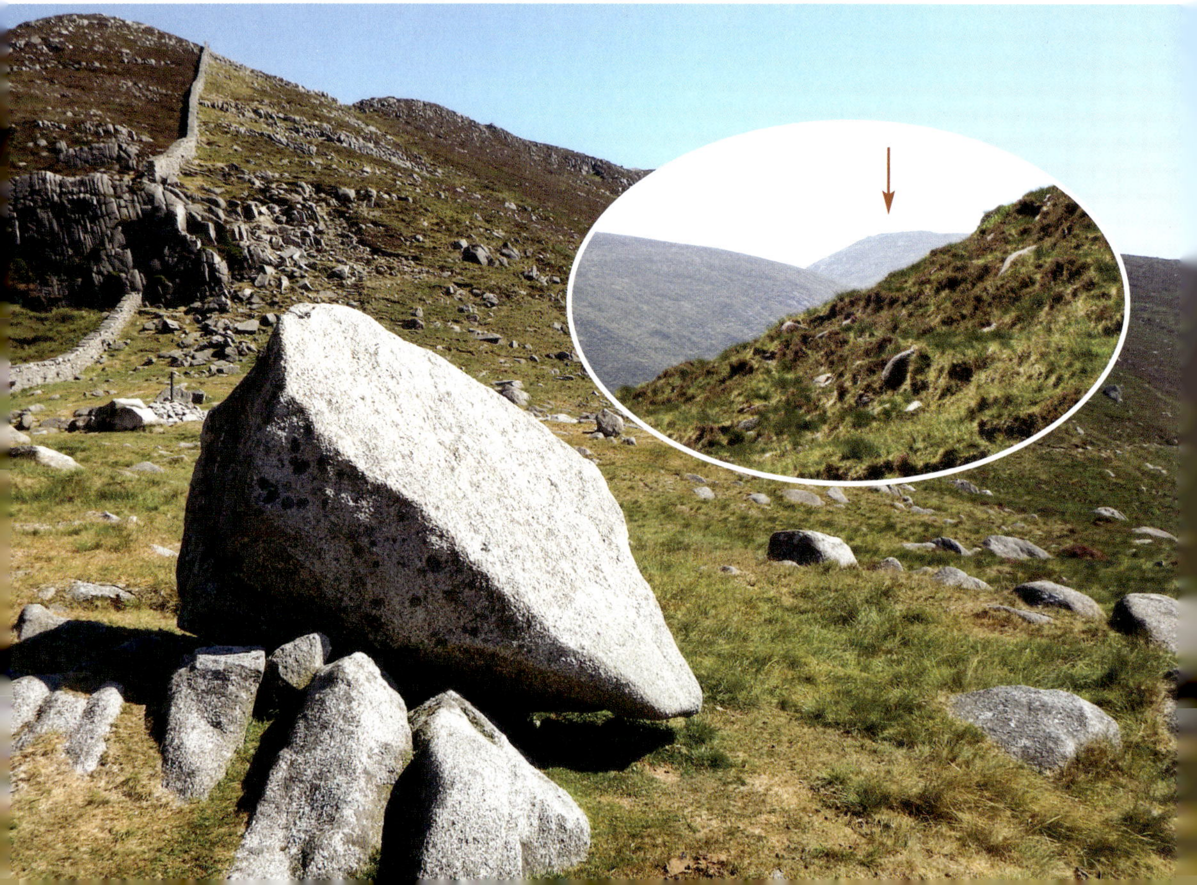

Top opposite: This large mirror stone is to be found high on the west side of the Annalong Valley under Cove Mountain. It faces where winter solstice light will make an appearance from behind Chimney Rock Mountain.

Lower opposite: This mirror stone is to be found at the col of the Hare's Gap, GPS:
N. 54° 11. 390'
W. 005° 58. 451'   Elevation 443m.
It is a beautiful representation of a whooper swan, a bird that is still a winter visitor to Dundrum Bay. Unfortunately the 'eye' of the swan on this megalith is presently in shadow. The great flat 'mirror' surface measures two metres from top to bottom and is 1.5m across. Unless you looked carefully you would never know that this is also a fertility location. The megalith faces towards a 'penis in the vagina motif' beloved of the ancients who looked on the landscape in sexual terms. It is from this megalith that the tip of Slieve Bignian can just be seen, phallic like, in the landscape 'vaginal' notch formed between the descending shoulder of Slieve Bearnagh and the side of Slieve Lamagan. Bignian is marked with an arrow in the oval picture.

Top of this page: With a rucksack and water bottle to give scale, this is a very considerable mirror stone. It is found at the head of the Glen River Valley beside the trail up to Slieve Donard and is aligned to receive the first light of summer solstice sun. Indeed, this photo was taken at 5.27am on 14th June just a week before the solstice. Mercifully the defacing graffiti is beginning to degrade.

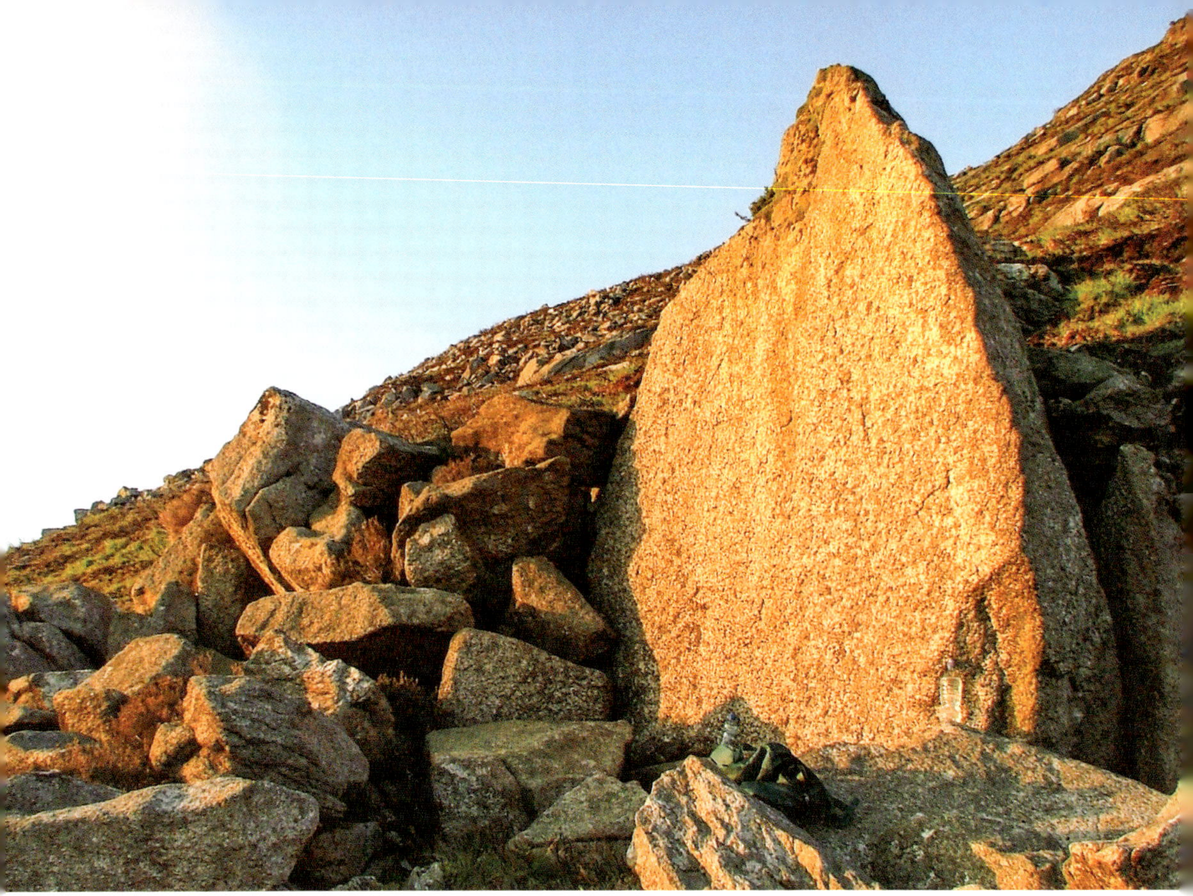
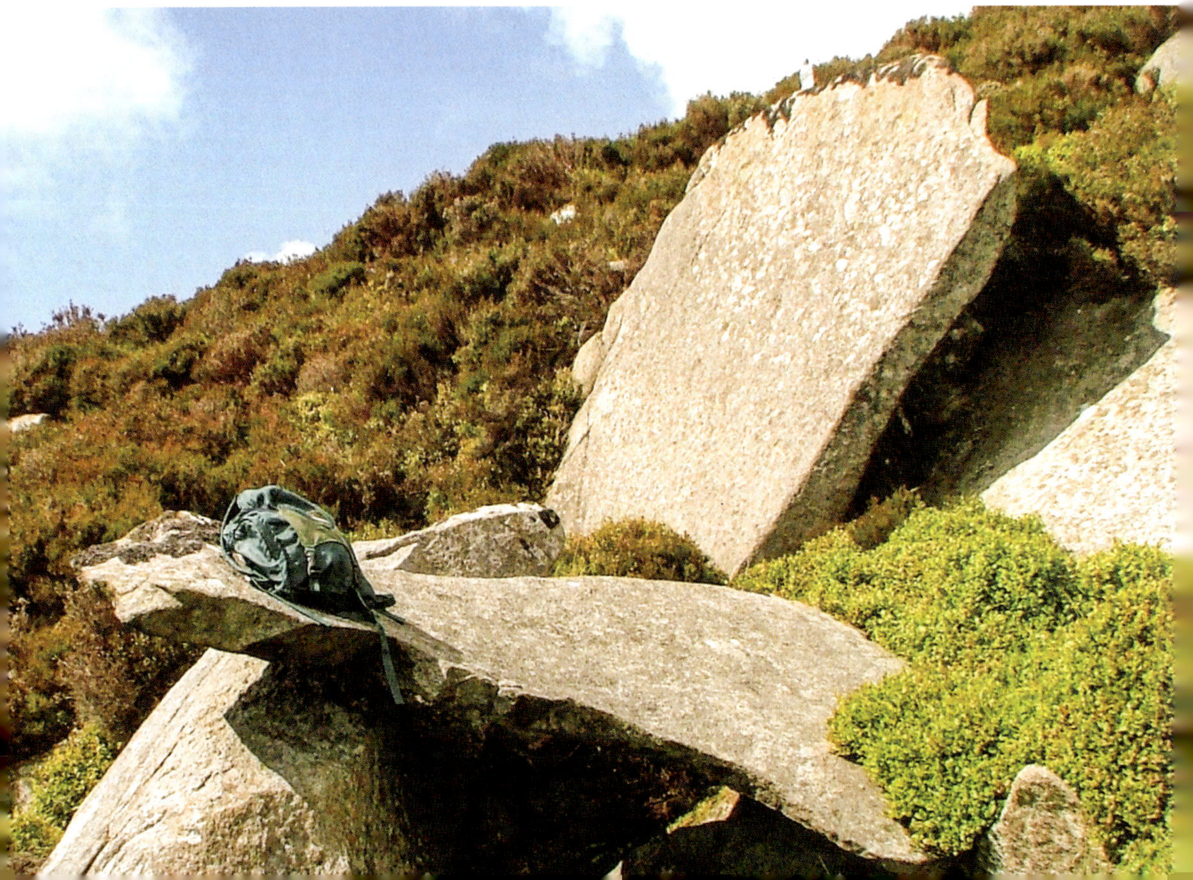

Top opposite: This mirror stone on the front of Thomas mountain was photographed at dawn a week before summer solstice. It is believed that this great 'headstone' of a monument gave Thomas mountain its name. It is a mnemonic of the Irish *Tuama*, 'a tomb'. When viewed from the seaward side this megalith has a remarkable resemblance to a breaching humpback whale with its huge flippers at its side.

Lower opposite: On the eastern flank of Thomas mountain the rucksack sits on a phallic stone pointing to where winter solstice sun will rise from the top of Millstone mountain. Behind it is a large mirror stone slab also ready to welcome the precious winter light. To the lower right is the edge of a second mirror stone. The importance of this arrangement is the gap between these two slabs. This illustrates what is known as a 'vaginal gap'; the two stones are the labial sides and the gap will only be illuminated at the other end of the year at summer solstice dawn. The moment of the sun's penetration to the back of the gap at solstice dawn was the notional moment of fertilisation.

Top of this page: This great mirror stone is to be found on a shoulder of Spellack overlooking the Trassey Valley. The GPS coordinates are:

N. 54° 11. 773'
W. 005° 59. 223'   Elevation 356m.

The substantial flat surface is presented to summer solstice sunrise. The point or 'nose' of the stone looks to the winter solstice sunrise at the side of Slieve Bearnagh. Across the top of the megalith a line has been gouged out to enhance the impression of a grim frowning eye. A superstitious dread long attached itself to the works of the ancients. This location is no exception.

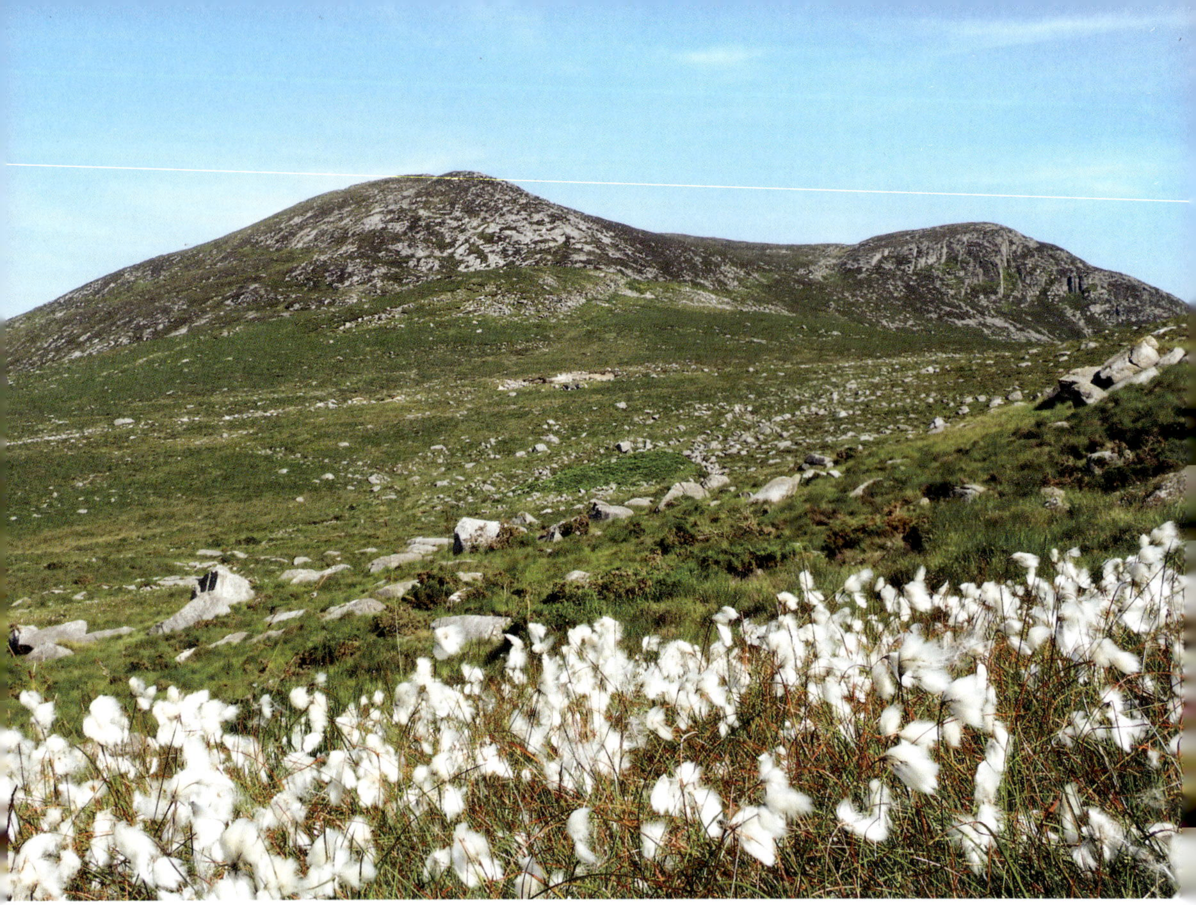

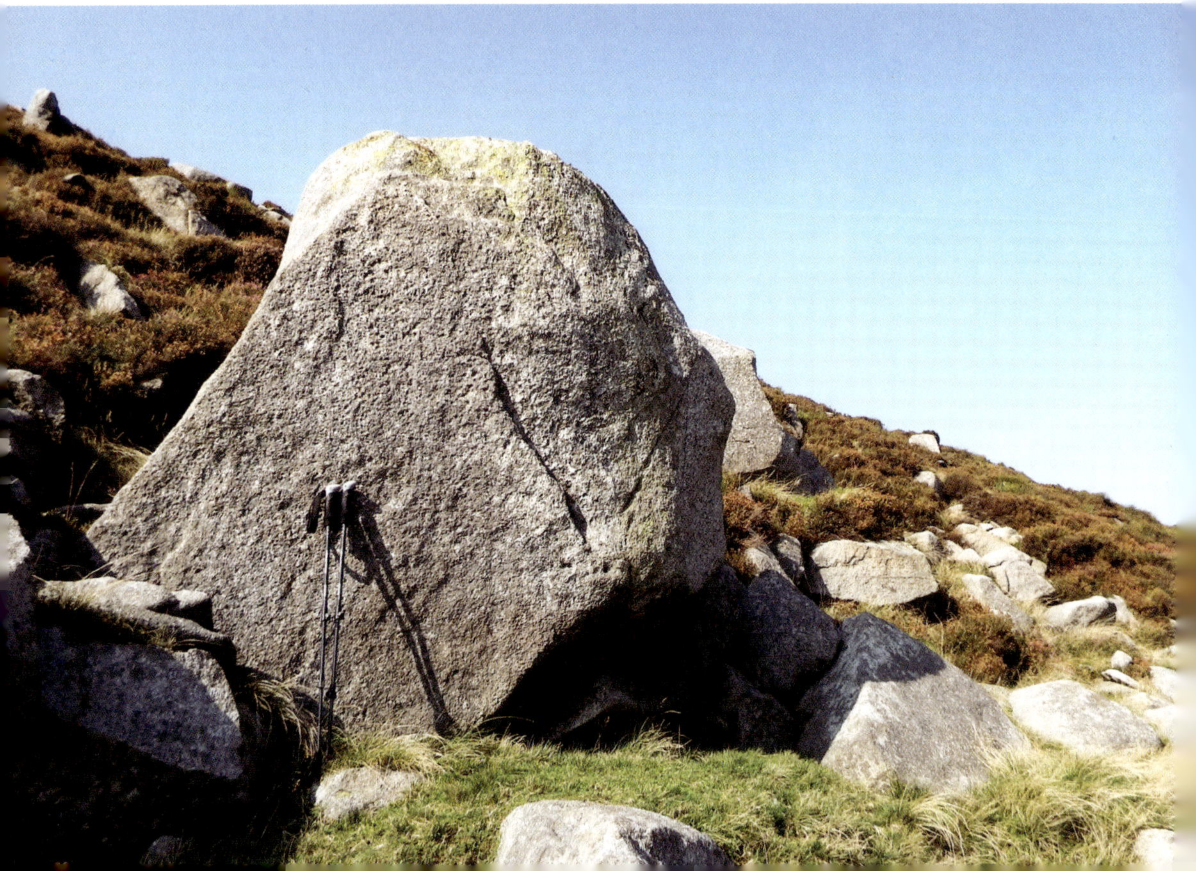

Top opposite: The grim frowning mirror stone, featured on the previous page, faces over towards Shimial mountain and summer solstice sunrise. In the photograph Shimial is the left shoulder of Slievenaglogh mountain. It is bound to be unfamiliar to some readers as it is not marked on the ordnance survey maps. This is hardly surprising given the pagan nature of its name. Shimial (J 325296) is from the Irish **Sidh Mí Áil**, 'blast of evil pleasure', a reference to an ejaculation and to the view southwards through the Hares Gap which depicted the landscape motif known as a 'penis in the vagina' an instance of which has just been illustrated in the oval picture attached to the Whooper Swan megalith already illustrated at the bottom of page eight.

Lower opposite: This brute of a mirror stone is to be found on the south-east flank of Slieve Bearnagh. This megalith was named *Óganach Scafánta* 'A Strapping Fellow' on account of its size. The stone is about 2.5 metres high by 3 metres across and it faces towards the appearance of winter solstice first light. The GPS is:

     N. 54° 11. 264'
     W. 005° 58. 487' Elevation 439m.

Top of this page: This little mirror stone is near the great wasp-like tor at the west end of Chimney Rock mountain. The flat surface is aligned to receive the early light of winter solstice dawn.

This boulder near the top of Spellack with its sleeping eye and pointy nose is a classic example of a 'face stone'. It is nearly two metres long, about one metre high and marks the start of a small spring, a fertility feature beloved by the ancients. The GPS is:

N. 54° 11. 759'
W. 005° 59. 513'   Elevation 493m.

FACE STONES

> They have mouths but they cannot speak;
> They have eyes but they cannot see.
> They have ears but they cannot hear;
> There is never a breath on their lips.
> Their makers will come to be like them
> And so will all who trust in them. (psalm 135)

When the topic of Face Stones of Mourne was first raised in *Prehistoric Mourne*, credit for first recognising them was properly given to Newcastle man W.H. Carson. In an appendix to his book, *The Dam Builders*, the story of the men who built the Silent Valley Reservoir, he included photographs of three stone faces above the Silent Valley. Certainly, were it not for pressure of space, he could easily have included more. When The Dam Builders was first published in 1981 the faces were unfortunately treated as an interesting oddity. Three photographs were not apparently enough to alert us to this treasure trove of early art. The purpose of this chapter, again showing face stones, is to demonstrate that this phenomenon is not an accident of nature but is deliberate, widespread and an art form worthy of serious appreciation and celebration.

The Mournes are indeed a treasure trove of the art of early man. With deceptive simplicity stones all across the hills have been brought to life by the addition of an eye and a mouth. The bigger the stone the more likely it will be found to have been given lines evocative of a face. Frequently the transformation of a boulder has been achieved by whacking the stone with an axe to impart a simple line to suggest an eye. Sometimes a stone maul has been used to hammer a hollow into the stone to create a shadow eye. Sometimes we have a drooped eyelid suggesting that a stone is asleep and at others it may be a deeply gouged shadow eye that looks most forbidding. Large stones often have a number of deeply indented cuts into the stone that allow the sun to cast shadows for eyes. Such shadows allow for various interpretations and for differing faces at different times as the sun moves around the heavens. It is not uncommon to have a number of faces on the same boulder, perhaps at either end or on either side. I have frequently found faces within faces. We are not talking about identifiable human faces but rather suggestive representations often using the shape of the stone in an imaginative fashion. Many of these representations are peaceful and tranquil but many others are grim and undoubtedly of malign intent.

The hills of Mourne are filled with thousands of artistic creations on rocks and cliff faces. Once you find a shadow eye it is just a matter of using the shape of the rock and your imagination to discern the intention of the ancient artist. Why such extensive efforts were undertaken are now lost in the mists of time. It may have been an attempt to impose control on the territory in which they lived, perhaps to placate imagined spirits, maybe to give honour to their dead, perhaps to give warning to any intruders or simply as a mark of ownership saying, 'this is our place'.

The skill of the ancients has seen them magically change inert lumps of granite to vibrant sculptures. In the following chapter we look at how skilfully and convincingly they portrayed the animals and birds around them. In this chapter, however, it is important to start with the simple concept of a 'face' that often has no more than a line for an eye, a corner of the stone for a nose and perhaps a crack representing a mouth. Anyone who walks in the Mournes will have passed many of these stones. They hide in plain view, overlooked by their commonness and by a previous presumption that the marks on the stones were accidents of nature, or weathering and thus meaningless. An awareness of these treasures and the joy of discovering them will add immensely to the pleasure of walkers and visitors. The diagram at the beginning of the book giving the compass points for the annual movement of the sun becomes important as it will be found that so many stones are more than just 'pretty faces'. The corners and sharp points on the stones will often be found directed with great accuracy to the appearance or setting of the sun at solstice. Once, at the Ballagh, having carefully checked by compass, a great stone spear point was found directed to the North Star. No doubt there will be other such discoveries to be made but at Mourne the essential interest seems to have been where the sun would appear at winter solstice and thereafter to a lesser degree the summer solstice.

Hammering granite is a dangerous occupation; sharp chips of stone frequently spall off when the granite is struck stinging hands and face. Nowadays workers wear protective goggles but in the past the great hazard was a blinding stone into the eye and many unfortunately suffered this fate. Working with great stones is an occupation fraught with peril and many a man has been caught unawares by the sudden shift of the huge weights and been crushed in hand or leg. Such accidents undoubtedly happened regularly in Mourne in ancient times. A folklore snippet about the ancient people, the *Fir Builg*, was previously thought to be a disparaging remark about a supposedly inferior conquered people but it can now be considered a fair comment on the tribe who, because they single-mindedly erected great megaliths in profusion throughout Mourne, must have suffered incredible injuries in the process. We are told that they were: '…hideous to behold, with single legs, single hands and single eyes…'* This catalogue of injuries sustained by the people would be consistent with frequent manipulation of huge stones of granite. When you get used to looking for eyes and mouths on rocks you quickly realise how productively busy the ancients have been. If we remember that the megaliths featured in this work are only a very small sample of the multitude to be found across the hills then the injuries suffered in their erection must have been equally prodigious. It is probably a mercy that we do not know the suffering involved in their creation.

* Page 49 of *Ireland in Pre-Celtic times* by R.A.S. Macalister, Maunsel and Roberts, Dublin 1921.

This sleeping beauty of a stone is near Meelmore summit on its eastern side. The roughly phallic shaped granite stone is about 1.3m long by 0.5m high. It has a lovely sleeping eye in the middle and the 'nose' points to summer solstice sunrise. The GPS is:

N. 54° 11. 562'
W. 005° 59. 902'   Elevation 644m.

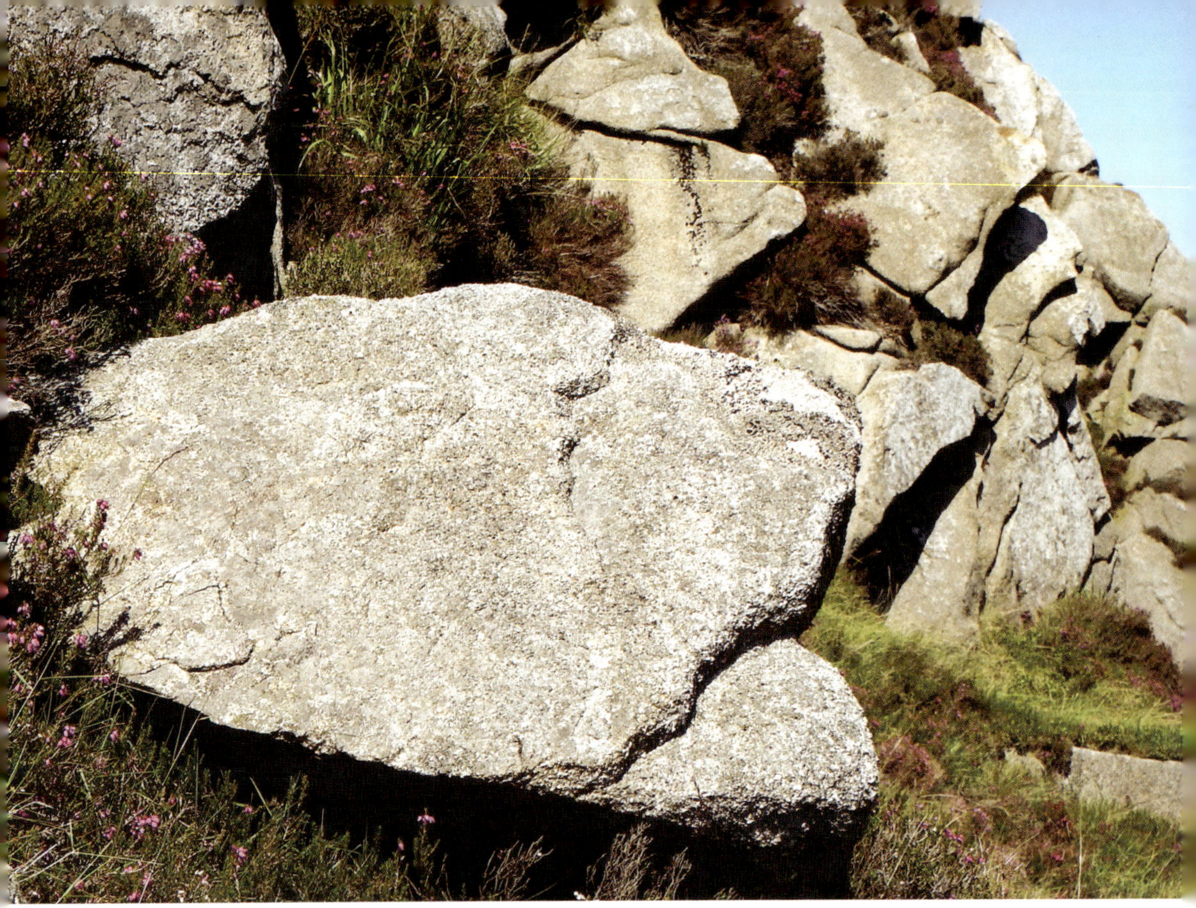
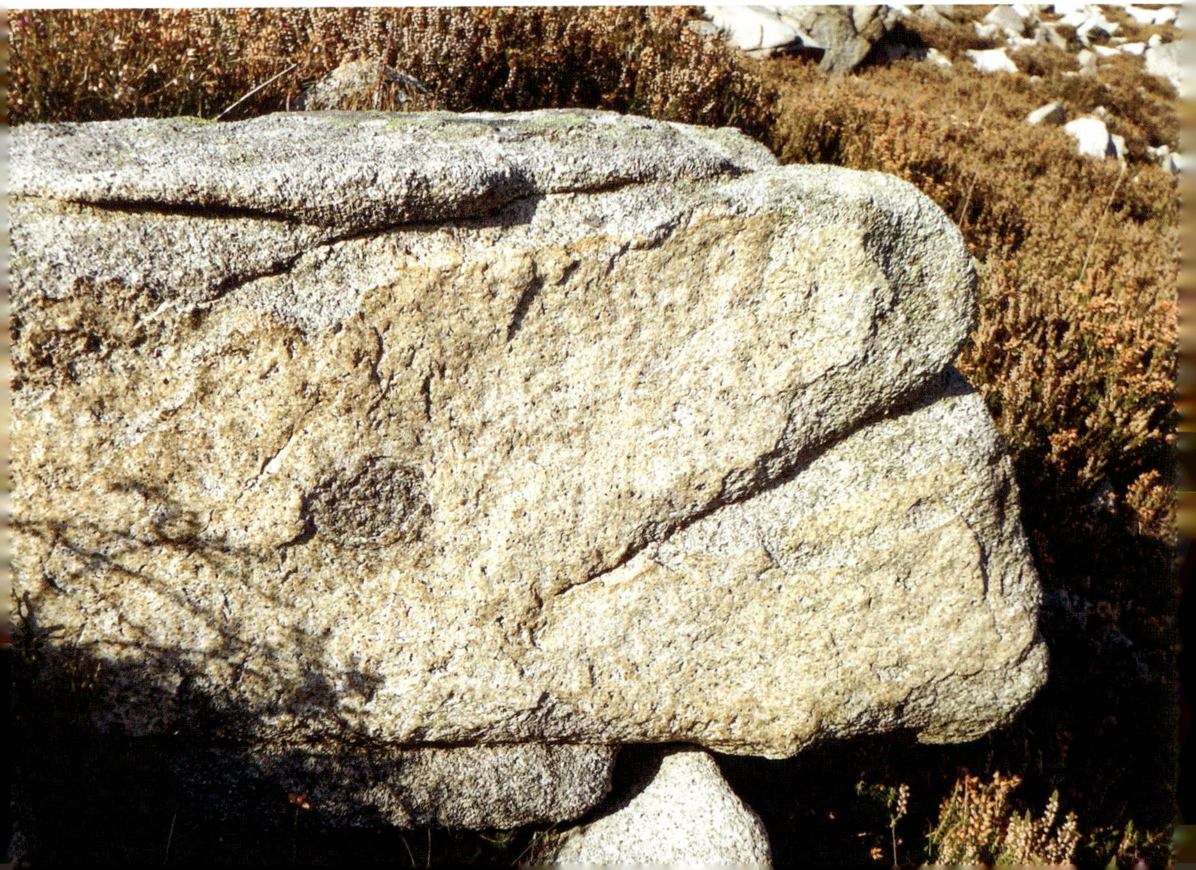

Top opposite: This little gem of a face is round the corner from
      N. 54º 11. 803'
      W. 005º 59. 331' Elevation 394m.
It is at the top of a very steep slope under Spellack overlooking the Trassey valley. It is a place rich in ancient artwork. Look again to see another little face in the background above.

Lower opposite: This low propped face stone is on the south east flank of Millstone mountain overlooking the Ballagh. The bulbous nose is aimed across Dundrum Bay to summer solstice sunrise. It may not be a big stone, being one metre long at the top, but the face gives it lots of character so it well deserves its recently bestowed Irish name of *Pláigheanach* 'A Mischievous Fellow'. The GPS for this stone is:
      N. 54º 11. 025'
      W. 005º 53. 619' Elevation 351m.

Top of this page: The 3.5m long granite boulder is located on the west side of the Annalong valley downslope from the Red Hand of Ulster, otherwise formally known as **Sliabh Snaib Báine**, 'mountain of the white end'. The small circular eye is certainly quite emphatic. GPS is:
      N. 54º 09. 879'
      W. 005º 56. 919' Elevation 296m.

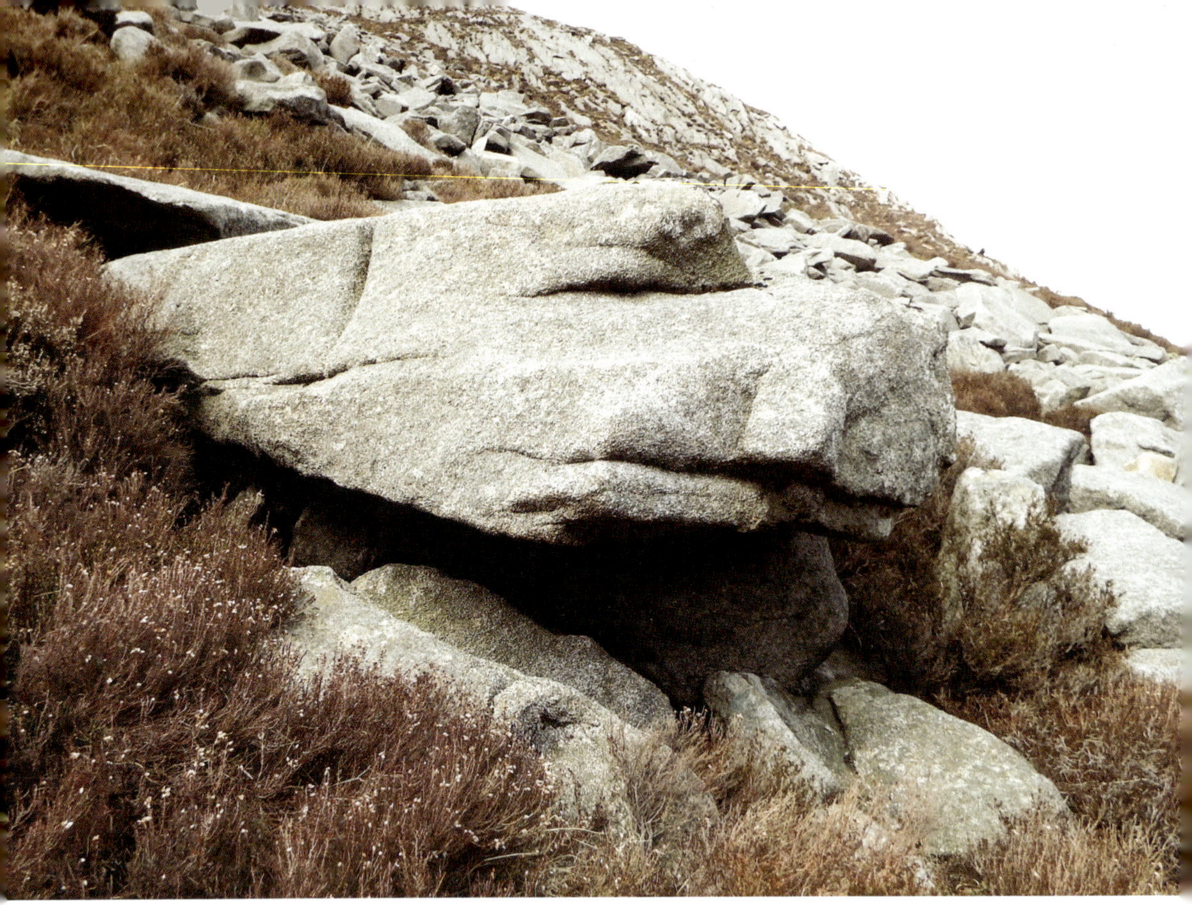

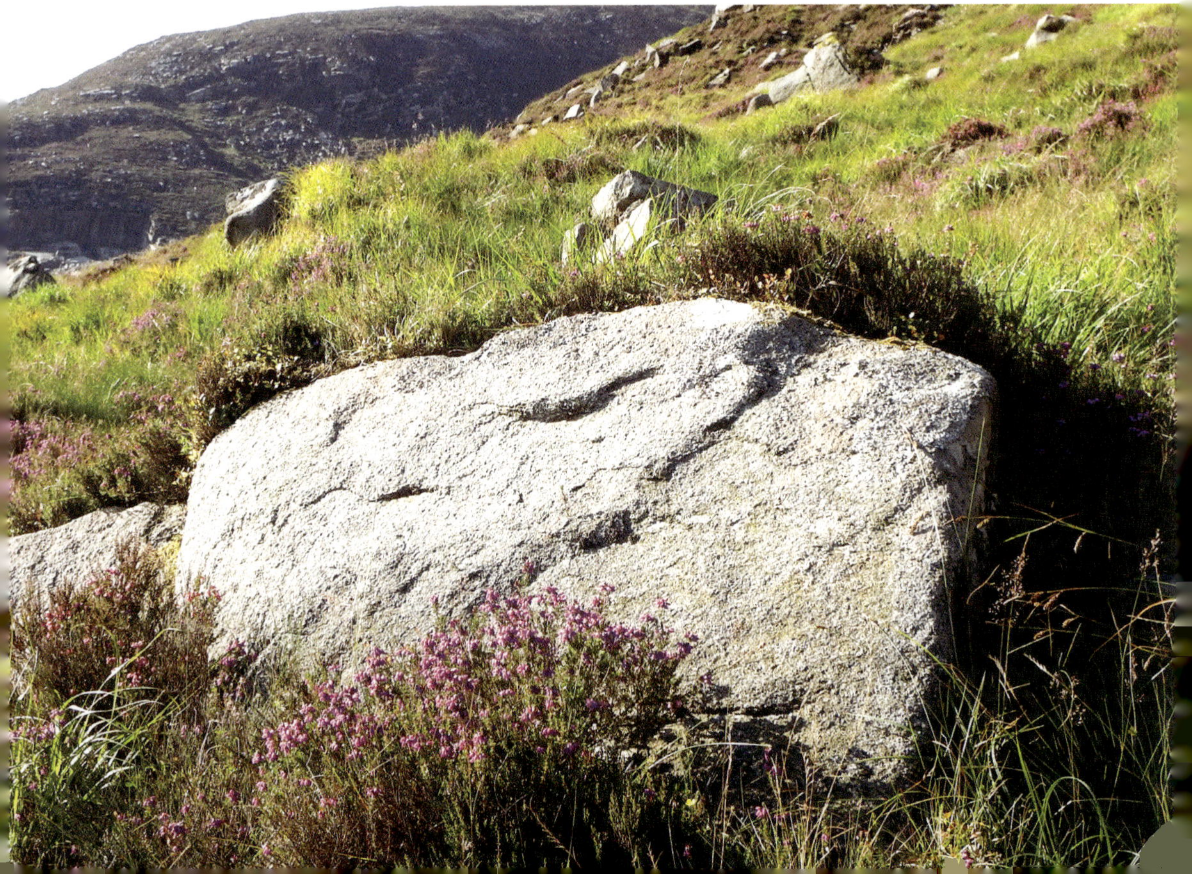

Top opposite: This megalith is to be found on the north side of Pollaphuca valley at the edge of a scree. It is a fine face, worthy of a mug shot. The stone is propped at the front and has a counter-balance stone at the back, the end point of which is directed to where winter solstice sunrise will appear. The GPS is:

N.   54º 11. 542'
W. 005º 59. 541'   Elevation 447m.

Lower opposite: A deep cut and rather formidable eye marks this megalith at the bottom of the southern rock slide under Spellack. It is about 200' above the path. GPS is:

N.   54º 11. 853'
W. 005º 59. 280'   Elevation 328m.

Top of this page: This delightful face stone overlooks Cove Loch. The location is:

N.   54° 10. 025'
W. 005° 57. 337'   Elevation 455m.

21

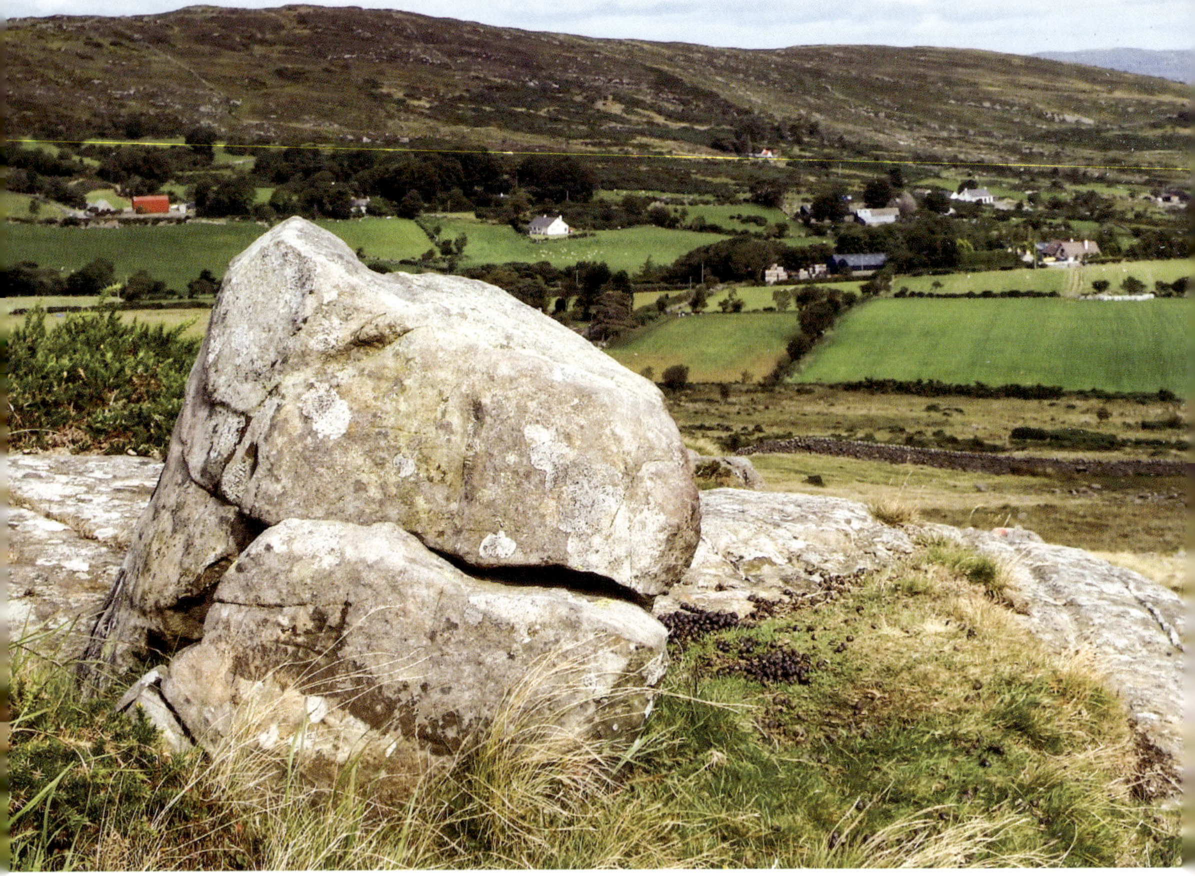

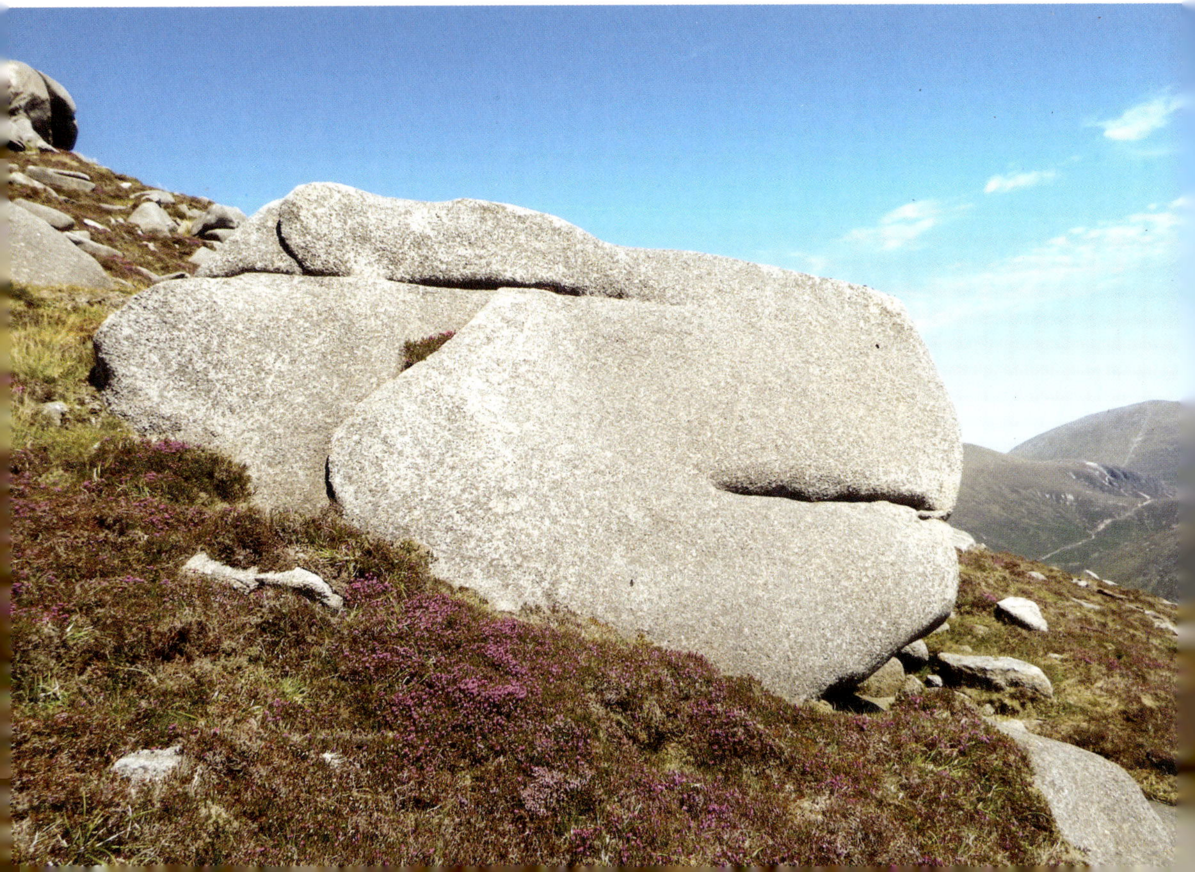

Top opposite: This low shale boulder that has a number of nice faces is in the lower Trassey valley on the north side of Slieve Meelmore. The GPS is:
>N.   54º 12. 100'
>W. 005º 59. 888'   Elevation 285m.

Round the side, and not in the photograph, the open mouth cavity is beautifully aligned so as to be illuminated by the summer solstice dawn. The nose of the stone points to the summit of Shimial mountain on the other side of the valley.

Lower opposite: Under Bearnagh's north tor a very large granite boulder, with a most imposing face, has its point directed to Slieve Donard. A substantial meatus groove at the point enhances the stone's phallic nature. The top flat surface is nearly 5m long and 2m across. A little bit of tongue sticks out at the front. This is a fertility location with a sliver of Seefin mountain in the 'vaginal notch' formed between Rocky and the descending slope of Lamagan. That view is probably the raison d'être for the stone's placement. The GPS is:
>N.   54º 11. 177'
>W. 005º 59. 117'   Elevation 711m.

Top of this page: You will find this large eyed stone near the Mourne wall and about twenty metres south of the stile atop Slievenaglogh at GPS:
>N.   54º 11. 564'
>W. 005º 58. 248'   Elevation 539m.

This is a location with magnificent views both over south Down and the Ben Crom reservoir valley.

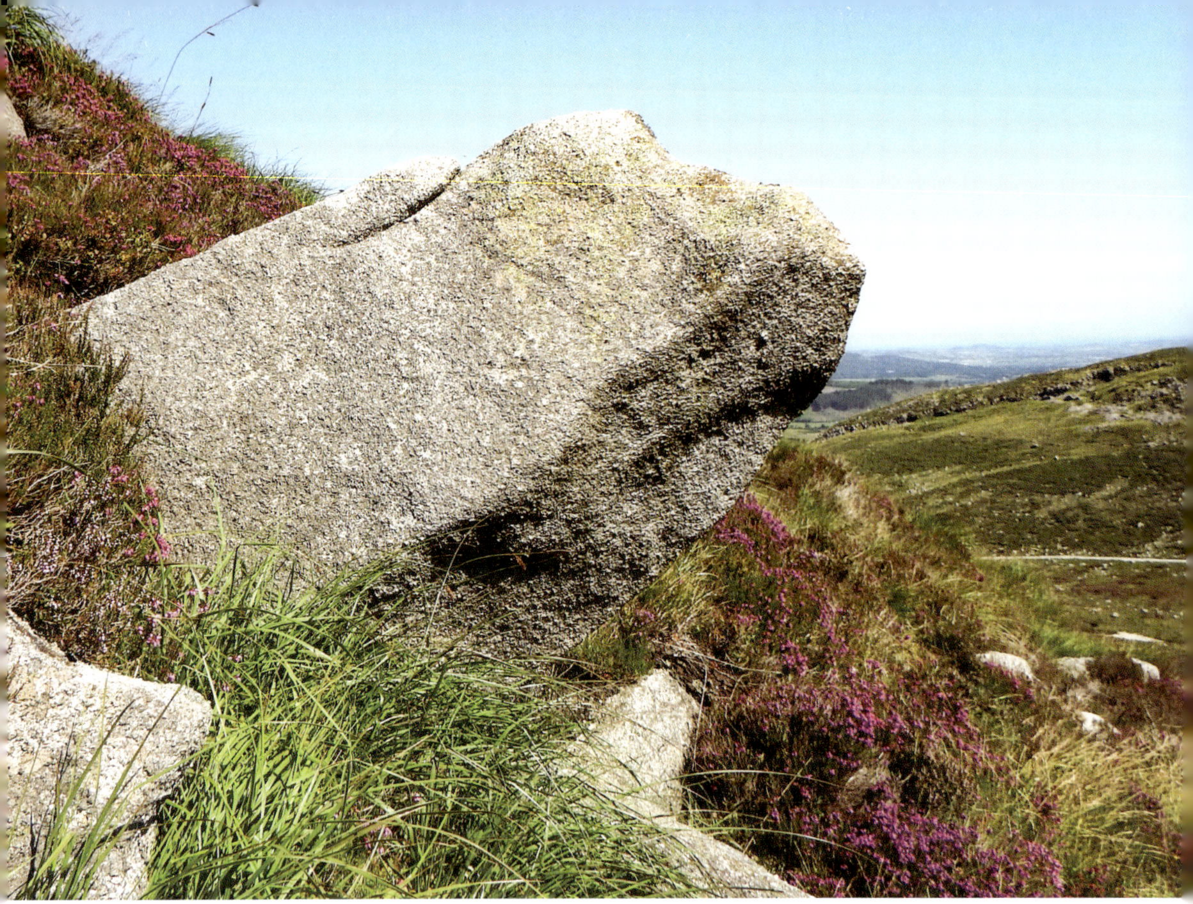

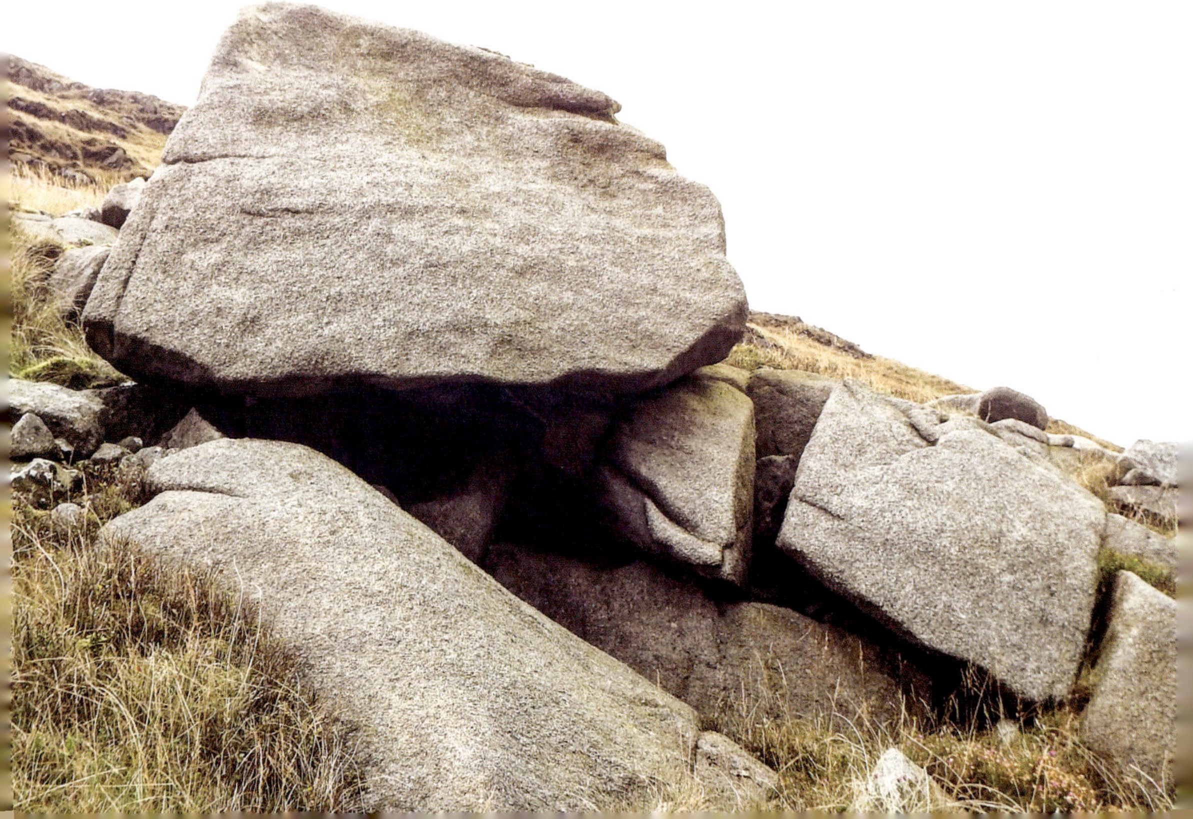

Top opposite: There is a grand face on this anchored phallic stone found on the corner of Spellack's southern shoulder and at the entrance to Pollaphuca valley. It is 1.6m long from tip to tail and about 0.5m thick and is found at:
N.   54º 11. 691'
W. 005º 59. 209'   Elevation 385m.

The tip of the stone points to summer solstice dawn over by Shimial mountain and a clever little curl at the tip of the stone funnels water to drip from the front in a symbolic act of perpetual fertility.

Lower opposite: You will find this big granite block high on the steep south slope of Happy Valley at GPS:
N.   54º 11. 405'
W. 006º 00. 863'   Elevation 463m.

The stone has faces to front and sides and indeed you would think it was frowning over towards Slieve Croob. Underneath is worth a look to see how carefully boulders have been placed to stop this brute sliding downhill. How they manipulated this great stone on such a steep slope is a source of wonder.

Top of this page: If you find this granite boulder half-way up the south side of Happy Valley with the huge eye on its south face, you will realise it is only part of a great vaginal fertility monument. This particular stone, one part of a labial side, is well supported and counterbalanced in its upright position. It is found at:
N.   54º 11. 422'
W. 006º 00. 855'   Elevation 433m.

25

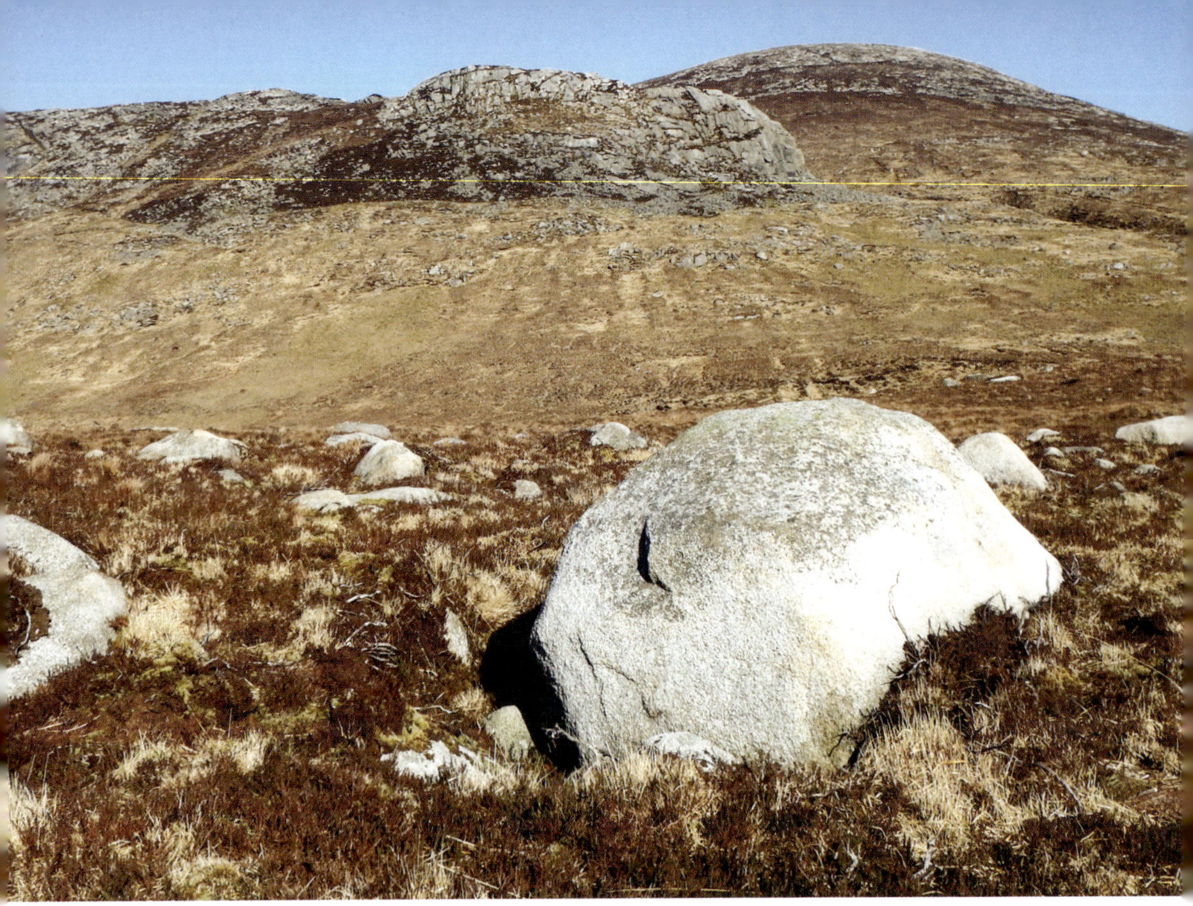

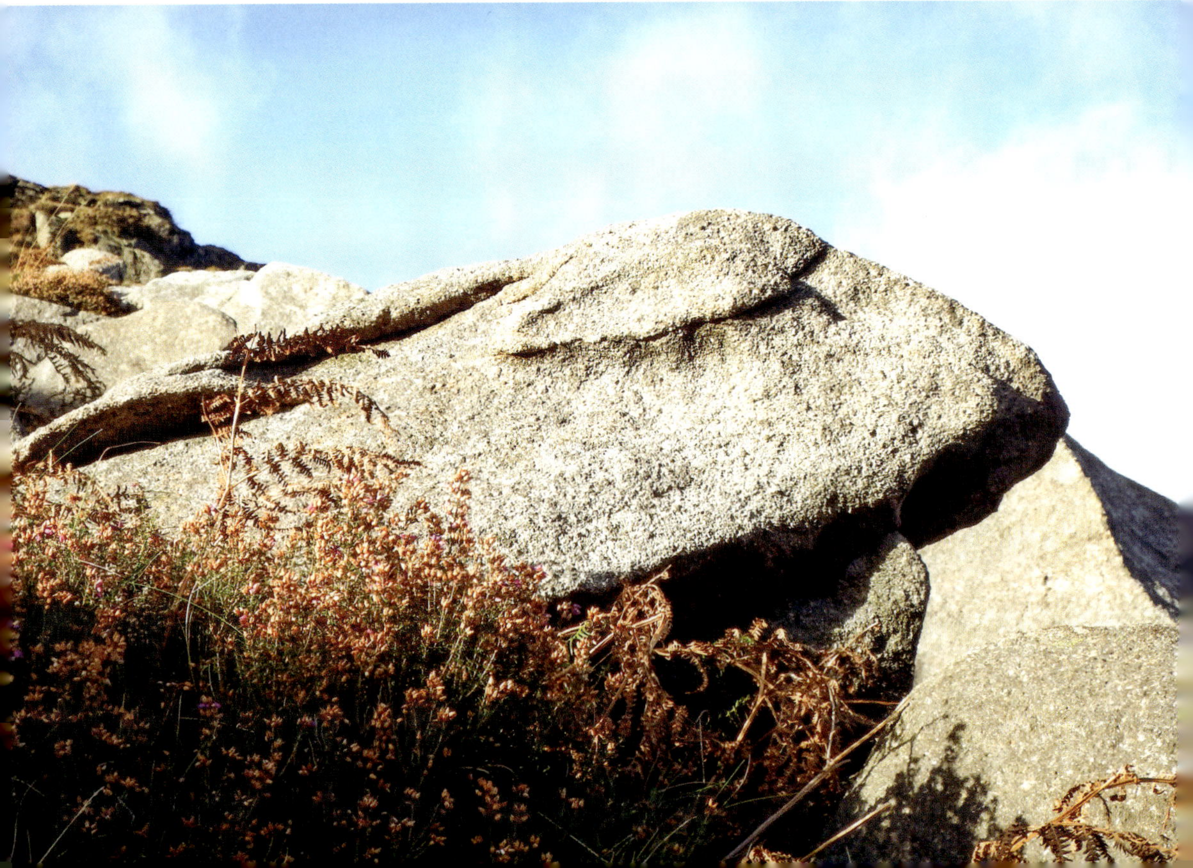

Top opposite: This face stone in the Annalong valley is a little work of art in itself. It has been 'animated' by the creation of a shadow eye and is a good representation of the many stones and boulders around Mourne that have been transformed into 'faces'.

Lower opposite: This drowsy eyed stone was found on Slievenamaddy. The tip looks towards summer solstice sunrise.

Top of this page: A great hooked nose and an emphatic shadow eye adorn this mighty boulder under the cliff face of north-east Bignian. Another shadow eye can be seen on the rock face at top right.

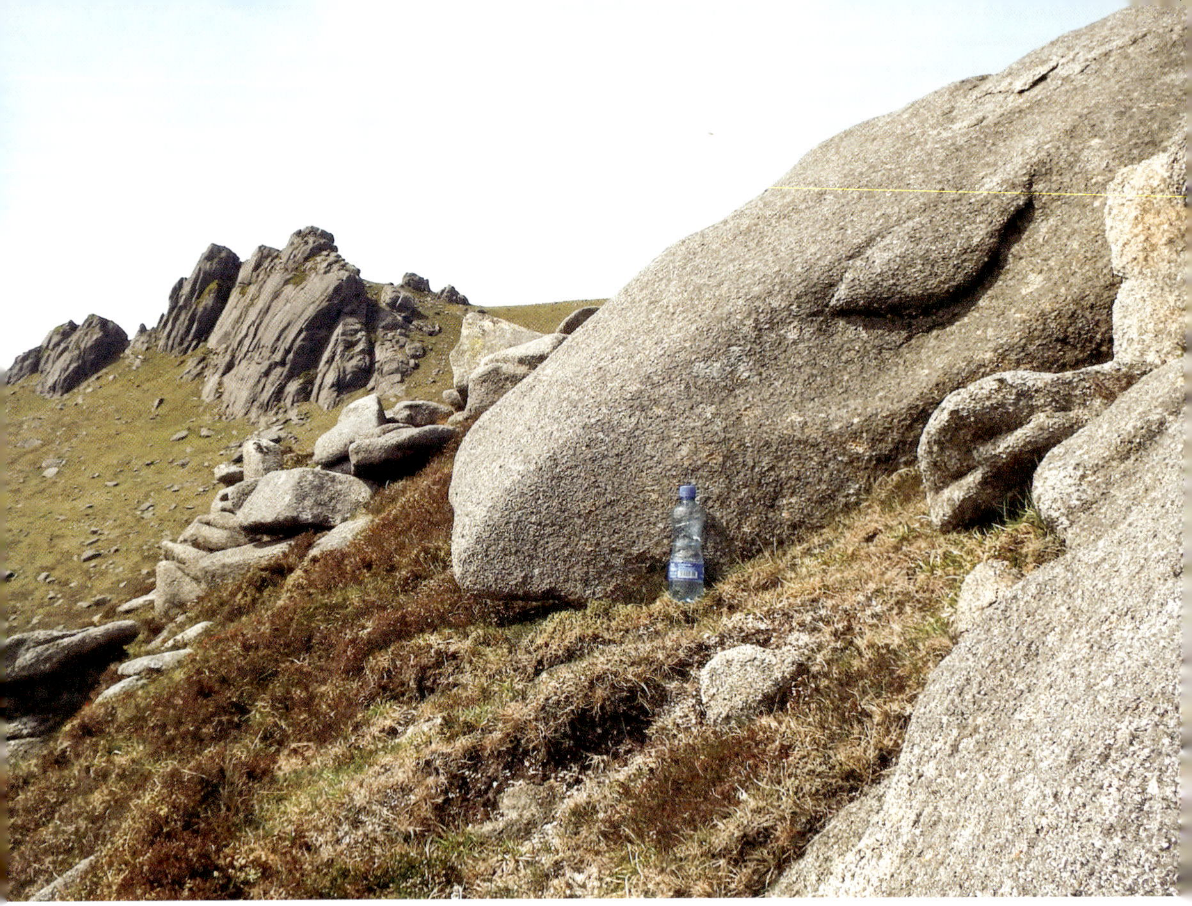

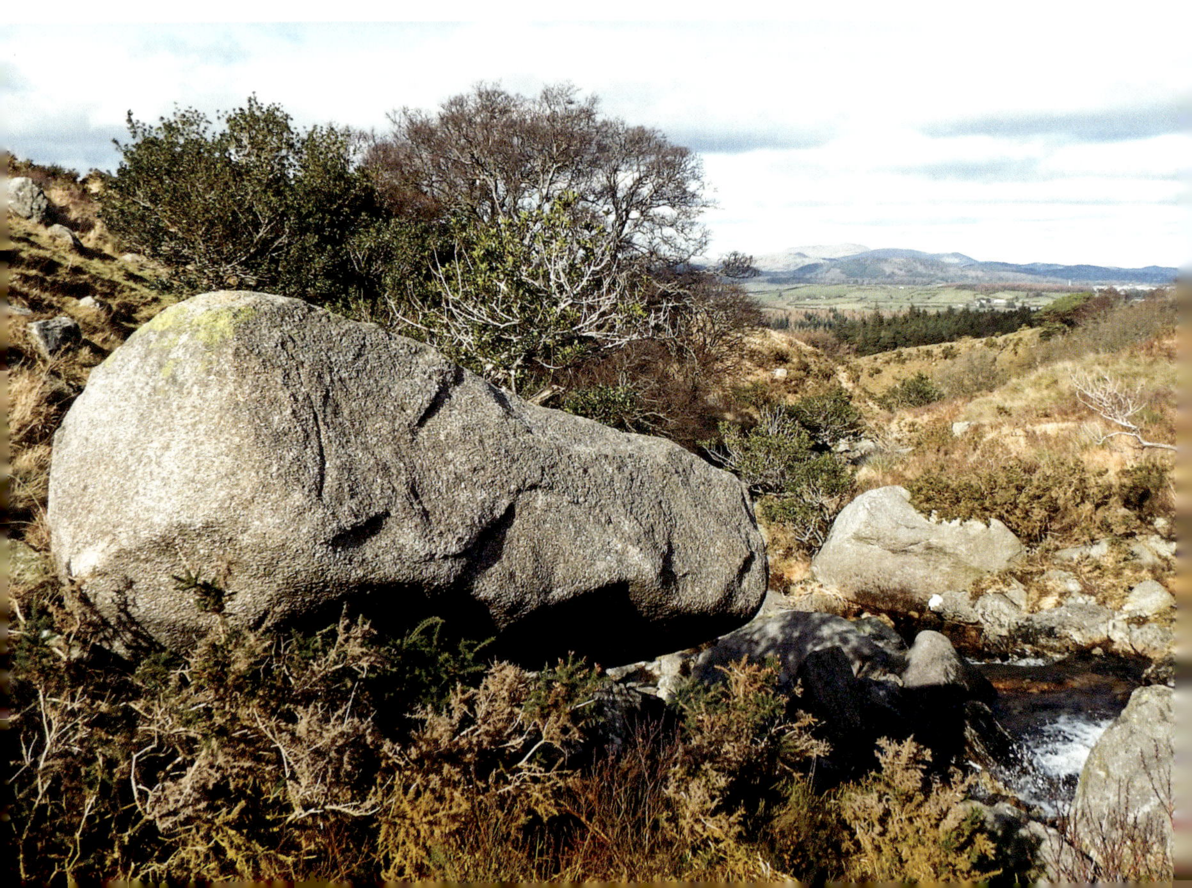

Top opposite: The north tor of Slieve Bearnagh is the place to find this low granite stone with its hooded eye.

Lower opposite: This boulder with its long muzzle is at the junction of the Cascade river and a tributary. No exact GPS is to hand but the sculptural masterpiece of the 'Great Hare', illustrated on page 84, is to be found scarcely sixty metres away on the other side of the river at GPS:

                    N.   54° 12. 416'
                    W. 005° 57. 181'   Elevation 220m.

Top of this page: There is a marvellous view over the whole of the Windy Gap valley from this location. Eagle mountain is at the back right. The top boulder has a second lesser face with an open mouth at the back and below. The large slab on the slope has also been decorated with a shadow eye.

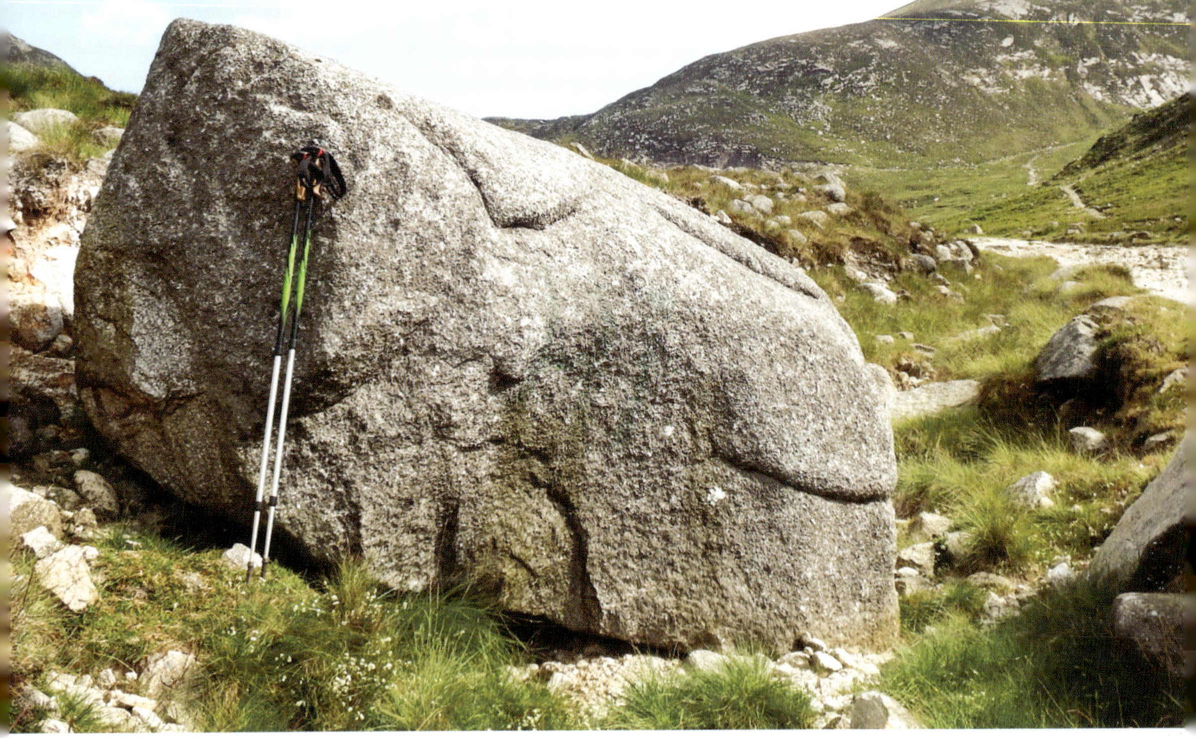

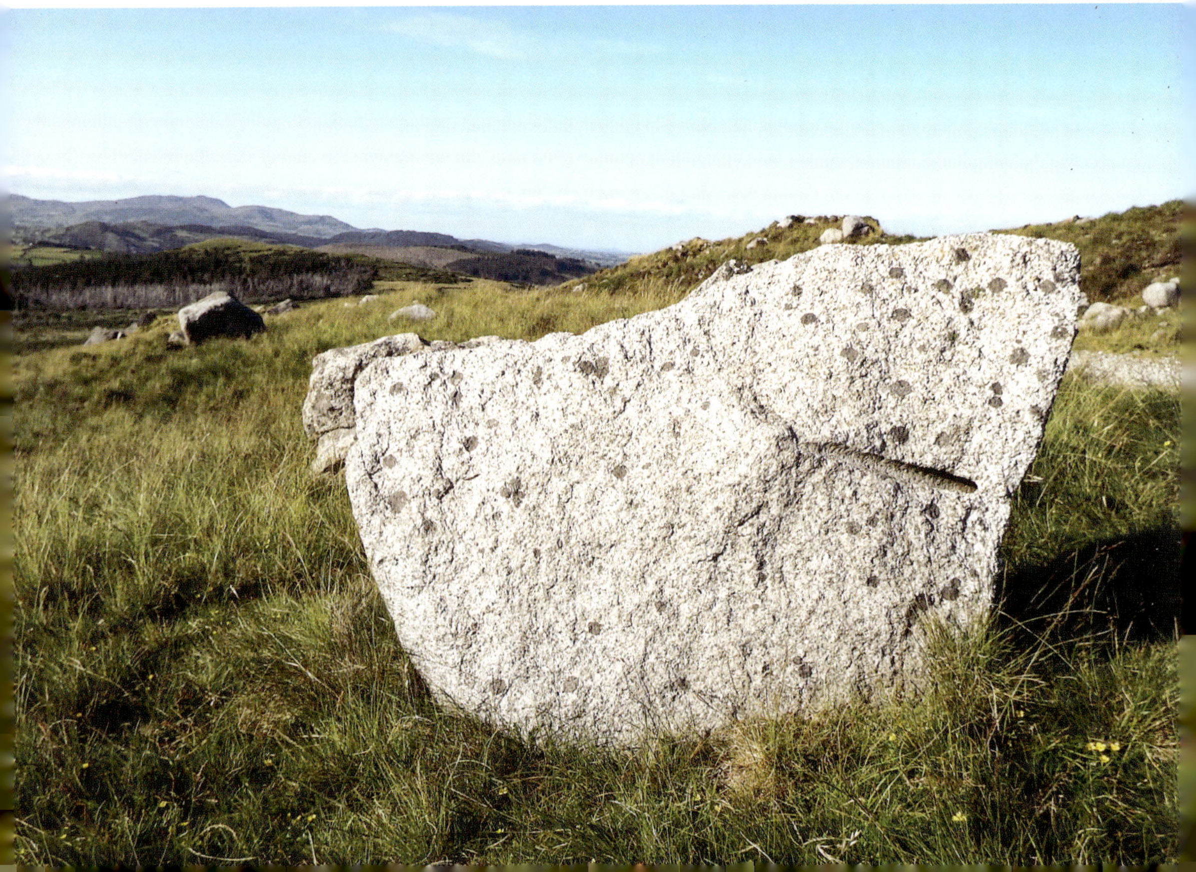

Top opposite: A peaceful dreamy smile, almost like the Mona Lisa, graces the front of the mighty face stone beside the Trassey track. It is a pity so many walk past this artwork in ignorance. The stone is hard to miss as it is nearly 3m from front to back and 1.75m high; it is seen here at 5.00pm at the end of June. The GPS is:

                N.   54º 12. 003'
                W. 005º 59. 238'   Elevation 292m.

Lower opposite: Two hundred yards further down the Trassey track from the previous entry is this item of 'modern' industrial archaeology. It sports a power drill hole for an eye, the stone having been pierced through from the back. The innovative use of a power tool to create an 'eye' testifies to the imagination of quarrymen after the war but its real significance lies in how enduring was the cautious respect that those men still had for the ancient beliefs. The stone is found at:

                N.   54º 12. 036'
                W. 005º 59. 248'   Elevation 285m.

Top of this page: Before the Mourne wall was built the rounded nose of this 1m long granite face stone on Slieve Corragh would have pointed to winter solstice sunrise. The wall, about ten metres away, now intervenes. A prominent round recess for an eyeball is a most distinctive feature of this stone and taken with the slim split line of a mouth gives the ensemble a distinctly skeletal look. The coordinates for the stone are:

                N.   54º 11. 633'
                W. 005º 58. 077'   Elevation 580m.

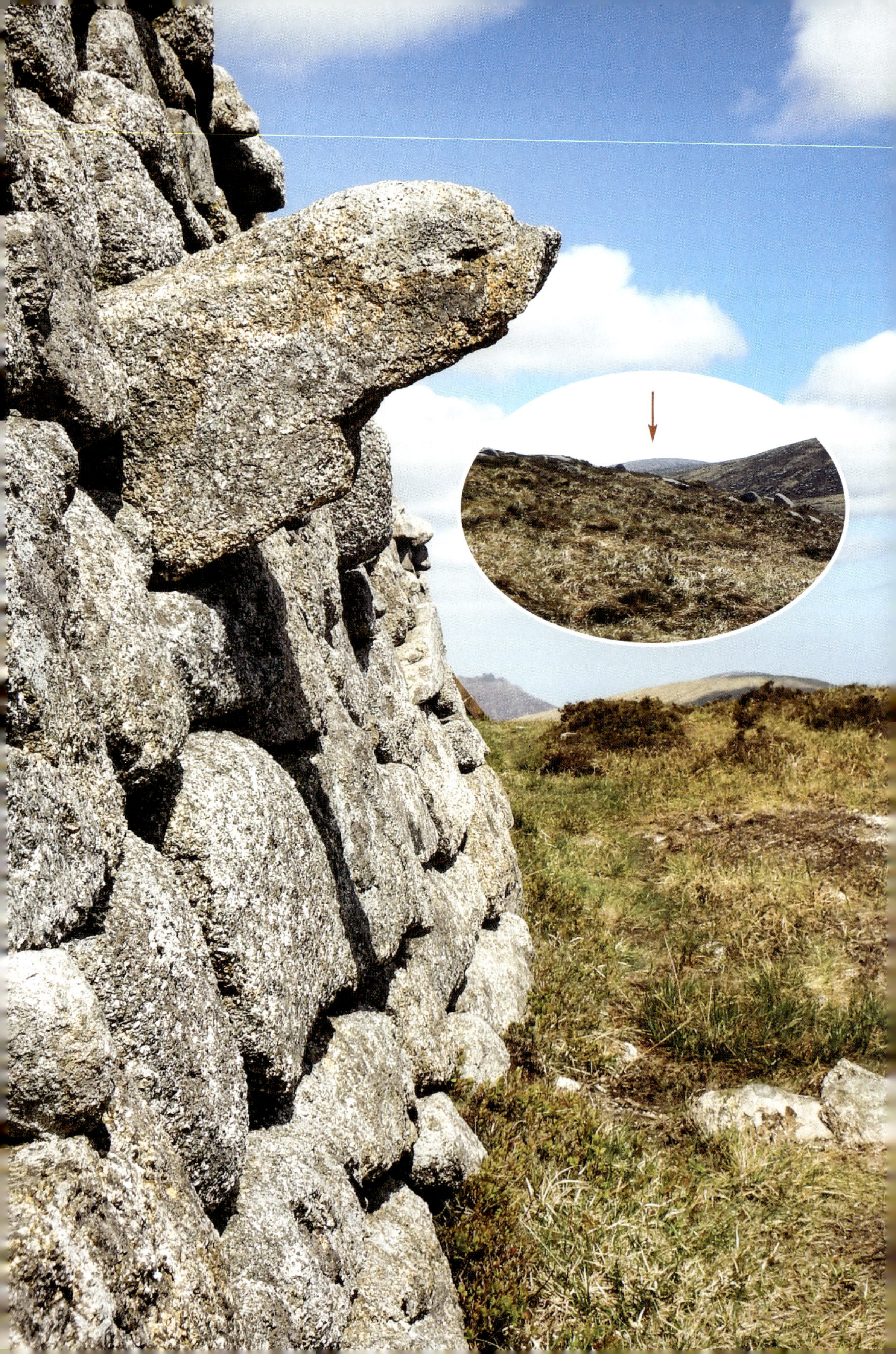

Opposite page: The men of Mourne who built this wall across the top of Eagle mountain respected and preserved the old traditions. This face stone was inserted prominently into the wall. The vicinity notices the old Mourne landscape motif of a penis in a vagina (shown in the attached oval). The motif is created by the distant top of Finlieve mountain peeping up between the 'labial sides' of Eagle mountain foreground and Shanlieve mountain on the right. It is very likely that this location is the 'lost mountain' known as **Sliabh Áine**, 'mountain of pleasure' that John O'Donovan marked on his map of Mourne as being beside Eagle Mountain. He mentioned that **Sliabh Áine** had been omitted in the Name Book. [p.50, Ordnance Survey Letters Down, edited by M. Herity.]

Top of this page: Beautiful views are to be enjoyed from this stone which is virtually a summit cairn on the hill across from the Benedictine monastery. Not in the photograph is the fertility motif on the south side of the boulder where a penile spear point is inserted between stone labial walls. The GPS is:

                        N.   54° 07. 859'
                        W. 006° 10. 443'   Elevation 279m.

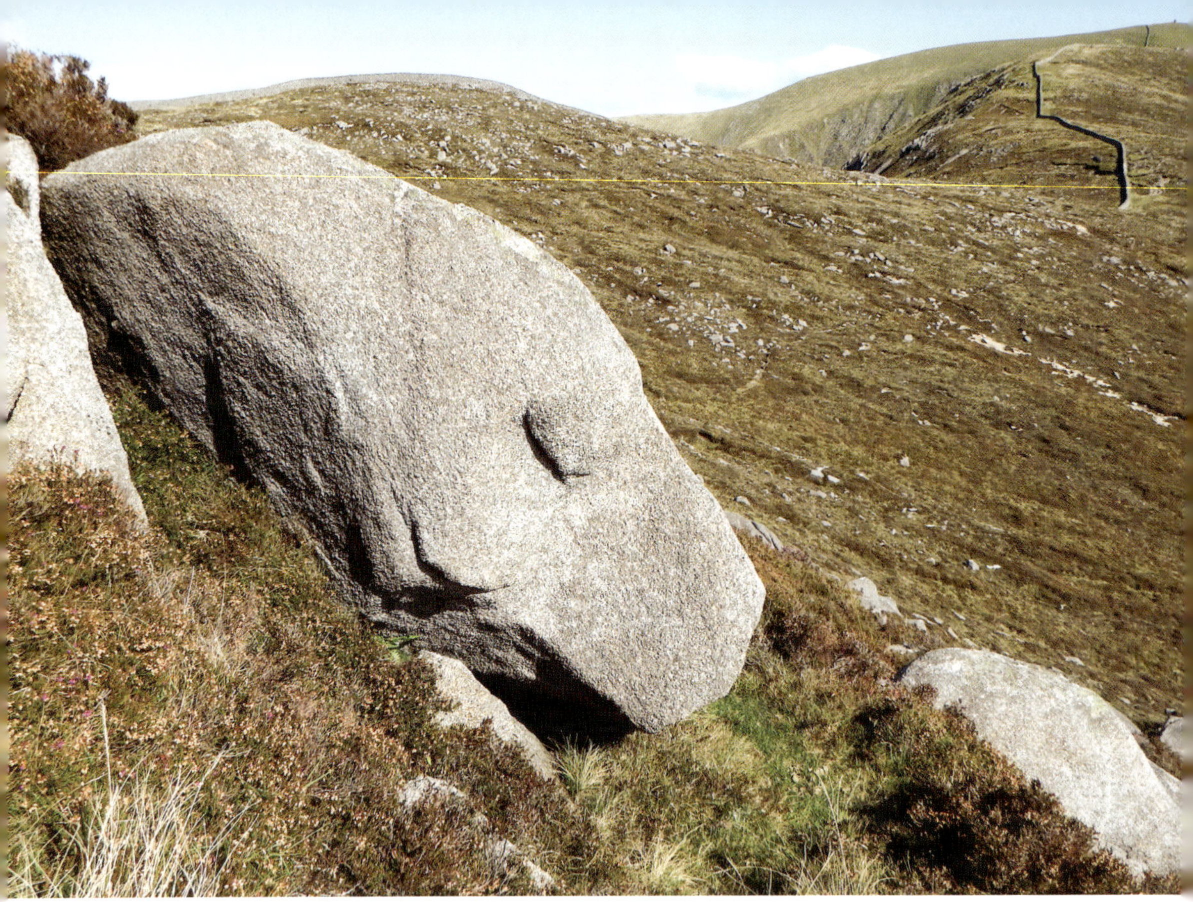
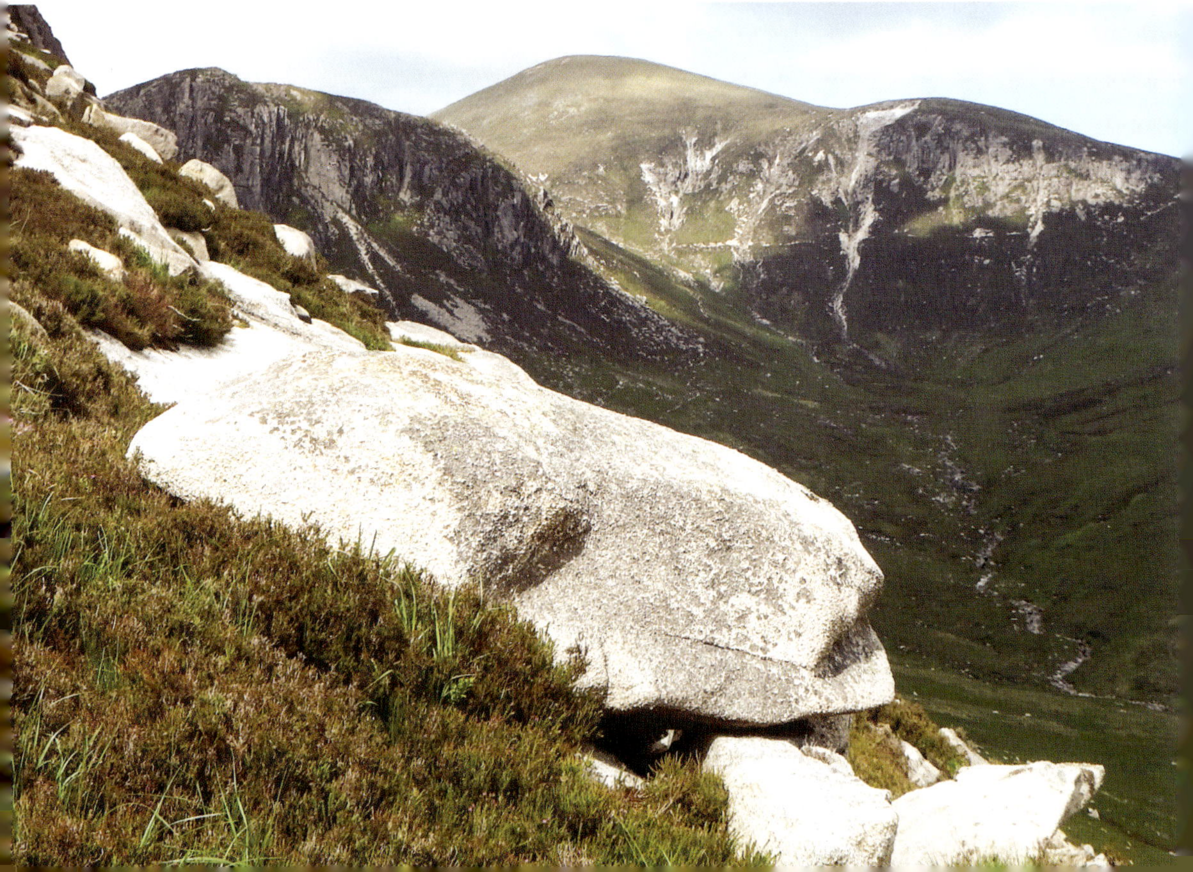

Top opposite: This three metre stone on the south-east side of Slieve Corragh, with its distinctive undercut eye, so beautifully suggested a sleeping creature that it was named *Néall Codalta*, 'A Wink of Sleep'. The GPS is:

      N. 54º 11. 572'
      W. 005º 57. 945' Elevation 543m.

Lower opposite: This marvellous face stone on the west side of the Annalong Valley caught my eye from a distance. Murphy's Law dictated that the sun should disappear by the time I finally got there. It was worth the wait however for the sun to reappear. The stone is about 2.5m long and has a nice point to winter solstice sunrise. The GPS is:

      N. 54º 10. 135'
      W. 005º 56. 947' Elevation 414m.

Top of this page: A real 'big boy' of a stone. It lies half-way up the western slope of the Annalong Valley and considering that the stone is easily 4m long, 2.5m across the top and not less than 1m thick, moving it would have been a real achievement. This erstwhile phallic length has been very precisely moved too. The side of the stone has been wedged up so that the spine on top is aligned with fertility intent directly to the rounded shape of Slieve Donard. There is also a tip of a tongue sticking out at the front. The GPS is:

      N. 54º 10. 132'
      W. 005º 56. 883' Elevation 356m.

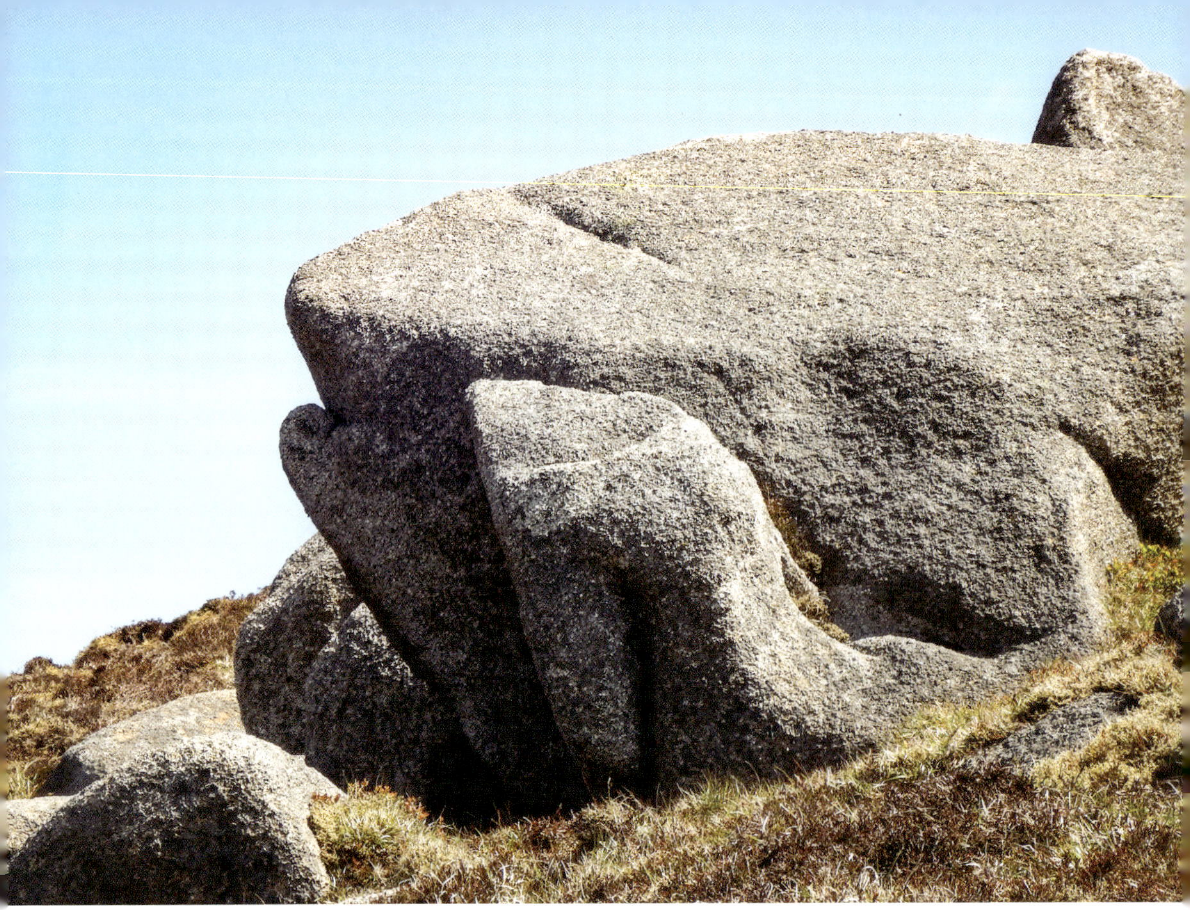

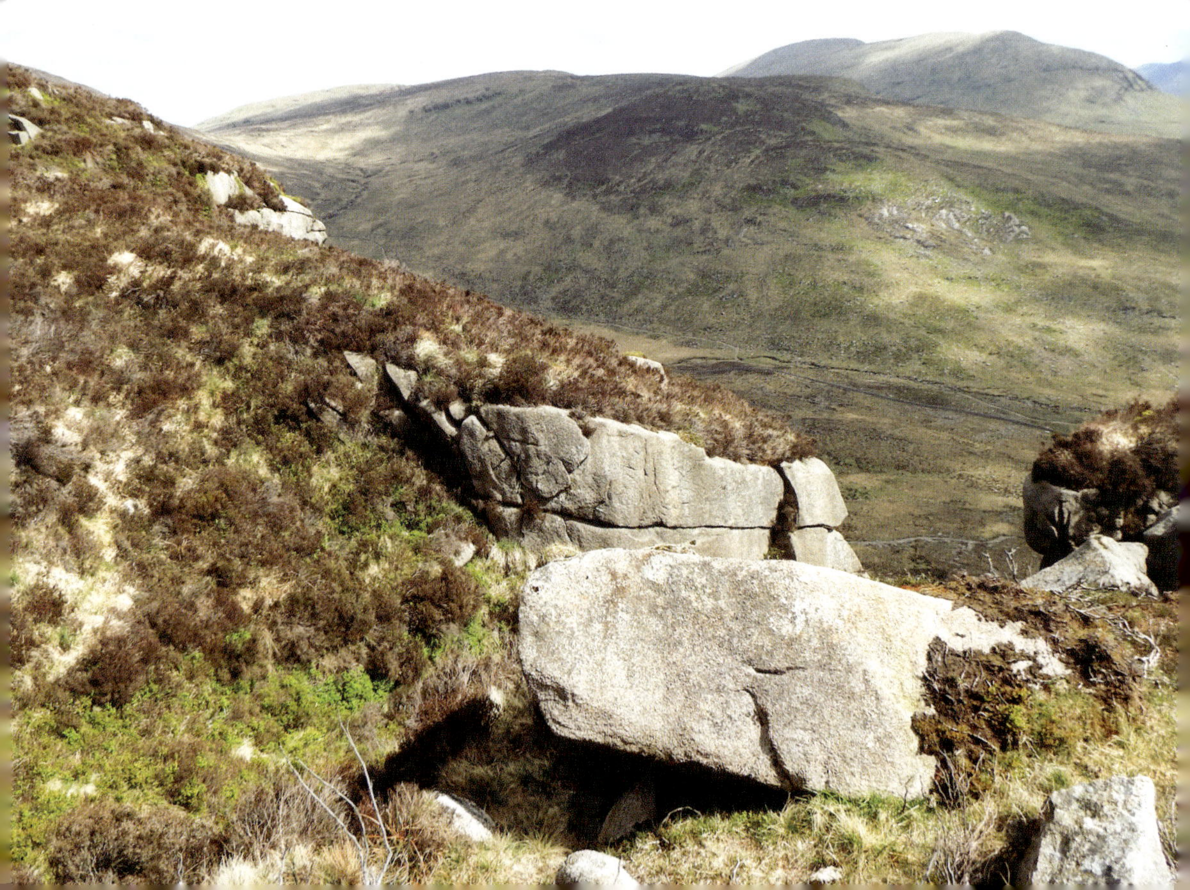

Top opposite: Besides the obvious eye on top, this hefty boulder on Forks mountain has a mouth that is slightly open. The delightful design of the stone gives every impression that it is a mother being pestered by its offspring for food.

Lower opposite: On Long mountain, overlooking the Windy Gap Valley, this substantial face stone guards the gully behind it that was treated by the ancients as a vaginal gap. The ridge overlooking the valley below is an area rich in megaliths and the beauty of the area probably had a lot to do with the proliferation of those huge stones.

Top of this page: Another unrecognised piece of ancient artwork. This granite block, with its deliberate eye and mouth, sits atop three or four largish stones about fifty metres above the granite trail serving Crossone and Glenfoffany and not far from the Bloody Bridge river, just above Crannog. The GPS is:
                    N.   54° 10. 386'
                    W. 005° 53. 632'   Elevation 221m.

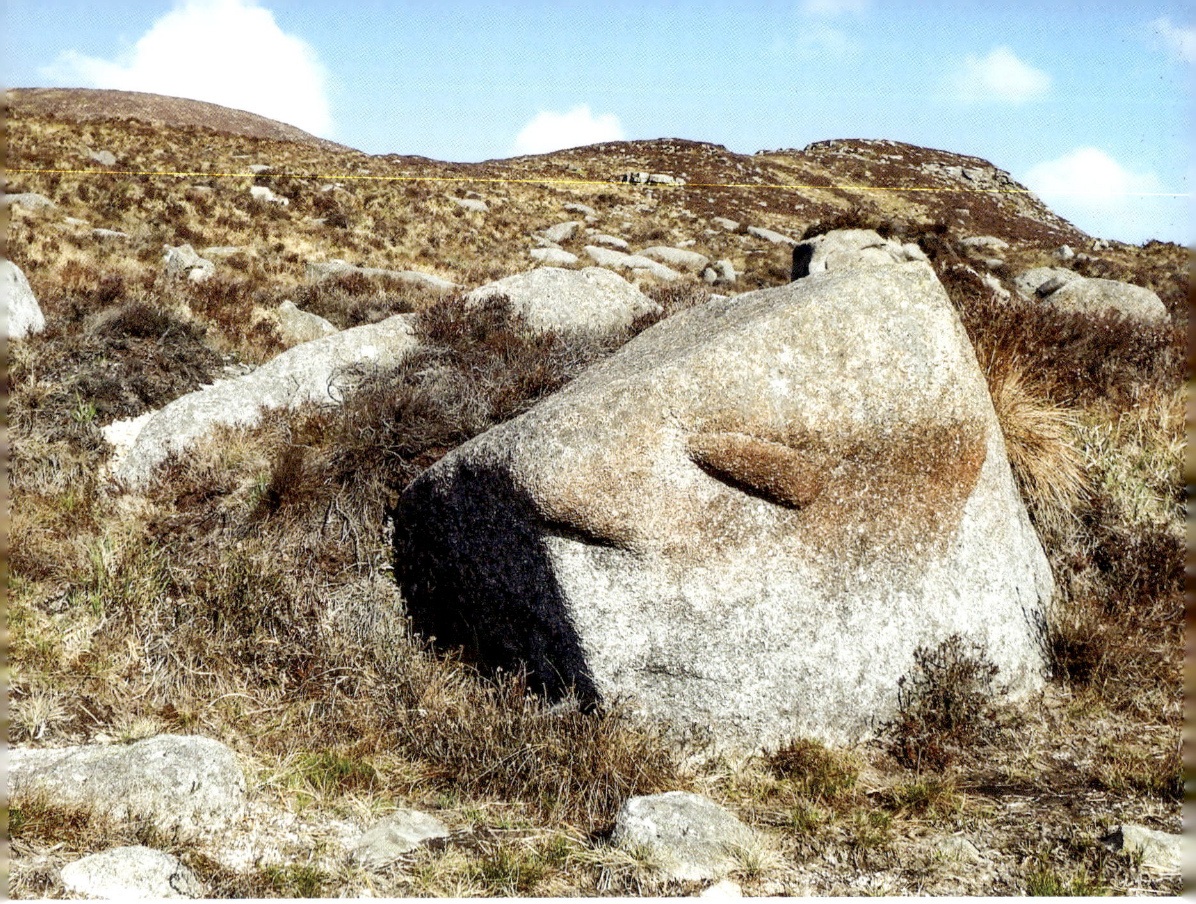

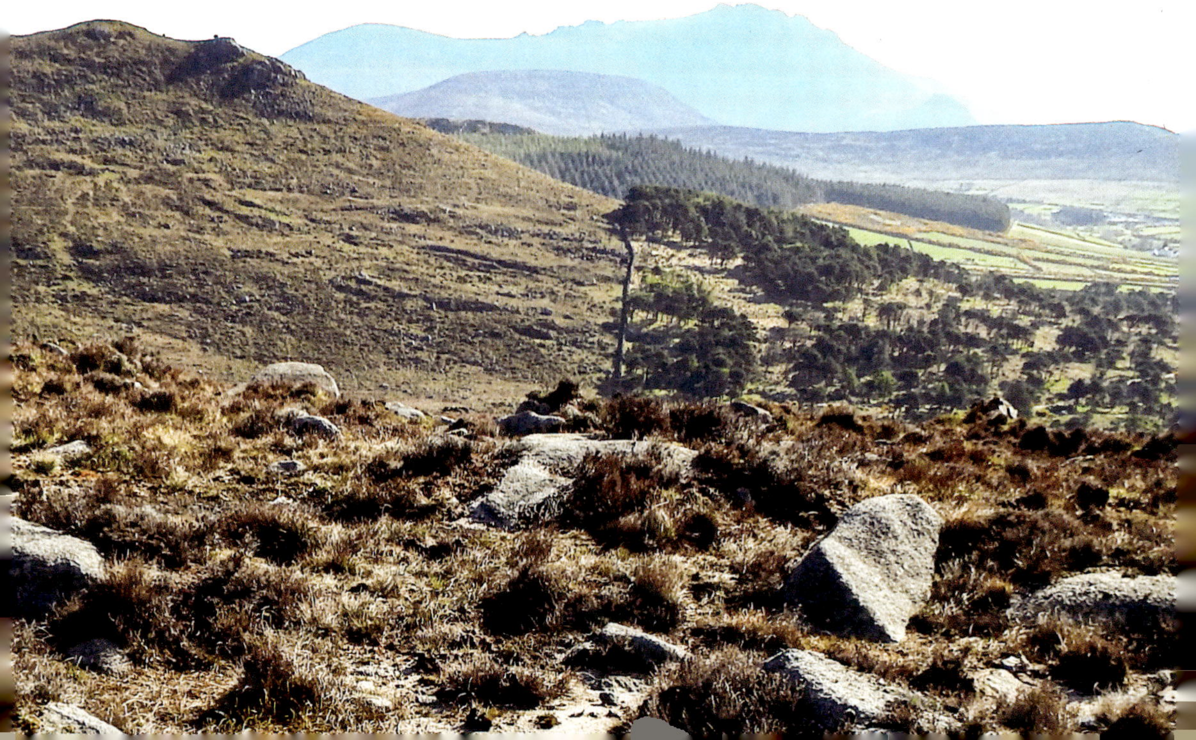

Opposite page: A granite block with a pouty face on the side. At 0.7m high I found it a convenient resting place after the climb up the hill of O'Hanlon's Ladder in the Windy Gap Valley. The stone is included here as much to locate the place-name of O'Hanlon's Ladder which is not on the ordnance survey maps. The name was happily supplied by a local farmer. O'Hanlon's Ladder is the slope immediately to the west in Windy Gap valley once you have passed up the lane beyond the last house and through the farmer's gate at the end. The name is a mnemonic of the Irish (*Tí na*) **h-Áine Láine Láidre**, 'place of the perfect powerful pleasure', a reference to the phallic profile of Slieve Bignian, shown beyond Slievemageogh in the accompanying photograph. The GPS of the face stone is:

        N.   54º 07. 393'
        W. 006º 04. 600'   Elevation 263m.

Top of this page: With its unhappy looking mouth, this stone earned the name 'grumpy'. It is in the Annalong valley on the north side of the little river coming down from Upper Cove plateau. The back of the boulder is covered in heather but we are still looking at a stone 2m from front to back and about 2.5m across by 1.5m high; yet another big megalith. The GPS is:

        N.   54º 09. 999'
        W. 005º 56. 897'   Elevation 321m.

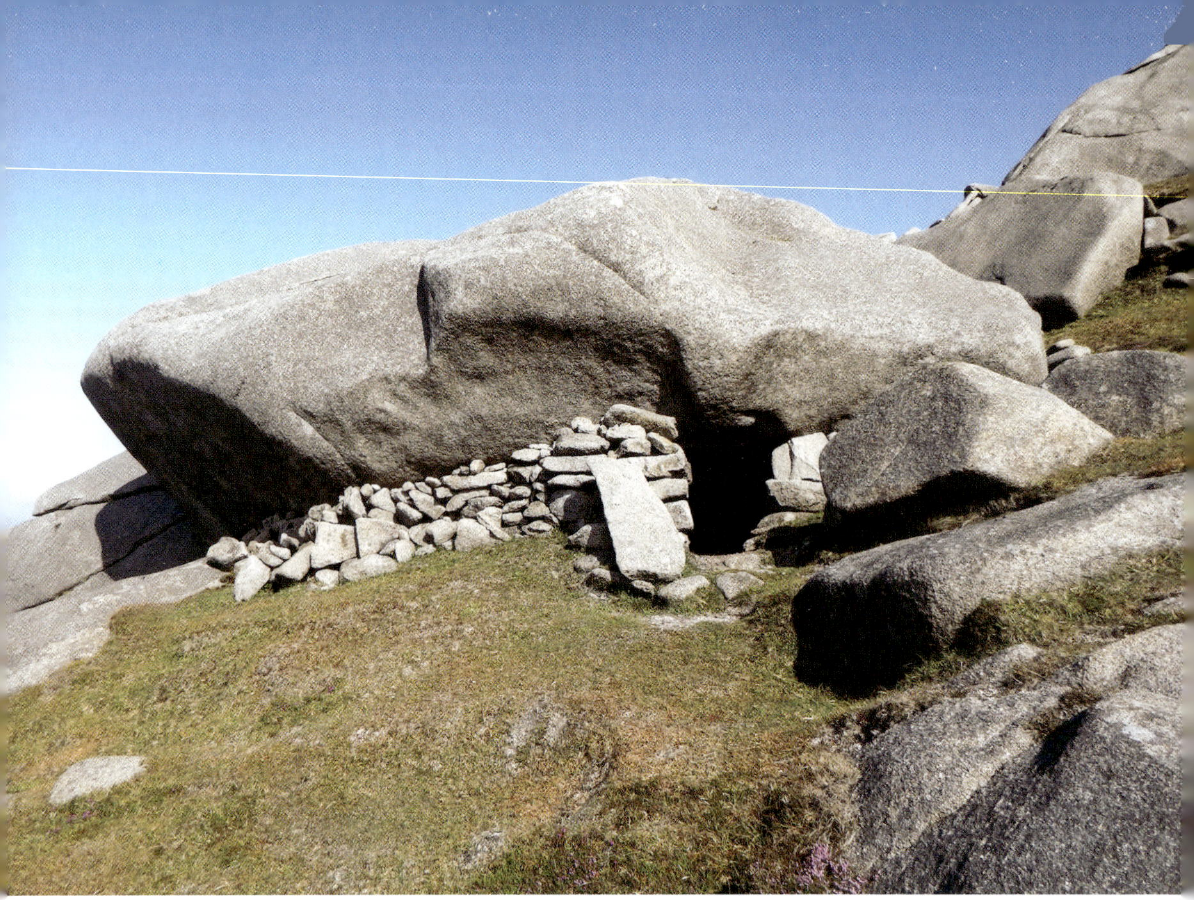

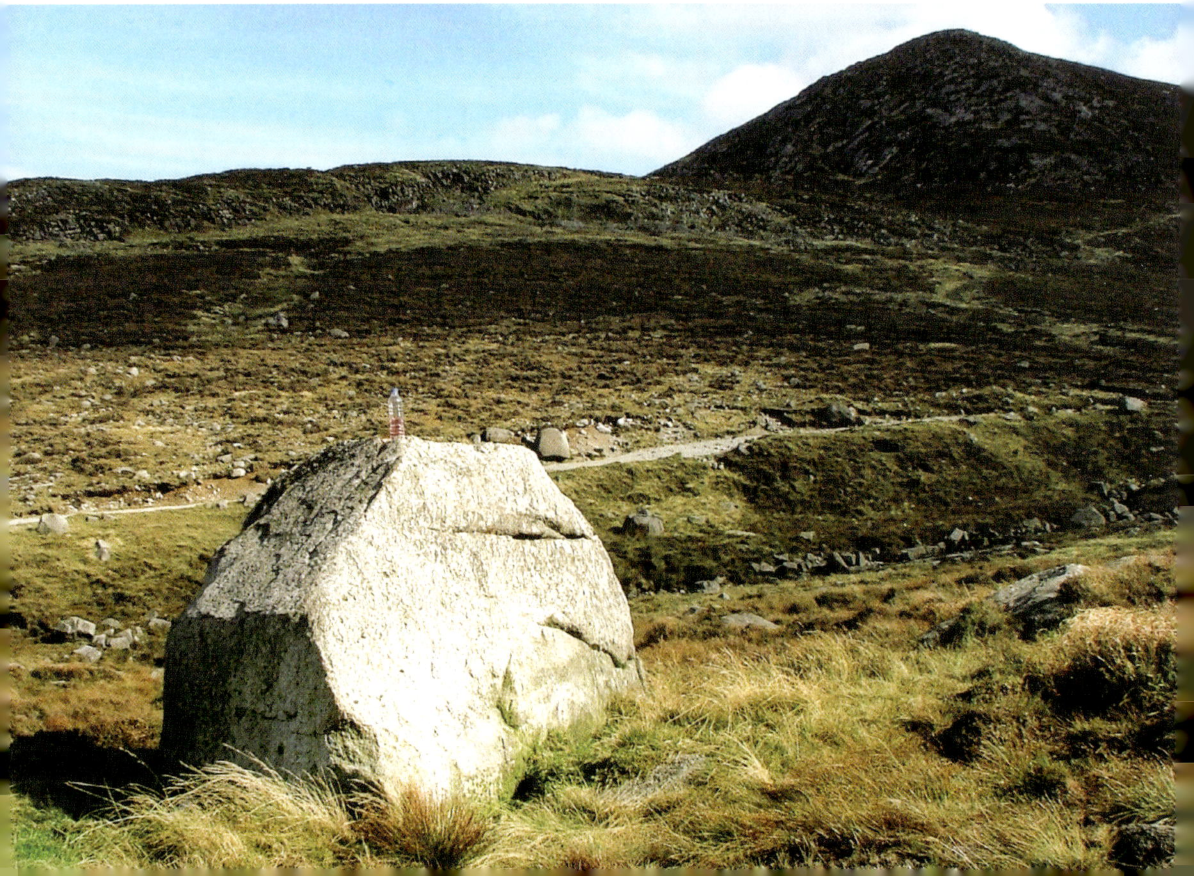

Top opposite: This truly immense stone worthily deserves the name ***Bothán Sléibhe***, 'A Mountain Shelter'. It is to be found under Slieve Bearnagh's North Tor at GPS:

N. 54º 11. 174'
W. 005º 59. 181'   Elevation 689m.

Stones have been piled up around the bottom to create a shelter underneath. The door faces the mountain shoulder where summer solstice sun will appear. It is more than likely that the builders of the Mourne Wall availed of shelter here while they worked on Bearnagh. You could crawl into the cavity underneath if you were desperate for shelter but there is no height at all and you would need to bring a lot of heather to make the slightest semblance of a shred of comfort. This mighty shelter stone is about 10m long, say about 4m high and nearly 5m across at the door; it is a monumental stone that would have required a comparable mighty effort. Indeed, this is probably how the 'North' tor of Bearnagh got its name. It derives from the Irish ***Neart*** meaning 'physical strength' and the raison d'être for the stupendous efforts likely lies with this being a fertility location marking where winter solstice sun declines onto the perceived phallic summit tor of Bearnagh casting its shadow across the distance in between.

Lower opposite: This scowling face stone sits at the corner of Spellack. It has a well worked shadow eye. The Trassey track is in the background and brooding Shimial mountain is on the right. Shimial mountain is not marked on the ordnance survey; it is from the Irish ***Sidh Mí-Áil***, 'blast of evil pleasure'.

Top of this page: A big granite block on the western slope of the Annalong valley has a good face and a nose pointed to Chimney Rock. It is both a counter-balance to the boulder below it and, with its up raised nose, doubles as an erect phallic stone. The GPS is:

N. 54º 10. 156'
W. 005º 56. 958'   Elevation 413m.

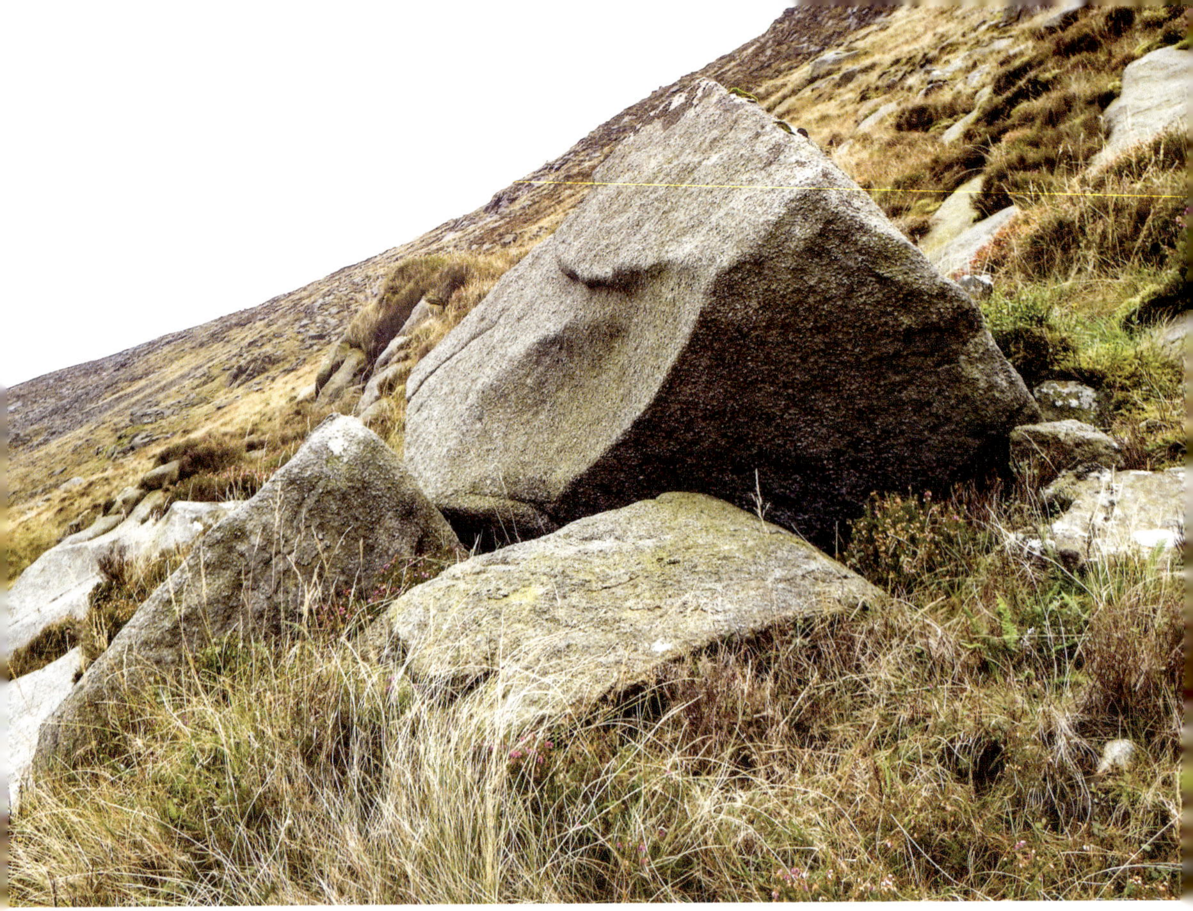

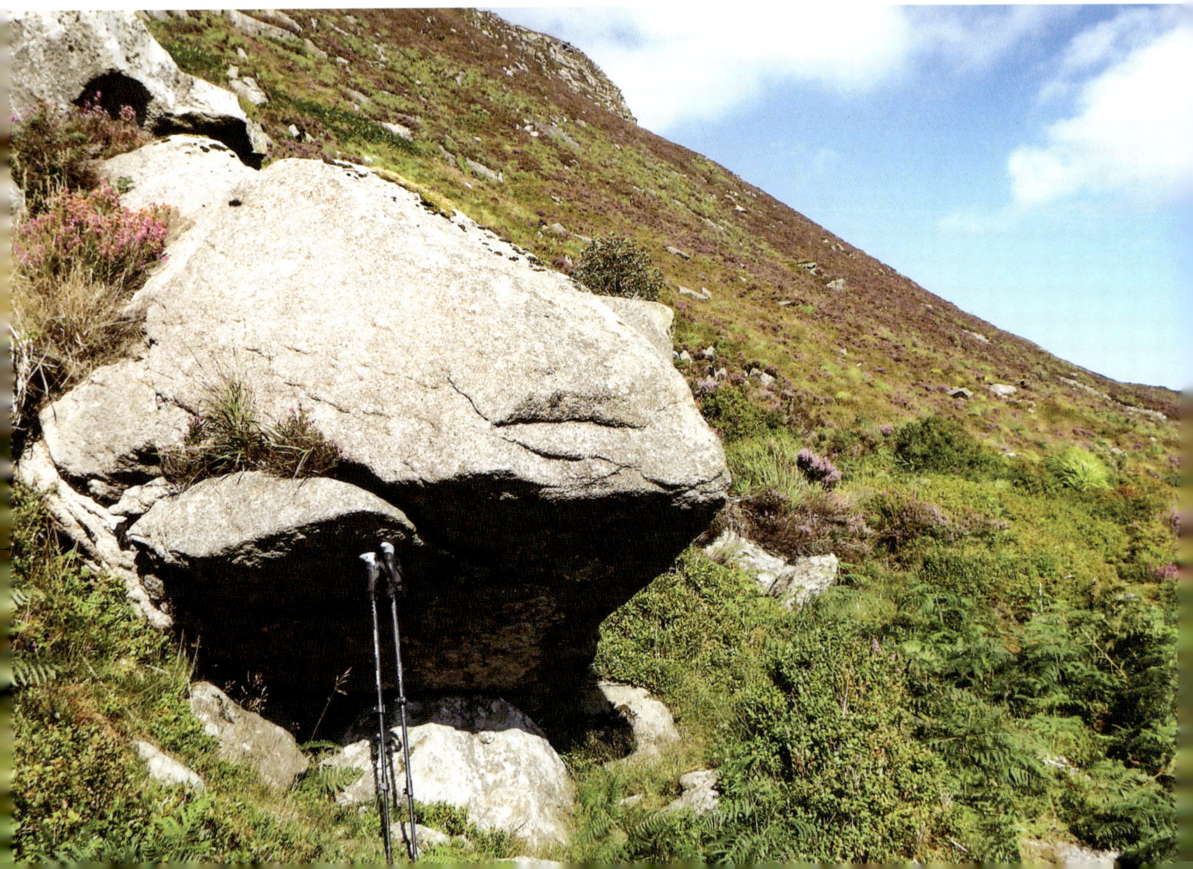

Top opposite: The brooding face on this great granite boulder looks out over Happy Valley from its place high on the south slope. Not for the first time the steep slope causes wonder at how such a weighty boulder was manoeuvred; there must have been lots of skill, daring and brute strength. The GPS is:

N. 54° 11. 407'
W. 006. 00. 856'   Elevation 447m.

Lower opposite: This is a gigantic face stone found in the south side of the Windy Gap valley at a place known as the 'Hole of the Scar'. It is only one of a number of awesome creations at this location. 'Hole of the Scar' is from the Irish (*Tí na*) **h-Olla-Scairbhe**, '(place of the) huge hardness', a reference to the phallic profile of Slieve Bignian.* This is quite distinct from another 'Hole of the Scar' found on Slieve Muck. Phallic Bignian was deemed to come to sexual climax as the sun rose at dawn of summer solstice. Nothing less could warrant the prodigious physical effort expended here. At the top left of the photograph can be seen part of the masterful monument 'The Hawk', which is looked at in the next chapter. It is an even bigger creation and there are other glorious monuments as well that collectively leave one astounded and humbled at the magnitude of labour and exertion involved.

Top of this page: A deep hooded face stone on the slopes of Slievemageogh overlooks the Moyad Road.

* See pages 313 & 314 of *Places-Names of Beanna Boirrche*, published 2021.

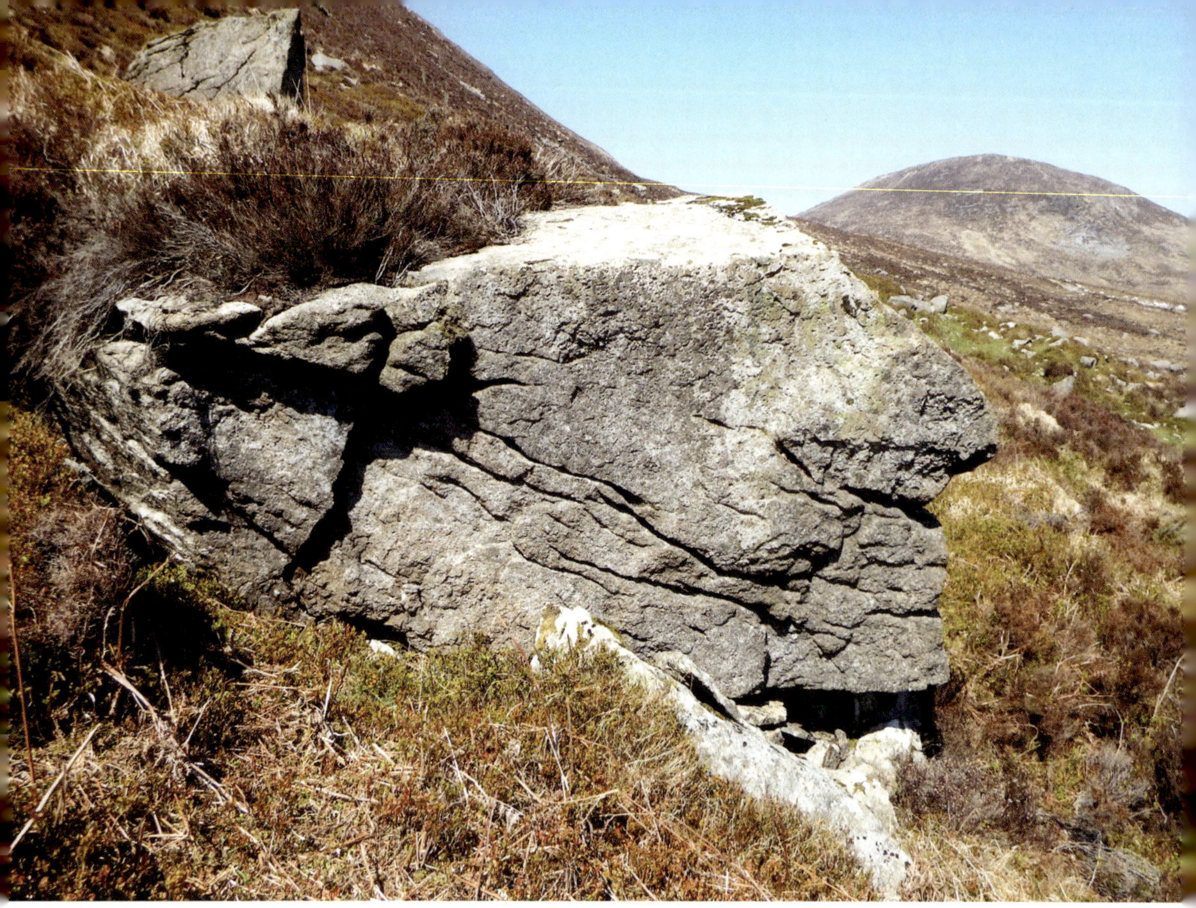

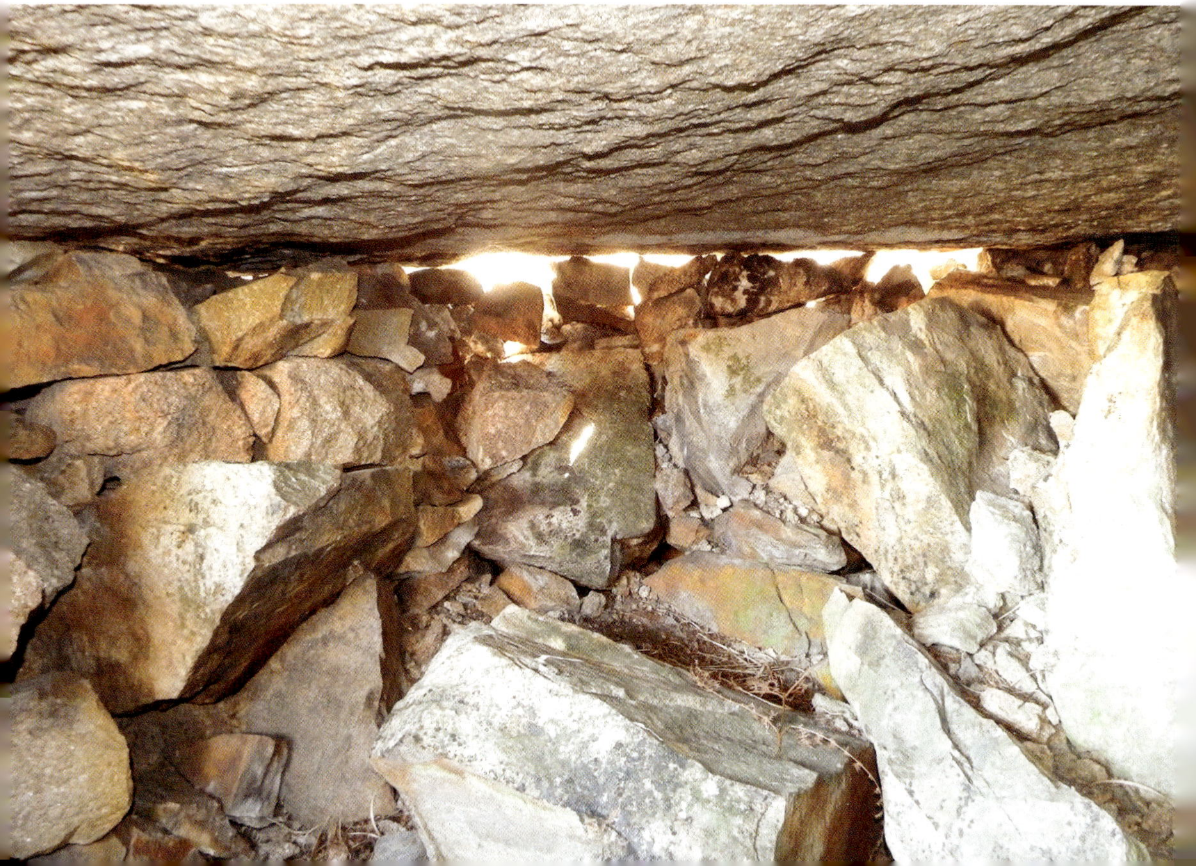

Opposite page: Here is another mighty block with a profusion of faces. It is found at the 'Hole of the Scar' area on the west side of the Windy Gap valley. This monster stone is at least 5m long. The back is all overgrown with heather and grass so it could be even longer. It is 3m across at the front and a comfortable 2m high; a most substantial stone indeed. Enormous work would have been required in the moving. The stone has been named **Carraig na gCaidhe**, 'Rock of the Space Underneath' as this is the main feature. The space below has obviously been used and the accompanying photograph shows how chinking stones have filled in gaps around the bottom edges. The space is not particularly great. There is no question of standing up, stretching out or getting really comfortable but it has the great redeeming feature of being absolutely bone dry. If you get to examine this treasure then note the little phallic stone horns made on the upper surface edge. The GPS is:

      N. 54º 07. 925'
      W. 006º 05. 082' Elevation 270m.

Top of this page: Like a hen brooding an egg the back end of this face stone sits on top of a little boulder as it surveys the magnificent panorama of the Windy Gap valley below. The photo is deceptive as, at 3m, this is actually quite a long phallic stone. The business end points to the 'vaginal gap' between Slievemoughanmore and Pigeon. The GPS is:

      N. 54º 07. 684'
      W. 006º 04. 902' Elevation 359m.

Incidentally, the locals never use the OS name Moughanmore but invariably call the mountain Slimageen which comes from the Irish *Sliabh Magh-Geine*, 'mountain of the huge woman', a figure of speech, a synedoché, where the mountain was looked on as a vulva.

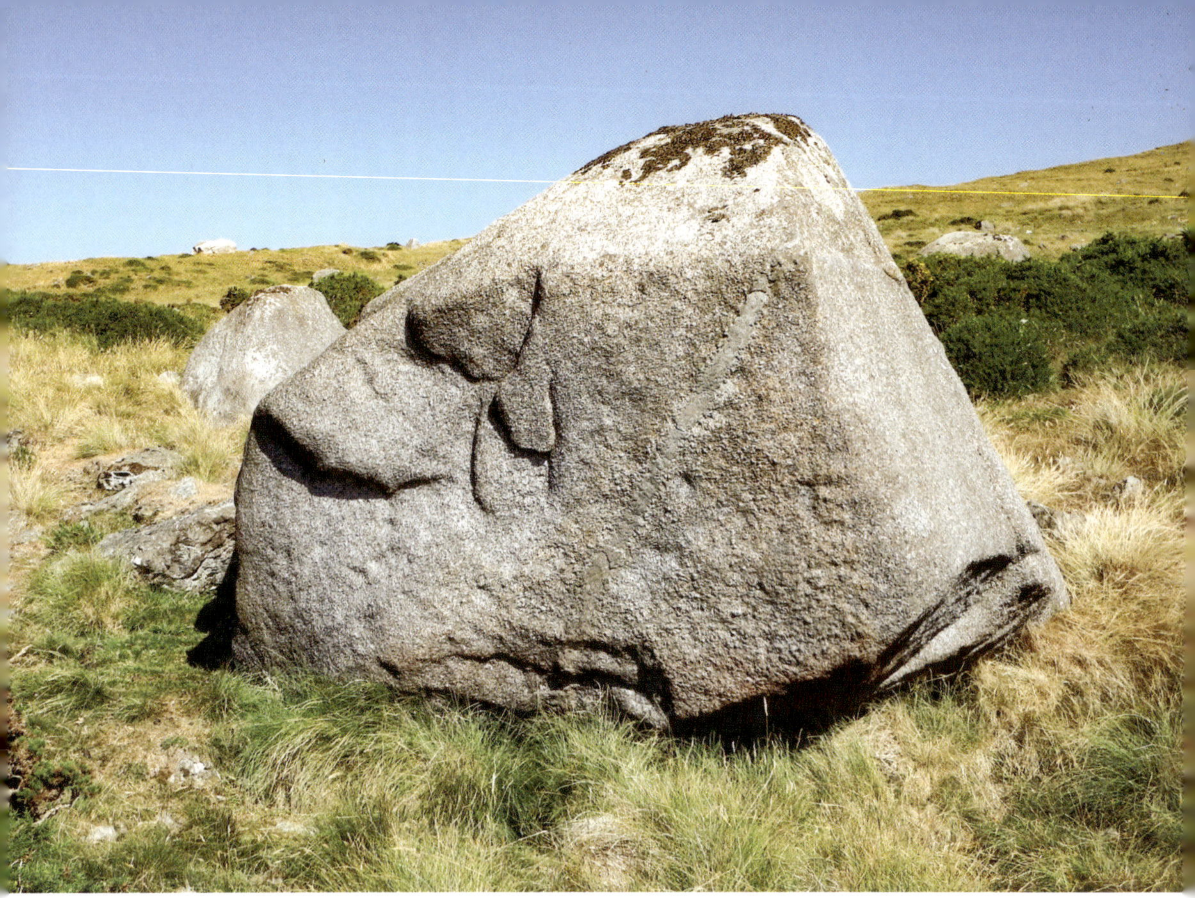
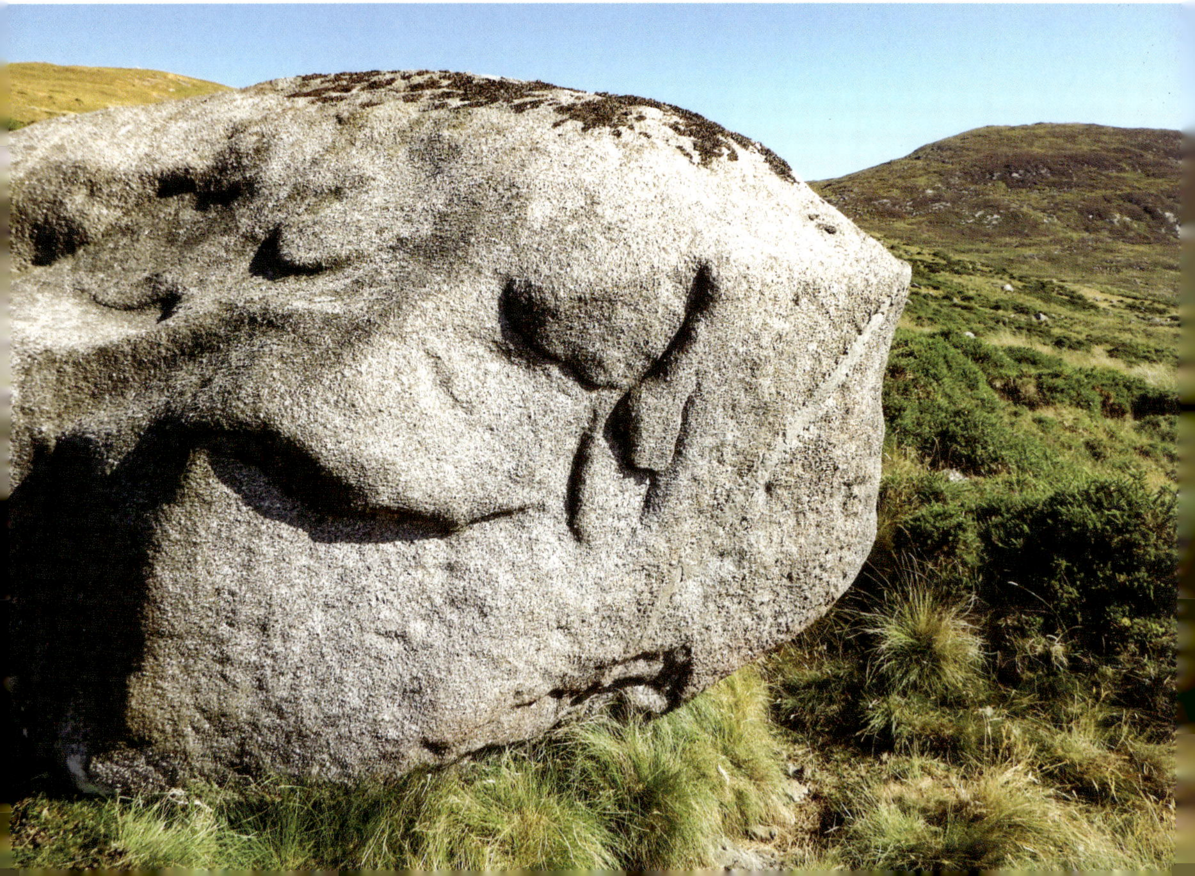

Opposite page: There are many other dog, canine or wolf depictions on rocks across the Mournes besides the three featured here. On the west side of Luke's mountain is a huge boulder with the muzzle on the side of mighty looking mastiff. To be correct there are two dogs depicted on this stone. On the other side, as shown in our second photograph, the head is turned round to look at the tiny 'pup' stone placed at the rear. The little low stone at the back (not shown) does not look much like a pup but it does have a 'face' on it. The boulder is roughly 3m long, 2.5m wide and 2m high. This is a megalith that is great in size, character and artistic representation. The GPS is:

        N.   54º 12. 542'
        W. 005º 58. 195'   Elevation 285m.

Top of this page: Another dog face megalith, this time to be found on the northern slope of Chimney Rock mountain. The image is found on the wide side of the stone. As the shadow suggests this is only a sliver of a granite stone. It looks out over Dundrum Bay and the nose of the 'dog' points to summer solstice sunrise. This is a phallic stone. It is not upright but set at a suggestive angle that is not discernible in the photograph.

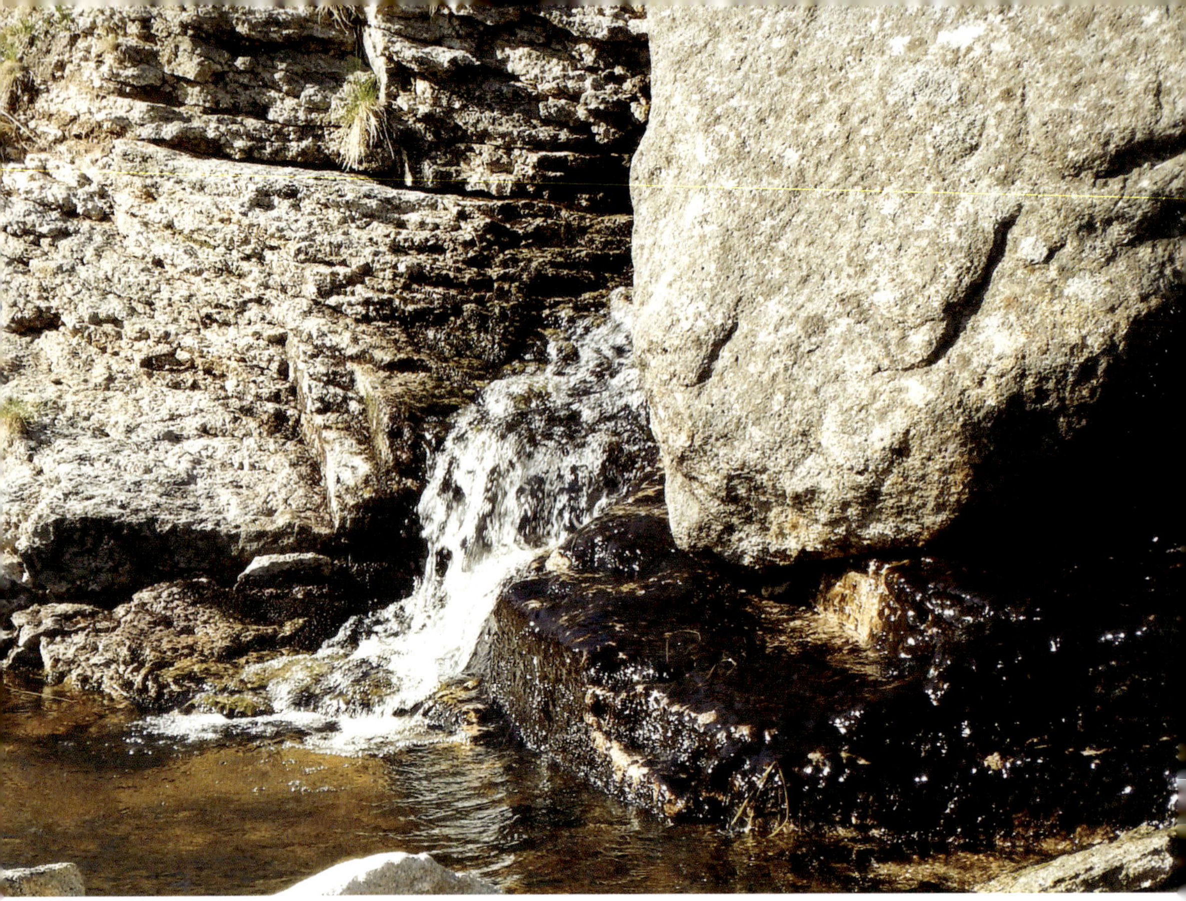

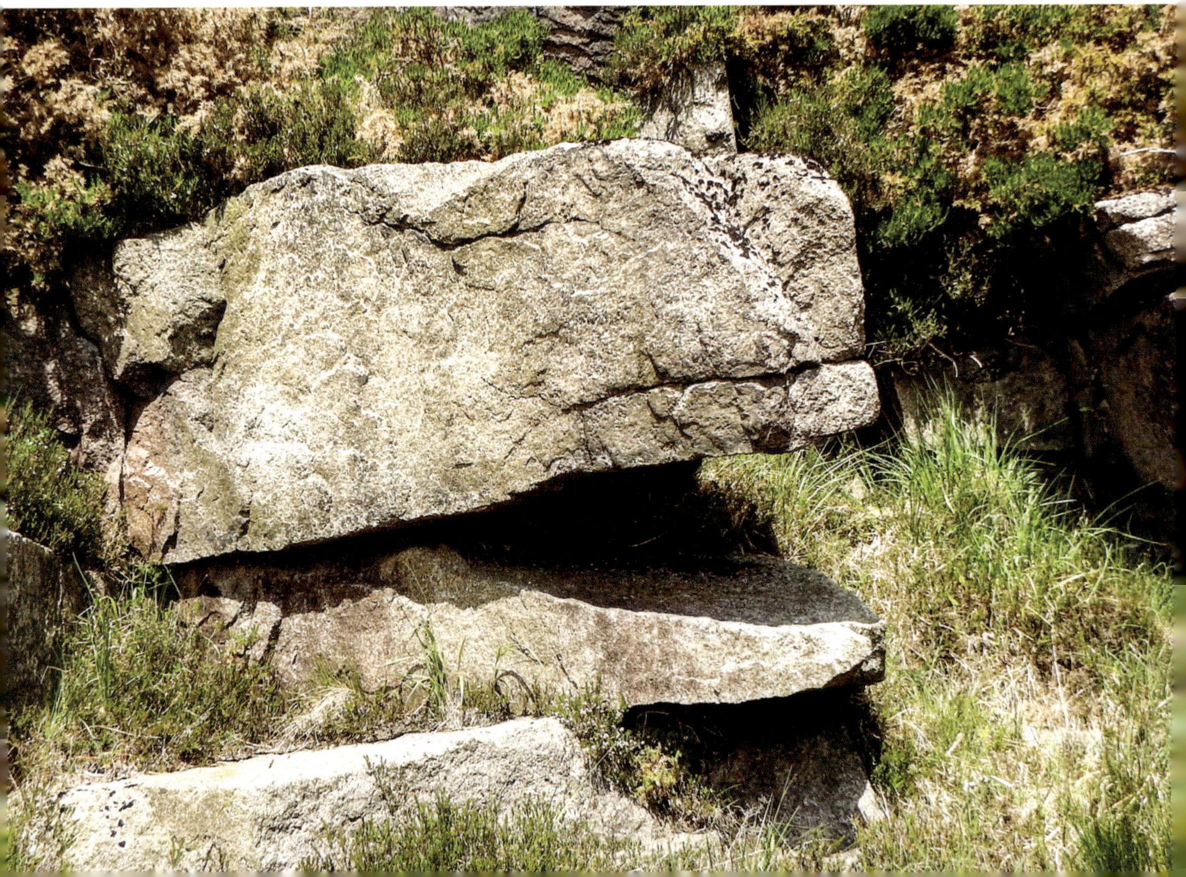

Top opposite: A beautiful representation of a feline having a drink is to be found along the Aughnaleck river. This is a small stone but the look of the cat-like creature is so good it certainly deserves attention. This is a masterful depiction.

Lower opposite: This image is on the west slope overlooking the Annalong valley. A projecting bit of granite that faces over towards Chimney Rock mountain has been skilfully decorated with a most realistic leonine face. The set of the lower stone that makes for an open mouth recalls a line from the great African novelist, Wilbur Smith, 'Even the bravest of men trembles the first time he hears the roar of the lion.' (The Burning Shore). The GPS is:

                      N.　54° 09. 993'
                      W. 005° 57. 023'　　Elevation 399m.

Top of this page: A very feline megalith atop Slieve Beg.

On Donard's south flank and above Crossone mountain, seen here at top right, are profile stones of a cat and mouse, an early version of Tom and Jerry. The rivals are about fifteen metres apart and, no doubt, are keeping a close eye on each other. You can't say the ancients didn't have a sense of humour. Both sides are shown of a slim megalith of a seated cat; nowadays we would think of the cartoon character 'Tom'.

Tom's view of Jerry up the slope.

MEGALITHIC MOURNE

These photographs, showing a pig on a shoulder, all recall the tale of the Otherworld in *Togail Bruidne Dá Derga* (The Destruction of Da Derga's Hostel) where the lord of the feast was sometimes represented as a man carrying a pig on his shoulder. This Irish tale belongs to the Ulster Cycle of Mythology and is part of the 'Book of the Dun Cow'. It is considered one of the finest Irish sagas and comparable to the better-known *Táin Bó Cúailnge*. The Book of the Dun Cow (*Lebor na hUidre*) is an Irish vellum manuscript dating to the 12th century but these images in stone are likely far earlier and may have played a part in the formation of the story's oral tradition. There are a surprising number of 'pigs on shoulders' in Mourne and others will still likely be discovered.

MEGALITHIC MOURNE

Opposite page: This boulder is on the western top of Chimney Rock near the great summit tor. The outline of a pig can be seen below the shadow eye.

Below: Another instance of 'the pig on the shoulder' can be seen nearby etched onto the side of Chimney Rock's summit tor (shown here in the circle). Two pigs heads would seem to be in play, one facing each way. The tor itself was transformed into a great representation of a wasp. This interpretation is sustained in the strange phrase 'The top of ye mountain fote' in Mercator's map of Ulster 1595. All becomes clear when we realise that 'fote' is really the Irish *Foithe* meaning 'wasp'.

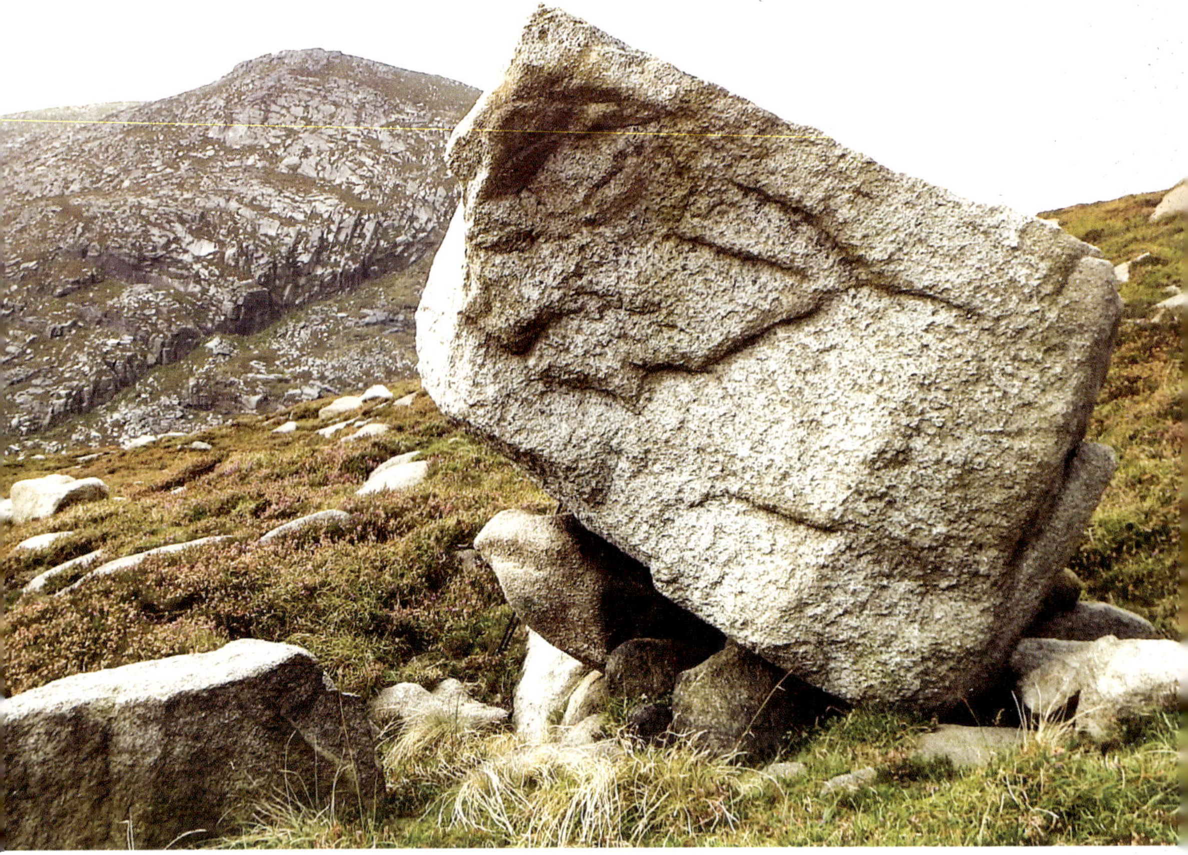

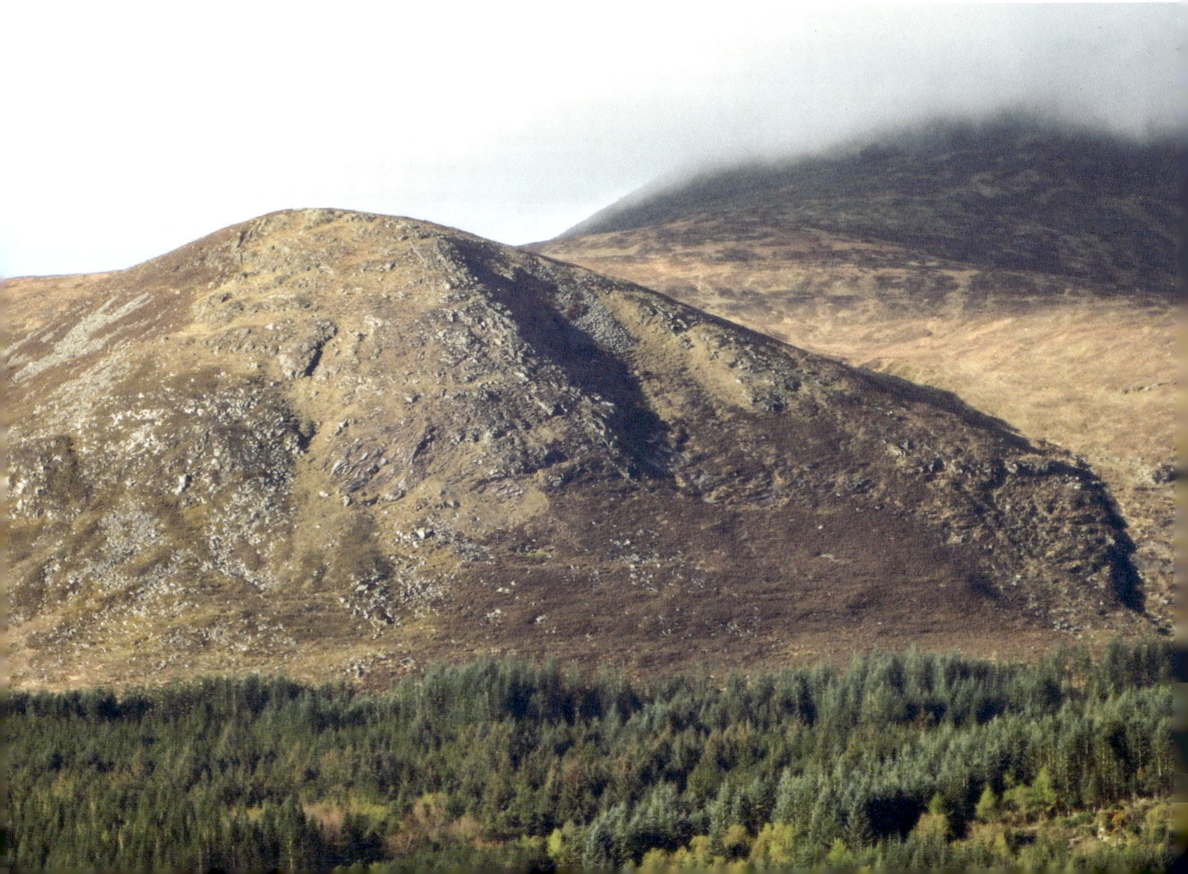

Top opposite: This is a propped phallic stone with the business end pointing to Bignian. It is on the plateau below upper Cove. The first obvious impression is the linear eye in the middle of the stone and a corresponding line for a mouth below. Look again at the upper left side to see the pig on the shoulder with its snout facing downwards. Walk round to view the south side of the stone and it transforms into the profile of a frog. The GPS for this boulder is:

N.   54º 10. 296'
W. 005º 57. 036'   Elevation 483m.

Lower opposite: By the expedient of creating a shadow gully high on the slopes of Slieve Thomas, the ancients transformed the whole front of the mountain into the impression of a boar's head with the snout over at the Black Stairs waterfall to the right. Thomas mountain thus becomes a pig on the shoulder of Donard.

Top of this page: The north tor of Slieve Bearnagh has been shaped like a great boar's head, with a heavy brooding eye and a snub snout. This view is from Slieve Meelmore.

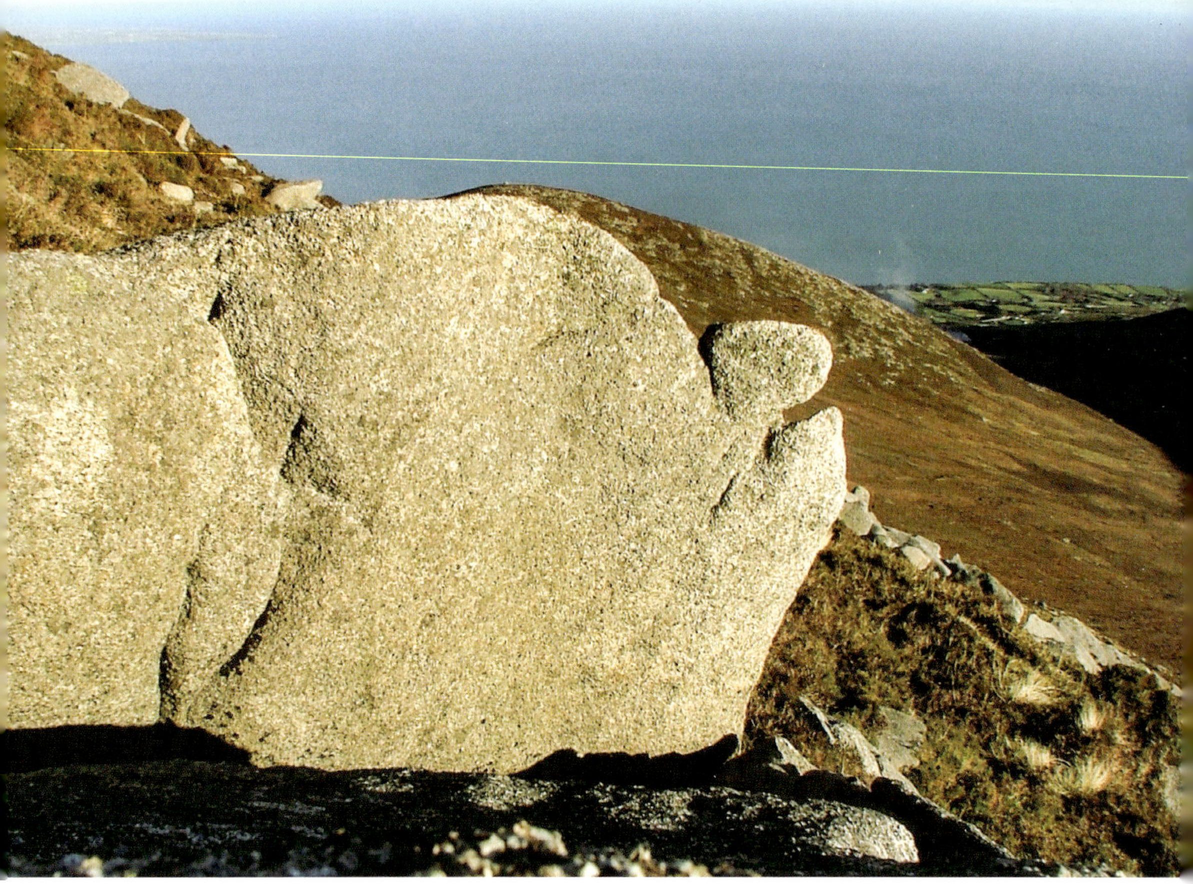

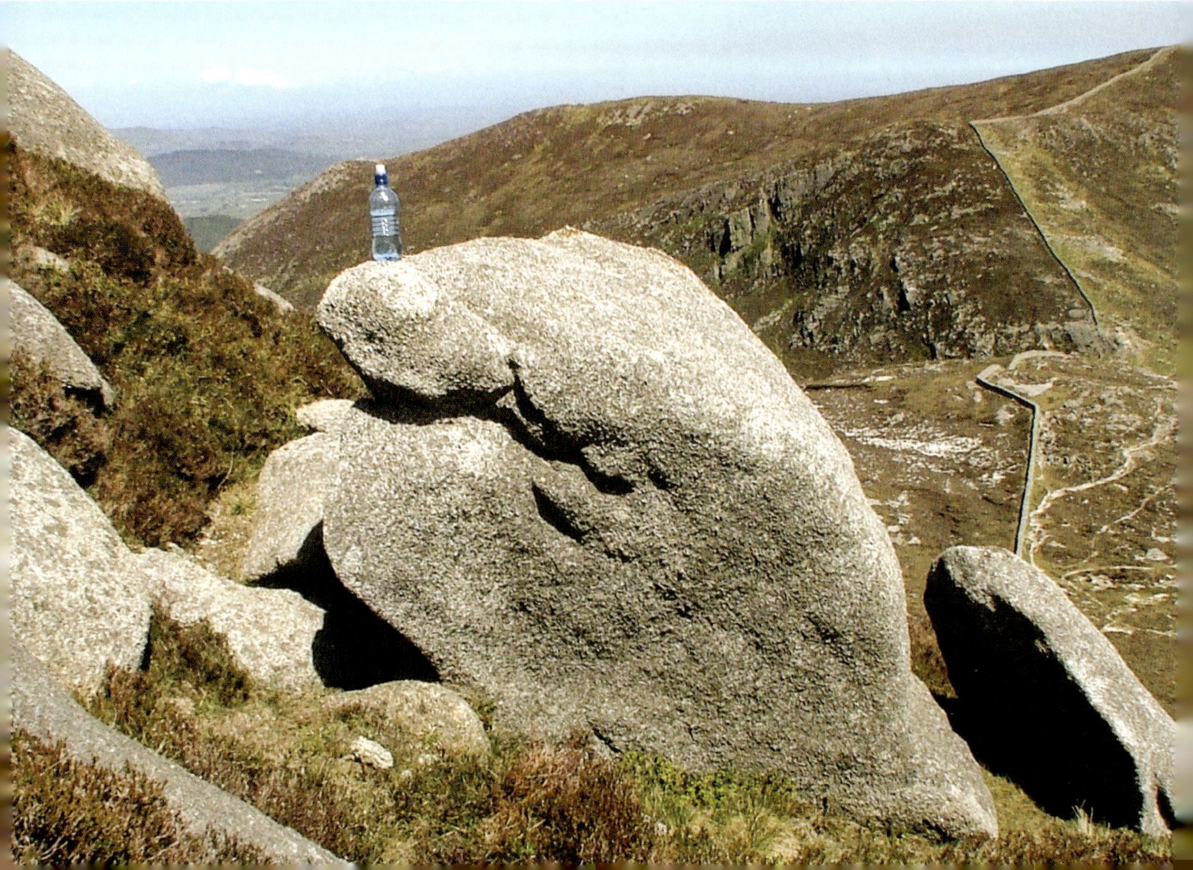

Top opposite: A selection of sore noses found around Mourne. This example of a cauliflower nose is on the south slope of Slieve Donard. Crossone mountain is seen in the background.

Lower opposite: This megalith is found of the eastern slope of Slieve Bearnagh. The poor guy's greatly swollen nose has certainly seen better days. The megalith is to be viewed in conjunction with the shadow slab behind and below. The swollen nose stone is only one labial side of a 'vaginal gap' aligned on summer solstice sunrise. The slab below is the other 'vaginal side'. It is at solstice sunrise that the gap is 'pierced' and notionally fertilized by the sun.

Top of this page: A 2m high spear stone sits on the ridge-line on the south-west side of the Windy Gap valley. A piece of the stone has been broken off to make an open or screaming mouth. Above the mouth is a bulbous cauliflower nose. The GPS for this fighting face is:

N. 54º 07. 701'
W. 006º 04. 914'   Elevation 362m.

Overleaf: we have a block of granite 4m long by 1.75m thick near the front of Cove mountain. It shows the face of a man with a cauliflower nose carrying, at the back, a little pig on his shoulder. The GPS is:

N. 54º 10. 205'
W. 005º 56. 998'   Elevation 452m.

57

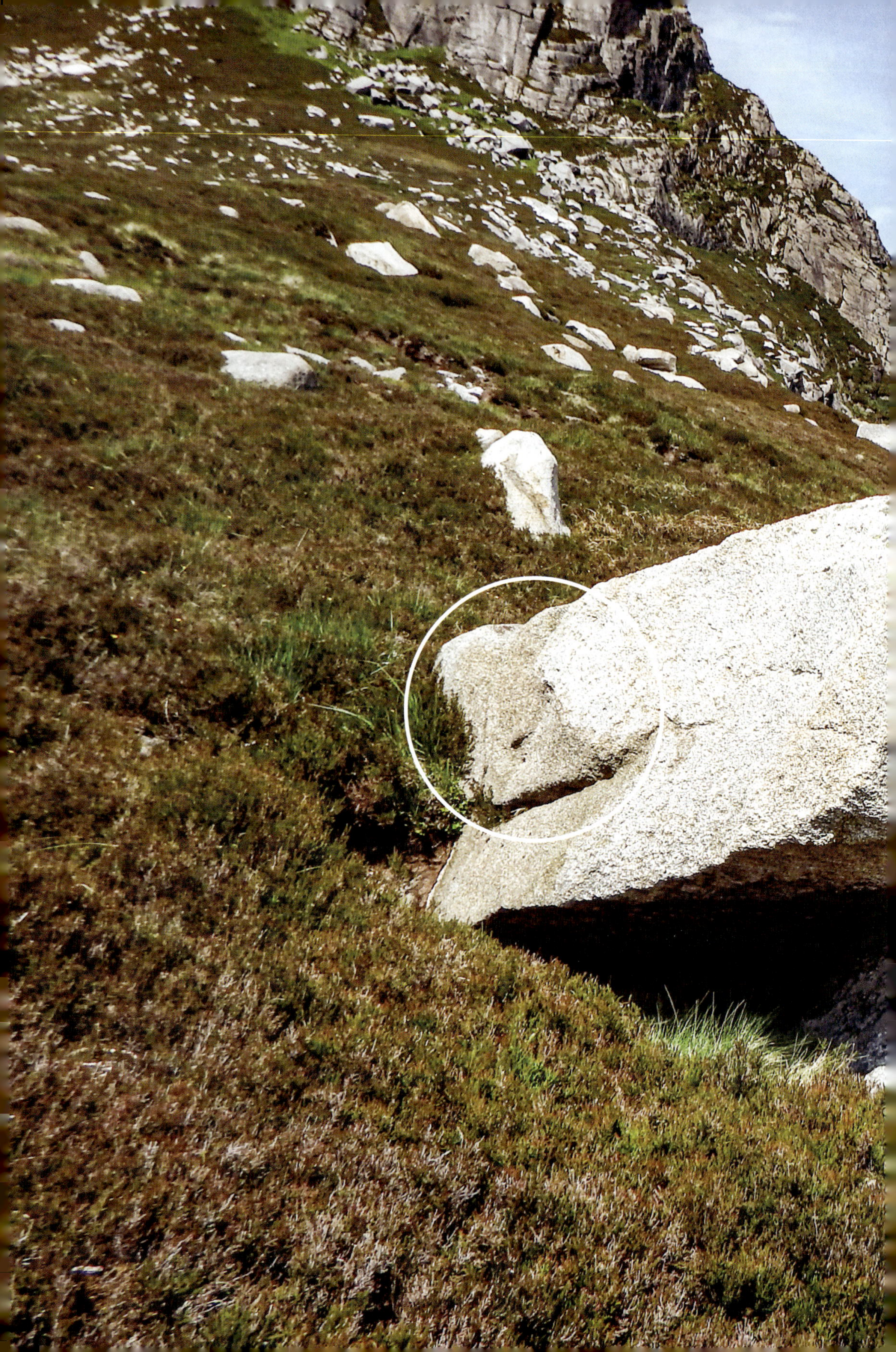

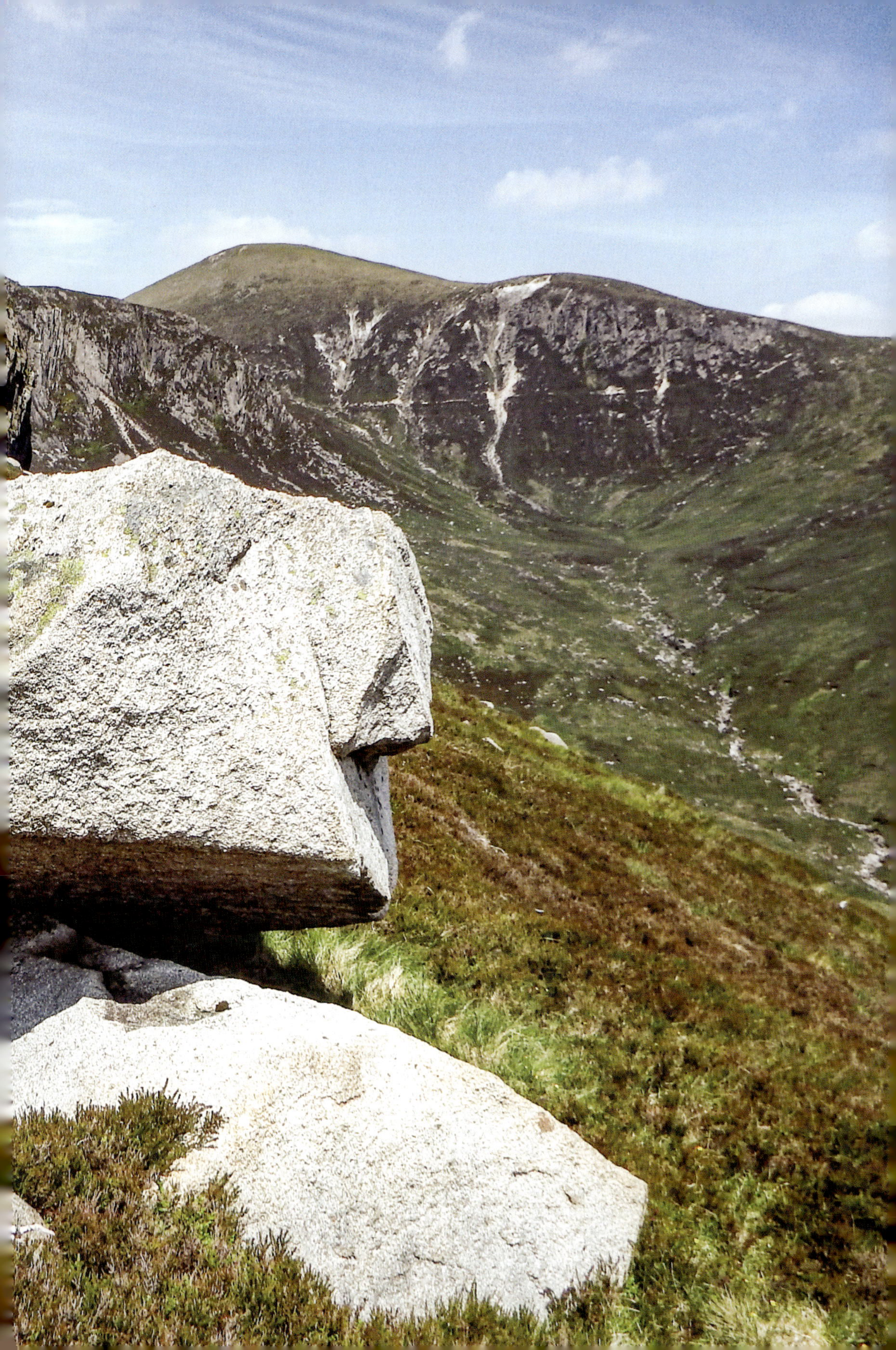

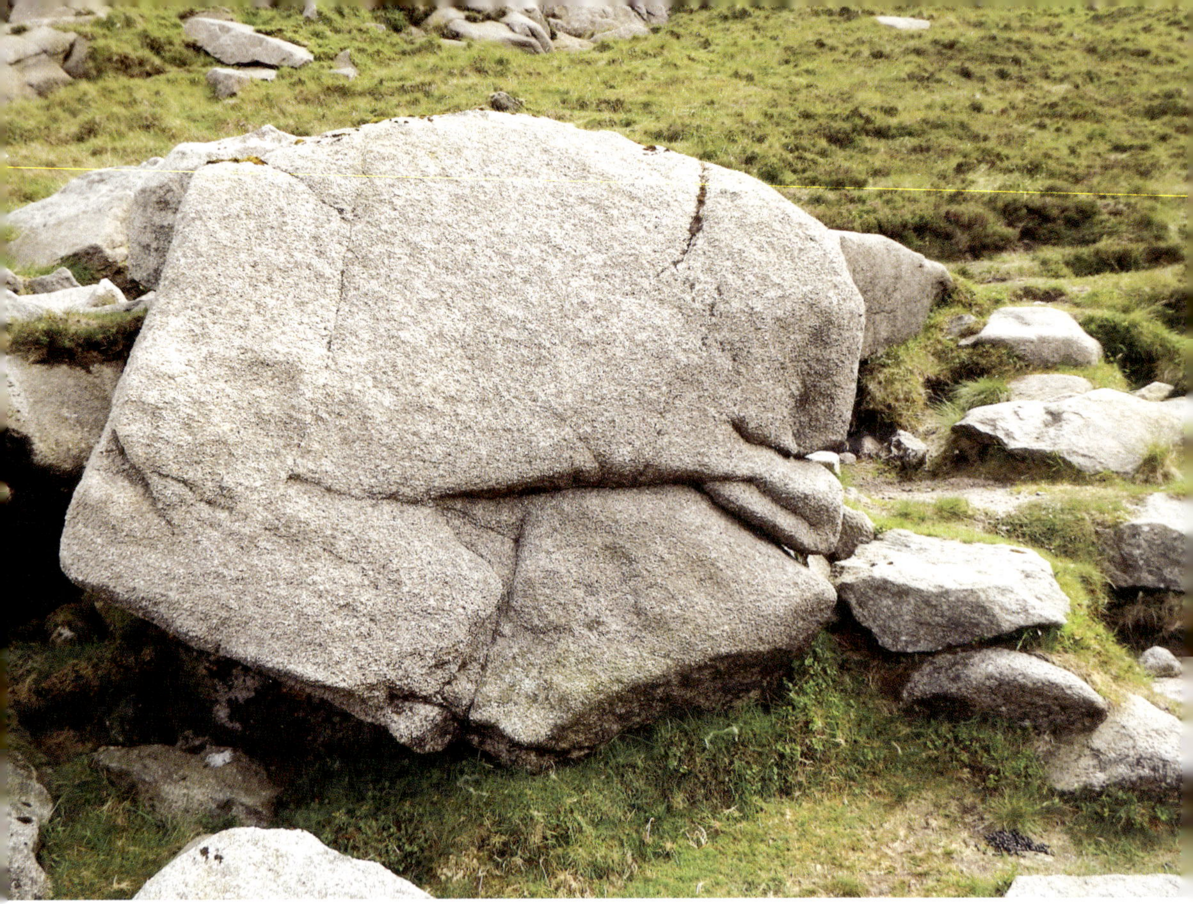

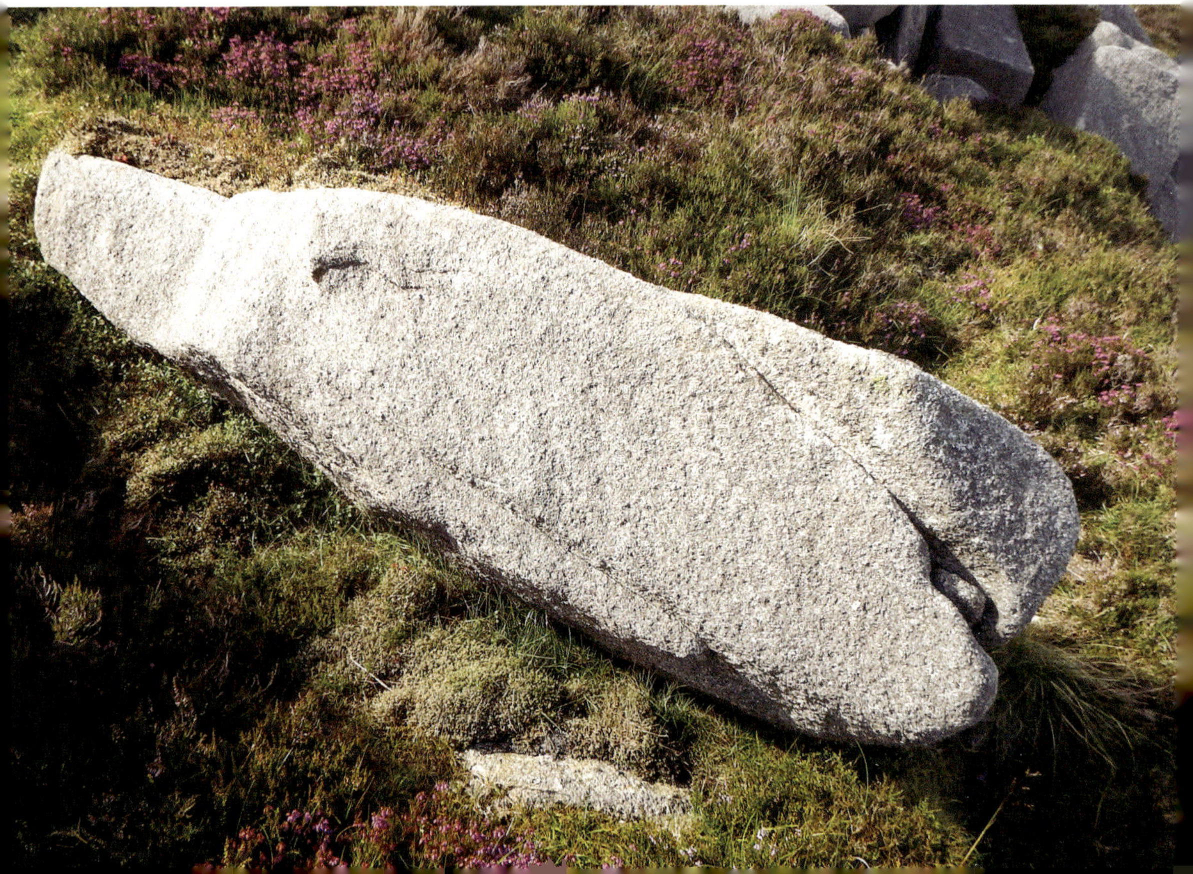

Top opposite: A few pages showing megaliths with tongues sticking out. This face stone with its juicy appendage is up under the slabs of Bearnagh at the upper end of Pollaphuca valley near the Mourne wall. The GPS is:

N. 54° 11. 182'
W. 005° 59. 656'   Elevation 525m.

Lower opposite: This 2.3m single granite stone is to be found high on the southern slope of Meelmore. The carefully crafted little protruding tongue is quite appealing. The stone's lower end points, with phallic import, to Slieve Donard and it also marks the start of a seep or tiny spring, intended no doubt to suggest that this was a remarkable fertile stone indeed.

N. 54° 11. 519'
W. 005° 59. 832'   Elevation 625m.

Top of this page: A great spear of a stone measuring over 3m long by 2m wide is found up on the south side of Happy Valley. It was recorded both on account of the dominant eye as well as the little tongue peeping out. There is also a small delicate eye making another face on the other side. If you get this far then note the extended counter-balance above of a bird at lift-off which has such a pointed nose it is reminiscent of the cartoon image of Margaret Thatcher used for many years by the Times. The GPS is:

N. 54° 11. 411'
W. 006° 00. 861'   Elevation 451m.

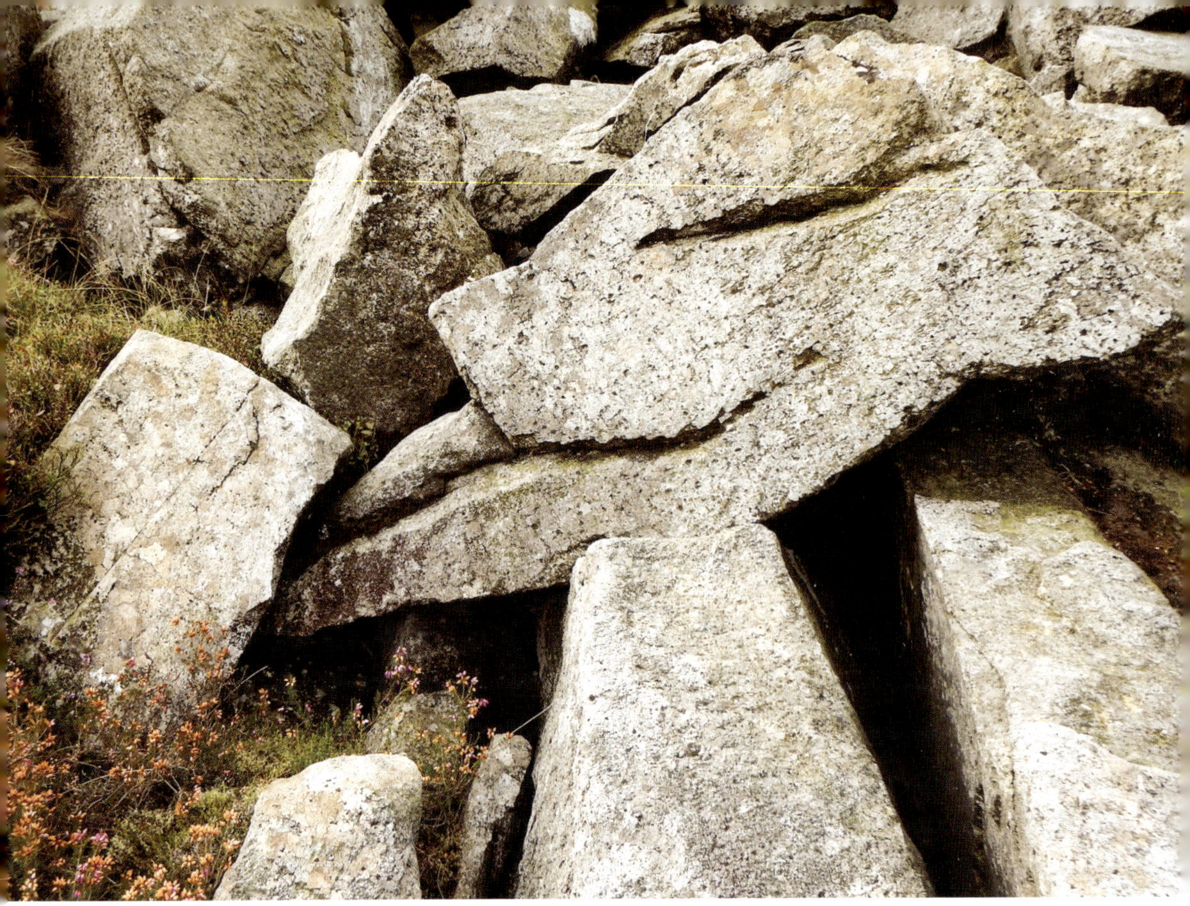

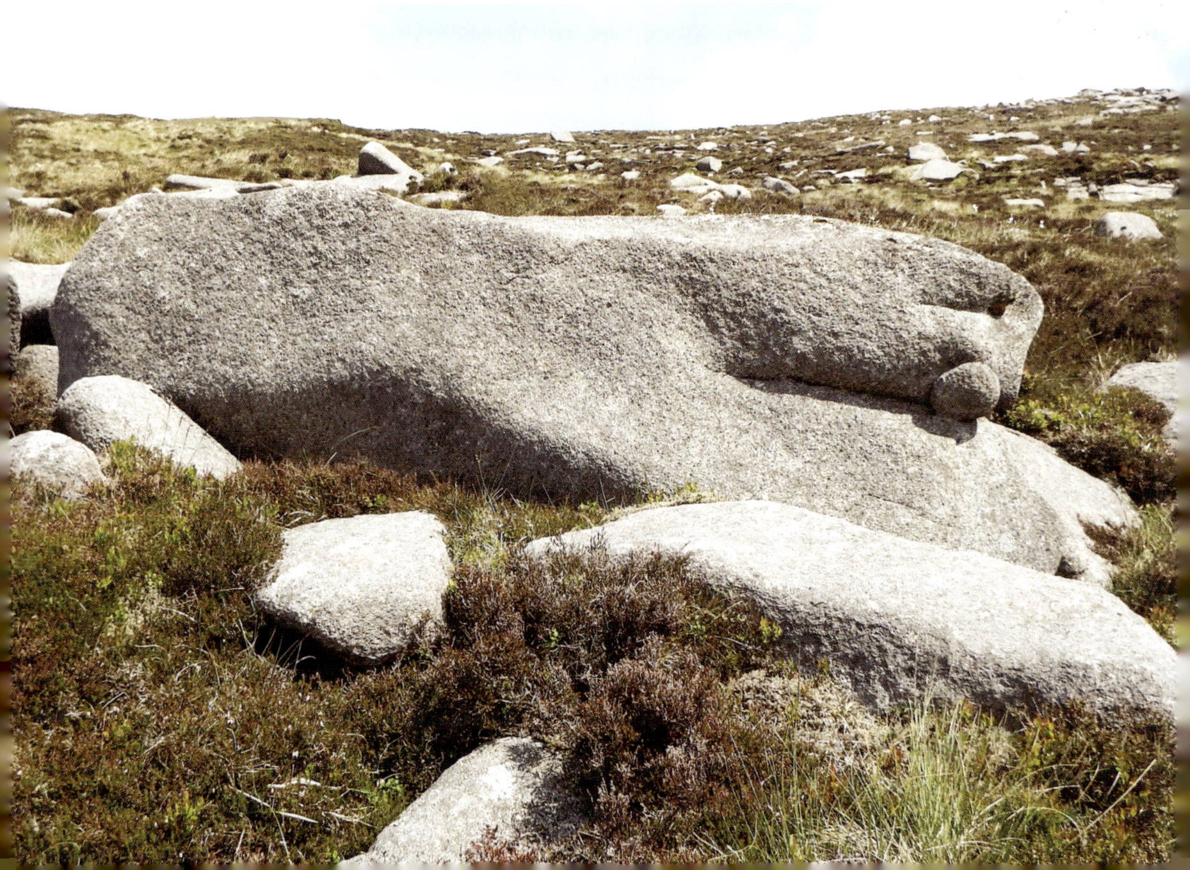

Top opposite: This cheeky stone is under the north corner of Spellack. It is a sculptured face with its tongue out licking the little phallic stone placed in front of it.

N. 54º 11. 992'
W. 005º 59. 456'   Elevation 337m.

Lower opposite: A delightful piece of rock art on a 2.8m long stone showing a face licking its lips. It is on the top north side of Happy Valley also known to the shepherds as Bug Hollow. Note the up-thrusting phallic spear stone on the left background. The GPS is:

N. 54º 11. 260'
W. 006º 00. 251'   Elevation 596m.

Top of this page: There is no mistaking the image on this stone on Slieve Bearnagh's summit tor. It has been given the name **Cloch Lighreac**, 'Stone of Licking'. A deep shadow eye compliments the stuck out tongue. Quarrymen have had a nibble from the back end of the tongue stone for the adjacent Mourne Wall but fortunately without doing damage to the 'head'. The GPS is:

N. 54º 11. 091'
W. 005º 59. 420'   Elevation 739m.

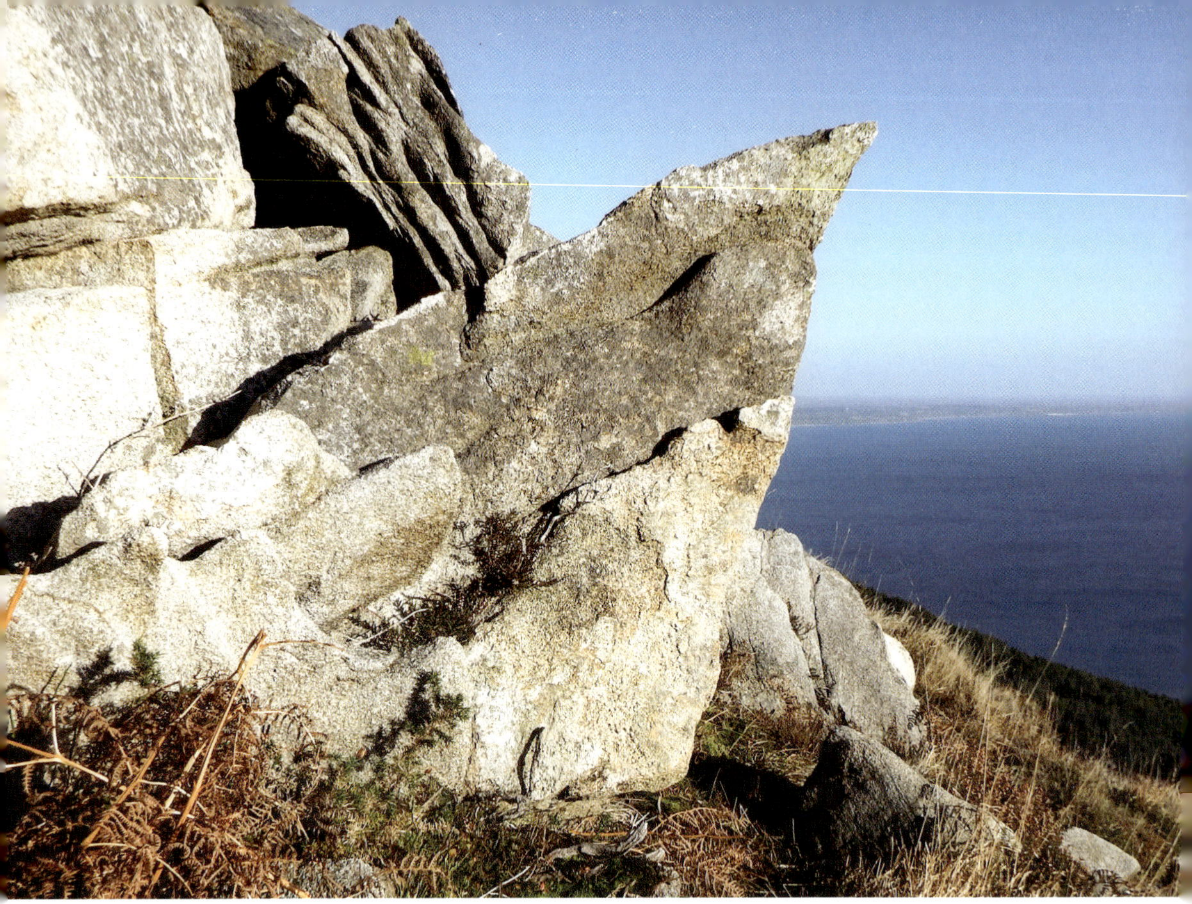

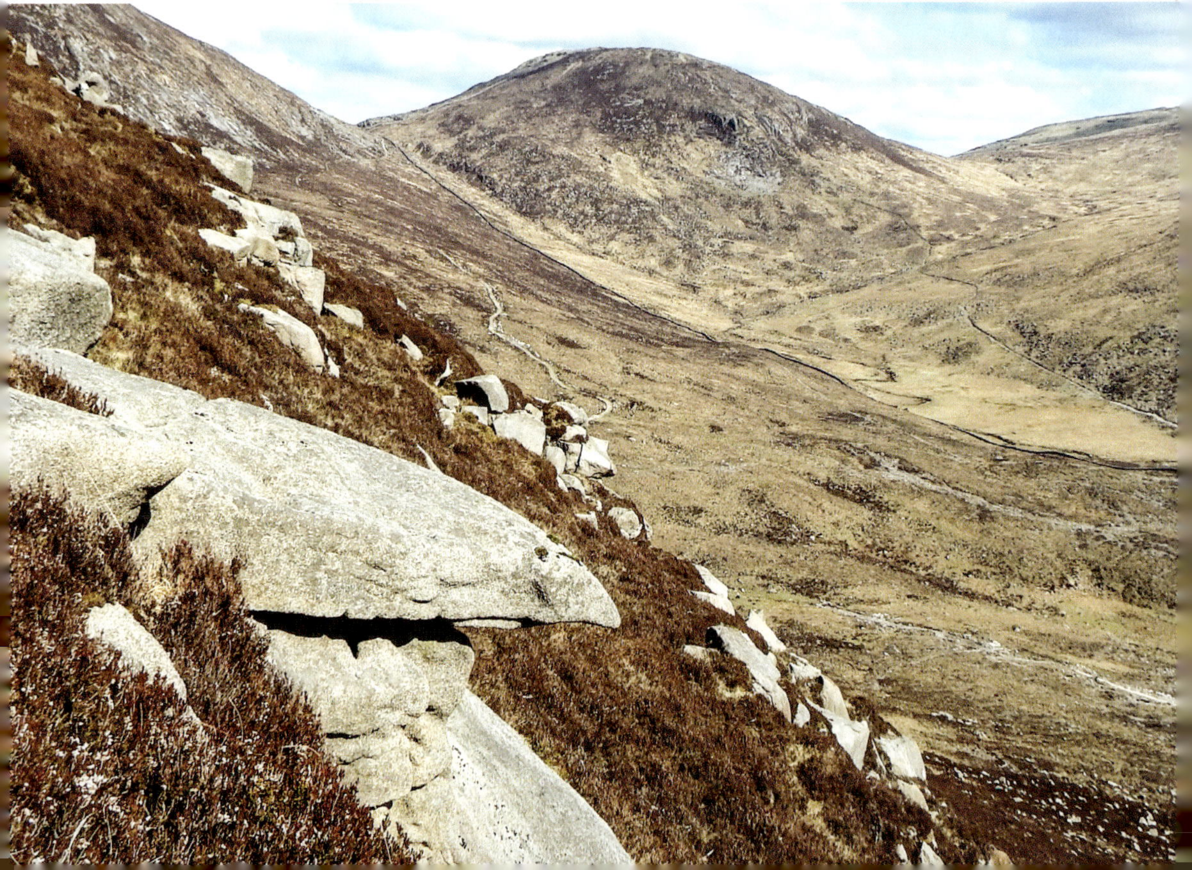

Top opposite: These next number of photographs show birds at the moment of taking to flight. The first 'bird' with its emphatically pointed beak is on the south-east slope of Millstone mountain. The highest tip of the stone is directed to winter solstice sunrise. The GPS is:

                      N.   54º 11. 042'
                      W. 005º 53. 589'   Elevation 338m.

Lower opposite: You have to see this face from the side to appreciate the artwork at the tip as it is not visible from the top of the stone. The oeuvre shows the head of a hawk-like bird about to launch itself off the top of the cliff. Such a stone is known in Irish as a **Leachtán** and has no single word equivalent in English. It refers to a slab that has been pushed out over the edge of a cliff and they usually have fertility symbolism. There are many **Leachtán** in Mourne and this one is along the crest of Long Mountain on the south-west side of Windy Gap valley. The GPS is:

                      N.   54º 07. 682'
                      W. 006º 04. 899'   Elevation 359m.

Top of this page: This large granite block on the south-west slopes above the Aughnaleck river depicts a bird ready to launch itself into flight. The beak points over beyond Pigeon mountain where the summer solstice sun declines.

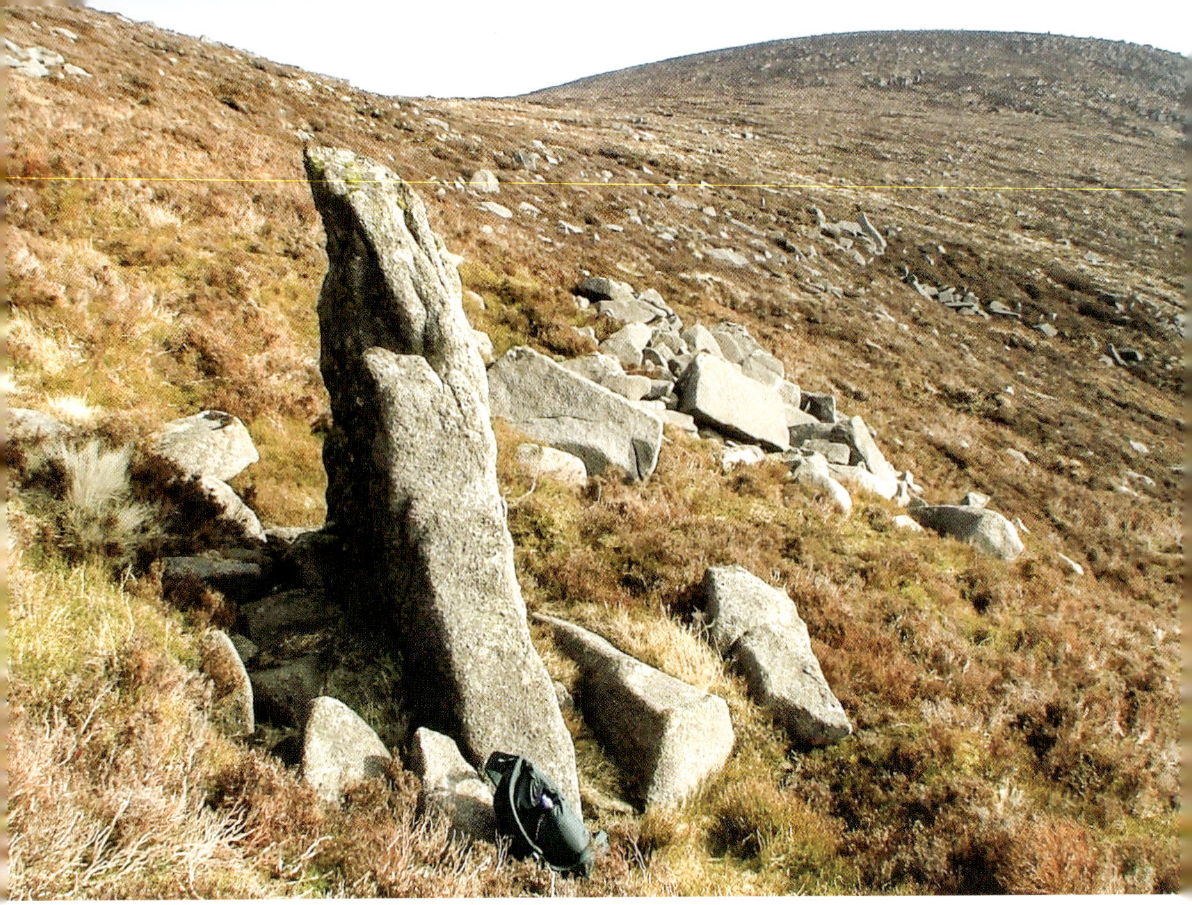

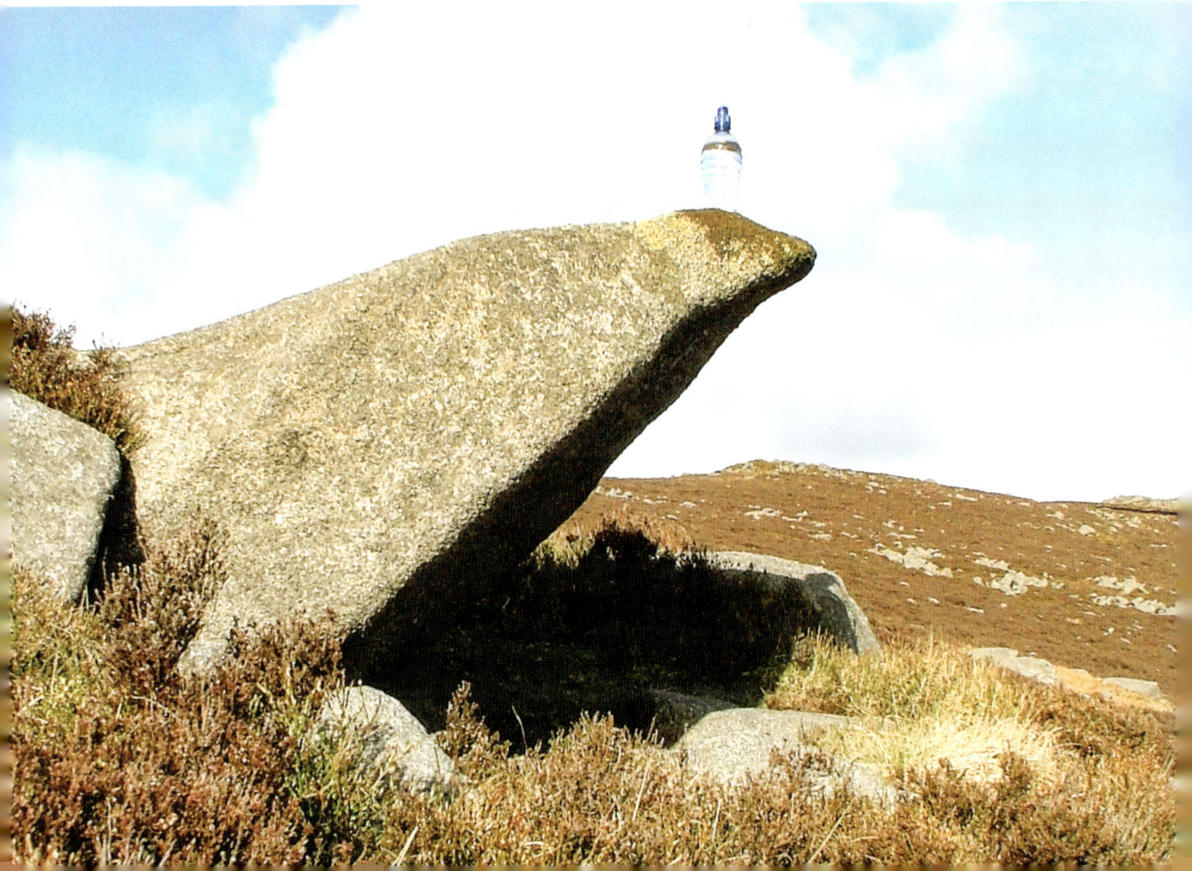

Top opposite: A large triangular spear stone, with a hawk's head remarkably like the nose of Concorde, can be found on the southern flank of Chimney Rock mountain in the act of taking flight. The location is believed to mark where the winter solstice sun sets on one of Bignian's tors.

Lower opposite: This stone is found on the northern flank of Chimney Rock mountain. It's shape is evocative of a bird propelling itself off the ground. The beak of the 'bird' points to summer solstice sunrise across Dundrum Bay.

Top of this page: This might be a bird about to take off but somehow it appears more like a fledgeling with an open maw looking to be fed. The rounded eye and upward pointed beak make a marvellously realistic piece of ancient sculpture. It is found near the crest of Slievemageogh overlooking the Moyad Road.

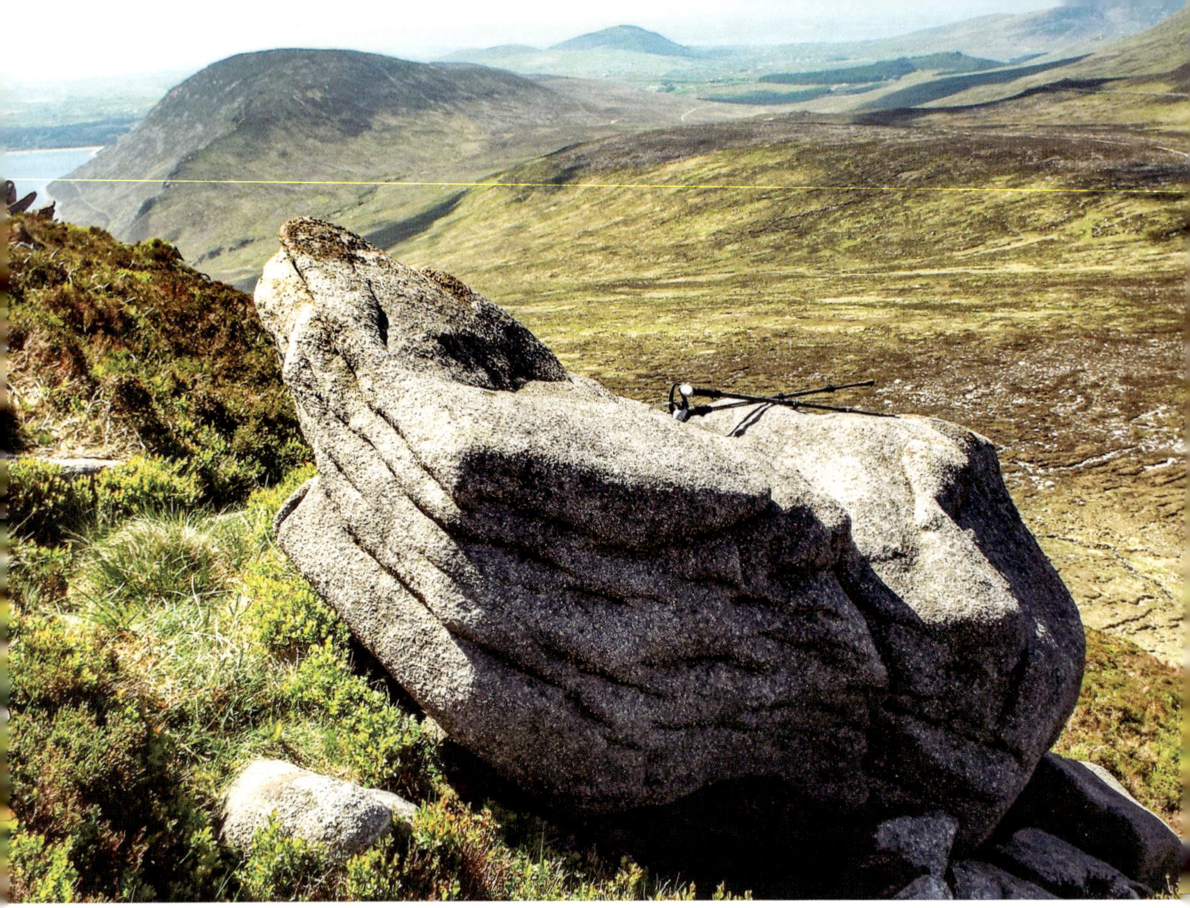

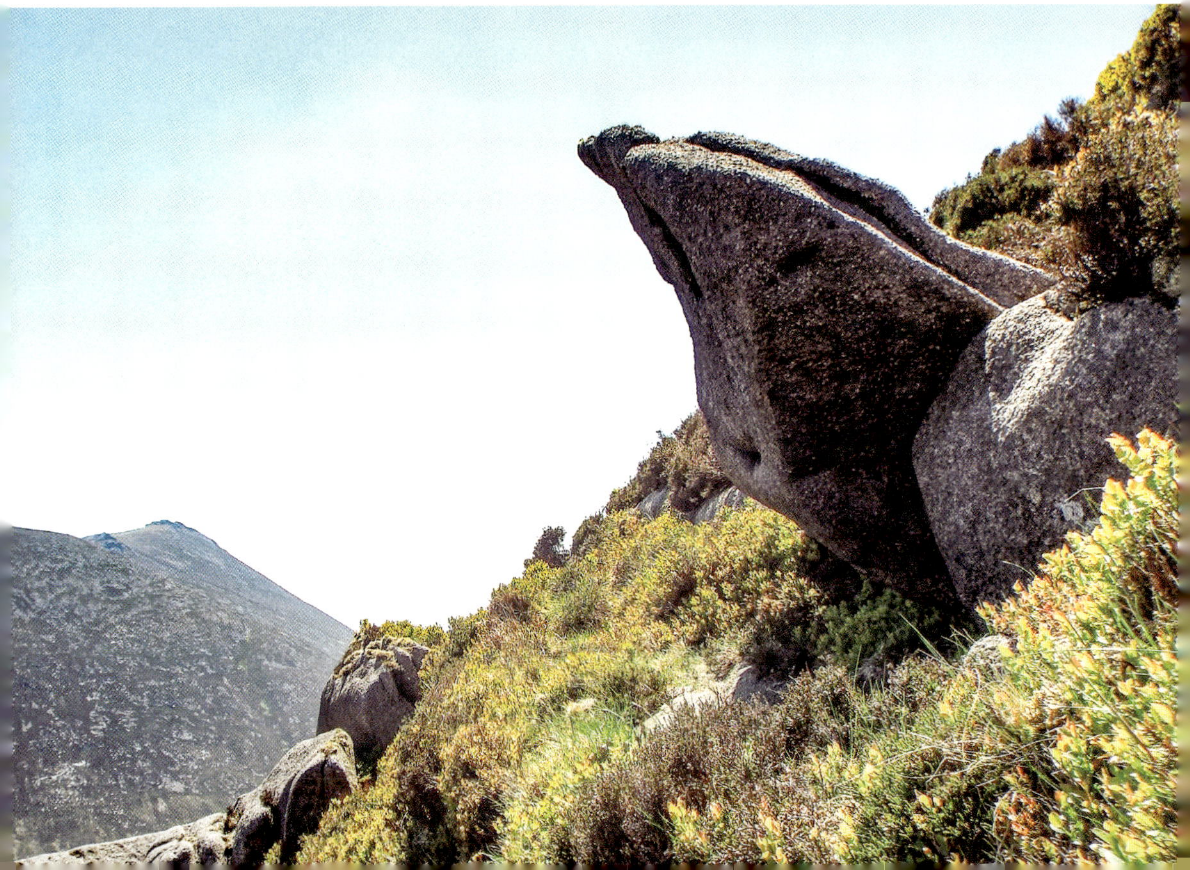

Top opposite: On the south side of Doan mountain clever use is made of the grooves on this granite block to suggest a bird unfurling its wings for flight. The trekking poles on top are a metre long and show this to be a very substantial stone indeed.

Lower opposite: On the steep northern side of Doan mountain this stone bird is almost airborne. But for the anchor stone wedging it in place below it probably would be tumbling downhill. The artist has captured the moment the wings are swept back ready for flight. In its very simplicity this is a masterful creation.

Top of this page: This propped stone of a bird about to take flight is on the north side of Pollaphuca valley. The beak points to summer solstice sunrise. The GPS is:

N. 54° 11. 418'
W. 005° 59. 641'   Elevation 471m.

This sensitive piece of early rock art shows a mother cat tenderly looking after its kitten. It is found on the south-east summit of Slievemageogh overlooking the Moyad Road. The GPS is:
N. 54° 07. 735'
W. 006° 03. 776'   Elevation 316m.

SCULPTURAL TREASURES OF MOURNE

> The most striking quality common to all primitive art is its intense vitality. It is something made by a people with a direct and immediate response to life.
>
> (Henry Moore)

Such is the wealth of sculptural treasure found across Mourne that the day will surely come when the area will join Ireland's three other UNESCO world heritage sites, namely, the Giant's Causeway, Brú na Bóinne/Newgrange and Skellig Michael. Presently there are other contenders for the honour of inscription such as, Tara, Rathcroghan, Dún Ailinne, the Hill of Uisneach, Cashel, Kerry's transatlantic cable area around Valentia Island and the Passage Tomb landscape of County Sligo. Mourne's early settlers have left behind such a profusion of their art, sculpture and megaliths that this area of South Down will hold its head up with any of them. It certainly would be a worthy and natural extension of the region marketed by the Irish Tourist Board as Ireland's Ancient East.

The stone treasures hide in plain sight. Walkers and explorers in the Mournes pass them by daily without recognition. They cannot be blamed for any oversight as the Irish names that formerly identified so many of these faces and megaliths were lost with the disappearance of Irish. It has been a labour of love to retrieve and save some of these names fortunately still found in the local knowledge of a few shepherds and farmers. Two such magnificent monuments are *Carraig a tSeabhaic* (Rock of the Hawk) and *Carraig na gCuilm* (Rock of the Pigeon) both illustrated in this chapter. The names were recorded on John O'Donovan's map of Mourne in 1834 but have only now been located and photographed.*

The identification of these two megaliths only underscores the sad disappearance of so many other names that once abounded on every hill and shoulder of the mountains.

---

* For O'Donovan's map of Mourne see page 70 of *Ordnance Survey Letters Down*, edited by the late Michael Herity (he died 23rd January 2016), published by Four Masters Press, Dublin 2001.

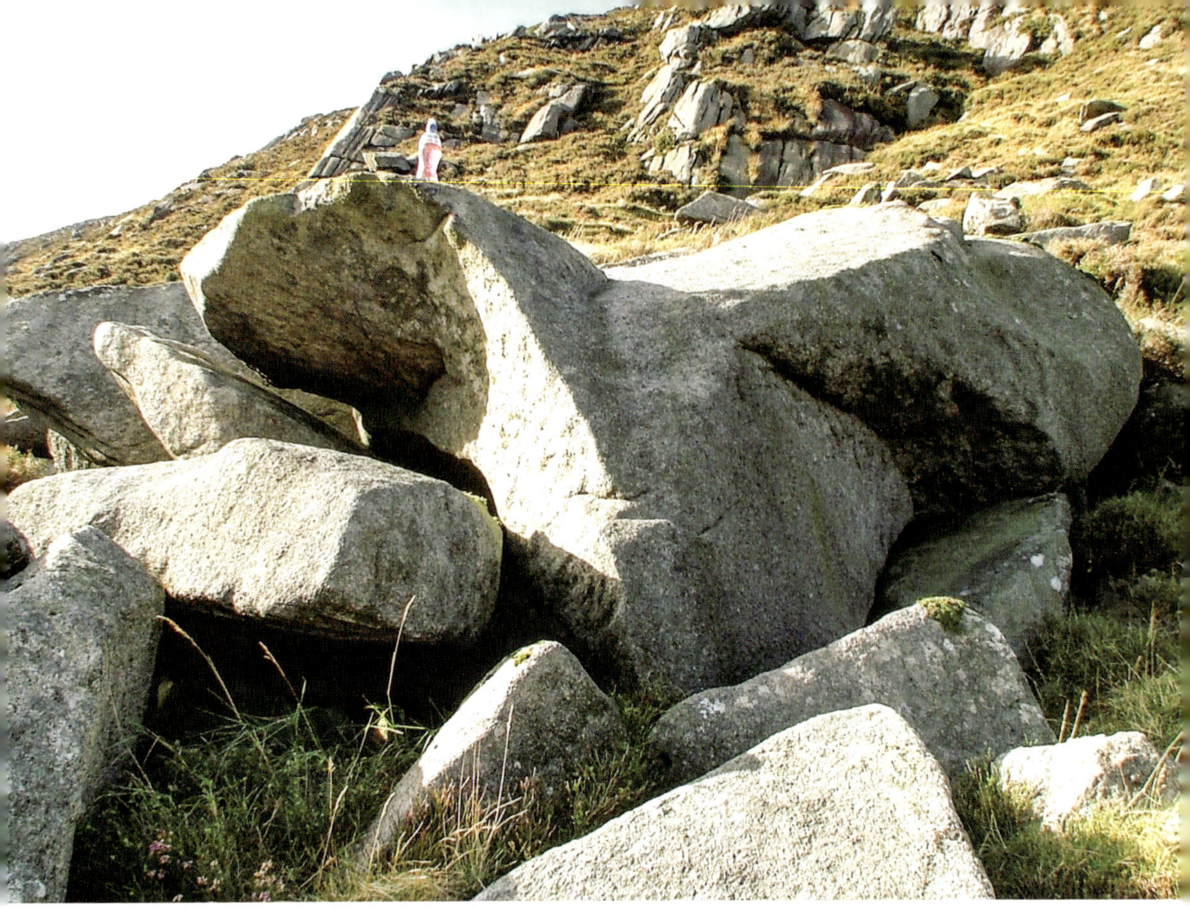

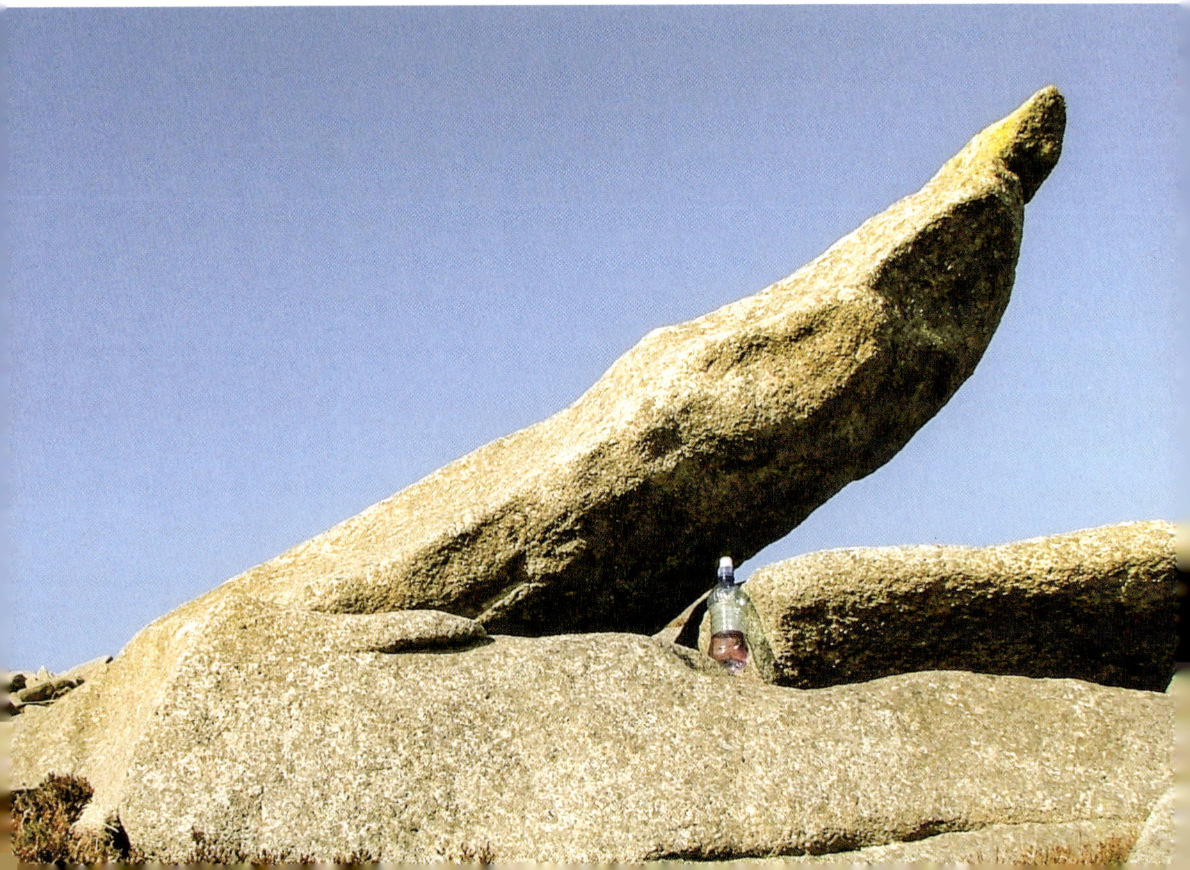

Top opposite: **The Attacking Squid**
A giant squid seizes its prey. This beautifully observed sea creature measures nearly four metres from front to back and just over two and a half metres wide and is found on the northern side of Pollaphuca valley. Its GPS is:

        N. 54° 11. 498'
        W. 005° 59. 560'   Elevation 467m.

Lower opposite: **The Shrew**
The 'Shrew' megalith, with its long tapering 'nose' is found on the south flank of Slieve Donard at

        N. 54° 10. 550'
        W. 005° 55. 304'   Elevation 693m.

This is also a decidedly phallic monument over three metres in length and aligned to the landscape 'vaginal notch' on the hills of the Isle of Man. A subtle little twist at the tip of the stone points to winter solstice dawn.

Top of this page: **The Elephant Bull Seal**
On the south side of Slieve Bearnagh's summit tor you can look up to see *An Rón Mór*, 'The Big Seal'. It is a marvellous sculpted recollection by an early artist of an elephant bull seal complete with prominent proboscis. The animal would only have been found far south from Ireland's coasts. The GPS is:

        N. 54° 11. 050'
        W. 005° 59. 377'   Elevation 711m.

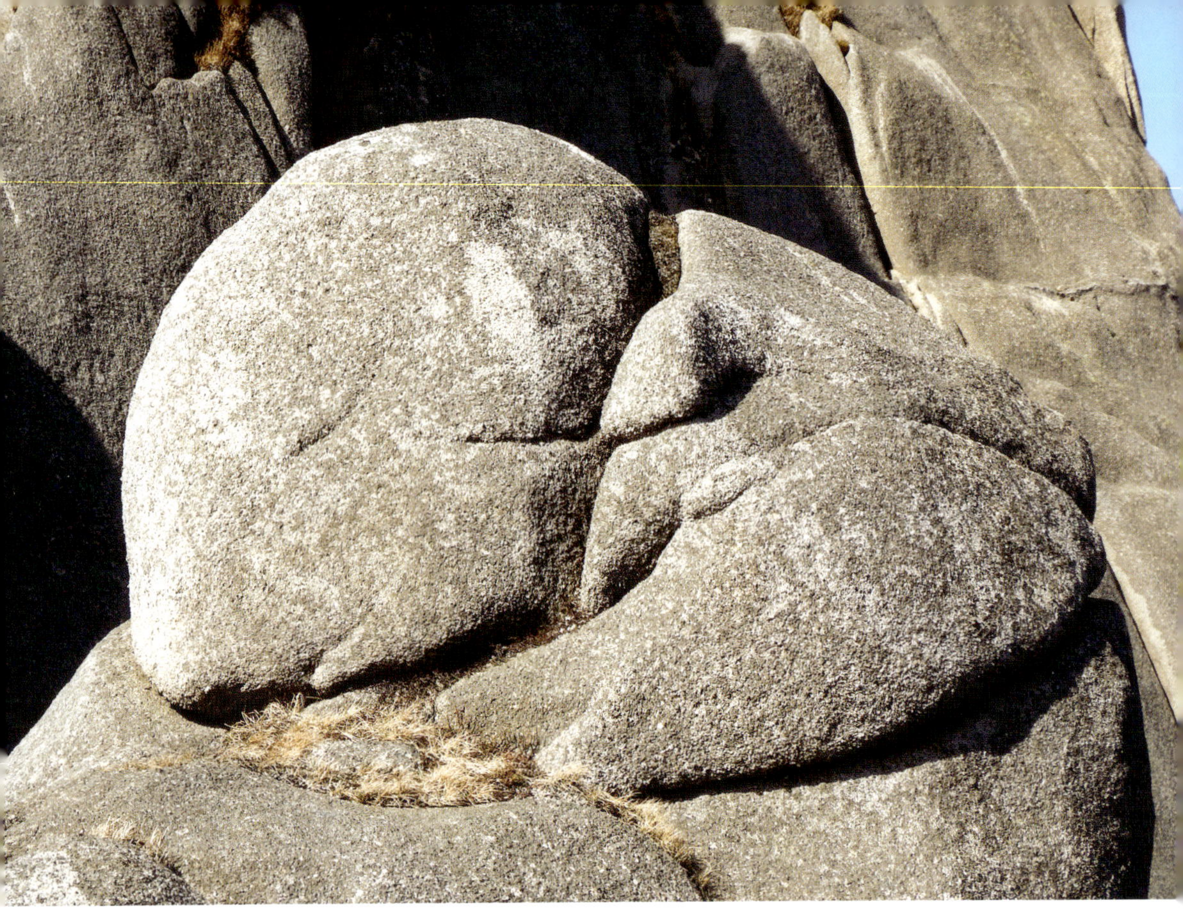

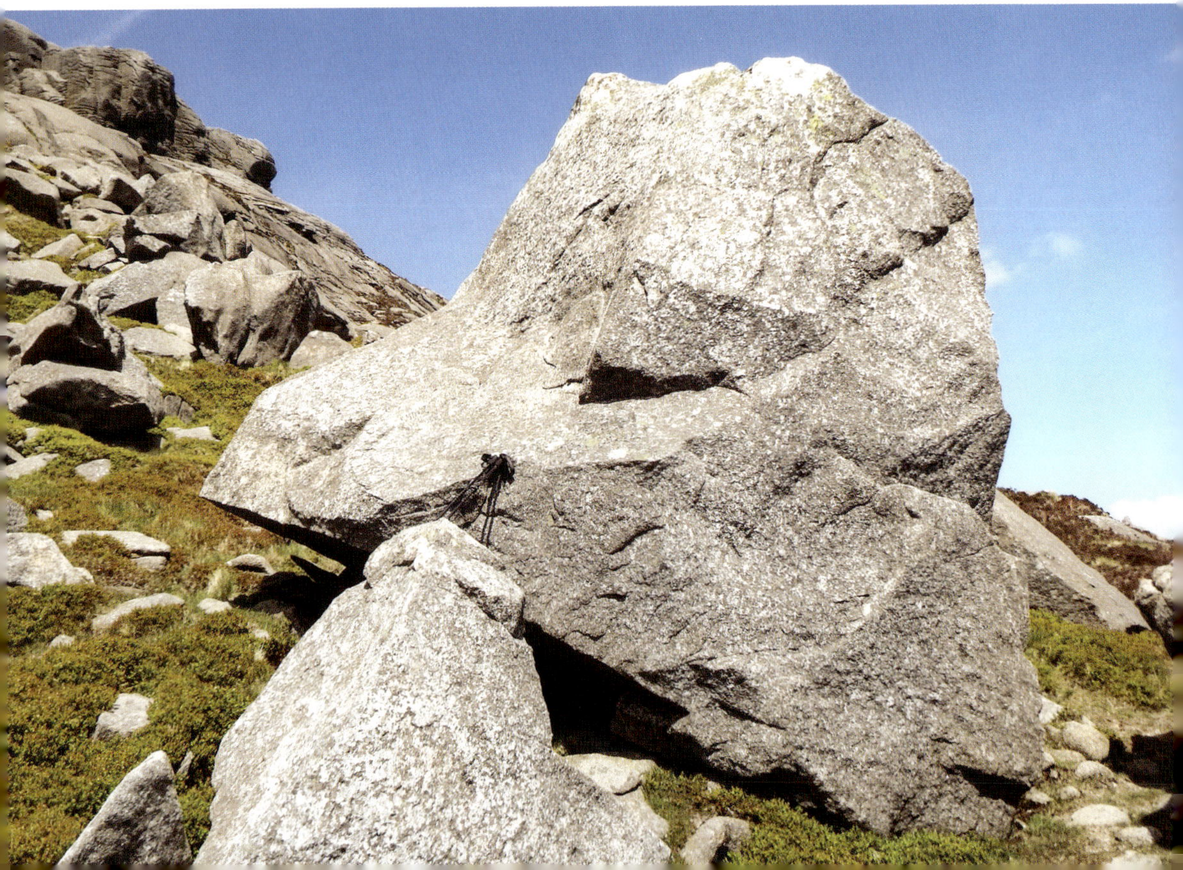

Top opposite: **The Sleeping Baby Mouse**
Tá sé 'na leo-leo-ín (He is fast asleep). This little sleeping baby mouse is found on the south side of Slieve Bearnagh's summit tor. Count the limbs and you have four legs and a tiny penis. GPS is:

$$\text{N. } 54°\ 11.\ 012'$$
$$\text{W. } 005°\ 59.\ 335' \qquad \text{Elevation 719m.}$$

Lower opposite: **The Hen**
The trekking pole handles are nearly lost against this huge megalith on the eastern side of Slieve Bignian's south tor. The three metre high boulder has a fair resemblance to a Hen and it may have been inspired by the multiple tors above giving a likeness to the comb of a Hen's head.

Top of this page: **Feeding Time**
When you realise that the top stone is close to 3.5metres across by over 2m from top to bottom, you can begin to appreciate the remarkable achievement of manipulating this mighty boulder, along with so many others, to perch it high on the treacherous stony slope of south-east Lamagan. The artist depicts what is probably a bird caring for its young. It is found at:

$$\text{N. } 54°\ 09.\ 616'$$
$$\text{W. } 005°\ 57.\ 679' \qquad \text{Elevation 377m.}$$

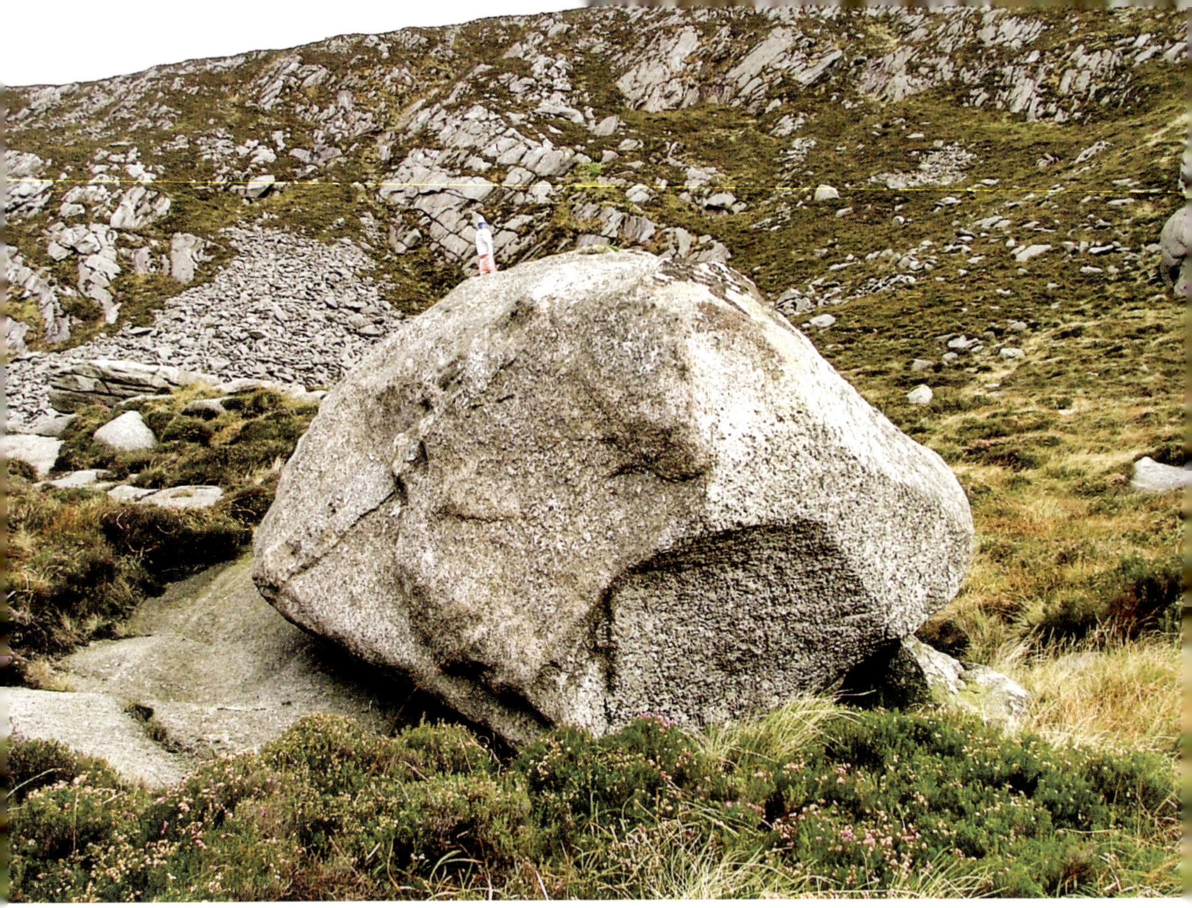

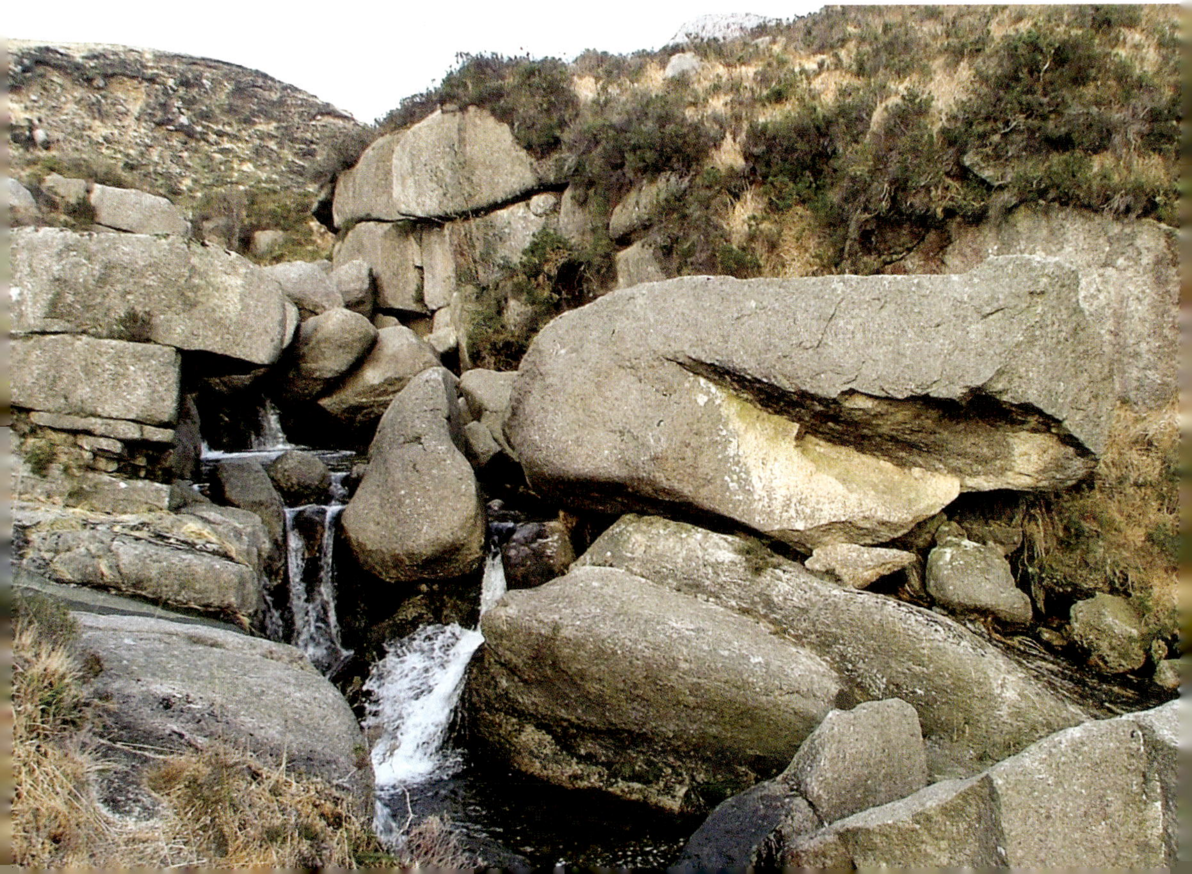

Top opposite: *Liamhán* **(Basking Shark)**
This beautiful rendition of a feeding basking shark with its mouth typically open is found on the north side of Pollaphuca valley. Note the lines on the right side of the mouth showing where the stone has been spalled in the creation of this work of art.
The GPS is:	N. 54º 11. 413'
	W. 005º 59. 555'	Elevation 439m.
The location marks the tip of Slieve Commedagh appearing in the 'vaginal notch' between Slievenaglogh and the shoulder of Bearnagh.

Lower opposite: **Basking Shark in the Annalong River**
The ancients certainly had a sense of humour when they placed a substantial representation of an ocean going basking shark on the bank of the little Annalong River. The shark boulder is close to five metres long and is well propped in place. The creation has a prominent 'nose' and a large lower part has been spalled off to make a wide open mouth. The GPS is:	N. 54° 09. 363'
	W. 005° 57. 031'	Elevation 231m.

Top of this page: *An Liamhán Beag* **(The Wee Basking Shark)**
This three metre long granite boulder on the north side of Pollaphuca Valley is aligned to the appearance of winter solstice sun on the shoulder of Slieve Bearnagh. A ridge along the top of the boulder points towards the fertility feature of the tip of Commedagh appearing, phallic-like, in the vaginal notch formed between Slievenaglogh and Bearnagh. The GPS is:	N. 54º 11. 399'
	W. 005º 59. 621'	Elevation 450m.

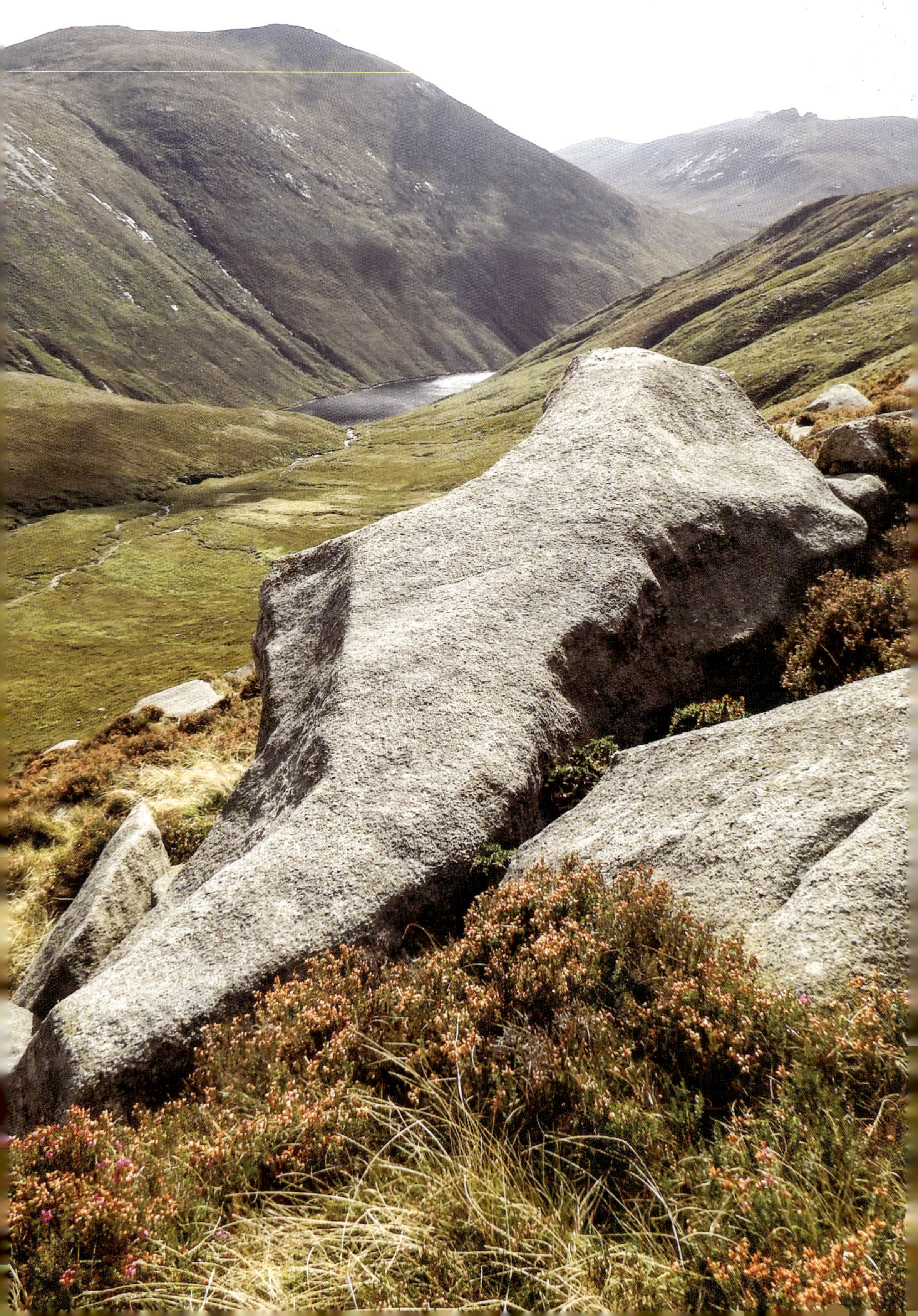

Opposite: The Sinuous Common Lizard
On the east slope of Slieve Bearnagh is this huge twisting megalith evocative of the turns of a common lizard. The head is turned to the right side as if looking back behind it. This monument is a particularly large creation being five to six metres in length. The stone has a little horn at the end pointing to Lamagan and to where winter solstice sun will appear. An approximate GPS is given. The Lizard will be found about 100 metres south and about 20 metres below:

        N.   54° 11. 136'
        W. 005° 58. 665'   Elevation circa 456m.

Top of this page: The Bat
It is really only when viewed from above that this placement of stones at the north-easterly end of Chimney Rock mountain can be recognised as a beautiful rendering of a bat.

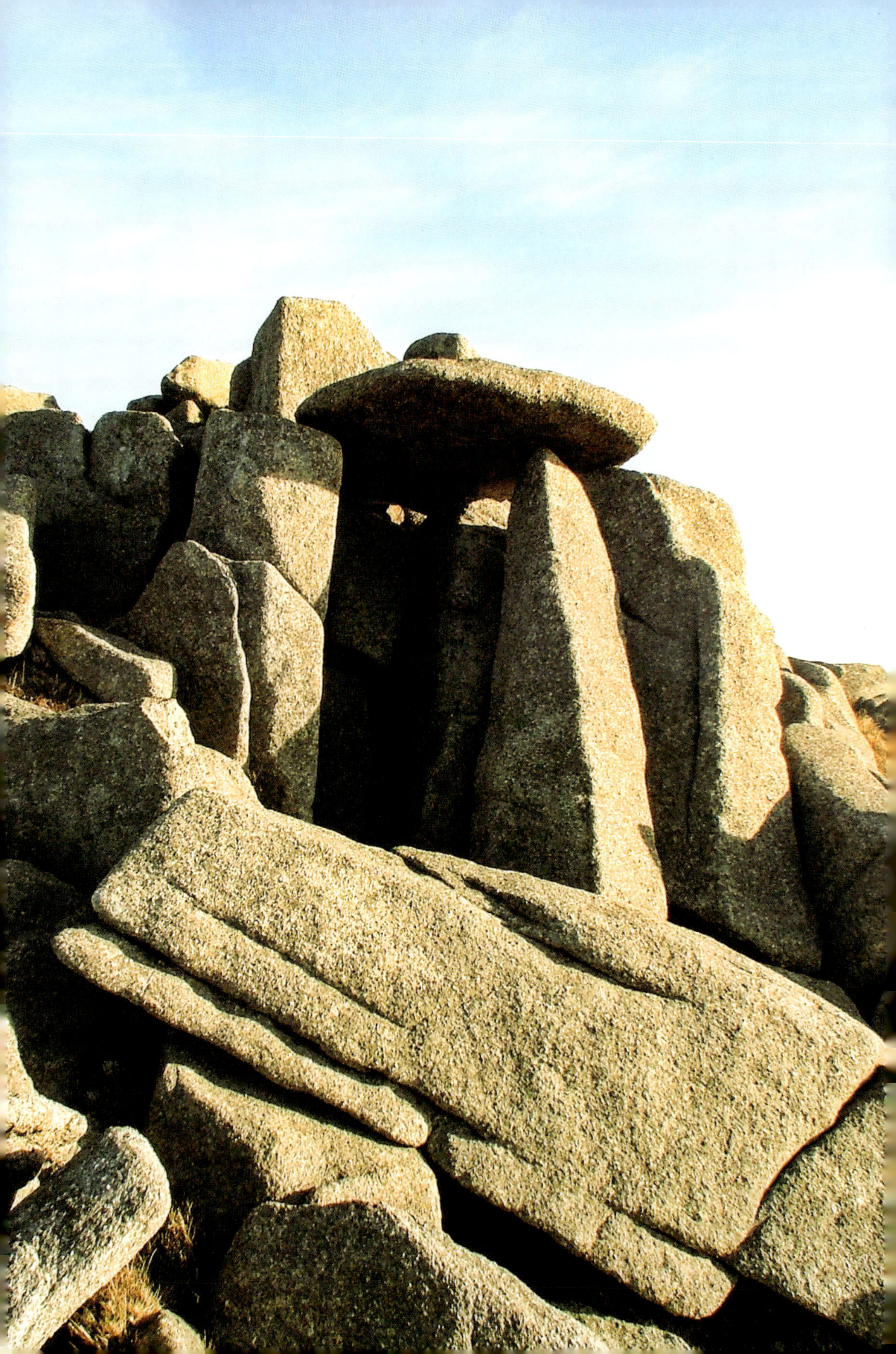

Opposite: The Sleeping Guard-Dog
At the eastern seaward end of Chimney Rock mountain is this delightful domestic scene of a rather large guard-dog sleeping across the threshold of a 'door'. Definitely a case of 'let sleeping dogs lie'.

        N.   54° 11. 136'
        W. 005° 58. 665'   Elevation circa 456m.

Top of this page: The Coiled Snake
On the western edge of Slievenamiskan summit is this low granite boulder roughly 1.5 metres across. The boulder makes for a very pleasant seat from which to appreciate the wonderful view over County Down below. When viewed from the south side however the boulder turns out to be a well sculpted coiled snake. Like the Lion megalith at the Hares Gap, this stone is another instance of the earliest settlers, the *Fir Builg*, recalling notable creatures they were acquainted with from the Iberian peninsula. In the past the very tip of the snake's head was apparently knocked off, presumably to rob the megalith of any dangerous power. The GPS is:

        N.   54° 10. 731'
        W. 006° 04. 309'   Elevation 441m.

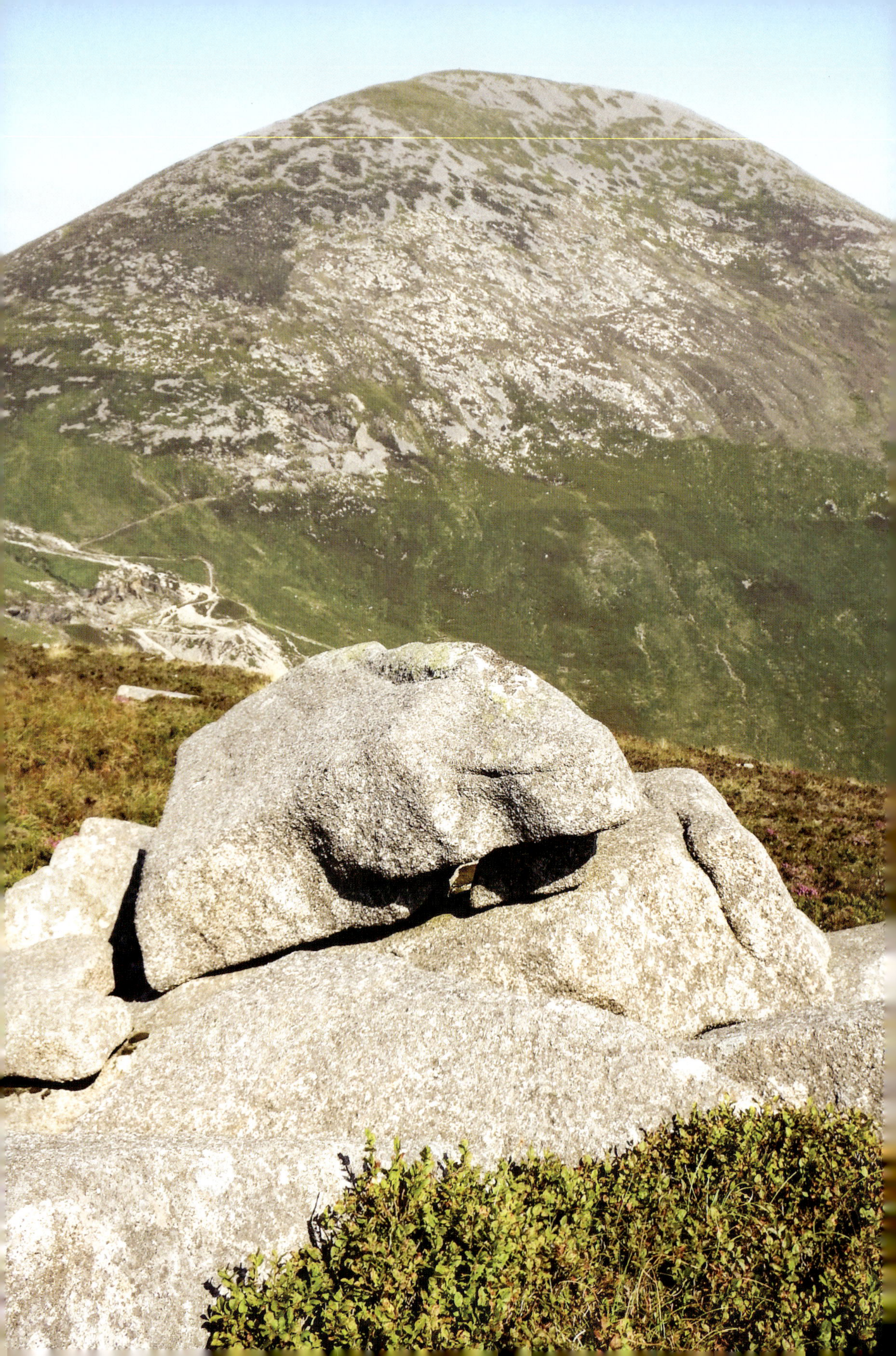

Opposite: **The Dormouse**
Along the middle of Chimney Rock mountain is this boulder shaped into a representation of a hazel dormouse with its cheeks already stuffed with food. The sculpture has even been given a stone under its 'mouth' both as a prop and a notional hazelnut. There are no dormice in Ireland except those recently imported in hay for horses at the Curragh, Co. Kildare. Perhaps the ancient artist was showing back then how widely travelled he was.

Top of this page: **The Fat Mouse and its Mousehole**
The natural rock just below the summit of Doan Mountain has been decorated with a face of a fat mouse. This rock is about four metres long and two metres high. The fissure to the right is the notional mousehole. You can't say the ancients didn't have a sense of wit. The GPS is:

                        N.   54° 10. 127'
                        W. 006° 00. 410'   Elevation 591m.

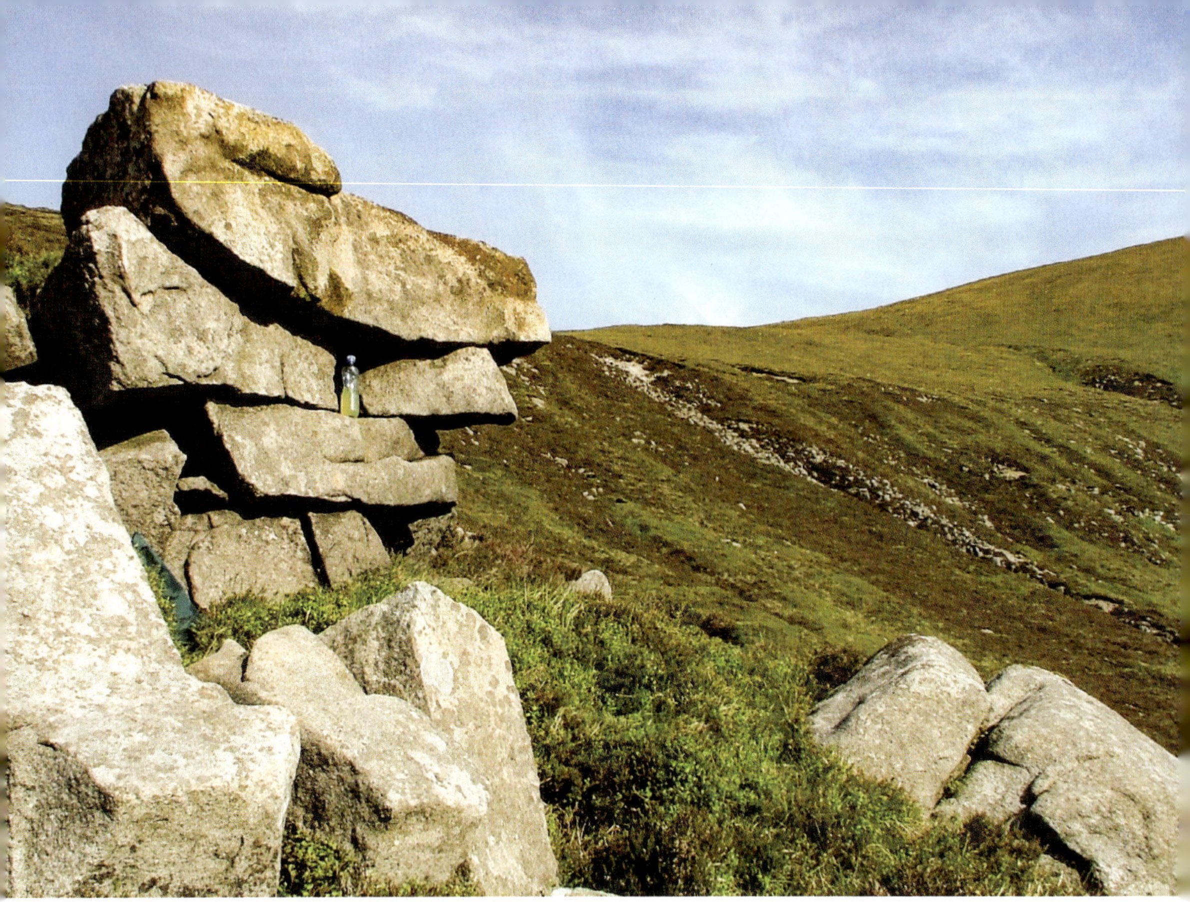

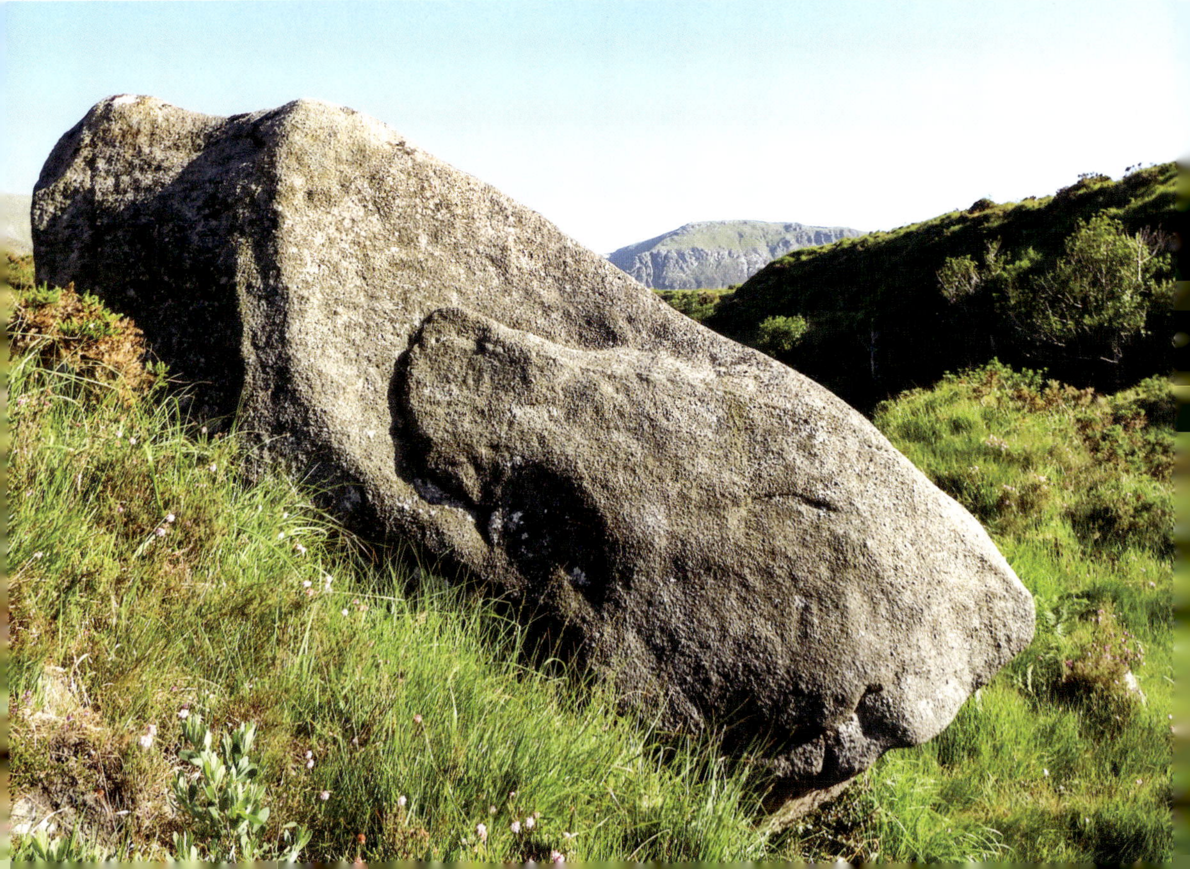

Top opposite: The Warning Beast
High on the cliff and looking menacingly down the length of the Glen River Valley this grim faced compound megalith of a rather fierce looking beastly creature was probably raised up and placed in this dominant position to warn, threaten or intimidate early intruders coming into Mourne. In this respect it could be said to compliment The Lion megalith at the Hare's Gap.

Lower opposite: The Great Hare
This glorious rendering of *An Míol Maighe*, 'The Great Hare', sits beside the Cascade river near a tributary junction. The sculpture well deserves the description 'Great' for this granite boulder is a good four metres long and rises nearly three metres between front and back. The GPS is:

        N.   54º 12. 416'
        W. 005º 57. 181'   Elevation 220m.

Top of this page: The Howling Wolf
Before it was toppled, this magnificent monument of a Howling Wolf, with its head lit by the first rays of summer solstice dawn, graced the summit of Millstone Mountain. The stone is still there.

    The Down Recorder, 5th November 1921, records somewhat sceptically the legend of the extermination of a she wolf and litter in the Mourne range as late as July 1820. The GPS is:

        N.   54° 11. 286'
        W. 005° 53. 913'   Elevation 452m.

The Lion
This impressive sculpture is found under Slievenaglogh on the east side of Trassey Valley, about 200 metres from the Mourne Wall at the Hare's Gap and level with it in height. The leonine shaped boulder is about 2.5 metres high by 4 metres long but is surprisingly slim being only .75m across the top. The chopped eye also comes in at .75m in length. The Lion may have been placed here as a guardian or protector of the pass and as such would be similar to the dog-like carnivore, (probably a wolf) that looks down another important entrance into Mourne, the Glen River Valley. There are, of course, no lions in Ireland. Along with other stones like the cobra, coiled snake, sharks and the vulture, this Lion stone speaks of the earliest settlers, the *Fir Builg*, remembering the animals they were familiar with from the Iberian peninsula and the north African coast. The GPS is:
N. 54° 11. 472'
W. 005° 58. 481'   Elevation 440m.

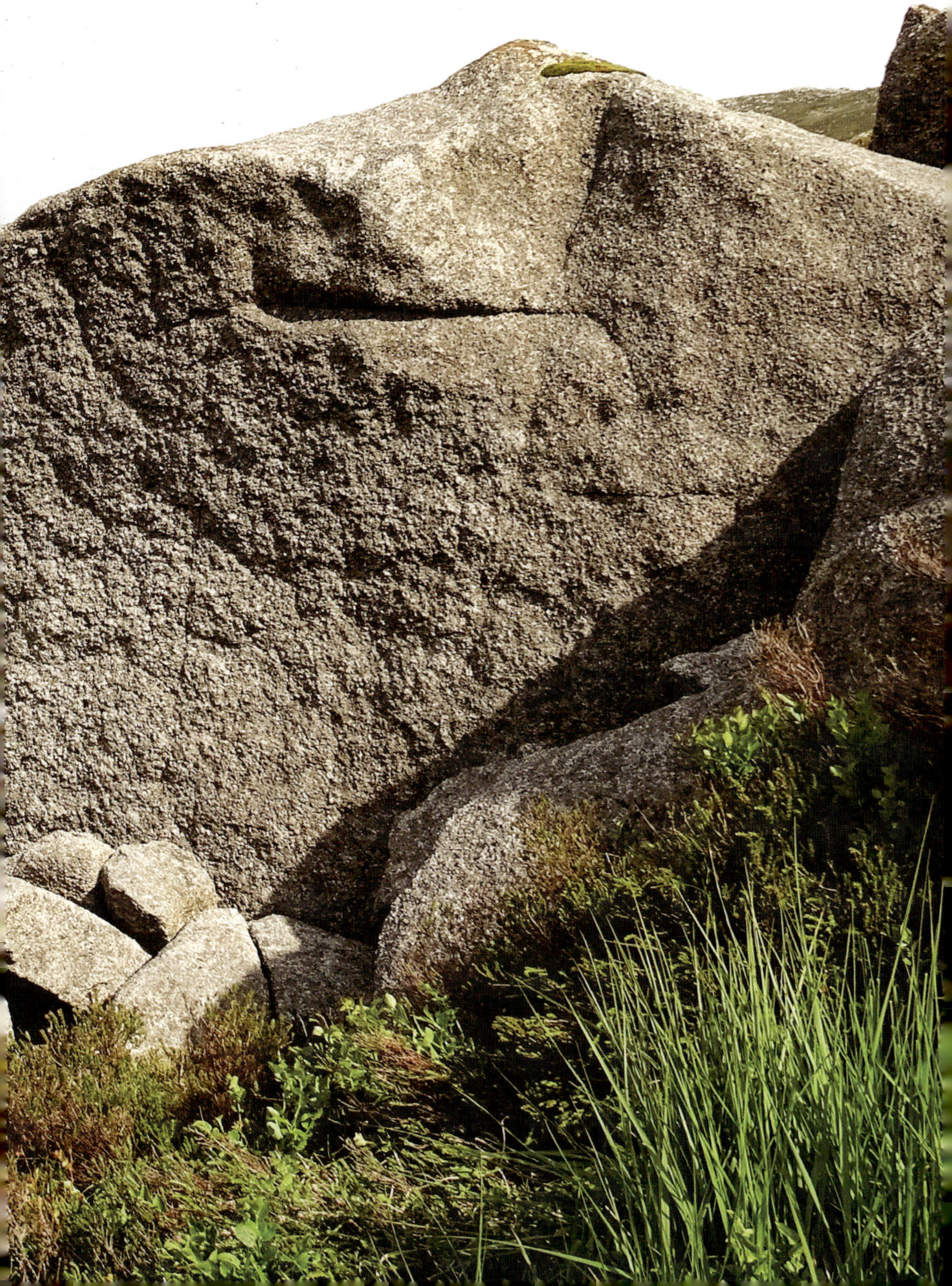

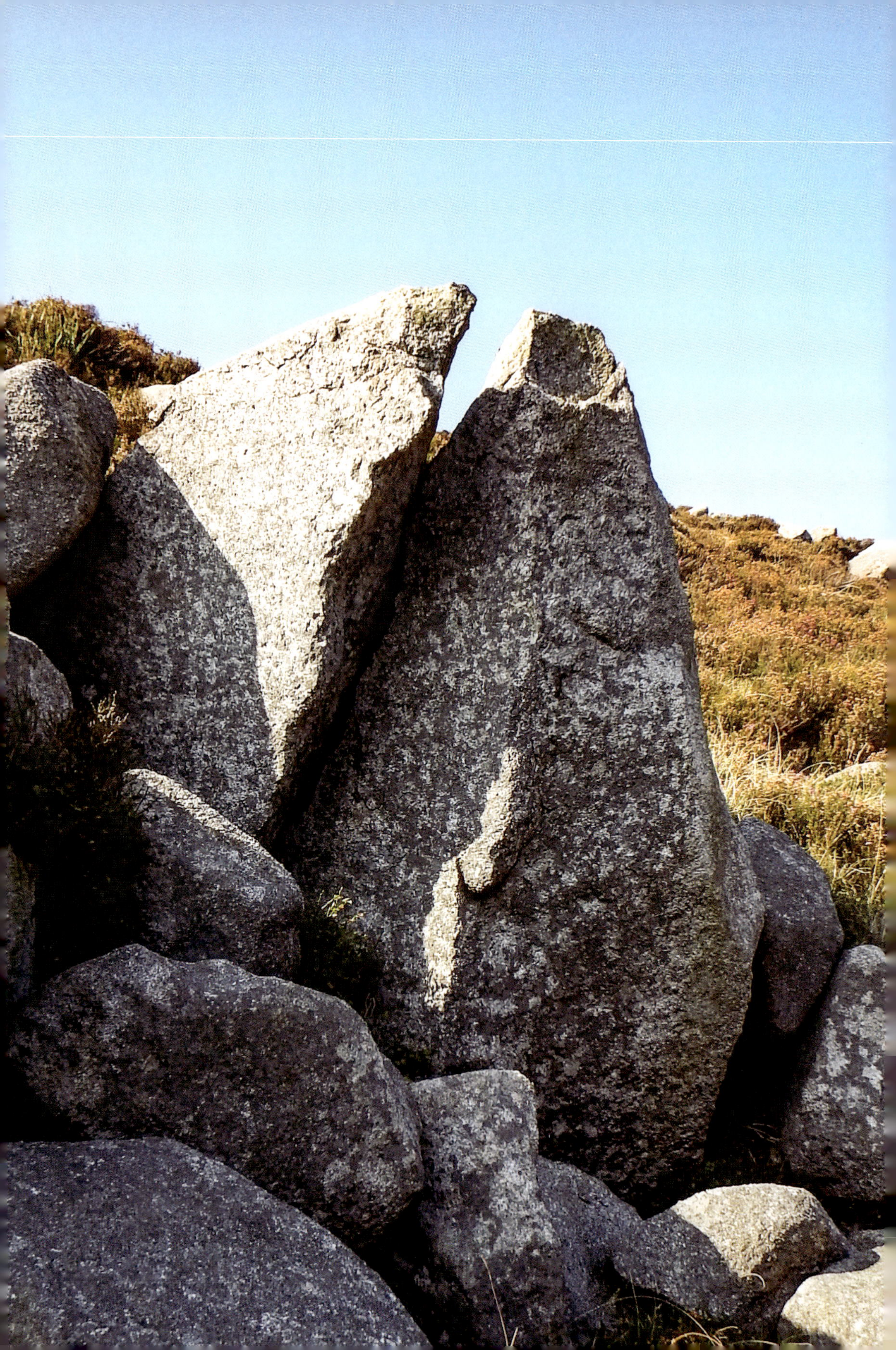

Opposite: The Fighting Seals
These upright stones on the eastern slope of Slieve Bearnagh are a beautifully observed instance of two male seals fighting for dominance. The stones are nearly three metres high (there is a lot down below). Rock has been spalled off at the top of both uprights to represent open mouths. There is also a subtle placement in that the [V] shaped opening between them represents a female opening aligned for fertilization to early winter solstice sunrise. The location is:

                     N.   54° 11. 260'
                     W. 005° 58. 491'   Elevation 450m.

Top of this page: The Seal Pup
On the more northerly slope under Spellack is to be found this chubby rendering of a seal pup. The photo was taken at 1.30pm in late September. The slopes under Spellack are a rich hunting ground for face stones and creations of the ancient settlers.

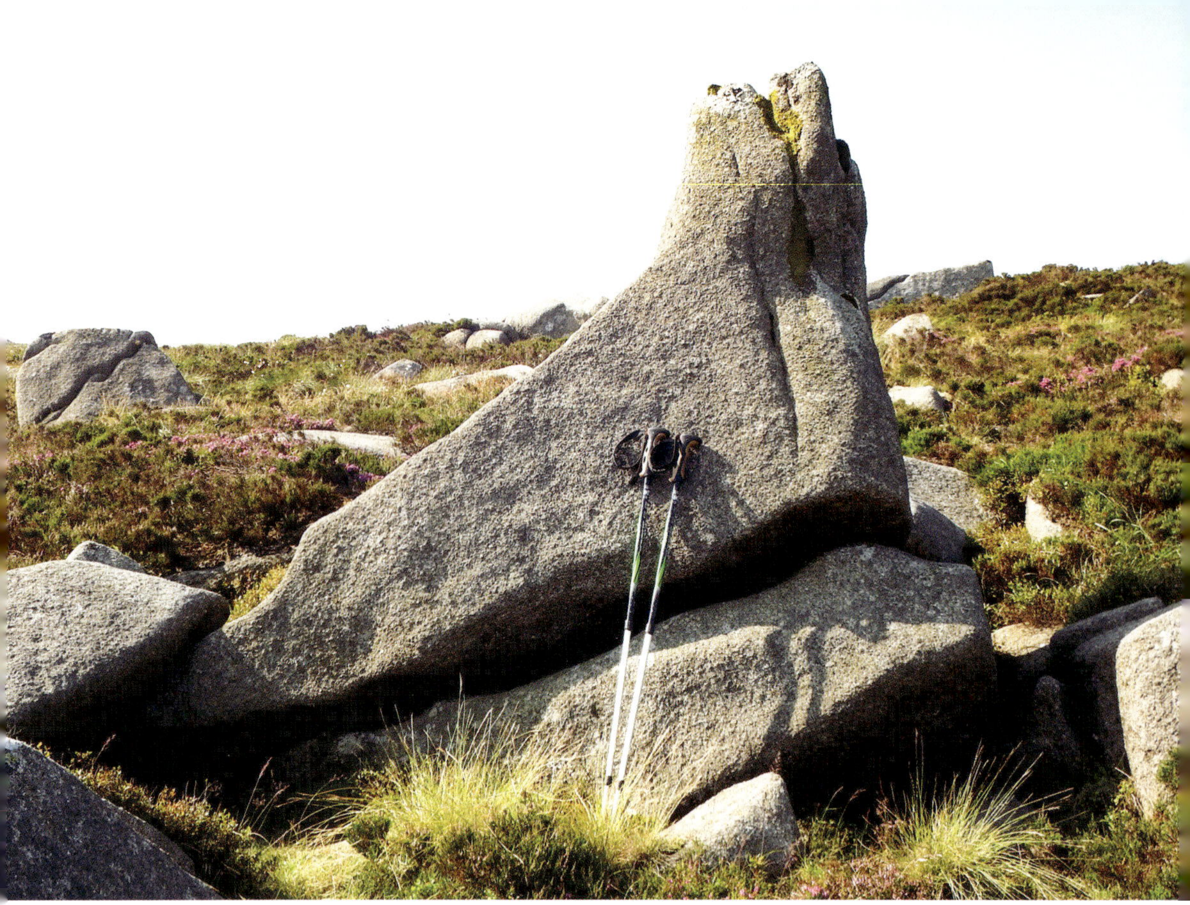

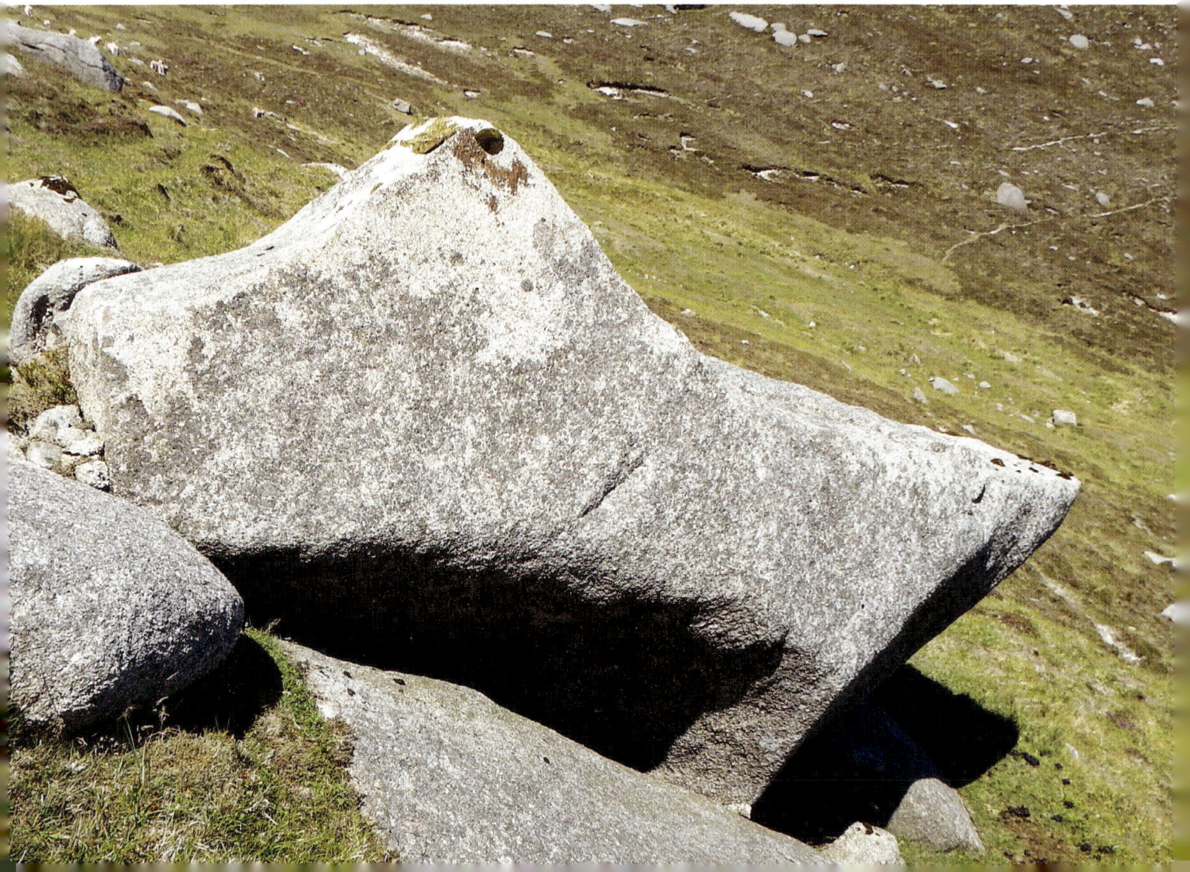

Top opposite: The Mating Seals
Along the top of Chimney Rock mountain, and more towards the northern slope, is this portrayal of two seals in the act of mating. The male is shown apparently at the rictus moment of climax. Scale can be gauged from the trekking poles which are approximately a metre long.

Lower opposite: The Shark
You would think that the triangular stone dorsal fin would have been a big enough hint but it was actually quite some years after taking this photograph that the connection was made with an ancient sculpture of a shark. The marine creature is found on the east side of Slieve Bearnagh's summit tor crafted out of a four metre long boulder. The GPS is:

$$N. \ 54° \ 11. \ 064'$$
$$W. \ 005° \ 59. \ 244' \quad \text{Elevation 659m.}$$

Top of this page: *Faoileann Mór* (The Great Seagull)
What a magnificent rendering of a seagull! The base of the stone is well imbedded below ground but even so the monument is about three metres high and the same lengthwise. It is found on Wee Slevanmore, the southerly shoulder of Slieve Meelmore. The GPS is:

$$N. \ 54° \ 11. \ 190'$$
$$W. \ 005° \ 59. \ 966' \quad \text{Elevation 592m.}$$

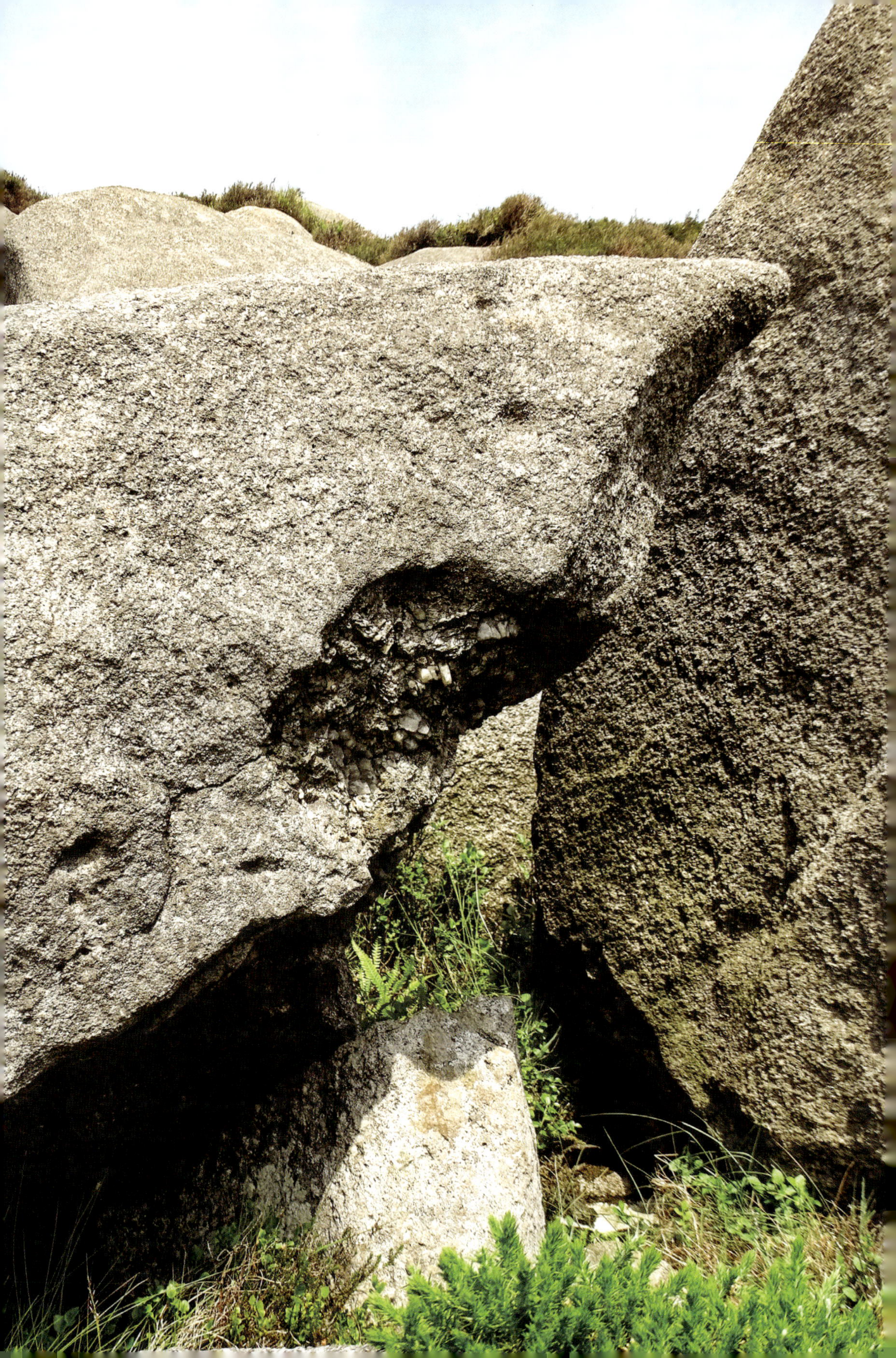

Opposite: **Jaws**
This fearsomely realistic representation of an attacking shark on the east slope of Slieve Bearnagh is further evidence that the early settlers who came to Mourne were experienced mariners and quite familiar with the denizens of the deep. The genius of this sculpture is the way the mouth has been chopped to reveal the white crystals within and using them to represent the shark's teeth. The GPS is:

N.　54°　11. 166'
W.　005°　58. 565'　　　Elevation 434m.

Top of this page: **The Breaching Humpback Whale**
On the lower front of Thomas Mountain, with a superb view over South Down, a Humpback Whale bursts forth. This is another view of the solstice facing mirror stone already featured on the top of page 10. The creators were obviously knowledgeable sea-farers quite familiar with marine life. The interpretation of the whale's great flippers down the side of the stone are a work of genius. This is a large tombstone of a monument. It is likely the source of the mountain's name, Thomas being a mnemonic of the Irish *Tuma*, 'a tomb'. The GPS is:

N.　54°　11. 632'
W.　005°　54. 353'　　　Elevation 326m.

93

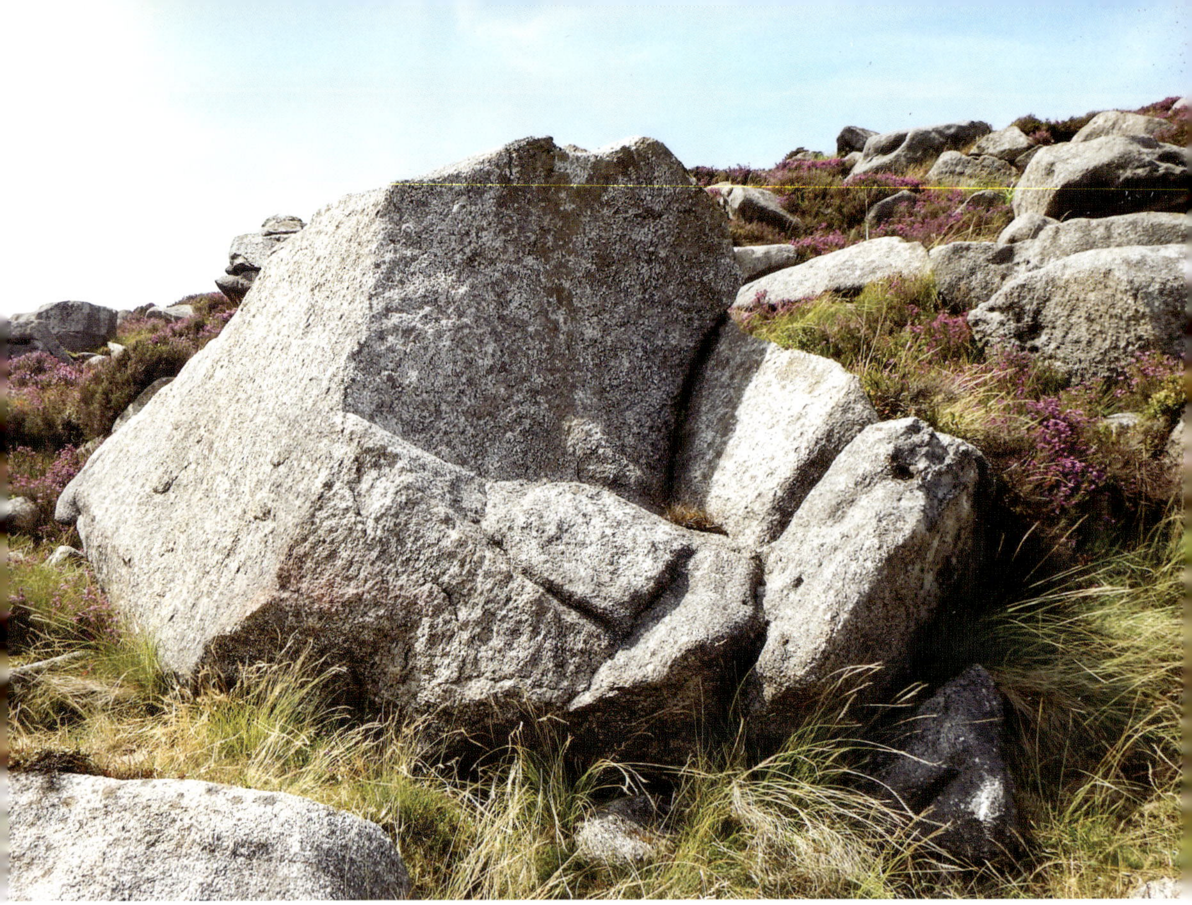

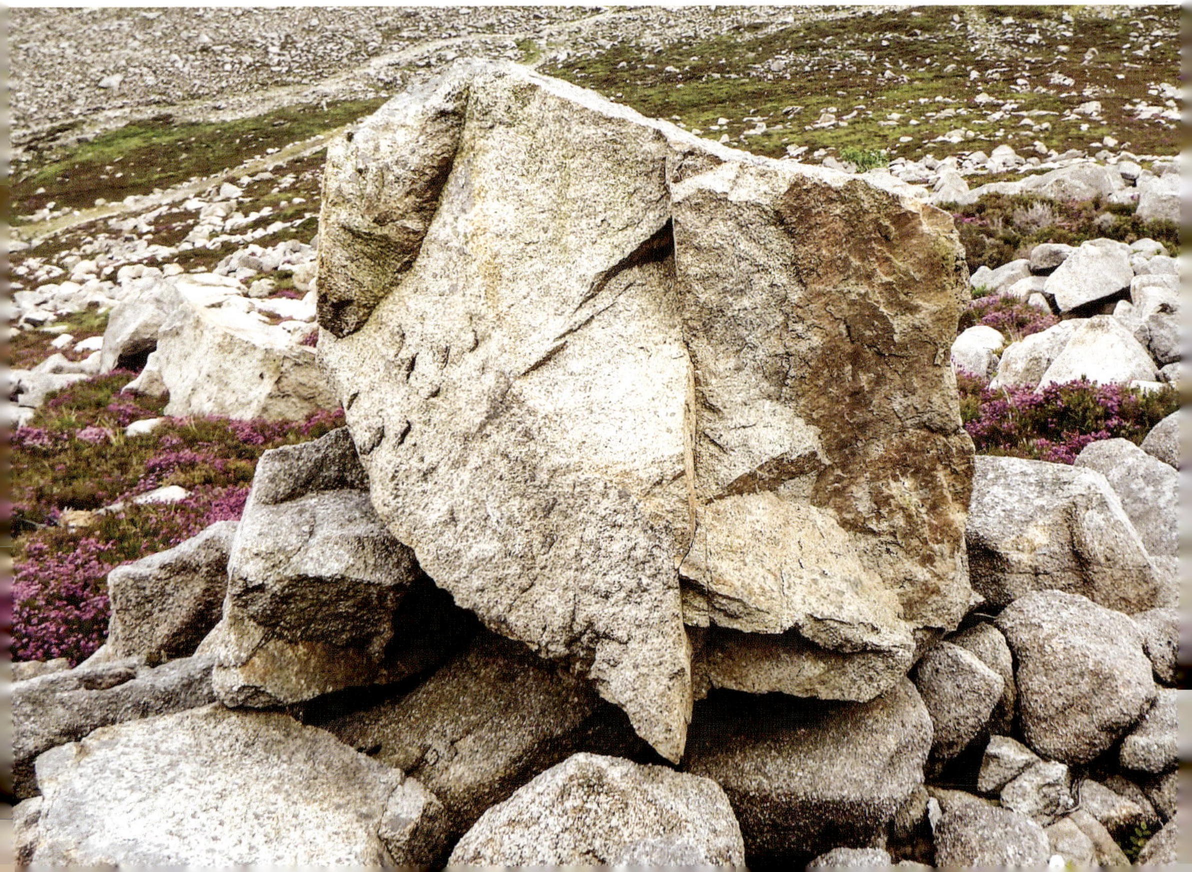

Top opposite: **The Crab**
This brute of a boulder on the south-east flank of Slieve Bearnagh measures a good four metres in length. The northerly end that looks to summer solstice sunrise has been formed into a striking likeness of an alert crab with its head raised. The GPS is:

      N. 54° 11. 267'
      W. 005° 58. 487'   Elevation 446m.

Lower opposite: **The Diving Hawk**
A large prominent boulder on the south-east side of Slieve Lamagan, when looked at closely, reveals itself to be a finely observed sculpture of a diving hawk with wings folded behind it as it comes to snatch its prey. The indenting of the rock on the left to denote fluffed feathers is a particularly nice touch. The stone is found at:

      N. 54° 09. 623'
      W. 005° 57. 720'   Elevation 385m.

Top of this page: **The Fleeing Duck**
Below the 'Hole of the Scar' in the middle south side of Windy Gap valley is a great compound megalith the bottom of which is a large granite block pointing to Bignian's profile. Behind this is an interesting small dry cave. Our interest lies in the sculpture of a fleeing duck on the side of the spear stone lying on top of the granite block. The duck is fleeing from the Hawk megalith found a little further uphill. The GPS is:

      N. 54° 07. 913'
      W. 006° 05. 072'   Elevation: circa 270m.

Carraig a tSeabhaic, 'Rock of the Hawk'; found at
N. 54º 07. 904'
W. 006º 05. 085'   Elevation 288m.

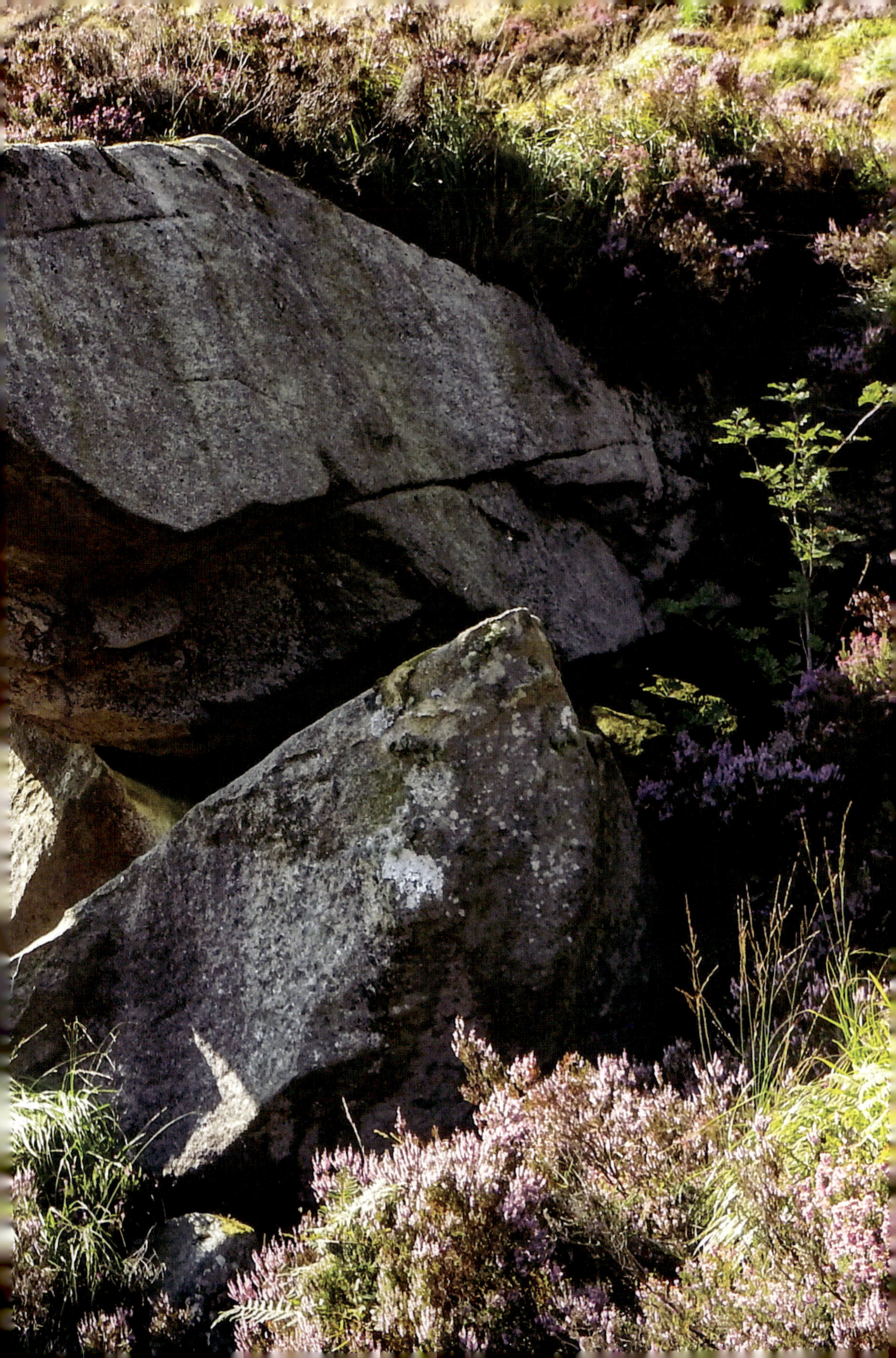

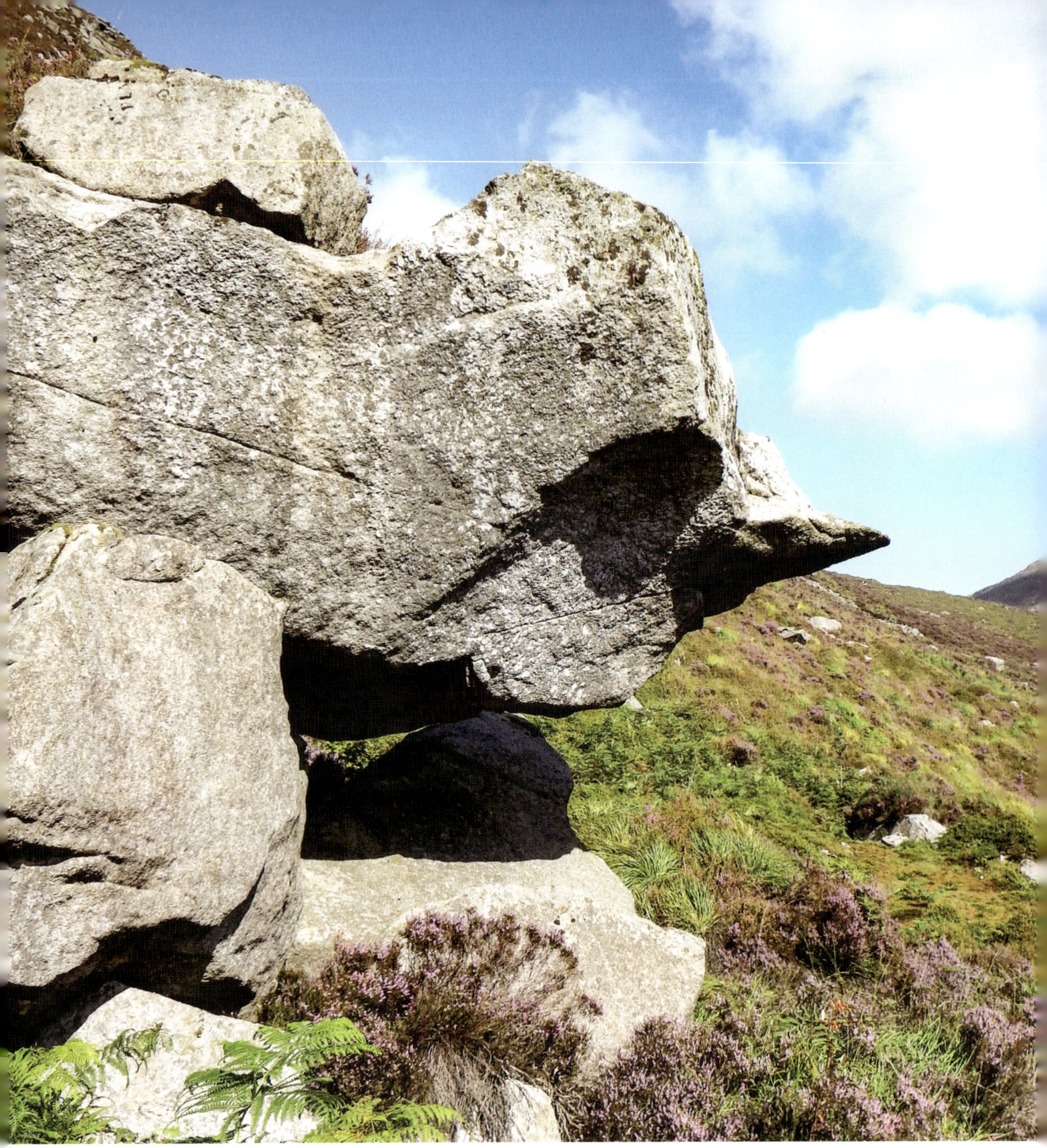

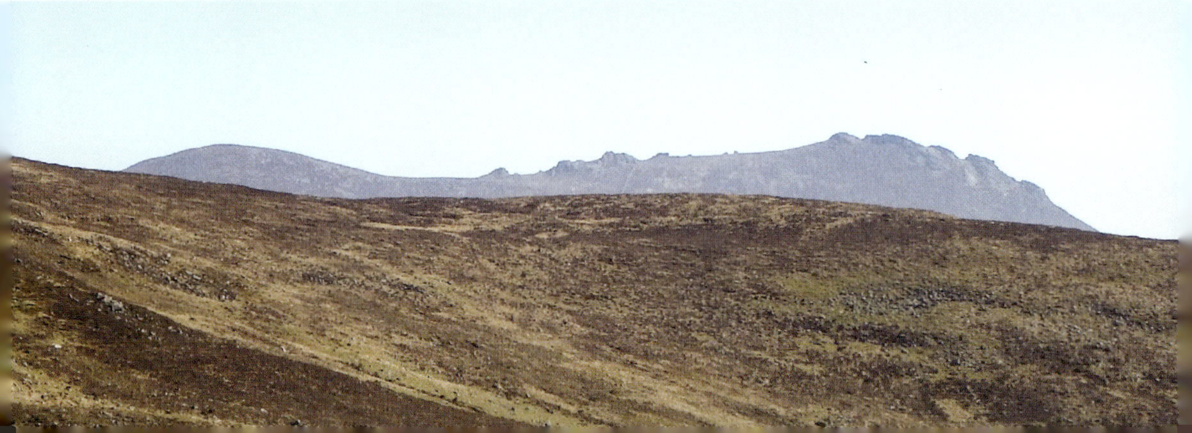

Carraig a tSeabhaic, 'Rock of the Hawk'
Until the building of the Silent Valley Dam no man-made monument in Mourne would have been greater than this awesome ancient achievement. It is located on the south side of the Windy Gap valley at the epicentre of the place formerly known in Irish as (*Tí na*) **h-Olla-Scairbhe**, '(place of the) huge hardness', or in phonetic English as 'Hole of the Scar'. The location name was a reference to the phallic profile of Bignian to the East North-East. The monument's name, *Carraig a tSeabhaic,* 'Rock of the Hawk', was recorded by John O'Donovan on his map of Mourne circa 1834 but is not named on present ordnance survey maps.

The great boulder shows the 'Hawk' at the moment of launching itself into the air. The beak points to Bignian's phallic profile which was deemed to come to sexual climax with the rising sun of summer solstice. Nothing less could warrant the prodigious efforts behind the construction of this treasure of Mourne. The stone is close to ten metres long and the front must be nearly twenty feet in the air. There are multiple huge stones used in the making of the base. This is a monument that has required truly impressive and extraordinary physical effort. The GPS is:

N. 54º 07. 904'
W. 006º 05. 085'   Elevation 288m.

The photographs show the monument from either side, from underneath and also the distant phallic profile of Slieve Bignian.

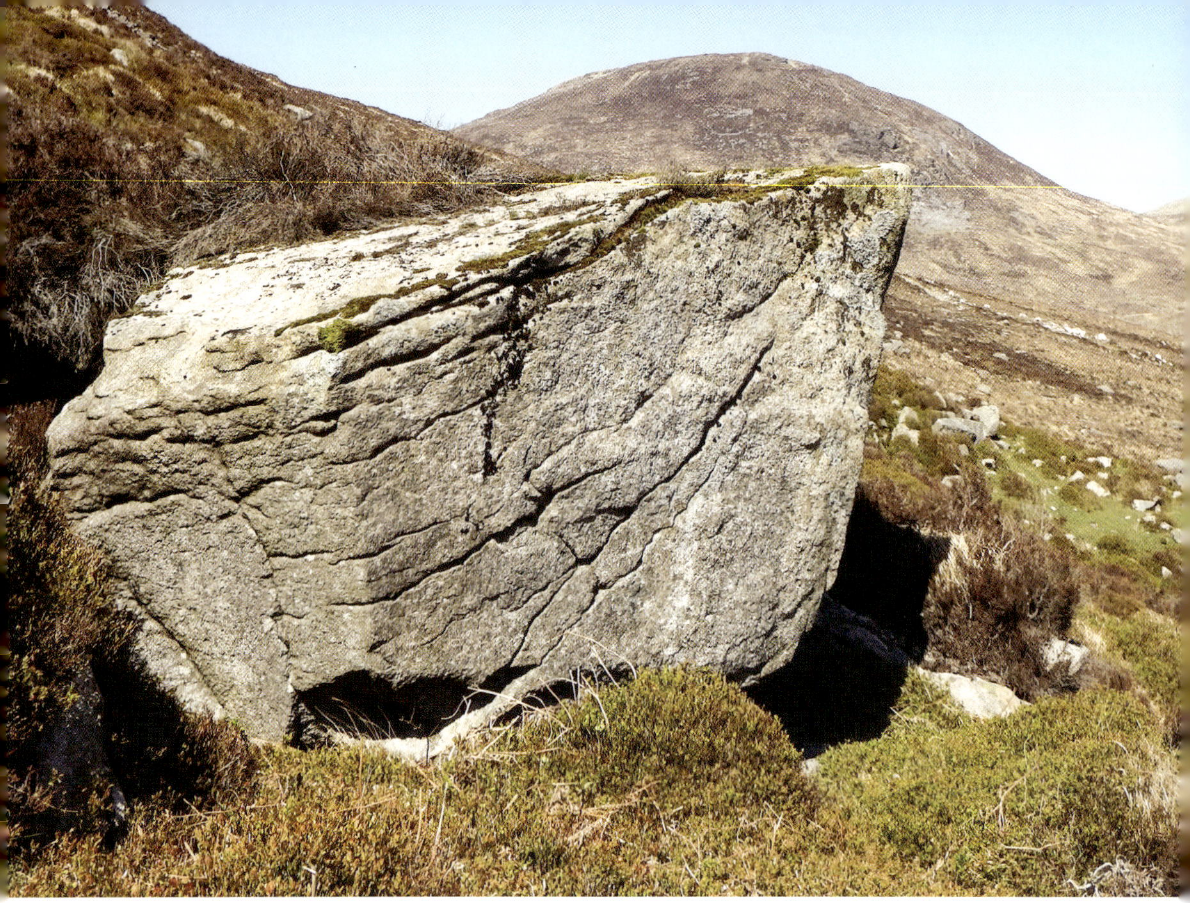
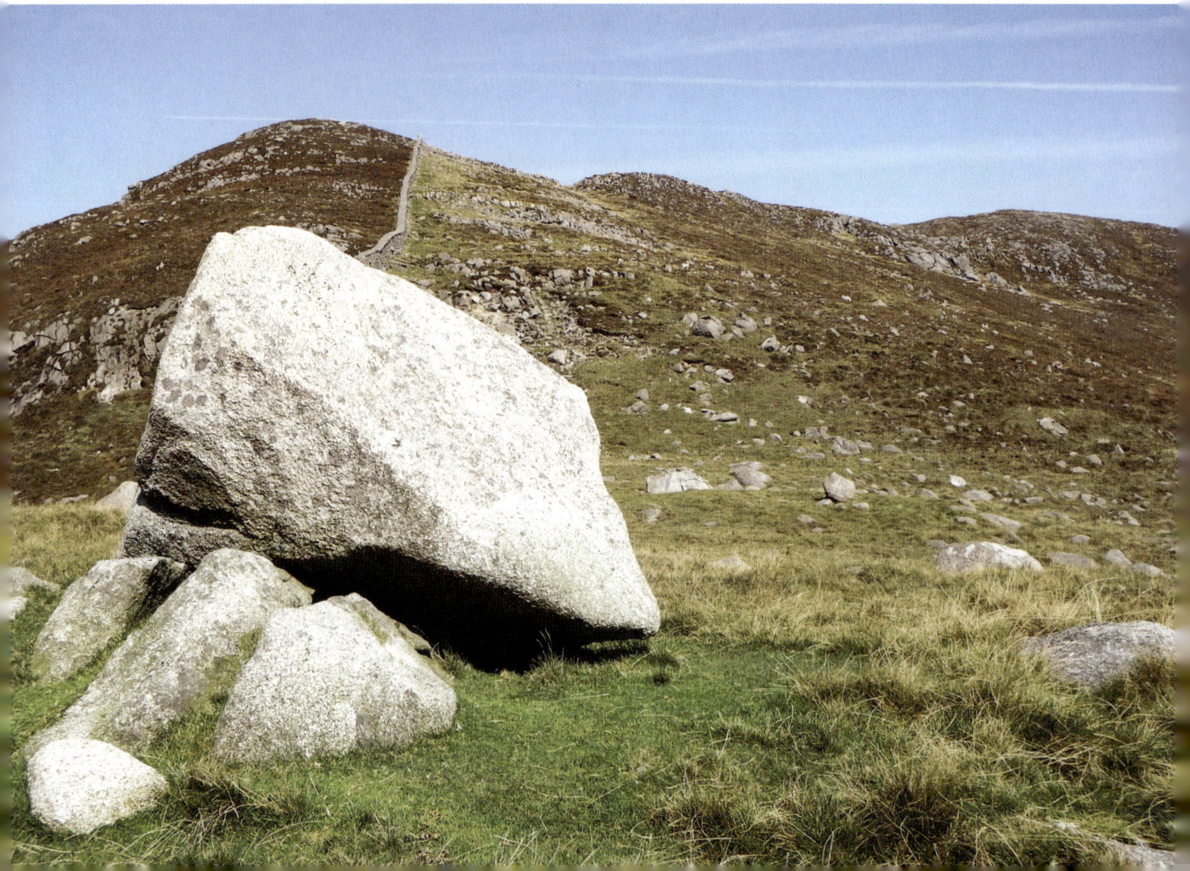

Top opposite: *Carraig na gCuilm* (Rock of the Dove)
Just a little below and to the side of its great companion megalith *Carraig a tSeabhaic*, 'Rock of the Hawk', is this two metre up-thrusting spear point that also looks across the Windy Gap valley to the phallic profile of Slieve Bignian. It was this phallic profile that saw the slope named 'Hole of the Scar', a mnemonic of the Irish *(Tí na)* **h-Olla-Scairbhe**, '(Place of the) Huge Hardness'. This part of Mourne was originally such an important fertility area that John O'Donovan placed these megaliths on his map of Mourne in the 1830's. See also the nearby 'Fleeing Duck'. The GPS for *Carraig na gCuilm* is:

        N. 54° 07. 929'
        W. 006° 05. 086'   Elevation 277m.

Lower opposite: **The Whooper Swan**
Another illustration of the Whooper Swan megalith at the Hare's Gap previously illustrated on page eight but this time showing the eye at the side.

Top of this page: **The Mute Swan**
This head of a Mute Swan is to be found on the seaward side of the Mourne Wall as you ascend Slieve Bignian from the Annalong Valley.

101

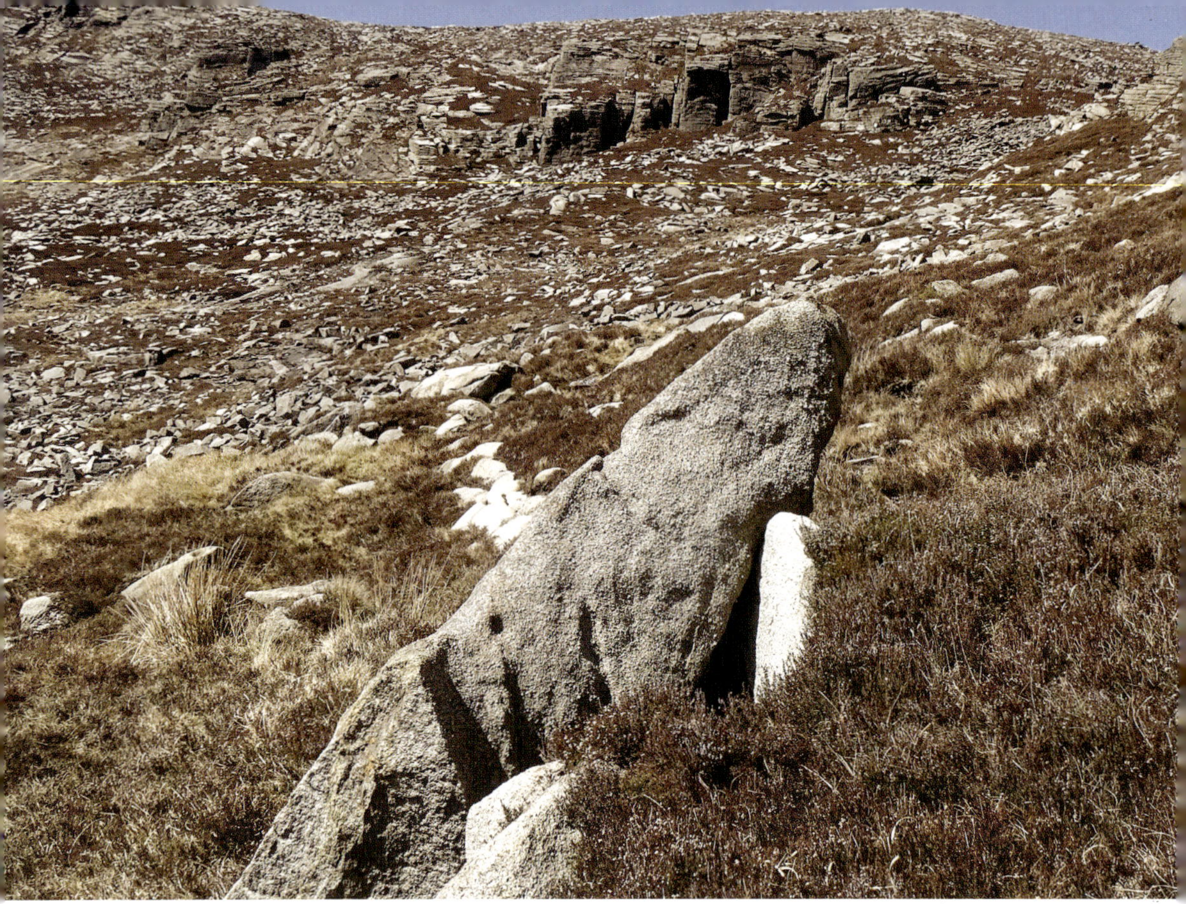

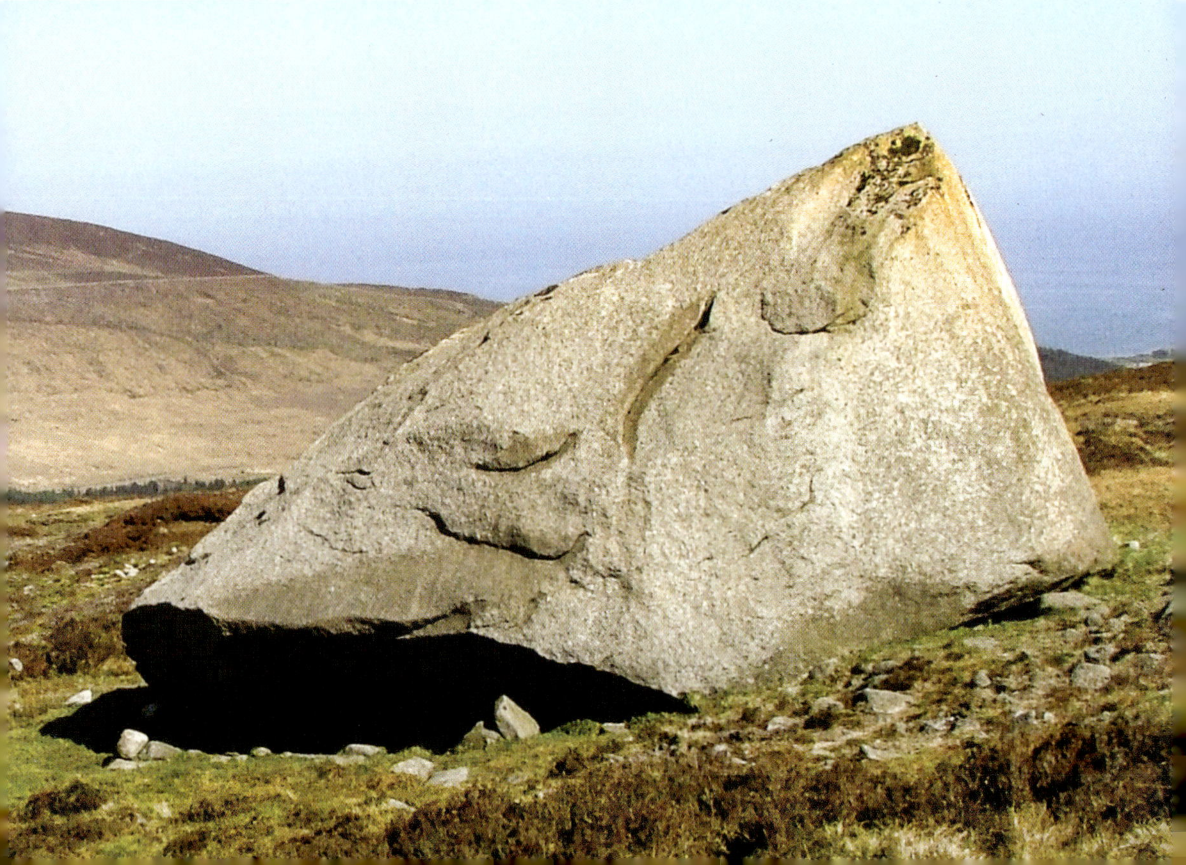

Top opposite: The Rat
Despite the quarrymen having damaged this three metre long megalith and taken a chunk off the bottom, this sculpture under Lower Cove still retains its form of a rat gnawing on a scrap. The representation is made all the more effective by the difference in colour between the grey granite of the rat and the much lighter granite, perhaps a notional bone, which the rat is chewing on. The GPS is:

N.   54° 09. 946'
W. 005° 57. 340'   Elevation 385m

Lower opposite: The Boar's Head on Douglas Crag
On this mighty boulder at the back of Douglas Crag, the closed eye and gouged tusks of a boar have been carved into the rock on the Bignian side. It is a really large boulder, measuring near five metres long by almost four metres in height. The GPS is:

N.   54° 08. 907'
W. 005° 58. 266'   Elevation 469m.

Top of this page: Nesting Bird on Donard
This nesting bird is to be found on the southern flank of Slieve Donard. The 'bird' has even been given a little egg to incubate. The GPS is:

N.   54° 10. 597'
W. 005° 55. 352'   Elevation 739m.

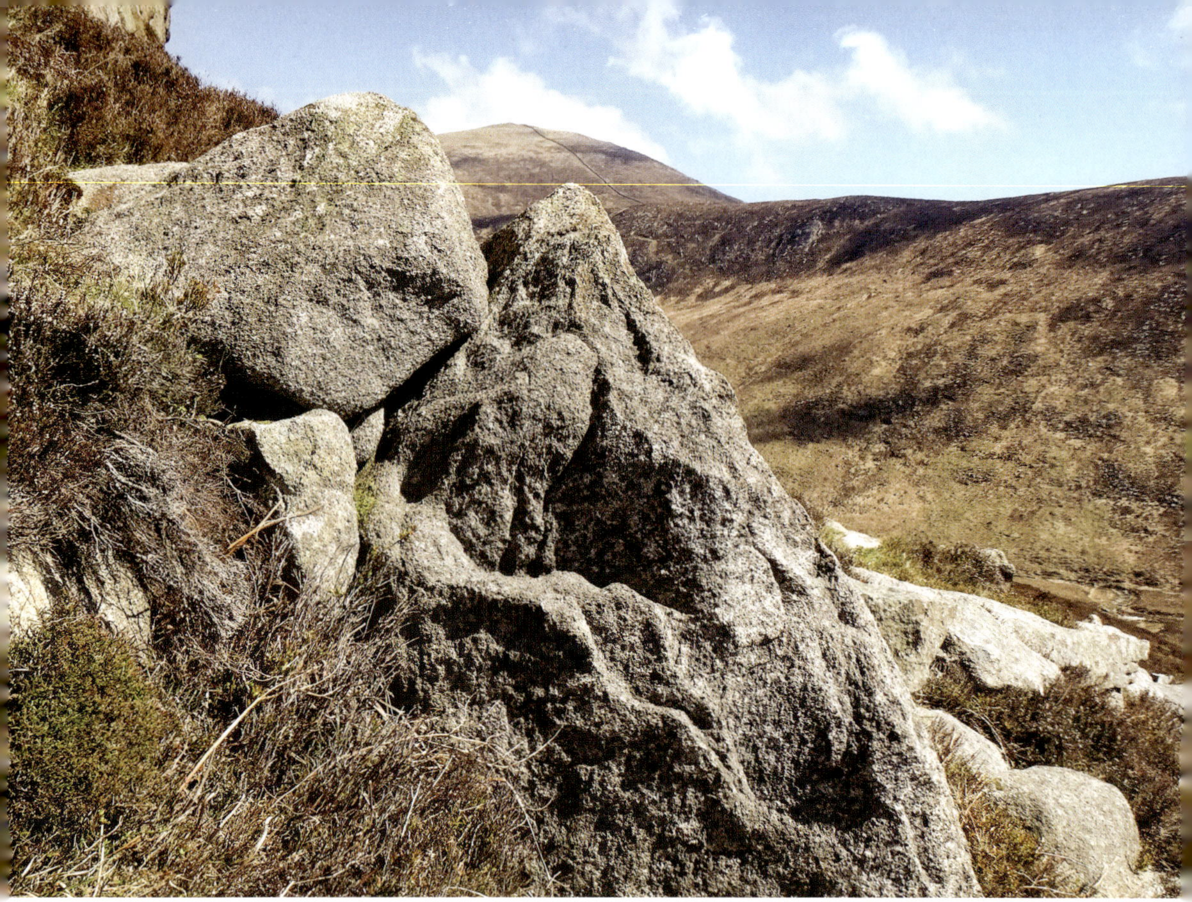

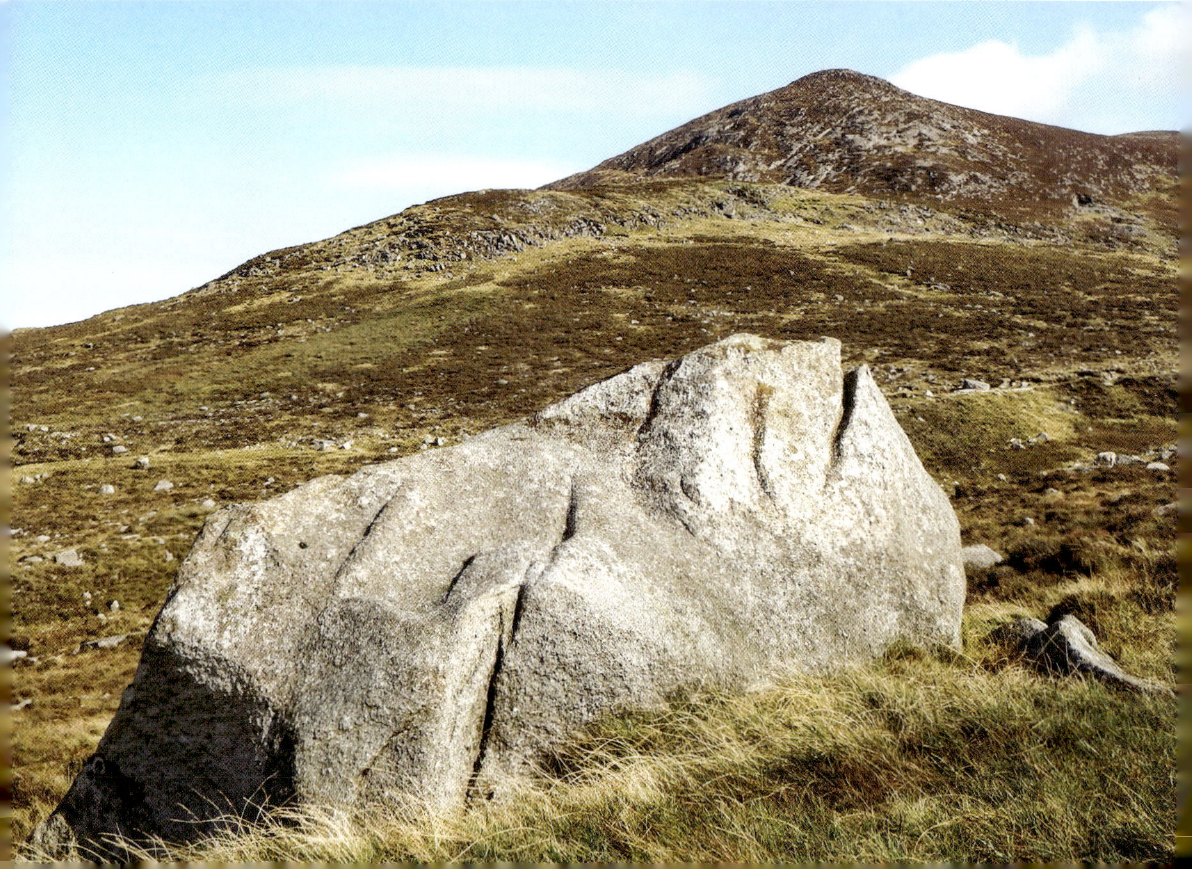

Top opposite: Feeding The Cuckoo
At the cliff corner of Lower Cove and the Annalong Valley, a large three metre mirror stone doubles as a large open-mouthed hungry cuckoo being fed by the much smaller parent bird. The GPS is:

        N.   54° 09. 902'
        W. 005° 57. 089'   Elevation 359m.

Lower opposite: The Cuckoo
On the north side of Spellack, a chunky granite boulder, roughly four metres long by two high by two again across, shows itself to be a sizeable sculpted cuckoo. This is a fertility location. The Cuckoo megalith marks the protruding tip of Cove mountain in the landscape 'vaginal' notch of the Hare's Gap. The GPS is:

        N.   54º 12. 030'
        W. 005º 59. 365'   Elevation 292m.

Top of this page: Common Lizard
This monument on the south-east flank of Slieve Bearnagh is of a Common Lizard and shows the skin folds behind the head. From below this is a mighty slab. It stretches over three metres across the top. The GPS is:

        N.   54º 11. 161'
        W. 005º 58. 582'   Elevation 435m.

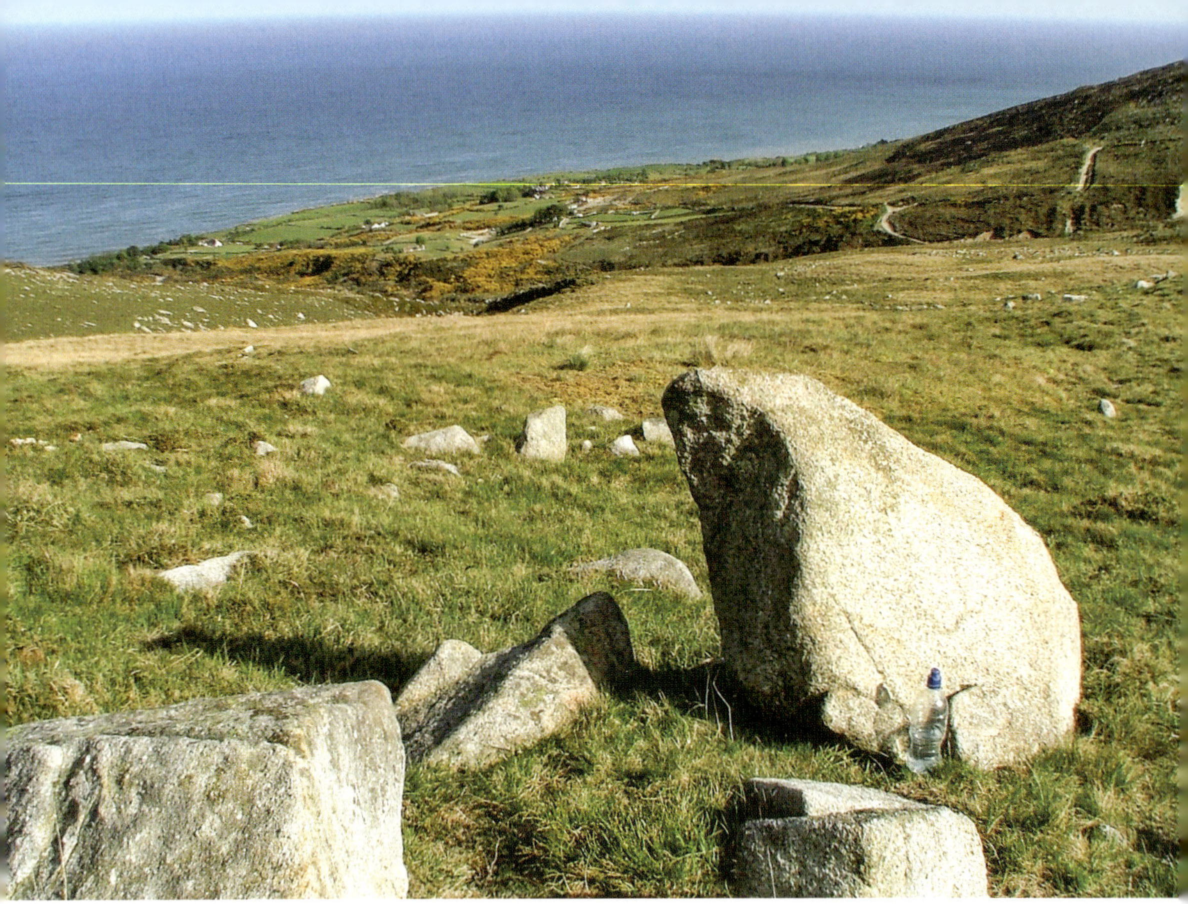

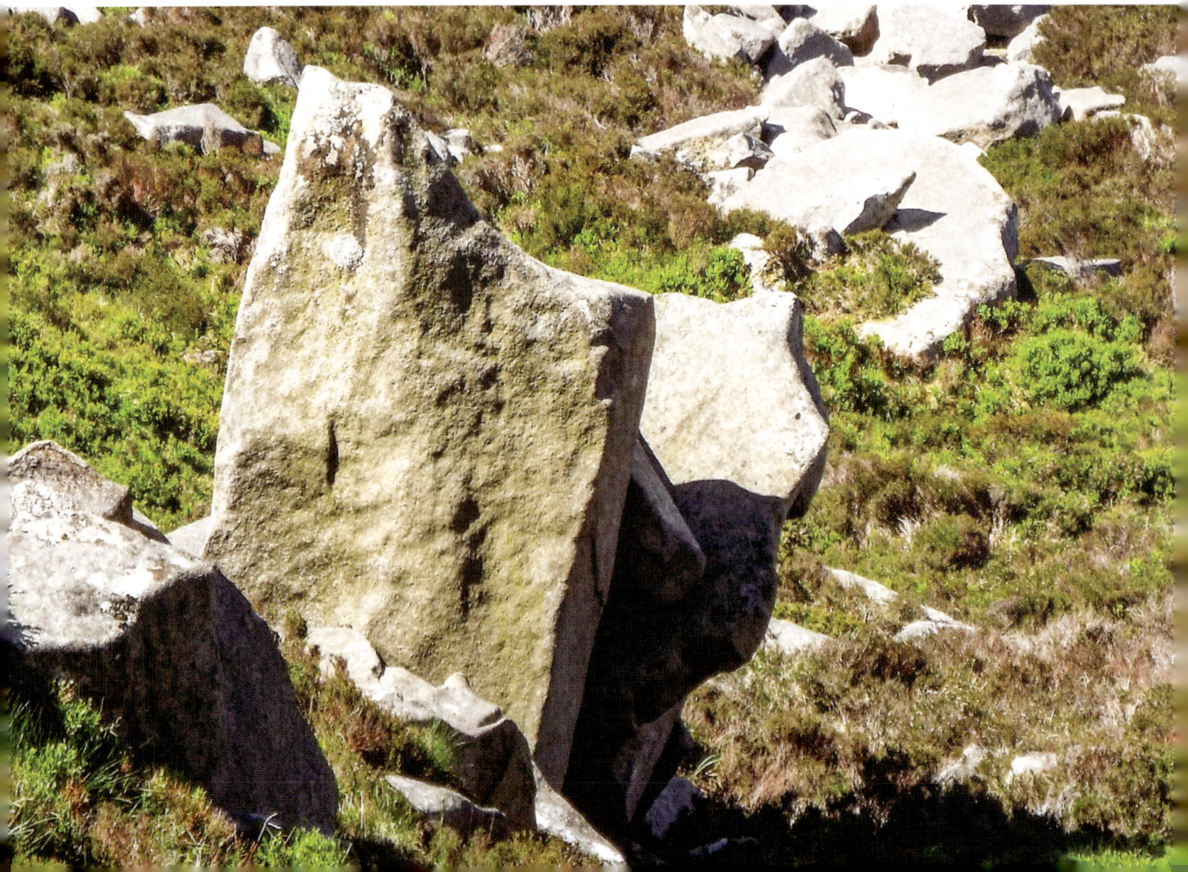

Top opposite: **The Little Frog**
A little frog sits on the lower seaward slope of Crossone mountain and above Glen Fofanny valley as it looks out over to the Isle of Man.

Lower opposite: **The Feeding Whale**
On the south side of Doan, and unfortunately not easy of access, is this remarkable creation of a feeding whale coming up from the depths with its mouth wide open. Only experienced mariners with a thorough knowledge of sea creatures and their habits could have made this striking monument. Definitely one of Mourne's noteworthy treasures.

Top of this page: **The Cobra**
Being conditioned that there are no snakes in Ireland it was quite some years after this photograph was taken that it was realised the early *Fir Builg* settlers may truly have intended to depict a rearing cobra with its hood flared in warning. Endemic to Asia, the settlers from the Iberian peninsula would have been well aware of this venomous reptile and brought memories with them to Mourne. The 'cobra' hides in plain sight on the south side of Slieve Bearnagh's summit tor at GPS
                        N.   54° 11. 052'
                        W. 005° 59. 406'   Elevation 704m.

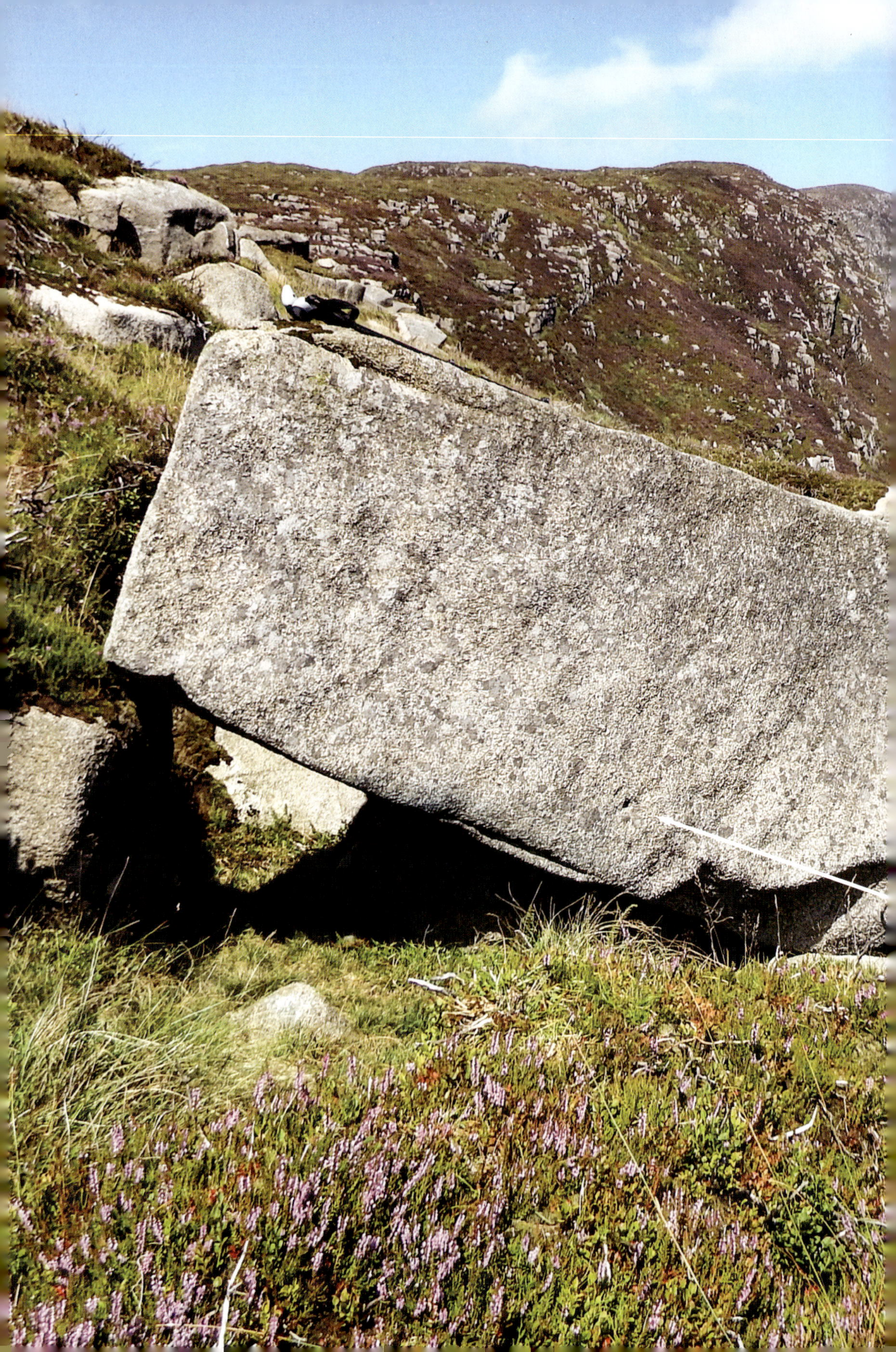

Sperm Whale
Along the crest of Long Mountain overlooking the Windy Gap valley is a propped granite stone the shape of which has ingeniously been used to represent the head of a sperm whale. With its mouth underneath and a tiny indent for a shadow eye, this imaginative creation is an artistic treasure of knowledge, skill and ability and, of course, a fair bit of strength to move and lift the stone to its present scenic position.

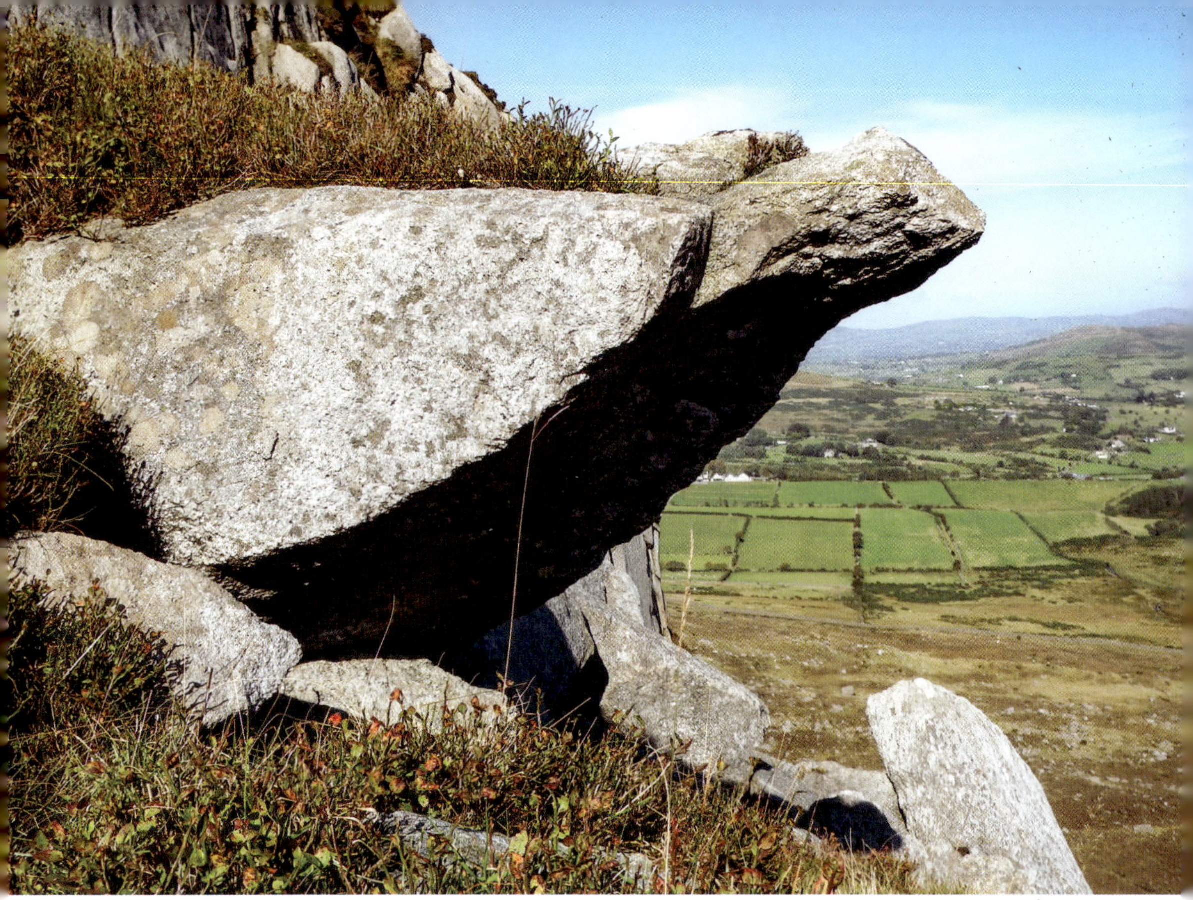

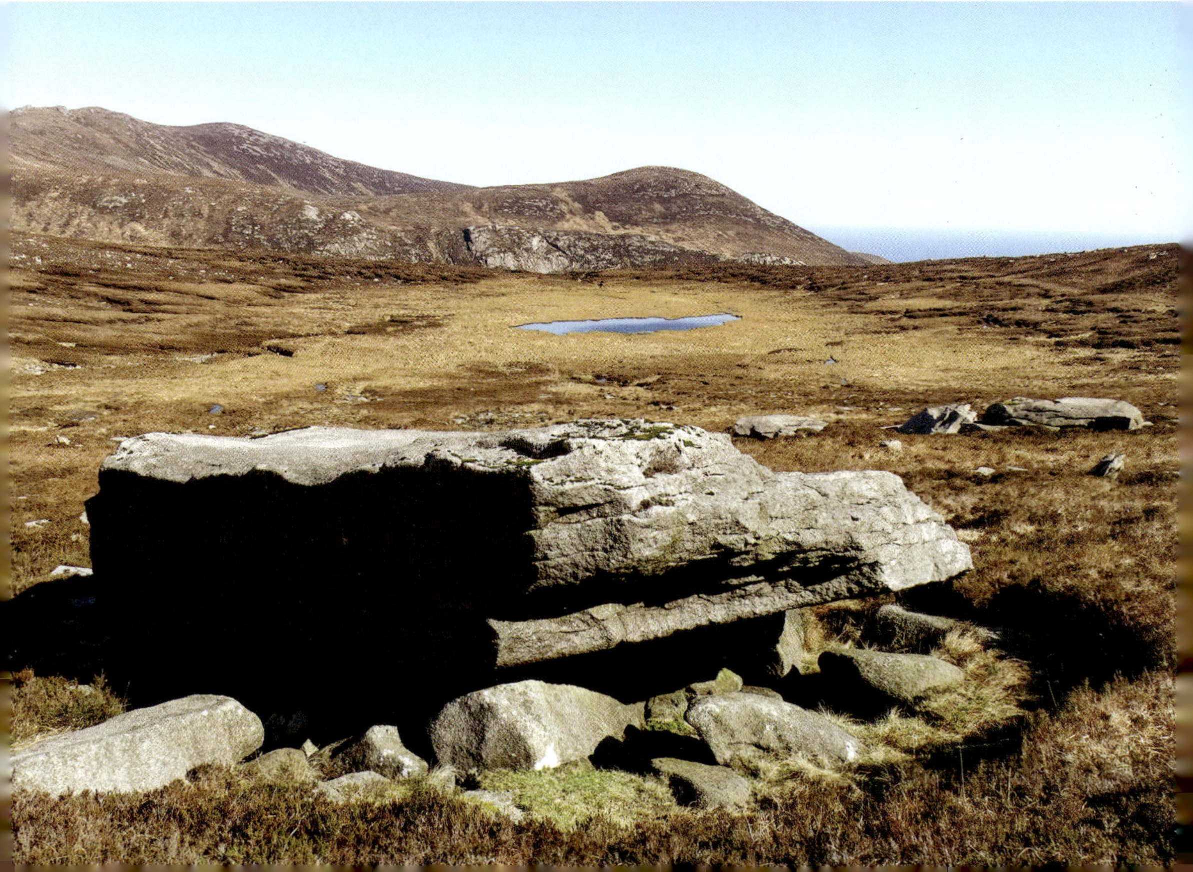

Top opposite: **The Spellack Turtle**
Among the slew of boulders at the north-east corner of Spellack is this propped granite stone of over two metres length that has a notable likeness to a turtle looking out from under its carapace. The stone is aligned on the tip of Shan Slieve to be seen in the landscape notch between Luke's mountain and Shimial mountain. The GPS is:

      N. 54° 11. 966'
      W. 005° 59. 443'   Elevation 352m.

Lower opposite: **The Great Turtle**
This stupendous slab, west of Cove Loch, is a representation of a great turtle with its head facing where winter solstice sun sets in the landscape notch between Bignian and Lamagan. The top surface of the stone was paced out at eight metres long by five and a half across. The slab is easily a metre thick and rests on at least three supports. Mighty men placed this megalith. The awesome stone is to be found at:

      N. 54° 10. 157'
      W. 005° 57. 398'   Elevation 452m.

Top of this page: **Luke's Mountain Turtle**
A substantial boulder on the west side of Luke's mountain, on the upper side of the peat trail, has been beautifully transformed into a turtle. The stone is perhaps two metres high by three metres long and the bottom part has been spalled off. The inset shows a close-up of the turtle's head. The GPS is:

      N. 54° 12. 502'
      W. 005° 58. 247'   Elevation 275m.

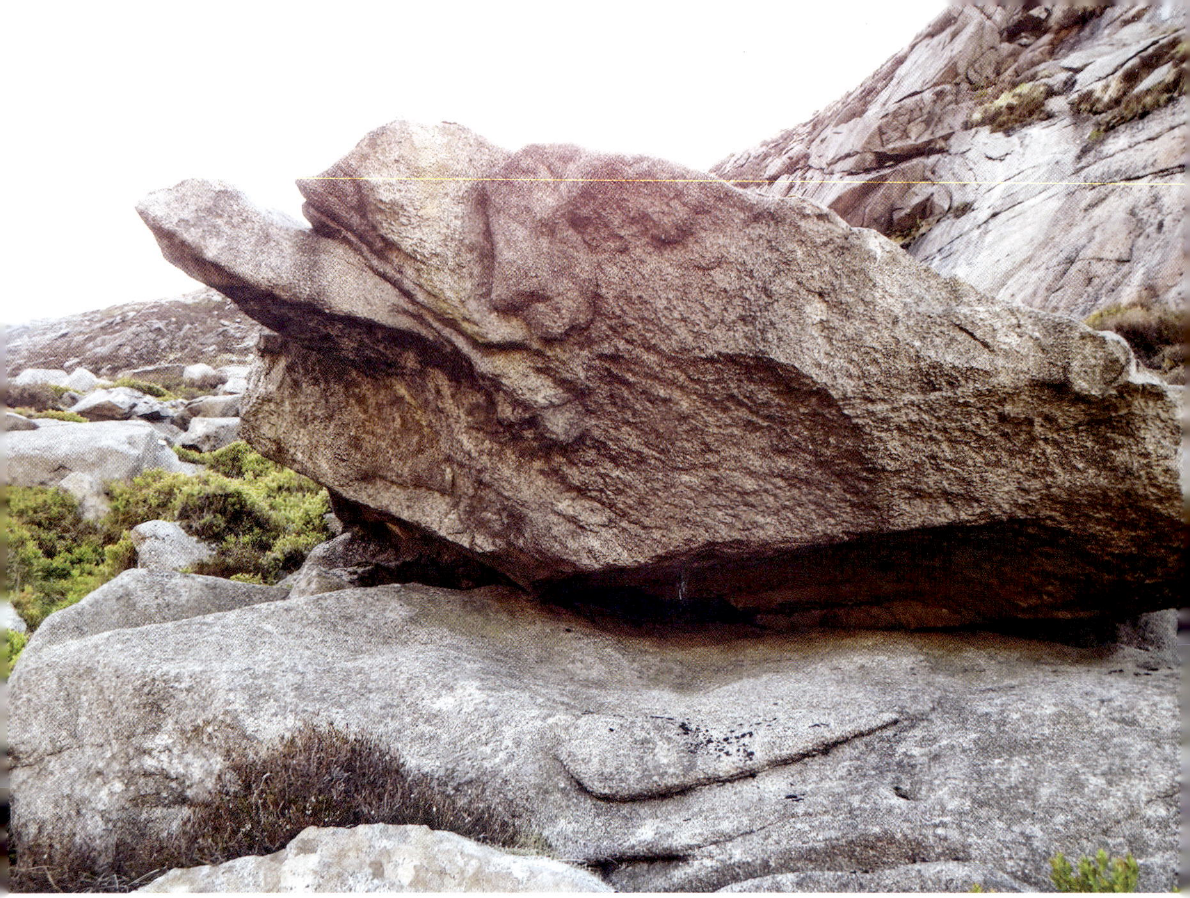

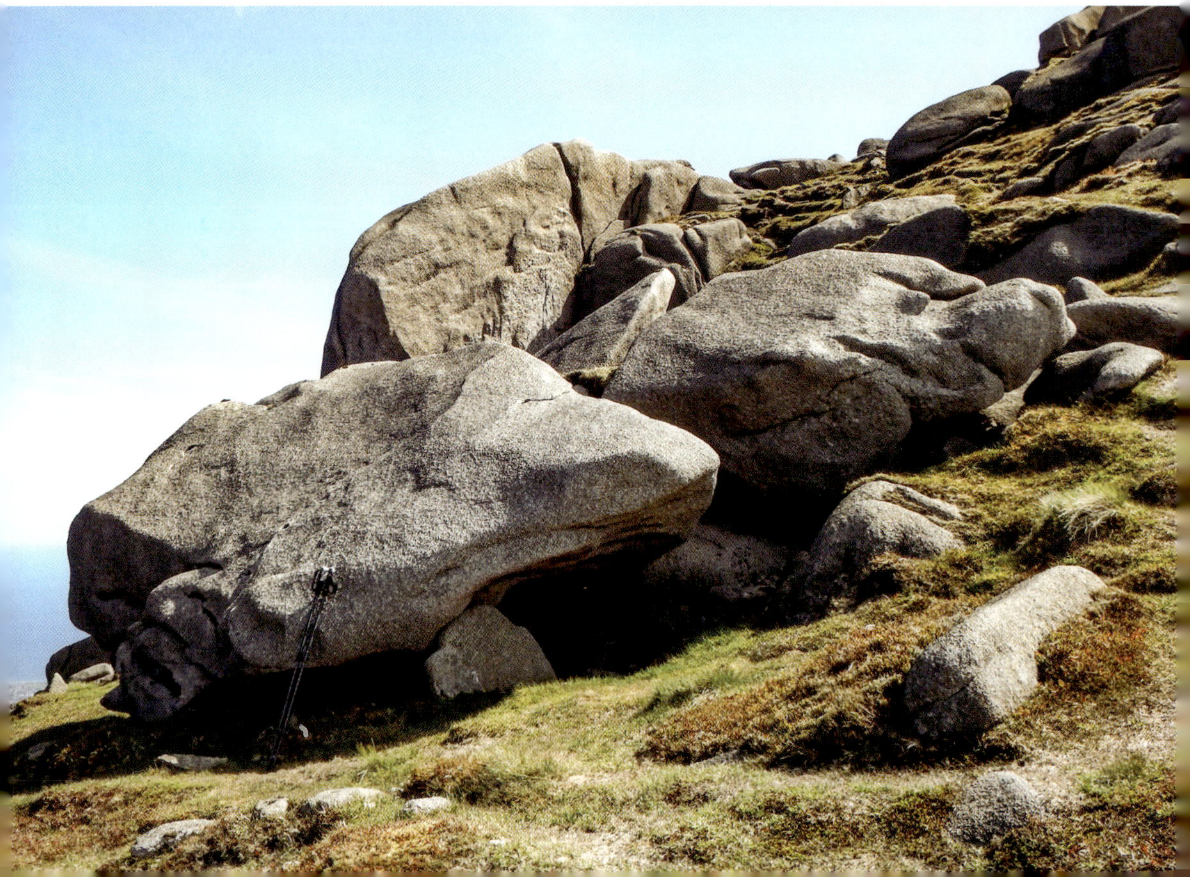

Top opposite: Pollaphuca Turtle
High on the eastern flank of Slieve Meelmore and on the north side of Pollaphuca valley is a great slab of about 3.5metres in length with a turtle head at the front pointing to Slieve Bearnagh's north tor. The GPS is:

                    N.   54° 11. 366'
                    W. 005° 59. 678'   Elevation 501m.

Lower opposite: Bignian Turtle and Dolphin
Near the eastern crest of Slieve Bignian these two rocks appear to depict a dolphin, on the left, and a turtle with a realistic flipper, on the higher right. The metre long trekking poles on the bottom left can be used to gauge how large these boulders are.

Top of this page: Donard Turtle
The water bottle gives scale to this little creature found on the southern flank of Slieve Donard.

113

The Eagle
On the south-west side of the Annalong Valley is to be found a cliff face carving that could easily be construed as an eagle. This is only part of a far more famous icon, namely the Red Hand of Ulster. The Eagle features under the first and second fingers. The GPS given below is about forty feet from the actual cliff face as this gives an overall better view.

N. 54° 09. 912'
W. 005° 57. 072'   Elevation 355m.

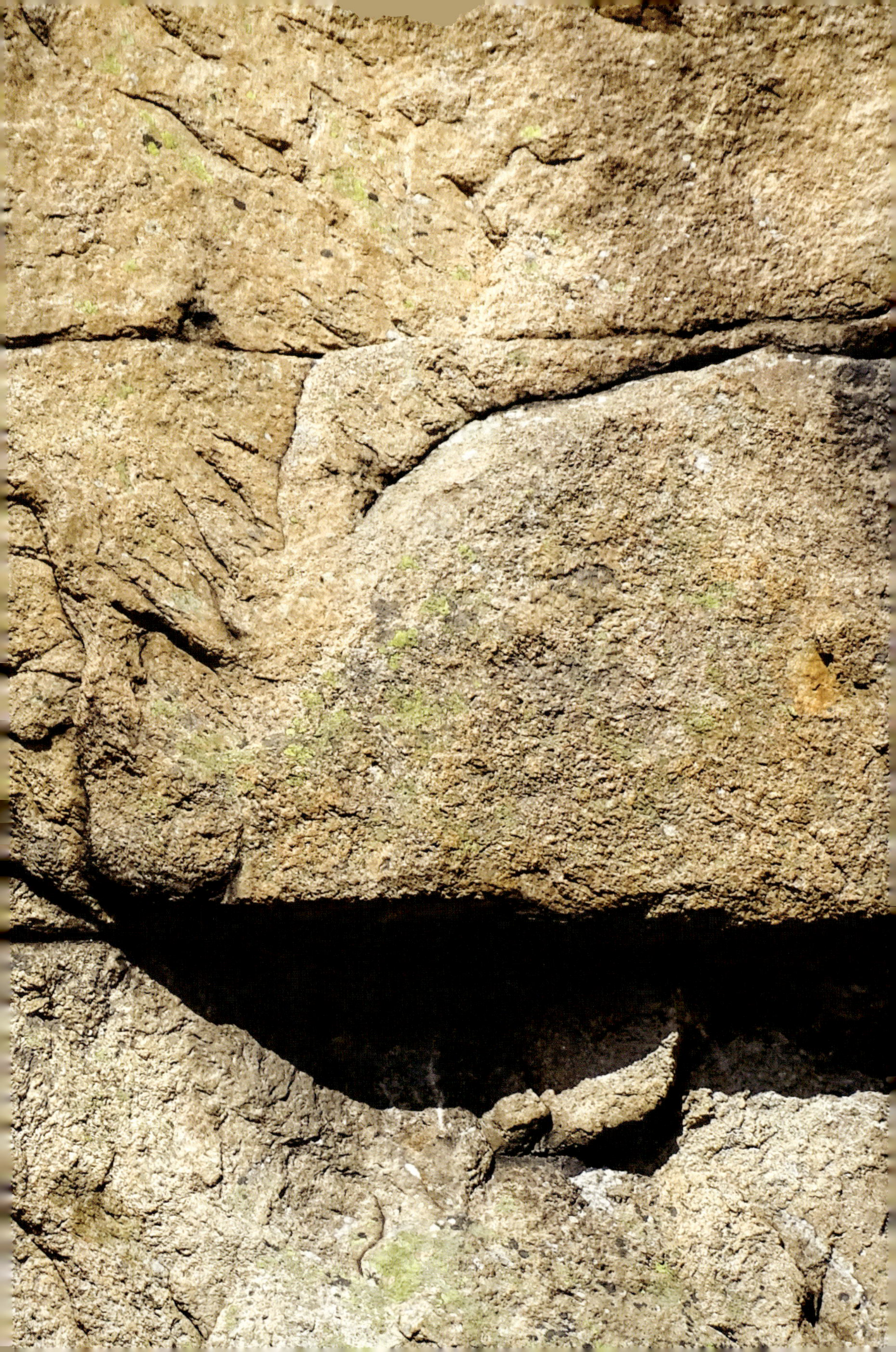

The Vulture
The rock formation on the second seaward buttress of Lower Cove cliff face has been skilfully used to represent an uncanny likeness of a vulture. The bird would have been another folk memory from the Iberian Peninsula. Above the sculpture, but not shown in our photograph, is the ritual stone chair of enchantment. This chair is illustrated on page 380 . The place-name of 'Upper' Cove derives from the Irish *Upthacht* meaning 'magic, sorcery, incantation, enchantment'.

The sculpture seems to show two vulture heads. The inset photo shows the lower vulture feeding what is presumed to be little chicks. The association of vultures with death gives rise to the ominous possibility that this location was a place of human sacrifice. It is probably no accident that the 'Rat' megalith is also to be found at the bottom of the buttress. The GPS is:

N. 54° 09. 929'
W. 005° 57. 148'   Elevation 420m.

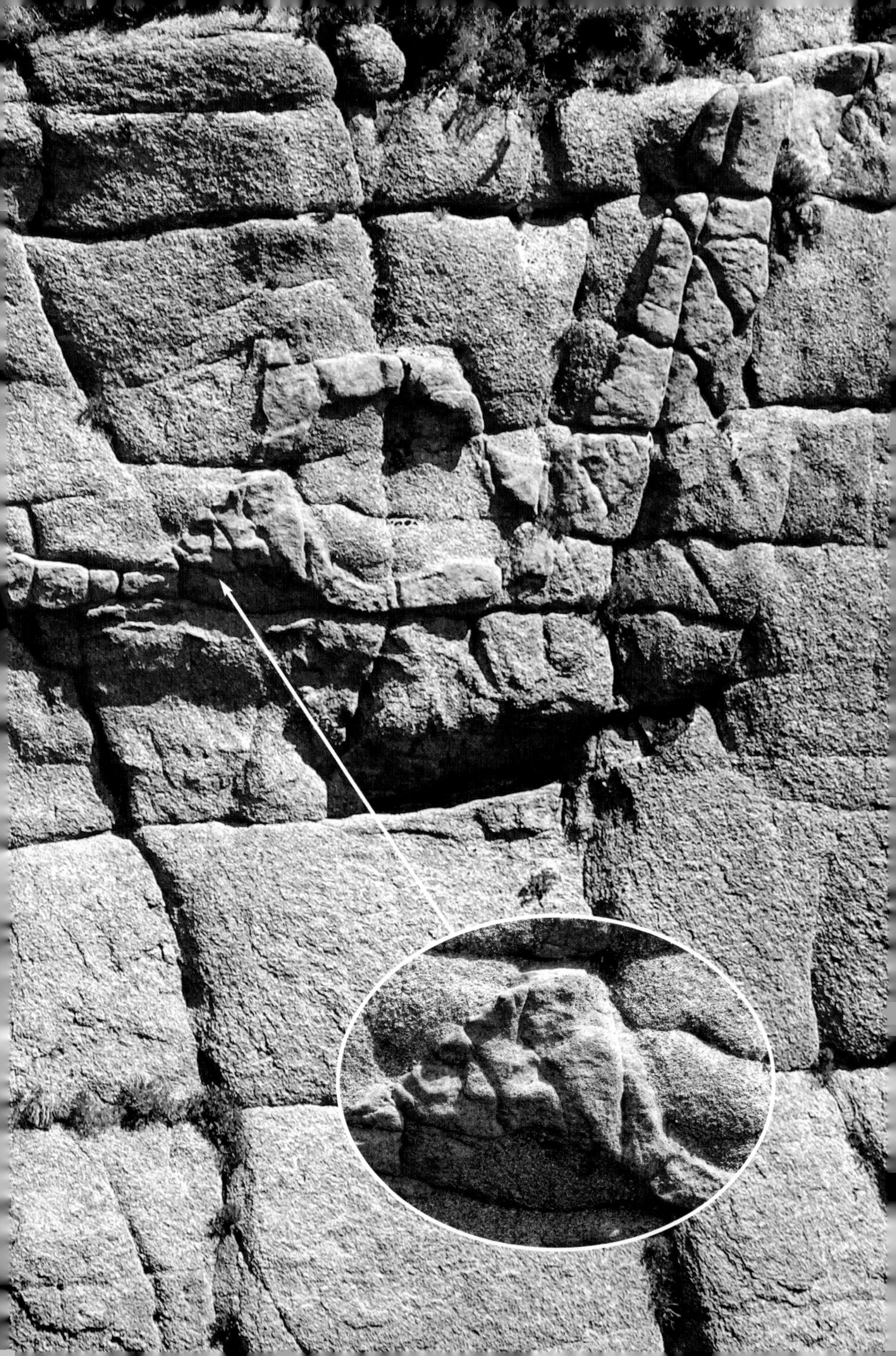

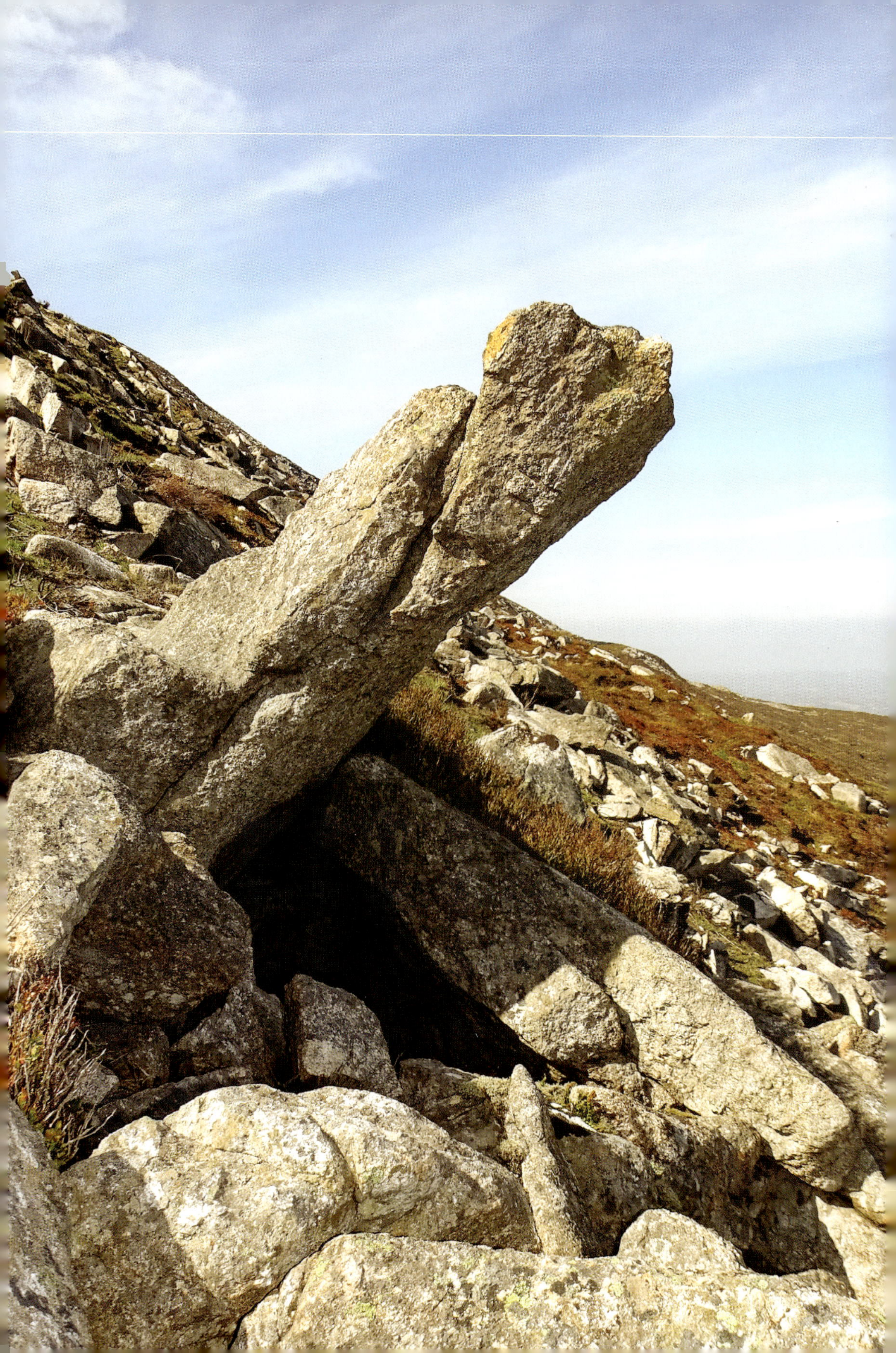

MALE STONES

**The truth a wonderful thing can be
Until it's found in the family tree.**

The sorry truth about Mourne is that our early ancestors were pagan. They worshipped the sun as the bringer of fertility. They placed a great multitude of megaliths in overt demonstrations of sexuality. You could say that they wore their sexuality on their sleeves almost like a badge of honour. They don't seem to have had any inhibitions or reserve. There was no sense of the usual codes of moral restraint that we take for granted after the coming of Christianity. Besides the plethora of male erections in stone, or the placement of slabs close together to represent a female slit, there is an extravagant abundance of great stones in the act of copulation or indulging in fellatio. In Irish the word for the act of begetting, or intercourse, is *Gein,* (gen.) **Geinte.** This has given rise to the mnemonic 'Giant' of which there are many instances in the folklore of Mourne. The last few decades have seen the resurgence and adaption of such stories as in the 'Wake the Giant' festival at Warrenpoint. Nowadays the mores of society frown on sexual 'unmentionables'. But the stones remain.

Winter solstice, the moment of the turning of the year, was of particular natural significance. Another sorry truth is that human sacrifices were made in Mourne. There is an old saying in Irish: *Lá na Sléibhe*. The literal translation is 'the day of the mountains' but the actual meaning is 'the Day of Doom'. The mists of time have mercifully blotted out the horrors of the sacrifices atop Ben Crom (recte: *Bean Crom*, 'the bent woman', the infamous fertility mountain 'penetrated' by the dawn light of winter solstice). The 'Day of Doom' was the fateful day when people, perhaps captives from battle, were led up the mountain to be sacrificed. All that is really left to remind us of the past horrors is the mnemonic name of nearby Miners Hole River which originated from the fact that in its early course it flowed

This great phallic projection on the seaward slope of Leganabruchan is aligned to winter solstice dawn. It is an impressively large stone. The back end buried in the hillside, and not shown in our photograph, is at least three metres long and a metre wide. There has been a lot of effort undertaken to manoeuvre this megalith into its present erection mode. The GPS is:

N. 54° 10. 863'
W. 005° 53. 523'   Elevation 315m.

MEGALITHIC MOURNE

towards Ben Crom as if yearning for what happened there. Miners Hole is from **Mian Áir Olc**, 'evil desire of slaughter'.

There is no doubt that human sacrifice took place at Mourne. Such is attested in *Bethu Phátraic* where the last king of Mourne was cursed by St Patrick. The king had two maidens tied to a rock on the shore until they were drowned by the in-coming waves for having offered their virginity to the Lord and for refusing to worship idols or marry.* Then we have the notorious sea chasm of Armours Hole. The very name Armour is its explanation; in Irish **Ár Mór** means 'great slaughter'.

When considering the great cliff called Spellach that rears over the Trassey river, we can only wonder if the real origin of the name comes from people being thrown off the cliff as in **Spealadh**, 'the act of shedding, flinging to waste, scattering abroad'. The same word also has the sense of 'cutting with the scythe'. The memory of the human sacrifices at Ben Crom is preserved even in one of the old names for Downpatrick. Rath Celtair is an old name for Cathedral hill. Standing in the graveyard at winter solstice you can see the sun setting on the shoulder of Shan Slieve and Slieve Corragh. If the sunset line of sight was projected further into the Mournes it would come to the great fertility mountain. The name of Rath Celtair refers to the sacrificial slaughter taking place out of sight in Mourne at Bean Crom at winter solstice. Rath Celtair is from the Irish **Ráth Ceilte Áir,** 'Rath of concealment of slaughter'.

This chapter shows another sorry truth of early Mourne namely the multitude of sexual megaliths erected by the *Fir Builg* settlers. Previously, in *Place-names of Beanna Boirrche*, we dealt with how their fertility beliefs influenced the names of the mountains; and very sexual names at that. It has annoyed some to hear of the sexual origins behind the names of Mourne such as Slieve Gluster, Ott, Meelmore or Shimial, to mention a few, but there is no changing the landscape from which they derive and it would be unworthy to dumb down or distort the Irish to try and assuage indignation. Comfort may be taken from the fact that the faith brought by St Patrick prevails. The pagan mindset behind the naming of the mountains has gone. While the mindset that viewed the landscape in sexual terms is

---

* The story of the 'Lighthouse' stone formerly sited on Glasdrumman shore, known in Irish as *Lia h-Iosa*, 'The Jesus Stone', was told and illustrated in *Prehistoric Mourne*, 2015, pages 487–489. This was the boulder believed to have been used in the drowning of the maidens. It is now deployed as a headstone in Bangor cemetery.

This is Slieve Gluster at the head of the Windy Gap valley. It is just one of many hills that were named from a sexual interpretation of the landscape. The phallic profile evoked the rhythm of intercourse and earned Gluster its Irish name of **Sliabh Gluaistighe,** 'mountain of moving'. The cliff edge seen on the very right is Craig Strucker. The name comes from the ominous Irish **Creag Stríocatha,** 'Crag of falling'. Neither name is presently listed by the ordnance survey.

now consigned to history, the sexual megaliths erected by the *Fir Builg* are still with us. They cannot be ignored. They are part of our patrimony. Indeed, it is the monumental work of erecting so many megaliths across the hills that lies behind the name of Mourne.

The Name of Mourne

The explanation as to how Mourne received its name has been made before but still bears repeating due to misunderstandings that have arisen since the disappearance of Irish. Mourne, as a name for the mountainous area of South Down, came into more common usage from the fourteenth century onwards. The account put forward over a century ago in the stories by Michael Crawford still prevails, namely that Mourne derives from a tribal name. He wrote:

> 'The three Collas came north and conquered Ulster in the third century, and from one of these '**Mughdhorn**' (Mourne), the clan MacMahon took their tribe-name, living in Cre Mourne, Monaghan, from which they migrated in the twelfth century to Beanna Boirche, and gave it their tribe name of 'Mourne'… (page 20: 'Boirche of the Benns', *Legendary Stories of the Carlingford Lough District,* printed by the Frontier Sentinel, Newry, 1913)

No need to look to Monaghan for the origins of the name of Mourne; Crawford was only following a mistaken Dindshenchas. We simply look to Irish and to what is found across the hills. '*Mughdhorn*' does not give us Mourne. '*More Mughorna*', as mentioned in QUB Place-names list of Mourne, comes from Neilson's Introduction to the Irish Language. It is a phonetic rendering of the Irish (*Sléibhte*) **móire Mudha h-Óirdnighe** which has been translated as 'mountains of renowned ritual killing'; yet another reference to human sacrifice in our sorry past.

The name of Mourne is a telescoped remnant of the Irish (*Sléibhte na*) **mBúir-na**, '(mountains of) very many roars'. The operative word is **Búir**, meaning 'a shout, a cry; a roaring, a bellow'. Allowing a short little grammatical explanation, it is because of the use of the definite article '*na*', before the word *Búir* that it has been eclipsed with [m]; that means the sound of [B] has been replaced by [M]. All that is heard nowadays is (*Sléibhte na*) **m_úir-na**, which has become our familiar Mourne. So many megaliths have been arranged by the ancients that the hills long echoed with loud shouts, roars and yells of effort and triumph. The stones featured in this work are only a very small sample of what is to be found.

The megaliths in this section have been ordered into the following general headings:

1. Spear Stones
2. *Leachtán*
3. Meatus Grooves (Anatomical: Penile orifice)
4. Use of infusions to denote penile coronal rings or semen
5. Stones of man's erect defining appendage (phallic stones)

One last little note. Where possible a GPS location is given with illustrations of megaliths. In some instances photographs of impressive stones were taken before a hand-held GPS was available. Also, to please be aware, hand-held GPS are not military grade and do not provide pin-point accuracy but come with a locational margin of error of roughly five or six metres so a bit of latitude is usually needed. The megaliths, however, live up to their Greek name of 'great stones' and are easily and quickly found across a hillside.

1. Spear Stones

Many of the phallic stones of Mourne are, what might best be called, 'Spear Stones'. The spear is one of the earliest hunting tools of mankind. The killing point, often meticulously shaped from flint, was the source of man's supremacy and dominance over animals. From earliest times when man lived by hunting, his spear was the source of his power and became, by extension, a representation of his own sexual prowess. It came to represent his erect sexual member in all its potency. In Mourne symbolical spear stones were erected in their hundreds. That there are so many is probably the accumulated work over many centuries. That they survived and remained undisturbed even after the arrival of Christianity was due to their remoteness up in the hills on land that could not be farmed and no doubt also to a strong superstitious dread that evil would befall anyone who interfered with them. In recent centuries when men made their livelihood from the granite of the hills, the point of a spear-stone was sometimes first broken off to rob it of any dangerous power before the stone was segmented for cribben or setts.

This flint spear head was found under Slieve Muck's escarpment.

Spear stones, as the name suggests, are stones with a pronounced point, the tip of which is usually directed towards a fertility feature like a rounded hill-top which would have been interpreted as a vulva; a fissure, crack or gorge which notionally became a vagina. Often the tip is directed towards a point on the horizon where the solstice sun rises or sets. Stones on the front of Millstone mountain, for instance, are found pointing either towards the breast-like summit of Drinnahilly, or out across Dundrum Bay to where the summer solstice sun rises, or again towards the distant phallic extremity of St John's Point. A phallic stone can also be spear shaped but is more overt in its sexual character or upward thrusting pose. The tip will invariably be found to point beyond itself to a place of fertility significance. There are a multitude of such stones to be found throughout Mourne and a rocky hillside is the surest place to look. Other sections illustrate how these spears have been pushed out over the void of cliffs and been endowed variously with meatus grooves, coronal rims and even deploying a light coloured rock suggestive of semen.

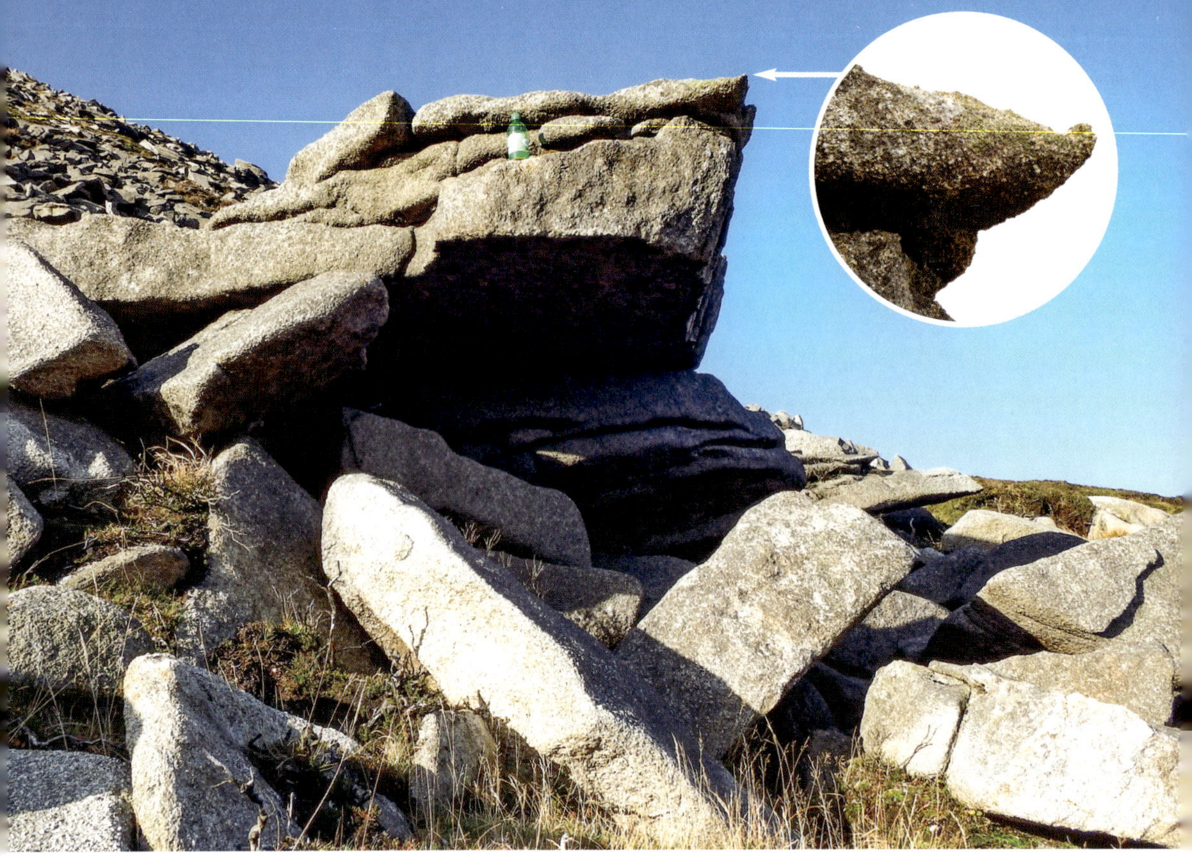

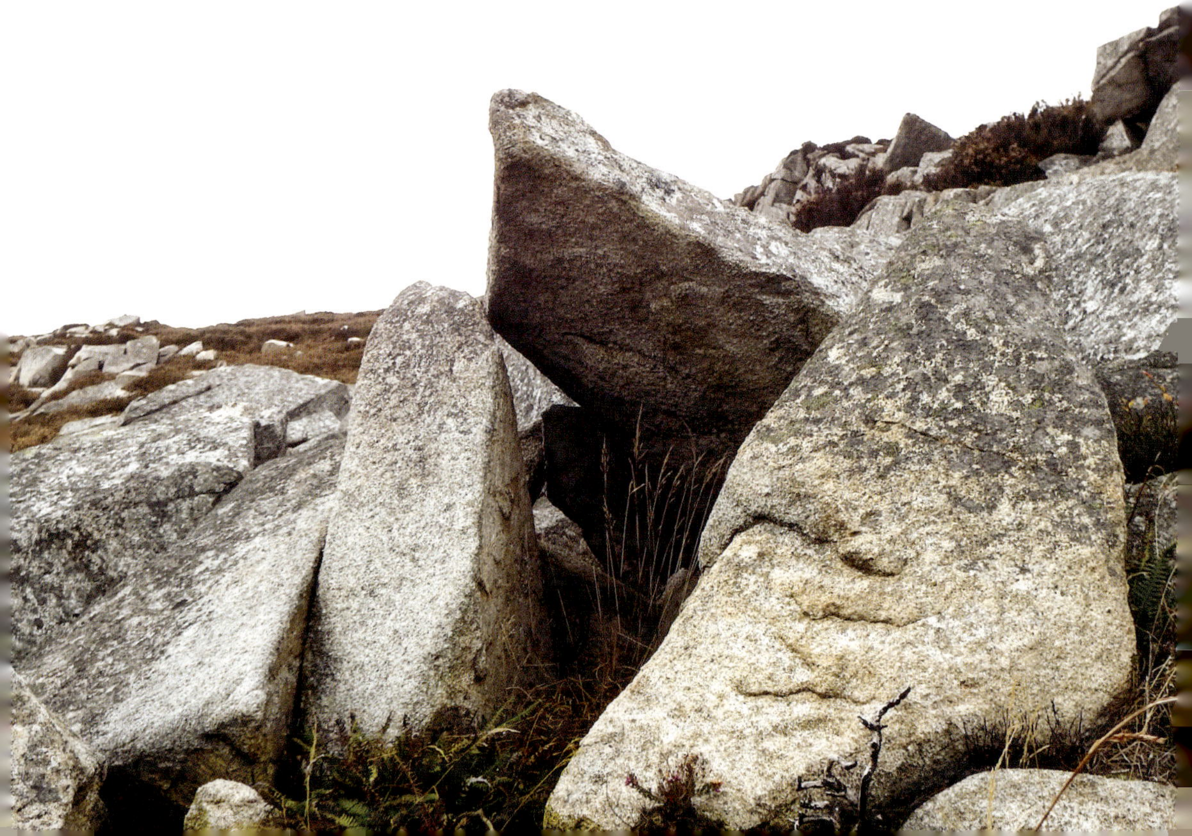

Top opposite: A mighty slab on Lamagan's eastern flank, overlooking the buttresses of Lower Cove, points to where the sun will rise at winter solstice. The inset shows the tip embellished with a tiny little phallic horn.
The GPS is:

                        N.   54º 10. 002'
                        W. 005º 57. 465'   Elevation 464m.

Lower opposite: On the south-east flank of Millstone mountain is this granite spear in erect phallic mode. The spear point is precisely aimed towards winter solstice sunrise. The 1.8m phallic spear is held in place by a counter-balance stone at the back. The two upright stones at the front form a vaginal gap under the spear for the solstice light. Neither of these uprights, however, support the spear although they are very close. The GPS is:

                        N.   54º 11. 046'
                        W. 005º 53. 597'   Elevation 354m.

Top of this page: Three substantial phallic spear stones strut their stuff in this commanding position near the top of *Uí Sliabh Bán Mór* which the shepherds refer to as Wee Slevanmore. It is the south eastern shoulder of Meelmore. This site has a magnificent view especially down the Silent Valley. The top stone, with its knobbly tip, points to the distinctive notch of Bignian's north tor. From the other side this knobbly tip suggests a bird about to take flight. The GPS is:

                        N.   54º 11. 193'
                        W. 006º 00. 025'   Elevation 624m.

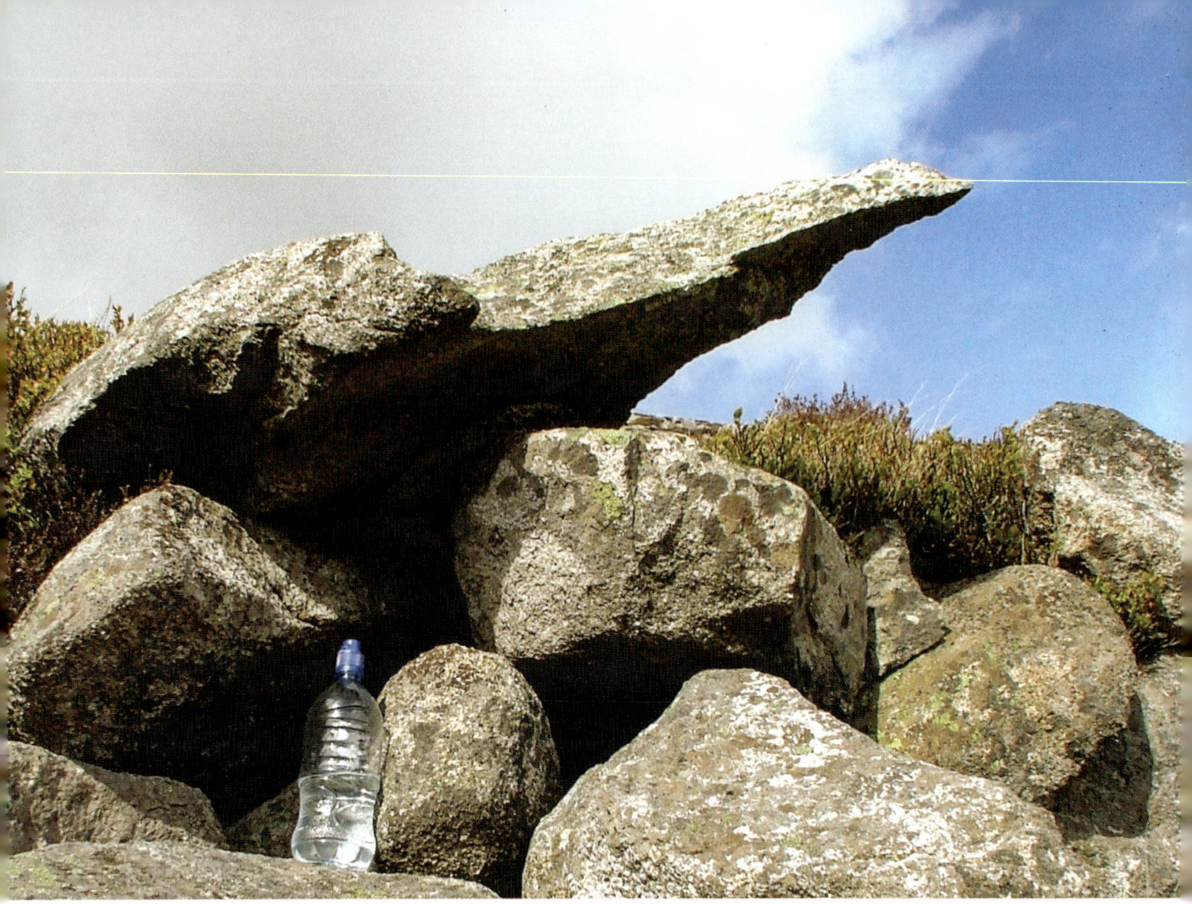

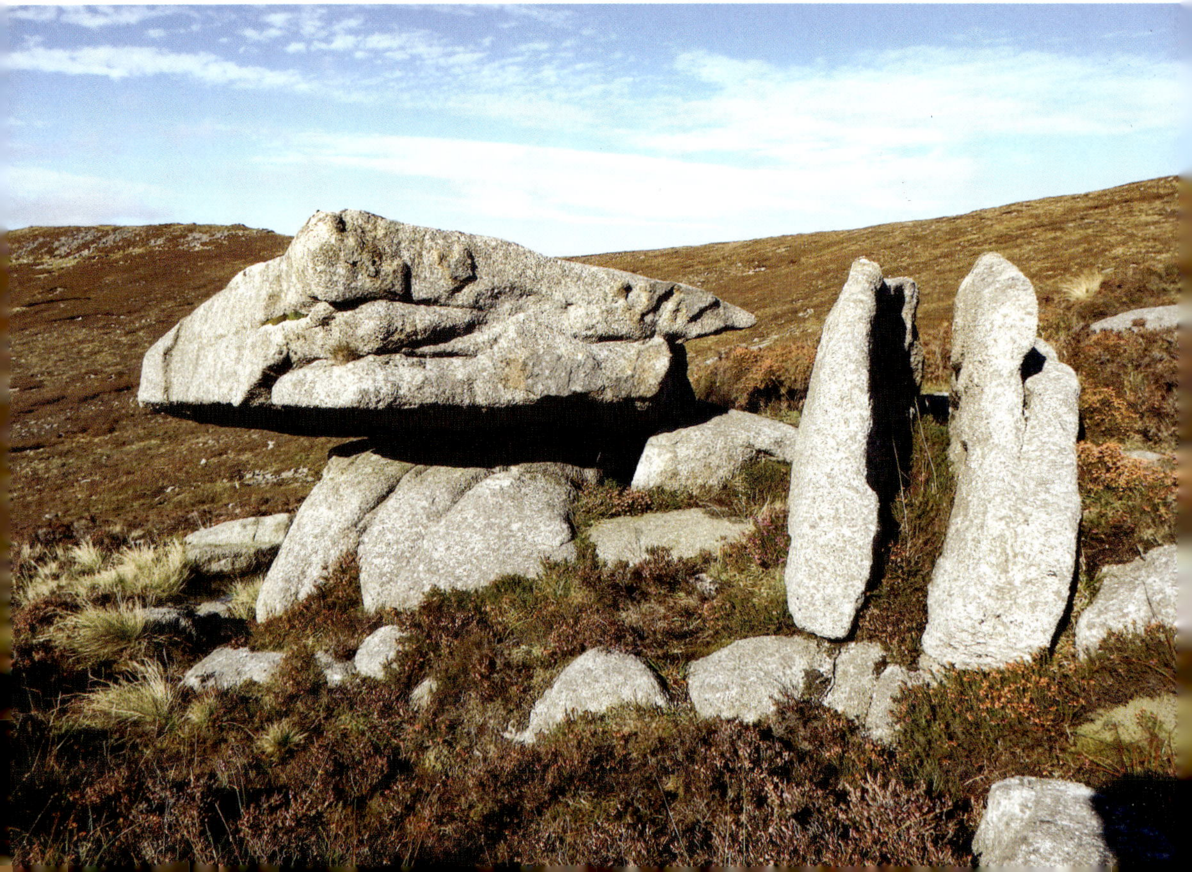

Top opposite: As the size of the water bottle shows, this stone on the southern slope of Crossone is not particularly large. It more than makes up for any shortcomings in size with its deadly tapering point. The tip is directed to winter solstice sunrise.

Lower opposite: The original name for this treasure of male and female stones unfortunately did not survive the disappearance of Irish so it has now been christened **An Rí Agus Banríon**, 'The King and Queen'. It is to be found at the northern end of Slievenaglogh cliff-top above the Trassey River. The 'King' stone is a triangle of spear points and the one on the right shows a 'face' with a rather pointy 'nose'. The 'Queen' is a classic female vaginal gap being variously 15cm wide at the bottom to about 40cm at the top. The two labial sides are about 1m high and vary in length. The important feature of the 'Queen' is its alignment to the landscape fertility feature of the Bearnagh/Meelbeg notch where it is believed winter solstice sun finally sets. The GPS is:

                N.   54º 11. 616'
                W. 005º 58. 389'   Elevation 515m.

Top of this page: The rucksack on top of this megalith under the north side of Bignian looks positively tiny. The near wedge shaped spear point looks back towards the appearance of the winter solstice.

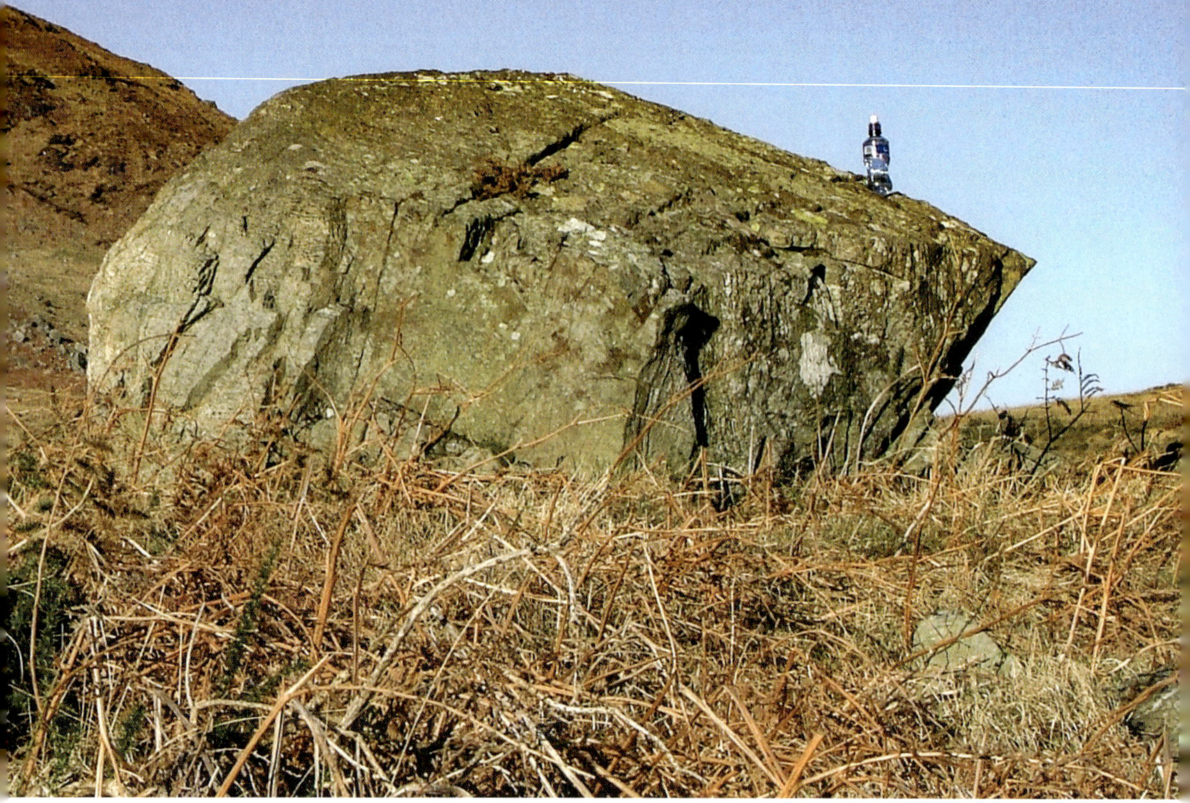

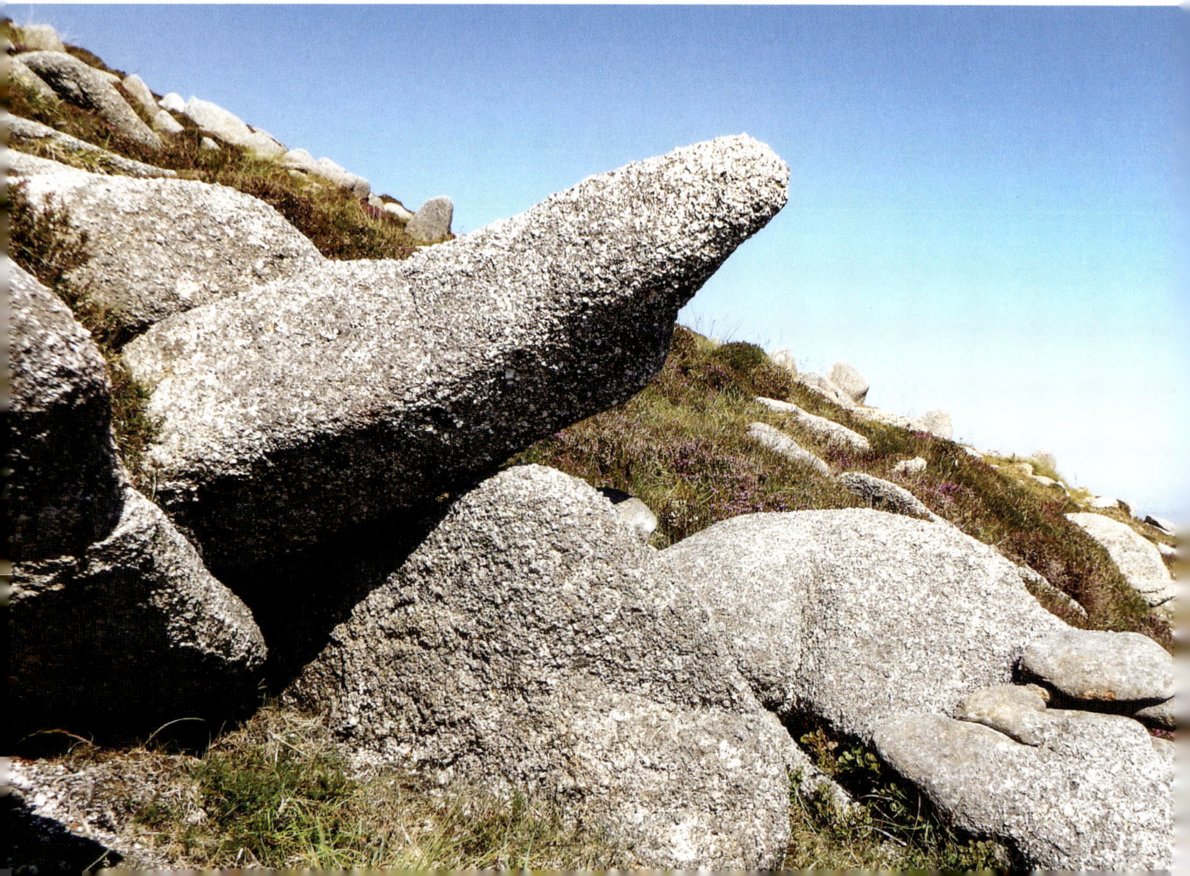

Top opposite: Given the propensity of shale to shatter the crafting of this exceedingly sharp spear point is an impressive work of skill and ability. If not by now overgrown by gorse, this metre high spear can be found at the mouth of the Curragh Ard Valley, 200 metres beyond the pump house atop a small rise. The GPS is:

                N.   54º 12. 496'
                W. 005º 55. 425'   Elevation 158m.

Lower opposite: This 1m propped phallic spear stone is on the east flank of Slieve Bearnagh's north tor. The GPS is:

                N.   54º 11. 198'
                W. 005º 58. 871'   Elevation 595m.

Top of this page: At three to four metres in length along the top this is a seriously impressive megalith. It is on the south-east flank of Slieve Bearnagh an area rich in the work of the ancients. The spear point is generally directed to the Beag/Cove landscape notch akin to winter solstice sunrise. The GPS is:

                N.   54º 11. 161'
                W. 005º 58. 582'   Elevation 435m.

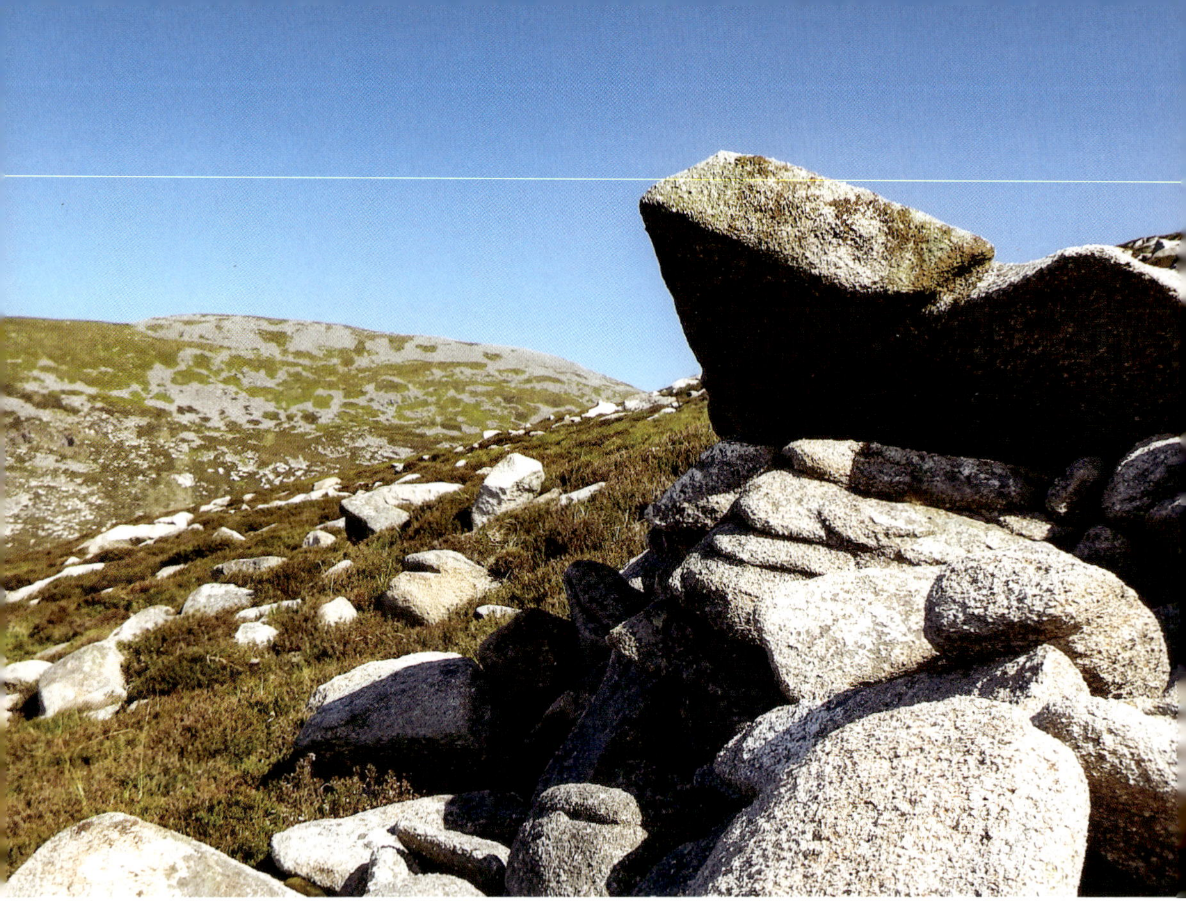

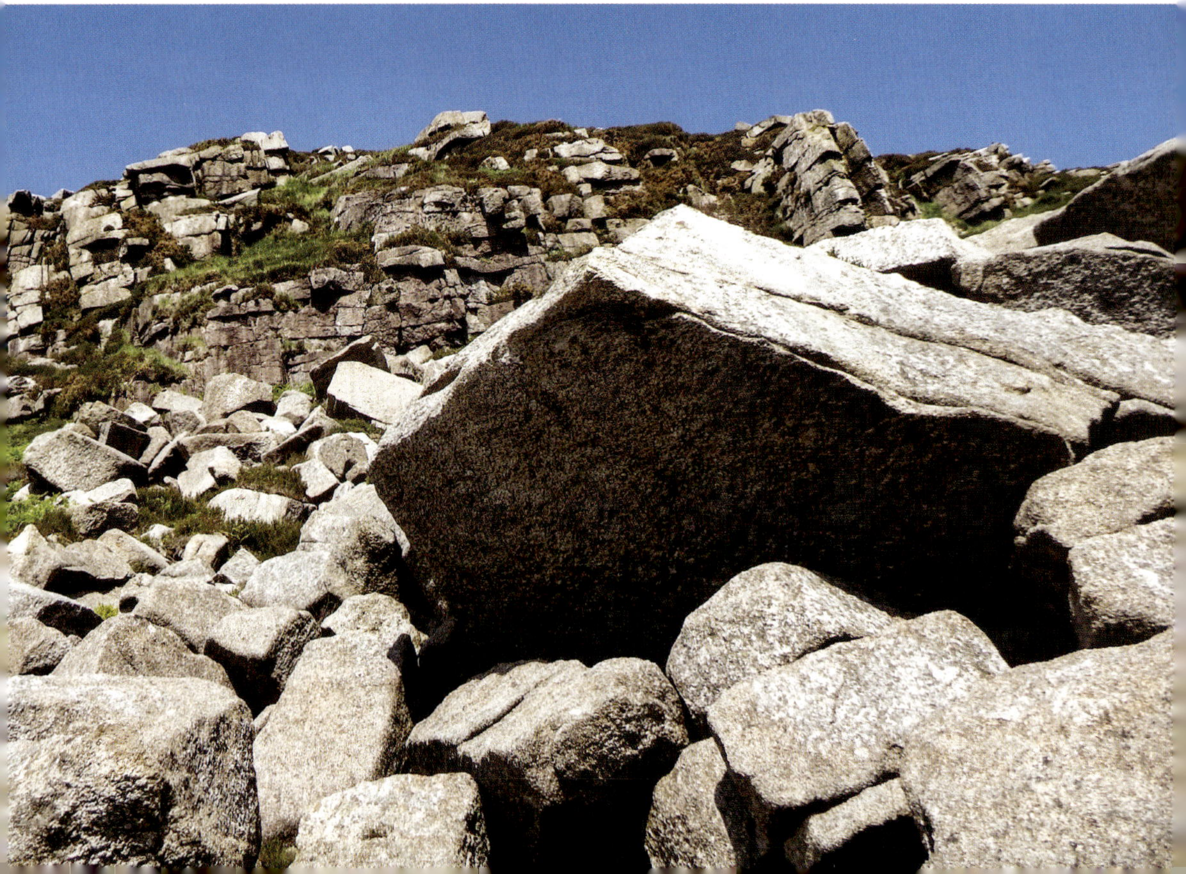

Top opposite: On the south flank of Crossone a number of smallish boulders have been piled up to support this dramatic phallic spear slab, the tip of which points to the end of Chimney Rock mountain. The GPS is:

    N. 54° 10. 498'
    W. 005° 54. 332'   Elevation 464m.

Lower opposite: The creation of this awesome megalithic that overlooks the Annalong Valley from its western slope would have taken very many men and strong men at that. This great propped spear stone is about four metres wide and easily a metre thick. The spear point notices the phallic profile of Chimney Rock mountain to the east. There is another propped spear stone at the back left. The GPS of the front megalith is:

    N. 54° 09. 971'
    W. 005° 57. 020'   Elevation 374m

Top of this page: A construction of at least a dozen granite blocks culminates in this large spear stone in erect phallic mode pointing to a vulva-like Commedagh. The side of the spear would be 1.4 metres long and .4m thick. It is just below the rim of Lower Cove lake plateau and overlooks the Annalong Valley. The GPS is:

    N. 54° 10. 063'
    W. 005° 56. 966'   Elevation 403m.

A beautifully crafted spear head, complete with barbs at either side, rests at the eastern end of Chimney Rock Mountain known to fishermen of old as 'The General'. The megalith overlooks the Mourne hill at J 3726 that was formerly known in Irish as *Glaise Drom Áine*, 'Stream of the ridge of pleasure' [Quite distinct from Glasdrumman village]. Due to an unfortunate mix-up in the past this hill seen in the background is now marked on maps as Slievenagarragh, a name which properly belongs to a megalith at the west end of Chimney Rock.

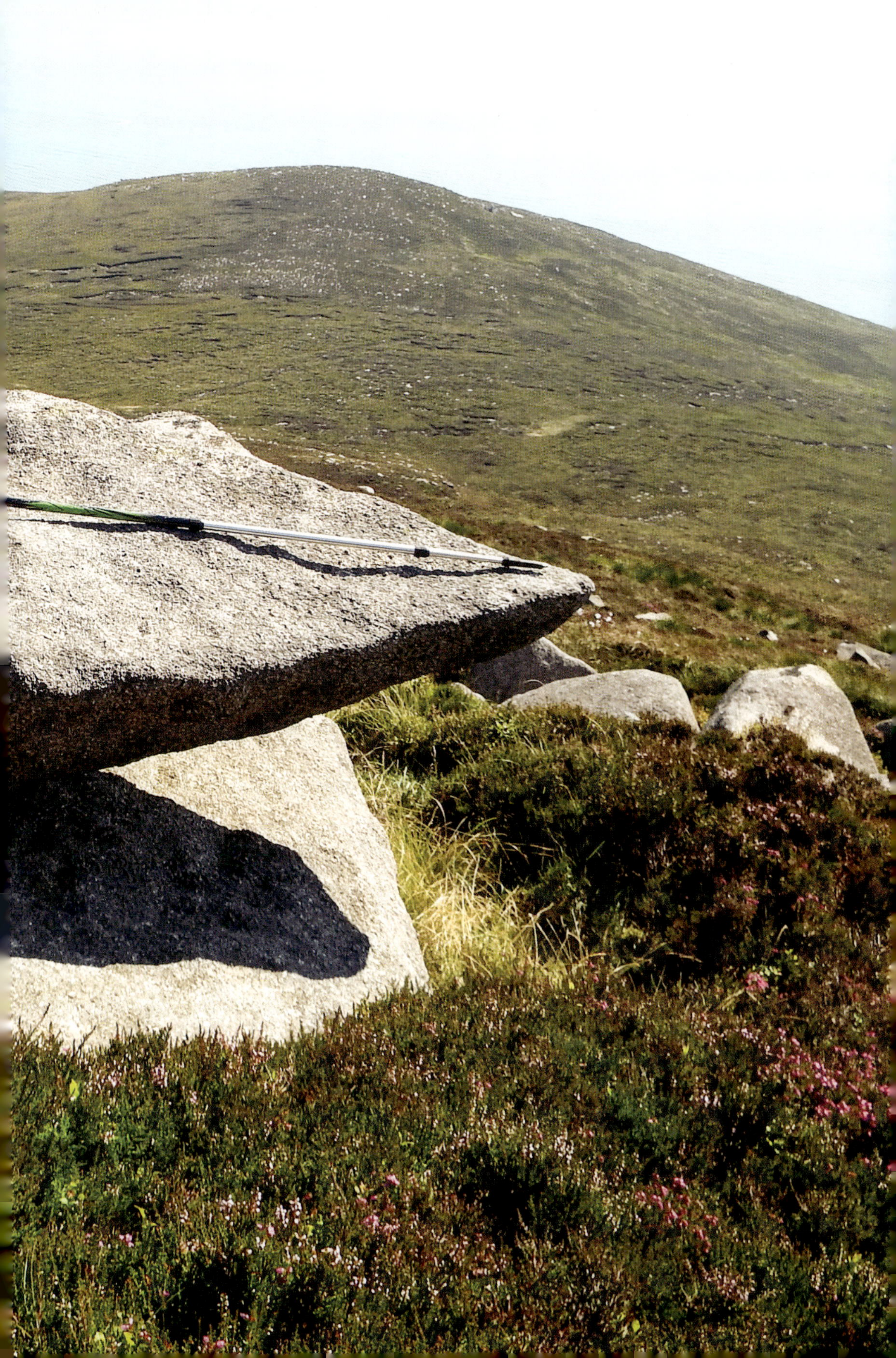

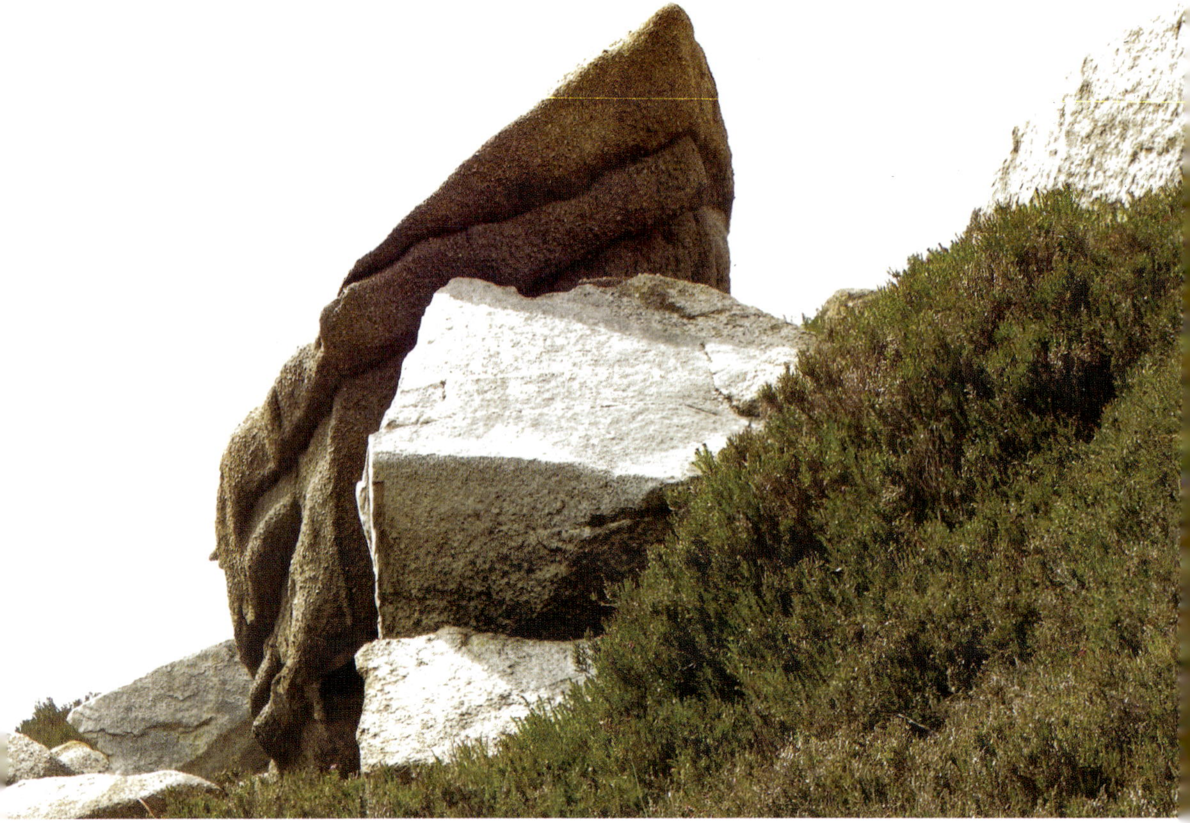

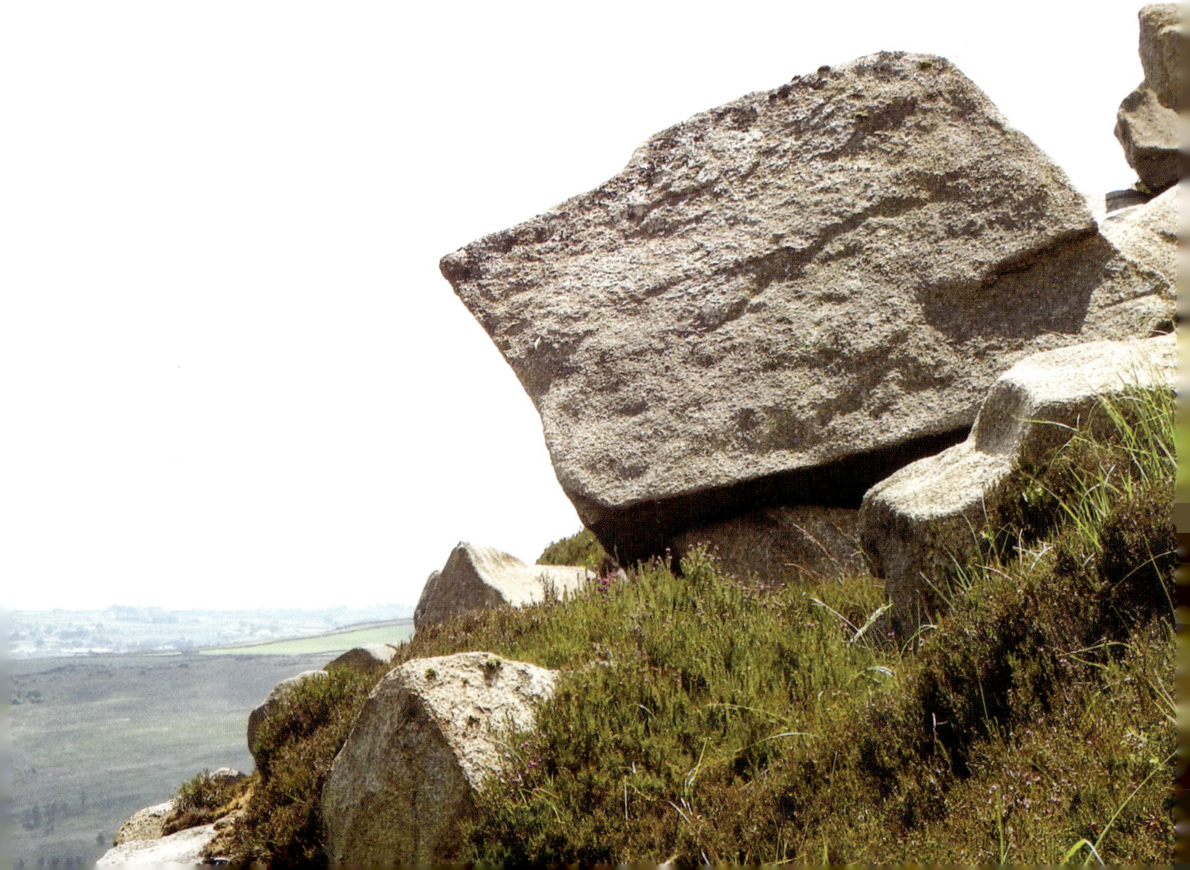

Top opposite: A 1.5m long spear stone overlooking the Annalong valley directs its emphatic point towards Slieve Donard. The stone is cleverly propped up into phallic mode by a tilted block underneath. The GPS is:

N.   54º 10. 051'
W. 005º 56. 971'   Elevation 399m.

Lower opposite: A pin-point sharp nose is the distinctive feature on this large boulder on the west slope of the Annalong valley close to Cove mountain. There is an open mouth face (not shown) on the other side. The GPS is:

N.   54º 10. 243'
W. 005º 56. 950'   Elevation 424m.

Top of this page: This significant boulder megalith, on the steep hillside of Shimial's northern slope was named **Duine as an gCéad**, 'One in a Hundred'. It overlooks the place known as 'Horse's Meadow'. The main corner in the photograph looks to summer solstice sunset but there is much more not shown. At the back you could look how the little chock stone raises the boulder substantially. See the little phallus carved in relief, complete with a penile corona and your imagination should also discern low at the back the representation of a little pig with its head down. The pig evokes the tale of the Otherworld in *Togail Bruidne Dá Derga*, 'The Destruction of Da Derga's Hostel', where the lord of the feast was sometimes represented as a man carrying a pig on his shoulder. The GPS is::

N.   54º 12. 070'
W. 005º 58. 542'   Elevation 346m.

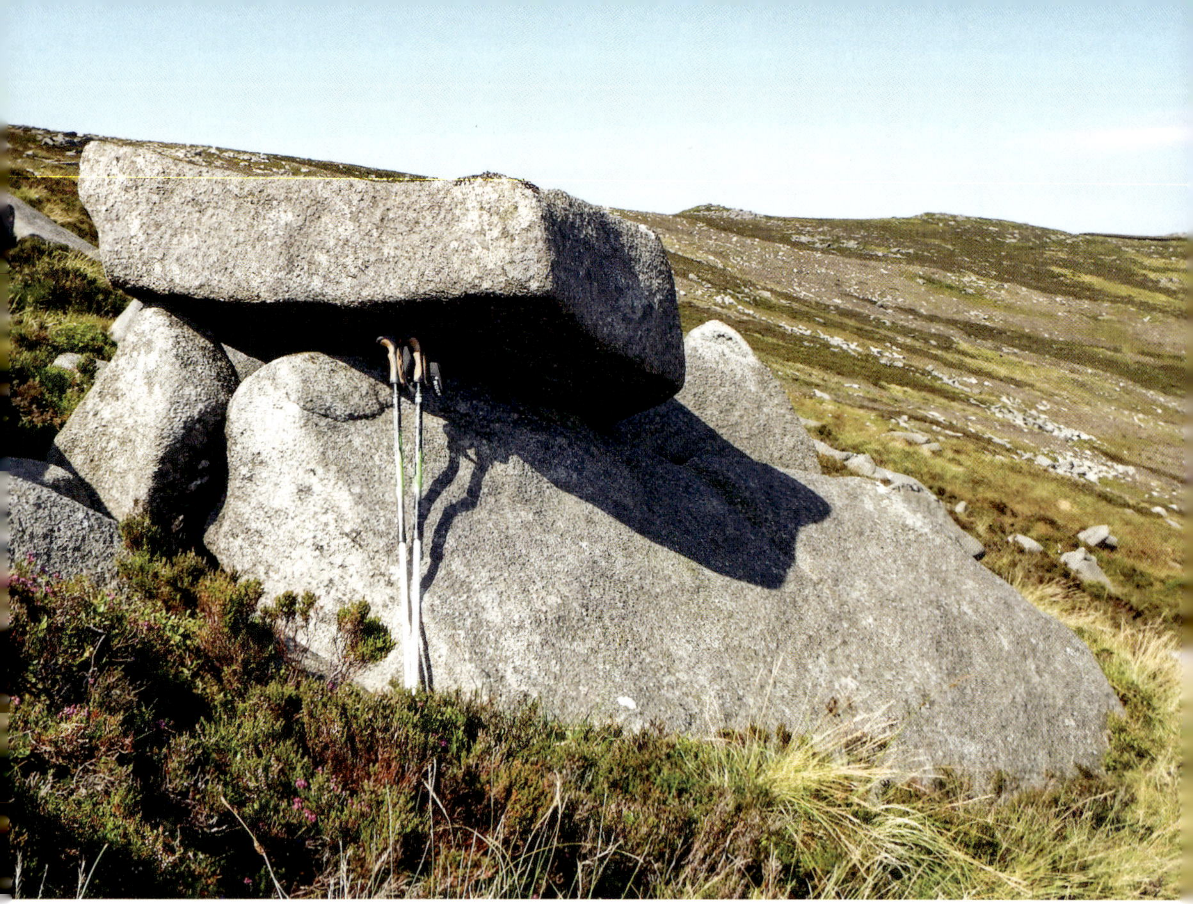

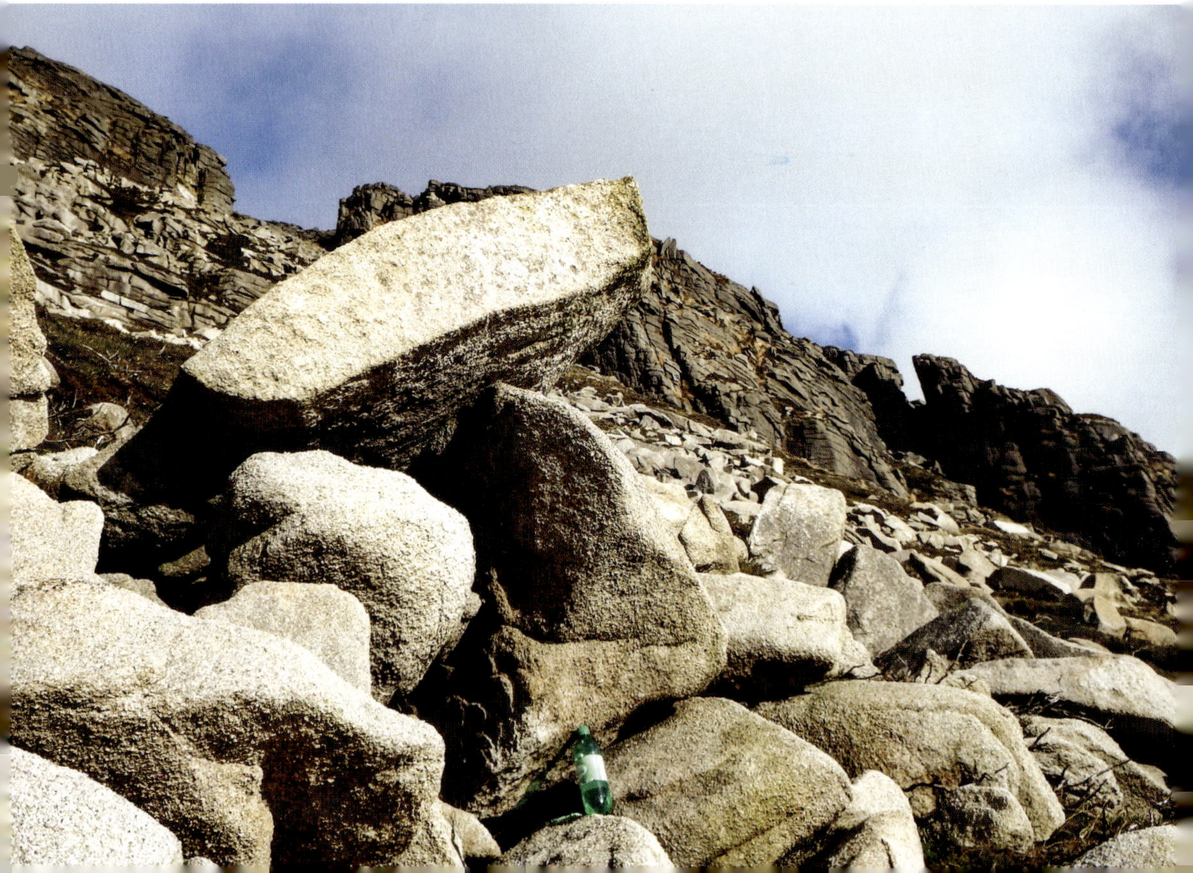

Top opposite: The trekking poles are approximately one metre long so you can imagine the effort involved in lifting this granite spear stone onto its two supports. This megalith on Chimney Rock mountain points towards summer solstice sunrise.

Lower opposite: This 2m long spear stone under the cliff of Cove is well thrust up as an erect phallus. Its point looks over to the vulva-like shape of Rocky mountain. It somehow reminds me of James Cagney at the end of the film *White Heat* (1949) and before the gas tank explodes, shouting, 'Made it Ma! Top of the World'. The GPS is:

    N. 54° 10. 346'
    W. 005° 57. 163'   Elevation 519m.

Top of this page: A 2m long granite slab on Wee Slevanmore, the south-eastern shoulder of Meelmore, has been propped up underneath into as an erect phallus. The featured spear point looks to Slieve Bearnagh's north tor. On the southern side, not shown, there is a great curve in the stone to denote an open mouth about to indulge in fellatio. The GPS is:

    N. 54° 11. 157'
    W. 006° 00. 086'   Elevation 629m.

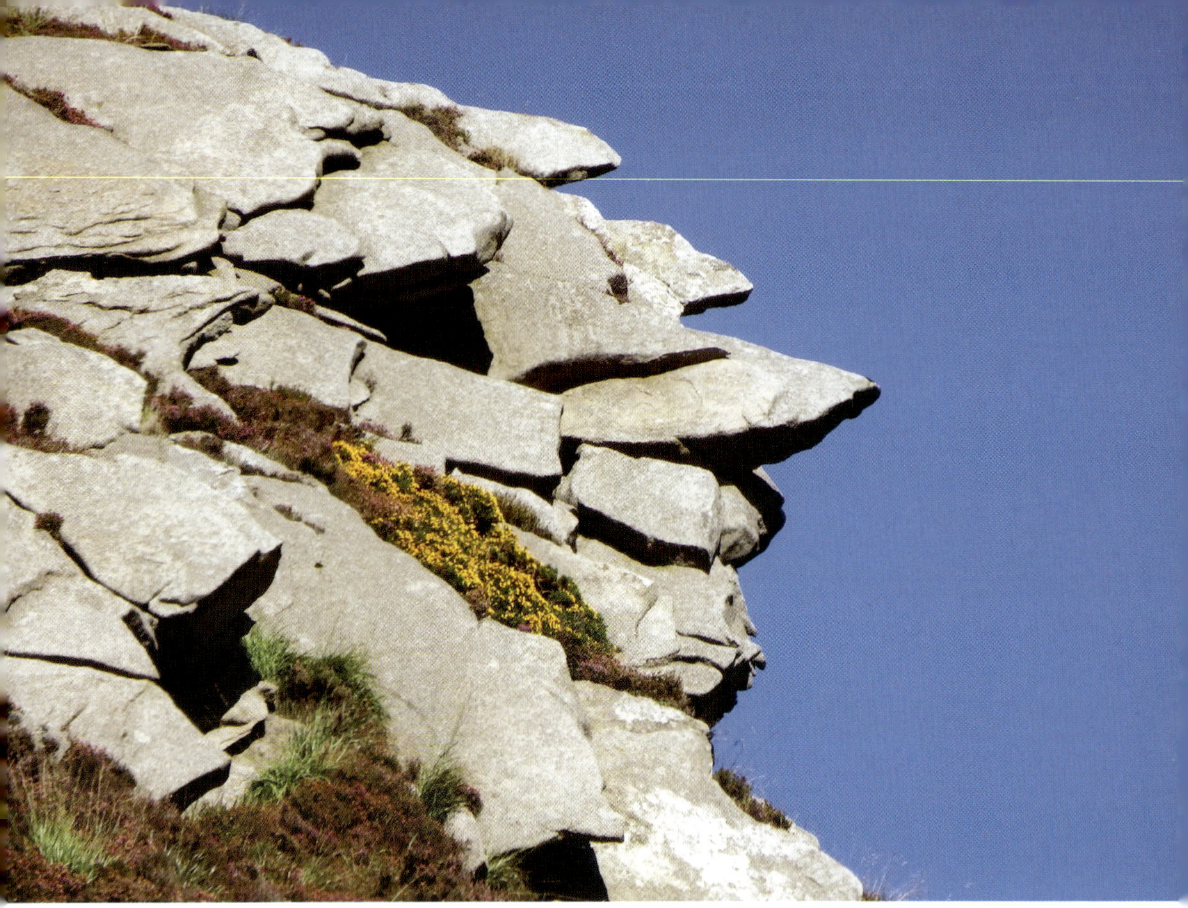

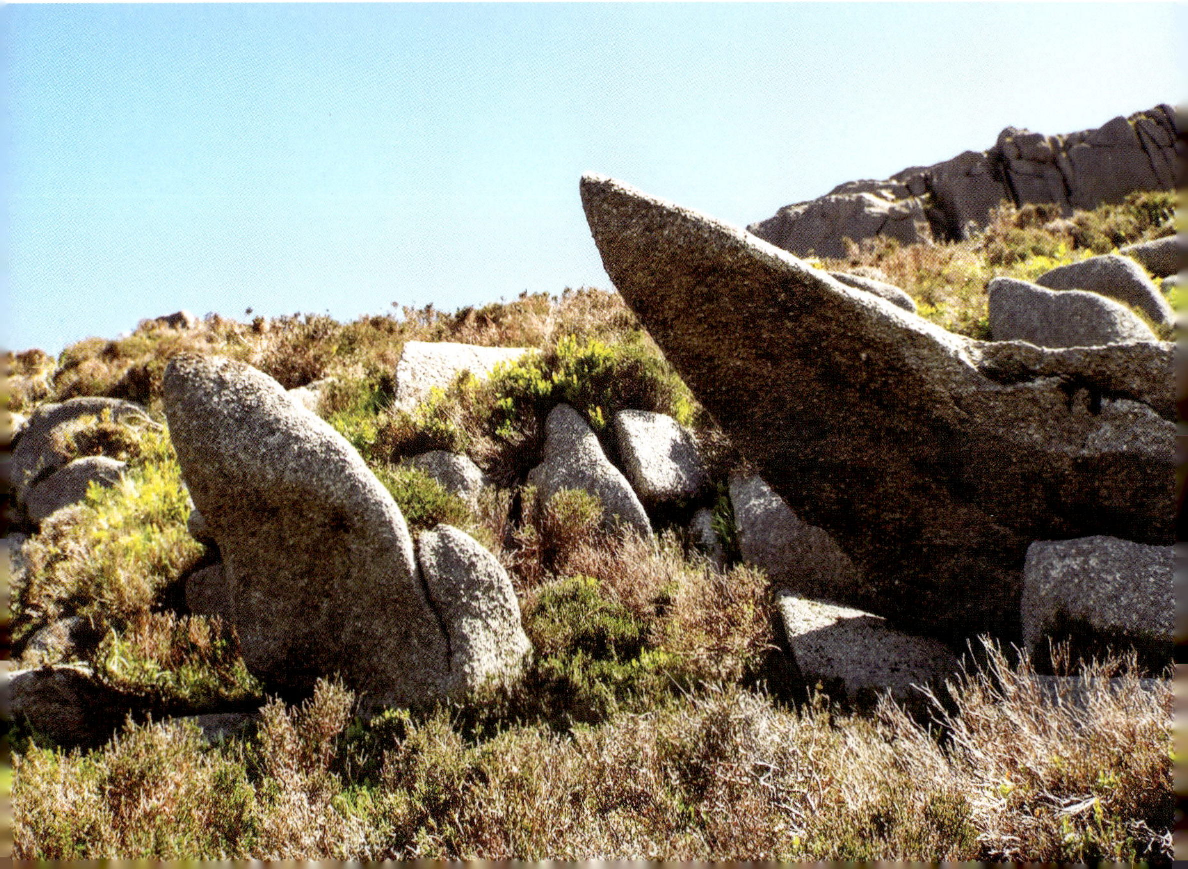

Top opposite: This is a telephoto shot of a series of spear stones high on the slopes of Meelmore mountain and overlooking Pollaphuca valley. They point presumably towards winter solstice sunrise beyond the end of Slieve Bearnagh. Some stones are not worth the danger to get either a GPS reading or to check the alignment of the spears towards solstice. They are a statement none the less of the commitment of the ancients to their beliefs in the importance of the sun. It may also be a case of the greater the danger the greater the glory redounding to the stonemen involved.

Lower opposite: A propping stone raises up the spear point into erect phallic mode while directing the tip towards winter solstice sunset. Lifting this megalith on Doan's steep slope is quite an achievement as there is a lot more of this stone out of sight to the right than features in the photograph. The left-hand stone shows, at the bottom, the suggestion of a little open-mouth pressed against the phallic shaft as if at fellatio.

Top of this page: This phallic spear on the west slope of Cove mountain notices a landscape vaginal notch (not shown) formed by the distant tors of Bignian. Slieve Bearnagh is in the background.

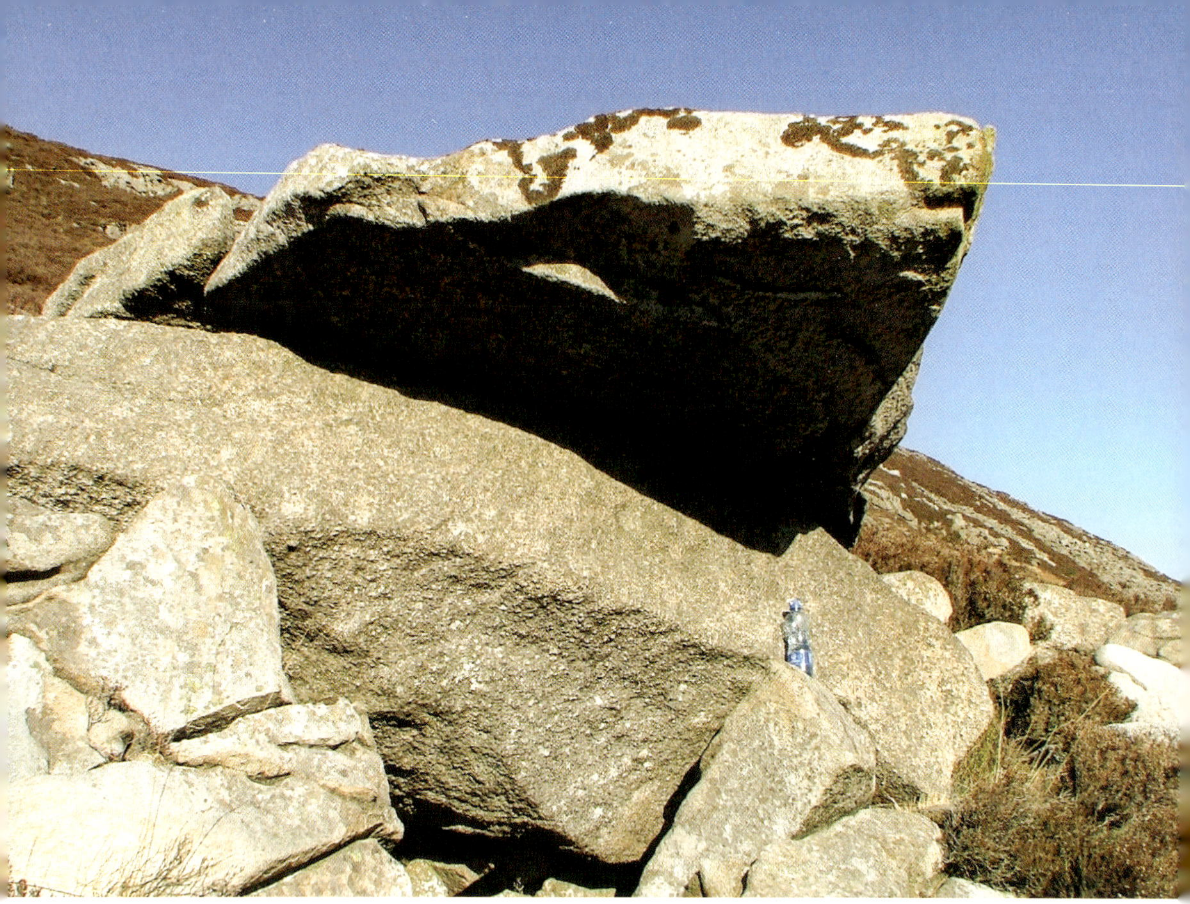

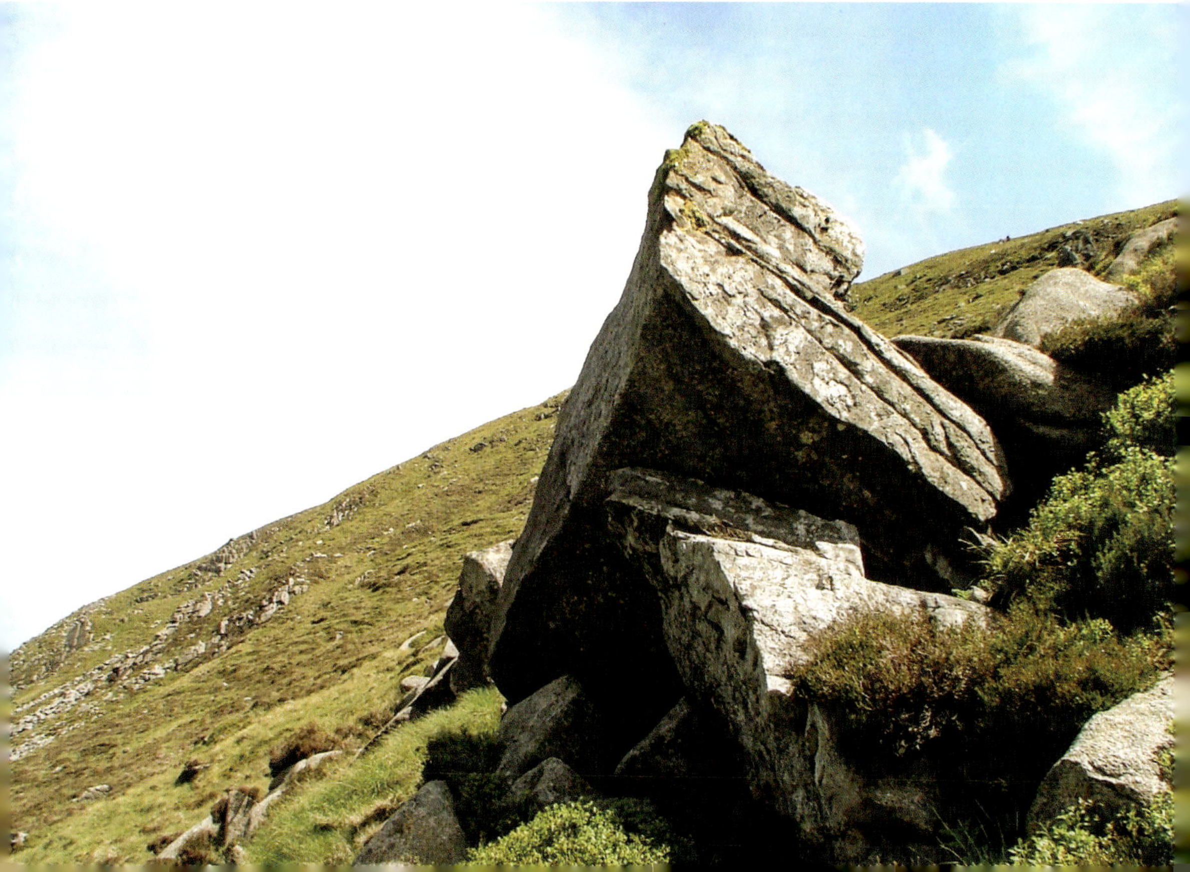

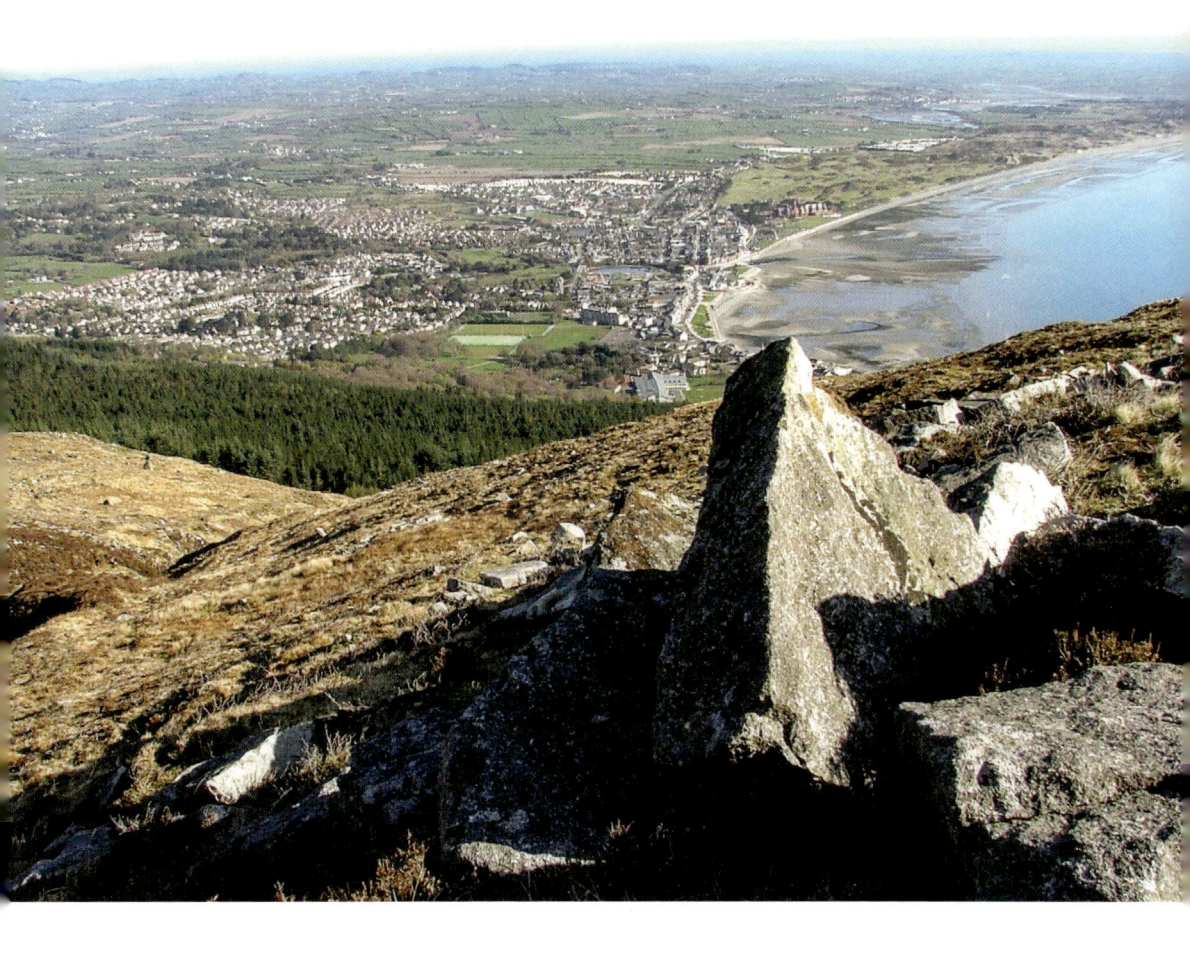

Top opposite: This spear point megalith on the south side of Slieve Lamagan points across the valley to Slieve Bignian's north tor. The water bottle underneath gives an idea of scale. When viewed from the side the slab is easily three metres or more in length. Towards winter solstice sunset Bignian casts its shadow across the valley onto the side of Lamagan. This phallic shadow was known as **Sleabhac**, 'a horn' but now, in English, it has morphed into the mnemonic Lamagan 'Slabs'.

Lower opposite: This very dramatic propped spear is found on the north-west slopes of Slieve Donard well above the Glen River path to Donard. There are two 'faces' on its southern side. Other substantial spear megaliths could be seen further up the slope and across at the edge of Eagle corrie but this find was more than enough and the energy levels at the end of the day made it more than it was worth to advance higher. The steepness of the slope makes one wonder how these considerable stones were manipulated. Even placing the counter-balance stones at the back would have been quite an achievement.

Top of this page: An April morning photograph of a spear stone on Millstone mountain. The spear is not too far above the Donard quarry yet on the seaward side of Amy's River. If memory serves, the tip of the spear looks to Slieve Croob but the near leading edge of the stone points beyond the Slieve Donard hotel to where summer solstice sun will rise.

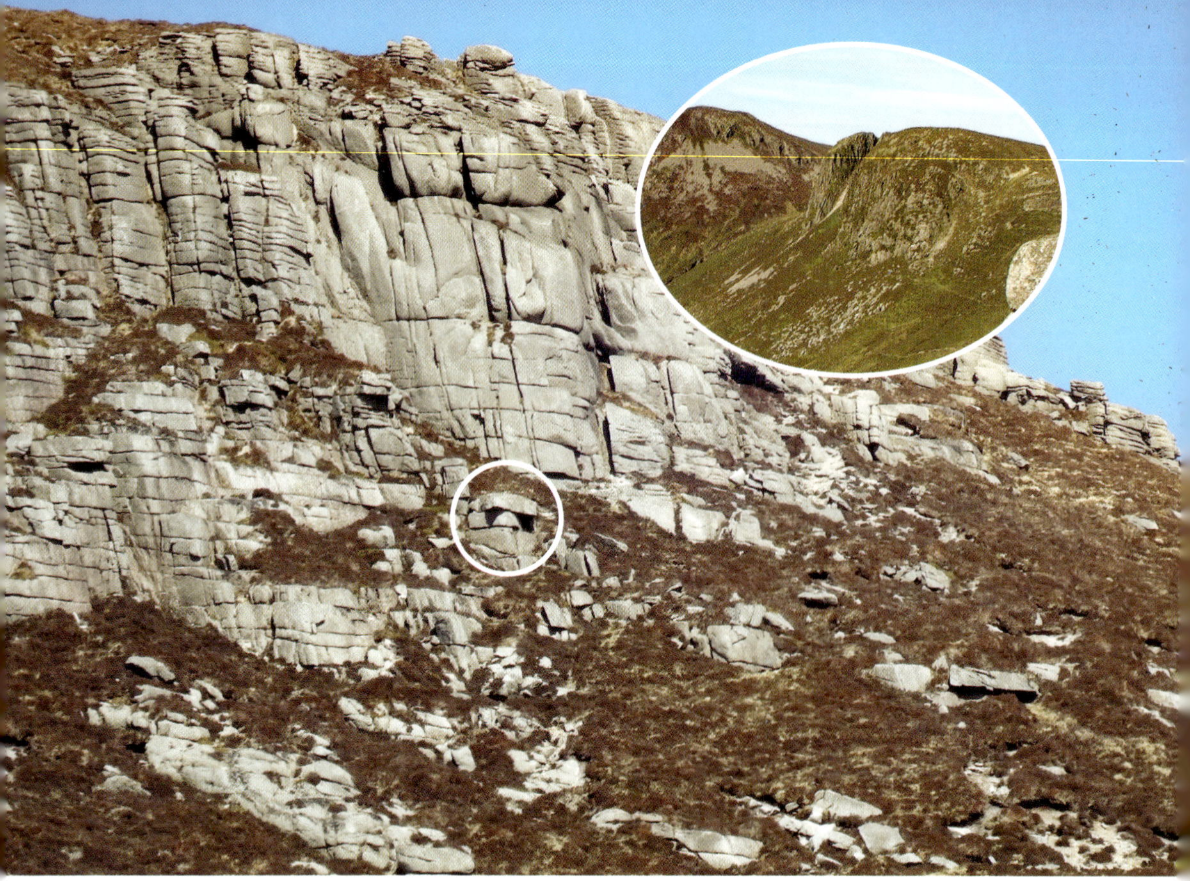

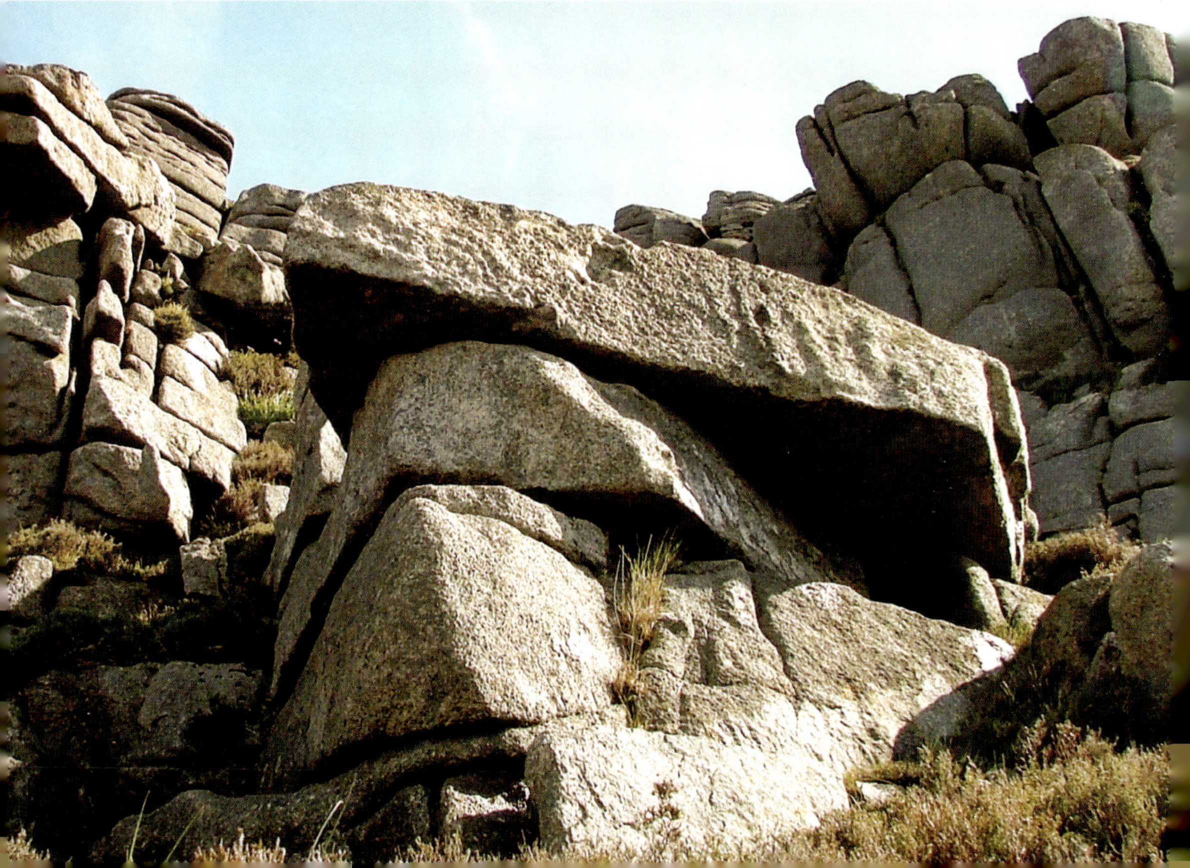

Opposite page: The small circle on the top picture at the Castles of Commedagh shows a spear stone of size and significance. The importance of this great slab is that the tip has been carefully arranged to point to where the setting winter solstice sun declines into the landscape vaginal notch at the top of the Devil's Coachroad. This is shown in the upper oval insert. Below opposite is a close-up view of the spear point slab. Other megaliths of interest can also be seen in the vicinity. If you come to sit on top of the slab then note the number of 'saucer cup marks' hammered into the upper surface.

The sun setting into the declivity of the Coachroad would have been a very potent fertility spectacle. The name of the Devil's Coachroad is from the Irish **Diabhail Cos Róide**, 'Devil's stem of force', a reference to the phallic like ridge up the centre of the ravine.

Top of this page: Under the cliff of Cove is this great slab about 2.5m to 3m long by 2m wide. It is propped up underneath enhancing its phallic credentials. The spear point is directed to the decidedly phallic profile of the Back Castles shown here in the oval inset. The GPS is:

N. 54° 10. 324'
W. 005° 57. 118'			Elevation 507m.

143

This is the cliff-face known as 'Upper Cove'. A deep fissure contains a spear stone arranged to point into the recess. For the fertility loving ancients, all such cracks, crevices, splits, slits or openings were evocative of female genitalia. That is why the ancients in millennia past have gone to extra-ordinary lengths to climb or abseil down the cliff to place this spear (symbolic of the male organ) into the fissure. The stone would have been fully illuminated at winter solstice sunset. Serious commitment as well as serious strength lies behind the placement of this fertility megalith. The ancients have demonstrated their courage and fearlessness by erecting a profusion of other mighty megaliths all along the edge of Upper Cove cliff-top. These are best admired from below

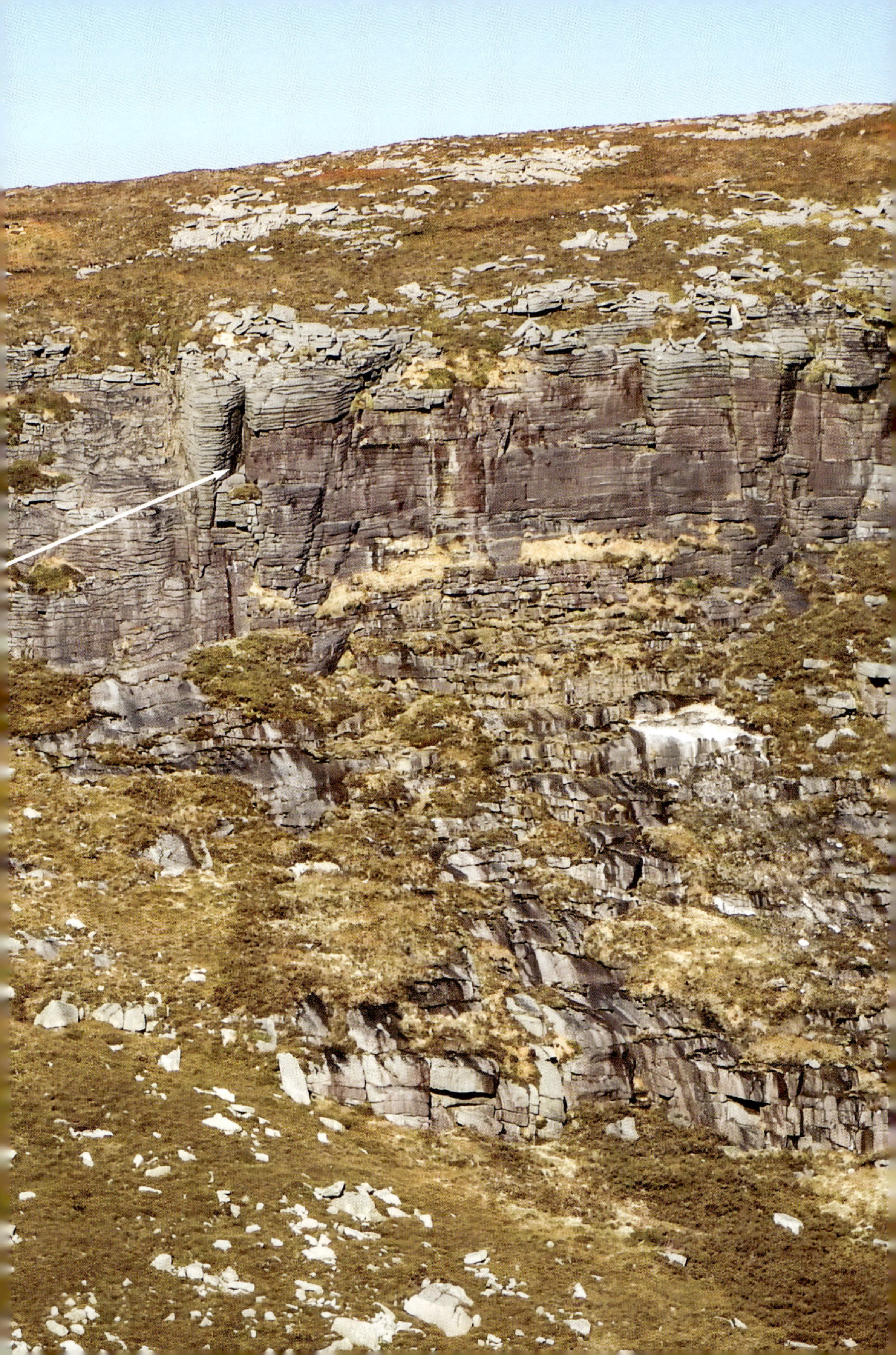

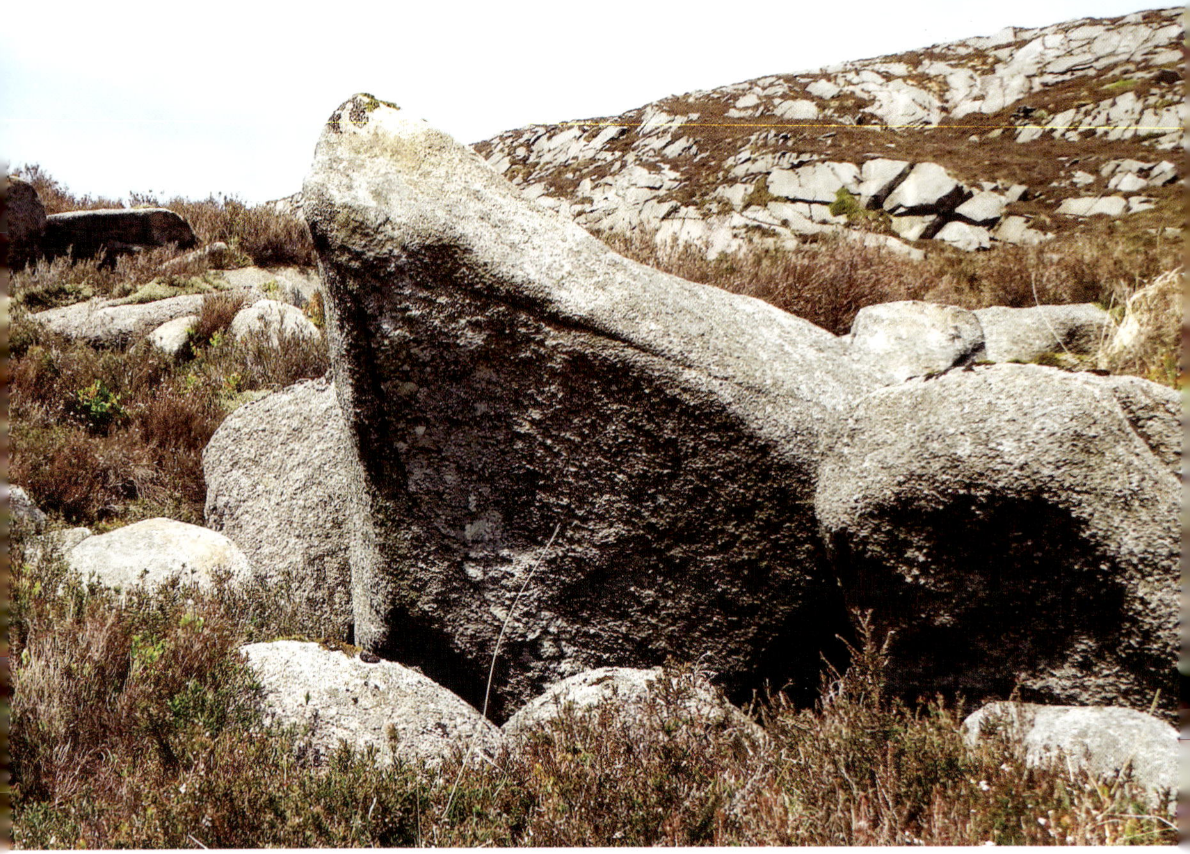

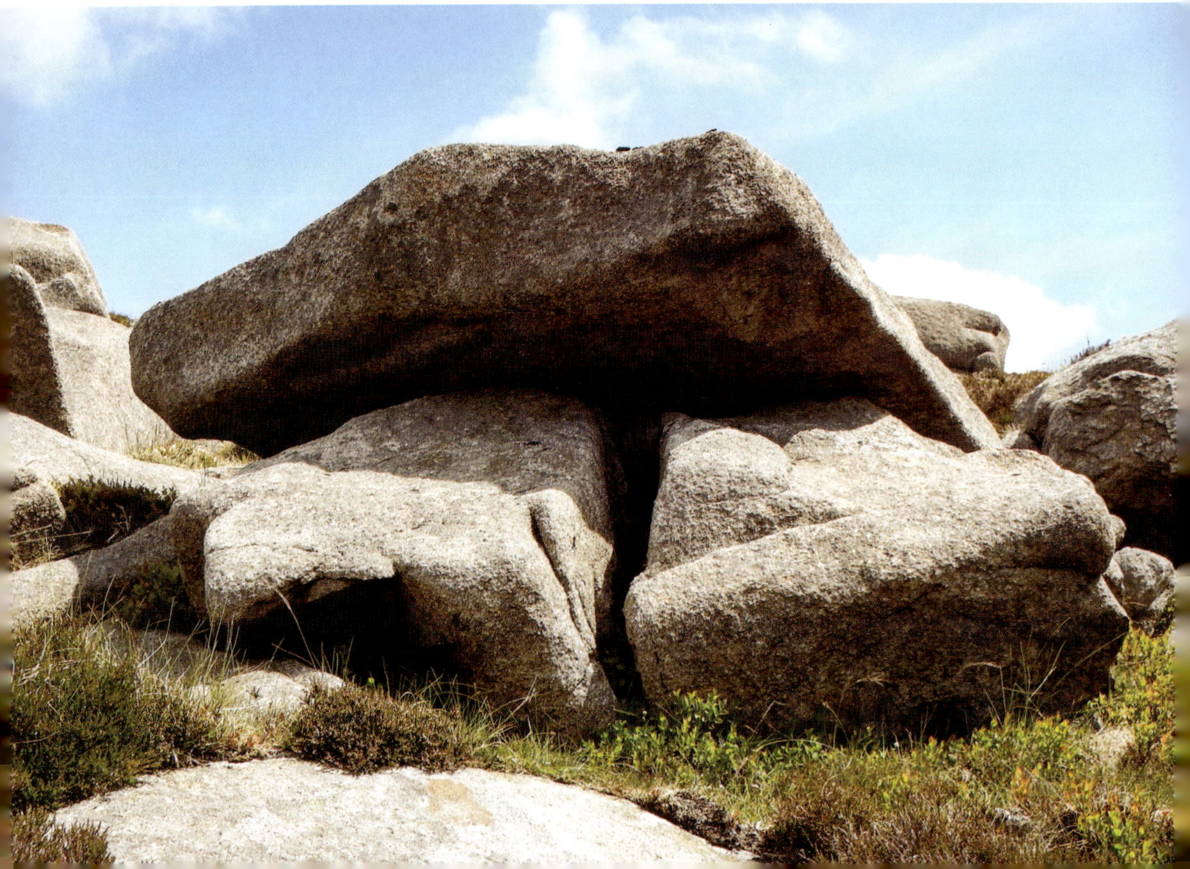

Top opposite: This two metre long granite spear stone on the middle north side of Pollaphuca valley is secured in its upright phallic position by stones underneath and at the side. It also has a counter-balance at the back. The well-defined phallic spear point is directed up to Slieve Bearnagh's north tor. Although not obvious in the photograph there is an infusion line of slightly lighter rock underneath the point. This would have represented semen running down the shaft of the phallus. It was on this account that the megalith was named **Damhán**, 'a young bull'. The GPS is:

                  N.   54° 11. 502'
                  W. 005° 59. 517'   Elevation 434m.

Lower opposite: In the upper reaches of Happy Valley a granite spear stone rests securely on its two supports as it points across the valley from its location on the side of Green Rigs, the northerly shoulder of Slieve Meelmore. The tip points to the intersection on the other side of the valley between horizon and descending shoulder of Meelbeg/Bug Mountain. The GPS is:

                  N.   54° 11. 262'
                  W. 006° 00. 255'   Elevation 593m.

Top of this page: On the Meelmore slopes and near the stile at the head of Pollaphuca valley is this great erect spear stone. The tip addresses a gully higher up the Meelmore slope, the gully being symbolic of the female opening. The GPS is:

                  N.   54° 11. 246'
                  W. 005° 59. 776'   Elevation 539m.

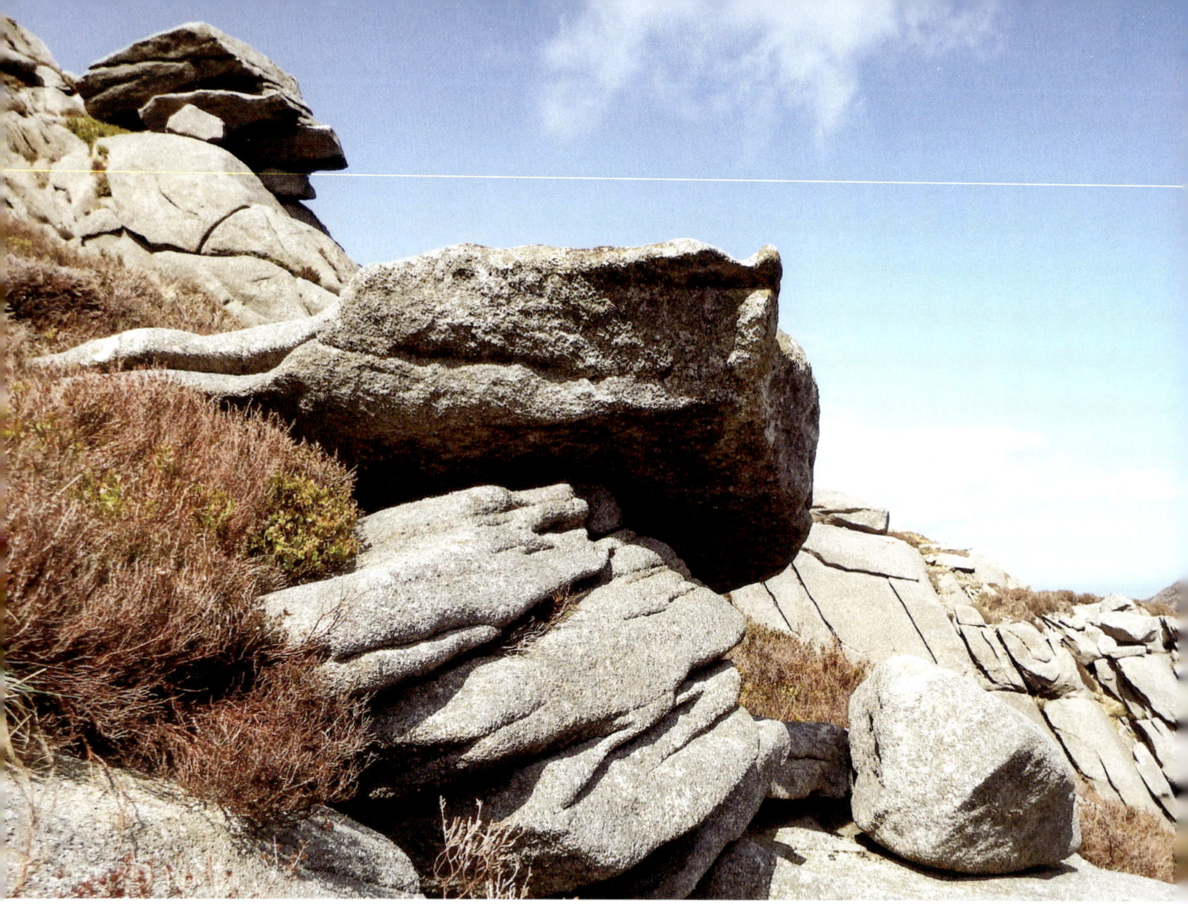

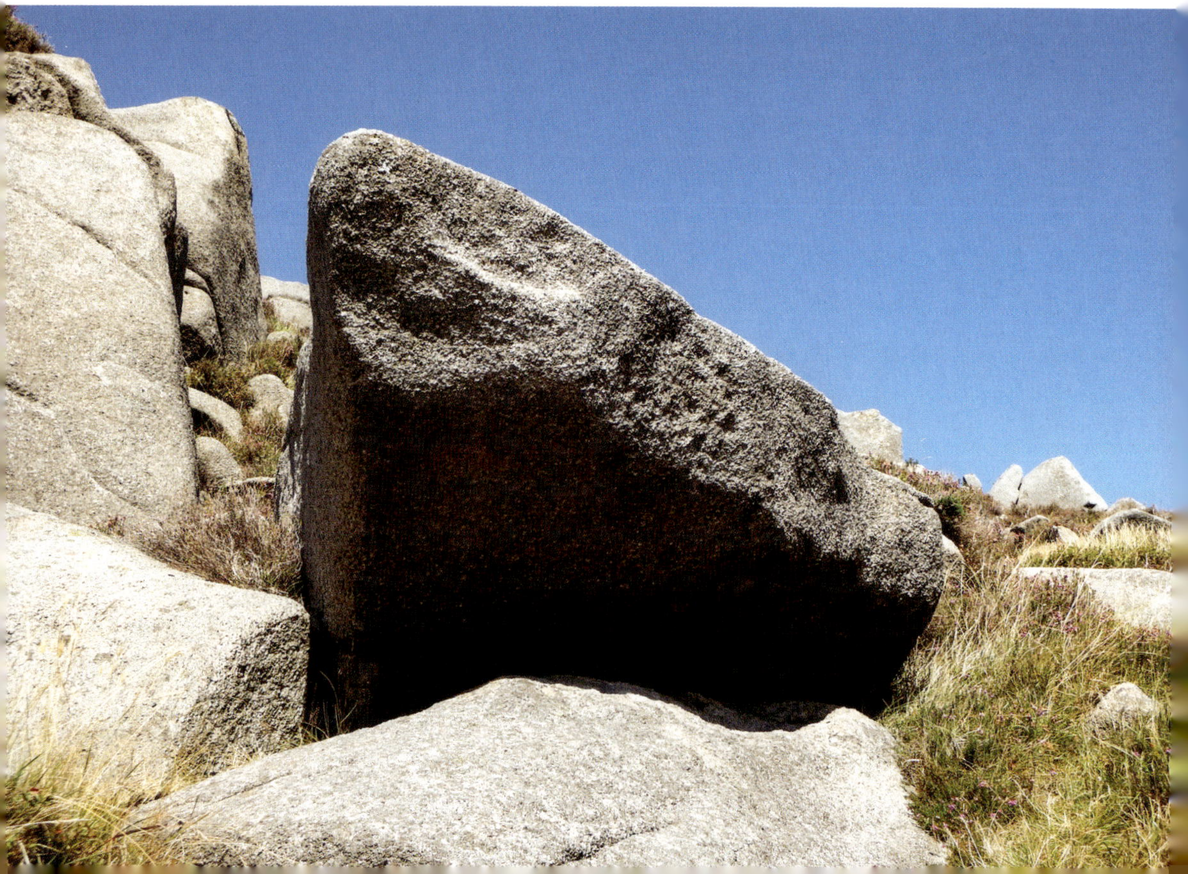

Top opposite: Two for the price of one. Our photograph shows two great compound megaliths on the north side of Pollaphuca valley. Though it doesn't look it, the near stone is secured in place by a minimum of six big stones and there are many more underneath. The megalith was named *Fidhchillín*, 'A Diminutive Person', on account of the little phallic point at the end of the spear. It aims at the notch at the head of the valley. The GPS is:

N.   54° 11. 425'
W. 005° 59. 631'   Elevation 472m.

Lower opposite: On the south-east flank of Slieve Bearnagh is this large propped spear stone. The rounded spear tip points to the summit of Slieve Lamagan and to the appearance of winter solstice sun. The GPS is:

N.   54° 11. 171'
W. 005° 58. 561'   Elevation 436m.

Top of this page: You will find this beautiful brute of a block beyond the Long Mountain quarry and up past two bothie shelters formerly used by the granite-men. The highest corner looks to Eagle mountain and the fine sharp point at the lower end of the megalith points to winter solstice sunrise. At 2.7m in length for the front downward slope, this is a seriously big spear. The GPS is:

N.   54° 07. 672'
W. 006° 04. 860'   Elevation 333m.

A Leachtán projects over the cliff-top in the Annalong valley.

2. *Leachtán*

The Irish word *Leachtán* is used for this category of megaliths as there is no single equivalent word in English. A *Leachtán* is a slab or large flagstone pushed part way out over a precipice. Sometimes the balancing act involved in a stone jutting out over a void is rather delicate and called for use of a counter-balance. Although the word *Leachtán* is now a single word in Irish, it derives from a merging of two Irish words, namely, *Leacht*, meaning amongst other things 'any monument' and also *Áin*, meaning 'pleasure, desire'. When projected out over a cliff the stone now represents a phallus and frequently was pointed towards sunrise on winter solstice. Many *Leachtán* in the Annalong valley point however to the rounded vulva-like shape of Slieve Donard.

On account of the danger inherent in approaching cliff edges no GPS are given for these stones. This is no loss as they look much more dramatic from the valleys below. Some of these creations seem so improbable, being on the side of sheer cliffs, that it brings about awe at their achievement. The monument high on the cliff of Cove is a case in point as is the second Devil's Coachroad monument on the cliff of Slievenaglogh. This last was mentioned by Prof. E.E. Evans on p.216 of his work *'Mourne Country'*. It also featured as the cover of *Prehistoric Mourne* (see end of book).

A Leachtán looks out over the Windy Gap valley

Leachtán in the Annalong Valley, like our close-up here of 'open mouth', often point to Slieve Donard.

Our close-up shows an impressive spear point Leachtán on the skyline of Cove mountain.

This is a most impressive Leachtán spear stone in the middle of Slieve Beg's southern cliff face. This large spear slab would weigh many tons. It was likely quarried from the cliff recess up behind it to the left. There is a little ledge behind the Leachtán but nevertheless manoeuvring this mighty slab on such a confined site half-way up a cliff must have been a daunting challenge.

Two Leachtán on the eastern crest of Slieve Beg.

The placing of this Leachtán and its two counter-balancing slabs on the eastern cliff of Slieve Beg is a truly amazing achievement. The stone seems to point to the appearance of winter solstice sun on Chimney Rock on the other side of the Annalong Valley.

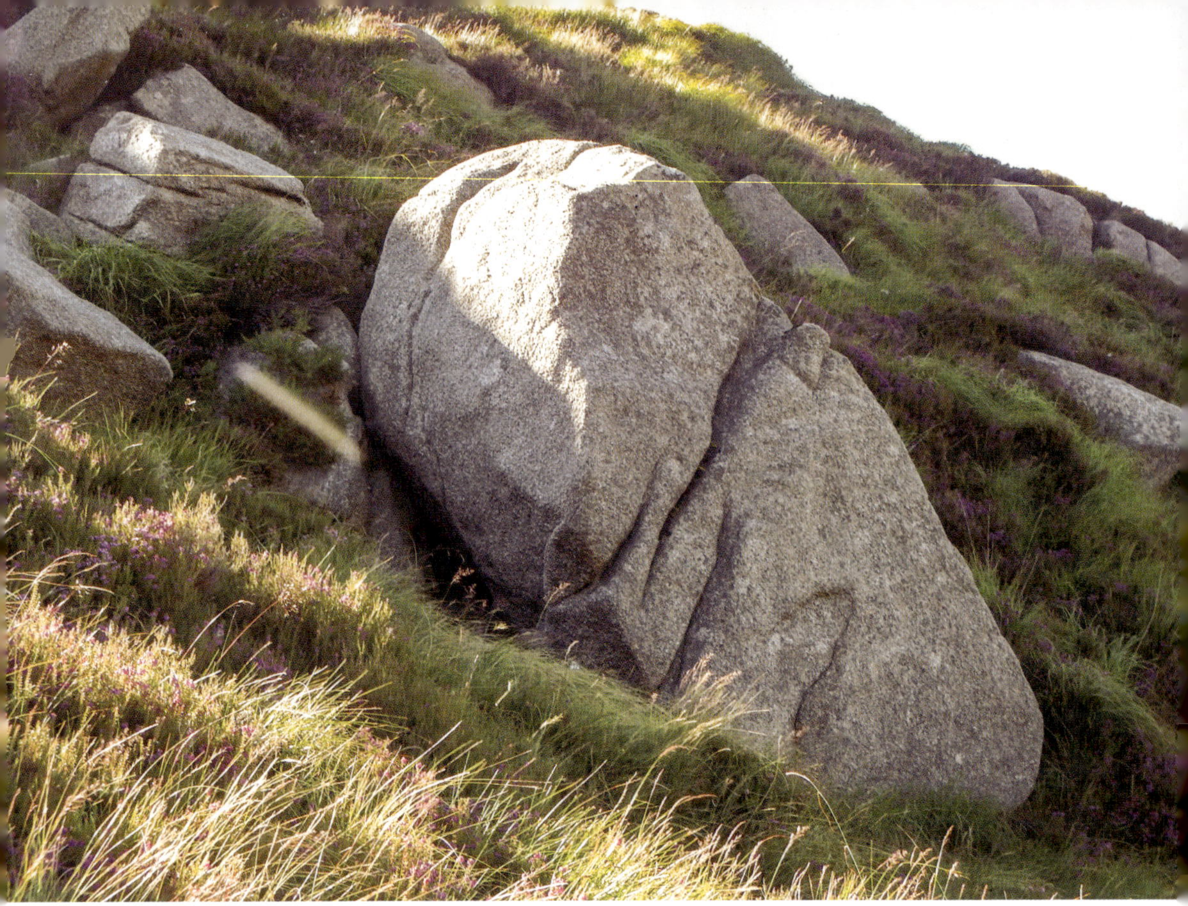

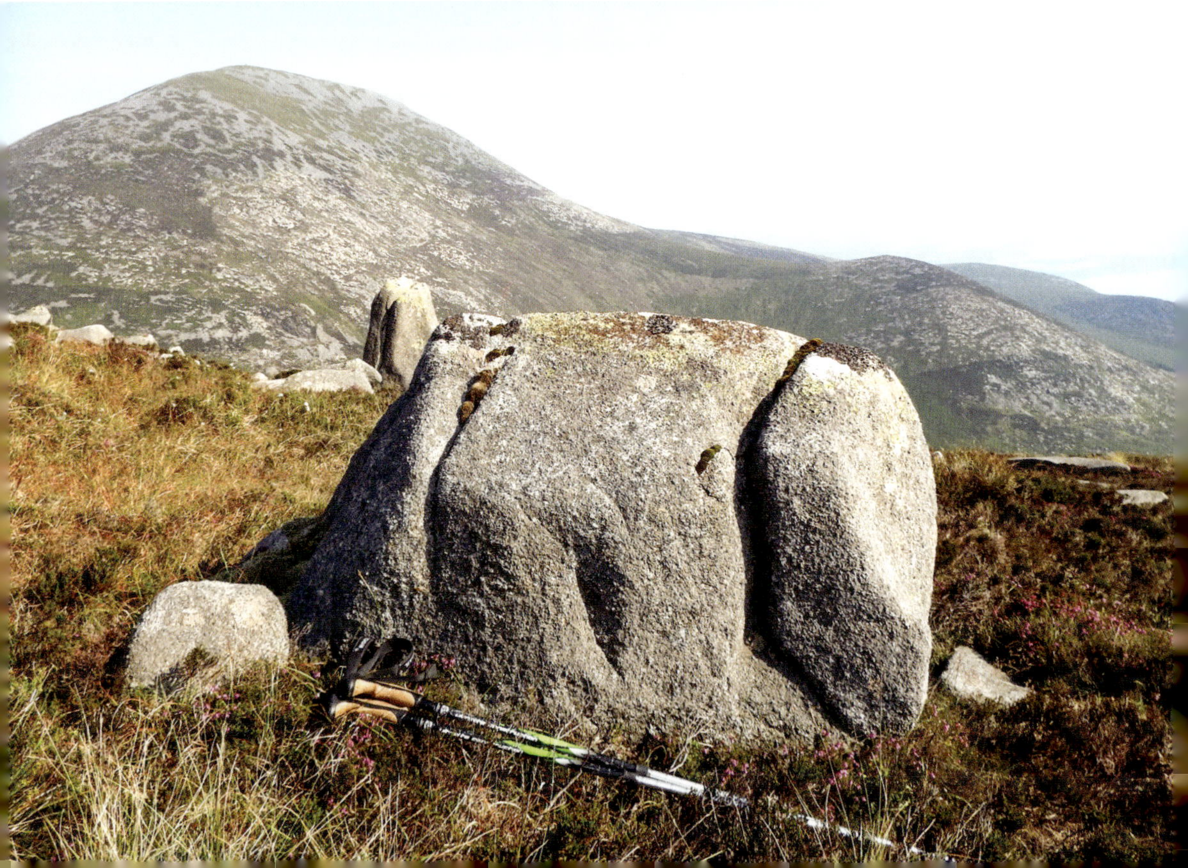

3. Meatus Grooves

A meatus groove is the convenient term used in the text to refer to the notch at the tip of phallic stones. Purists will say that the anatomical name for the slit at the end of a penis from which urine or semen is discharged would be a foramen while the meatus is the tubular opening or passage in the body behind it. The whole point of using such notches on suitably long stones or spears was to draw attention to their phallic nature or to enhance a stone's phallic credentials.

Top opposite: On the southern shoulder of Spellack mountain and just at the entrance to Pollaphuca valley, a great phallic stone in erection mode points towards Slieve Bearnagh's north tor. There is a distinctive deep meatus groove on the top of the megalith and a channel at the side making an imposing coronal rim. This is a seriously big stone standing at least three metres high by 1.5m thick and 2.25m wide across the lower bottom. The GPS is:

      N. 54° 11. 690'
      W. 005° 59. 204'   Elevation 373m.

Lower opposite: This is what would be called a 'penis in the vagina stone'. The central part of this stone on Chimney Rock mountain is the penis, sporting its meatus groove, while the channels on either side denote the labial sides of the vagina. Slieve Donard is in the background.

Below: This phallic boulder is to be found on the top of Cock & Hen mountain. It is about 1.3m long by .8m across by .8m high and it has a very distinctive meatus groove dipping towards the pool. A nice feature of this stone is the use of an infusion line, partly in relief, as a penile coronal line. The GPS is:

      N. 54° 10. 939'
      W. 006° 05. 717'   Elevation 323m.

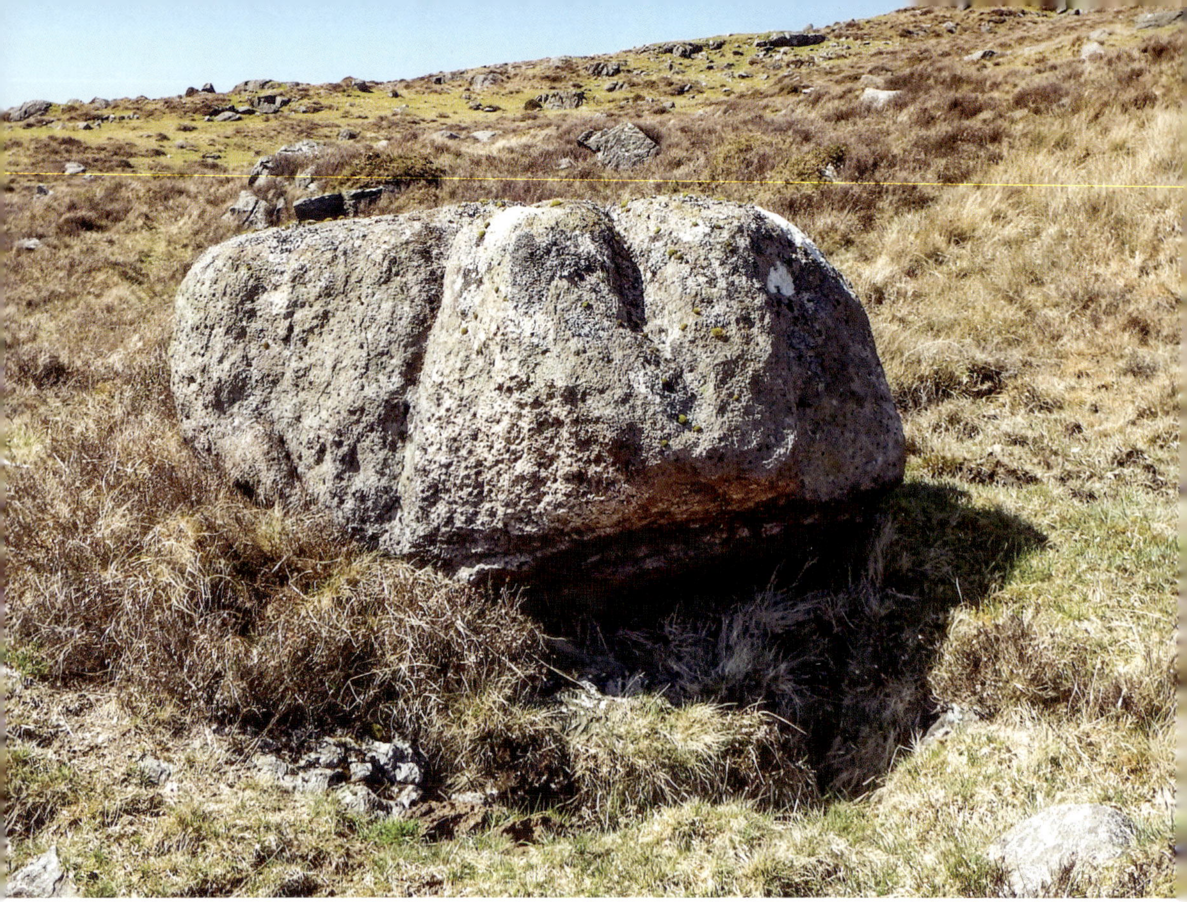
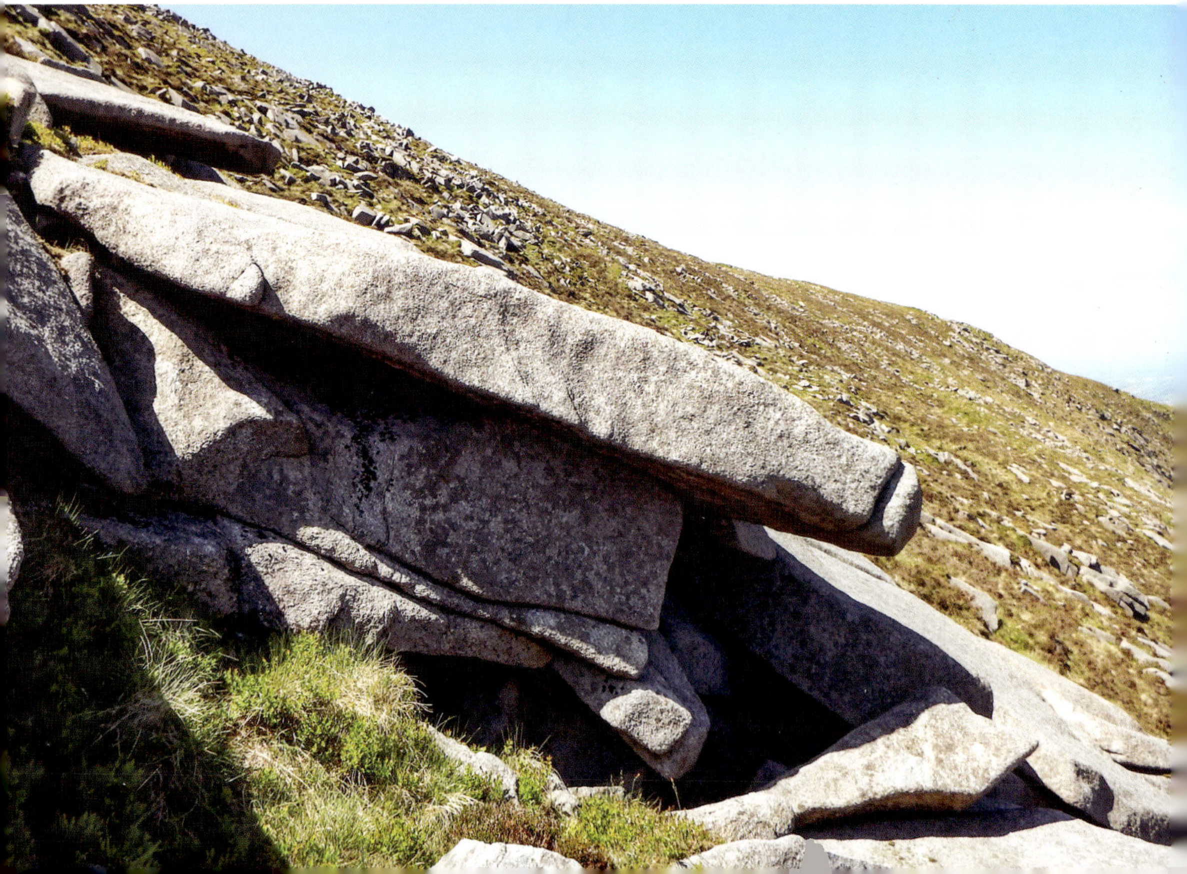

Top opposite: On the east side of Leckan More, in a place that gives great views, there is a noble phallic stone that has been given the name ***Cruaidh-Laoch*** (A Stout Warrior). The megalith has been deliberately brought here for it is a granite boulder atop shale bedrock. The stone is 1.5m long by 1m across and it makes a good seat; it has a very emphatic penile corona and meatus groove. The GPS is:

      N. 54º 07. 513'
      W. 006º 10. 875'   Elevation 235m.

Lower opposite: At four metres in length and over two metres across, this granite slab on the north slope of Meelbeg in the upper reaches of Happy Valley is certainly a most impressive phallic stone. It has quite a distinctive phallic tip, the meatus groove of which looks over to the tors of Slieve Bearnagh. The GPS is:

      N. 54º 11. 166'
      W. 006º 00. 494'   Elevation 610m.

Top of this page: This two metre spear stone, with its notable meatus groove, is on that shoulder of Slieve Meelmore known to the shepherds as Wee Slevanmore. The spear is propped up underneath so that the tip points to the side of Slieve Meelbeg where the winter solstice sun sets. The GPS is:

      N. 54º 11. 127'
      W. 006º 00. 061'   Elevation 584m.

Above: On the north-west side of Luke's mountain is this 1.5m high phallic stone with a meatus groove at the top. The many grooves and indents on the stone show signs of enhancement. At the very tip, the meatus crack is apparently transformed into the head of a little bird with its beak open. The GPS is:

                        N.   54° 12. 591'
                        W. 005° 58. 096'   Elevation 302m.

Opposite page: At 3.2 metres from tip to tail, 2 metres high and 1.5m across the back, this great phallic stone on the upper southern slope of Slieve Meelmore flaunts its meatus groove as it points uphill to where winter solstice sun declines. The second photograph of the same stone shows the coronal rim at the back (including a second, more proportionate rim, incised higher up). More importantly however is the fertility nature of the location and the reason for the stone's placement. The megalith marks where the distant tip of Forks mountain (circled) appears as a notional penis in a landscape vaginal notch formed between Slieve Bearnagh and Bignian. The GPS is:

                        N.   54° 11. 535'
                        W. 005° 59. 841'   Elevation 629m.

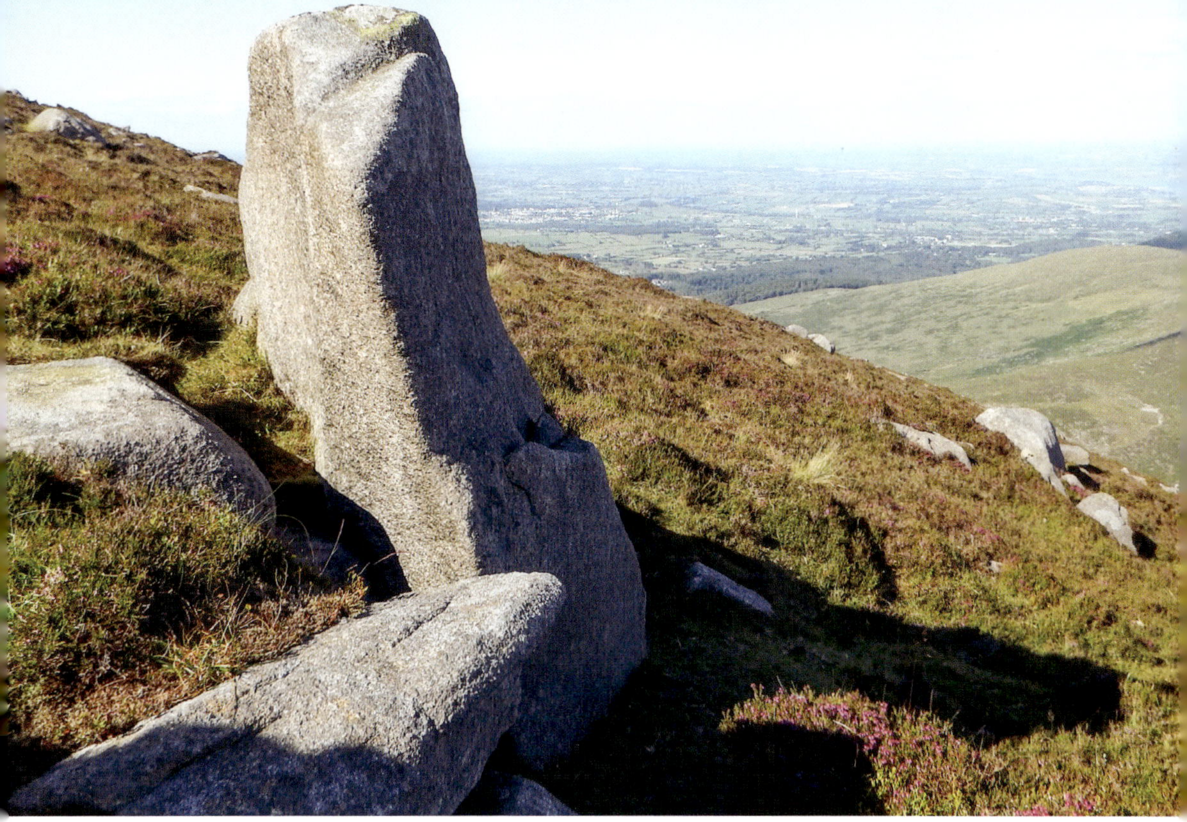

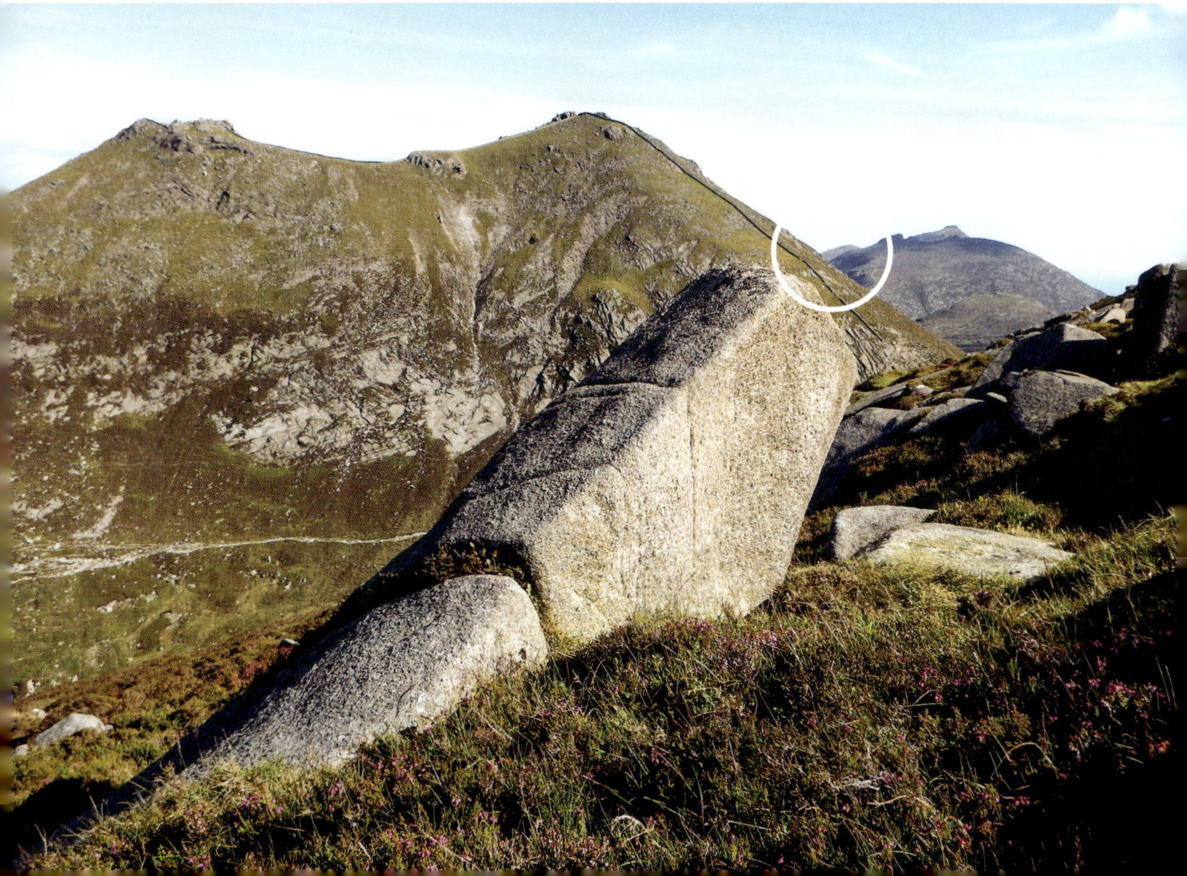

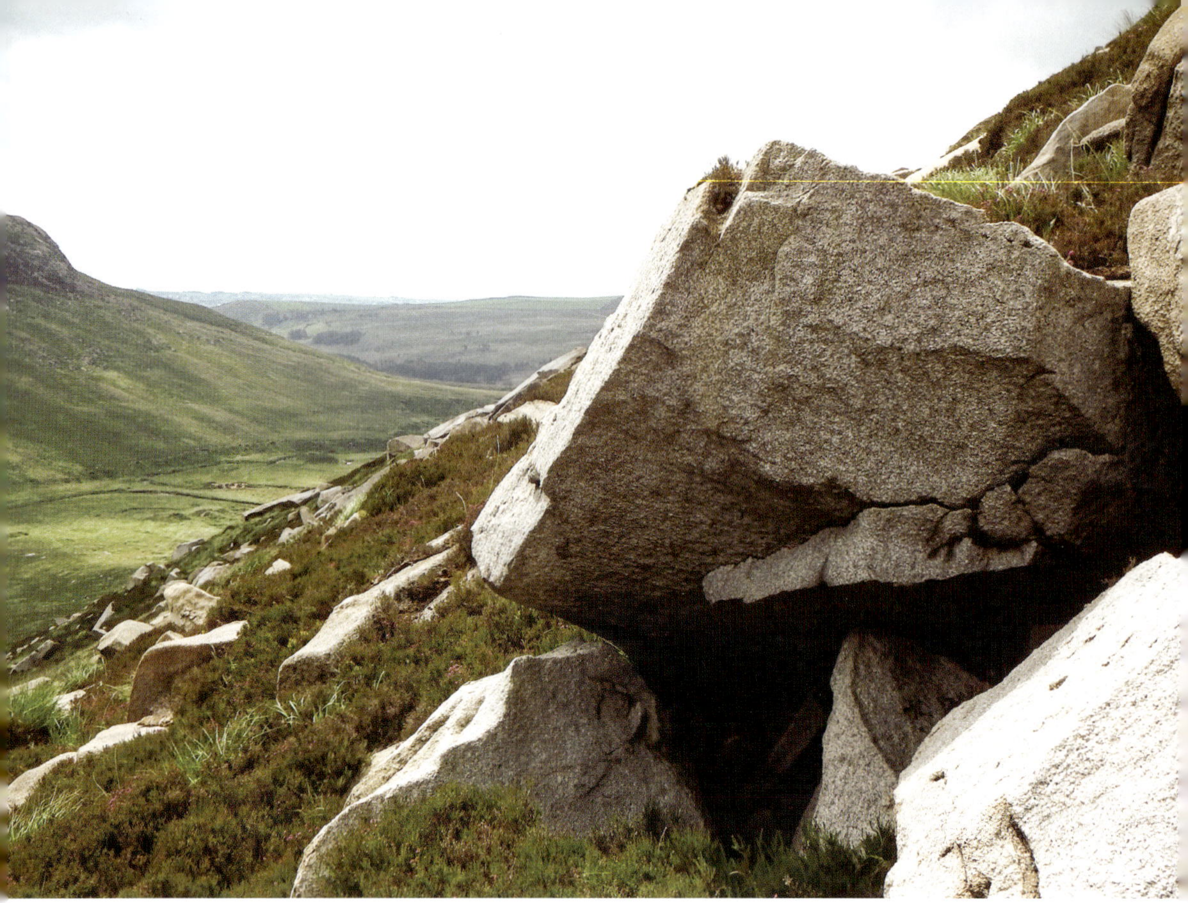

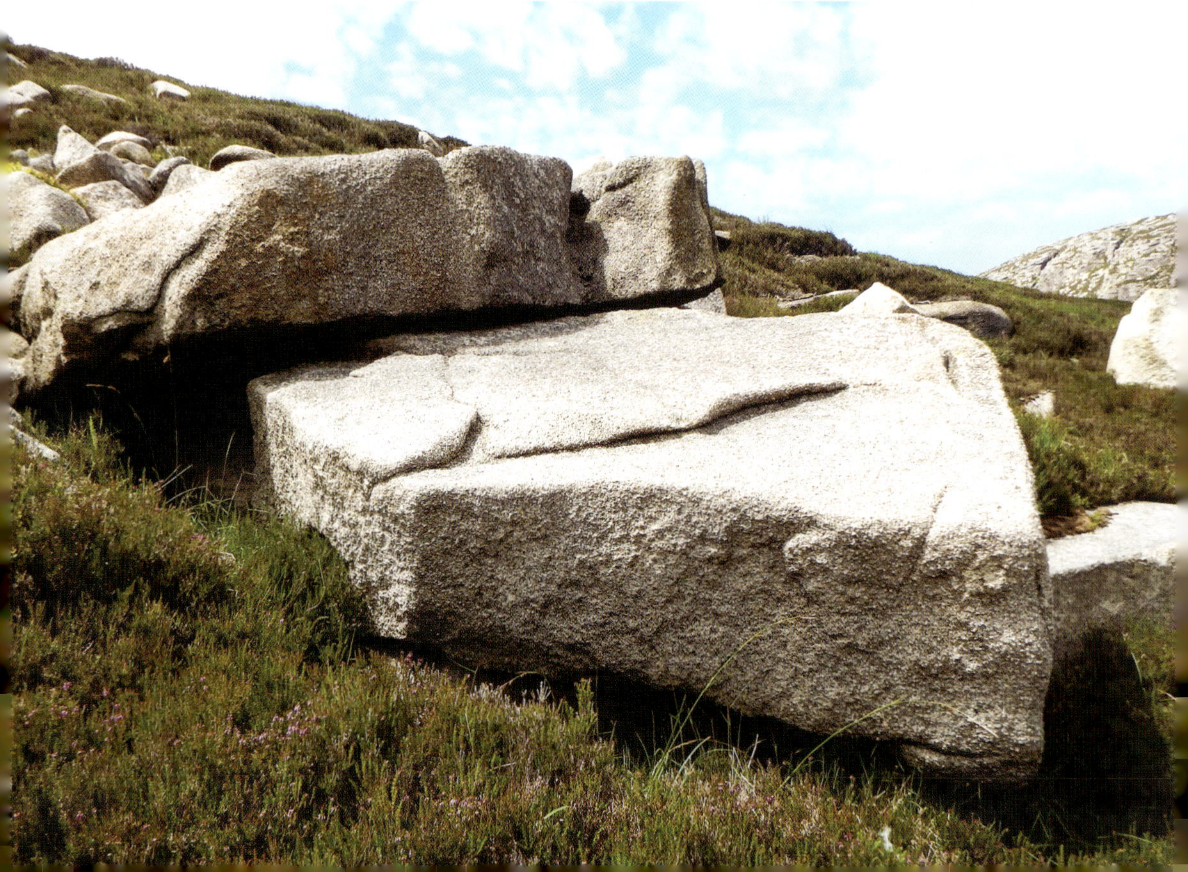

Top opposite: A great spear stone slab rears up on the west slope of the Annalong Valley. The prominent meatus notch at the tip of the stone points to the Slieve Commedagh/ Donard col. The GPS is:

       N. 54º 10 211'
       W. 005º 56. 921'   Elevation 380m.

Lower opposite: Along the west side of the Annalong Valley two large granite slabs have been placed in the act of copulation. The top slab is a mighty four metres long by three across by .6m thick. This is the stone with quite a generous meatus groove pointing towards Donard and the landscape notch to the right of it. There is also a tiny meatus groove at the top tip of the great spear stone slab below it though you would have to look hard to see it. The GPS is:

       N. 54º' 10. 076'
       W. 005º 56. 973'   Elevation 402m.

Top of this page: This 2m high stone near Leganabruchan's south side summit has a dribbling meatus groove at the top. Coming up-hill the profile of the stone resembles an open mouthed, wolf-like animal with its head thrown back as if howling. The oval shows the rounded, vulva-like, summit of Slieve Donard between Crossone and the slope of Leganabruchan to which the leading edge of the megalith points. The GPS is:

       N. 54º 10. 781'
       W. 005º 53. 578'   Elevation 332m

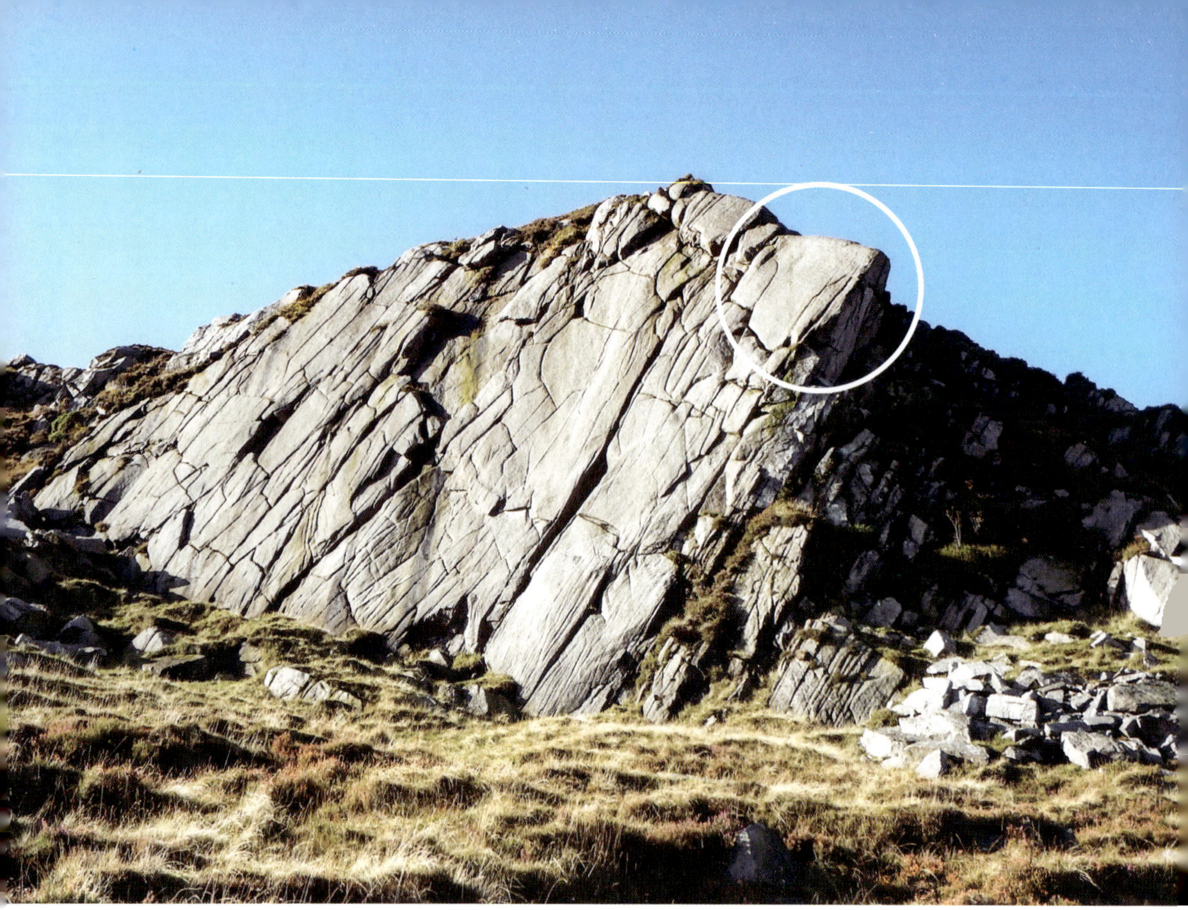

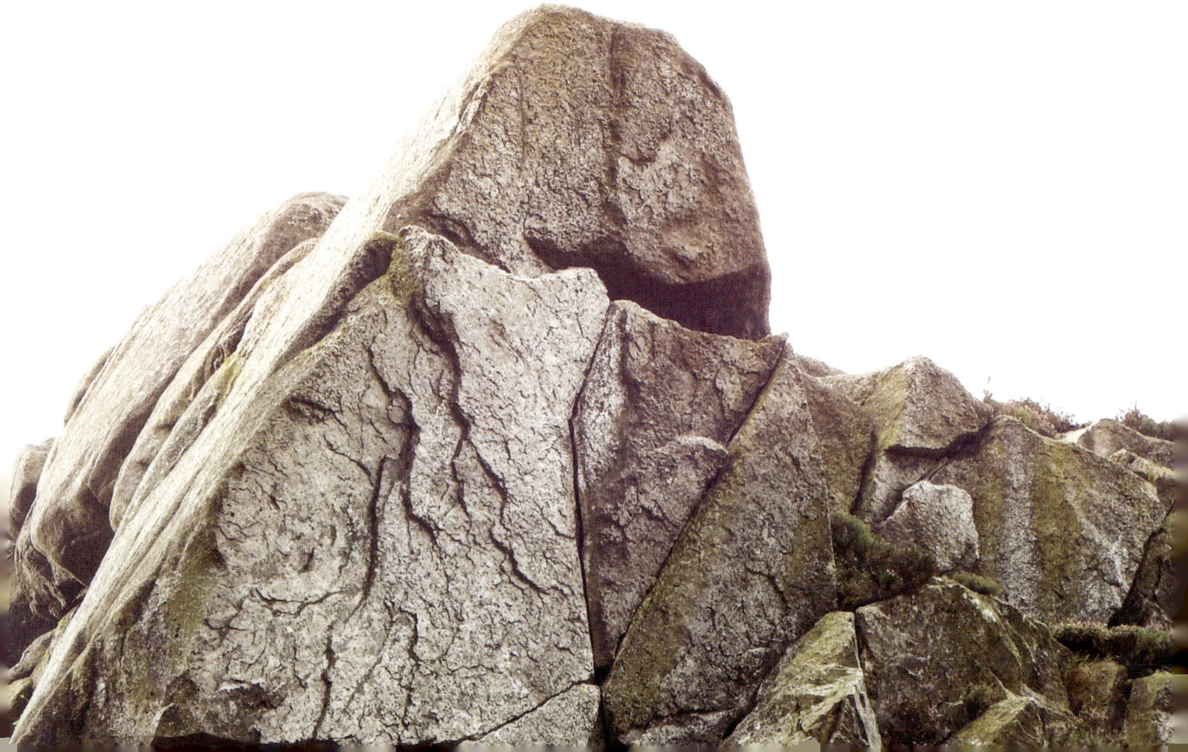

Opposite page: The circle shows a 'face' created at the very end of the cliff at Spellack's north-east corner. Cracks along the rock make for a mouth, a dark recess makes a shadow 'eye' and the very corner, or spear point, is the imaginary nose. Indeed, you could say that the whole cliff could be regarded as one great face on account of another 'shadow eye' recess being gouged into the cliff at the left end. The second photograph below shows how the spear point corner of the cliff has been treated as a huge phallus with a meatus groove chopped into the top of the rock. The GPS of the photograph is:

     N. 54º 11. 979'
     W. 005º 59. 454'   Elevation 335m.

Above: High on the upper south slope of Happy Valley an upright phallic granite boulder flaunts a pronounced meatus groove front and back. The stone is 1m in length and circa 0.2m thick. The stone is aligned to meet summer solstice sun appearing above the northern shoulder of Slieve Meelmore known to the shepherds as Green Rigs. This forms one side of Happy Valley and the name is from the Irish **Grian Righneálaidhe**, 'sun dawdler' on account of this hill being sheltered from the first light of winter solstice morning by the bulk of Meelmore mountain and not receiving the important light until later in the day. The GPS is:

     N. 54º 11. 408'
     W. 006º 00. 865'   Elevation 454m.

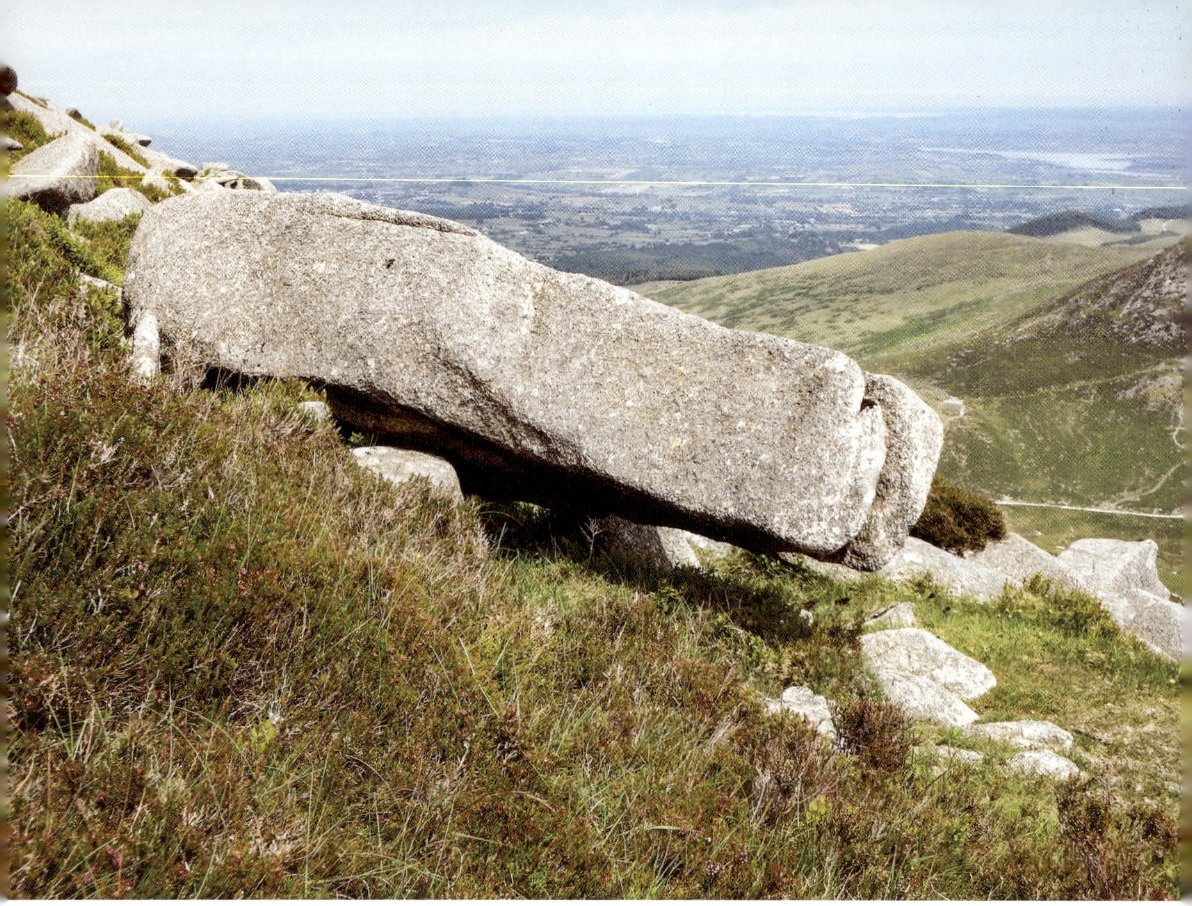

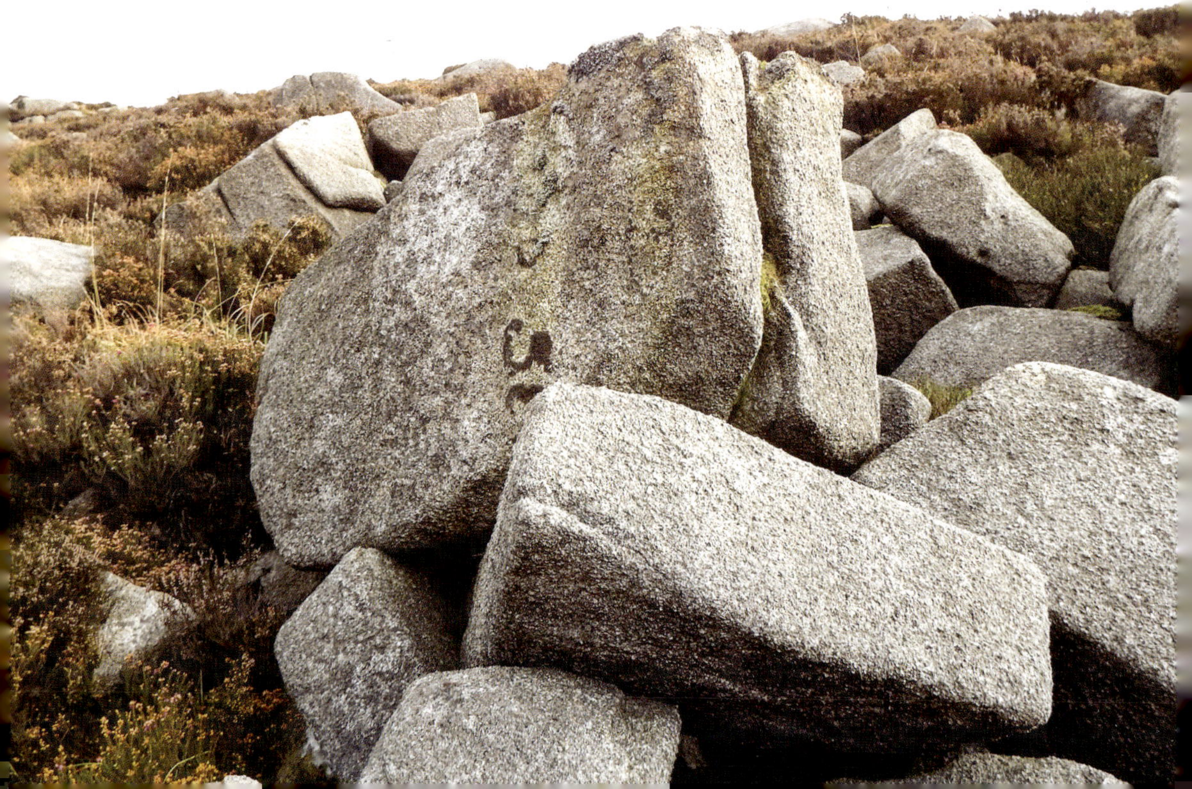

Top opposite: Overlooking the Trassey valley from the south-east slope of Slieve Meelmore, this 2.2m phallic stone has a large split at the tip for a meatus groove. The megalith is nicely propped and wedged in place by a stone on either side. An important feature of the stone is a 1m groove along the top that funnels rain-water to the meatus tip enhancing the symbolism of fertility. The GPS is:

     N. 54º 11. 437'
     W. 005º 59. 908'   Elevation 653m.

Lower opposite: A big split on the front of this granite boulder makes for a very sizeable meatus groove. The carefully propped megalith is on the north flank of Slievenaglogh. It measures about 1.6m long by 1m high by 0.4m wide and its tip points across the Trassey valley to a fissure on the side of Slieve Bearnagh where water has carved out a notional vaginal groove on the cliff face. The supporting spear stone below has a little mouth at its point that is directed to Meelmore summit. The GPS is:

     N. 54º 11. 770'
     W. 005º 58. 695'   Elevation 391m.

Top of this page: This spear stone on the southern flank of Slieve Beg points its meatus groove uphill to where the summer solstice sun will appear.

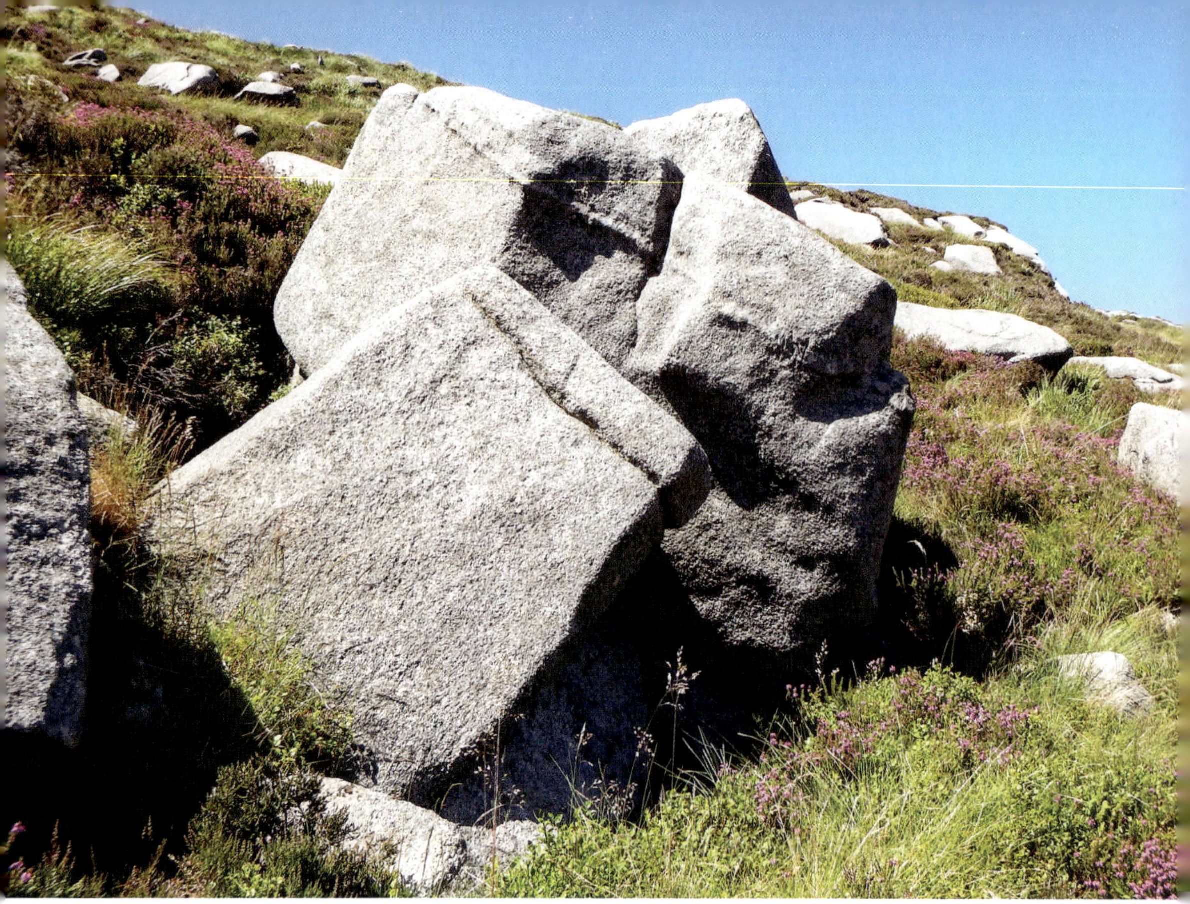

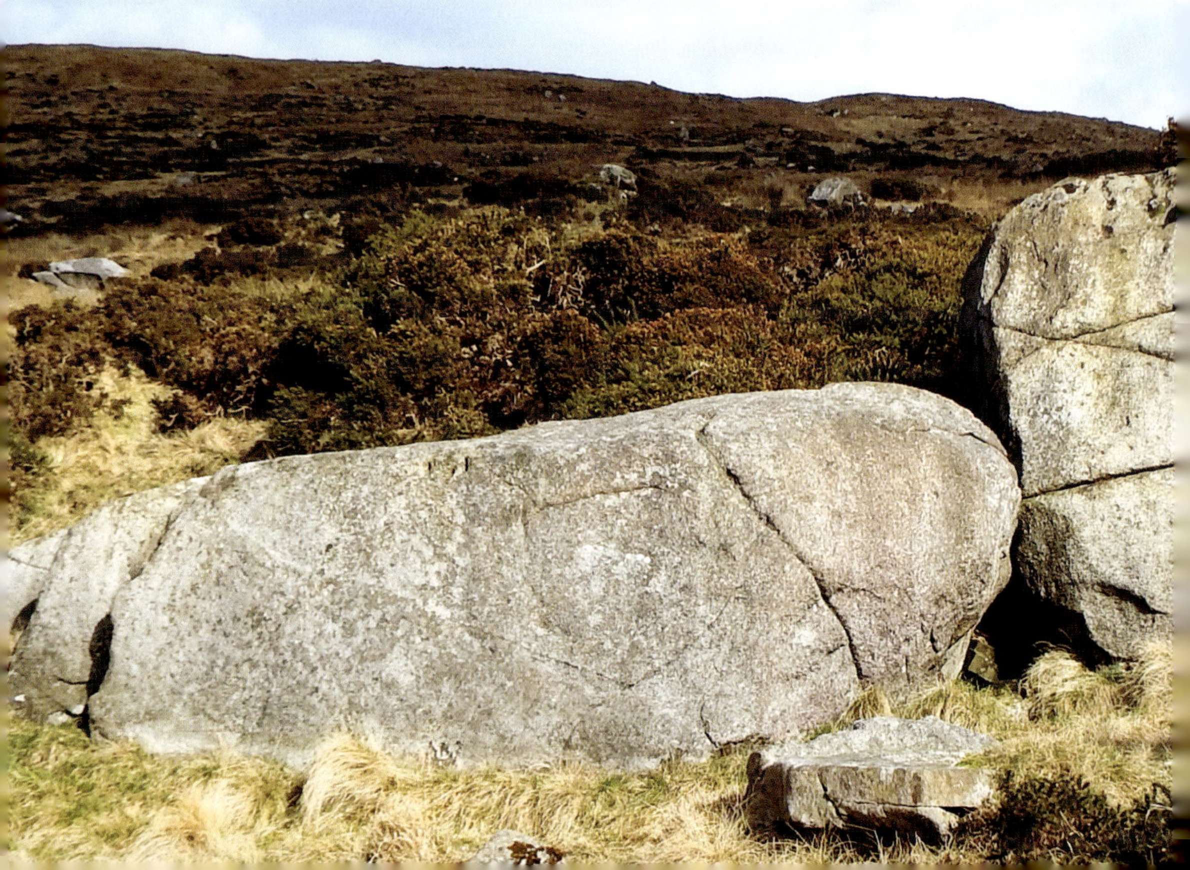

4. Infusion Lines, Coronal Rims and Semen Stones

The next series of photographs shows the genius of the ancients in utilizing infusion streaks in rocks to make them priapic. Sometimes grooves are cut into stones to create coronal rims but finding, shaping and then positioning stones that use infusions was probably a much harder proposition. The same could be said of some of the huge megaliths that feature lighter coloured rock representing a seminal discharge at the tip of the stone.

Top opposite: Apart from meatus grooves, a stone can be made suggestively phallic by giving it a coronal rim. This is usually done by enhancing a suitable natural crack in the rock or by chopping deeply into the crown of the stone. Our first photograph of a cluster of five large stones on the shoulder of Spellack mountain shows two types of coronal rims. The stone to the front left has an enhanced chopped coronal rim while the larger stone behind exploits an infusion band as a coronal rim and it also has a meatus groove. Five stones, you say? Yes, there is a lot more going on at the back that is not shown. The GPS is: N. 54° 11. 805'
W. 005° 59. 388'   Elevation 445m.

Lower opposite: This photograph on the west side of Luke's mountain and below the northern shoulder of Shimial, shows only one of two mighty granite boulders. This location is notable for the tors of Slieve Bearnagh peeping up over the shoulder of Shimial mountain. This featured megalith is six metres long, is decidedly phallic, has a crack as a penile corona and, although it cannot be seen in the photograph, has a light shale infusion tip to suggest semen. This colossal phallus is aligned to winter solstice sunset. It was given the name **Toll an Róid**, 'Get Stuffed!' on account of its perceived interaction with the great boulder in front of it. The GPS is:
N. 54° 12. 394'
W. 005° 58. 467'   Elevation 241m.

Below: Close-up of a 'semen tipped' megalith on Thomas Mountain.

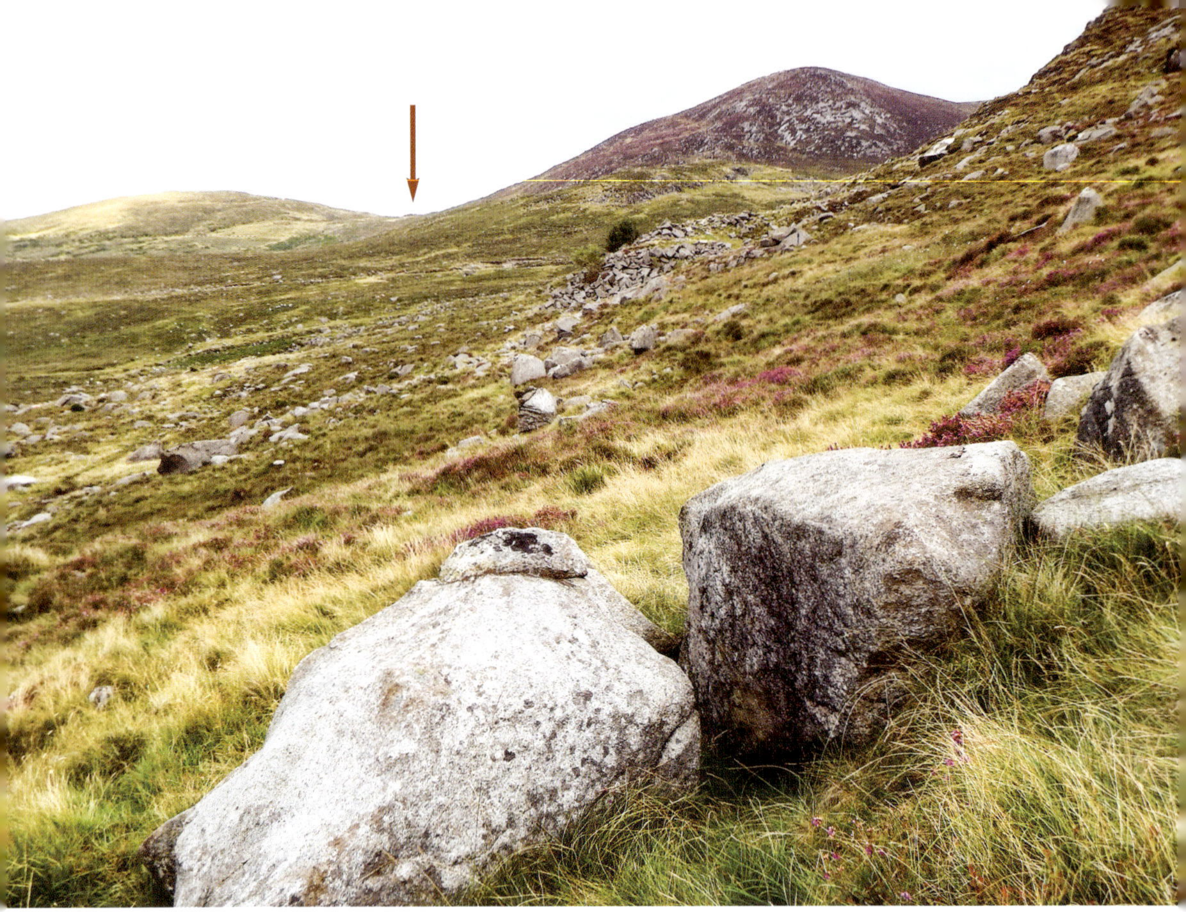

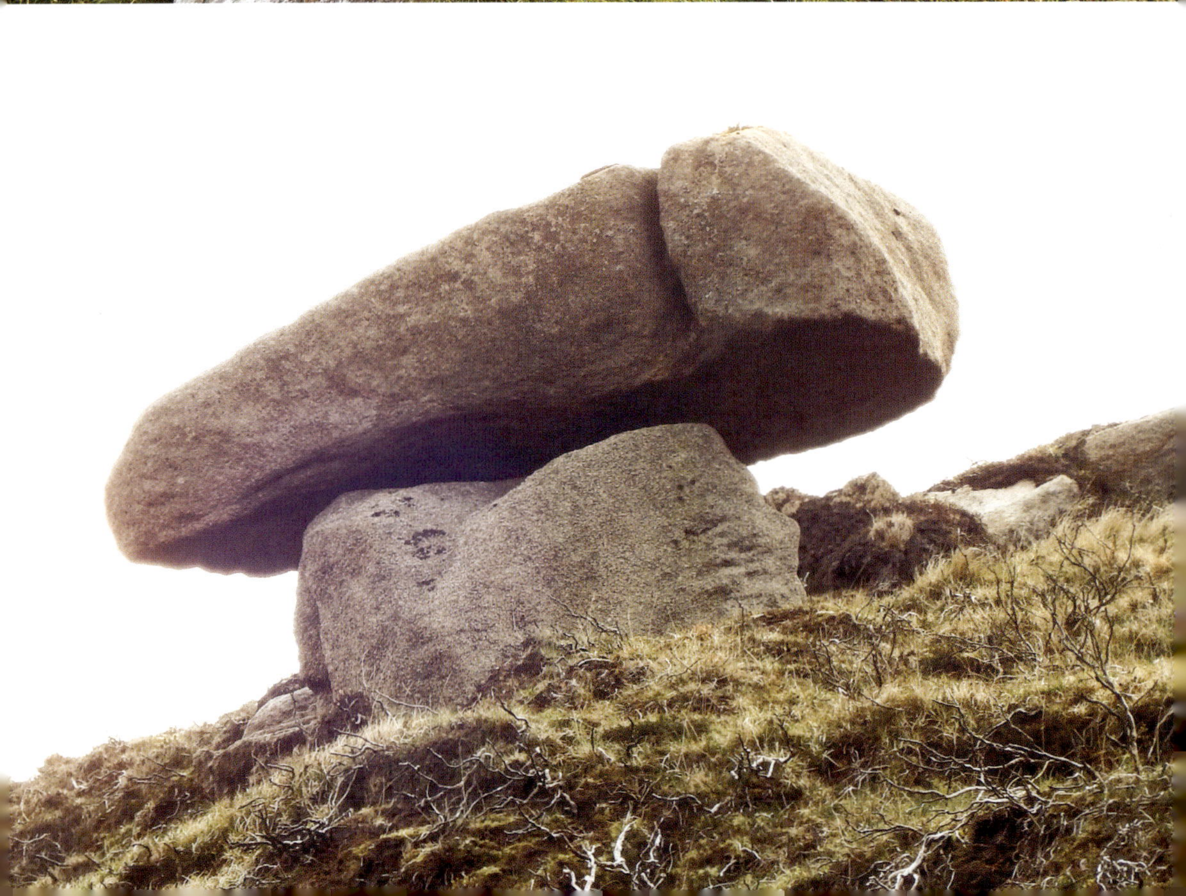

Top opposite: High up the northern side of Meelmore mountain is this knob-head stone. Sharp un-weathered chop marks around the top show how the phallic corona has been created. This is a fertility location. As arrowed, these stones mark the distant appearance of the tip of Shan Slieve between Luke's mountain on the left and darker Shimial mountain. Such a *'gein'*, or landscape begetting position, is referred to as a 'penis in the vagina', a motif beloved by the ancients. Unfortunately the scale of the photograph renders the tip of Shan Slieve scarcely visible. The GPS is:

        N.   54° 12. 055'
        W. 005° 59. 686'   Elevation 290m.

Lower opposite: With its impressive deeply gouged coronal rim, this phallic capstone along the crest of Long mountain overlooking the Windy Gap valley, certainly flaunts its fertility credentials. The magnificent capstone is circa 2.5m long, .9m thick, and 1.4m across. The dolmen type structure is at the top of a steep slope and begs the question of how the ancients managed to get the capstone in place. The GPS is:

        N.   54° 07. 729'
        W. 006° 04. 957'   Elevation 360m

Top of this page: On the south side of Leganabruchan is this spear stone with a pronounced coronal rim chopped down along the tip. If you get this far the rock-face a couple of metres up-slope also bears investigation on account of its suggestive artwork. The GPS is:

        N.   54° 10. 783'
        W. 005° 53. 557'   Elevation 333m.

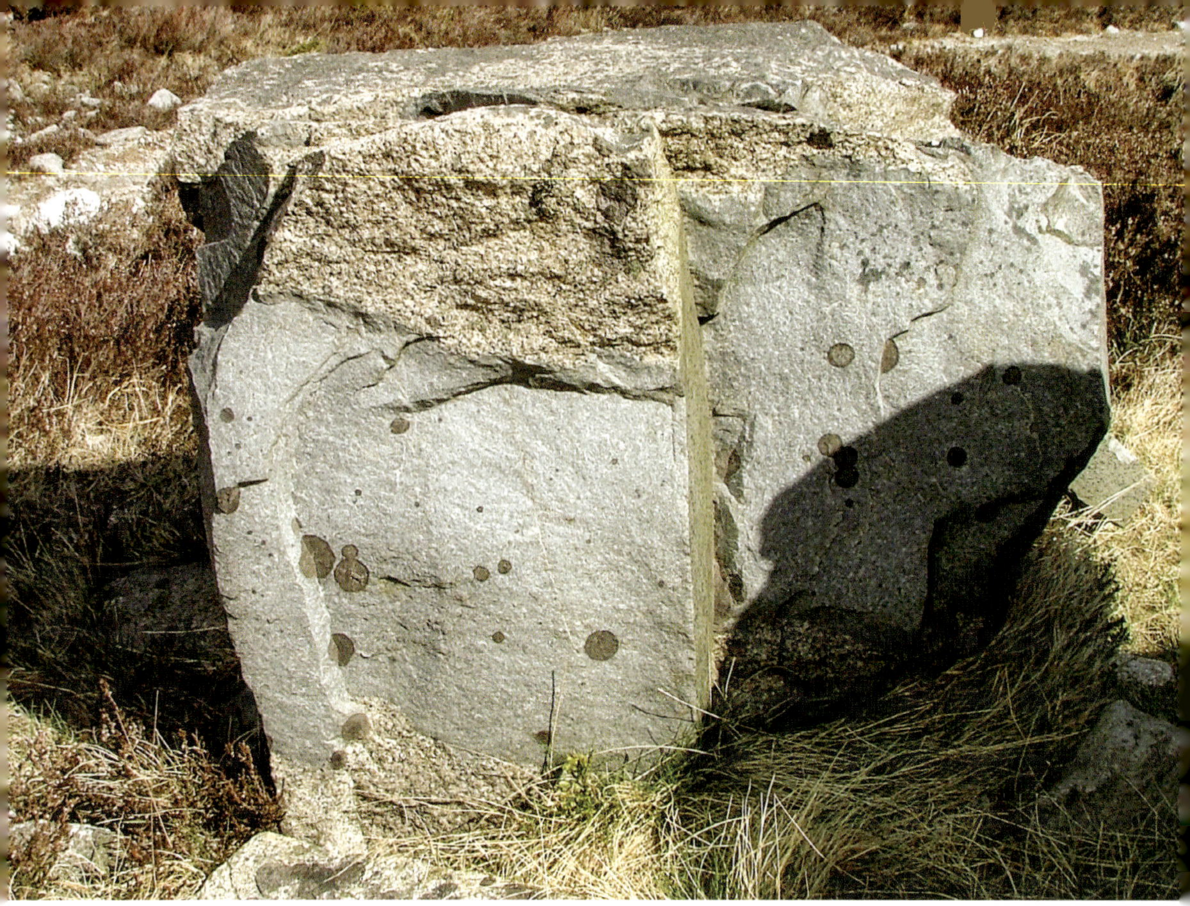

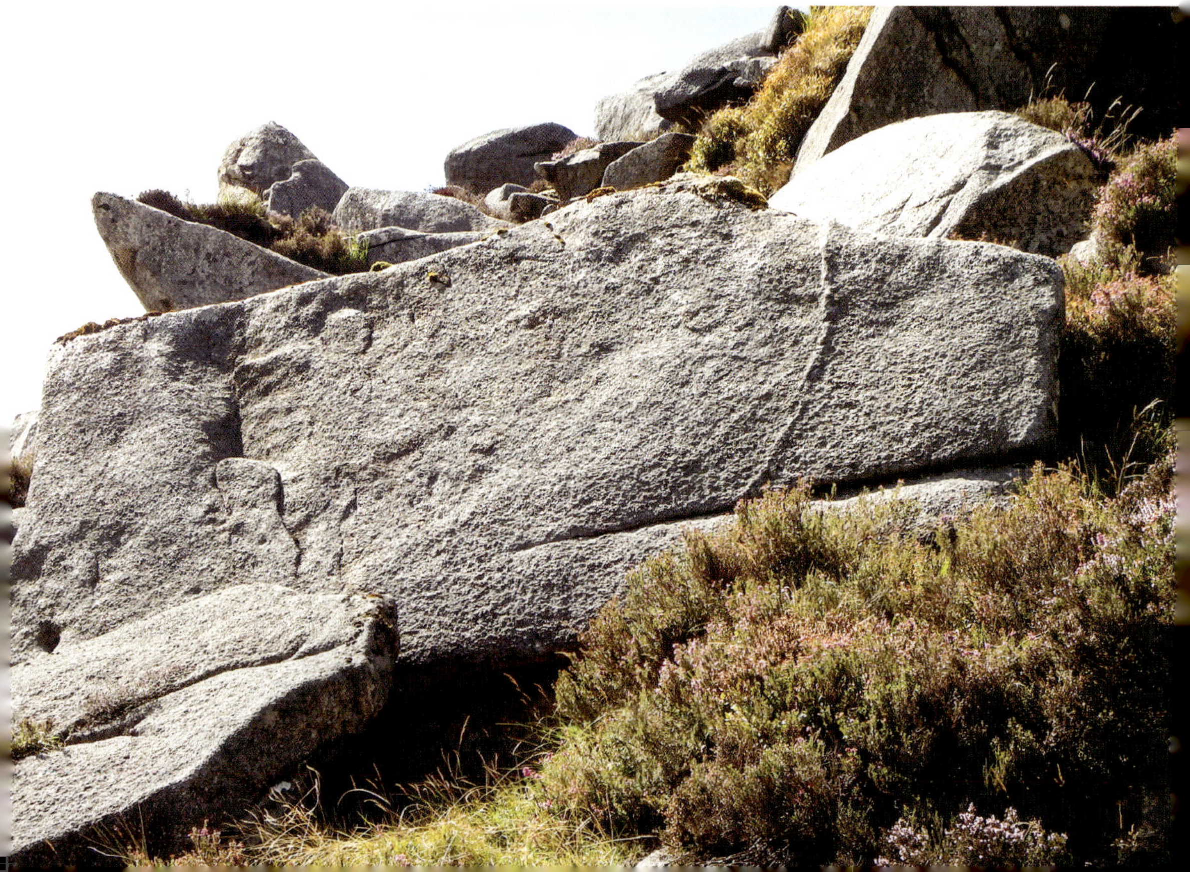

Top opposite: Beside the trail and near the quarry at the head of the Bloody Bridge valley is this self-explanatory fusion stone. The quarry-men did not tip this stone onto the spoil heap but carefully set it aside as such stones were long held important in Mourne. The fertility loving ancients looked on such fusions of igneous rock and granite as a metaphor for the human joining of male and female. The next series of photographs shows how fusion streaks have often been ingeniously used to depict coronal rims.

Lower opposite: On the south-east flank of Slieve Bearnagh, an area rich in megaliths and ancient art-work, is this granite stone, close to four metres in length, that has a nice infusion line near its tip as a coronal rim. The GPS is:
                    N. 54° 11. 129'
                    W. 005° 58. 630'   Elevation 442m.

Top of this page: This emphatic phallic megalith is up against the field boundary on the south side of the access path to Cock and Hen. It cannot be seen from the path, only from the field. It is a beautiful creation. It is 3.75m long by 2m high and artful use has been made of an infusion line across the stone to clearly represent a coronal rim. A passing shepherd told me that the stone had been moved by the owner of the field over to the fence. It probably wasn't moved too far as the location still reveals its fertility significance, marking as it does where two views of the 'penis in the vagina' motif can be seen in landscape notches, one on either side of Crotlieve mountain. One of the motifs is shown in the oval. The GPS is:
                    N.   54° 11. 009'
                    W. 006° 06. 425'   Elevation 141m.

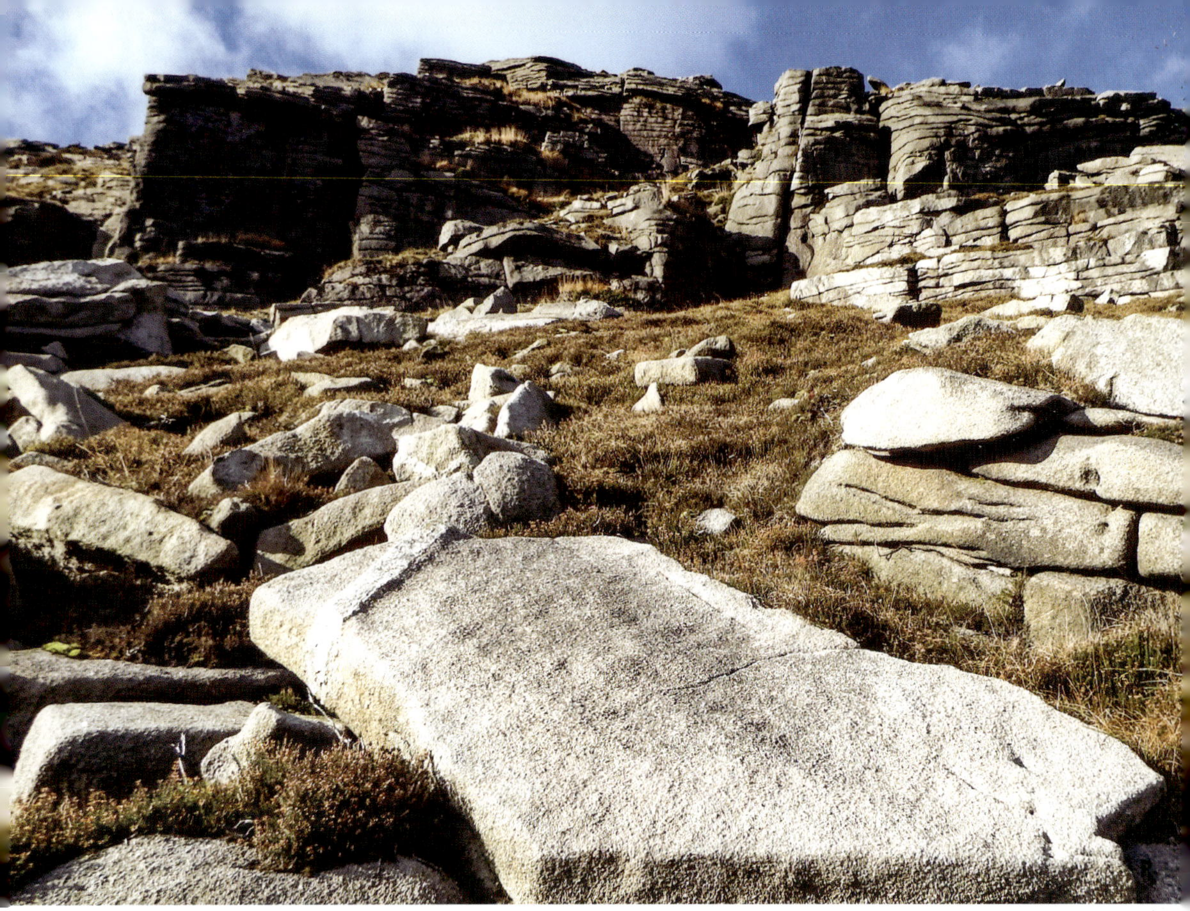

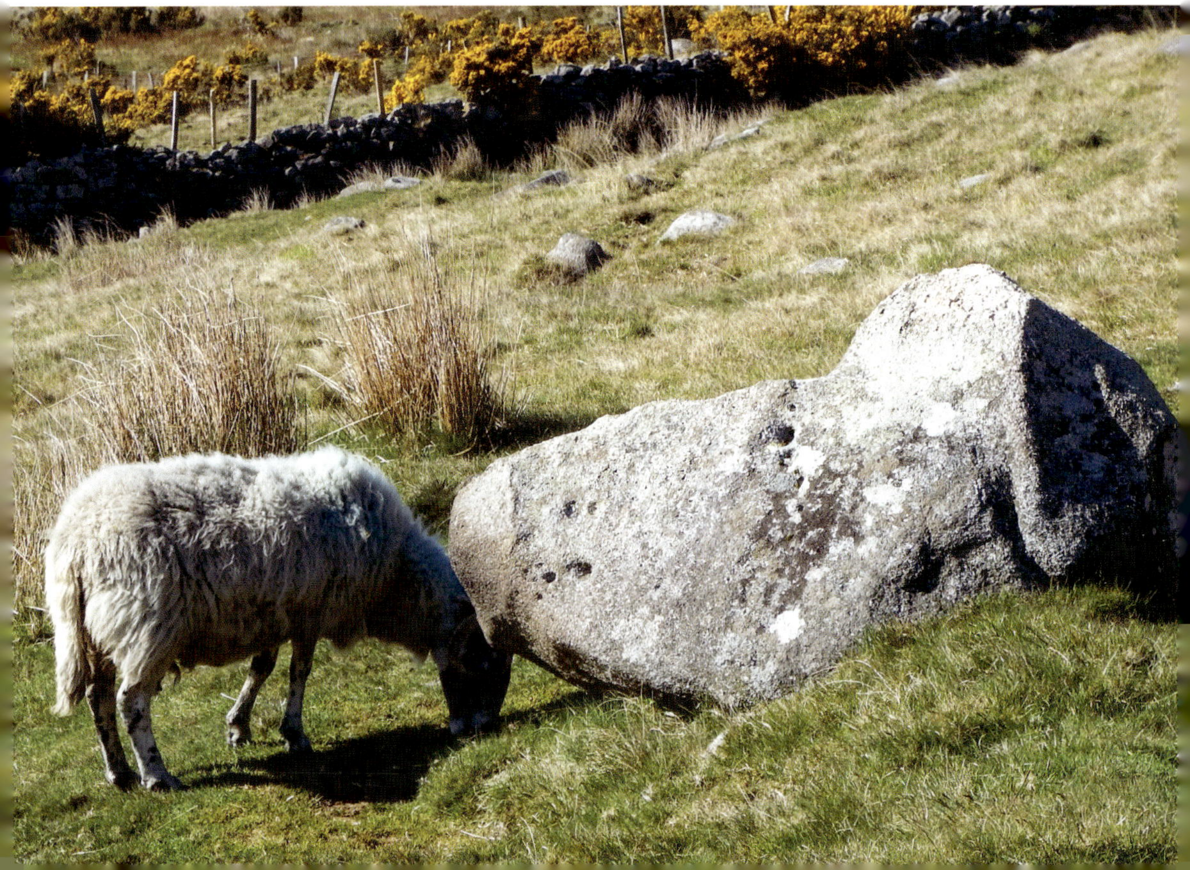

Top opposite: In the excitement of finding so many fertility stones here I entirely forgot to note the GPS after taking the photograph. The cliffs above should help you find the place on the eastern side of Lamagan, up above the path to the plateau of Cove Lough. The featured slab has a conspicuous raised infusion for a coronal rim. It also has a small open-mouth 'face' at the bottom of the stone.

Look again, just above the tip, two long granite stones have been laid in a shallow [V] shape symbolic of landscape vaginal notches. The granite stones represent the vaginal labial sides and between them is a cheeky little face stone as the penile insertion. Mourne is ill-served by those who myopically dismiss such creations as 'natural'. Time for the strategic placement of fertility stones, in all their many variations, to be recognised as an important genre in the archaeology of Northern Ireland.

Lower opposite: This lovely stone is beside the path up to the Cock & Hen. It is a phallic shaped granite boulder 1.5m long and the distinctive feature is the infusion line behind the sheep's head representing a coronal rim. The GPS is:

     N. 54° 10. 938'
     W. 006° 05. 146'   Elevation 172m.

Top of this page: Shadows clearly demark the slanted coronal infusion on this erect phallic megalith on the southern slopes of Chimney Rock mountain.

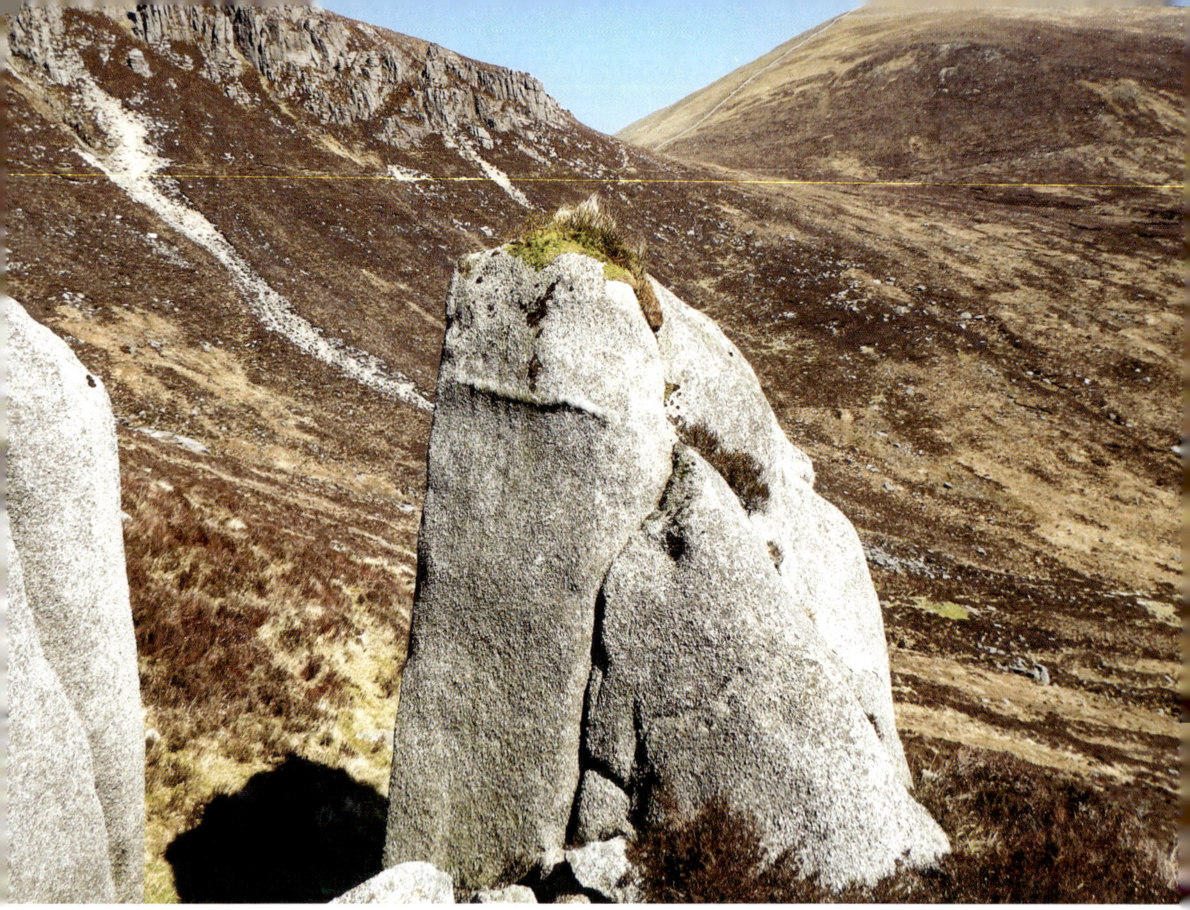

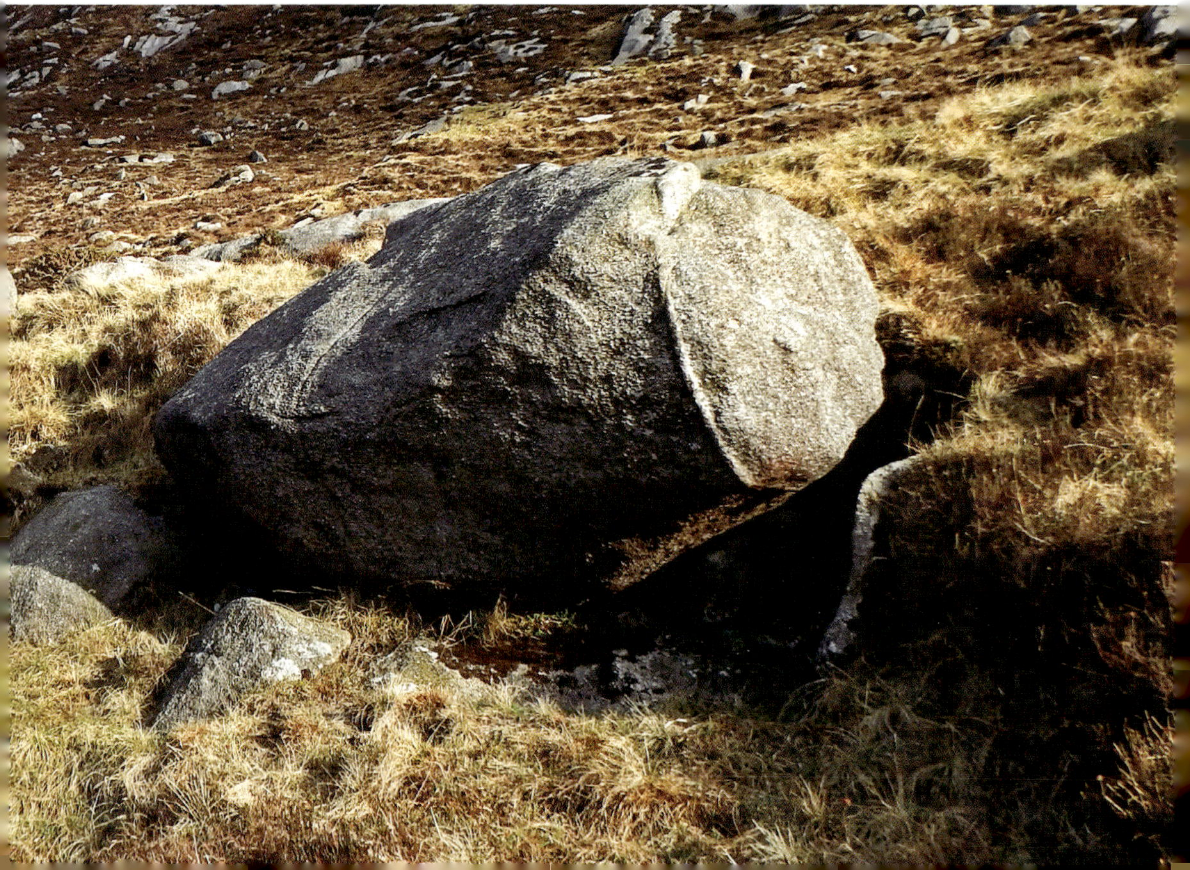

Top opposite: There is a lot going on here at this megalith near the head of the Annalong valley. The upright stone uses an infusion line near the top as a coronal rim while on its right side a shadow eye makes a face with a pointy nose. Chop marks on the stone that enhance the 'nose' show there was a deliberate intention to suggest fellatio. There is an intentional gap between this upright and the other upright on the left of the picture This gap would be penetrated by the light of early summer solstice to achieve notional fertility.

Lower opposite: The boulder field under the northern slope of Shimial mountain is a location rich in megaliths. This phallic stone with its distinctive coronal rim was photographed on an April evening.

Top of this page: Pierce's Castle is in the background. This phallic stone is beside the trail en-route to the summit. It skilfully uses two lighter coloured rock infusions to highlight both a coronal rim and a seminal discharge at the tip.

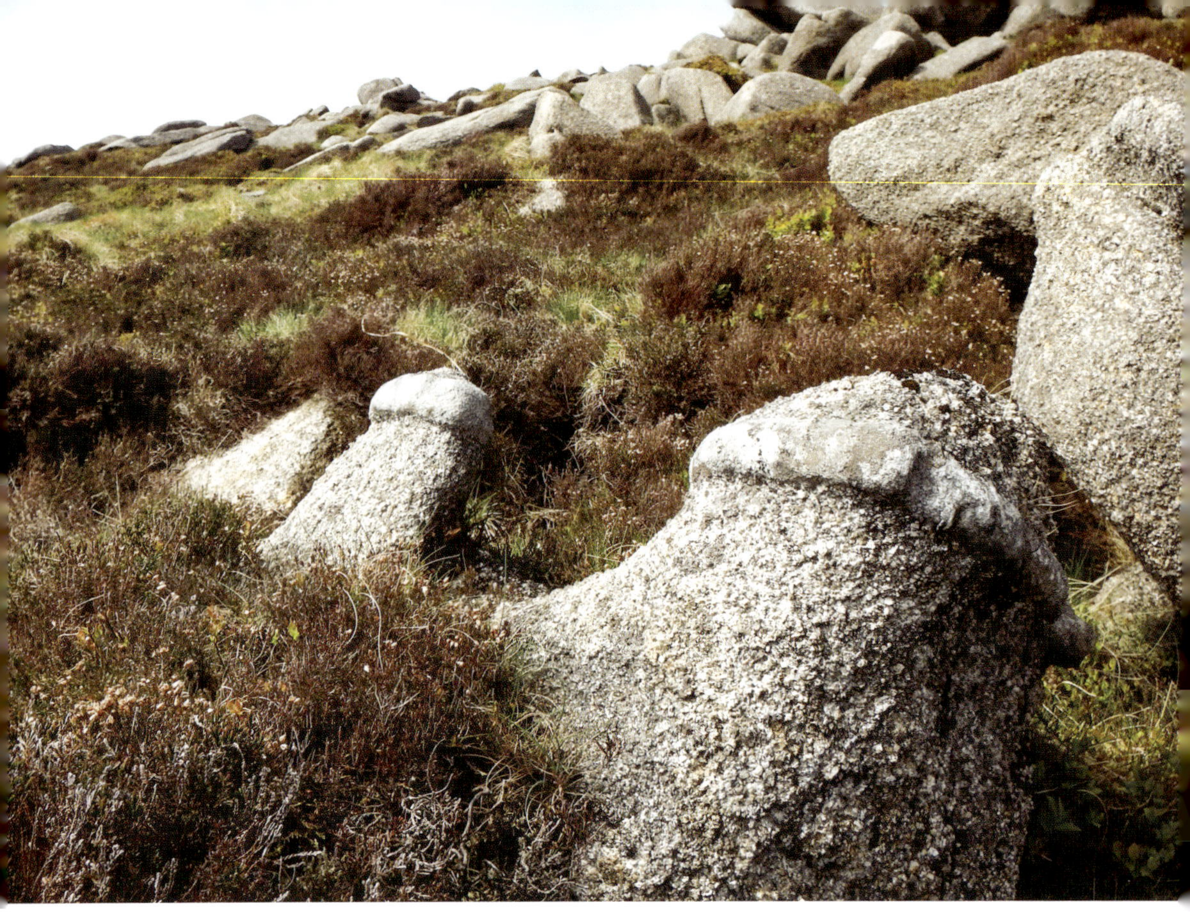

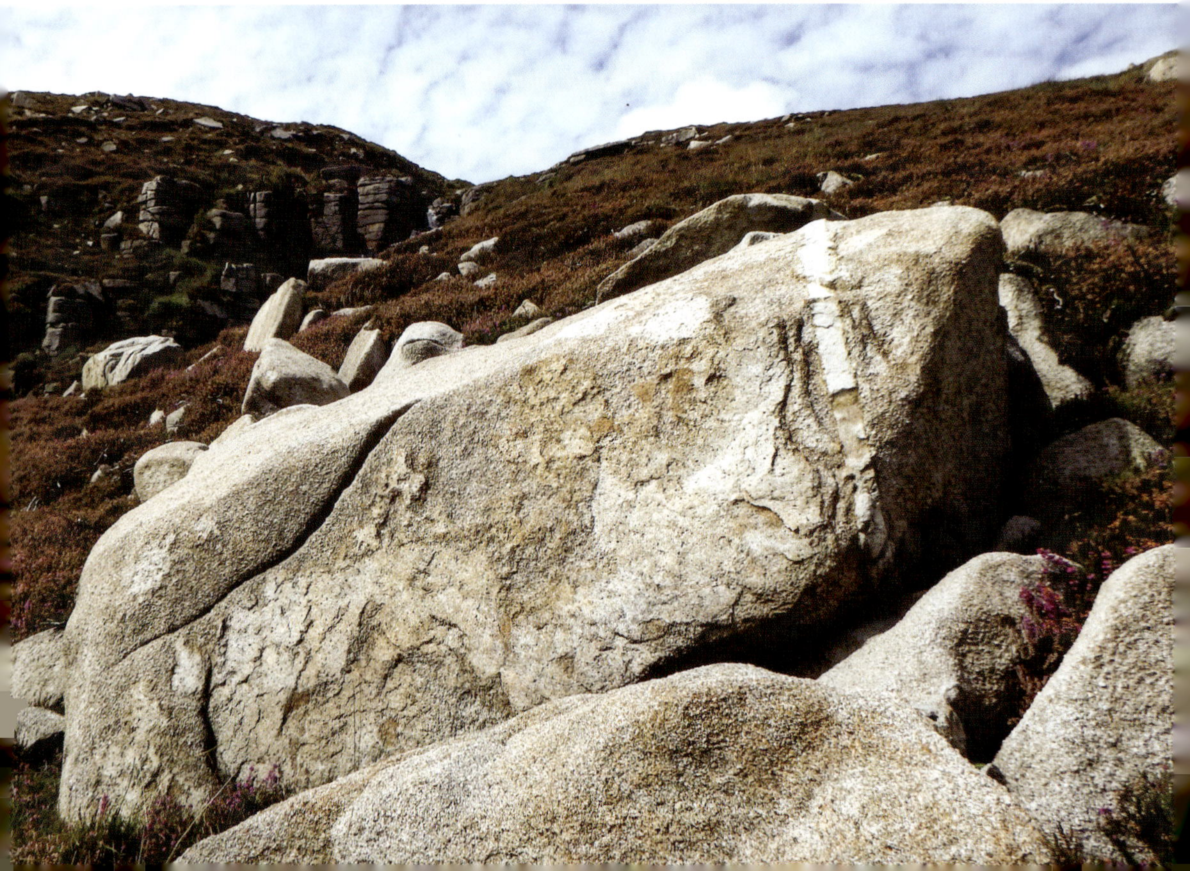

Top opposite: When it comes to the use of infusion lines as coronal rims you cannot get better than these stones on the east side of Bearnagh's north tor. In the excitement of the discovery the GPS was overlooked. However, it is a hardly two minutes above another megalith whose GPS is:

N.   54º 11. 187'
W. 005º 58. 842'   Elevation 586m.

These stubby phallic stones were previously illustrated in *Prehistoric Mourne* on page 262.

Lower opposite: High on the western slope of the Annalong valley and near the rim of the Lower Cove plateau is this mighty phallic stone approximately 3.5m long by 2m wide across the back and just over 1m thick. This is a big stone! The lovely feature of this megalith is how the ancients used a white infusion line near the tip of the stone to denote a coronal rim. The tip is towards the Castles and the infusion line across the top is around 5 to 6 centimetres wide. Beautiful. The GPS is:

N.   54º 10. 024'
W. 005º 56. 989'   Elevation 389m.

Top of this page: A number of megaliths are featured now showing how the ancients exploited infusion lines in stones to signify semen at their notional phallic tips.
This small granite megalith rests on shale bedrock beside a pond at the top of Luke's mountain. The distinctive feature of the stone is the light-coloured infusion band around the top of the stone most of which has been cut back but still leaving a white part protruding to emphasise the seminal exudation at the point. This highlighted point is directed towards summer solstice sunrise.

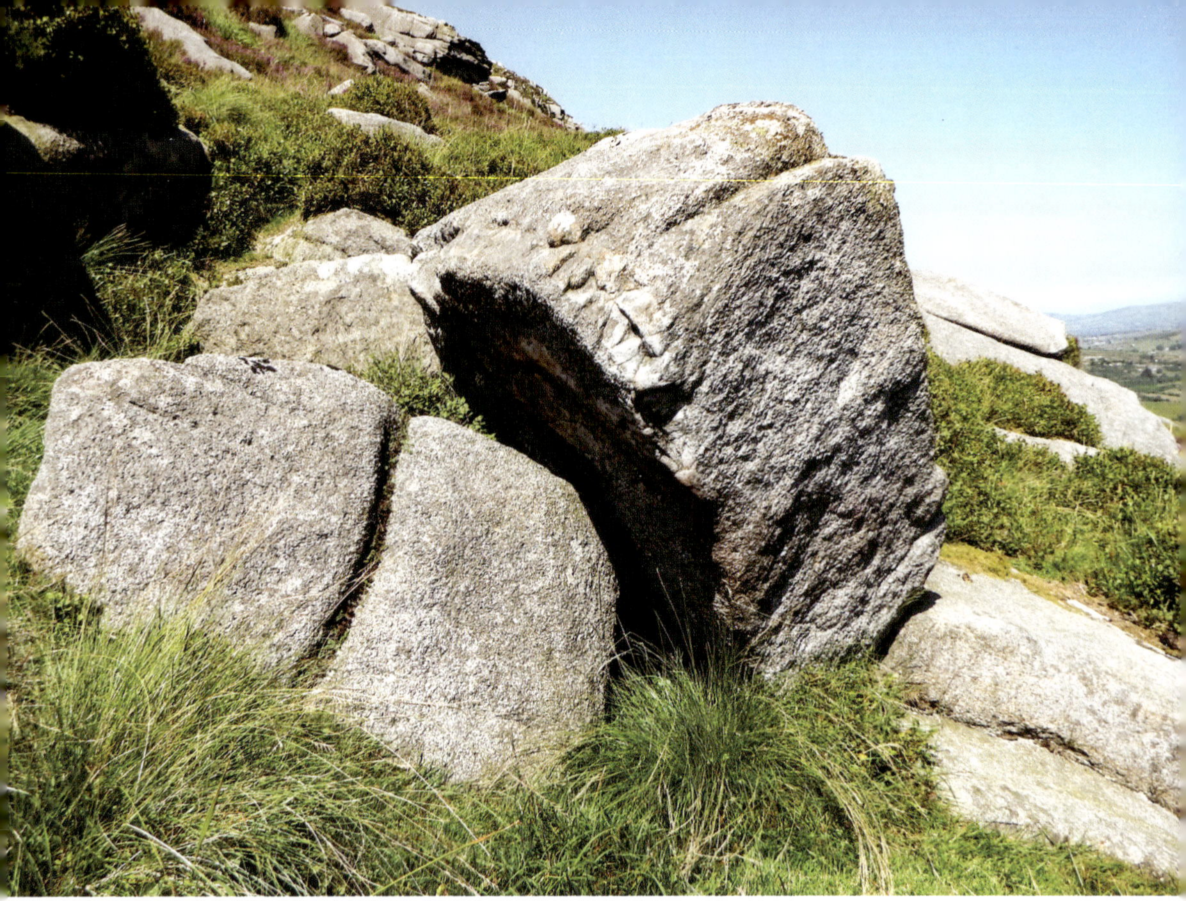

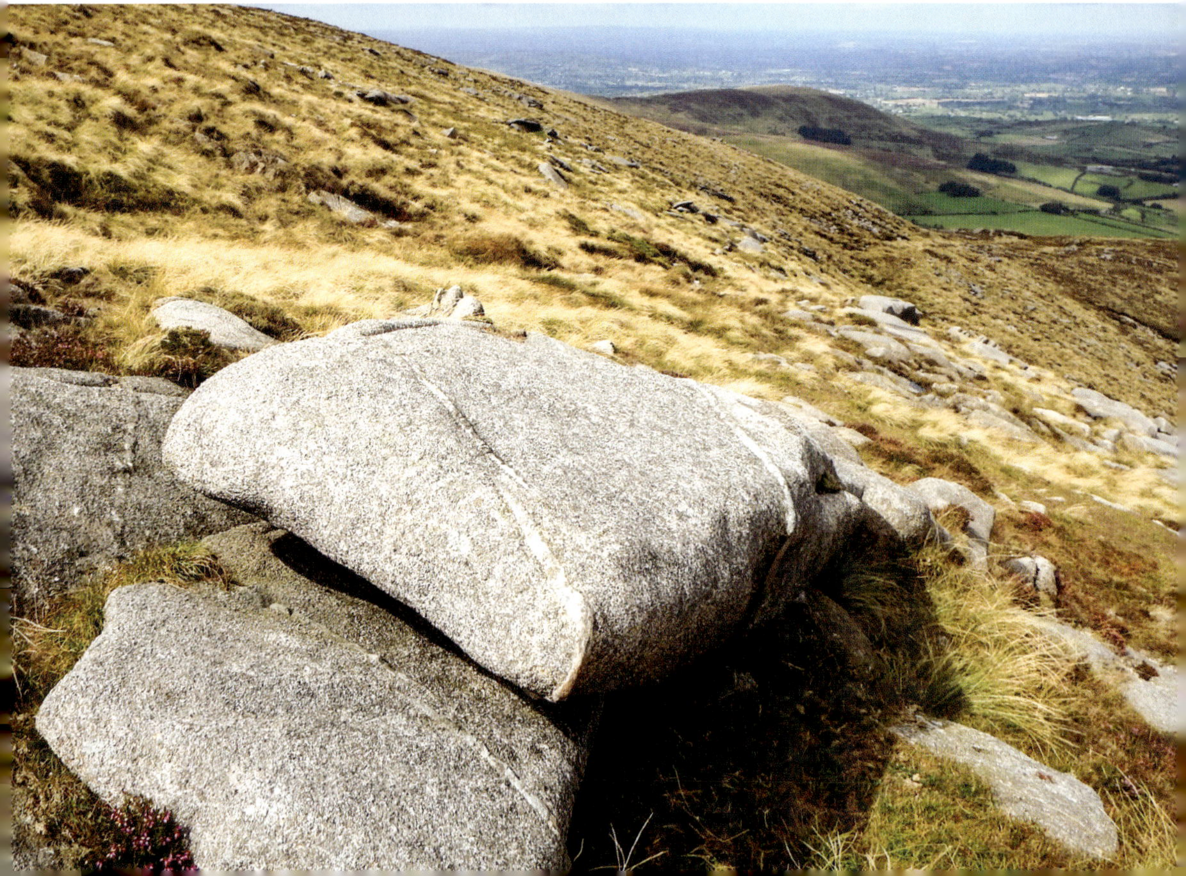

Top opposite: About half-way up the slope under Spellack a 1.4m long megalith is propped up in erection mode with its meatus groove facing towards Slieve Bearnagh and the appearance of winter solstice sun. Clever use has been made of a lighter coloured rock infusion in the granite to indicate semen at the tip. The GPS is:

      N. 54º 11. 853'
      W. 005º 59. 286'   Elevation 328m.

Lower opposite: On the top north-west side of Slieve Meelmore a 3.5m long granite block is nicely perched on a block below so as to raise its phallic tip. Skilful use has been made of the thin lighter infused streak to symbolise semen at the tip. The back right end of this stone is probably more important as it also has an infused band, this one acting as a coronal rim and a meatus groove aligned to summer solstice sunset. The GPS is:

      N. 54º 11. 637'
      W. 006º 00. 189'   Elevation 567m.

Top of this page: This semen tipped stone is in Happy Valley between the Mourne and Shepherd's walls. The end points to summer solstice sunset. The GPS is:

      N. 54º 11. 214'
      W. 006º 00. 278'   Elevation 577m.

5. Man's Defining Appendage

> No rest, no calm my soul may win,
> Because my body craves to sin;
> Till thou, dear Lord, thyself impart,
> Peace on my head, light in my heart.
> (Christian Hymn)

Such is the profusion of phallic stones across the mountains, the hardest part of preparing this section of Megalithic Mourne was what to leave out. There was only a limited amount of space available yet there was a distressing dilemma of choice. The many mighty monuments of Man's defining appendage may not be the most edifying to present to Christian souls but, welcome or unwelcome, the monuments are there in their hundreds. They cannot be ignored, denied or air-brushed away. For centuries their remoteness up in the mountains preserved them from destruction. Now, as an integral part of our ancient heritage, they deserve to be recognised. The hope is that these monuments will contribute one day to Mourne being inscribed by UNESCO as a World Heritage Site.

Another important reason for acknowledging these megaliths lies with the perpetual struggle within man's nature, the battle between good and evil. The stones are a reminder of what we are all capable of and for our constant need of *Aithrighe Truagh* (see p.387). We can hardly give full honour and glory to St Patrick, our national saint, unless we understand the enormity of the old pagan ways that Patrick had to contend with and overcome. It is a struggle from which we too are not excused. As we will see in the final chapter, St Patrick brought us all the way to cast out our own 'snakes'. Looking on the sexual monuments with disgust, denial, fear or anger is to overlook the need we all have to constantly ask the help of our Higher Power in our everyday efforts to do good. The day of stone idols may be gone but the struggle will continually remain with us not to replace them with money, power or some other transient obsession but to become people of love.

It is all too easy to leap to judgment on those who erected the monuments. It was a different time, a different mindset and calls for a different appraisal. Comments on the megaliths in this work are not endorsements. Evaluations have been made on the basis of the great size of the stones and the attendant huge efforts and likely dangers that have been involved. Proper judgement is best withheld until one has had the opportunity to walk all round the stones, to see them from more than one perspective, to examine them closely, to understand their '*sitz im leben*' and the influence of the surrounding landscape.

Under the north corner of Spellack a penile shaft has been sculpted on the side of a boulder that itself is part of a vaginal cavity. The light of summer solstice dawn would thus cast the fertilising shadow of the phallus into the back recess. The GPS is:

N. 54º 11. 989'
W. 005º 59. 423'   Elevation 335m.

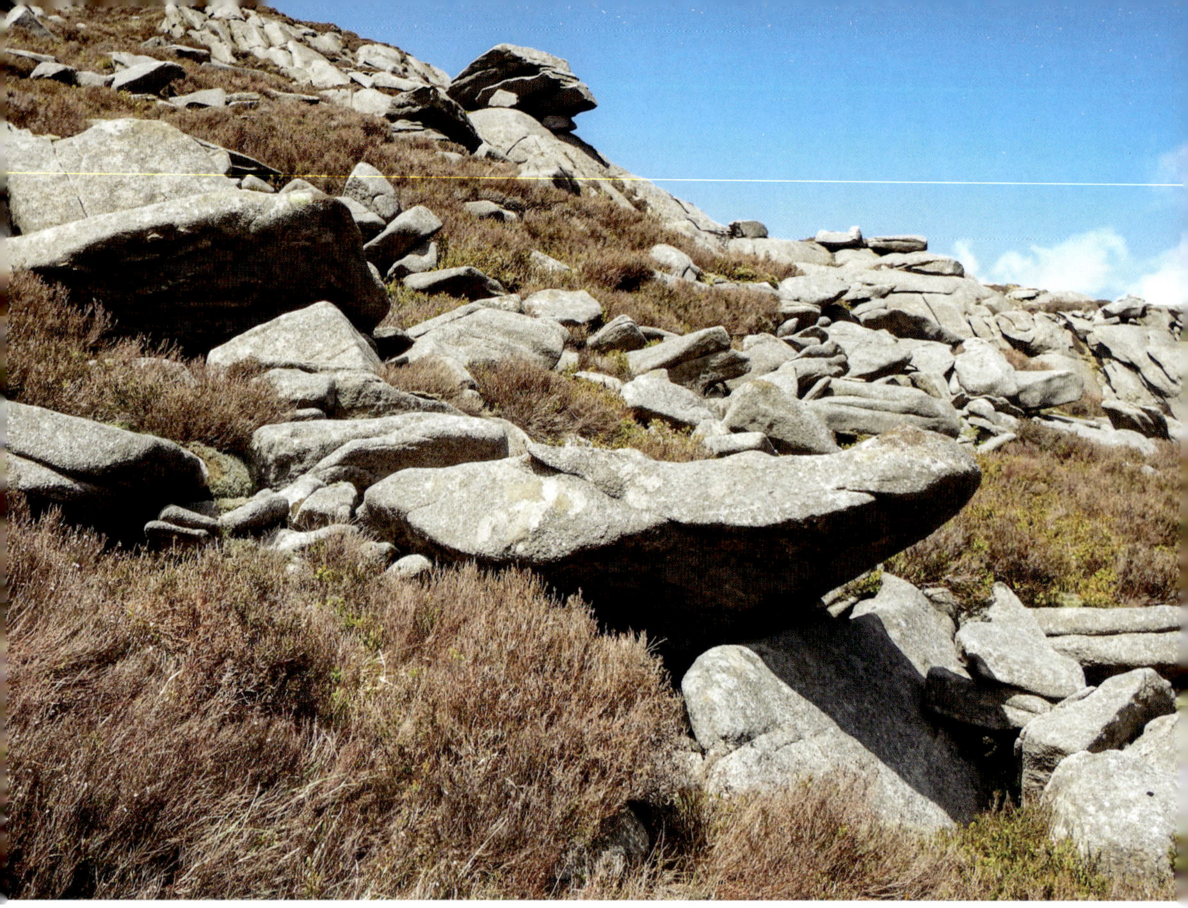

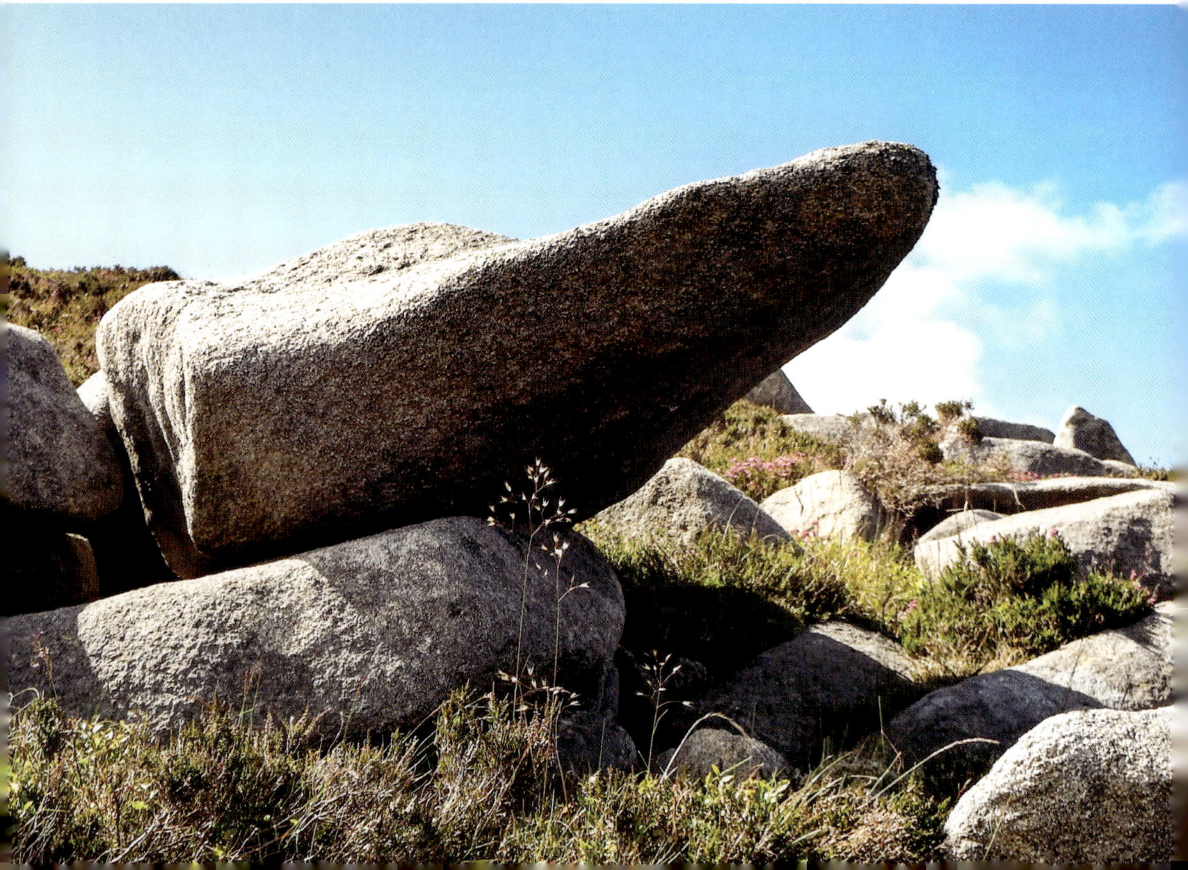

Top opposite: On the north side of Pollaphuca valley a substantial spear stone, comfortably 2m long, points to Slieve Bearnagh's north tor. The shape of the stone has an uncanny similarity to a seal, complete with a little flipper at the side. This location is rich in megaliths. Note the others in the background. The GPS is:

      N. 54º 11. 417'
      W. 005º 59. 629'   Elevation 463m.

Lower opposite: The vicinity around this phallic spear on the supper southern slope of Meelmore mountain hosts an overwhelming array of monuments. This horizontal spear looks to summer solstice sunrise. The GPS is:

      N. 54º 11. 514'
      W. 005º 59. 824'   Elevation 622m.

Top of this page: Above the upper path around Spellack shoulder at the entrance to Pollaphuca; a great phallic stone, with an impressive meatus groove, is tilted towards Slieve Bearnagh's north tor. The stone was in shade when first discovered and I remember being so impressed that there was no hesitation in returning another day to photograph it. The huge phallus stands at least 3m high, is 1.5 m thick and 2.25m wide across the lower bottom. This is a seriously big stone and an important megalith. The GPS is:

      N. 54º 11. 690'
      W. 005º 59. 204'   Elevation 373m.

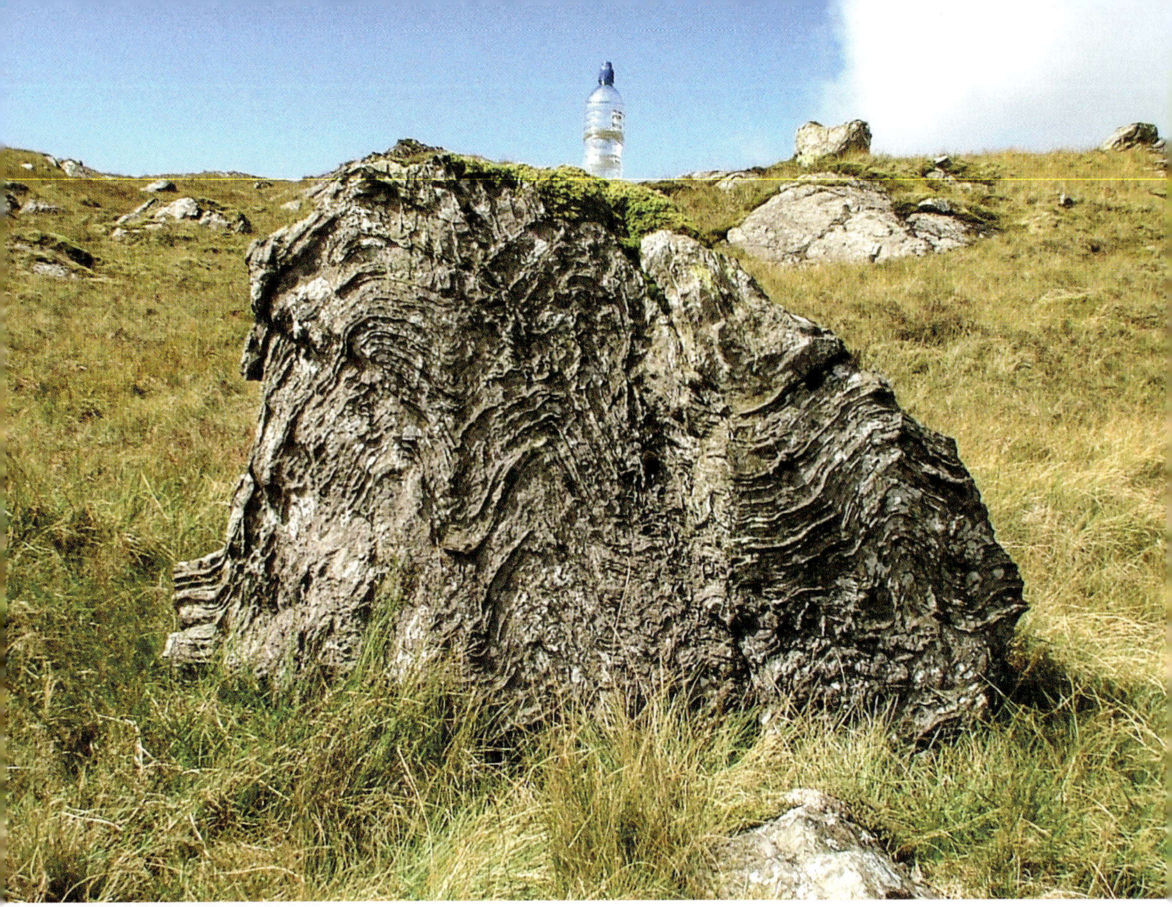

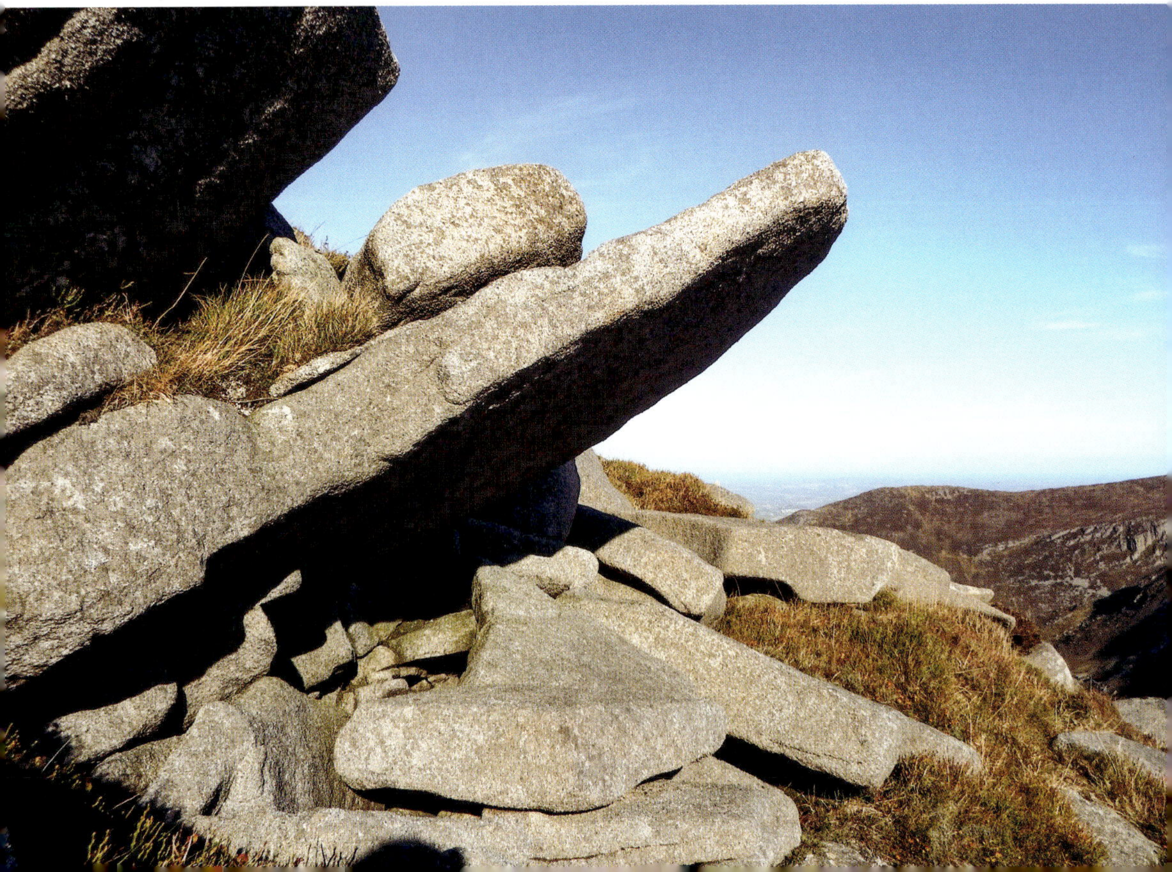

Top opposite: The use of the folded stratified layers in this shale boulder to suggest an upright phallus is an outstanding act of inspiration. The small boulder is found at the north end of Slieve Muck, even north of Far Top but a few hundred metres south of the shepherd's wall from Carn mountain. It has been placed to receive the early light of winter solstice. Brilliantly simple; the work of creative genius and yet you could pass it by so easily.

Lower opposite: On the east side of Wee Slevanmore a phallic granite slab, measuring 15cm thick at the tip, projects at least 2m from the hillside. The stone points to winter solstice dawn. There is a most suggestive intimation of fellatio from a stone with a great curved 'mouth' directly below the projection. The GPS is:

                N. 54° 11. 167'
                W. 006° 00. 021'   Elevation 609m.

Top of this page: This neat little phallic stone is on the east side of Slieve Bearnagh's summit tor. It is adjacent to an even larger phallic stone of 5m in length (but this one was more photogenic). The coronal rim on the stone is just about noticeable in the photograph. The rim is quite dramatic on the other side. The GPS is:

                N. 54° 11. 045'
                W. 005° 59. 234'   Elevation 651m.

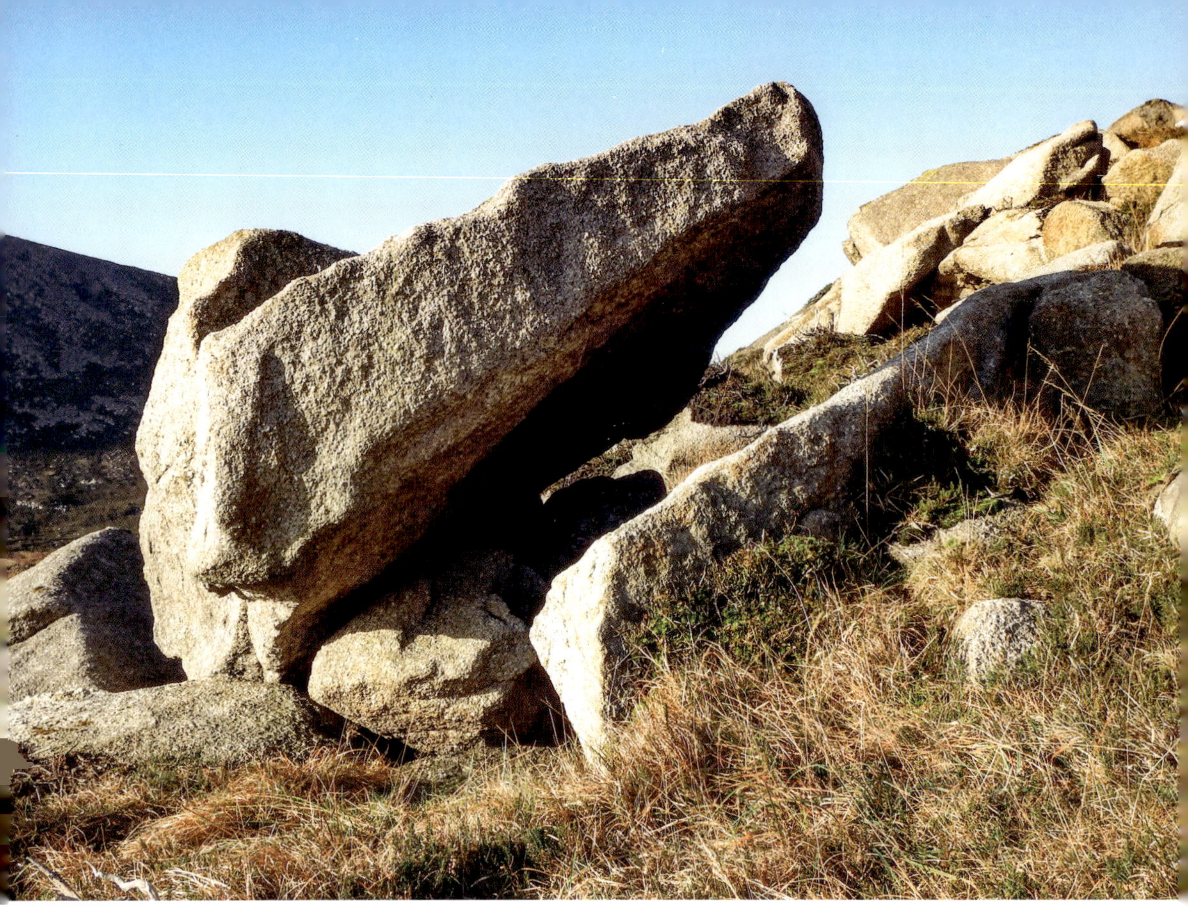

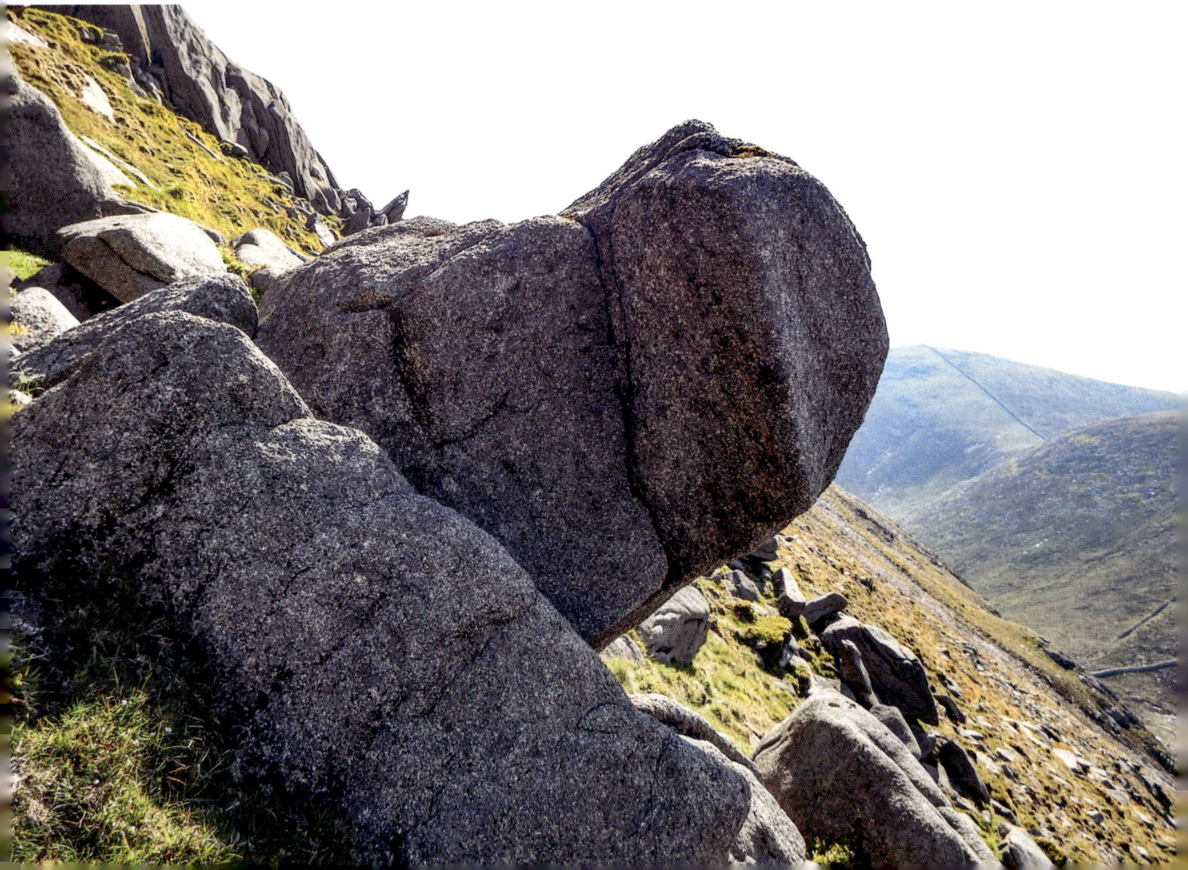

Top opposite: A beautifully raised phallic spear stone points towards summer solstice sun. If you look at the bottom left you will see how just the hint of a pig's snout and an eye has been given to the stone. The symbolism of the pig recalls the tale of *Togail Bruidne Dá Derga*, 'The Destruction of Da Derga's Hostel', where the lord of the feast was sometimes represented as a man carrying a pig on his shoulder. The monument is on the corner of Slieve Lamagan nearest to Percy Bysshe.

Lower opposite: There is no disguising the steepness of the slope on Slieve Bearnagh's north side where this monster of a phallic boulder has somehow been erected. It was named **Cloch Onchondachta**, 'Stone of Valour' to salute the brave men who raised it. The stone is roughly 3m long by 2.5 high by 2m across and elevated on large anchor stones. This is the work of mighty men. The GPS is:

                N. 54° 11. 216'
                W. 005° 59. 205'   Elevation 685m.

Top of this page: A vanity project if ever there was one. You can imagine a proud man boasting that his erection would be so hard and strong that it would support a great weight. Here on the south-east side of Slieve Lamagan the top stone has stayed secure on its penile perch for centuries. The GPS is:

                N. 54° 09. 630'
                W. 005° 57. 677'   Elevation 386m.

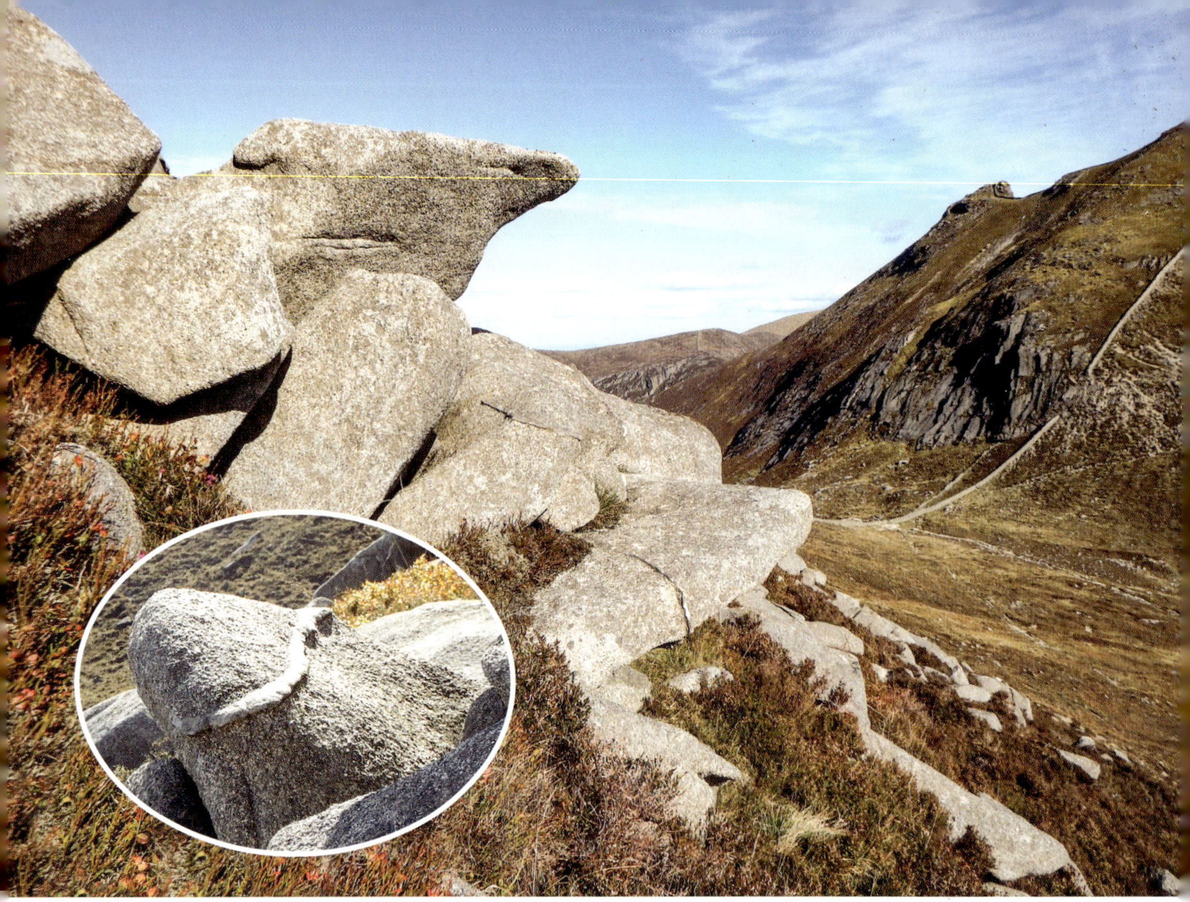

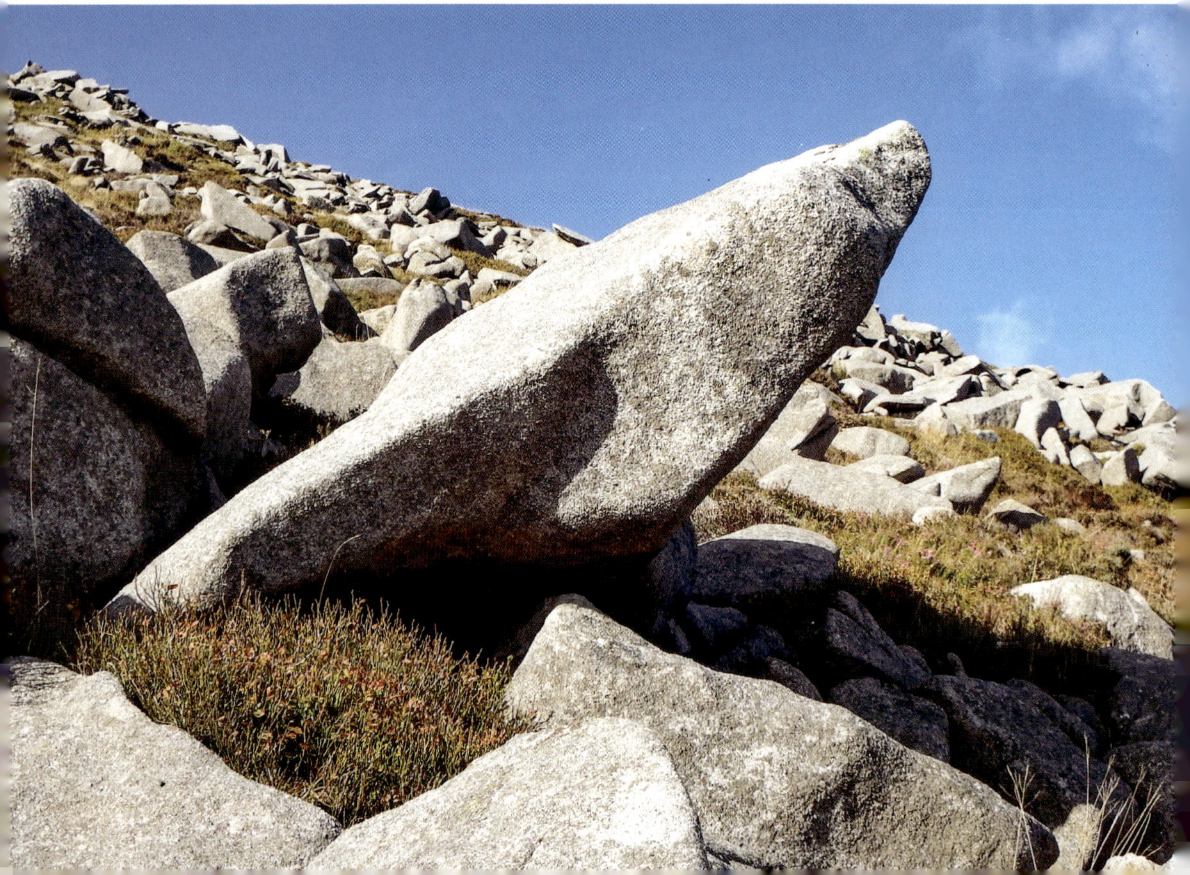

Top opposite: Carefully secured on the slope of Wee Slevanmore is this really beaky nose of a phallic face stone. The beak points to the Bearnagh/Lamagan landscape notch. The attached photograph shows the little phallic stone underneath sporting a magnificent infused corona. The GPS is:

                        N. 54º 11. 137'
                        W. 006º 00. 041'   Elevation 589m.

Lower opposite: This megalith enjoys the same GPS as the previous entry as it is only a step or two up the slope. It is no wonder that Slieve Meelmore and this, its shoulder, Wee Slevanmore, once enjoyed the Irish name of **Sliabh Meithle Mór**, 'mountain of great work gangs'. The ancients were certainly very busy right across these slopes.

Top of this page: This spear stone sits in phallic mode at the top of the Trassey Valley. The tip of the spear points to the summit of Spellack. Slievenaglogh is in the background and Shimial mountain (not marked on OS maps) is on the distant left. The GPS is:

                        N. 54º 11. 401'
                        W. 005º 58.' 502'   Elevation 438m.

Above: You will find this granite block in erection mode on the southern flank of Slieve Donard. The tip is directed to Greenore Point. The stone is over 1m long but the end is out of sight under counter-balance stones. An infusion line has been cleverly utilised to denote a penile coronal ring. The GPS is:

       N. 54° 10. 577'
       W. 005° 55. 333'   Elevation 726m.

Top opposite: A cluster of phallic spear stones looks out over beautiful scenery from the southern slope of Doan mountain.

Lower opposite: This monstrous erection is to be found roughly in the centre of Glenfoffany valley. What a monument it is! The huge slab is 3m from front tip to the back, about .8m thick and circa almost 3m wide. There is a large propping stone below helping to achieve the upright angle and the main alignment is to the vulva shape of Glasdrumman Hill (marked on OS maps as Slievenagarragh). The GPS is:

       N. 54° 10. 658'
       W. 005° 53. 853'   Elevation 335m.

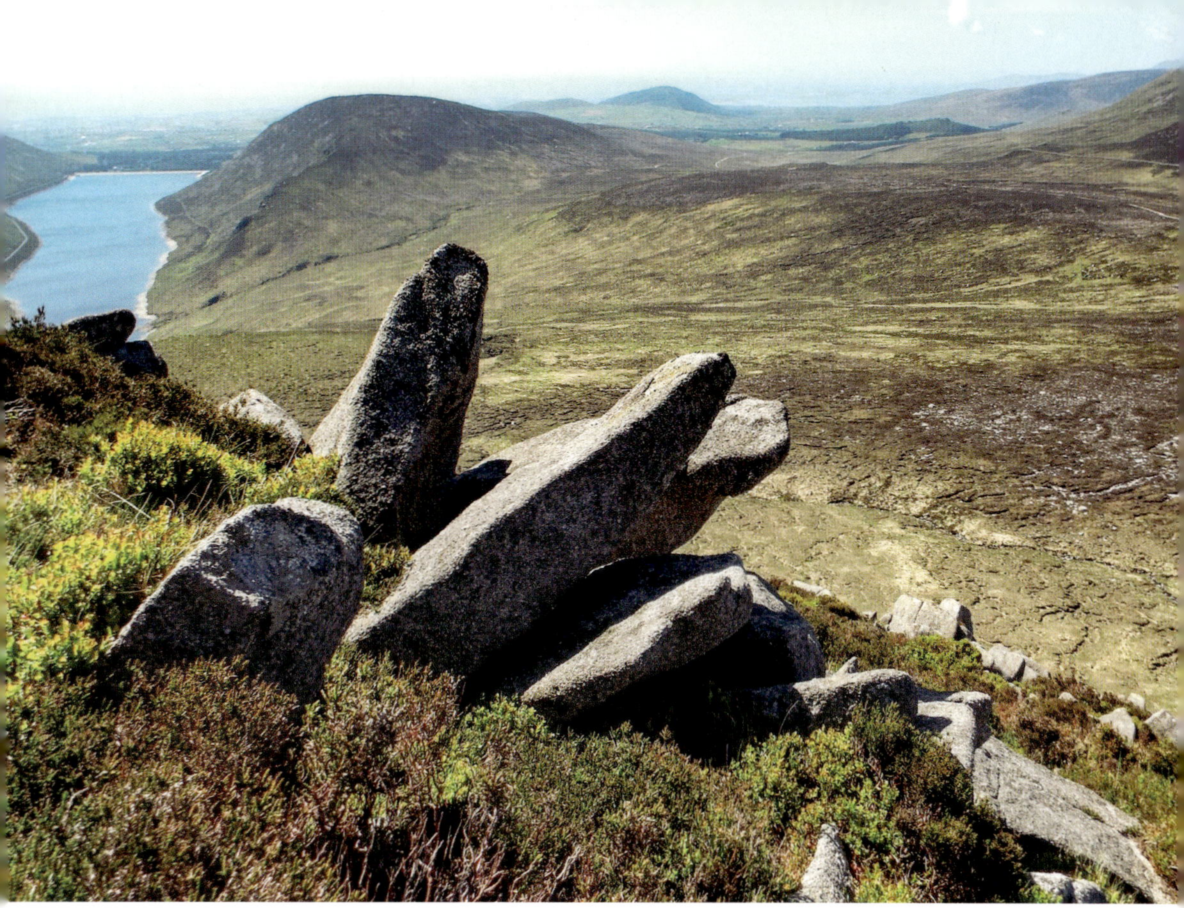

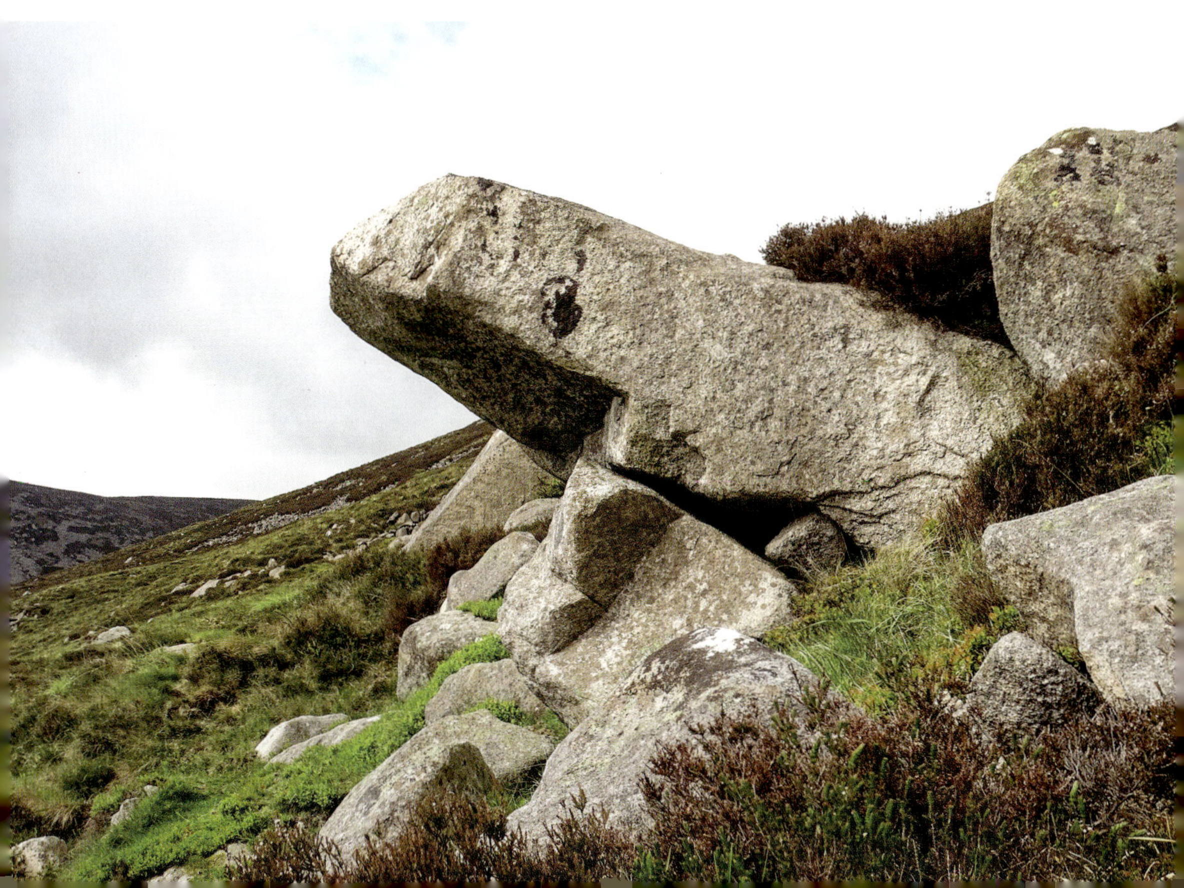

Above: A slab on the slope of Wee Slevanmore has been placed upright to show the lines on the rock of the classic fertility motif of a penis between two labial sides of a vagina. What makes this motif interesting is the further placement of a stone at the front left that has a little shadow eye and a deep split for a mouth; the stone has been strategically placed up against the central phallic shaft to denote fellatio. The same stone could be looked on as having a second face directed down towards another stone in the grass, again apparently with fellatio intent. The GPS is:

N. 54° 11. 179'
W. 006° 00. 026'   Elevation 621m.

Top opposite: A huge boulder 2m high by 2.5m across and 3m long is balanced (not propped) in erection mode. It is found in a field NE of Carrick Little track and is known by the mnemonic name of Carrick Big from its Irish name *Carraig Biach*, 'Rock of the Penis'. The location for this megalith is one of exceptional fertility for the megalith marks the appearance of Slieve Donard as the perfect 'penis in the vagina' between Rocky mountain and Chimney Rock. The GPS is:

N. 54° 08. 169'
W. 005°56. 188'   Elevation 209m.

Lower opposite: It was Canon Henry Lett who preserved the name of this great priapic megalith on the seaward heights overlooking the Annalong Valley. The Irish name is *Cnoc Goráin*, 'Rock of the Pimple', so called because it looks exactly like a pimple when seen on the skyline from the Annalong valley below. The megalith is believed to mark where winter solstice sun rises from the summit of Rocky mountain the tip of which can just be seen at the right of the photograph.

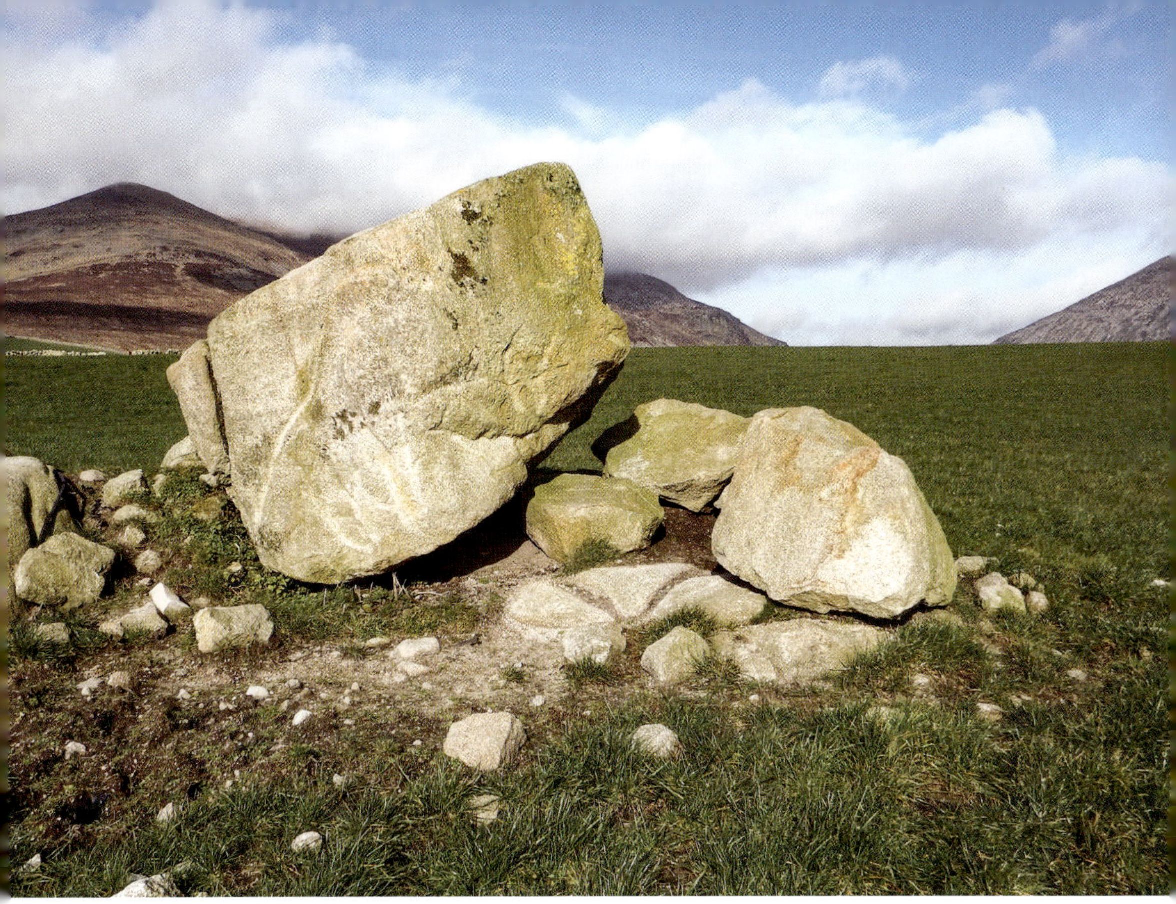

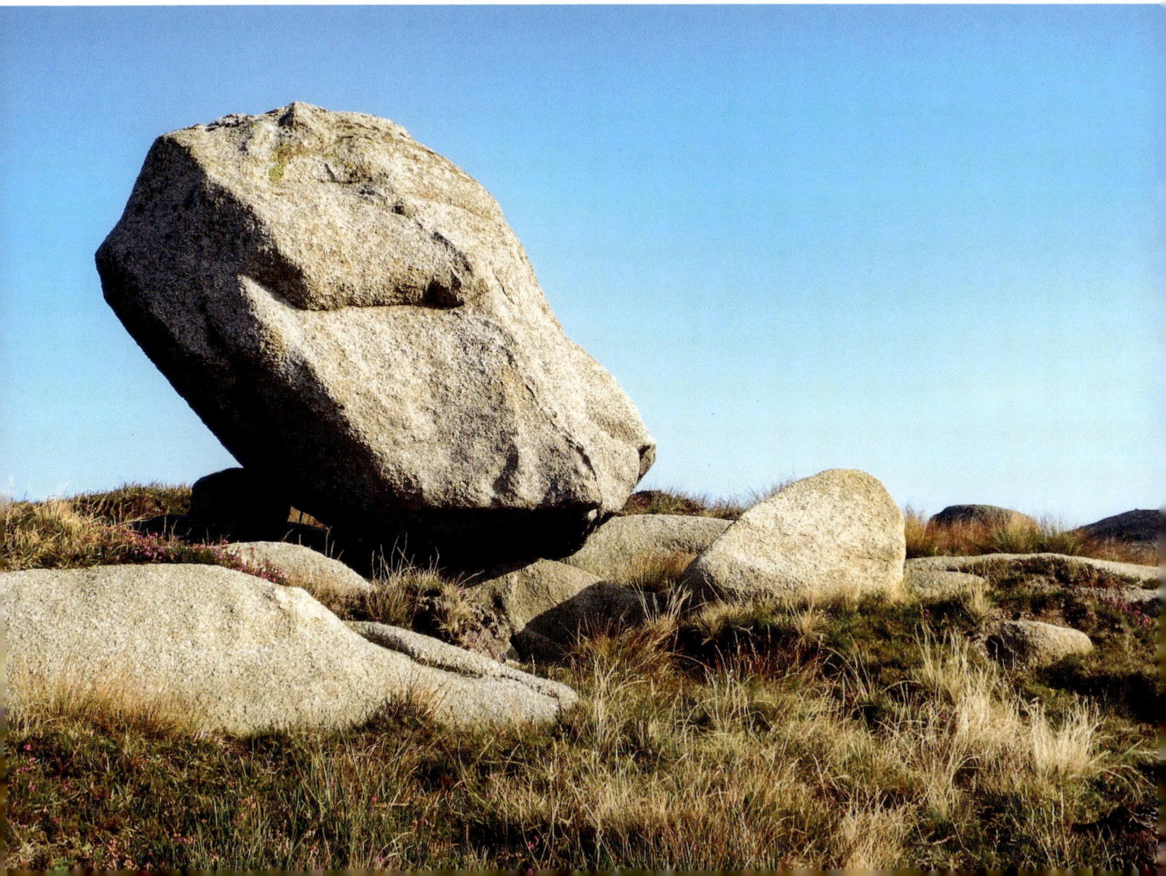

Above: This bold fellow is to be found high on the north side of Pollaphuca valley. The granite spear points its tip towards Slieve Bearnagh's north tor. The GPS is:

N. 54º 11. 437'
W. 005º 59. 668'   Elevation 505m.

Top opposite: The water bottle gives scale to this upright phallic stone, complete with testicles, not far from the summit of Ben Crom. Whatever is going on is left to your imagination but the real mystery might be how the top appendage has stayed secure and not been blown off by storms over the centuries. The location is one of special fertility. If the clouds were absent from the background then Donard would be seen as a 'landscape penis' between the labial sides of Lamagan and Bignian.

Lower opposite: On the seaward slope of Crossone mountain two granite slabs in erection mode also form an open mouth of .25m. The 'throat' is 1m deep. The ensemble would seem to be open mouthed with fellatio intent on the phallic sliver profile of Slievenagarragh (recte Glasdrumman Hill) to the south. The GPS is:

N. 54º 10. 710'
W. 005º 54. 162'   Elevation 443m.

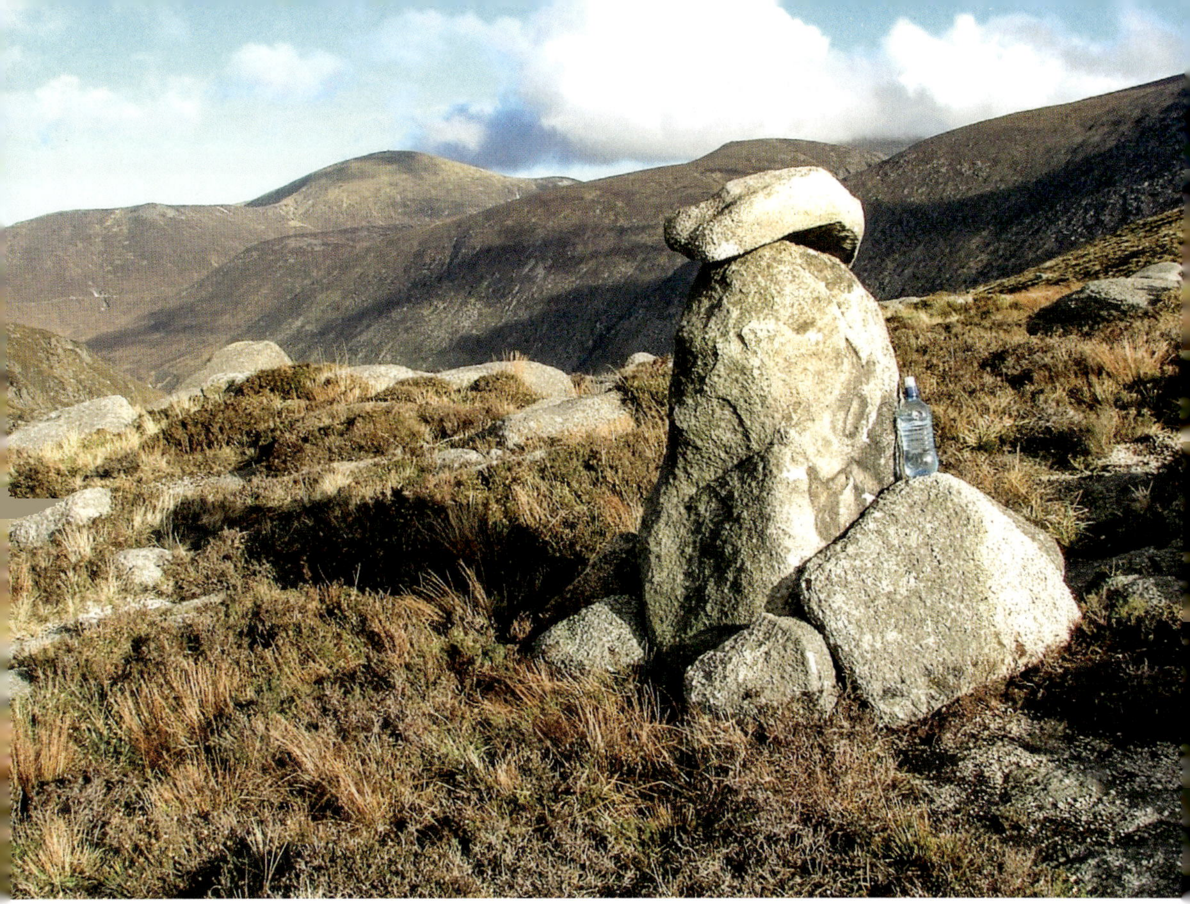

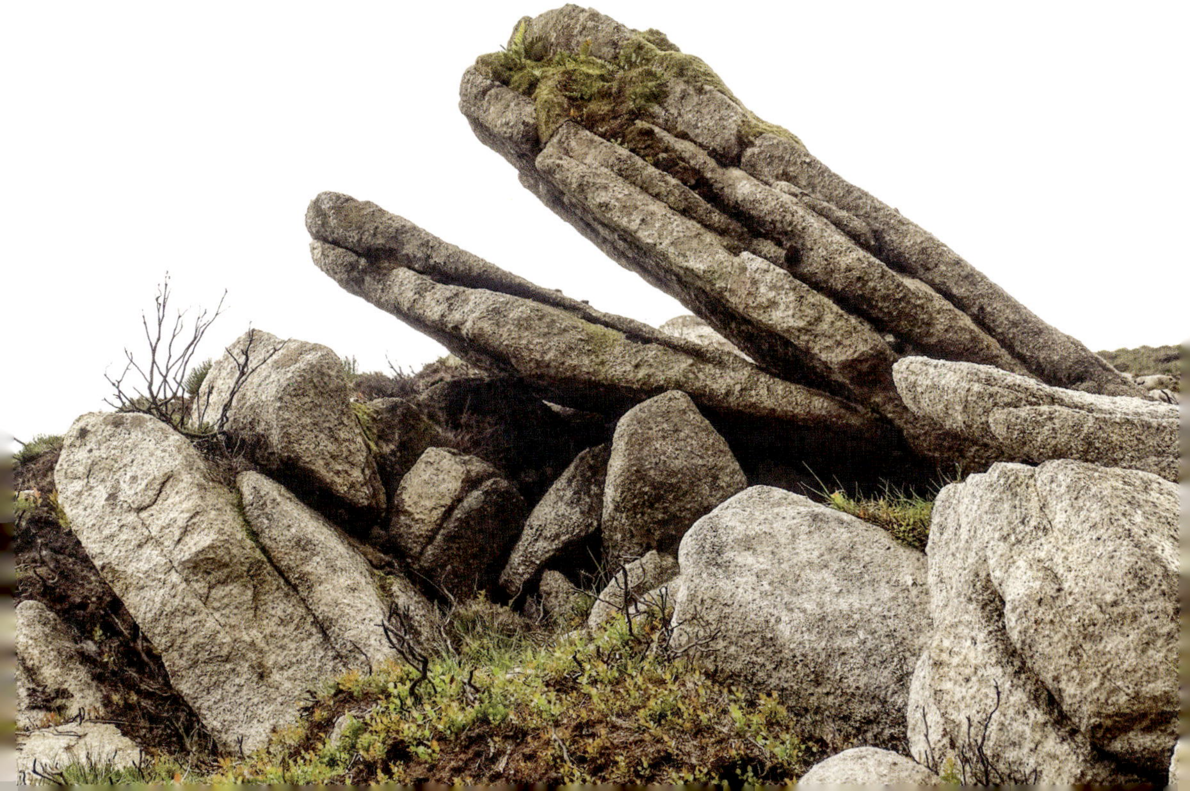

Above: The joy of noting this mighty propped spear stone half-way up the slope of Spellack was marred by my leg disappearing into a deep hole and a twisted ankle being sustained. Still, this magnificent megalith just had to be measured. It is 3.5m long and about 1.2m wide. The long shadow eye compliments the long pointed 'nose' and it should be no surprise that the stone was named Pinocchio. The tip is directed to the landscape notch between Wee Shimial and Big Shimial where the dawn light of summer solstice appears as if being born from the earth. The GPS is:

                  N.   54° 11. 851'
                  W. 005° 59. 296'   Elevation 336m.

Top opposite: This unambiguous bit of rock art is to be found at the NE corner of Cove mountain. The cliffs of Slieve Beg are partly seen in the background. The granite has been chopped away to leave an erection in relief on a rock outcrop.

Lower opposite: One of the most imposing and important megaliths of Mourne. This monumental phallus would be the stone that gave the valley its name, 'The Pole of the Puca'. It is on the north side of Pollaphuca valley well up the scree face, but worth the climb. At easily 3.5m high by about 2m across the base, it beggars belief how such an immense shaft was installed on this dauntingly steep slope. The GPS is:

                  N.   54° 11. 385'
                  W. 005° 59. 691'   Elevation 505m.

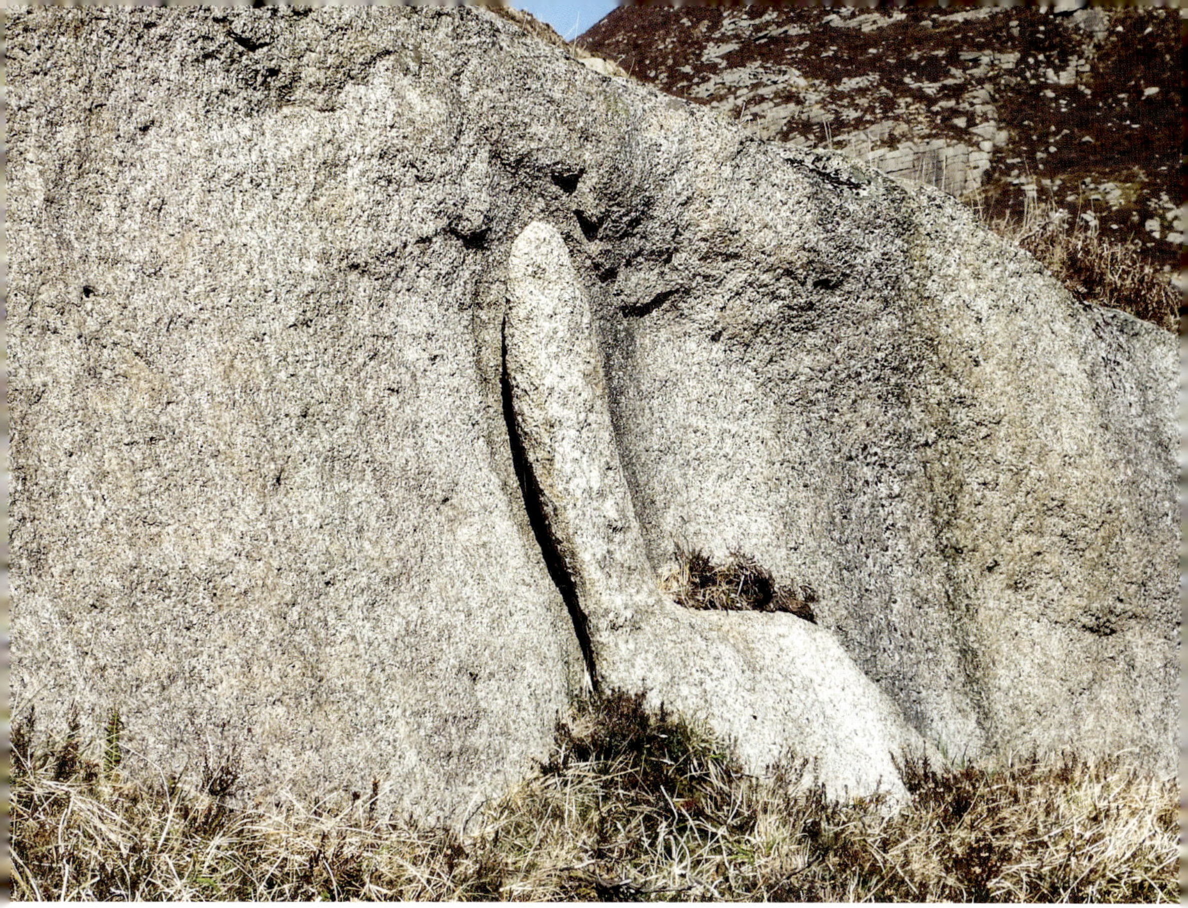

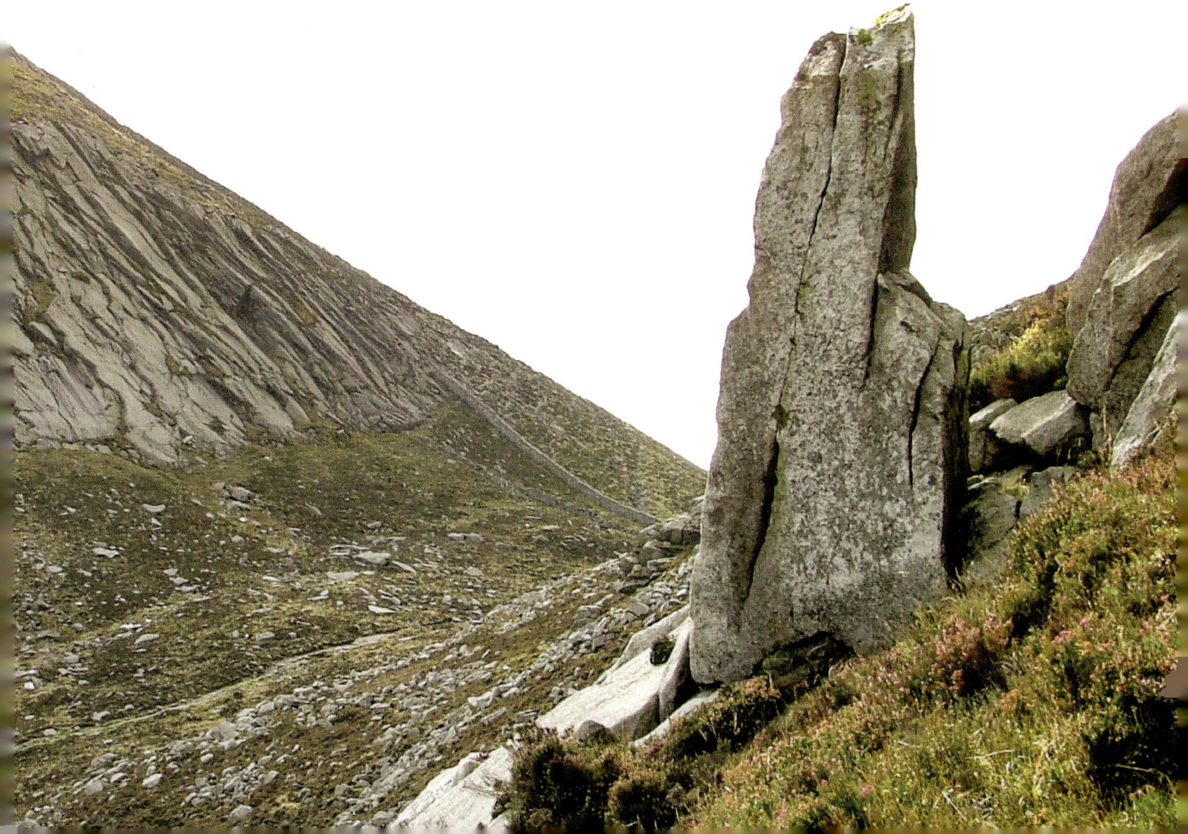

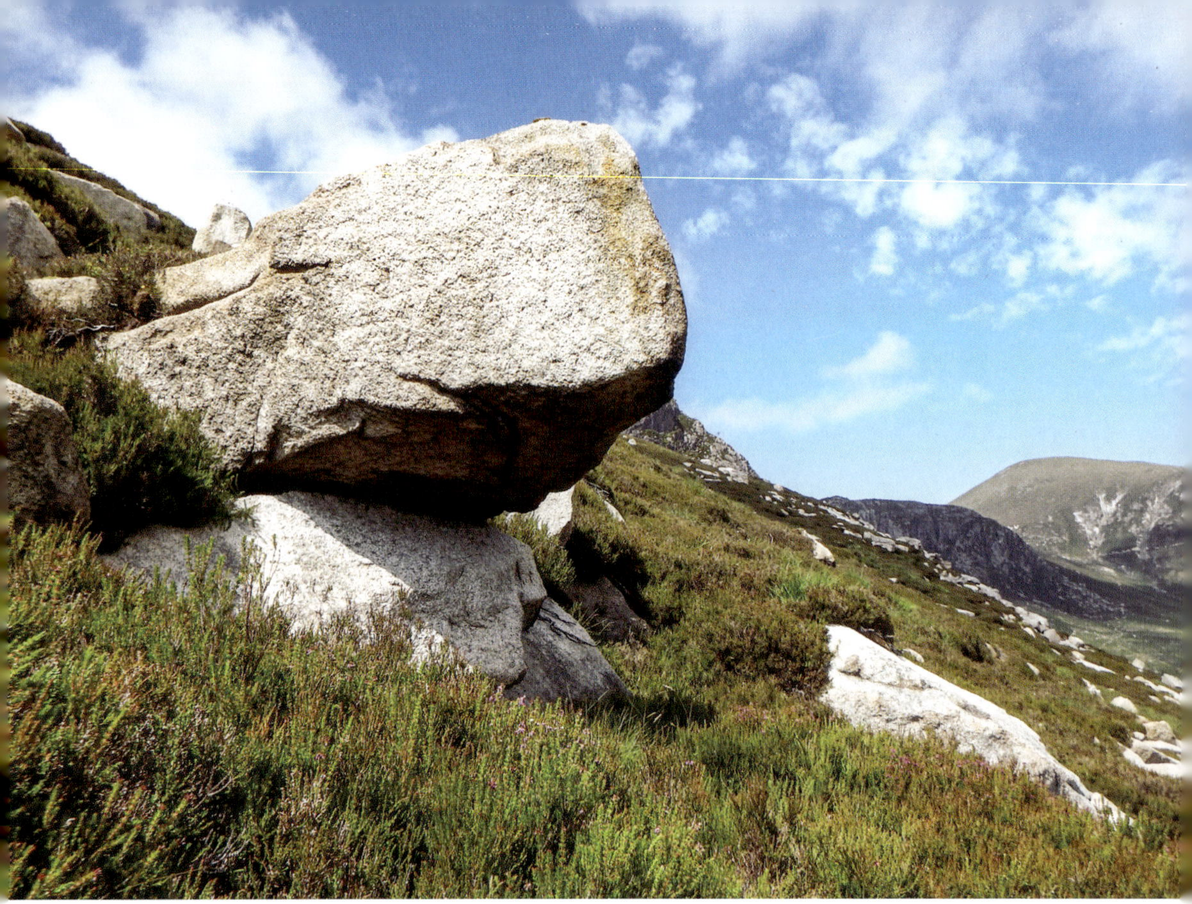

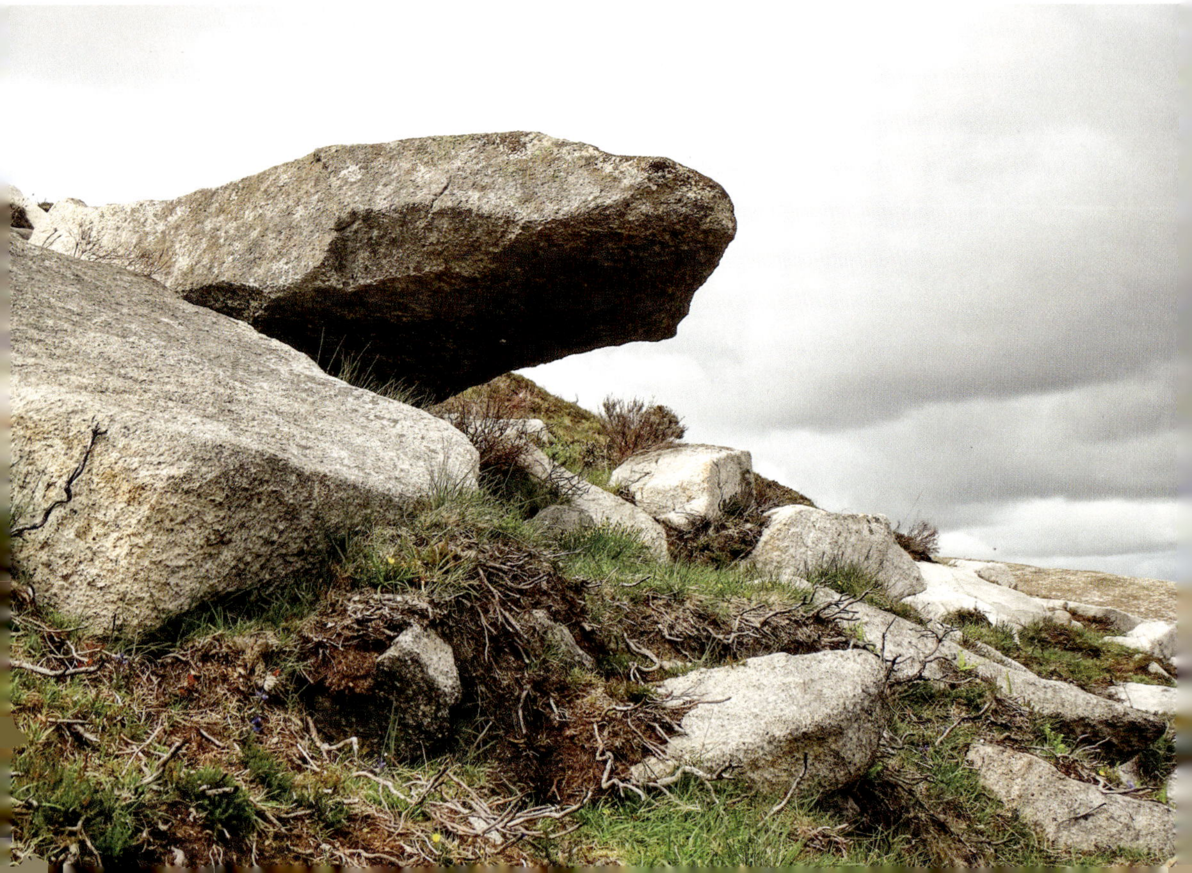

Top opposite: On the west side of the Annalong Valley a beautiful phallic stone, worthy of a wedding night, has been raised up with its point directed to a landscape notch across the valley. Even though the back of the megalith is hidden in heather you can still see a length of 3m and a width of 1m tapering to a sharpish spear point. There is a fine meatus groove at the top front though it cannot be seen in the photograph. The GPS is:

$$\text{N. } 54° 10. 075'$$
$$\text{W. } 005° 56. 966' \qquad \text{Elevation 396m.}$$

Lower opposite: On the seaward side of Crossone a 2m long propped granite phallic spear directs its point to winter solstice sunrise. The GPS is:

$$\text{N. } 54° 10. 670'$$
$$\text{W. } 005° 54. 208' \qquad \text{Elevation 487m.}$$

Top of this page: High on the east flank of Slieve Bearnagh will be found this massive phallic stone. The base is hidden in heather but despite that you can still see a length of 2.9m. Underneath the stone measures 1.9m across. The point of the megalith is towards the summit of Slieve Lamagan. The stone marks the landscape fertility feature of Chimney Rock appearing as a 'penis in the vagina' between the labial sides of Slieve Beg and Cove. The GPS is:

$$\text{N. } 54° 11. 124'$$
$$\text{W. } 005° 58. 826' \qquad \text{Elevation 553m.}$$

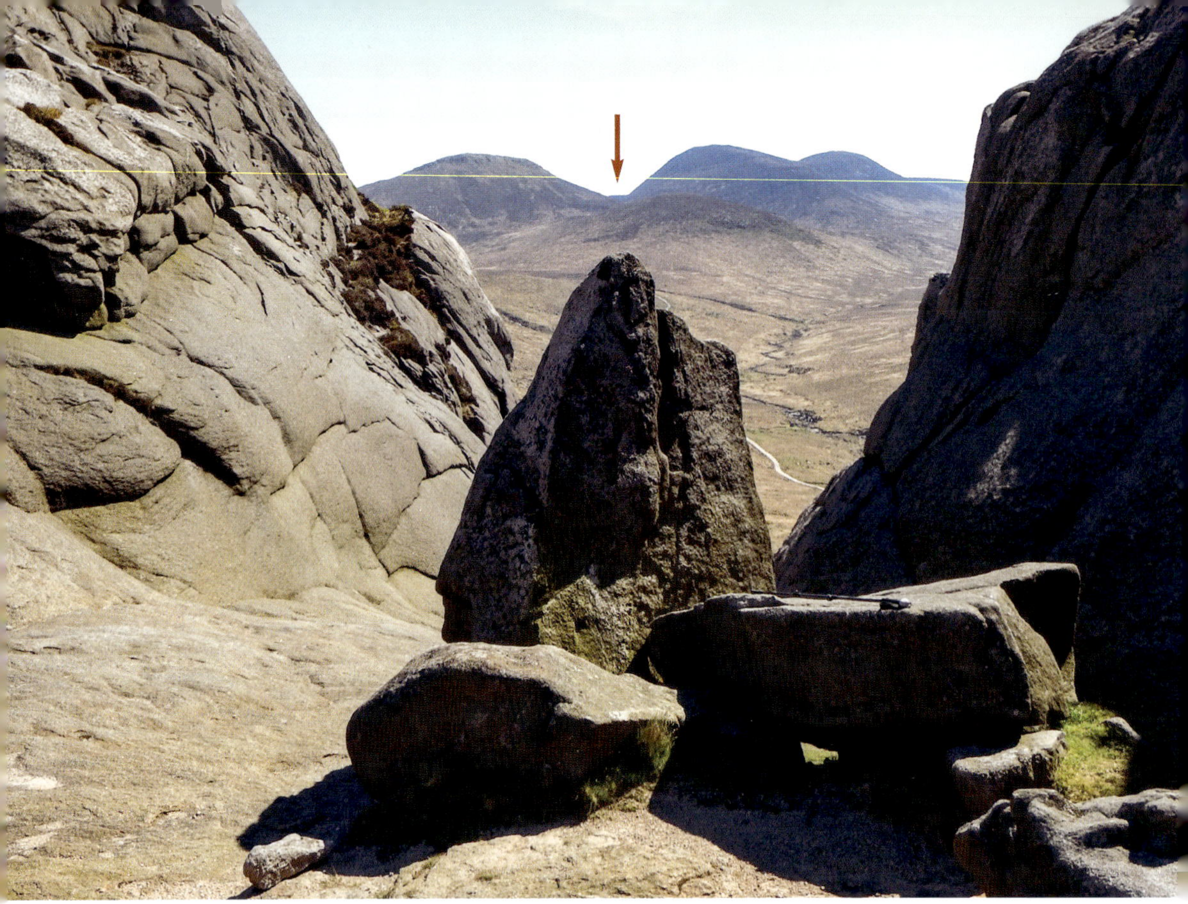

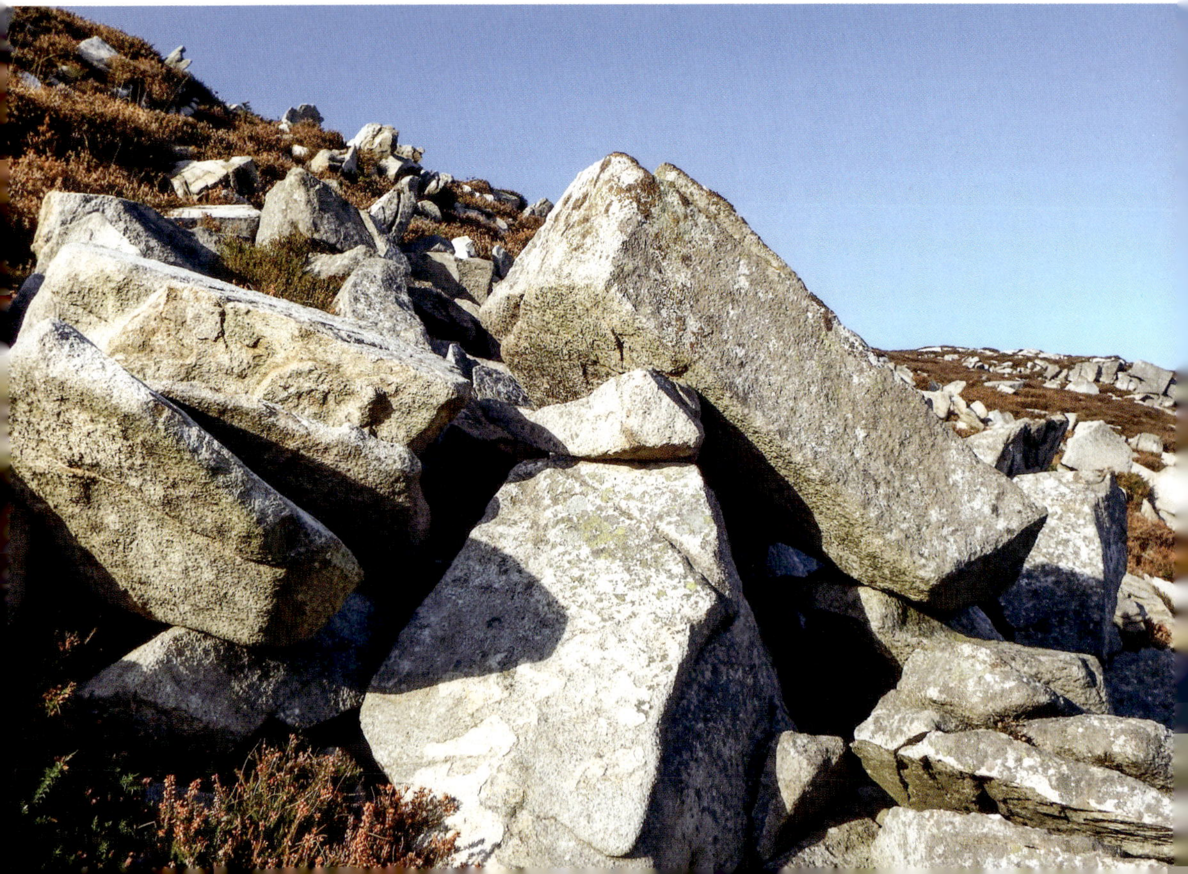

Top opposite: This great spear megalith in the gully at the top of Cock & Hen Mountain is one of the few for which we know the Irish name. The name of the phallic boulder was partially anglicised as 'Sleaghnekirk' on a map of 1682. The Irish name would have been **Sleagh na Círeach**, 'Spear of the Crest or Tuft'. The location marks the appearance of part of Long Mountain (arrowed) as the erstwhile phallic insert between Slievemoughanmore and Eagle Mountains. The presumption is that the 'crest' or 'tuft' referred to the distant projection of the mountain tip rather than one or more of the tors of the Cock & Hen. The GPS of the spear megalith is:

                N. 54° 10. 922'
                W. 006° 05. 774'   Elevation 321m.

Lower opposite: On the south-east flank of Millstone mountain a 1.8m granite spear has a well defined ridge-line on the top of the stone aligned to winter solstice sunrise. The GPS is:

                N. 54° 11. 031'
                W. 005° 53. 627'   Elevation 355m.

Top of this page: Welcome to 'The Boardwalk'. This phallic stone on the heights of Slieve Bignian has been aligned to winter solstice sunrise. It has long been a favourite place to take scenic photographs of someone standing out on the rock perhaps striking a dramatic pose. Note the shadow eye on the top surface.

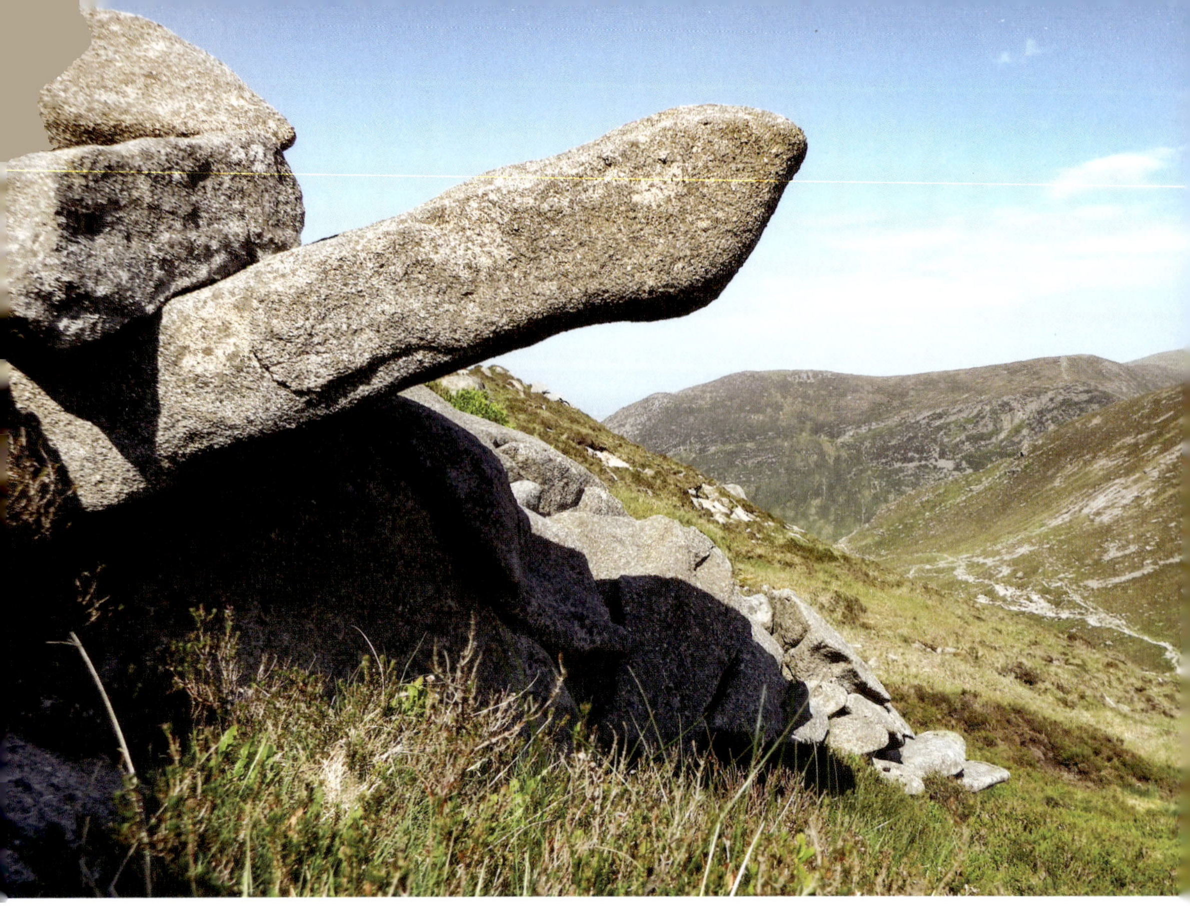

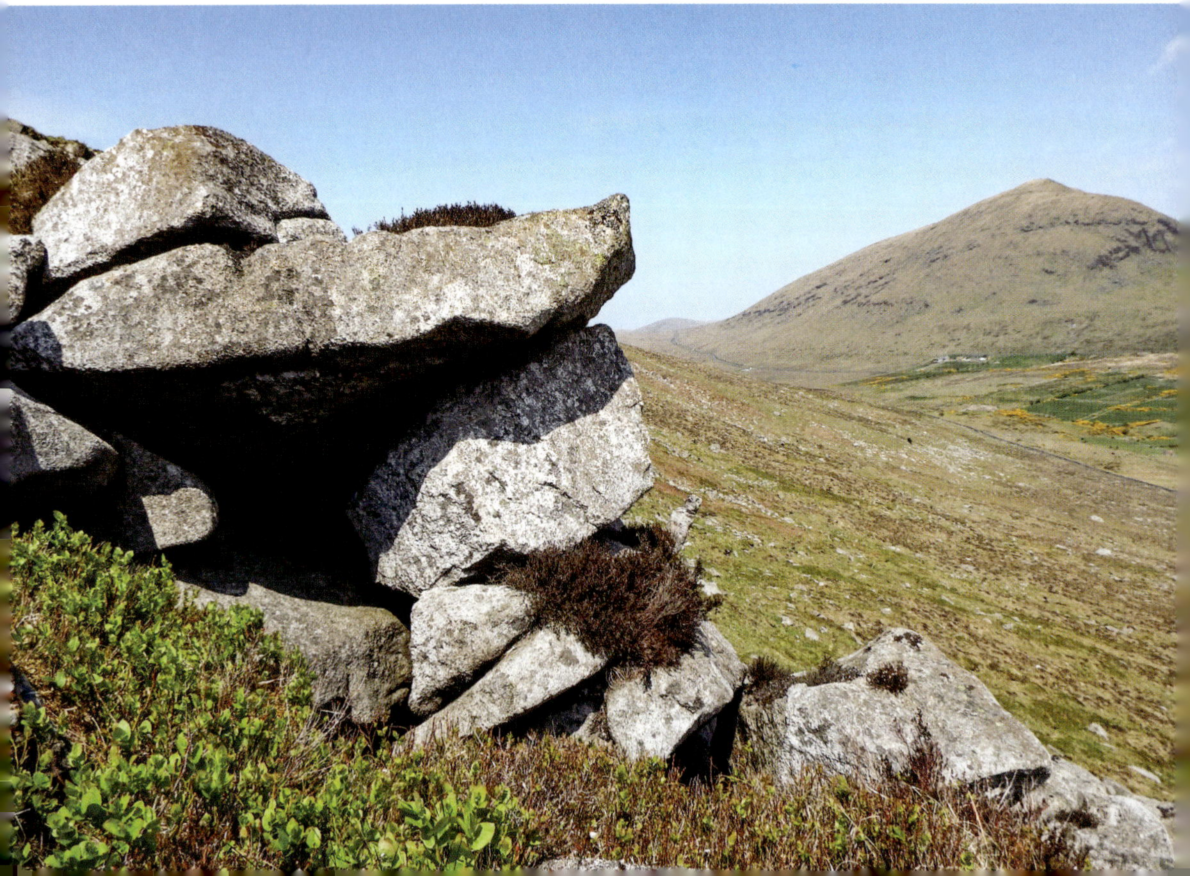

Top opposite: An up-thrusting 1.5m phallic shaft, near the stile at the head of Pollaphuca valley, points to Slieve Bearnagh's summit tor. The Lecarry Loanin track can be seen coming up the valley on the right. The counter-balance stone at the back is mischievously depicted as biting the shaft. The GPS is:

                        N.   54° 11. 253'
                        W. 005° 59. 783'   Elevation 547m.

Lower opposite: A carefully built up structure on the east slope of Slievemageogh makes a womb cavity to be penetrated by early winter solstice sun. The spear point capstone, with a noticeable little upthrust at the tip, is directed to Slieve Bignian and summer solstice sun appearance.

Top of this page: It sometimes happens. I believe this magnificent phallic stone is no longer in place. It was originally photographed at 4.58am a week or two before the summer solstice. The tip used to be illuminated by the rising solstice sun in a display of fertility. The elevation was 452m.

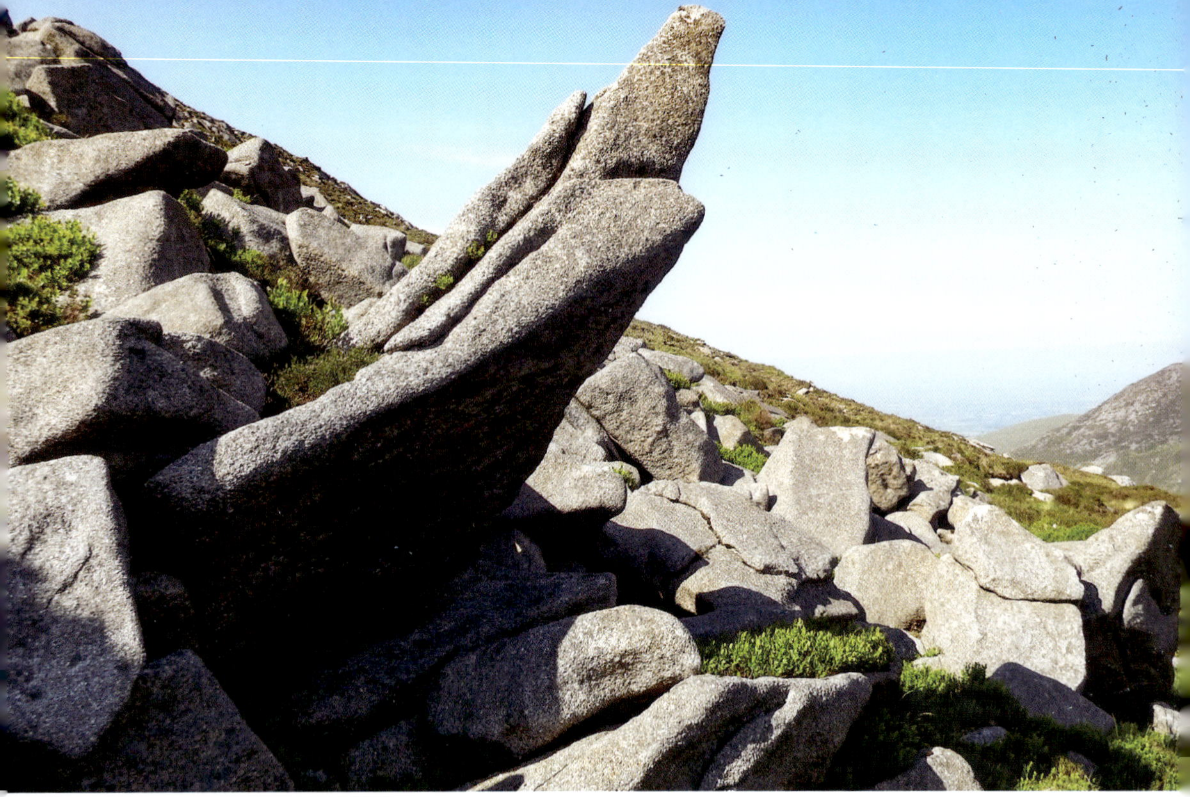

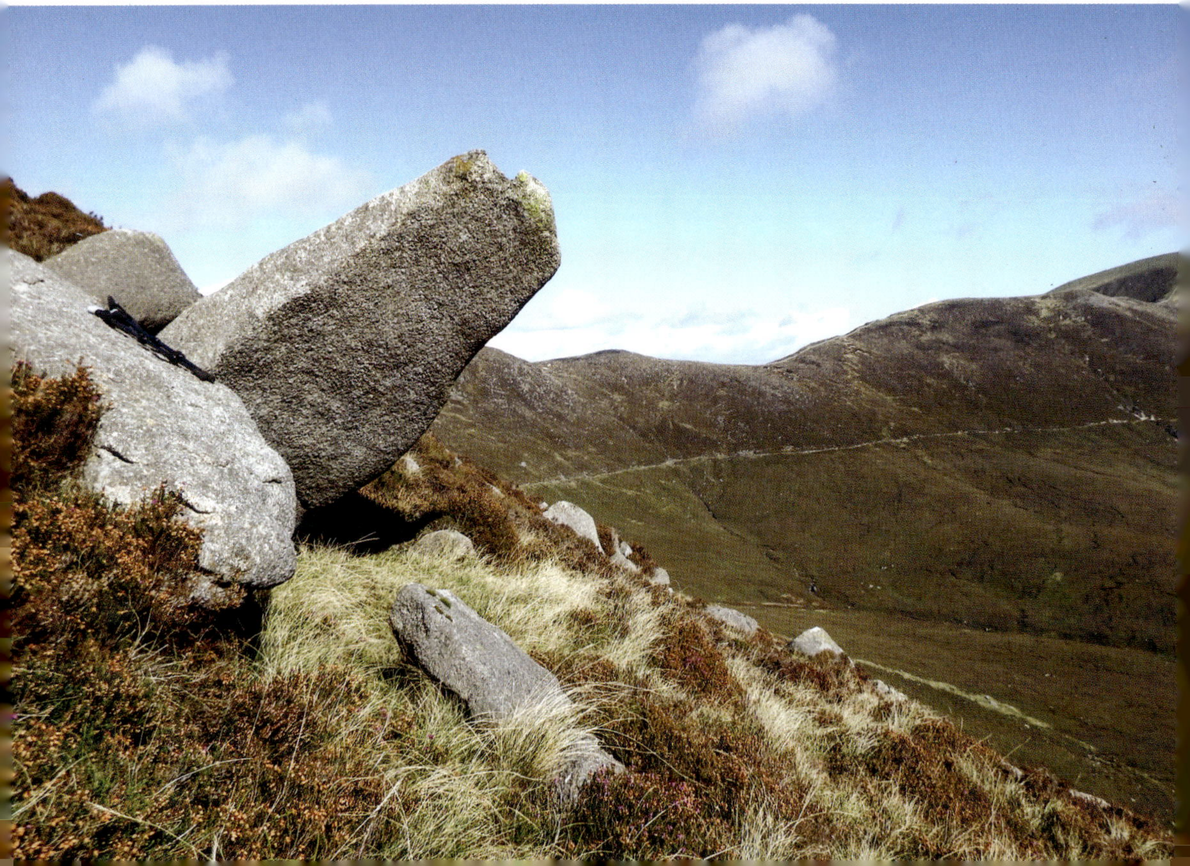

Top opposite: This remarkable rearing unmistakeably phallic stone, at least 3m long, happened to be entry number 666 in the field note-books and was unsurprisingly named *Ar Nós an Diabhail*. 'Like the Devil'. The tip of this rather shark-like megalith is to winter solstice sun appearance. The great stone is about 150m above the stile on Pollaphuca side of the Mourne Wall, which is about 5m away. It wasn't very auspicious that I nearly hurt myself getting over the Wall higher up the hill. The GPS of this most impressive stone is:

        N.   54° 11. 226'
        W. 005° 59. 769'   Elevation 540m.

Lower opposite: The line of the Brandy Pad cuts across the middle of the picture while this phallic stone on the east slope of Slieve Bearnagh looks to winter solstice appearance. The tip of the megalith has been given a notch to suggest it is 'crying out' as part of its sexual activity.

Top of this page: An awesome granite slab has been raised up in phallic mode on the east slope of Slieve Lamagan. The cliffs of Lower Cove can be partly seen in the background. The tip of the slab looks to the landscape notch between Bignian and Lamagan where it is thought the winter solstice sun declines. It is information such as this, that was formerly passed down from generation to generation, that was sadly lost at the time of the famine and by the decline of spoken Irish.

Above: It is breath-taking achievements like the erection of this awesome 3m phallic boulder on the top of Slieve Bearnagh's north tor that bring about a profound respect at how the ancients created such wonders on this dangerously steep slope. Even the counter-balance stones at the back are most substantial; and how did they secure them in place without toppling the phallic stone in the process? The GPS is:

       N. 54° 11. 202'
       W. 005° 59. 221'   Elevation 680m.

Top opposite: You will find this 2m well raised phallic stone on the summit tor of Slieve Bearnagh. Part of Ben Crom dam can be seen in the background. The megalith was named ***Damhaireacht***, 'excitement'.
The GPS is:

       N. 54° 11. 071'
       W. 005° 59. 417'   Elevation 722m.

Lower opposite: This construction is in the gap between the two most southerly of Slieve Bearnagh's summit tors. A lovely spear stone, 2.5m long by 1.9m across, straddles the small col between the tors. The stone is well propped up in phallic mode and has a counter-balance at the back. The GPS is:

       N. 54° 11. 002'
       W. 005° 59. 338'   Elevation 713m.

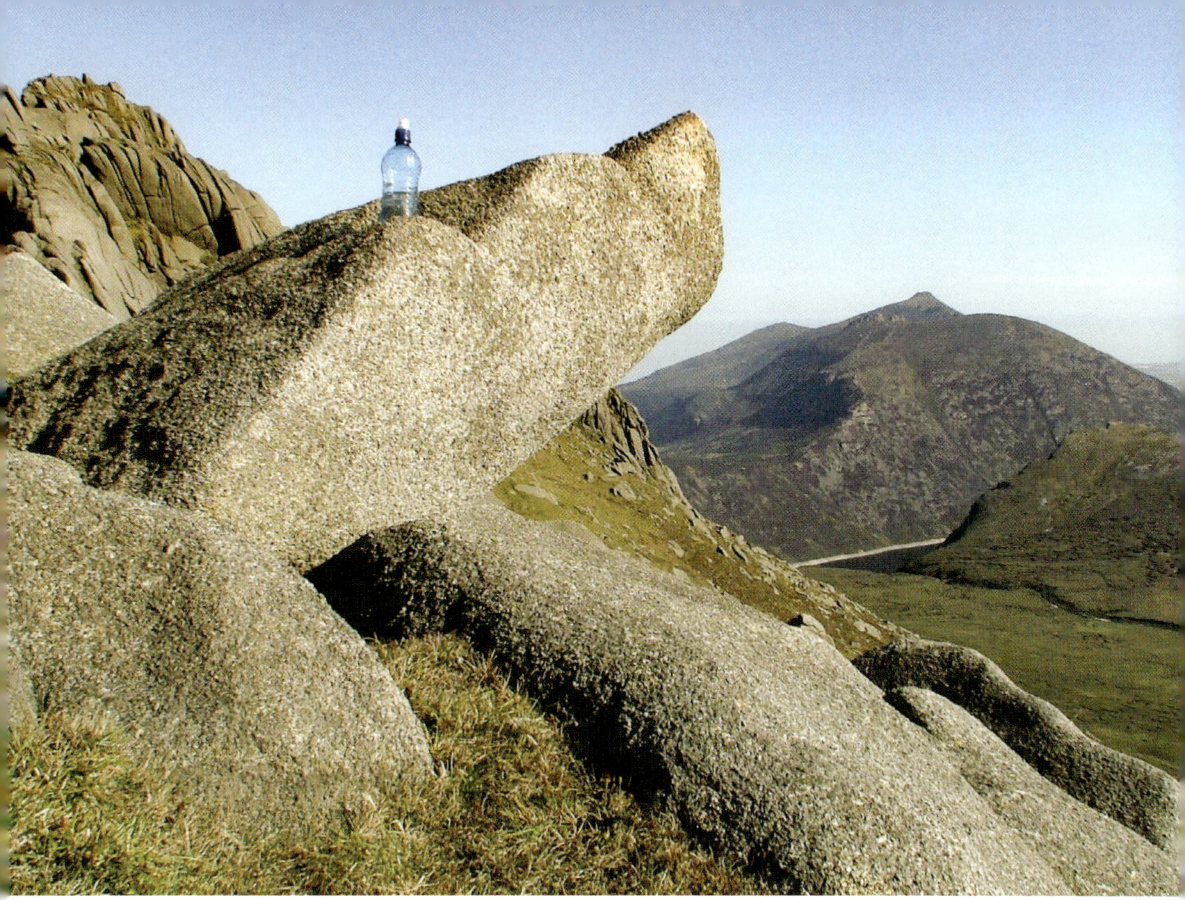

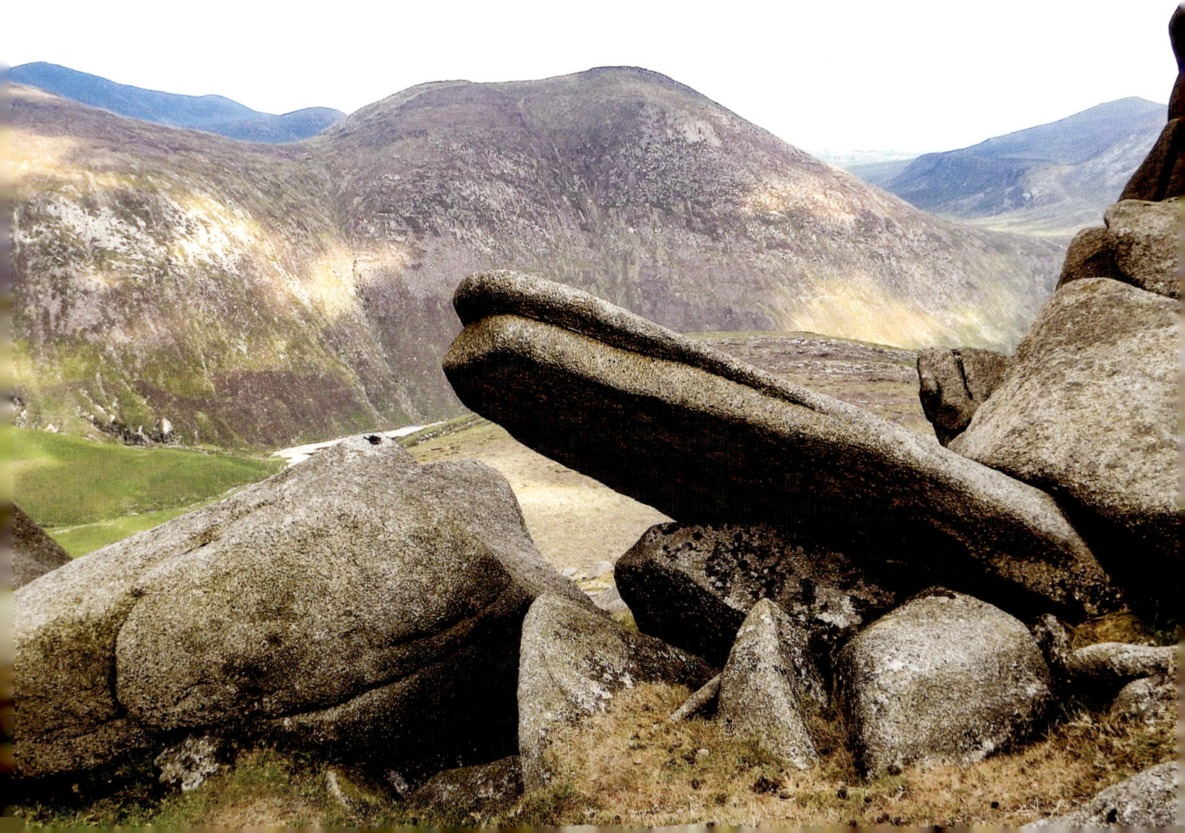

Above: This massive erection stone is found on the east side of Slieve Bearnagh's summit tor. The megalith was assessed at a serious 7m in height. Tall as it is, the stone has been very precisely positioned for the thin straight ridge line at the very top points perfectly to winter solstice sunrise between the tip of Long Mountain and Rocky Mountain. It well earns its name of *Is Fiú Ór*, 'It is Worth Gold'. The GPS is:

                N.   54° 10. 976'
                W. 005° 59. 276'   Elevation 670m.

Top opposite: One photograph is scarcely enough to do justice to this erection stone on the south-west side of Slieve Bearnagh's summit tor. It happens to be only one side of a filled vaginal gap. Another view-point shows the inserted stone with its 'head thrown back', its 'mouth' open and calling out as if at the moment of sexual climax. On that account the megalith was named 'The Rictus Rock'. The GPS is:

                N.   54° 10. 945'
                W. 005° 59. 328'   Elevation 660m.

Lower opposite: This beautiful phallic spear stone on the southern slope of Chimney Rock is believed to mark the setting of the winter solstice sun on one of the tors of Bignian. The megalith was photographed in the early days before I had a GPS. I still recall, however, that the footing underneath the heather in that locality was quite treacherous. Perhaps it is best admired from a distance.

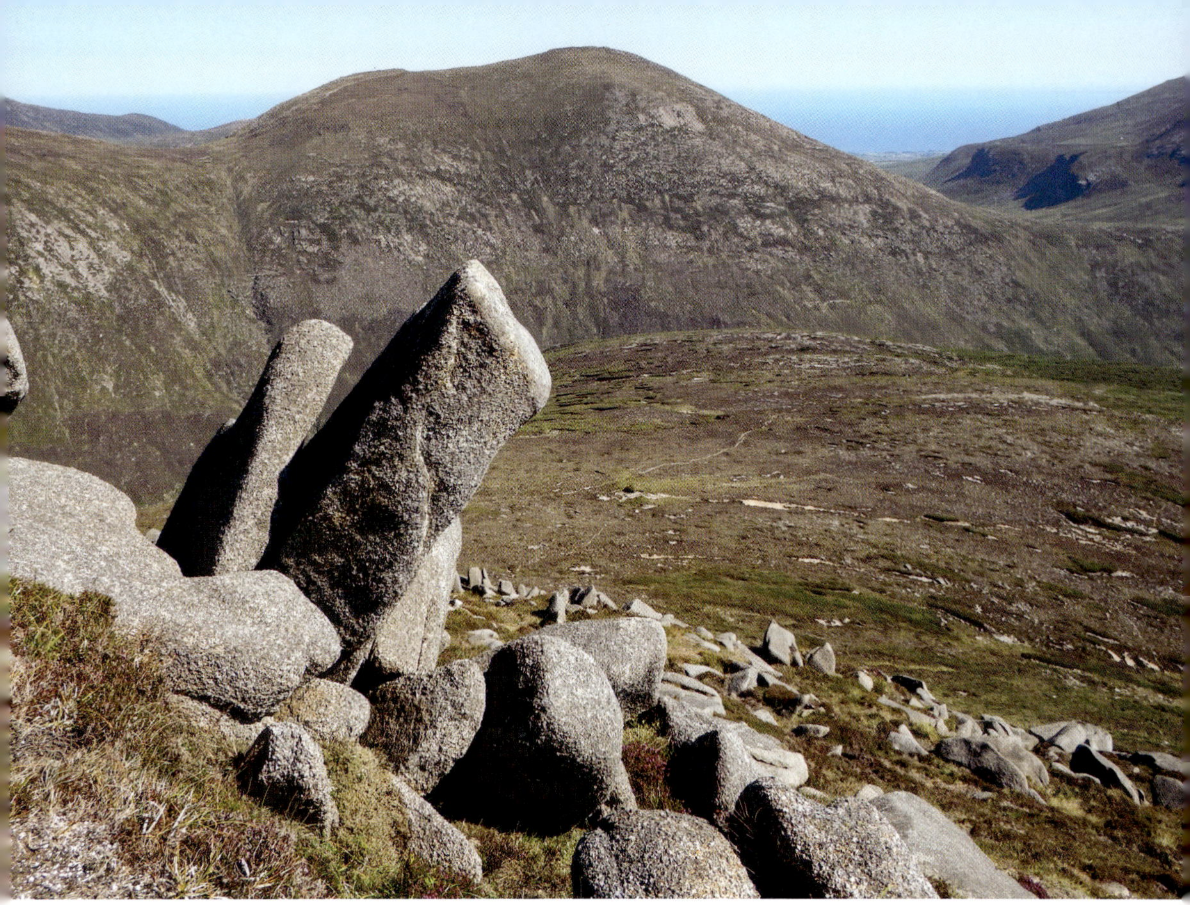

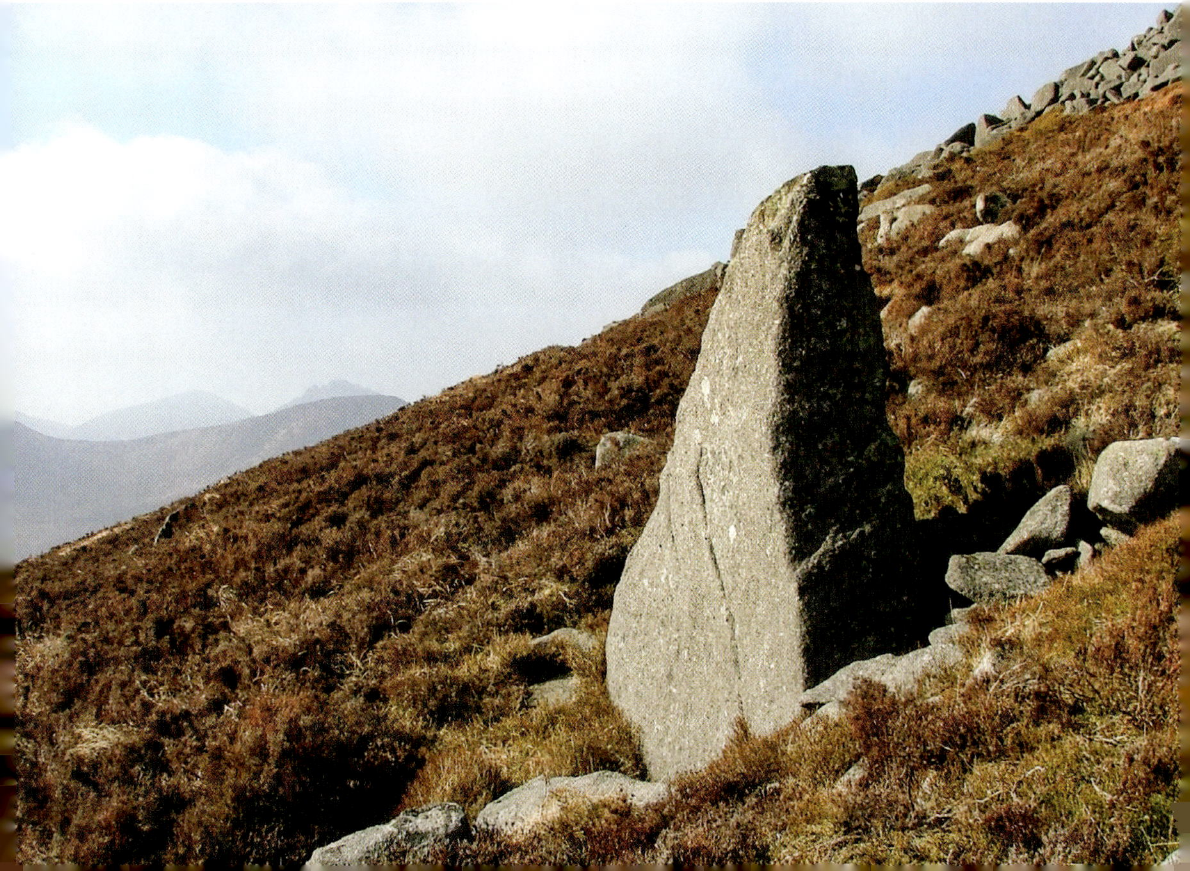

Above: At about 4.5 metres long from tip to base and 2m across, this is certainly a huge and very impressive phallic stone. It is found on the southern shoulder of Meelmore overlooking the Pollaphuca valley and the tip points to summer solstice sunrise. The other side reveals the construction to be a vaginal gap also awaiting the fertilising sun. Again on the other side the stone has a groove representing a penile corona. The GPS is:

      N.   54º 11. 755'
      W. 005º 59. 455'   Elevation 465m.

Top opposite: Over 150m higher than the previous entry on the southern slope of Meelmore rears another most imposing phallic stone. It is also over 4m from tip to toe, 1.2m wide at the lower end and tapers to an authoritative point. The vicinity abounds with other examples of phallic stones. The GPS is:

      N.   54º 11. 514'
      W. 005º 59. 824'   Elevation 622m.

Lower opposite: Still on the upper southern slope of Meelmore and overlooking the Pollaphuca valley, a phallic spear stone. about 1.2m, points to the declivity junction between Commedagh and Shan Slieve. The GPS is:

      N.   54º 11. 532'
      W. 005º 59. 765'   Elevation 598m.

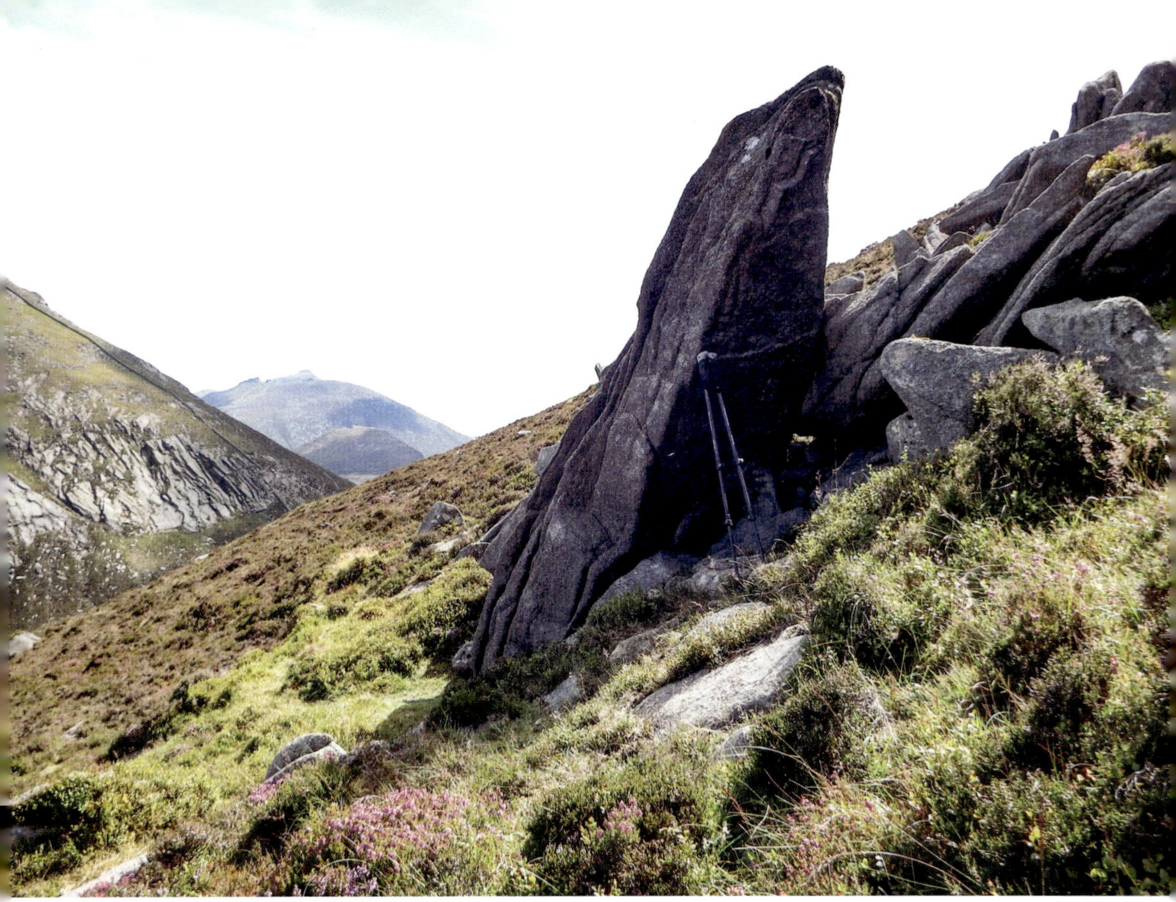

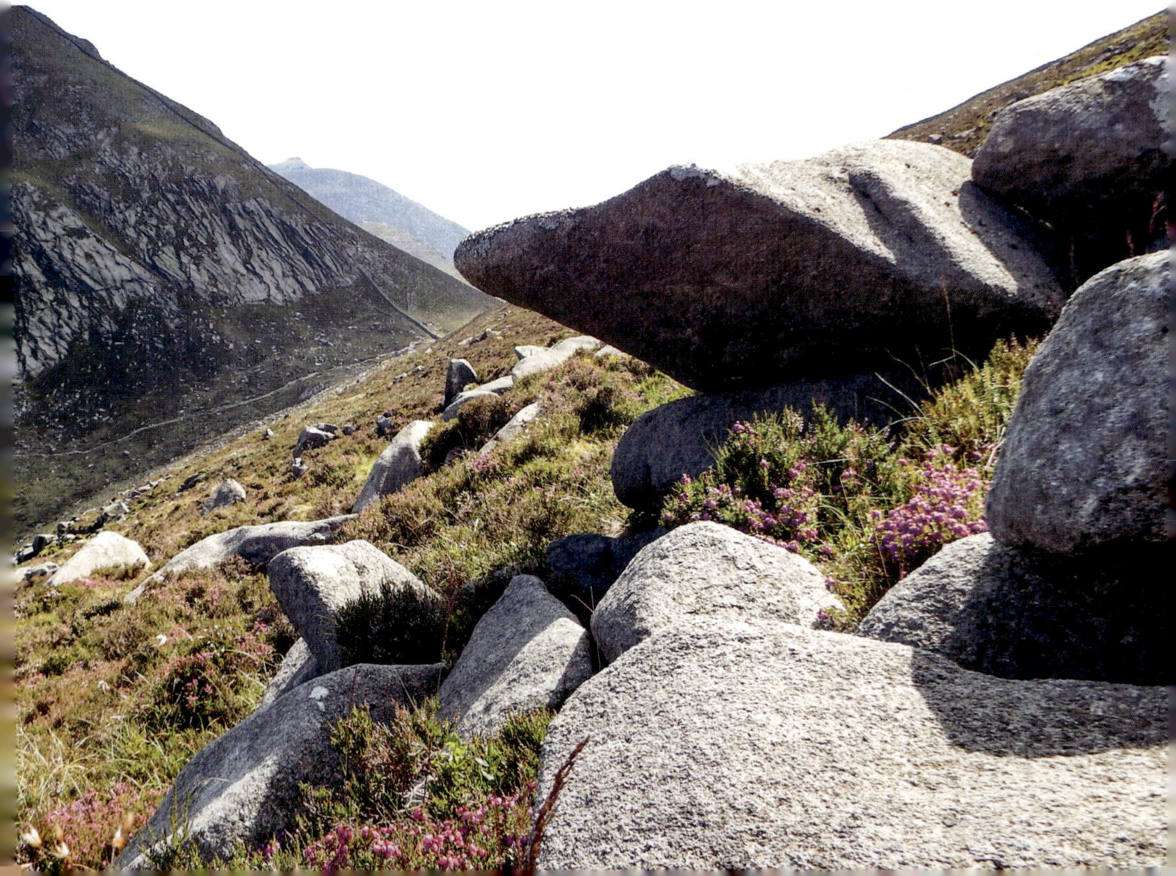

Above: Say hello to *Faraire*, 'A brave fellow'. The top surface of this mighty spear stone, on the slopes of Wee Slevanmore, was paced out at almost 5m in length. The point of the incredible stone looks to Doan mountain. There is a phallus etched out on the top surface. The counterbalance which holds the spear in place does so with a very light touch. It doesn't need to lean heavily as it is also a mighty stone, easily 5m as well. This is a place of prodigious effort. The GPS is:

                N.   54° 11. 191'
                W. 005° 59. 962'   Elevation 590m.

Top opposite: Another instance of the humour of the ancients. This phallic stone on the east slope of Slieve Bearnagh, having an indent for a penile corona and a crack to denote a meatus groove, is immediately obvious. It is the little fellow at the bottom centre who rather steals the show. With a shape suggesting a head thrown back and a mouth wide open, he appears to have a remarkable ambition for fellatio.

Lower opposite: A 2m high phallic stone on the south side of Crossone might not seem particularly remarkable but it has been most carefully placed and shows how seriously the ancients watched the landscape at dawn of winter solstice. The compass reveals the location's secret. The stone marks where winter solstice sun rises at the landscape notch formed between horizon and the shoulder of Slievenagarragh. The rising sun would probably appear to 'roll up the hill'. The GPS is:

                N.   54° 10. 407'
                W. 005° 54. 277'   Elevation 382m.

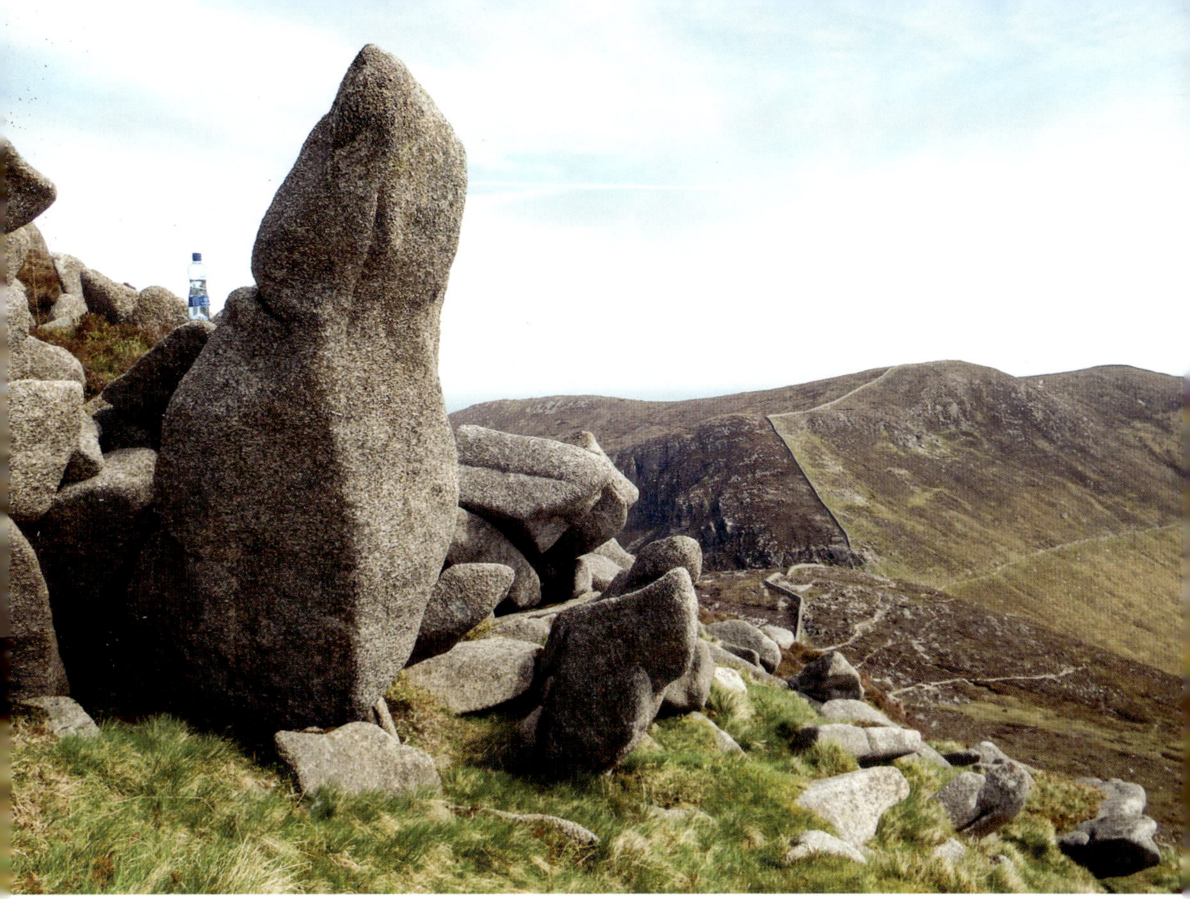

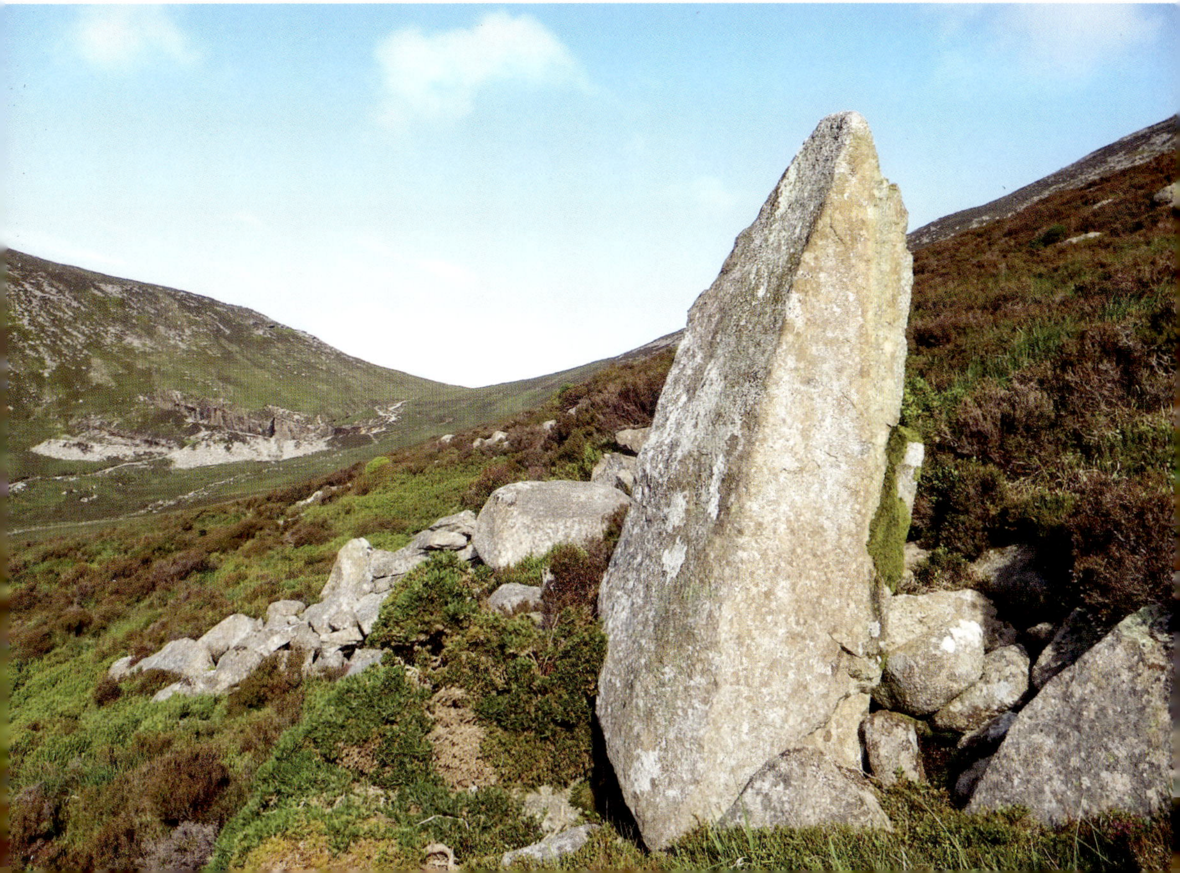

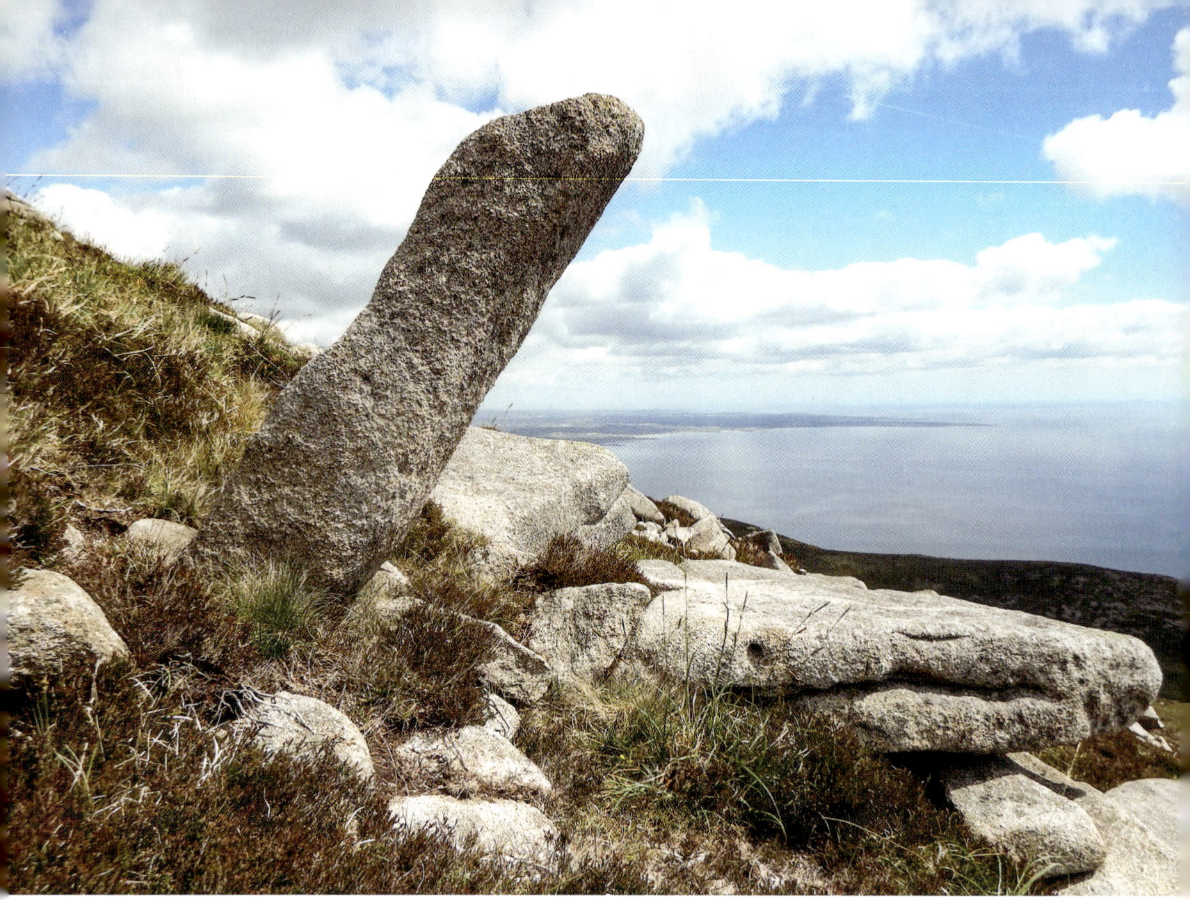

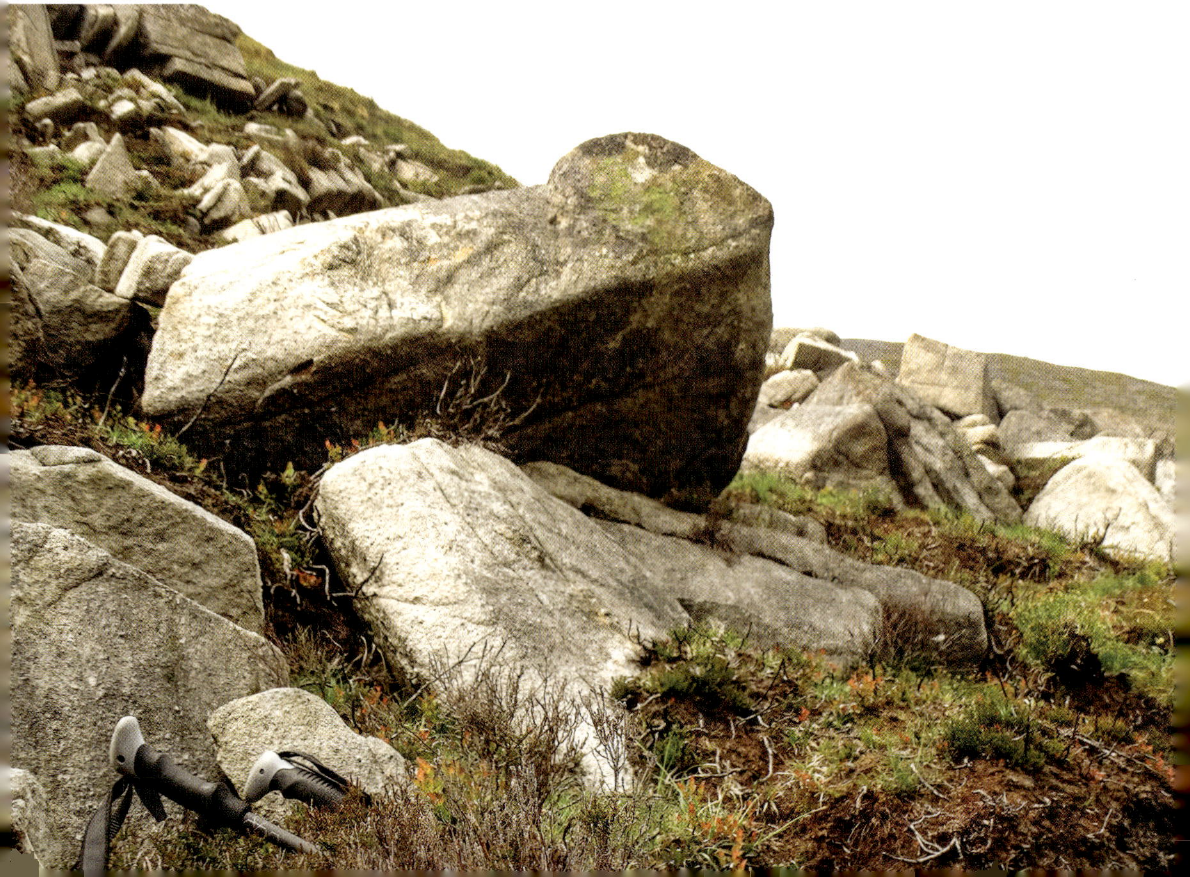

Top opposite: We are looking at a pronounced phallic stone just over one metre in height on the south-east flank of Donard. The rather snub or blunt tip is towards winter solstice sunrise. The GPS is:

      N. 54° 10. 786'
      W. 005° 54. 738'   Elevation 601m.

Lower opposite: Up on the seaward slope of Crossone mountain a 1.4m granite block rests on a thin prop stone as it directs its phallic tip to the vulva shape of Millstone. It was only afterwards that the thought occurred that the megalith might also mark where summer solstice sun would rise from the top of Millstone. As the saying goes, 'leave something for the angels'. The GPS is:

      N. 54° 10. 715'
      W. 005° 54. 141'   Elevation 431m.

Top of this page: A little north and below the great summit tor of Chimney Rock is this raised megalith. It sits askew on four boulders but the placement seems quite deliberate as the winter solstice sun can penetrate underneath at the back or lower end. Crossone mountain is in the background.

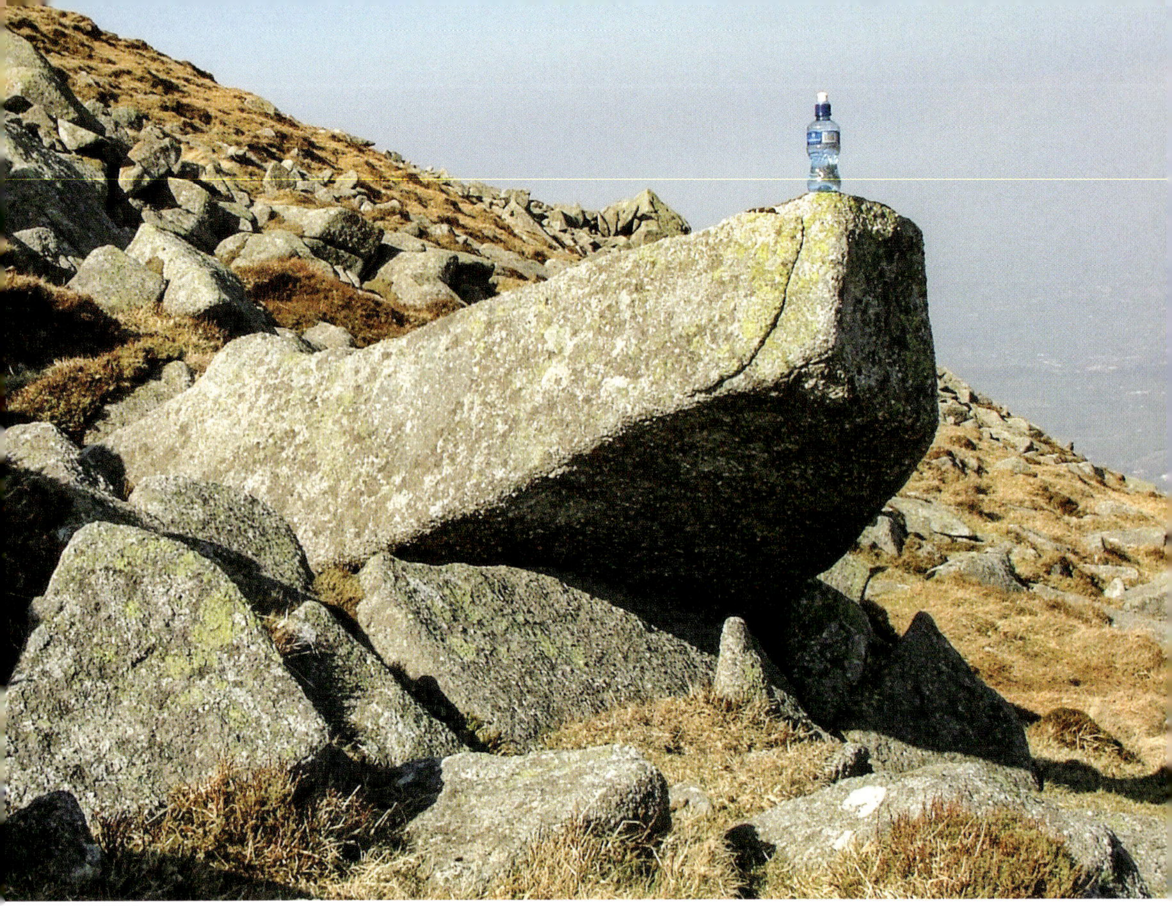

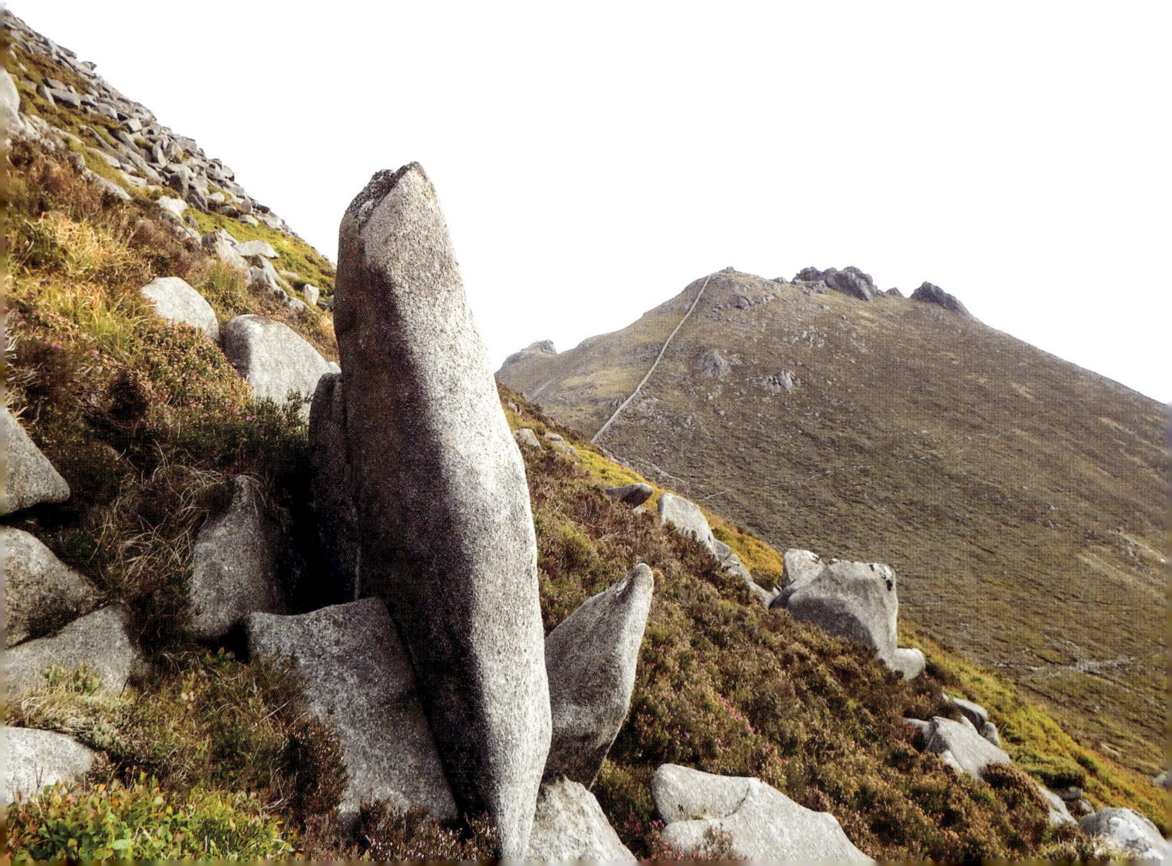

Top opposite: The top corner of this propped phallic stone on the eastern slope of Slieve Donard has been arranged to point to winter solstice. From the heights of Donard there is a clear unimpeded sight out to sea to the horizon and the dawn of that auspicious morning.

Lower opposite: This is **Cloch Dúilmhireachta**, 'Stone of strong desire'. A thin slab on Wee Slevanmore has been skilfully used to make an erection with the point directed across the col to Meelbeg summit. It is beautifully wedged at the front and stones have been packed in at the back to keep it upright. The GPS is:
N.   54º 11. 107'
W. 006º 00. 156'   Elevation 570m.

Top of this page: The shadow eye and the flat pig's snout on the middle part of this important phallic monument are enough to again evoke the tale of the Otherworld in *Togail Bruidne Dá Derga* (The Destruction of Da Derga's Hostel) where the lord of the feast was represented as a man carrying a pig on his shoulder.

Perched on a shoulder of Chimney Rock this megalith overlooks the upper reaches of the Bloody Bridge valley and from below it was regarded as a 'spike'. The Irish for 'spike' has given us the names of Slieve Neir (not on OS maps) and Ballaghanery. There is a small level turf platform at the low end likely used for ritual at winter solstice. The 'bony haunches' at the bottom end resembled the back end of a cow and earned the locality the further name of Slievenagarragh, 'mountain of the great-granddaddy cow'. The vertical dark crack representing a penile meatus groove can be seen at the top end of the stone.

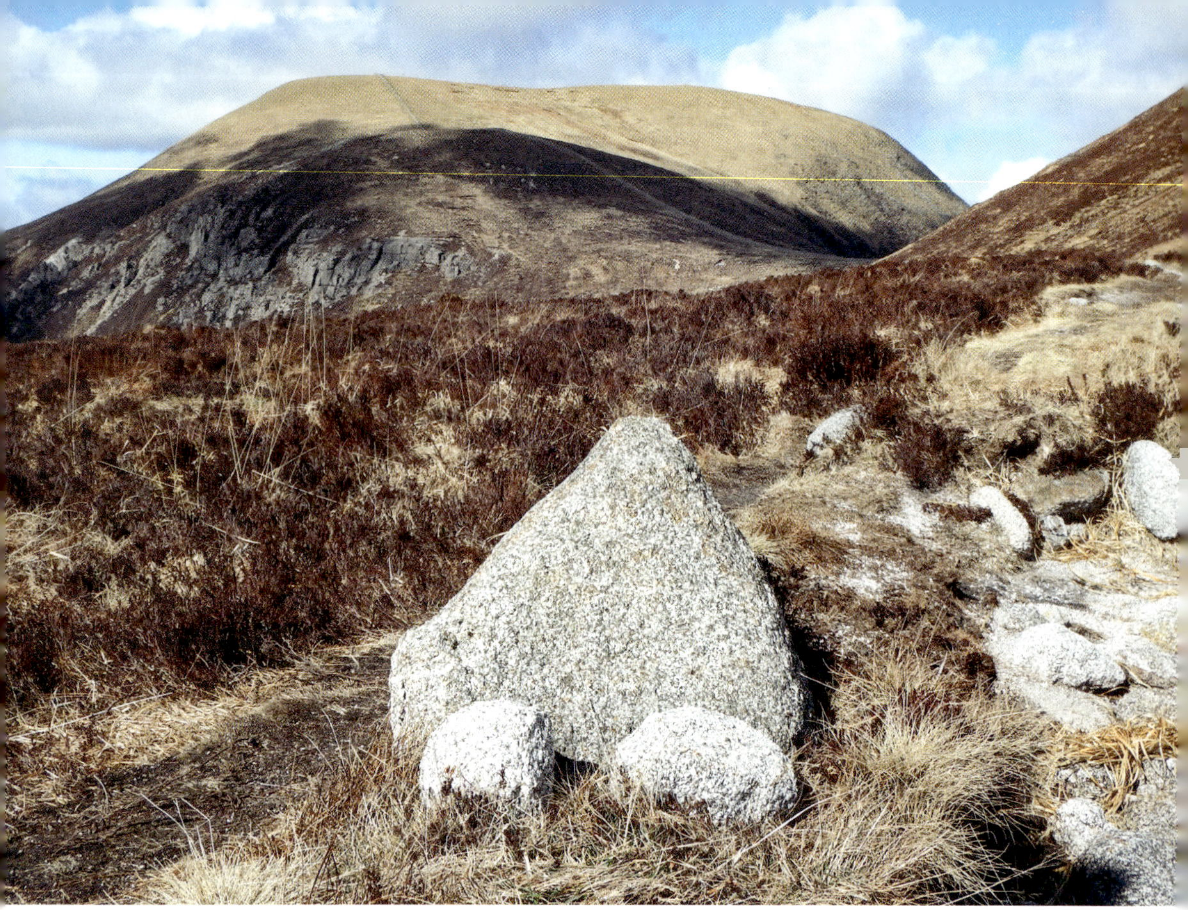
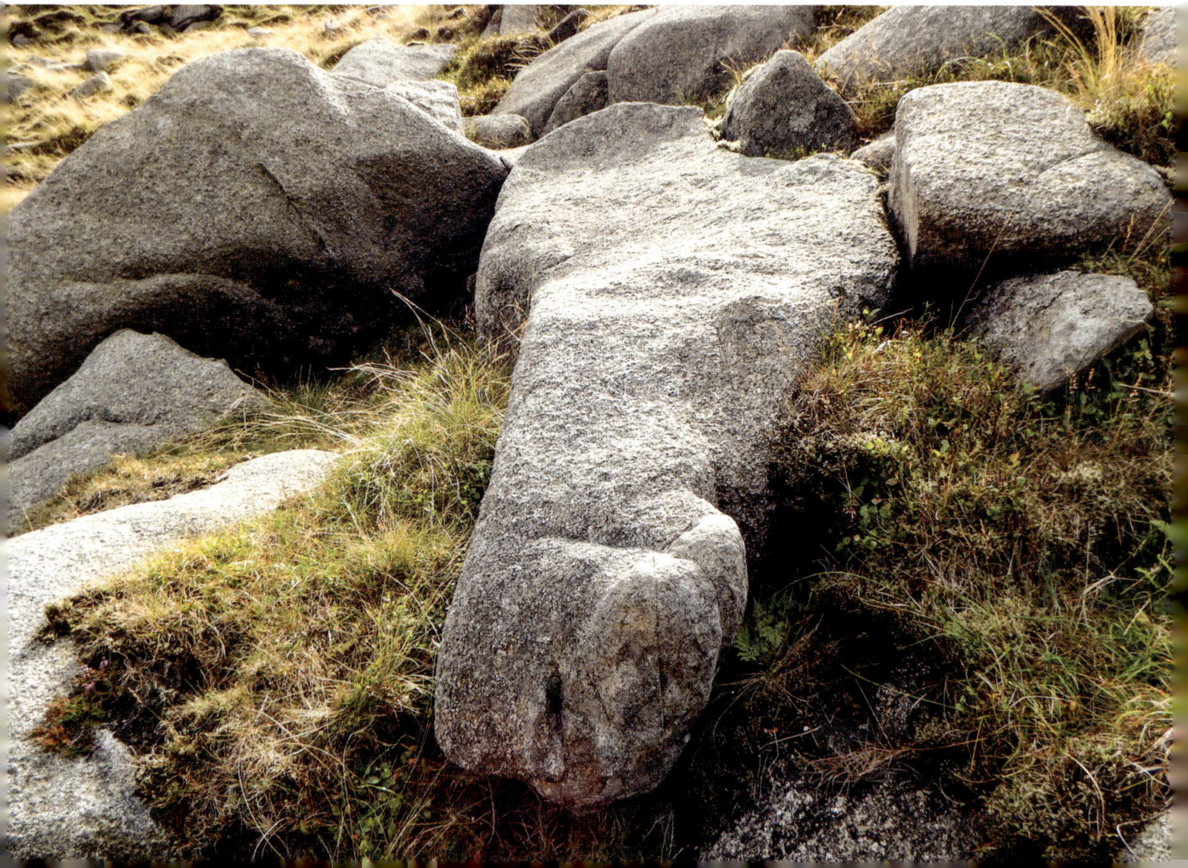

We feature now a few photographs of penis stones and their testicles.

Top opposite: It was a surprise to find this remnant of the elder faith right beside the Brandy Pad at the back of Slieve Donard. The worn trail can be seen to the left of the stones. Fortunately the little spear phallus with its stone testicles has remained undisturbed across the centuries. The photographer wanted the mass of Slieve Commedagh in the background but if the viewpoint had moved slightly over to the left it would probably be found that the point of interest of the spear-point was the landscape 'vaginal notch' between Commedagh and Donard.

Lower opposite: This 2.55m long granite phallic shaft will be found on the top northwest side of Meelmore. The maker seems to have indulged in a bit of artistic license by allowing a kink or twist at the tip but this was to take advantage of an infusion in the rock to suggest semen. The meatus groove addresses summer solstice sunset. The GPS is:

N.   54º 11. 643'
W. 006º 00. 165'   Elevation 571m.

Top of this page: On the shoulder of Meelmore and above Happy Valley will be found this 1.6m phallic shaft with a rounded knob at its tip. The shaft points to the summit of Meelmore. The GPS is:

N.   54º 11. 637'
W. 006º 00. 362'   Elevation 554m.

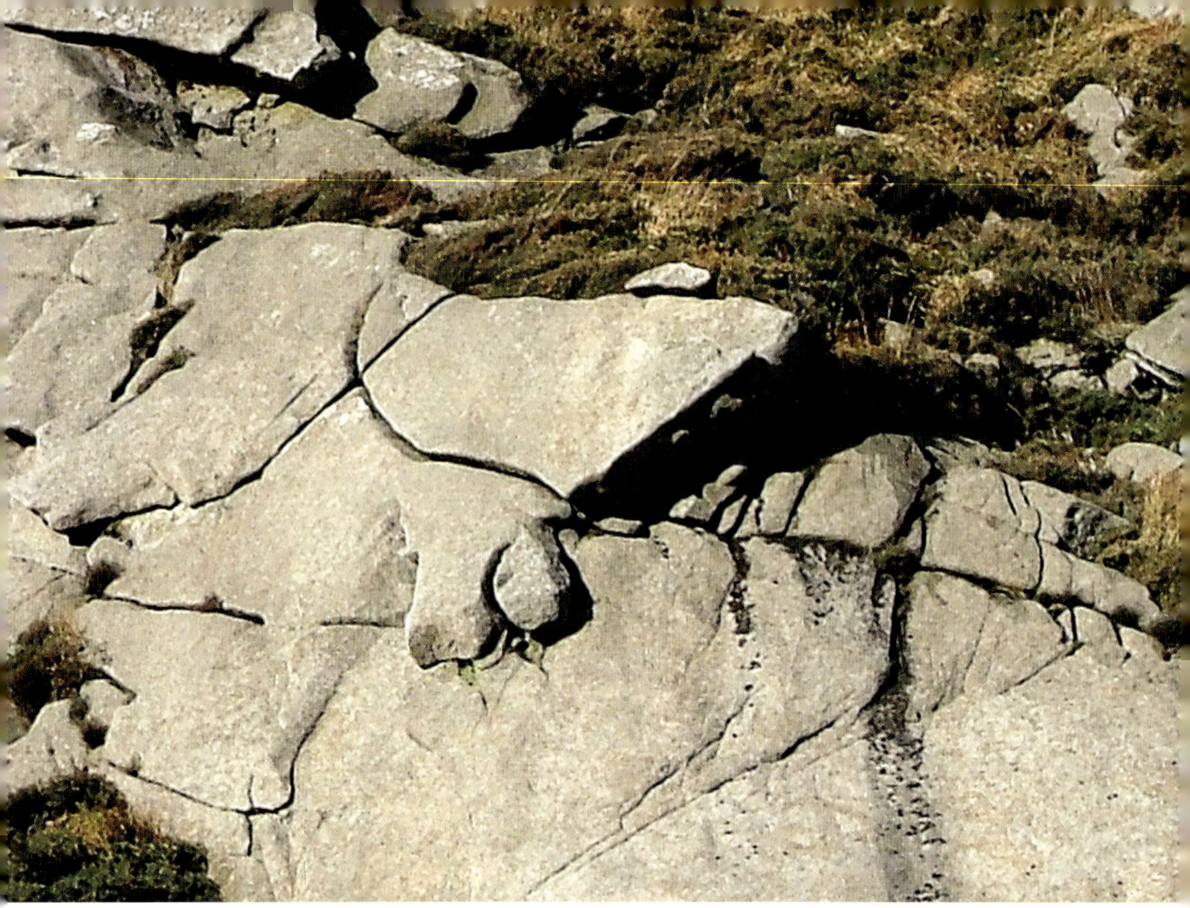

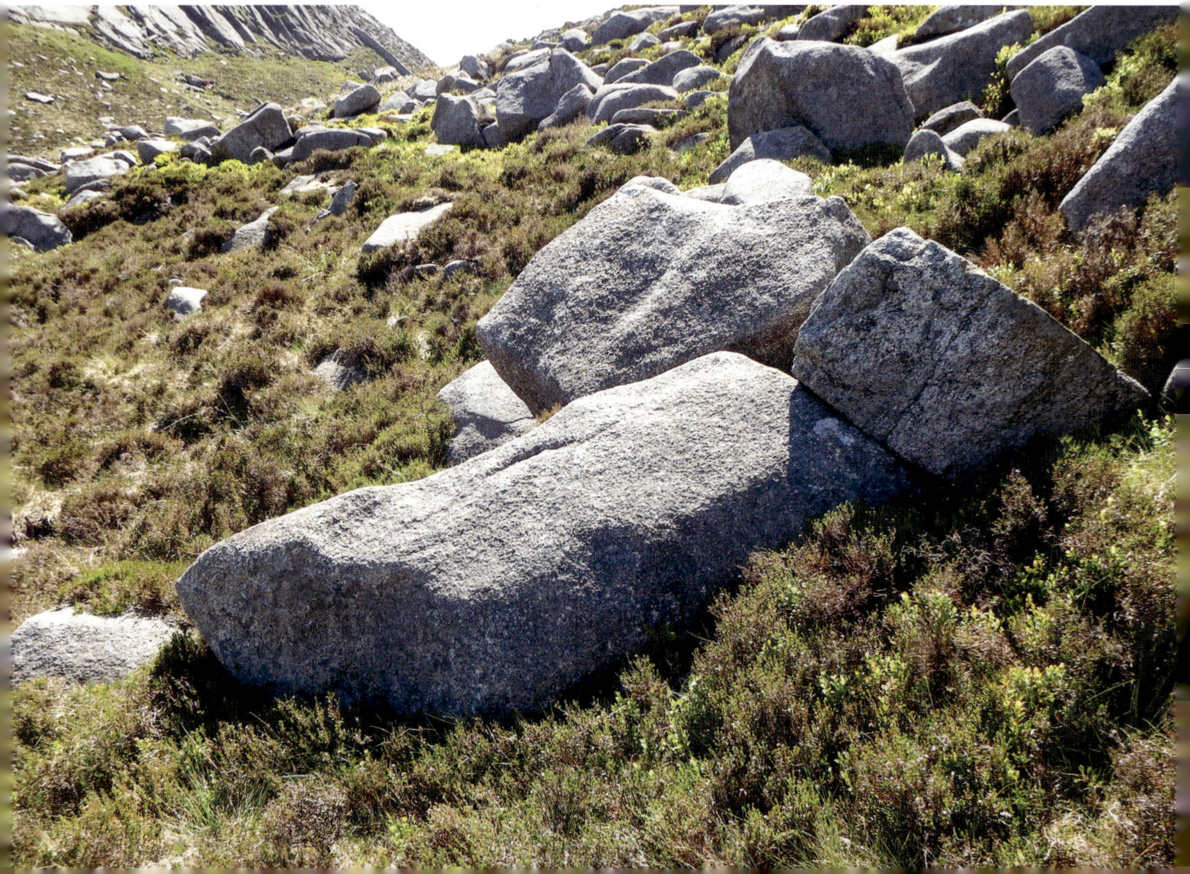

Top opposite: First note the natural drainage stain on the rock face at bottom right. This feature was exploited to suggest abundant fertility through perpetual ejaculation when the early artists reshaped the rock face as spear shaped male genitalia complete with two distinctive testicles. This rock sculpture is on the north slope of Slieve Meelmore in Pollaphuca valley. The GPS was taken from below and is only approximate:

      N. 54º 11. 505'
      W. 005º 59. 579'   Elevation circa 469m.

Lower opposite: This construction of genitalia was named **Briogún**, 'A Skewer'. You will find it in the upper reaches of Pollaphuca valley. It is a granite shaft about 1.8m long with two large boulders at the back as testicles. The alignment of the shaft is to winter solstice sun appearance. The GPS is:

      N. 54º 11. 278'
      W. 005º 59. 679'   Elevation 495m.

Top of this page: Near the Mourne Wall in upper Pollaphuca valley are found these three stones representing a penile shaft and two testicles. The tip of the shaft points towards the summit of Meelmore. It measures 1.9m in length. The GPS is:

      N. 54º 11. 222'
      W. 005º 59. 628'   Elevation 516m.

The cliff face at Douglas Crag shows that a spear stone, at the upper left, has apparently been detached from the top of its pillar and swivelled around to point, with fertility intent, into the erstwhile vaginal cavity in the rock face. How did they do it?

Having talked about the prodigious efforts of the ancients in raising awesome megaliths across Mourne, it is fitting to finish this section with prodigious efforts of more recent times, namely the making of 'lazy beds'. Our photo shows most extensive old rills across the hill of Dromena. These ridges were all dug long ago so that potatoes could be planted. They are now being reclaimed by nature.

It is long past time that a correction is made to the erroneous term 'lazy beds'. Professor E.E. Evans, in his acknowledgements in *Mourne Country*, referred to *'mis-named lazy beds'* as he reflected on the vast amount of labour involved in digging the ridges and then fertilising them with wet wrack that likely had been carried over slippery rocks.

The name in English is quite nonsensical. When treated, however, as a mnemonic of Irish, a quite different sense is revealed. 'Lazy Bed' is from the Irish (*Tí na*) *Laise Béad*. This means (Place of) **the Lash of sorrow**, an altogether more meaningful expression for the back breaking, tough and demanding physical labour needed to heap up the soil.

The Irish is *Lais*, (gen.) **Laise**, meaning 'a lash', and **Béad**, 'a deed; crime, injury; **sorrow**, ill-tidings or doings', giving us 'the Lash of sorrow'.

On a different note a correction could similarly be made to 'St Patrick's Bed', a name given to the hill overlooking Struell Wells outside Downpatrick. Hosts of pilgrims once used to come to the wells looking for relief from sufferings. Others used the gathering as an occasion for indulgence. Such were the degrading and immoral orgies that the hill opposite was known as 'St Patrick's Sorrow' or in Irish *Béad*. The shenanigans ended as the clergy forbade their people to go to the wells.

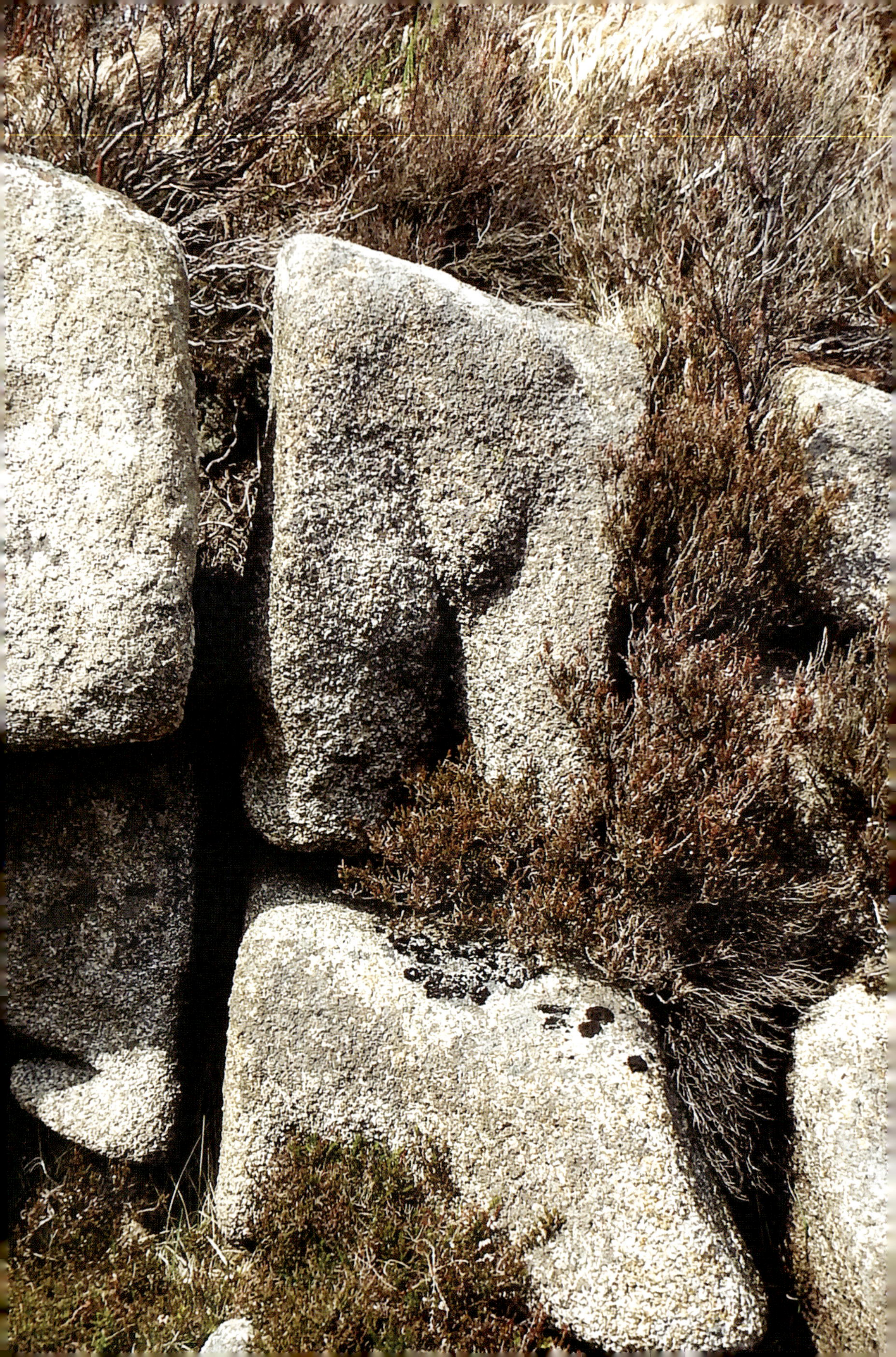

FEMALE STONES

Given that quite a number of the mountains of Mourne have been named after female sexual anatomy is should be no surprise that the hillsides also abound with megaliths displaying similar pronounced female characteristics. The early settlers, the *Fir Builg*, 'men of the womb', were well named. They were sun worshippers with a fierce passion for fertility. The turning of the year at mid-winter saw the returning of the sun to make the grass grow and bring fertility to the earth. The settlers demonstrated this by arranging megaliths into slits and holes evocative of female openings that would be illuminated and deemed 'penetrated' by the sun at solstice. The epitome of these beliefs is the world heritage site of Newgrange at *Brú na Bóinne* where dawn light of winter solstice penetrates the long passageway to illuminate the inner chamber. Mourne has its share of great stones that also welcomed the solstice light. This chapter illustrates numerous instances of 'vaginal gaps' most of which are oriented towards receiving first light of solstice. Many of these gaps are shown to be 'filled'. In such a case a stone is placed between the two labial sides as representative of a penile insertion. Recognition of this genre of megalith will bring a deeper appreciation of Mourne's heritage to those who explore our beautiful hills.

A reminder first of a few of the 'female' mountains which were previously illustrated and explained in *Place-names of Beanna Boirrche*. There was the front of Slieve Bignian known to the quarrymen as the *Broinne Nó*, the 'famous breast'. As they quarried granite from the mountain the men envisaged they were 'sucking from the famous breast'. In Irish this was **mBiadh Súighteán Broinne Nó**, which was made famous in the song 'Maid of the Sweet Brown Knowe'. Above Newcastle there is the rounded shape of Slievenamaddy. The declivity near the top ensured it was regarded as a vulva and thus had the name of **Sliabh na mBáidhe**, 'mountain of love'. Likewise Formal mountain (J 2316) to the east of Cassy Water valley was regarded as a vulva and was known in Irish as **Foirm Áil**, 'shape of pleasure'. Slievemeel (J 2120) with its rounded summit easily lent itself to

---

Opposite page: A generous vulva is displayed as a centrepiece on a rock outcrop on Long Mountain. The outcrop is north-west of the hillside known as 'O'Hanlon's Ladder' and near the old quarry that overlooks the Windy Gap Valley. The GPS is:

N. 54° 07. 553'
W. 006° 04. 837'   Elevation 329m.

the gynaecomorphic interpretation of being a vulva especially when seen from the Kilbroney valley below. The mountain has its name from *Sliabh Mí-Áil*, 'mountain of evil pleasure'. Two more mountains with the same Irish root were thought of as vulvas. These were Slimageen at the head of the Windy Gap valley and Lamagan. Both names in Irish are a figure of speech, a synecdoche, where the whole woman is mentioned but only a part is understood, namely her vulva. Slimageen at Windy Gap is from the Irish *Sliabh Magh-Geine*, 'mountain of the huge woman'. On ordnance survey maps this mountain is named Slievemoughanmore but the usage of Slimageen is still preferred by the locals. Also looked on as a mighty vulva was Slieve Lamagan so named from the Irish *Sliabh Lab a Geine*, 'mountain of the considerable lump of a woman'. The corruption of the present name being spelt with an [M] stems from the time of Walter Harris' 1744 work *The Antient and Present State of the County of Down*. However, the great Irish naturalist, Robert Lloyd Praegar, in his guidebook for the County Down Railway, drew attention to the local pronunciation of 'Lavigan' which was closer to the original Irish. Lamagan's name arose from the shadow of Bignian's north tor casting itself, with phallic intent, onto the side of Lamagan at winter solstice sunset. Another two mountains had their names from female anatomy but now only the landscape, rather than written sources, prevail to suggest that Slievenaglogh mountains, at Trassey and overlooking the Silent Valley, were originally *Sliabh na Glotan*, 'mountain of the slit' rather their present banal and meaningless translations of 'mountain of stones'.

Top opposite: The great vertical gash on the side of Slievenaglogh at Trassey would have been regarded as a vagina and likely responsible for an earlier Irish name of *Sliabh na Glotan*, 'mountain of the slit' that has now morphed into the banal *Sliabh na gCloch*. Unfortunately there are no written sources extant for verification; only the landscape remains.

Lower opposite: A view of Slieve Builg from Slievenaglogh summit cairn. The name of Slievenaglogh at Silent Valley is likely a corruption from *Sliabh na Glotan*, 'mountain of the slit'. The Slit is the arrowed 'stripe' down the side of Slieve Builg which was perceived as a vulva. Slievenaglogh has its name therefore, not from being a mountain of 'rocks' but rather from the summit view. The name of Slieve Builg is not mentioned on the ordnance survey maps.

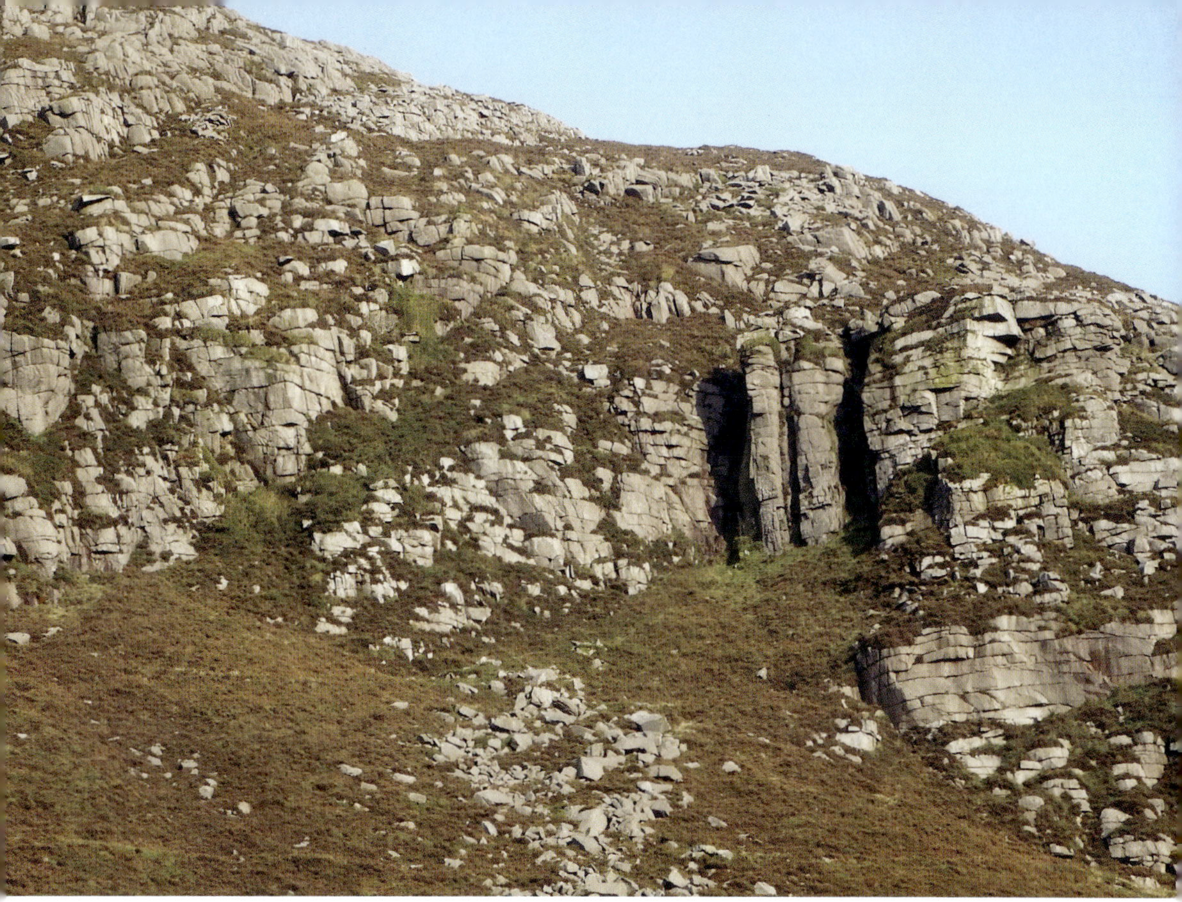

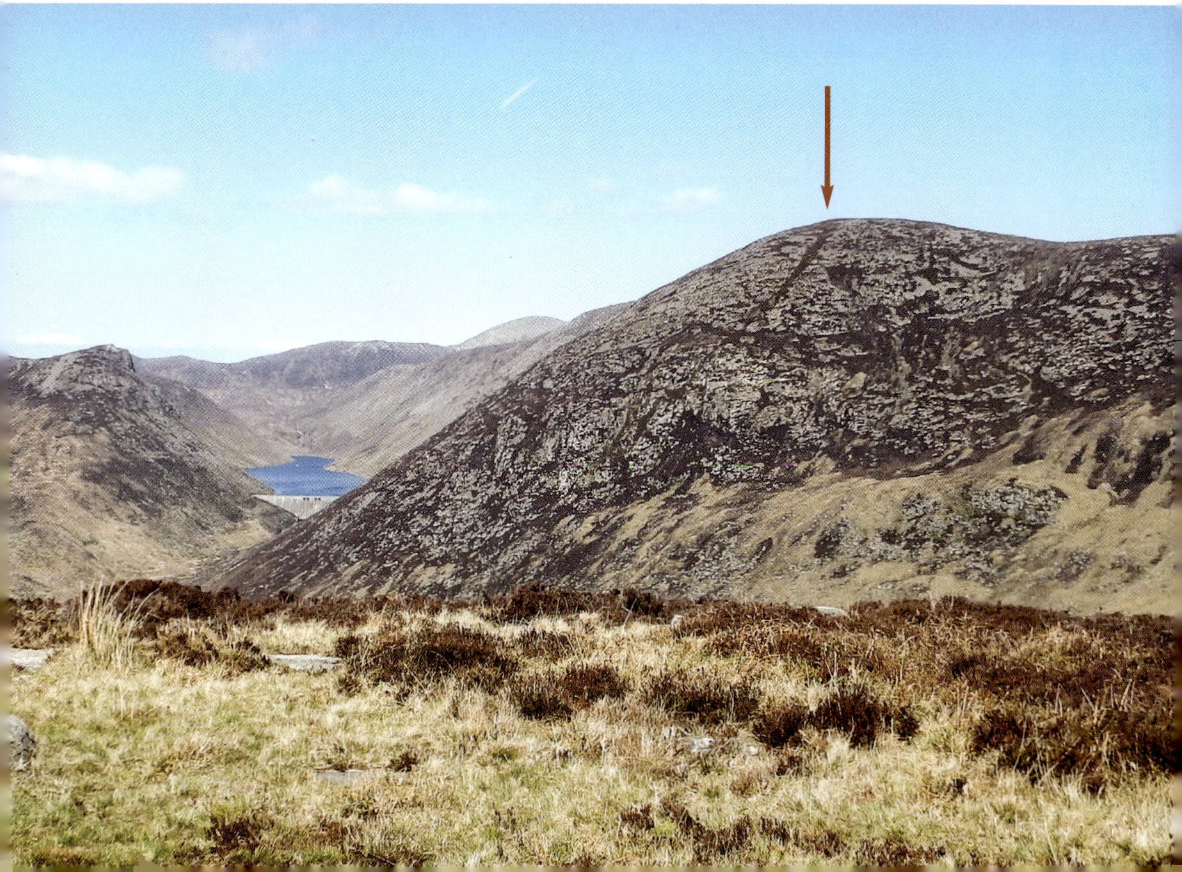

Above: This is a beautiful representation in stone of female genitalia. The two granite slabs, about 2m long, form a classic vaginal gap and after checking with the compass the gap was found to be sweetly aligned to summer solstice sunrise. Accordingly the monument was named **Dílseog**, 'A Faithful Sweetheart'. It is to be found on the east side of Wee Slevanmore. Note the propped phallic stone in the background. The GPS for *Dílseog* is:

      N. 54° 11. 177'
      W. 006° 00. 015'   Elevation 610m.

Top opposite: This arrangement of vaginal gap stones on Long mountain has been placed at the very edge of a steep drop. The female opening is deliberately aligned towards the landscape notch at the head of Windy Gap valley. Note how the right-hand labial stone has been carefully propped in place. The right-hand mountain, with the quarry workings in the middle, is known as Slimageen.

Lower opposite: On the west flank of Slievemageogh, and overlooking the Windy Gap valley, is a vaginal gap construction aligned on the notch between Eagle mountain and Slimageen (marked on OS maps as Slievemoughanmore). The diagonally slanted gap is about 0.3 metres wide. It not only looks to the landscape notch but also to where summer solstice sun sets. The GPS is:

      N. 54° 07. 706'
      W. 006° 03. 801'   Elevation 319m.

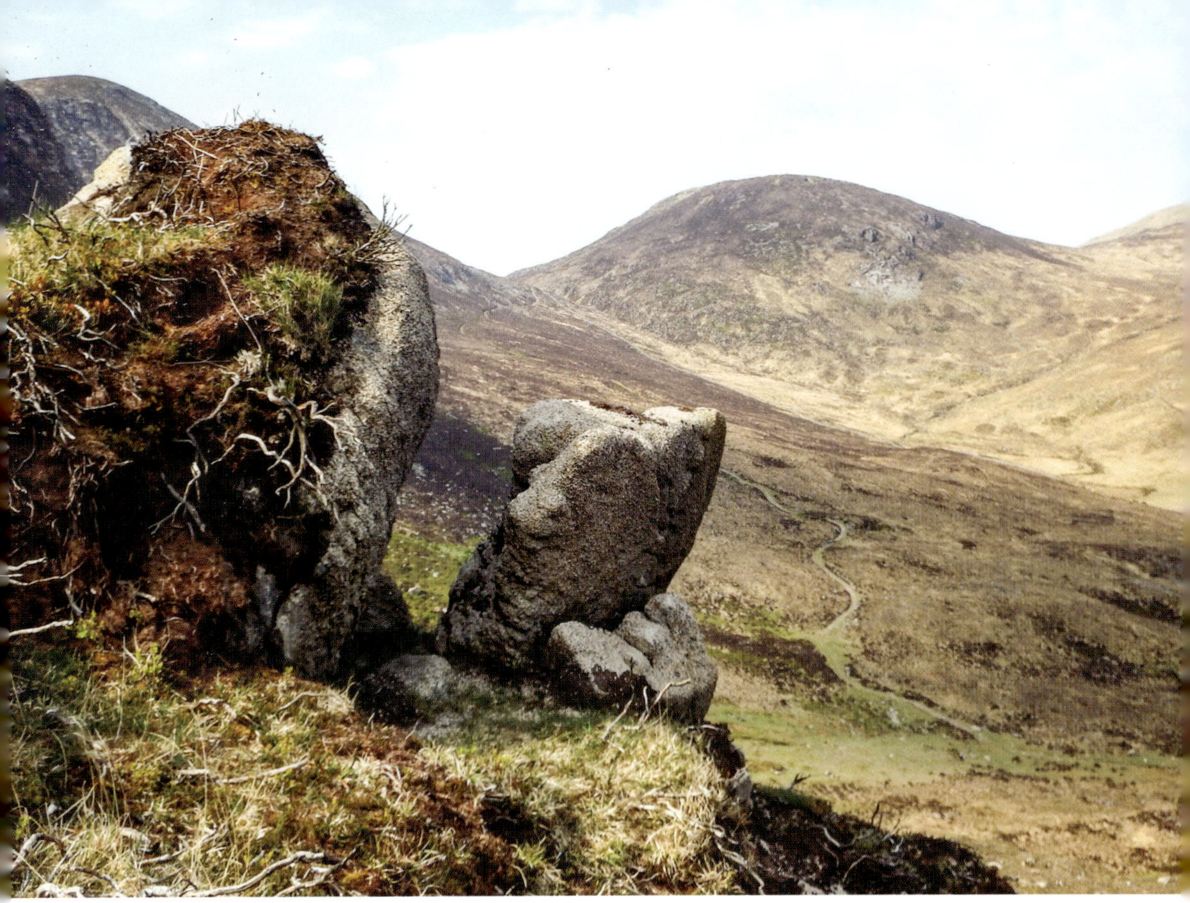

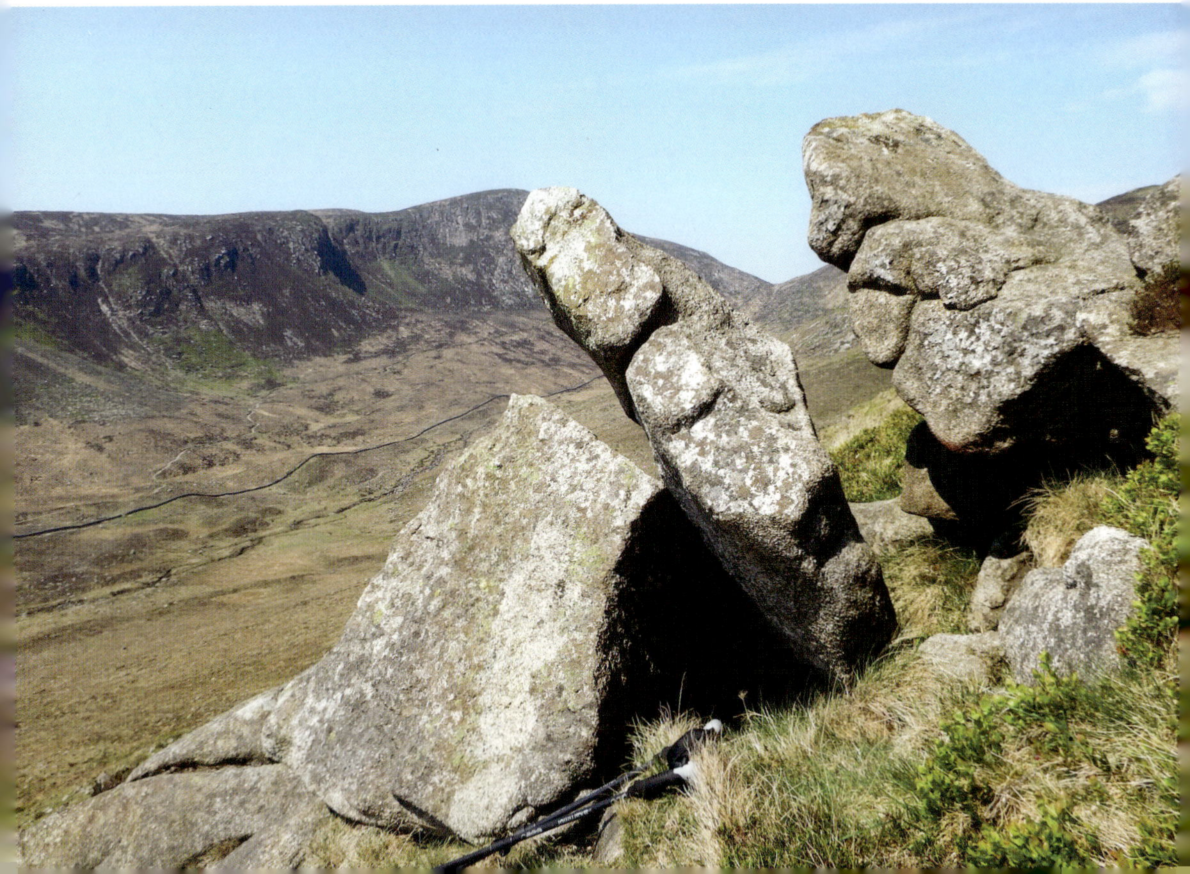

Above: Two great stones were placed close together in the col between the north and summit tors of Slieve Bearnagh to create a vagina. The arrangement allowed the fertilising first light of winter solstice dawn to shine directly into the 20cm gap between them, that was until the Mourne Wall was built behind them and thereafter blocked that light. The GPS is:

      N. 54° 11. 192'
      W. 005° 59. 213'   Elevation 691m.

Top opposite: On the northern corner of Spellack is a rather androgynous megalith. On one hand two projecting granite stones, propped provocatively on top of a monstrous three metre boulder and firmly wedged at the back, could be regarded as phallic. On the other hand the 15cm slit between the two stones marks that opening as a vagina. The tips of the stones, as well as the slit, address Shimial mountain across the valley. The GPS is:

      N. 54° 11. 975'
      W. 005° 59. 380'   Elevation 317m.

Lower opposite: Walkers on Chimney Rock mountain will recognise the mighty rock on the right as part of the mountain's western summit tor. Its phallic profile could be seen by fishermen far out at sea and they named it (*Tí na*) **h-Oiris Méin**, (Place of the) 'Landmark of Pleasure', which later became in English the mnemonic 'Horsemen'. The mountain has its Irish name of **Shimleadh Roc**, 'pretended gap' from the two metre opening between the summit tor and the megalith boulder deliberately placed in front of it. This gap was an imagined vagina that would be 'inseminated' shortly after dawn on winter solstice

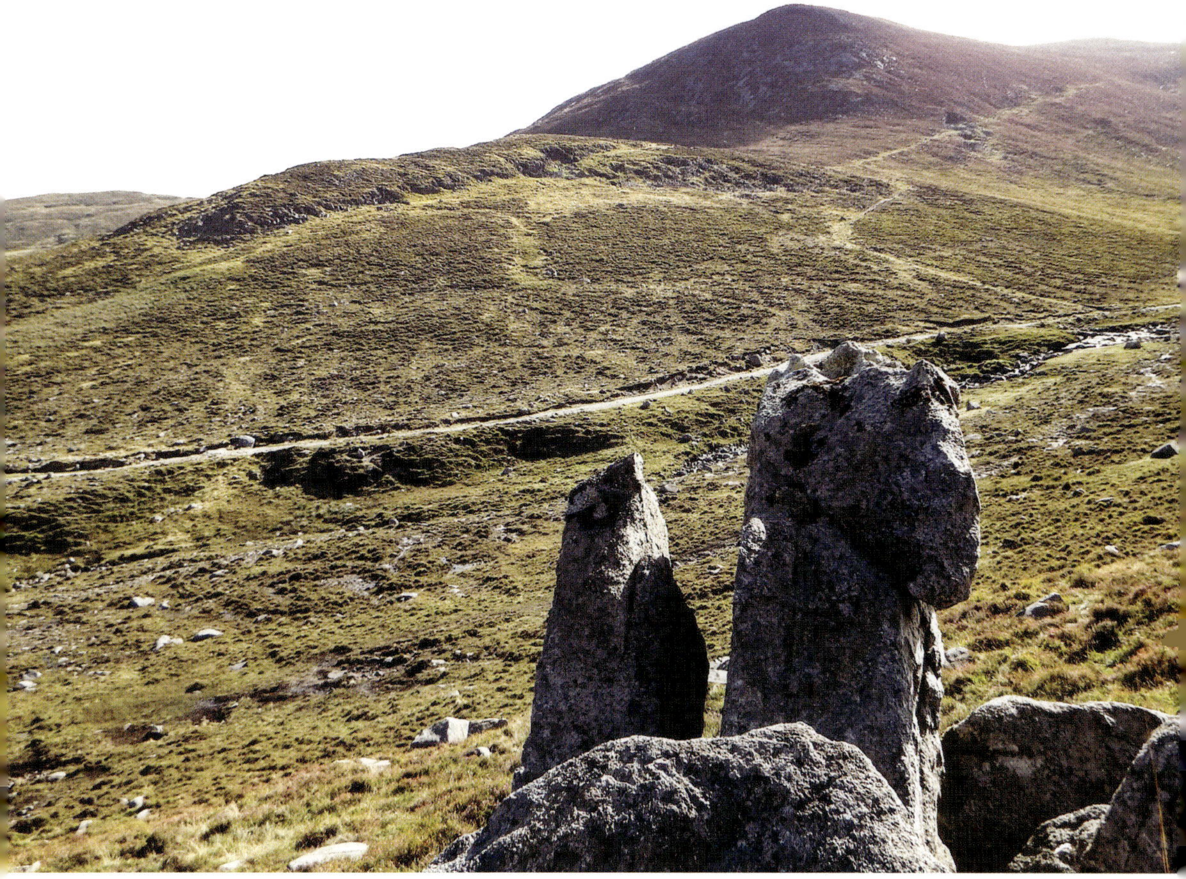

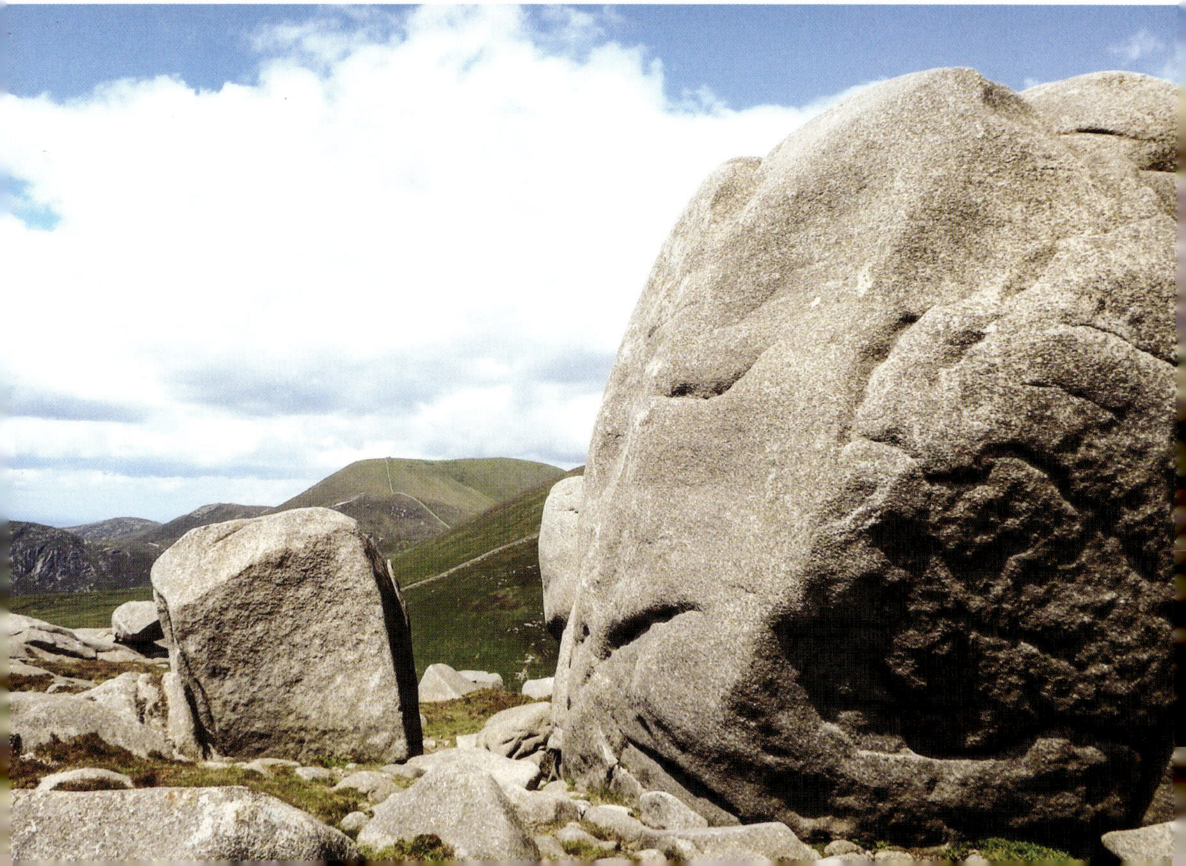

Above: On the slope of Meelmore mountain overlooking Pollaphuca valley is this important structure built with many stones. Two large slabs form a vaginal gap specially arranged to be deeply illuminated at summer solstice sunrise. The gap is about 30cm wide but is nearly two metres high. There are chopped eyes for faces on the inside of the labial slabs. The ensemble is topped with a pancake-like capstone about 1.4m wide. Note the phallic stone sticking out on the left side. It points to Shimial mountain. The GPS is:

>N. 54º 11. 653'
>W. 005º 59. 504'   Elevation 456m.

Top opposite: This very pleasing construction is at the top of the valley on Slieve Meelmore's northern flank. A shale boulder is carefully propped up adjacent to a shale outcrop to form a vaginal gap aligned towards summer solstice sunrise. The gap between the rocks is about 0.25m at the top. The GPS is:

>N. 54º 11. 933'
>W. 006º 00. 265'   Elevation 371m.

Lower opposite: Under the north corner of Spellack a large 1.8m long granite boulder, and another slightly smaller beside it, rest on a boulder base and form a tapering vaginal crack varying in width from 0.25m at the bottom to only 2 to 3cm at the top. This gap awaits penetration by sunlight at summer solstice dawn. The GPS is:

>N. 54º 11. 965'
>W. 005º 59. 402'   Elevation 340m.

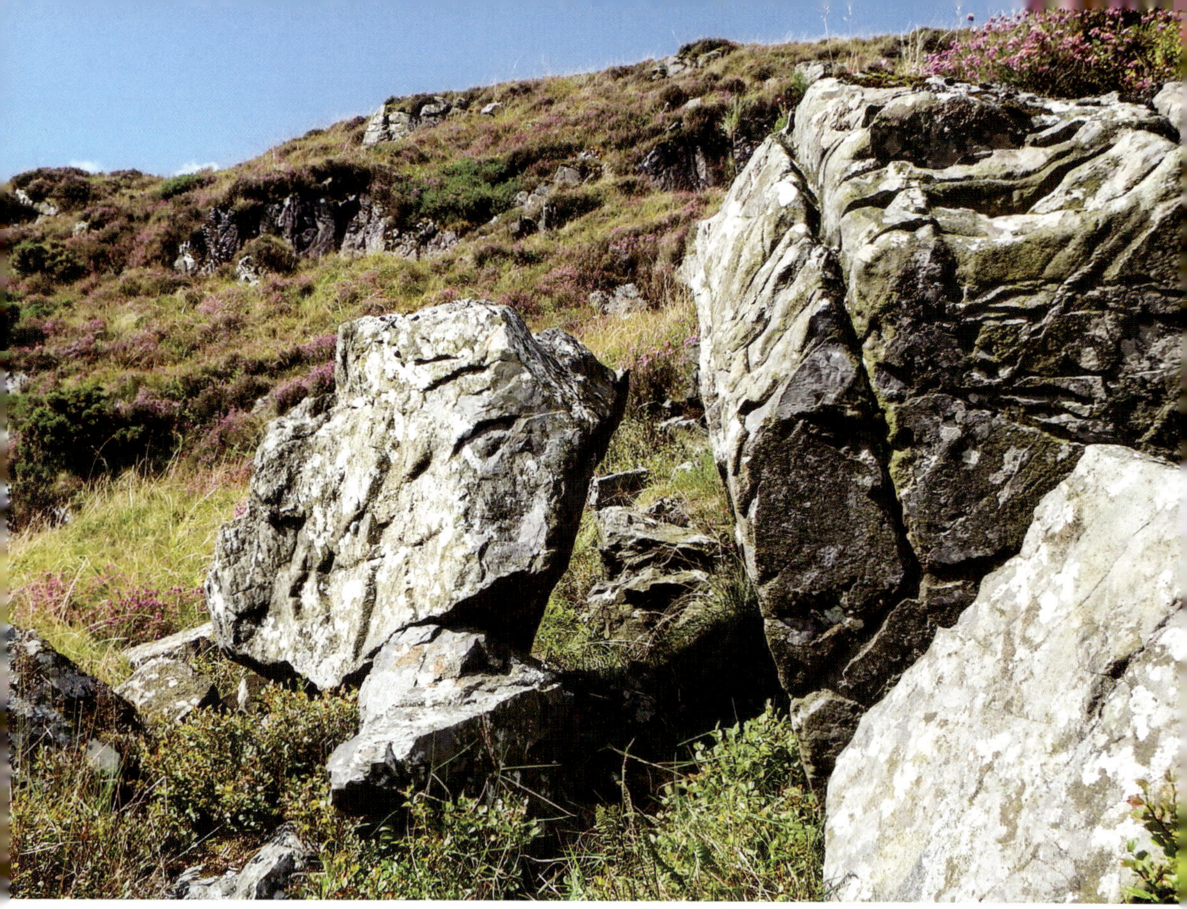

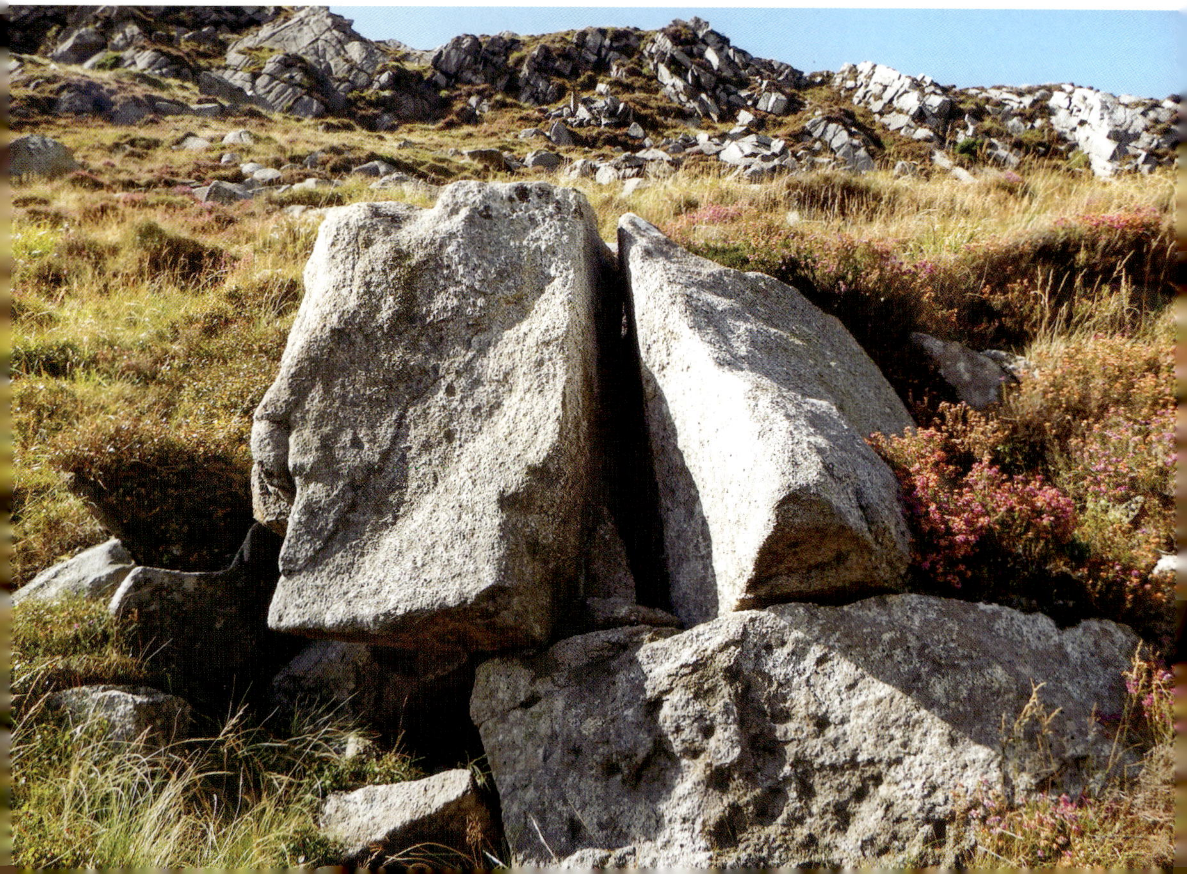

Above: On the east side of Slieve Bearnagh's north tor a pillar has been split to form a vaginal opening. Its placement and wide opening would seem to allow penetration of early sunlight at both summer and winter solstice. The megalith was named **An Brillín Óg**, 'The Young Clitoris' on account of this being a 'recent' creation by a stone-man, though one with a respect for the old gods. Jumper holes can be seen in the rock where plug and feathers were used to split the stone. Professor Evans reckoned that the use of steel 'plug and feathers' was not used in Mourne before 1860. The GPS is:

N. 54° 11. 230'
W. 005° 58. 749'   Elevation 514m.

Opposite: This fabulous construction of huge granite stones is found in the lower Trassey valley. It was named the 'double vagina' as there are two great notches slicing through the stones allowing the notches to receive solstice light at both summer and winter. It is well worth a walk round the monument to appreciate how the slit openings are aligned towards the various peaks of Luke's mountain, Shimial and Slievenaman. There are rich possibilities in trying to interpret the meaning of the many chopped surfaces on the rock. This is a masterly treasure both in conception and execution. The GPS is:

N. 54° 12. 094'
W. 005° 59. 441'   Elevation 265m.

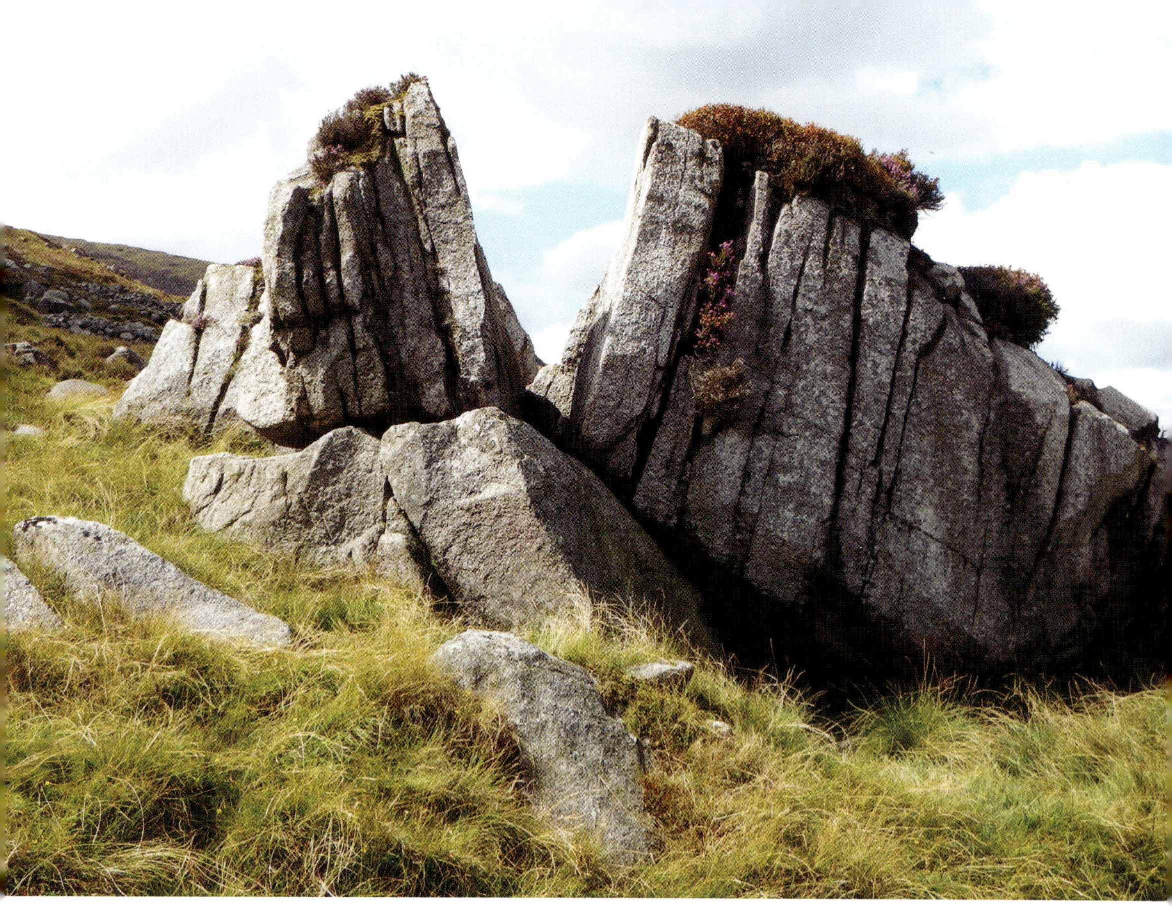

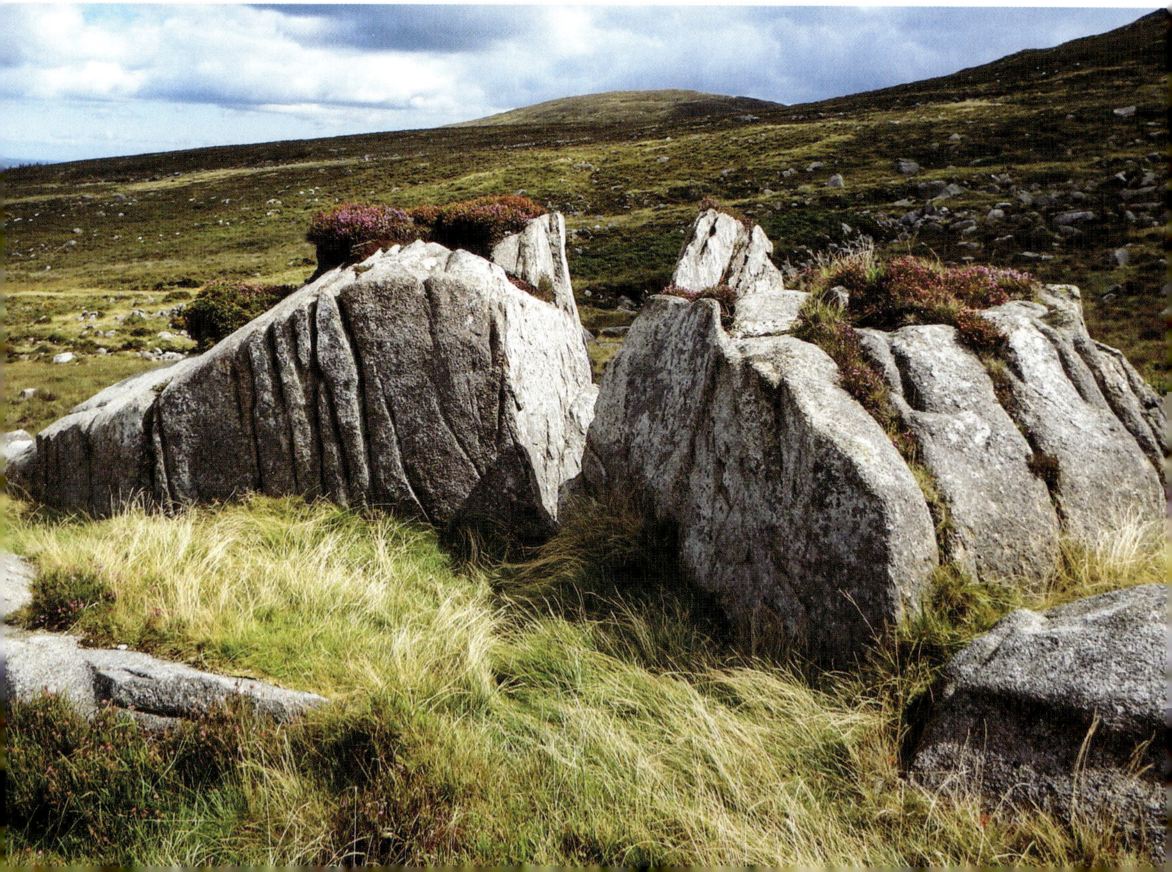

Above: A nice example of vagina stones on the upper reaches of Spellack/Meelmore shoulder overlooking Pollaphuca valley. The stones are beautifully aligned on summer solstice sunrise. On that auspicious morning the sunlight will pass between the stones and bestow fertility. The GPS is:

                N.   54º 11. 743'
                W. 005º 59. 502'   Elevation 489m.

Top opposite: A granite boulder on the seaward side of Leganabruchan has been split down the middle to give a gap of 0.5m at the top and tapering to a much narrower opening of 12cm at the bottom. The stones have been arranged so that the notional vaginal gap thus formed is pierced at dawn of summer solstice. The GPS is:

                N.   54º 10. 716'
                W. 005º 53. 542'   Elevation 288m.

Lower opposite: The boulder strewn slopes under the cliff of Slieve Beg at the head of the Annalong valley are a rich hunting ground for stones arranged by the ancients. Here granite stones have been aligned so that the gap between them will be penetrated by the summer solstice sun as it clears the landscape vaginal gap between Commedagh and Donard.

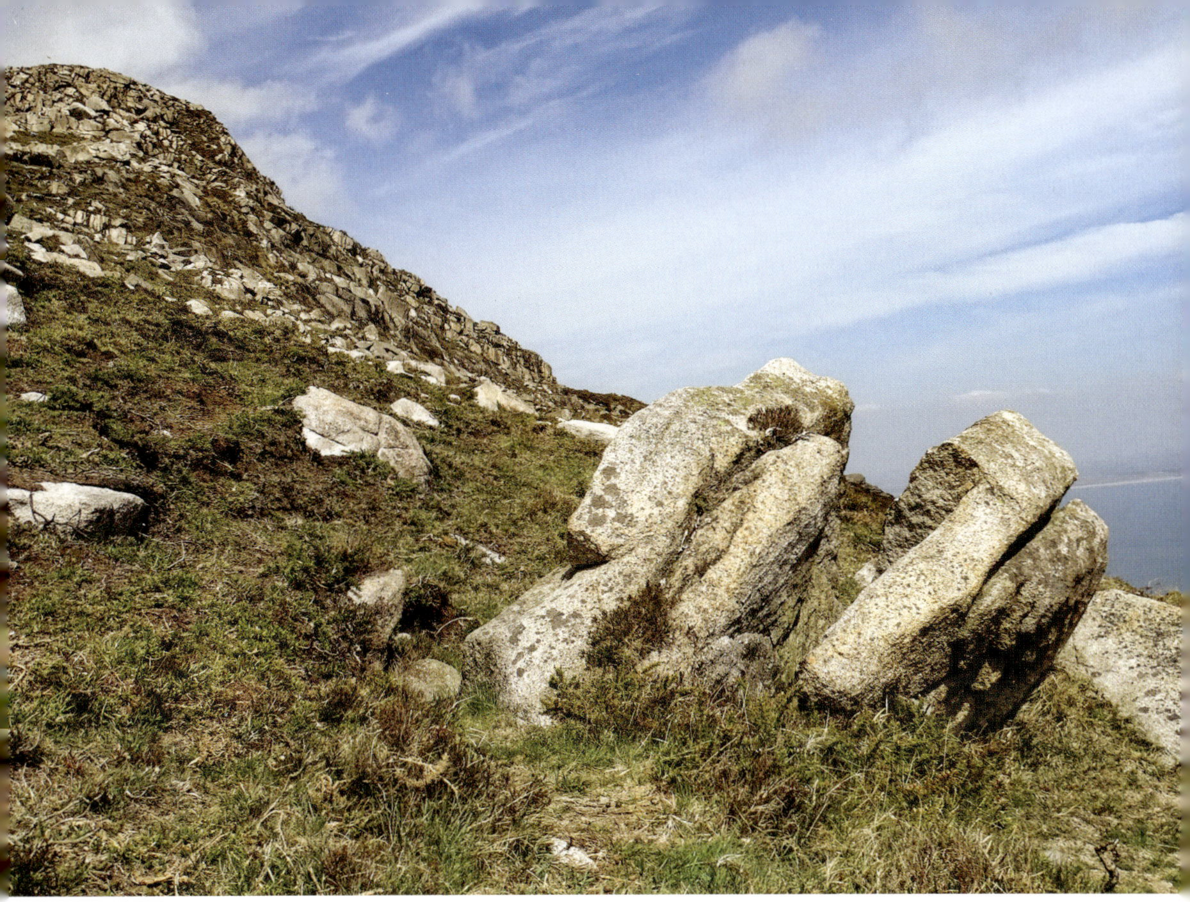

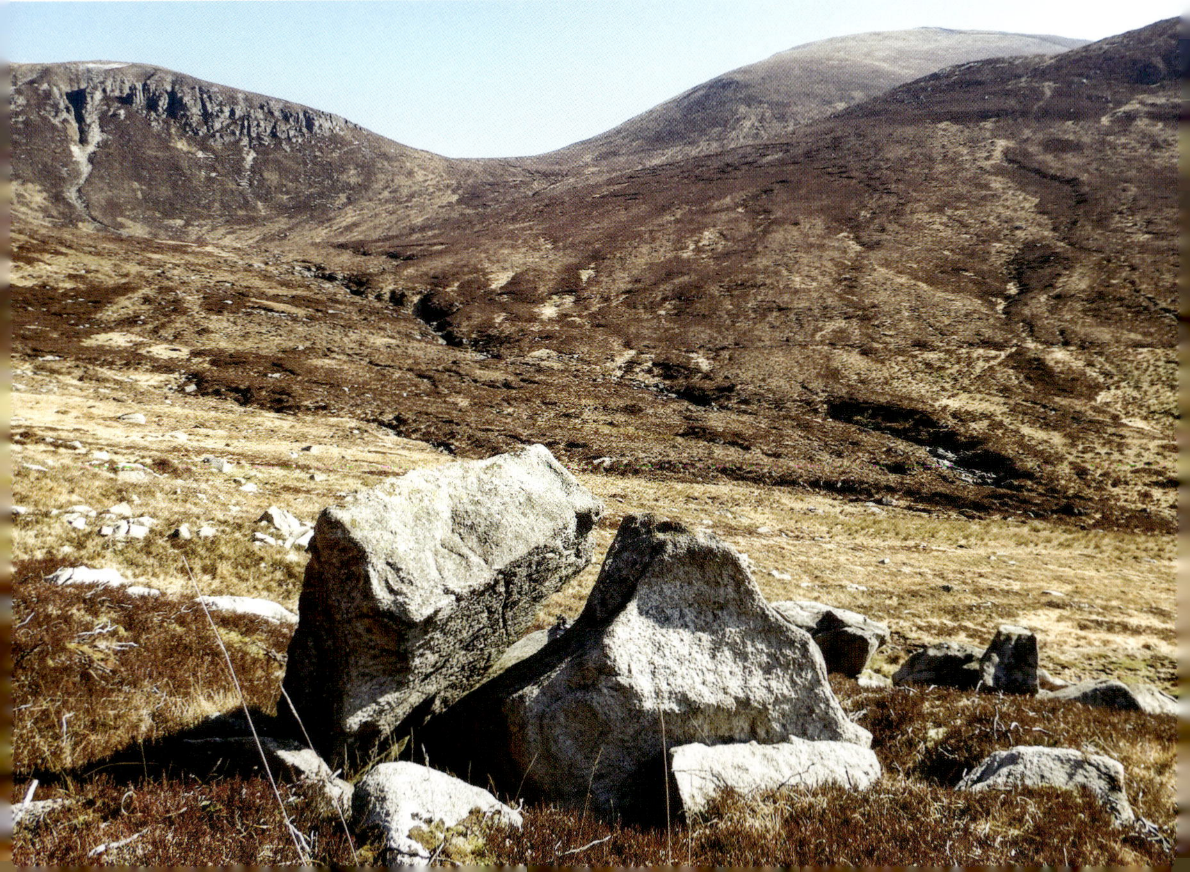

Above: This is a magnificent expression in stone of a vaginal gap much prized by the fertility loving ancients. It is on Millstone mountain. The red item on top of the right-hand stone is a compass that was used to confirm that the alignment of the stones was faithful to summer solstice sunrise. The stubby block in front of the stones has a barely visible light coloured infused line as a coronal rim. As the solstice sun would rise and strengthen this block would cast its shadow into the gap in simulation of copulation. The phenomenon was referred to in Irish as **Dúid lia Scáth**, 'Fertility stone shadow'. [Further examples and an explanation given in the appendix under Diddly Squat].

Top opposite: High on the side of Slievenaglogh and overlooking the Hares Gap is this truly impressive vaginal gap construction. The massive boulder representing the left-hand labial side is delicately balanced on top of a smaller stone. Note the little phallic projection with the infused coronal rim sticking out into the shaded area from the left. Its fertilising shadow would be cast into the present dark gap as the sun set; this is another instance of **Dúid lia Scáth**.

Our second photograph is of the same construction but taken from behind. It shows the top of a pointed priapic Slieve Bearnagh complete with a dimple meatus groove at its summit. Towards winter solstice sunset, and with the sun now behind Bearnagh, the summit notionally 'came to climax' to inseminate the opening between the stones. This creation is one of Mourne's gems. The pity is that the slope is perilously steep and really should be avoided. The danger of the location only adds to the wonder of the monument's assembly.

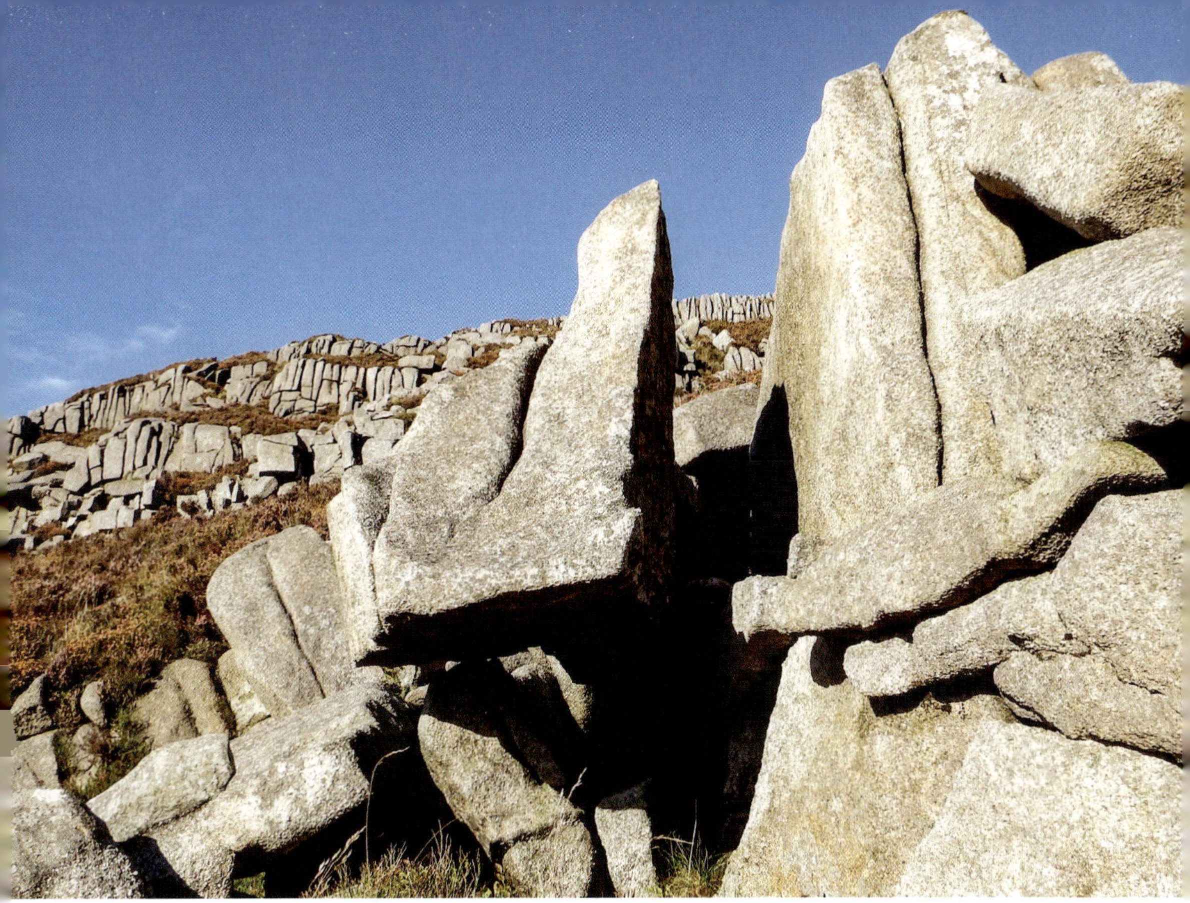

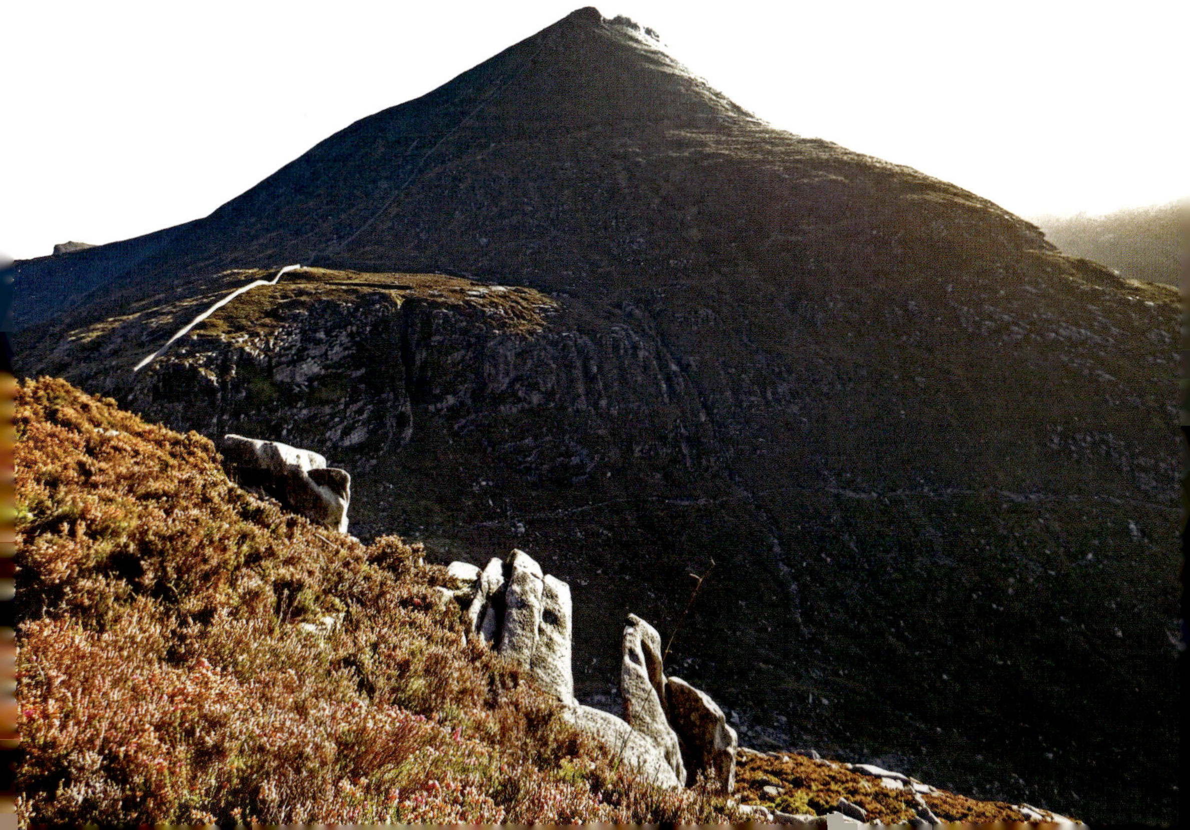

Above: This vaginal gap monument is in the middle of the Glenfoffany valley. The holly tree makes the location easy to find. The tree in the photograph hides a spear stone at the back pointing to winter solstice. The gap between the two large boulders is aligned to be penetrated and notionally inseminated by the sun on winter solstice. The star attraction here, however, seems to be the huge 3.2m spear stone in the middle of the photo which is propped up in erection mode. The GPS is:

       N. 54º 10. 658'
       W. 005º 53. 812'   Elevation 306m.

Top opposite: Two granite boulders, north of the Red Moss river, are placed side by side but leave an all-important gap between them for the early light of summer solstice dawn that will appear over by distant Slieve Bignian.

Lower opposite: On Douglas Crag plateau a big rock has been split into two pieces and these have been placed side by side creating a 60cm gap at its smallest yet aligned to receive the first light of winter solstice dawn. There is evidence of a long iron drill hole at the top inside left stone making this quite a 'recent' creation. This is important in showing that adherence to the old beliefs lasted up until the demise of Irish and long after the arrival of Christianity. The GPS is:

       N. 54º 03. 985'
       W. 005º 57. 980'   Elevation 447m.

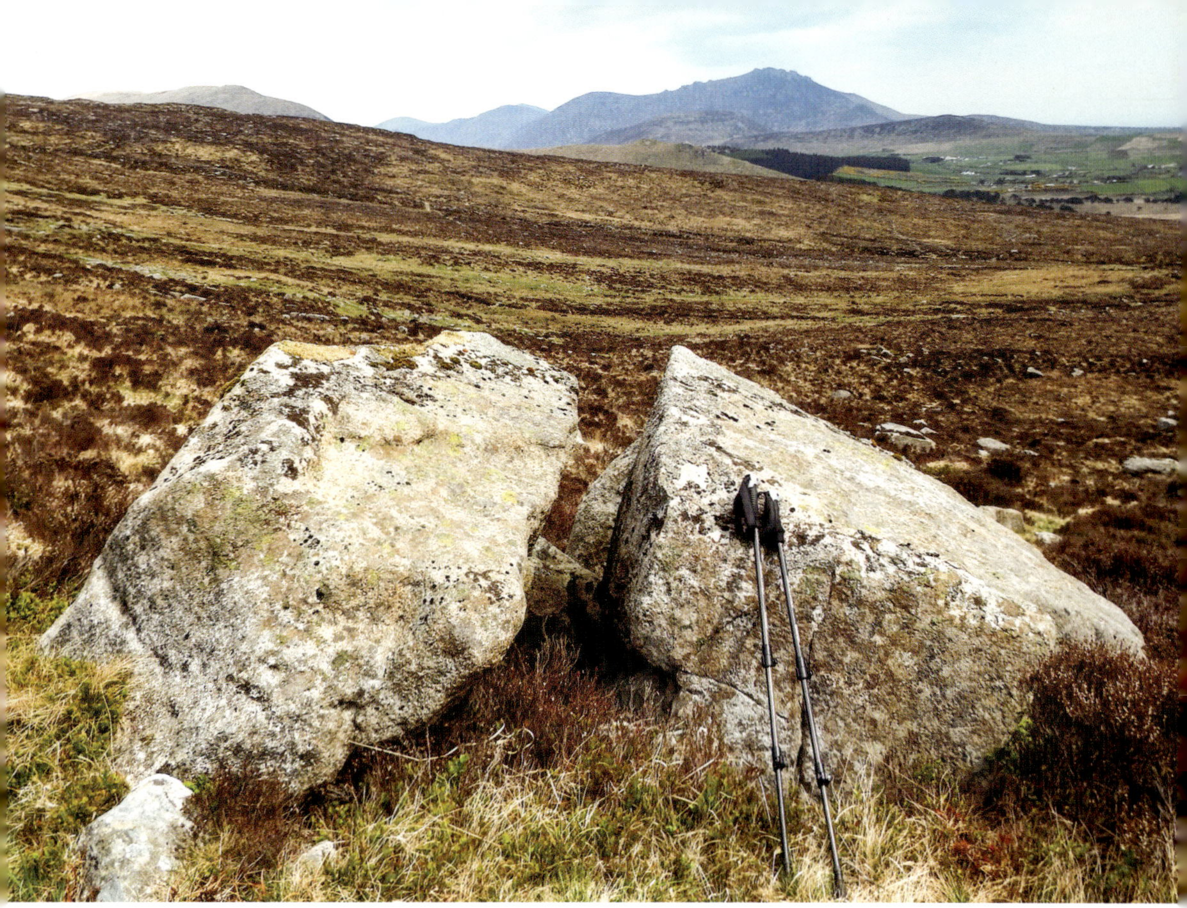

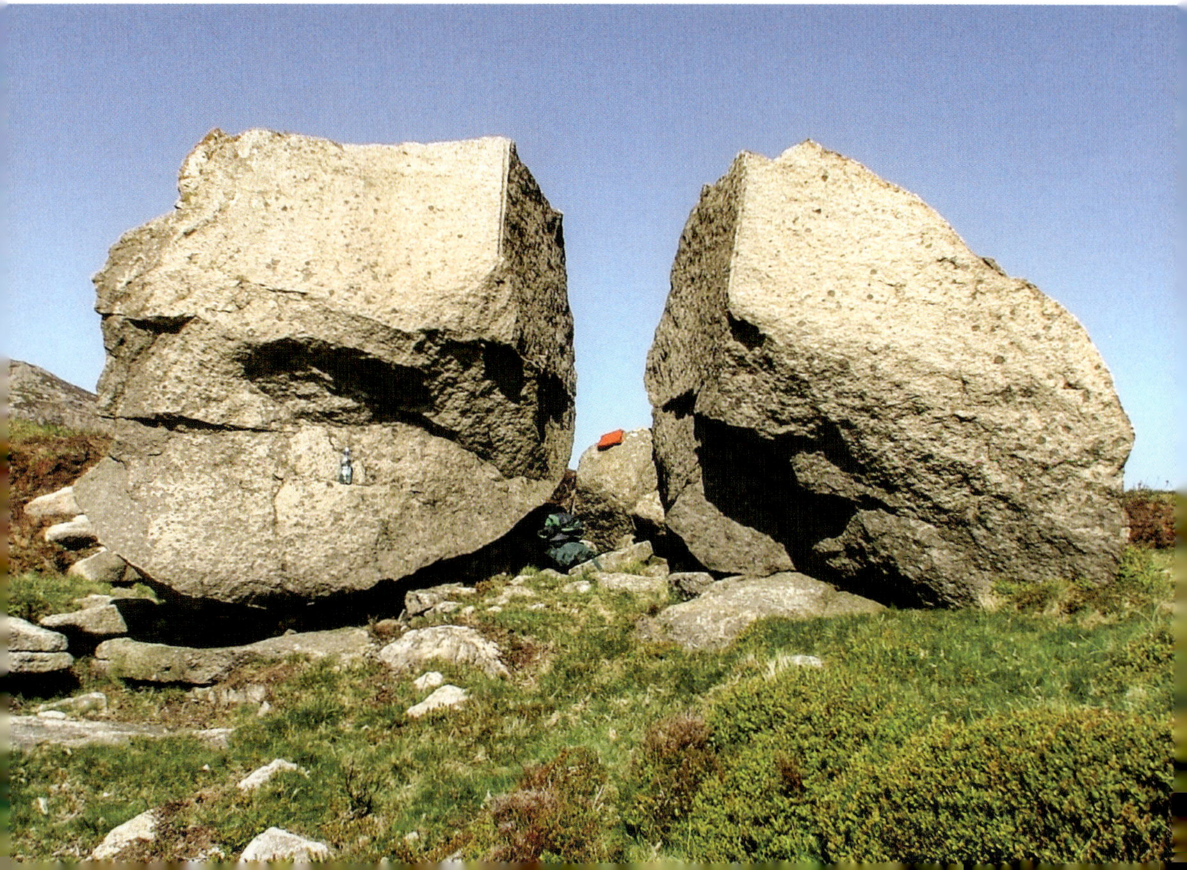

Above: This pair of vagina stones, in shale, are under the cliff on the north-west corner of Shan Slieve. You can see the shepherd's wall in the background. The right-hand stone in the photograph has been propped up at the front making it dual-purpose. As a female stone it acts as one labial side, whereas being propped up it becomes a male erection. The unique feature of the megalith is on the top of the stone. Here, as shown opposite, the tiniest phallic horn has been crafted. It is only a sliver but it is beautifully done. Given the propensity of shale to shatter, the making of this tiny penis is a remarkable work of skill and proficiency. The GPS is:

      N. 54° 12. 106'
      W. 005° 56. 831'   Elevation 333m.

Lower opposite: The mountain heather is slowly engulfing this pair of vagina stones on the crest of Long Mountain overlooking the Windy Gap valley. The opening is aligned with summer solstice sunset. Slieve Gluster is in the middle background.

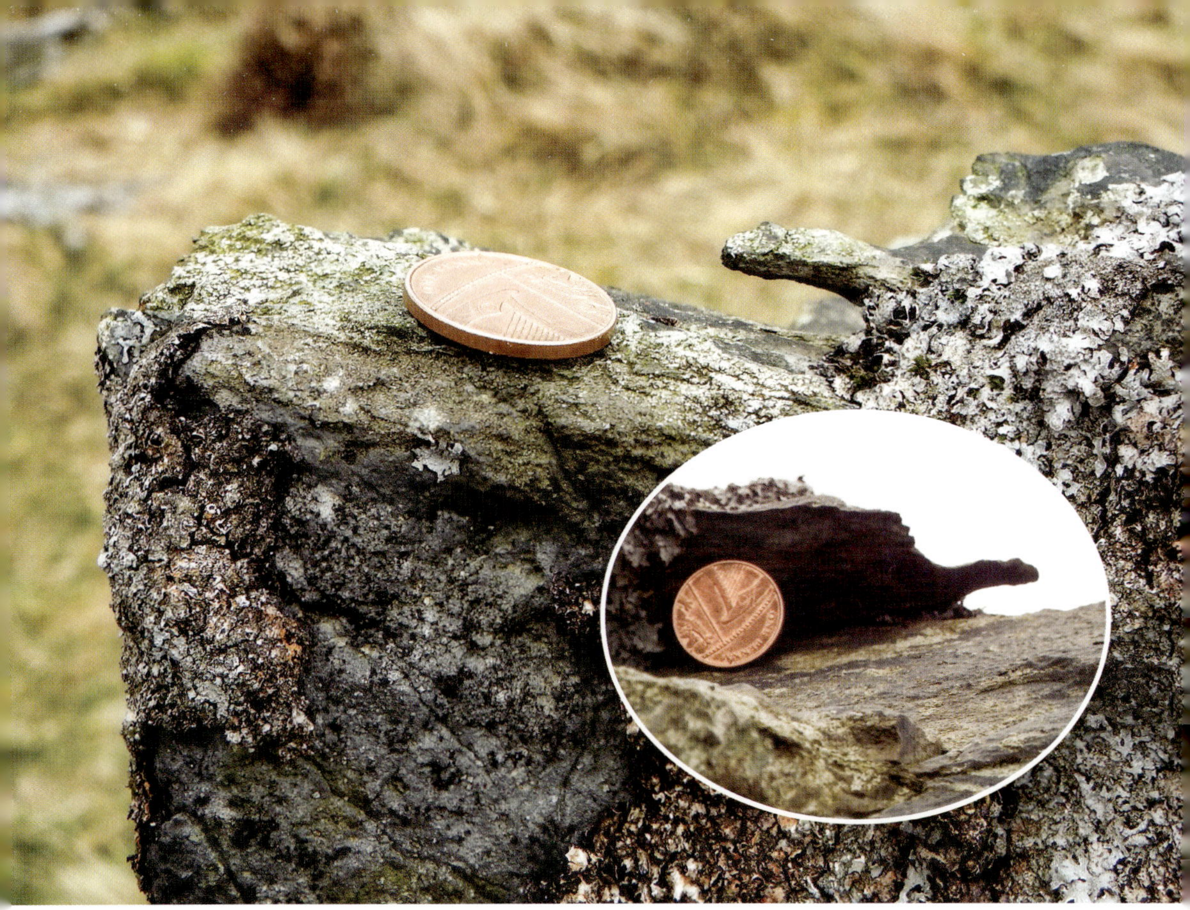

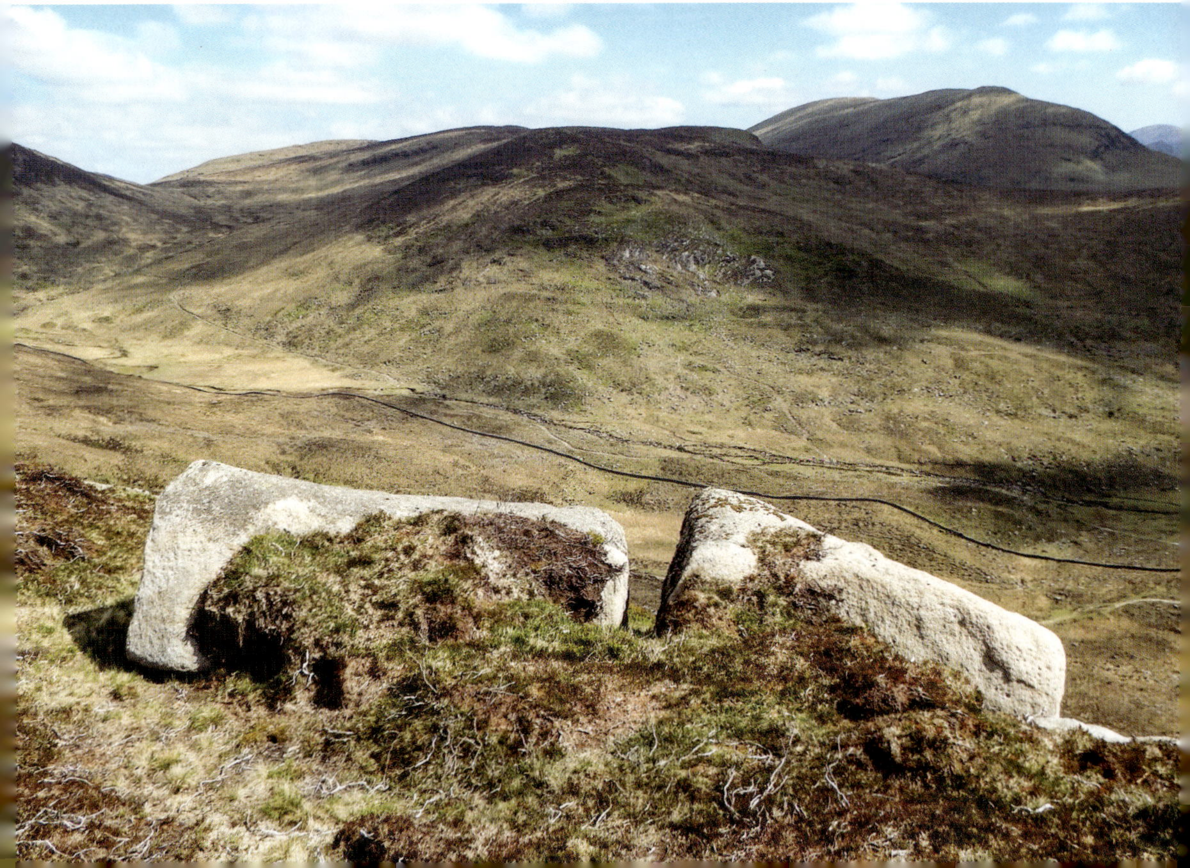

Above: A classic example of vagina stones filled with a phallic insertion. They are found under Slieve Bearnagh slabs, just above the Lecarry Loanin' path and not too far from the stile at the head of Pollaphuca valley. Look sideways at the right-hand stone to see the closed eye and the slightly open 'mouth' at the top, suggestive of a sexual climax. The GPS is:

      N. 54° 11. 369'
      W. 005° 59. 308'   Elevation 454m.

Top opposite: Situated on the east flank of Slieve Bearnagh's north tor this vaginal gap monument certainly enjoys magnificent scenery. The gap, which is no wider than my closed fist, is aligned towards summer solstice and has a penile insert stone jammed in the crack towards the top. The GPS is:

      N. 54° 11. 203'
      W. 005° 58. 778'   Elevation 535m.

Lower opposite: These two large boulders are found under the southern shoulder of Spellack. The left stone is at least three metres long, base to tip. There are six or seven small boulders in the vaginal gap in-between whereas normally there would be a single insert stone. If the monument is a grave for a woman perhaps the smaller boulders are representative of her children? It certainly is a most substantial structure. The GPS is:

      N. 54° 11. 827'
      W. 005° 59. 279'   Elevation 345m.

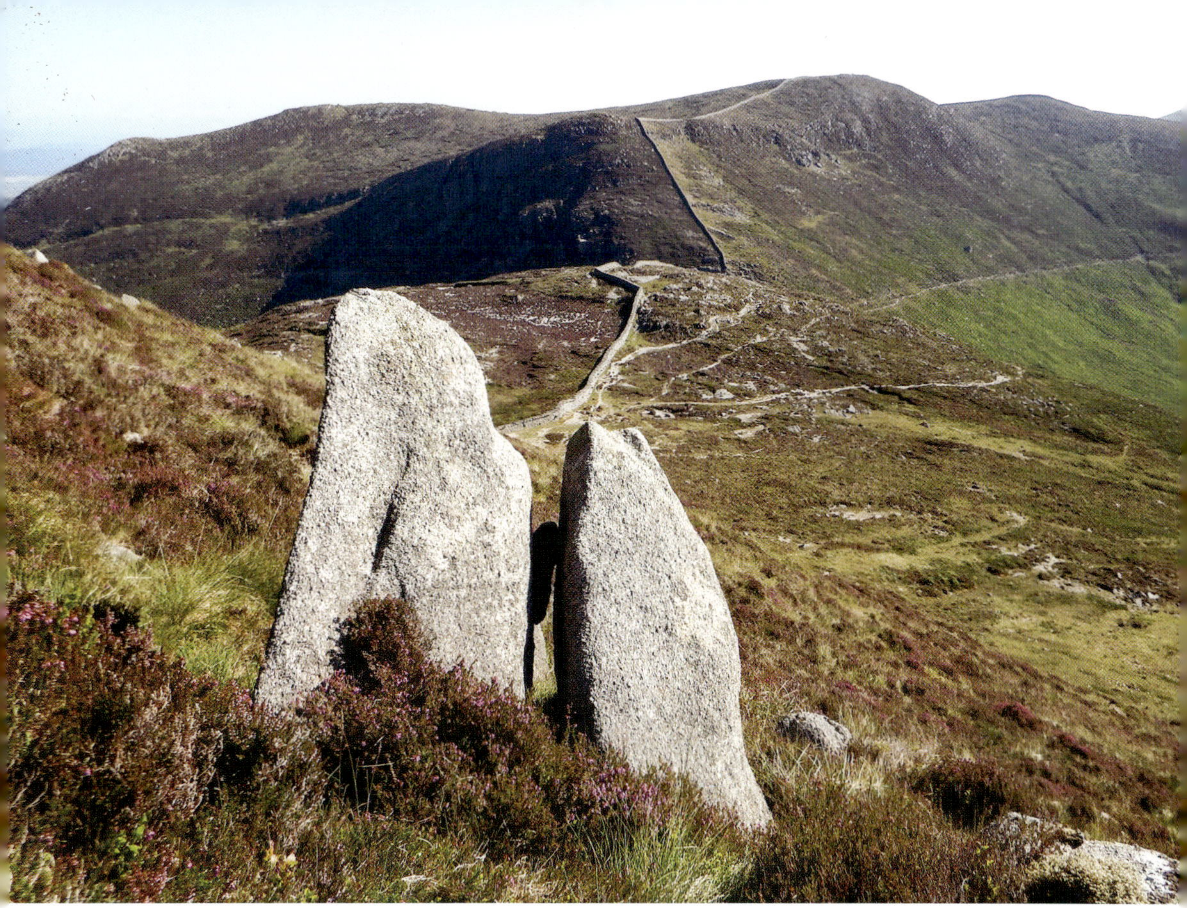

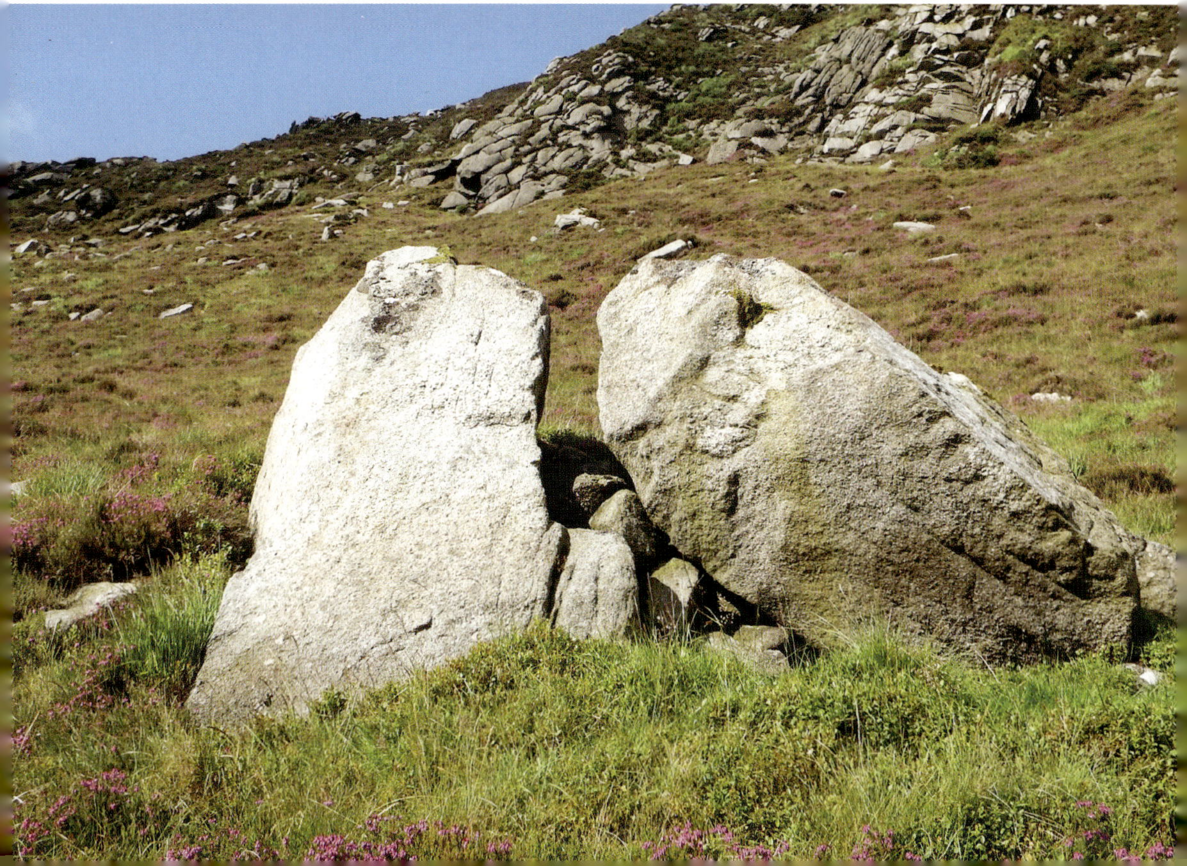

Above: This female monument is only one of many on this south facing slope of Meelmore mountain overlooking the Pollaphuca valley. The gap faces the shoulder of Slieve Bearnagh and the appearance of winter solstice sun. By comparison with the labial sides the little phallic insert seems almost an afterthought. The GPS is:

>   N. 54° 11. 740'
>   W. 005° 59. 472'   Elevation 467m.

Top opposite: On the top north west side of Meelmore two granite slabs; the biggest being 1.4m long, are arranged with a 'V' shaped vaginal gap between them. At the bottom of the gap, which is oriented to summer solstice dawn, is a small boulder to represent the male insertion. The GPS is:

>   N. 54° 11. 638'
>   W. 006° 00. 166'   Elevation 574m.

Lower opposite: Three large granite stones form a 'filled' vagina and stand near the very lip edge of the Pot of Legawherry with commanding views over South Down. The compass shows that the gap between the stones is perfectly aligned to summer solstice sunrise. The GPS is:

>   N. 54° 11. 460'
>   W. 005° 57. 200'   Elevation 632m.

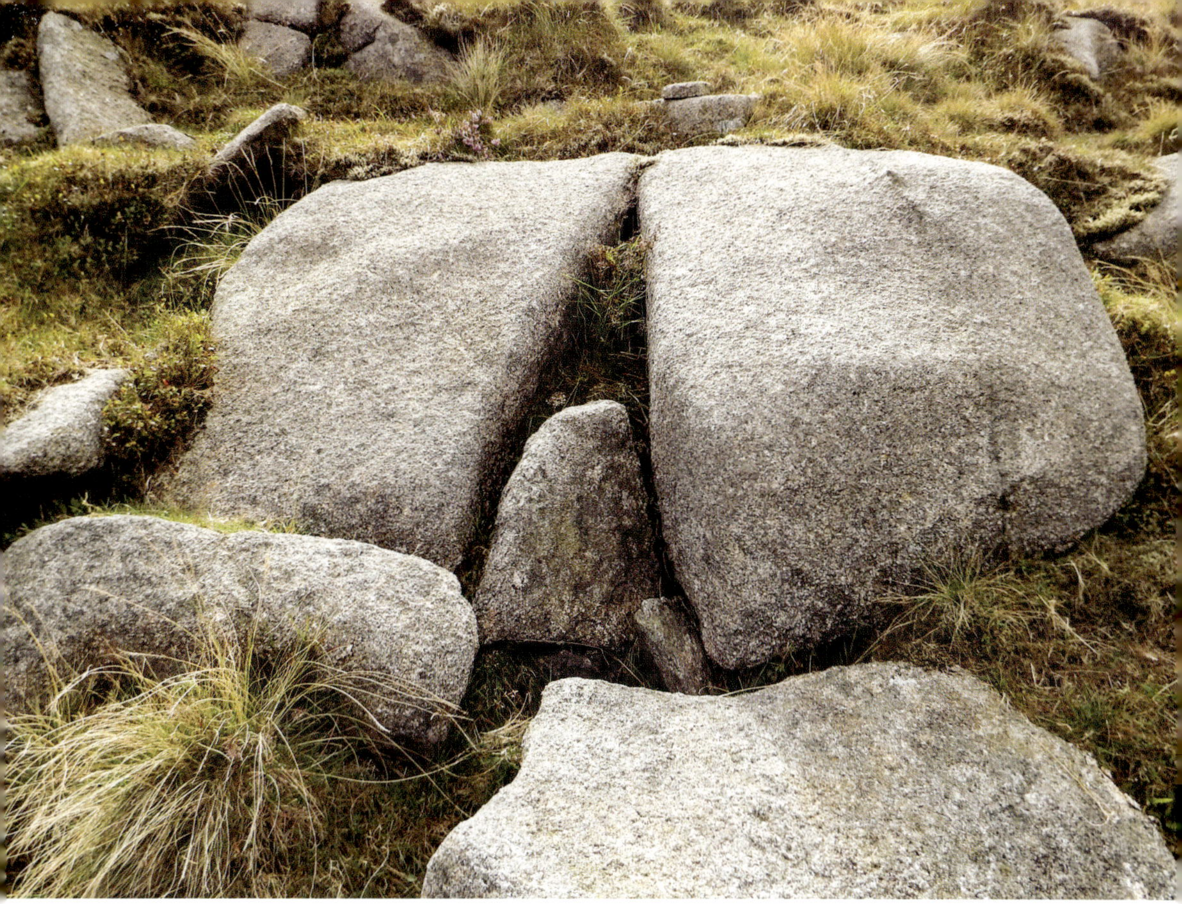

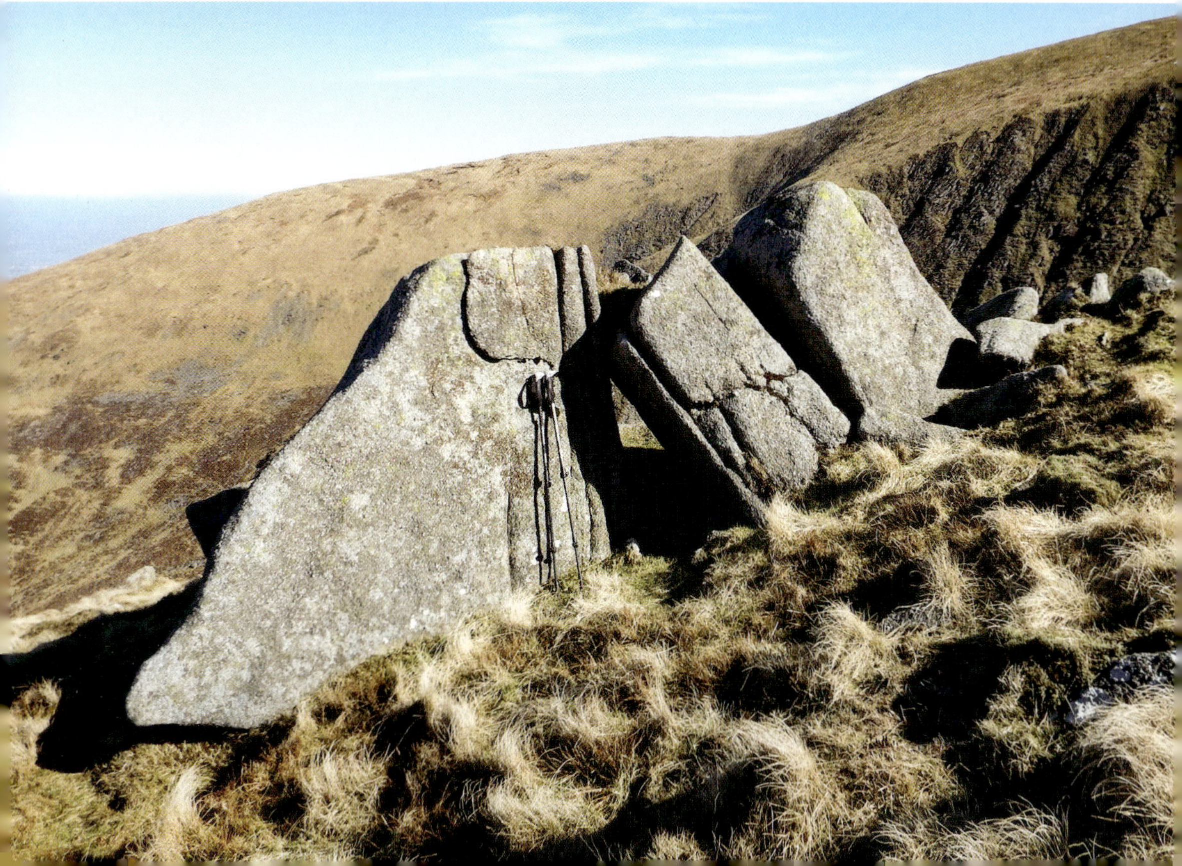

Above: This is a 'filled vagina' with a difference in that it uses shale and granite rocks to symbolise the fertility union of male and female. The formation is to be found on the lower side of the Trassey track just across from a sand quarry. The quarry pit is a good guide as this creation cannot really be seen from the pathway. Two large shale stones represent the female labial sides and between them is a 1.2m wide granite boulder to represent the male insertion. The shale stones have likely been brought here from Green Rigs, the northerly shoulder of Slieve Meelmore. The GPS is:

N. 54° 12. 072'
W. 005° 59. 249'   Elevation 284m.

Top opposite: A particularly deep vaginal construction has been created on the corner of Spellack's southern shoulder by the entrance to Pollaphuca valley. Large granite stones form the labial sides which open towards Shimial mountain and the direction of summer solstice sunrise. The low back recess can be considered a 'womb cavity' as the depths couldn't be reached even with the trekking pole. Note the two vertical lines on the rear stone. This is another variation of the 'penis in the vagina motif'. The GPS is:

N. 54° 11. 705'
W. 005° 59. 202'   Elevation 374m.

Lower opposite: Only about ten metres from the Trassey river on the Meelmore side is this delightful little construction of granite vaginal stones. It features a generous gap to receive the light of summer solstice sunrise and the upright male insertion. The GPS is:

N. 54° 12. 161'
W. 005° 59. 431'   Elevation 246m.

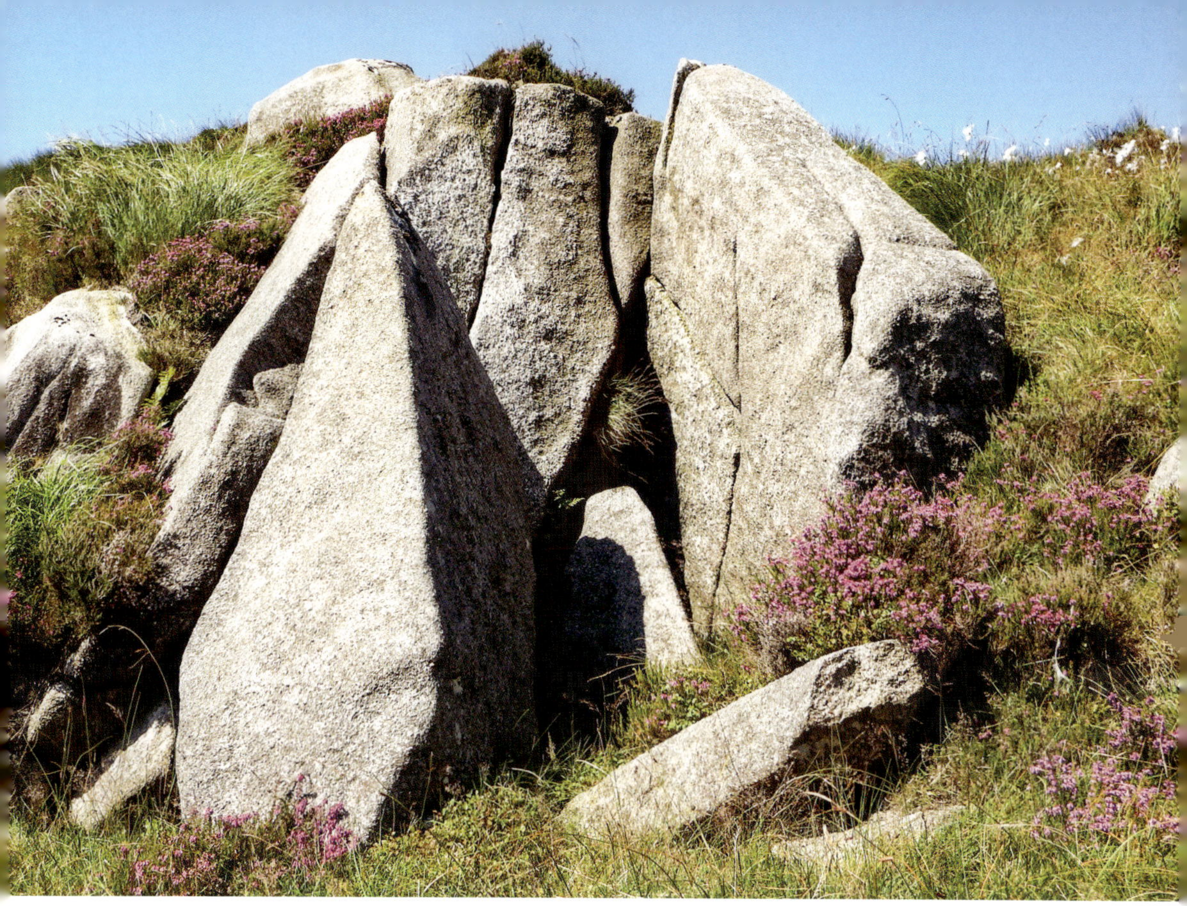

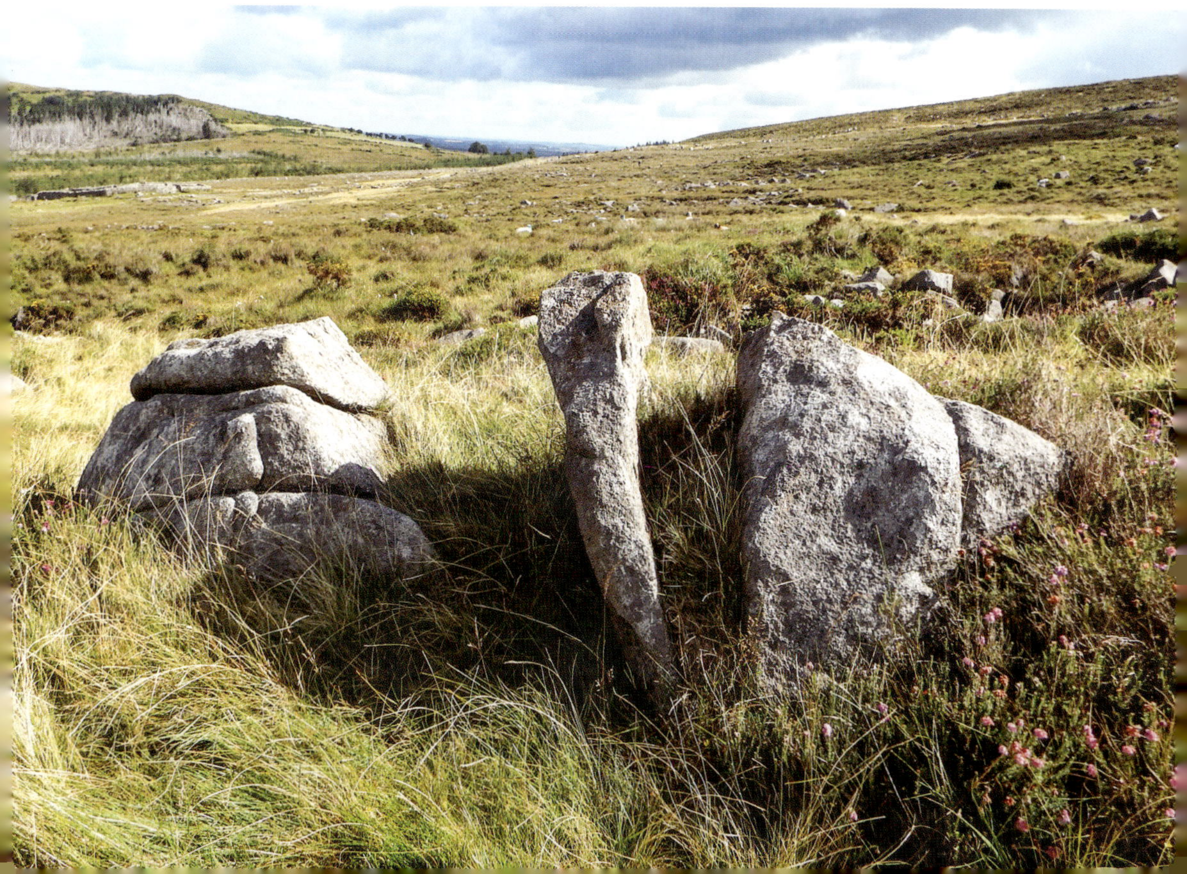

Above: A classic example of the fertility motif of a penis in a vagina. It is to be found below the eastern granite trail on the side of Slievenaglogh overlooking the Trassey. Thin as the penile insert is in the middle, it has a meatus groove on its west side towards the setting solstice sun. The GPS is:

N. 54° 11. 709'
W. 005° 58. 514'   Elevation 442m.

Top opposite: About half-way up the seaward side of Chimney Rock mountain you will see this filled vaginal construction. The opening is aligned to the distant landscape notch between the hills on the Isle of Man where the sun apparently rises at the equinox. The smaller spear stone at the top back, however, has its point firmly to winter solstice sunrise out at sea. The GPS is:

N. 54° 09. 996'
W. 005° 54. 335'   Elevation 515m.

Lower opposite: Climb the granite trail above Newcastle harbour and you emerge above the tree-line just below Lynn's quarry and on the north flank of Millstone mountain. Here above the quarry will be found three great granite stones forming a filled vagina oriented to summer solstice sunrise. The middle stone represents the male insert. Again, the fertility idea is duplicated with a much smaller phallic insert stone between the two on the right. On the left-hand stone note the shadow eye and wide open 'mouth' intent on fellatio. The GPS is:

N. 54° 11. 448'
W. 005° 53. 820'   Elevation 324m:

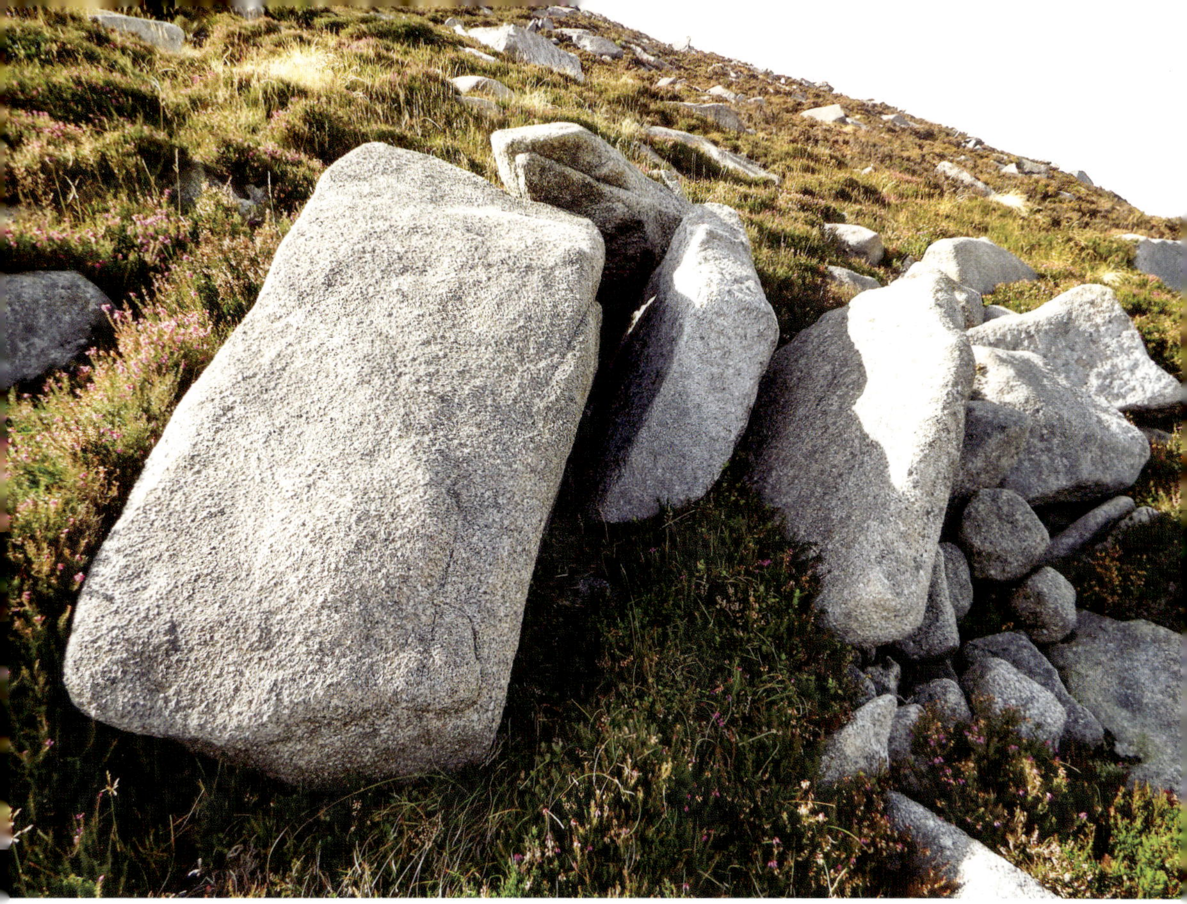

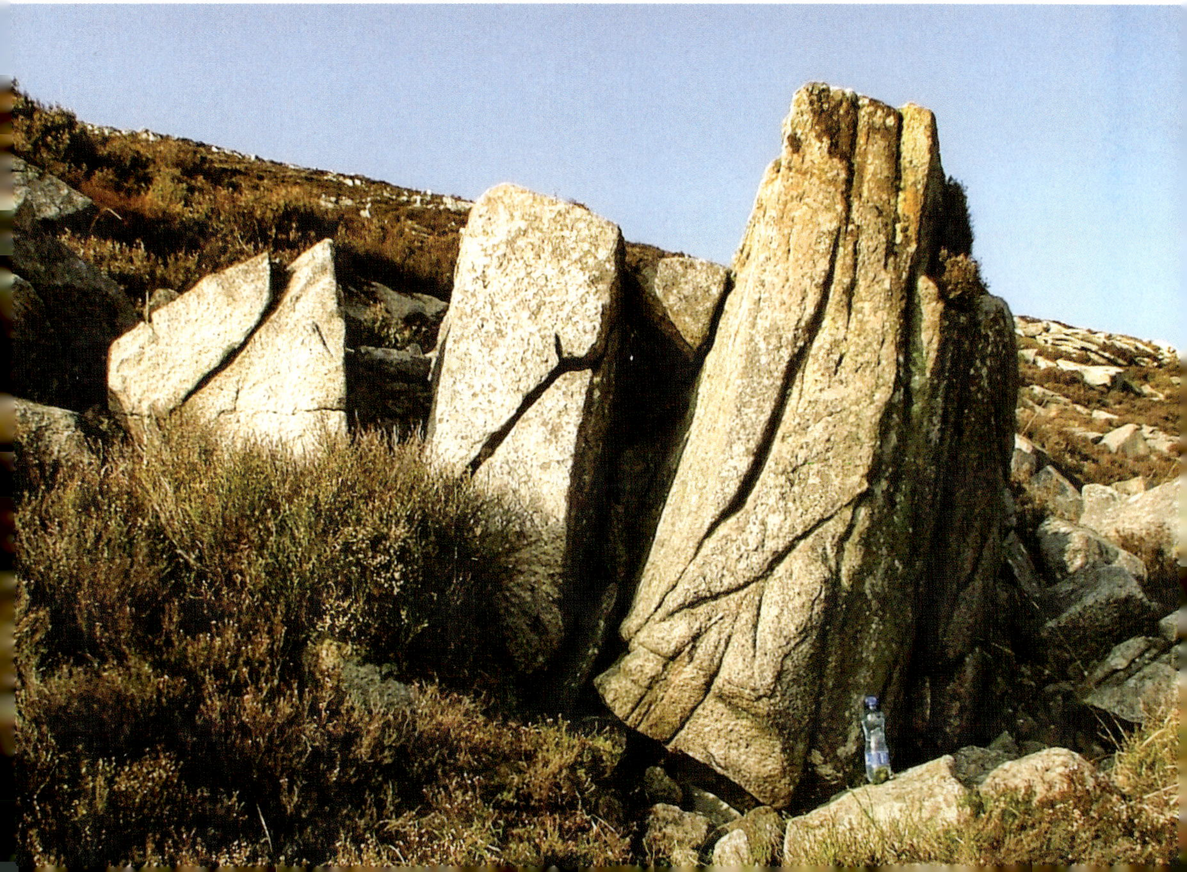

Above: We begin here with a look at a series of really large Female megaliths in Mourne. The first is a truly magnificent creation found under the north tor of Slieve Bignian. It is a fertility site par excellence, a site of prodigious labours and what surely has to be the site of the greatest man-made vagina (arrowed) either in Mourne or elsewhere. The sheer size of the monstrous boulders used as labial sides indicates how important this site was to the ancients. How many tons do these boulders weigh? How far did they have to drag the stones to get them to this location? How many men would have been needed to move the stones on this mountain slope?

Top opposite: This shows the view south to the Back Castles on the spine of Bignian. From this location the phallic profile of the Castles in unmistakable. The raison d'être for the immense efforts undertaken here becomes apparent on winter solstice morning when the sun emerges at the phallic tip. The earth was thus blessed and fertilised again with a great burst of solar insemination as the mountain tip 'came to climax'. This is how the Back Castles got their name. The Irish behind the mnemonic is **Biach Caise Tál**, meaning, 'pouring forth of the penis stream'. **Biach**, means 'erect penis'. In Padraig Dinneen's Irish/English dictionary this was delicately translated into Latin as *'membrum virile'*. **Caise**, means 'a stream, a current, a flood', and **Tál** has the meaning of the 'act of yielding (as milk, juice, sap, etc.), flowing, issuing, pouring forth'. The sunrise spectacle was a magnificent demonstration of fertility.

Lower opposite: A close-up of the enormous boulders used to create the great vaginal gap on Bignian.

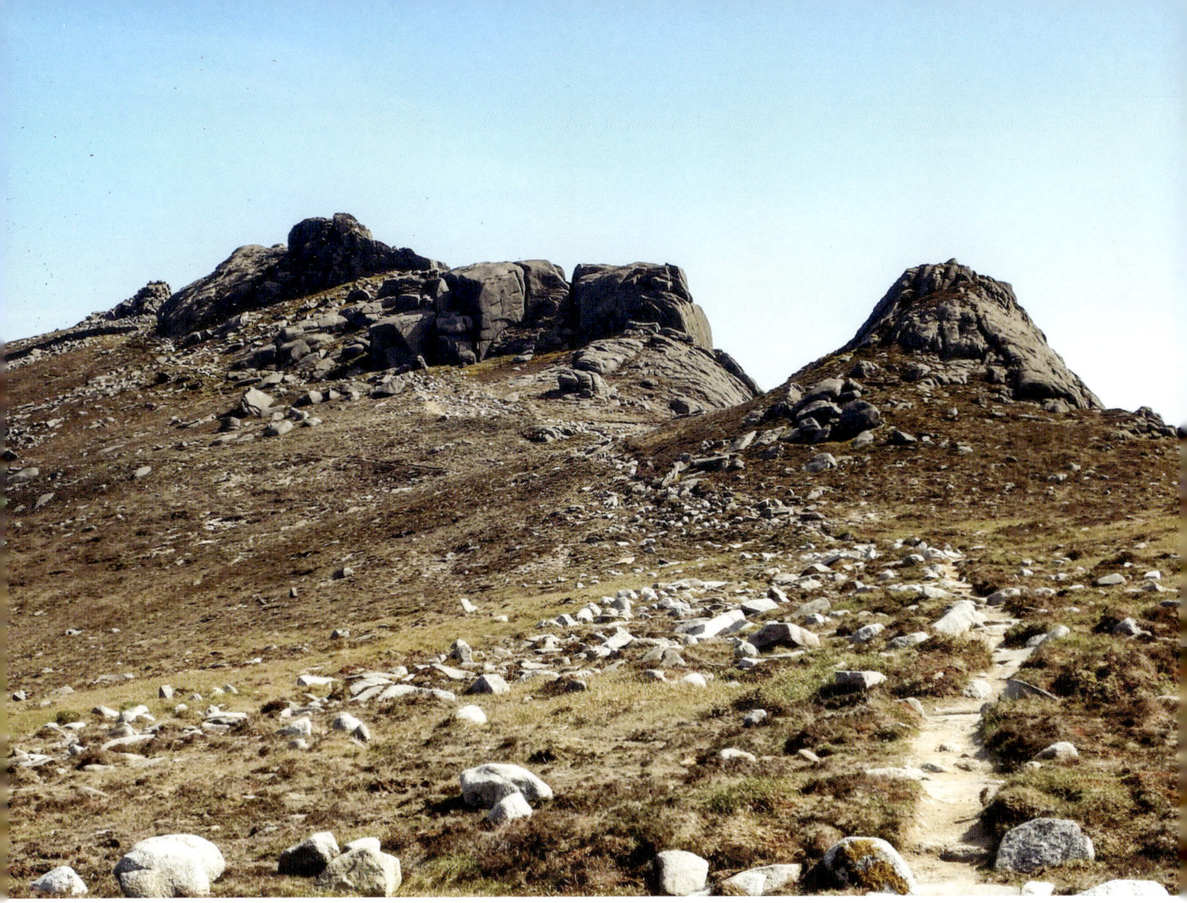

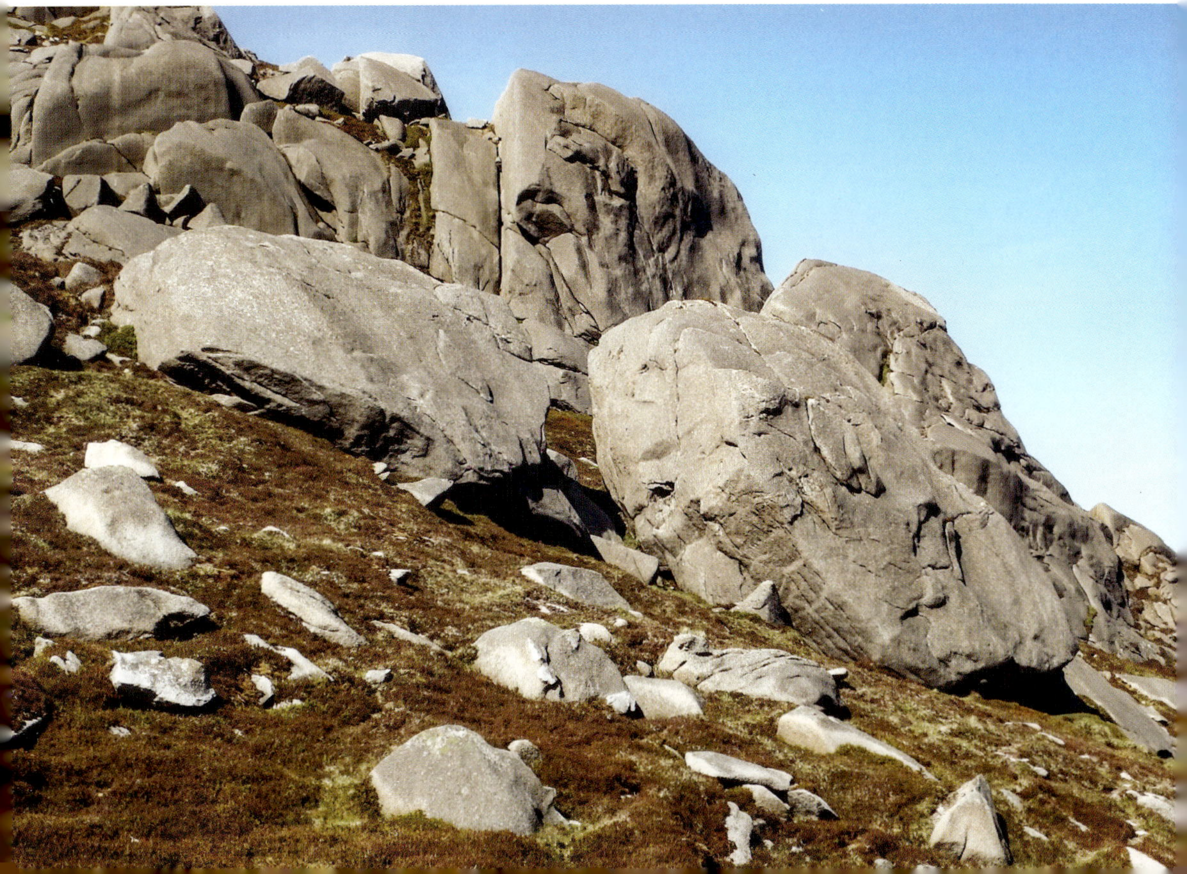

Above: This is the view looking back through the gap towards the Back Castles. The low stone in the foreground is a ***Dúid lia Scáth***, At the other end of the year, at summer solstice sunset, this stone acted as a penile substitute so that its shadow would be cast into the gap. ***Dúid lia Scáth*** means 'Fertility stone shadow'.

Top opposite: One of Bignian's north tors. Note the granite stone chair on the platform to the left of the photograph. This ritual location had a commanding view of the sunrise. A line of stones has been deliberately placed across the gap between the tors. The consequence is to raise the sight of sunrise onto the top of Ben Crom rather than lower down the Ben Crom cliff face. It all added to the drama of the occasion especially as the appearance of the sun in the landscape fertility notch would likely have been the notorious moment for human sacrifice. [see, Miners Hole River from the Irish ***Mian Áir Olc***, 'Evil desire of slaughter', page 44, *Place-names of Beanna Boirrche*, 2021.]

Lower opposite: A fire bowl has been gouged into the top of a nearby boulder. No doubt these bowls would have been filled with fat or fish oil to burn brightly during the vigil chants and incantations preceding the solstice dawn. This is just one of a number of fire bowls in the vicinity.

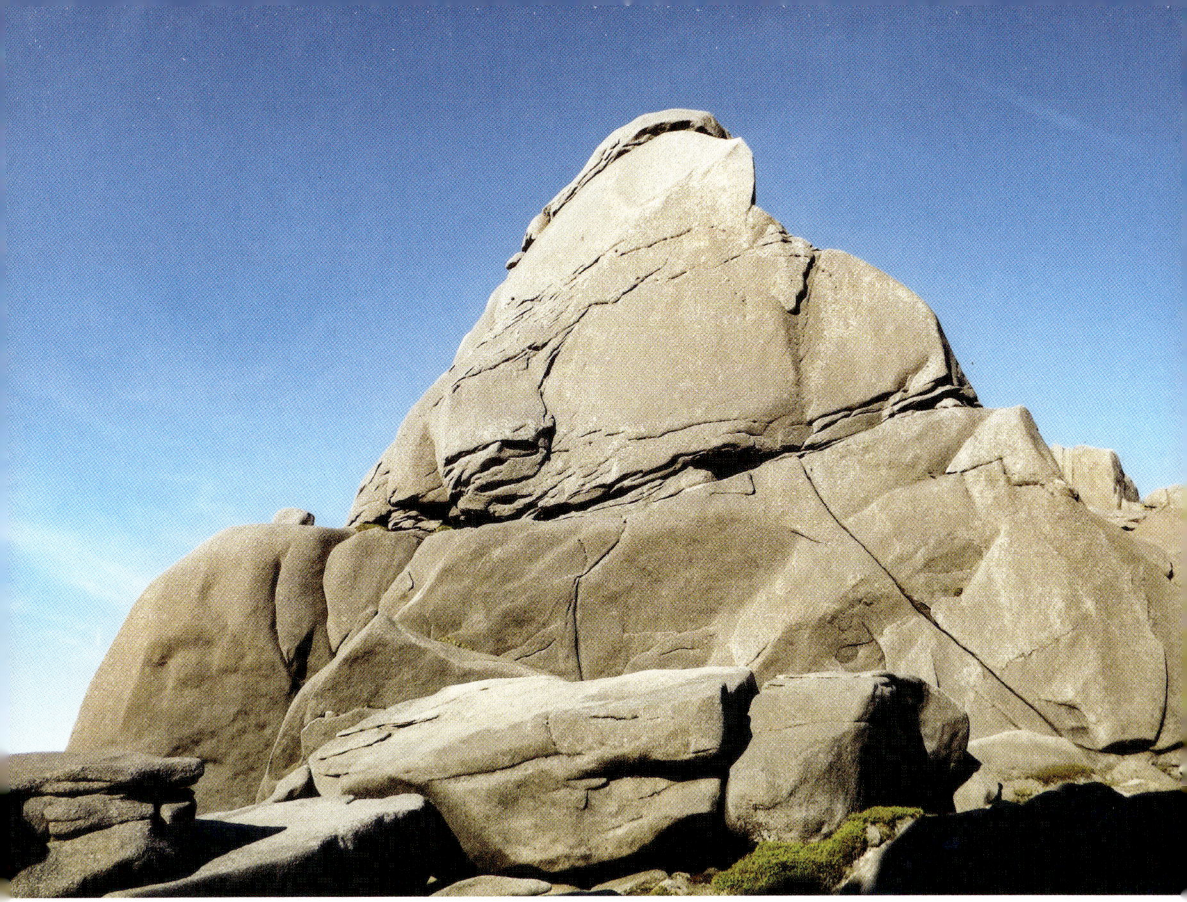

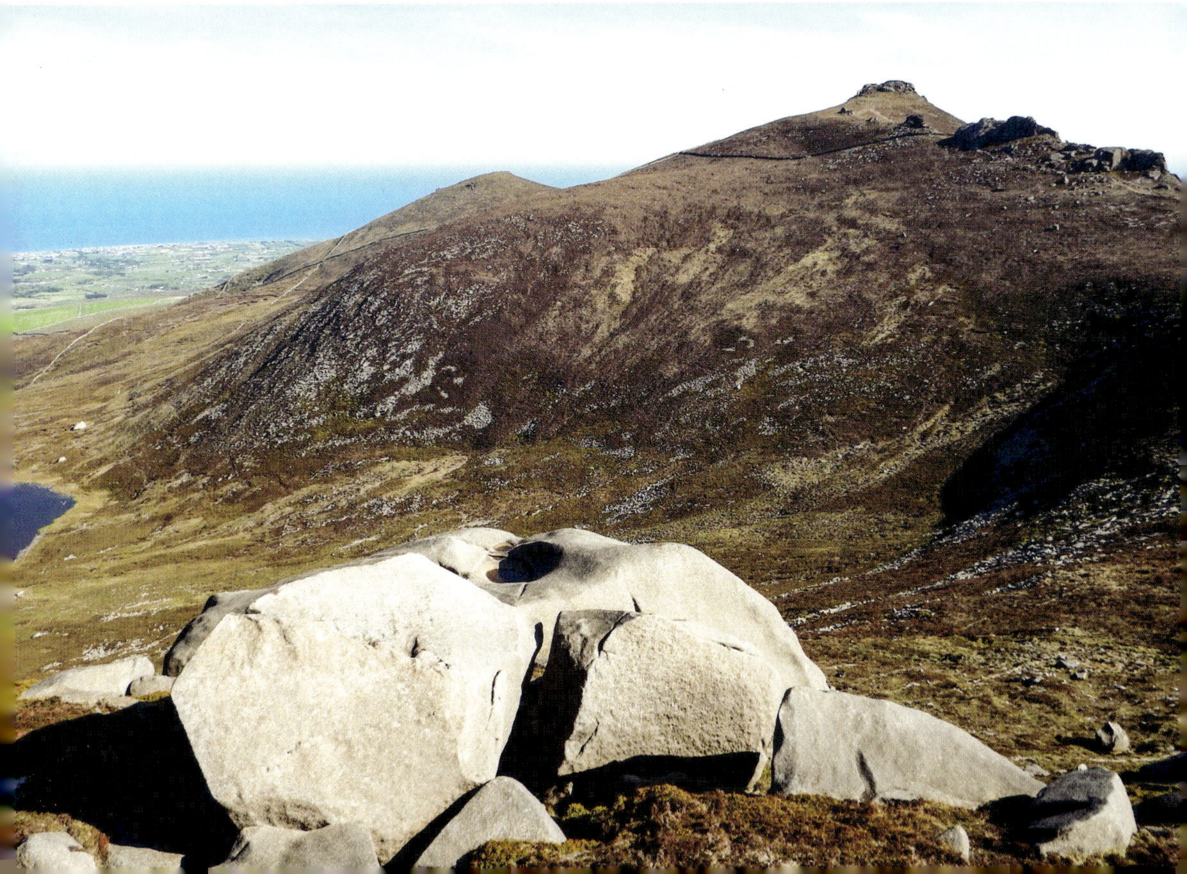

Sunset at winter solstice was deemed to cast a fertilising shadow into the mighty vulva on the east slope of Slieve Bearnagh.

    The monument was discovered at the start of July 2018 while climbing the east flank of Slieve Bearnagh checking large stones as one went along. The parallel line of stones was the first intimation of something special, quickly followed by noticing the shadow eye and mouth of a 'face' on the upper stone that would have made it worthy of a great whale. There was an awe-struck moment of stunned disbelief at the sheer size of the monument. The scale of its construction was a totally different order of magnitude from the usual run of discoveries. The gap between the parallel stones that was to represent the vagina was a staggering four metres wide! That is some opening! The upper labial stone with its gigantic face was a good eight metres long. The drooping eye at its northern end was itself one metre long. One felt small standing beside the monstrous upper stone for, at about two and a half metres in height, it certainly towered above me. At about four metres in height the stone for the lower labial was even higher; it was also an impressive six metres long. This was truly a mighty vulva made with enormous stones!

In the middle of the vaginal gap there was a little upright spear stone placed there as a penile insert. By comparison with the labial sides it was only a perfunctory token, almost an empty symbol, a joke. This was a construction built to honour the Female. I used the upright stone as a seat while taking the GPS measurements. The monument is to be found on Bearnagh at:

$$N.\ 54°\ 11.\ 065'$$
$$W.\ 005°\ 59.\ 192' \quad \text{Elevation 631m.}$$

The reason for the monument's placement and phenomenal efforts behind its construction lie with the surrounding landscape at solstice.

This particular location features at least three special fertility events. To the east can be seen the tip of Rocky mountain appearing, phallic-like, between Cove and Lamagan. It is arrowed on the photograph on the next page. This is the important 'penis in the vagina' motif beloved by the ancients and already referenced in this work on a number of earlier pages. Significant as this motif was to the sun worshipping ancients, it must have instilled astonishment when the landscape projection of Rocky mountain, the notional penis, 'came to climax' on the most auspicious of mornings. At dawn of winter solstice the sun rises from the top of Rocky mountain. This was the ultimate of fertility spectacles. The way the ancients saw it, the sun was again bestowing its fecundity and abundance on the earth.

At the seaward side of the monument, note the level platform specially made with built up layers of turf under the sheltering bulk of the megalith. It is prudent to be cautious before shouting, 'Ritual Platform', but in this instance the events of solstice dawn would merit it gold status.

The second reason behind the placement of Bearnagh's mighty vagina becomes apparent as the sun declines to disappear behind Slieve Bearnagh at the end of winter solstice day. The great female opening of the stones is aligned to receive the fullness of the sun before it recedes behind the rock outcrop at the top of the hill.

The third reason for the stupendous efforts undertaken at this location lie with the landscape at summer solstice. On that morning the sun rises from the landscape notch formed between the descending slopes of Bearnagh and Shan Slieve. A second, much smaller, vaginal gap has been prepared to receive the sun's early light from this different direction. The level ritual platform, already referred to, was also wide-open to this summer sunrise. The massive megalith is a gift that keeps giving. Note the artwork on the inside of the lower labial. A 'face' with a shadow eye is preparing to suckle from a nipple. It only echoes the tip of Rocky mountain in the distance behind it. This is a magnificent monument in scale and conception. It is a glorious achievement for the ancients and a superlative treasure of Megalithic Mourne.

Above: The view eastwards shows the tip of Rocky mountain (arrowed) as the 'penis in the landscape vagina'. A compass check shows that at winter solstice dawn the sun rises from the tip of Rocky mountain as if the mountain was coming to climax. This spectacle bestowed fertility on the earth.

Top opposite: The carefully levelled ritual platform at the front of the megalith was open to dawn of winter and summer solstice. A similar turf made platform is to be found in front of the important Slievenagarragh megalith on Chimney Rock mountain, the huge stone that sticks up on the skyline and dominates the upper reaches of the Bloody Bridge valley [This was illustrated on pages 350–351 of *Place-names of Beanna Boirrche* and has appeared in this work on page 219.]

Lower opposite: The view through the four metre wide vaginal gap shows the tiny phallic spear stone sticking up in the middle. The real 'insertion' was the final full illumination of the winter solstice sun before it declined behind the rock outcrop in the background.

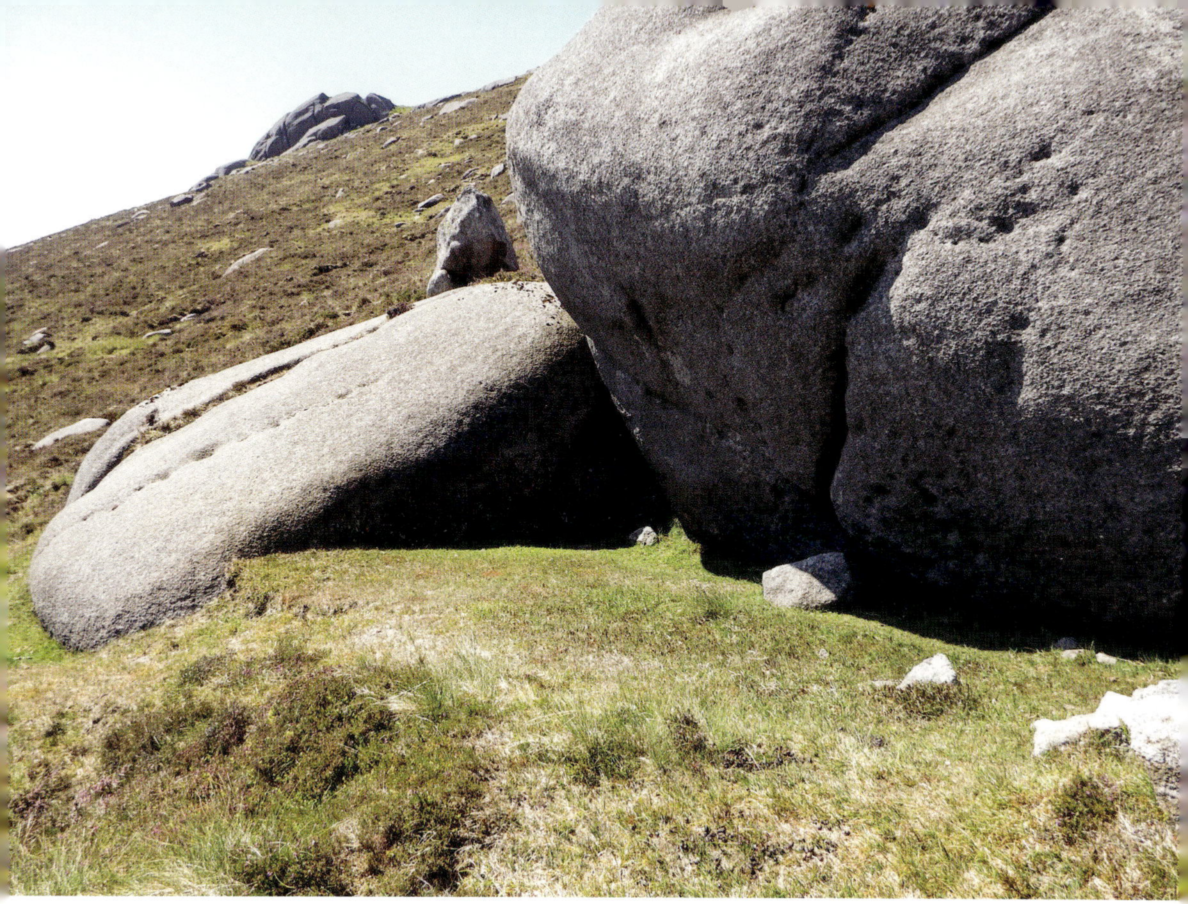

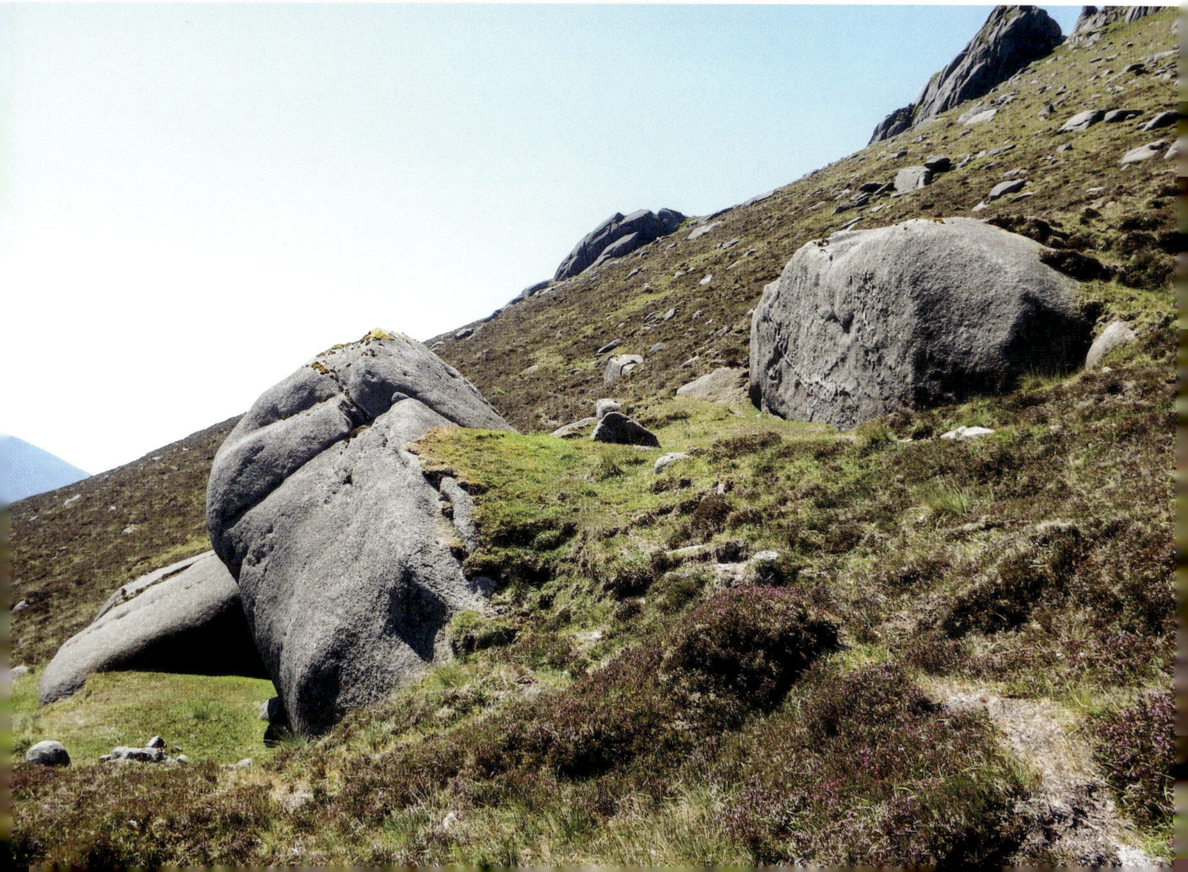

Above: The great face on the upper labial is a wonder indeed. The 'sleeping' eye on the right is deceptive in its genius; the design means it can double as an eye to either end of the megalith. The back of the stone is buried in the hillside but enough shows to confirm this stone is a real giant many metres wide. It is certainly much bigger than the vertical sarsen standing stones at Stonehenge which are each around 4 metres high, 2.1 metres wide and weigh around 25 tons. And don't forget that, unlike Stonehenge, these great stones on Bearnagh were manoeuvred on a challenging steep slope!

Top opposite: With a deep little shadow eye and a faint line for a mouth, a 'face' on the right of the photograph is ready to suckle from a nipple. This artwork only enhances the Female credentials of this huge vulva and echoes the landscape tip of Rocky mountain in the distance behind it.

Lower opposite: A second vaginal gap in stone has been prepared to receive the fertility light of summer solstice dawn as the sun emerges from the distant landscape vaginal gap, arrowed. The multiple interactions with the sun at the solstices made this location a unique and specially favoured place of fecundity. This is reflected in the monstrous size of the stones used and the attendant awesome labours that would have been needed to source and align them.

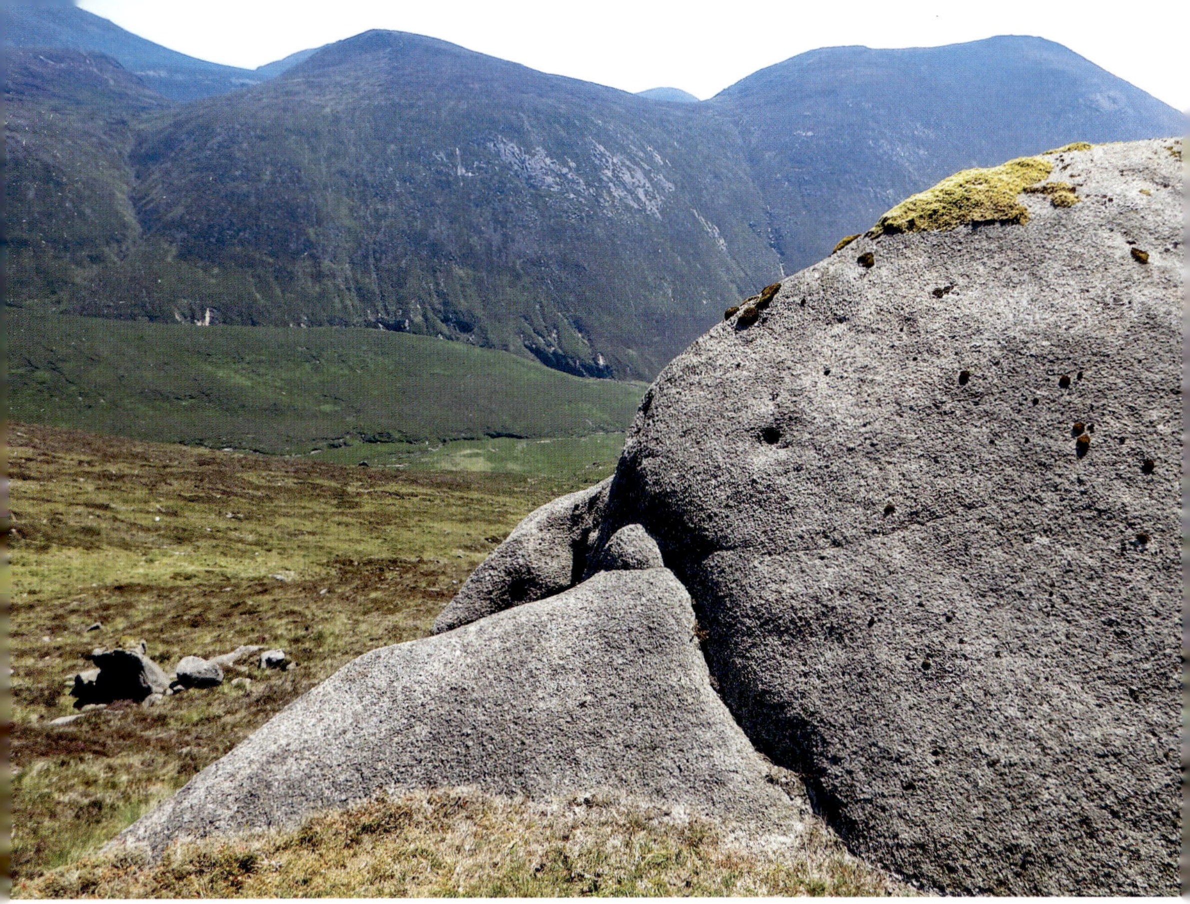
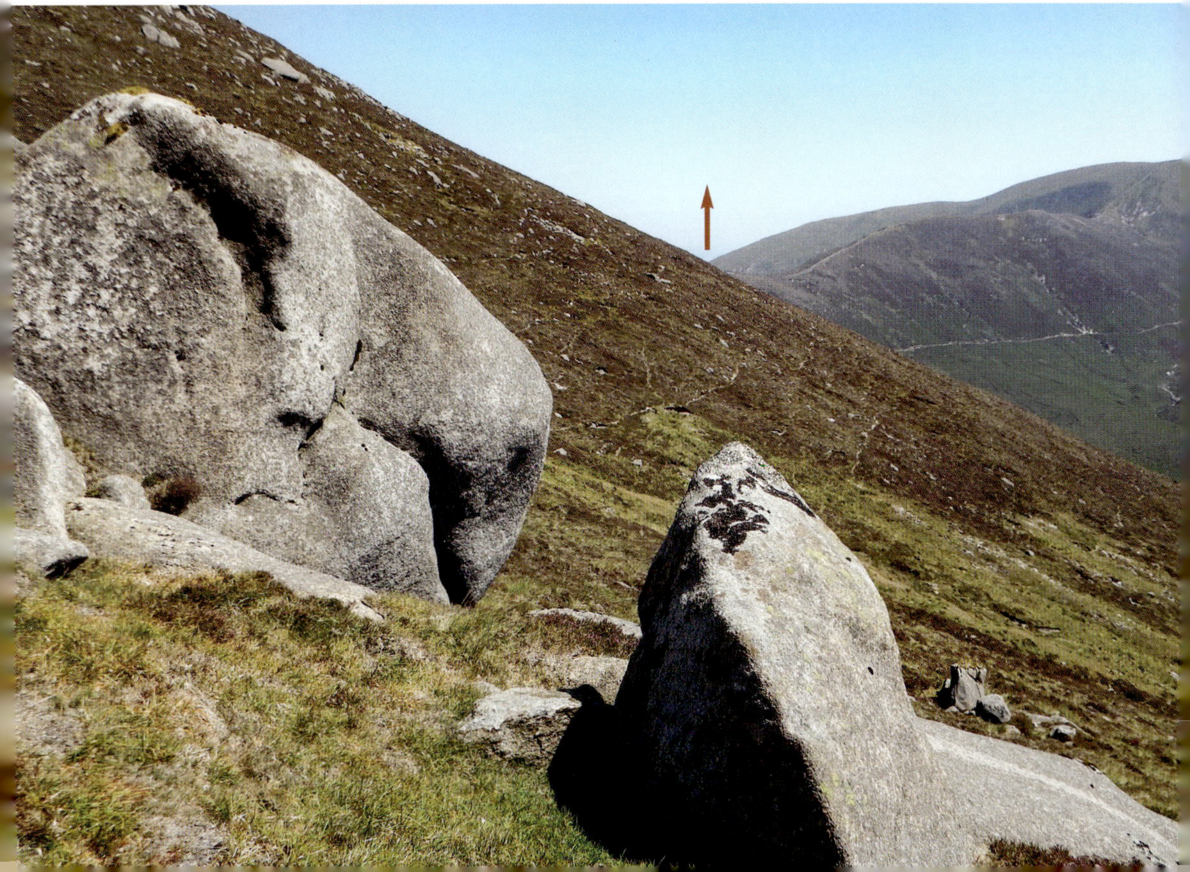

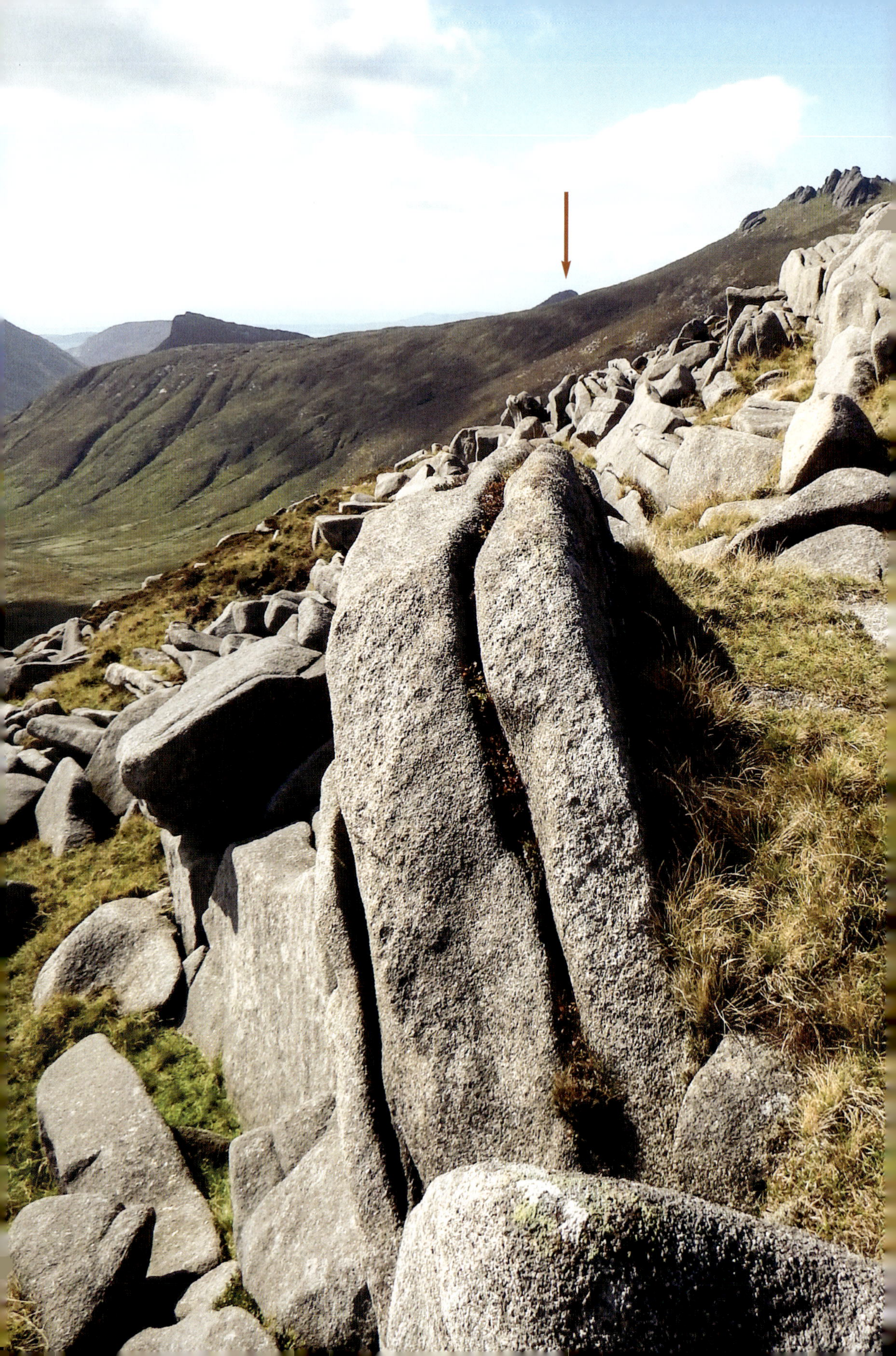

Our look at particularly large female themed megaliths continues with this colossal stone on the east side of Slieve Corragh. It is Lord and Master over any other stone nearby. At 5 metres long, by 2.5m high and nearly 1m wide at the top, this is certainly a giant of a megalith. The reason for the deployment of such an enormous boulder at this location lies with the fertility interpretation of the landscape.

   In the large photograph opposite, it can be seen that the megalith is oriented towards the tip of Doan (arrowed) which peeps up, phallic like, over the shoulder of Slieve Bearnagh. A compass reading shows this is the likely setting place of the winter solstice sun. With the solstice sun touching the perceived phallic tip of Doan, the mountain would notionally 'come to climax' making this spot one of very special fertility and justifying the astonishing physical efforts behind bringing such an impressive stone here and aligning it to the sunset. The stone was given the name **Sanntughadh Doan**, 'Desiring Doan'.

   The megalith is rather androgynous as the slits at either end can represent the male meatus groove or the female opening. One end of the stone is open to dawn of summer solstice and the other, as mentioned, to winter solstice sunset. But there is more. There is another fertility feature to be noted at this location. This special spot marks the appearance of the tip of Rocky mountain, also phallic-like, between Slieve Beg and Cove mountain; (Rocky mountain is shown in the oval).

   The top of the megalith is also worthy of attention as the two grooves along the upper surface separate that plane into three sections forming the beloved symbolic motif of a penis between two labial sides. The GPS is:

N. 54° 11. 609'
W. 005° 57. 923'   Elevation 578m.

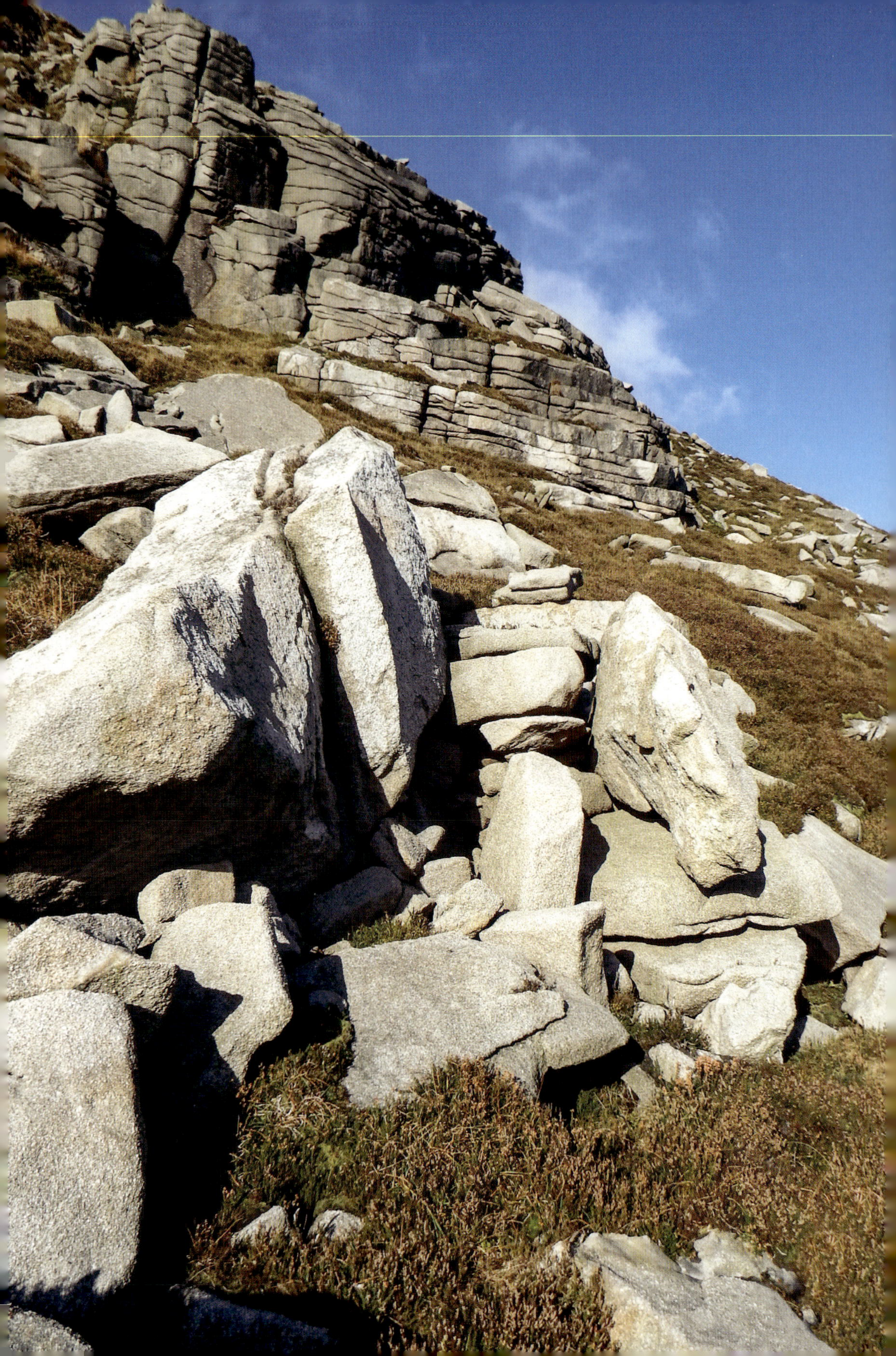

There is something quite fitting about the mountain known as a 'considerable lump of a woman', in Irish **Lab a Geine**, and in English, Lamagan, hosting this most impressive vaginal gap creation on its slope above Lower Cove. Start with the small upright slab just below and right of centre. Compared with the rest of the monument this slab representing the male insertion is exceedingly modest. Indeed, the scale of the stone only emphasises the overall importance and dominance of the Female. The gap between the labial sides is nearly two metres across. The stone of the upper labial side is a gigantic seven to eight metres in length and a step break in the middle gives the impression of a kiss taking place. The higher part of this stone, shown in the photograph above, has a great 'face'. The bottom left corner of this picture shows just enough of a pig's snout to evoke the Otherworld tale in *Togail Bruidne Dá Derga* (The Destruction of Da Derga's Hostel) where the lord of the feast was sometimes represented as a man carrying a pig on his shoulder. The alignment looks south at circa 170°, presumably to a headland down the coast that was too hazy to discern. Such seaward projections of the land in the ancient past were often regarded as phallic. The GPS is:

N.   54° 09. 994'
W. 005° 57. 510'   Elevation 496m.

One of the most important ritual platforms in Mourne is mentioned here as it has so many connections to the Female. It is found on the southern flank of Slieve Donard. The location enjoyed the name of 'Bishop's Seat' and for a while it was attributed to the ruined chapel of St Mary's, Ballaghanery. However, this name is only a mnemonic of the Irish (*Bealach na*) **bPis Óibhéala Seata**, meaning '(Pass of) the wide open vulva of the harlot'. A name that would have mortified any bishop. The picture shows a great male insertion, complete with meatus groove, in the middle of the 'harlot's vulva'. This is the background to the ritual platform below.

Our second photograph shows the 1.5m long granite chair placed at the edge of the platform. The centre of gravity of this great boulder has been placed with such exacting care that the stone jerks up and down when you sit on the western most end. The phallic knob at the other end, measuring 90cm high, then jolts up in simulation of sexual movement.

The third picture is a view WNW from the platform. It is the important fertility sightline through the indent of the Devil's Coachroad [*Diabhail Cos Róide*, 'Devil's stem of force', ie. a penis] and on towards the landscape vaginal notch between the tors of Slieve Bearnagh. This is the line Professor O'Kelly noted on the famous kerbstone of K1 at Newgrange. As explained in Prehistoric Mourne, K1 is a stylised map of Mourne. The GPS for **bPis Óibhéala Seata** is:

        N.   54° 10. 510'
        W. 005° 55. 393'   Elevation 668m.

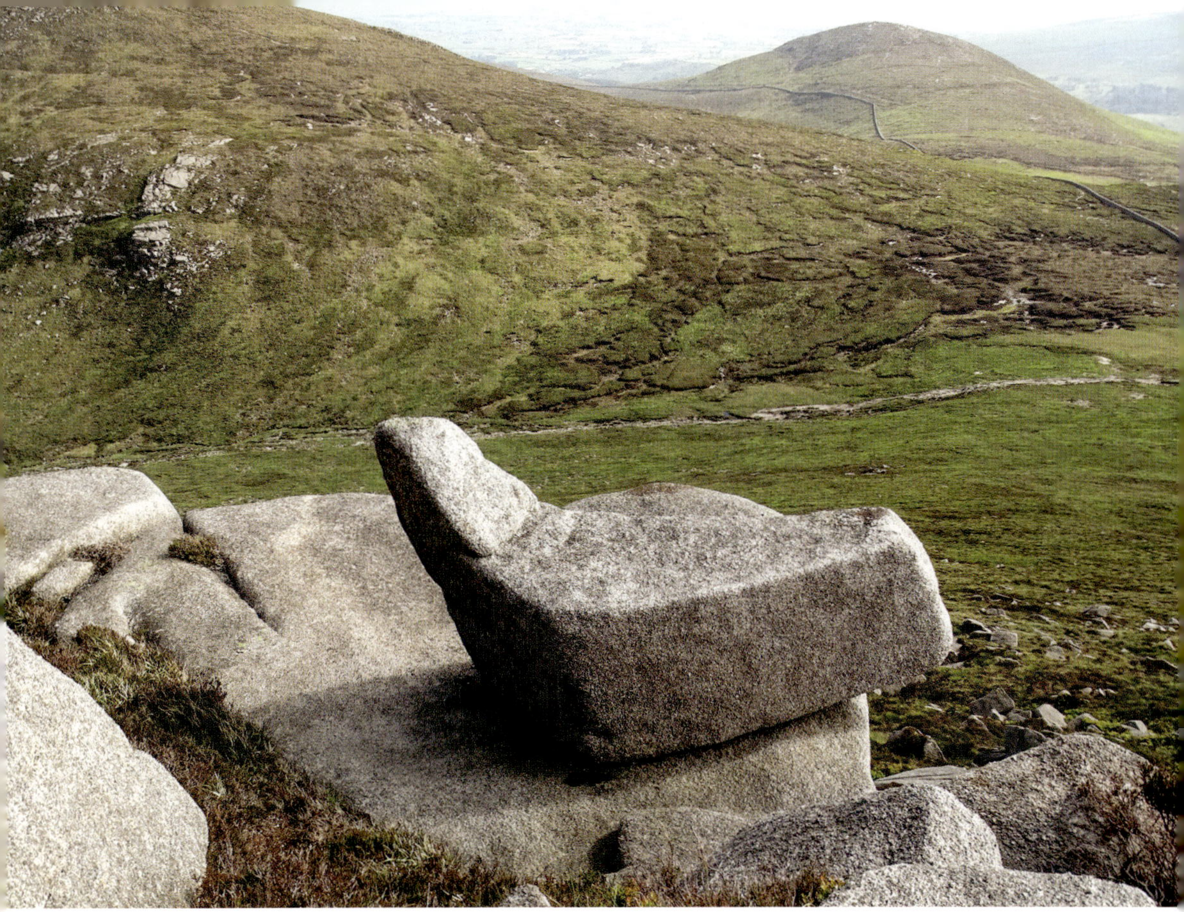

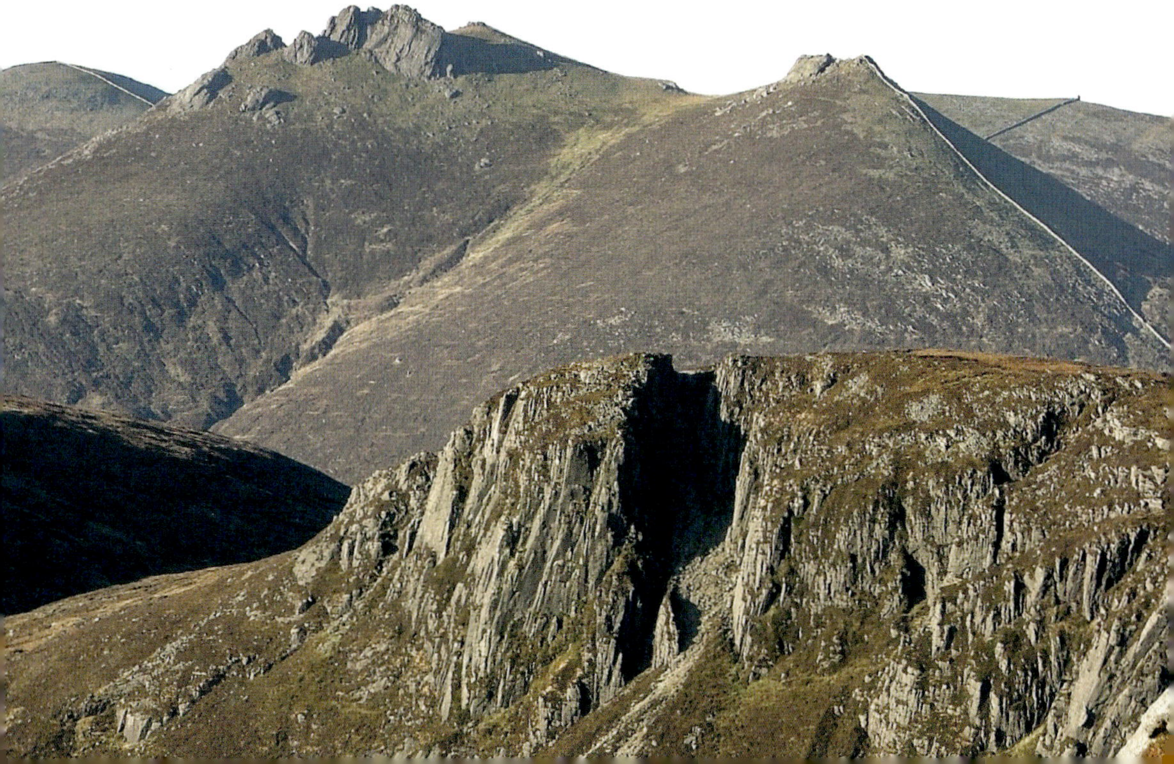

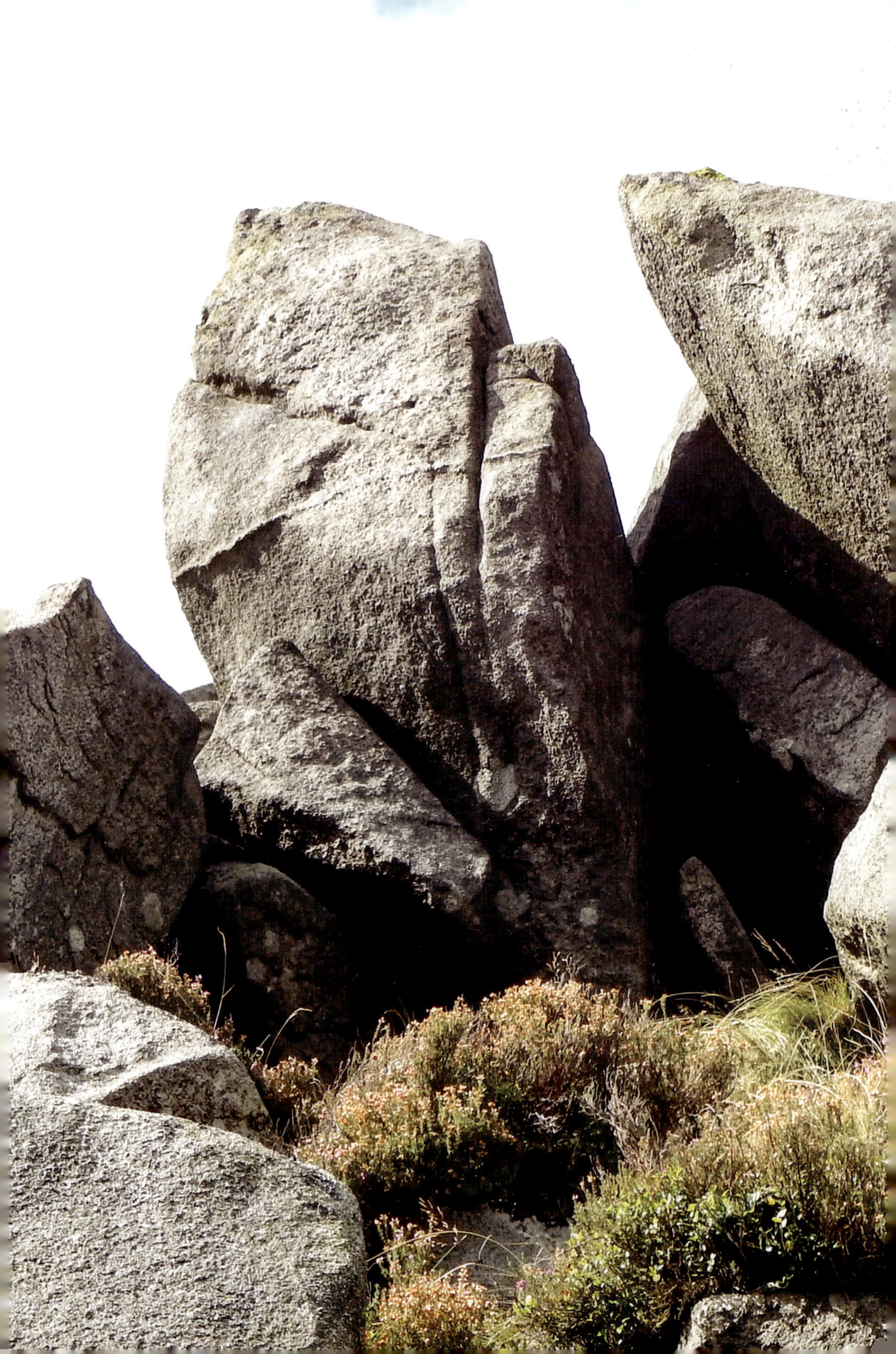

Continuing our illustrations of exceedingly large female megaliths, this immense construction on the south-east flank of Slieve Bearnagh displays the all-important vaginal gap. The opening alignment is, as expected, to the light of winter solstice dawn. The bottom of the gap has a long slab that is both a support for the labial spear above and also a penile insertion. Climbing round the monument one got the impression of a feeding frenzy of sharks. The left-hand stone certainly looks ready to take a bite. The GPS is:

N. 54º 11. 129'
W. 005º 58. 638'   Elevation 446m.

There is definitely no GPS with the vaginal gap construction shown on these photographs. There have been too many unfortunate accidents on this side of Bearnagh. It is not a safe slope to venture onto. The photos were taken from adjacent Slieve Meelmore.

This is surely one of those 'how did they do it' monuments. You are looking at two great boulders on the exceedingly steep north flank of Slieve Bearnagh. The stones have been arranged so that the vaginal opening between them is presented to the early sun of summer solstice sunlight.

As shown in many other instances, the ancients seemed to revel in placing monuments in particularly dangerous and difficult locations like cliff-tops and steep slopes. The greater the difficulty involved the greater the sense of achievement and consequent glory on completion. The stones cannot tell us of the cost in human lives but many accidents surely happened on this treacherous slope. Perhaps a slip, a bit of wet grass, a breaking rope, a wobbly stone underfoot, exhaustion in moving a great weight, a moment's inattention; it doesn't take much for things to suddenly go wrong. The workers striving to place the boulders would not have known of momentum formula, such as momentum = mass x velocity, but they triumphed none-the-less. These are not the only monuments on Bearnagh's northern flank but these stones, in their open location, are perhaps the easiest found.

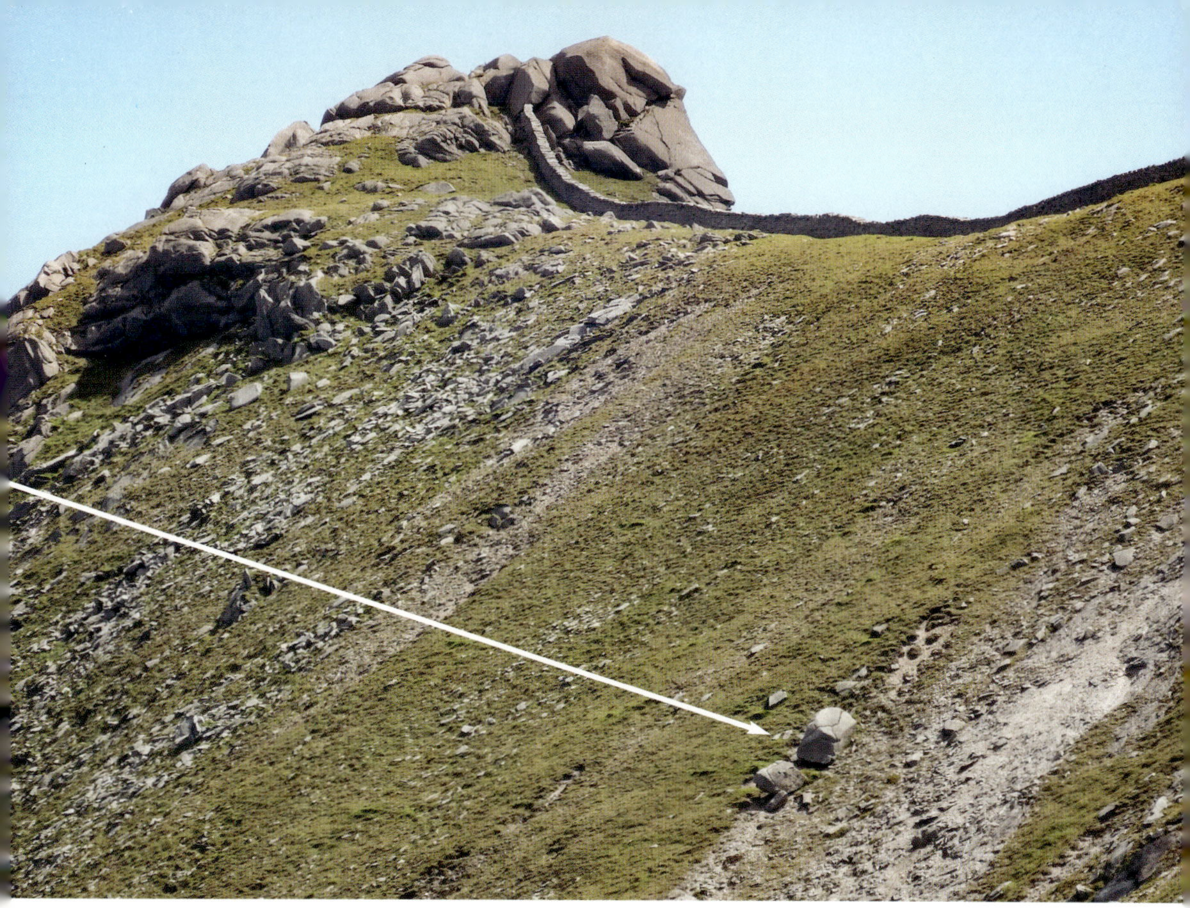

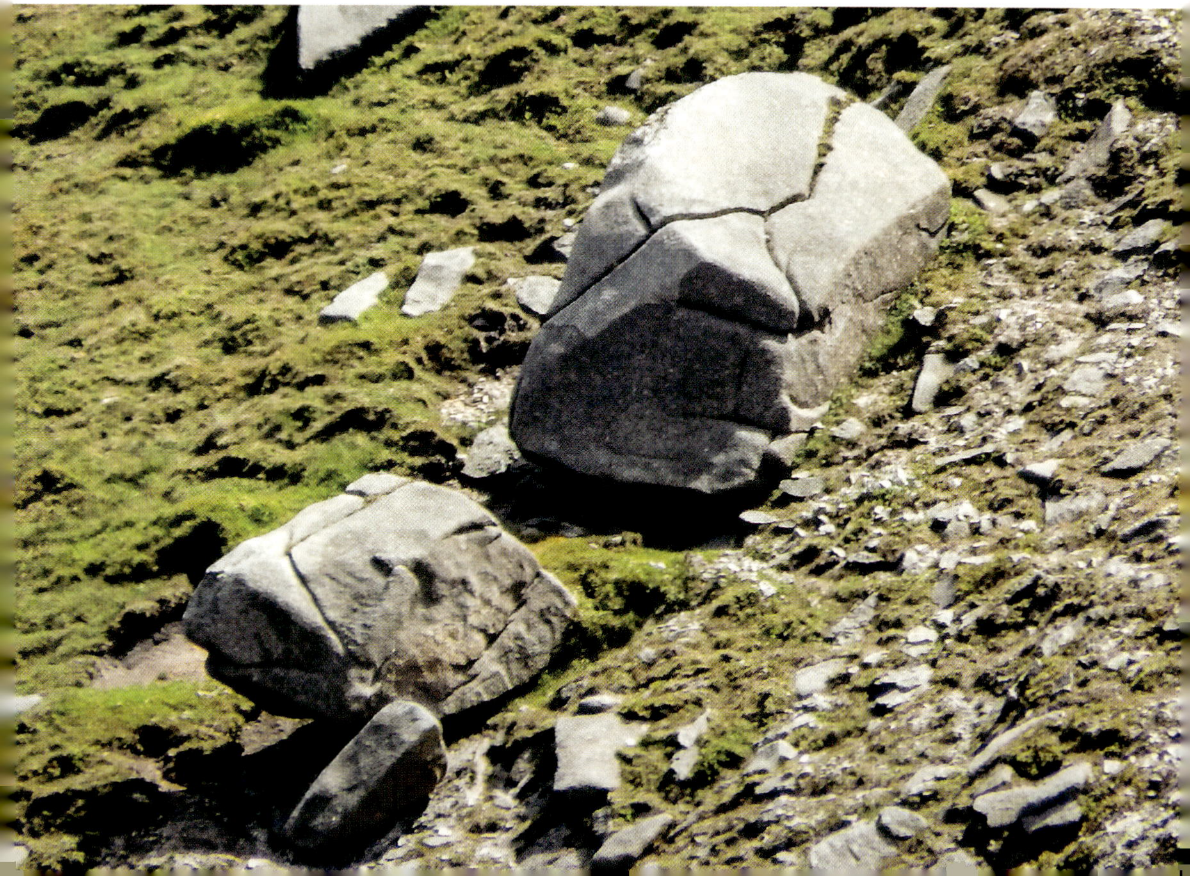

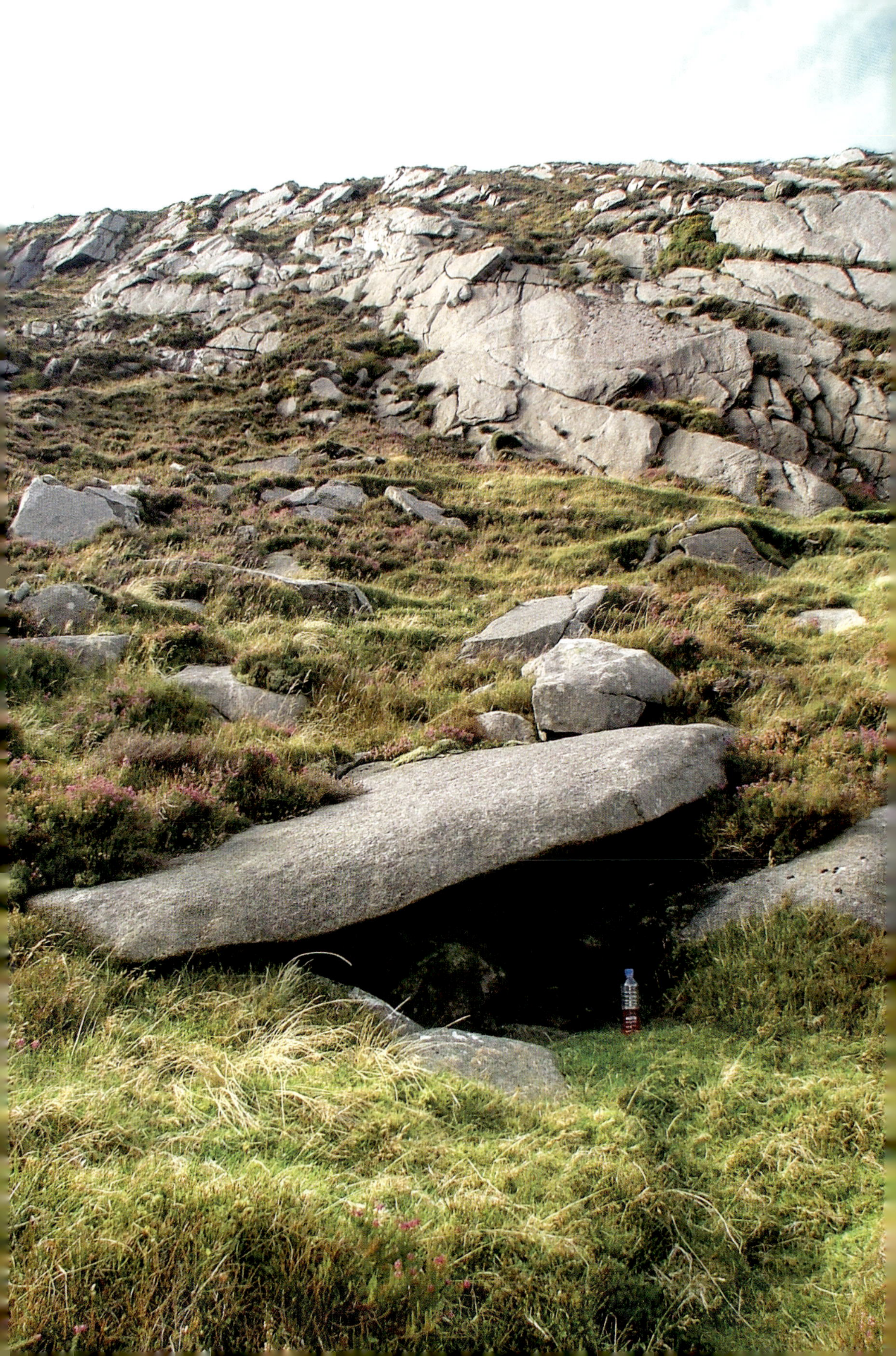

WOMB STONES

When considering Womb Stones, thoughts turn to some of the tales of the *Filidh*, the early poets, philosophers and historians of the native learning. Their training was to commit to memory the legends, battles, striking events, dynasties and historic deeds of ancient ancestors. So much of this has been lost with the disappearance of Irish. Even if we view the surviving traditions and oral poetical accounts with a more prosaic eye there will always be a kernel of truth. Perhaps discerning that kernel is not always so easy.

The story of the various colonisations of Ireland is given in a seventh century work *Leabhar Gabhála*, 'The Book of Invasions'.[1] Here a place is found for the magic chants of Amergin of the 'Children of Mil' against the Tuatha Dé Danann who were of the same stock as the *Fir Builg* who occupied Mourne. The two forces met in battle and the Dé Danann were routed with great slaughter. The conclusion was later told as follows:

'The survivors fled into the remote hills and into the caves. Possibly the glimpses of some of these fugitive hill-dwellers and cave-dwellers, coupled with the seemingly magical skill which they exercised, gave foundation for the later stories of enchanted folk, fairies, living under the Irish hills.

A quaint tale preserved in the ancient Book of Leinster says that after (the battle) it was left to Amergin, Milesian poet and judge, to divide Eirinn between the two races, and that he shrewdly did so with technical justice – giving all above ground to his own people, and all underground to the Dé Danann.'[2]

It has been wondered if the kernel of truth about the *Dé Danann*, or fairies, living underground could possibly derive from the womb monuments they left behind, the most famous of which would be *Brú na Bóinne* at Newgrange. Womb stones were not erected as living spaces but more as memorials to the dead. The thinking behind the erection of the monuments

---

1 This is part of The Book of Leinster a medieval Irish manuscript compiled circa 1160 and now kept in Trinity College, Dublin, under the shelf-mark MS H 2.18 (cat. 1339).
2 Page 10, *The Story of the Irish Race*, by Seumas MacManus, New York, 1921.

Opposite: A classic womb stone invariably has a large raised slab or capstone over an opening aligned to receive the light of solstice dawn. This stone on the north side of Pollaphuca valley is arranged towards summer solstice. **An Magairle Árd**, 'The High Testicles', on the centre of the cliff face above will help in finding this location.

was likely analogous to the sun bringing new growth and life to the earth after solstice. As the sun penetrated deep underneath the womb stones at solstice, so it would bestow a similar blessing of life to the remains committed there.

The notion of the fairies living underground was strong in Mourne and has given us the name for the Trassey River. The Trassey, the name for both river and valley, is only a contraction of the Irish **Trasna Sídhe**, 'across the home of the fairies'. In its early stages the Trassey river flows across the mouth of Pollaphuca valley. This was where the fairies lived. This valley is particularly abundant with womb stones, especially in the upper reaches, with the openings arranged to receive the fertilising light of summer solstice. In more superstitious times it was these dark recesses under the rocks that were fearfully regarded as entrances to the fairy world. Such fear was only compounded with awe at the immense effort needed to place the great granite capstones in place. It was dread like this that probably lay behind the Bearnagh quarry-men breaking off the front of the capstone closest to their quarry to break the power of the *Sídhe* who they believed lived there. They didn't break the stone out of any commercial interest for they left the sectioned granite behind them beside the dark hole of the entrance.

Incidentally, the word 'fairies', *na daoine maithe*, 'the good people', would seem to be from the Irish *Fáirbre*, plural **Fáirbrí** (the soft [b] sound being virtually silent) meaning 'a notch', 'a welt'. As befits the fertility loving people, the 'notch' would have been a reference to female genitalia. The Fairies, unsurprising therefore, could be known as 'The People of Notches, or (sexual) Holes'.

Nowadays the superstitious dread about fairies is long gone and is more likely to be replaced by levity as was shown some years ago in a letter to a paper.

Sir, – What is wrong with drones using Dublin Airport?

Are the 'little people' not entitled to a holiday? Yours.

Top opposite: The quarry on the side of Slieve Bearnagh as seen from Slieve Meelmore.

Lower opposite: This womb stone under the slope of Slieve Bearnagh is noteworthy for its huge capstone and the opening underneath. The hole under the capstone was the home of the fairies. *Púca* in Irish means 'a hobgoblin, bogey, a sprite or ghost. They were not to be trifled with.

The saying was in Irish, **Chughat an Púca** – 'beware of the pooka', or 'be on your guard'.

The quarrymen took no chances and they split off the point of the capstone to rob it of any power. Those pieces of broken capstone can be seen in the grass on the bottom left. The granite capstone is still a substantial 6m by 4m across the top and is a good 1m in thickness. Actually there are two capstones although the second stone is not so large. Moving such prodigious stones would have been a real achievement. The GPS is:

N. 54° 11. 418'
W. 005° 59. 200'   Elevation 440m.

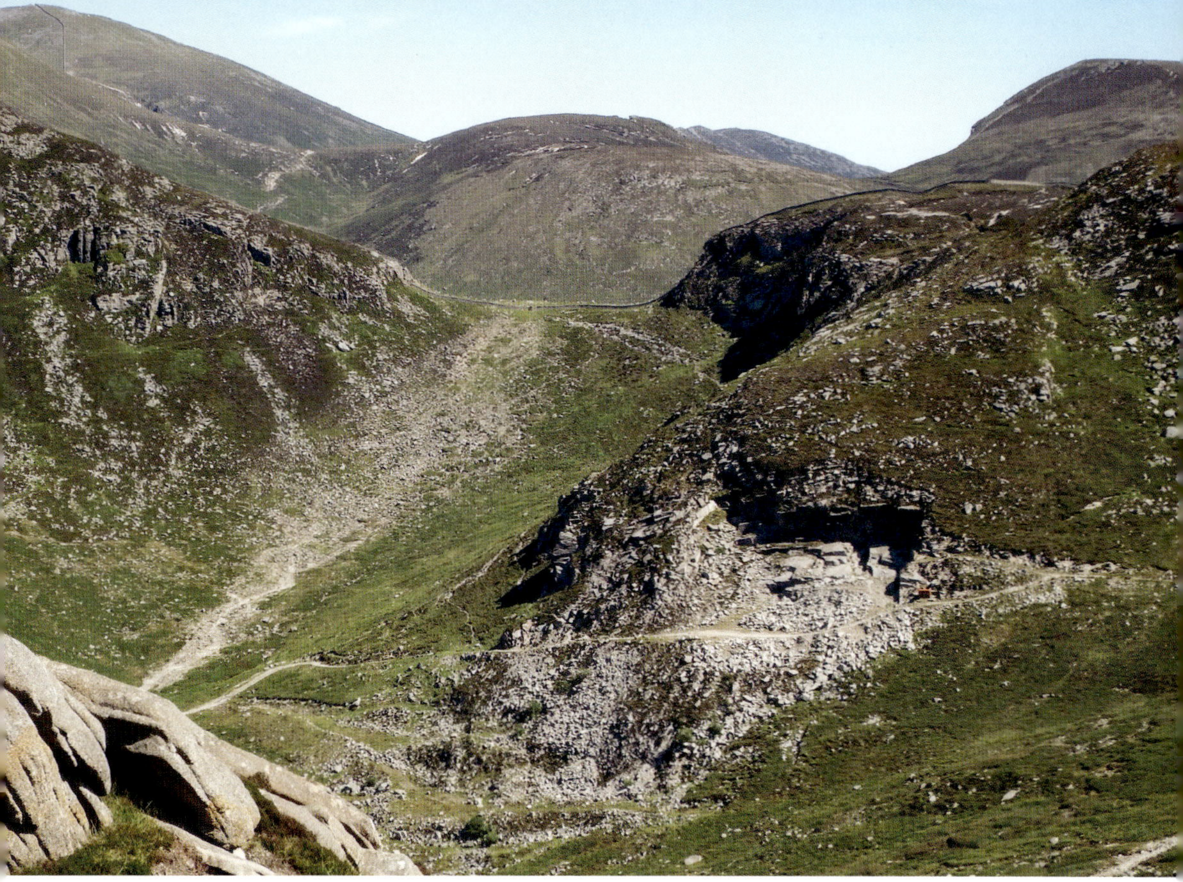
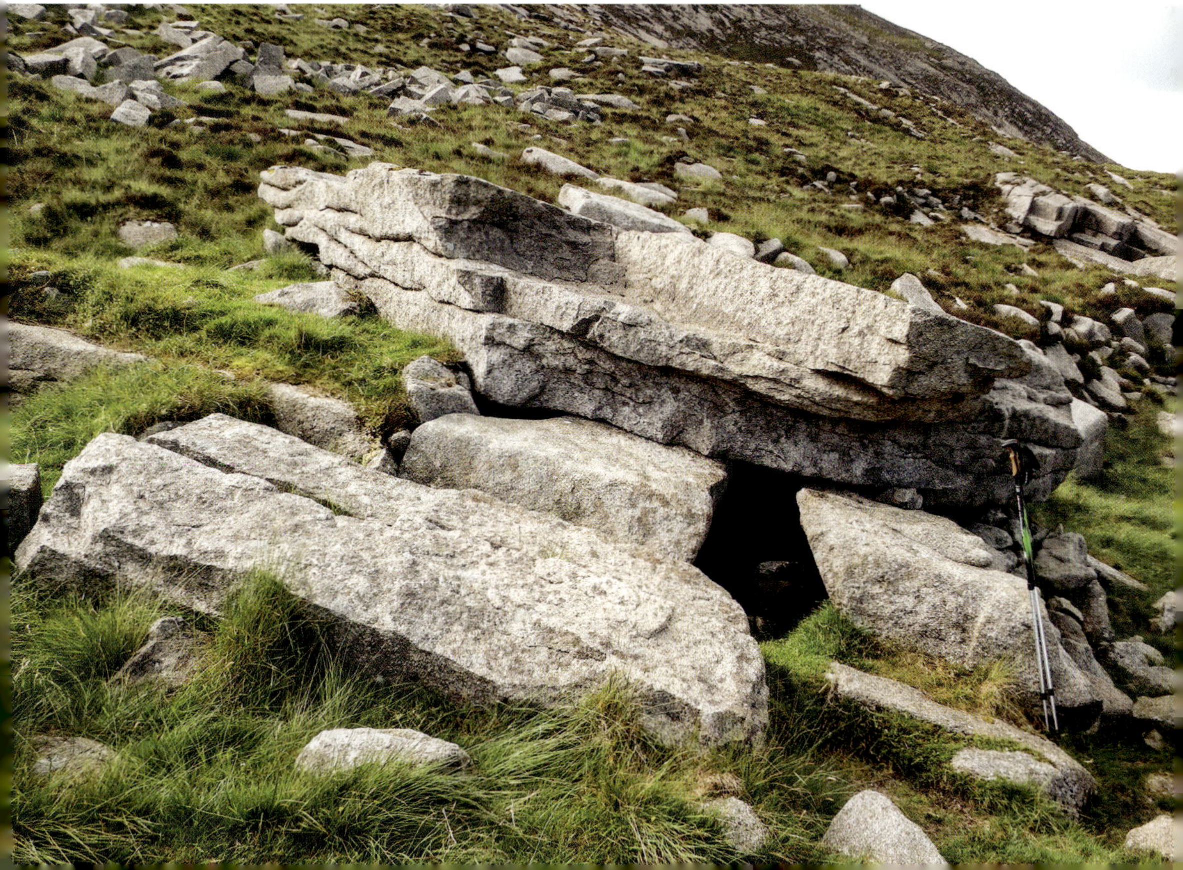

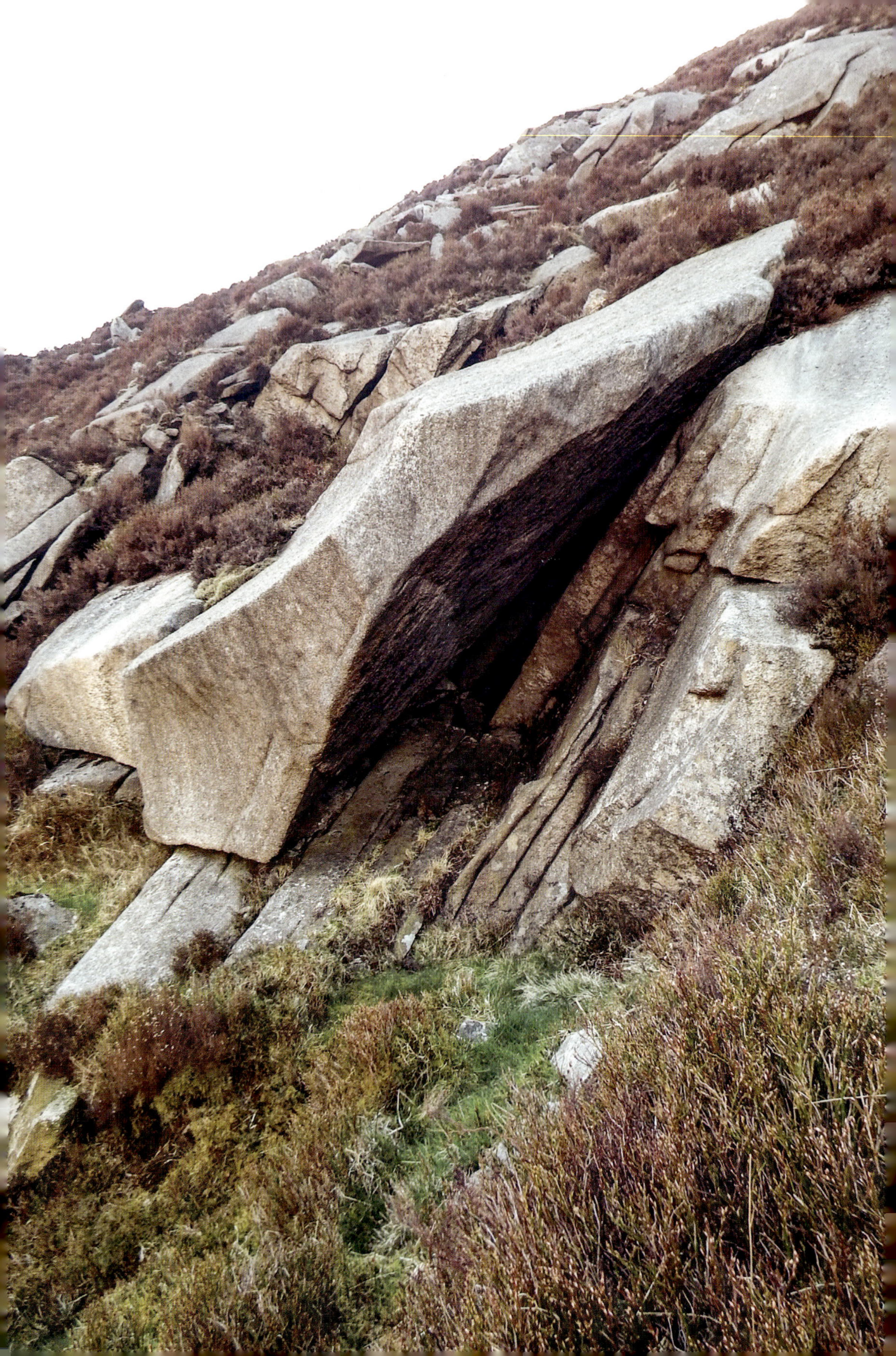

It was late on an April evening when this magnificent womb creation was found high on the southern slopes of Slieve Meelmore. The important discovery brought a moment of wonderful excitement. The monstrous cap stone must be at least 4m long, 1.5m thick at the bottom and maybe 3 to 3.5m across. The opening awaits the fertilising light of summer solstice dawn. It was named **Cithinseach Mná**, 'a beautiful woman' because the Irish has a particular sense of a woman of fine physique and this womb megalith conveys such symbolism in spades. Remember, the vaginal opening at the side of the great capstone is a synecdoche for the whole woman. Note, by the way, the shadow eye on a downward looking 'face' to the right of the entrance.

You can go right into this recess crawling or well stooped and then you find to your delight that the ancients have laid out a flat slab making a sheltered refuge and a dry rest-place. The smaller photograph shows a slight part of the interior. The stone slab rocks slightly. It is a lovely little womb cave and the only later regret was that a flash photograph of the rest of the interior had been overlooked. The slab is evocative of funerary bowls used in Newgrange and Knowth passage graves and was probably where the remains of a beloved were originally laid to rest. I think a coin was respectfully left behind as a memento. The place certainly deserves further examination. The GPS is:

               N.   54º 11. 395'
               W. 005º 59. 712'   Elevation 506m.

Above: This compound megalith, christened 'Wombs Galore', is on the north side of Pollaphuca valley. The top is a triangular womb creation placed to receive the light of summer solstice dawn. The location also marks the landscape fertility notch filled with the tip of Slieve Commedagh. To left and right are further cavities to receive that important solstice light. The little up-thrusting phallic spear stone towards bottom left will throw its shadow into the womb at solstice. In the background, is yet another large capstone making a further womb. The GPS is:

                  N. 54º 11. 377'
                  W. 005º 59. 657'   Elevation 468m.

Top opposite: At the east end of Pot hollow, under Pigeon mountain, a massive stone is propped up on a 1m boulder to create a large cavity for the winter solstice sun rising from the top of Slievenagore. Above the prop stone the pointed corner is directed to the vulva shape of Aughrim hill. The GPS is:

                  N. 54º 08. 692'
                  W. 006º 03. 688'   Elevation 293m.

Lower opposite: This beautiful arrangement of stones in Pollaphuca valley provides two recesses, or wombs, for both summer and winter solstice. The star of the show is the tilted boulder in the middle with the rather phallic pointed tip. The arrangement ensures that this tip will cast its shadow into the dark womb recess left of centre at dawn of summer solstice in a notional act of insemination. The GPS is:

                  N. 54º 11. 468'
                  W. 005º 59. 551'   Elevation 456m.

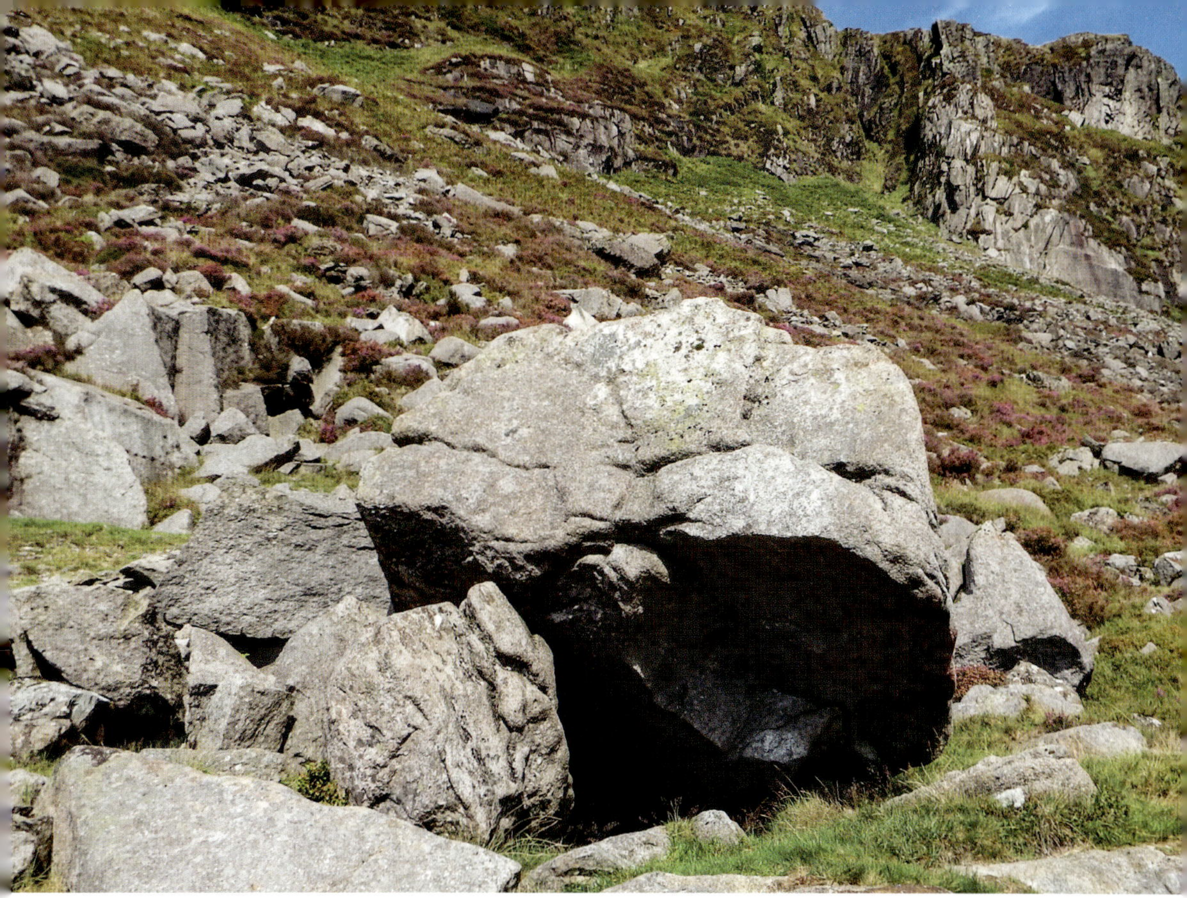

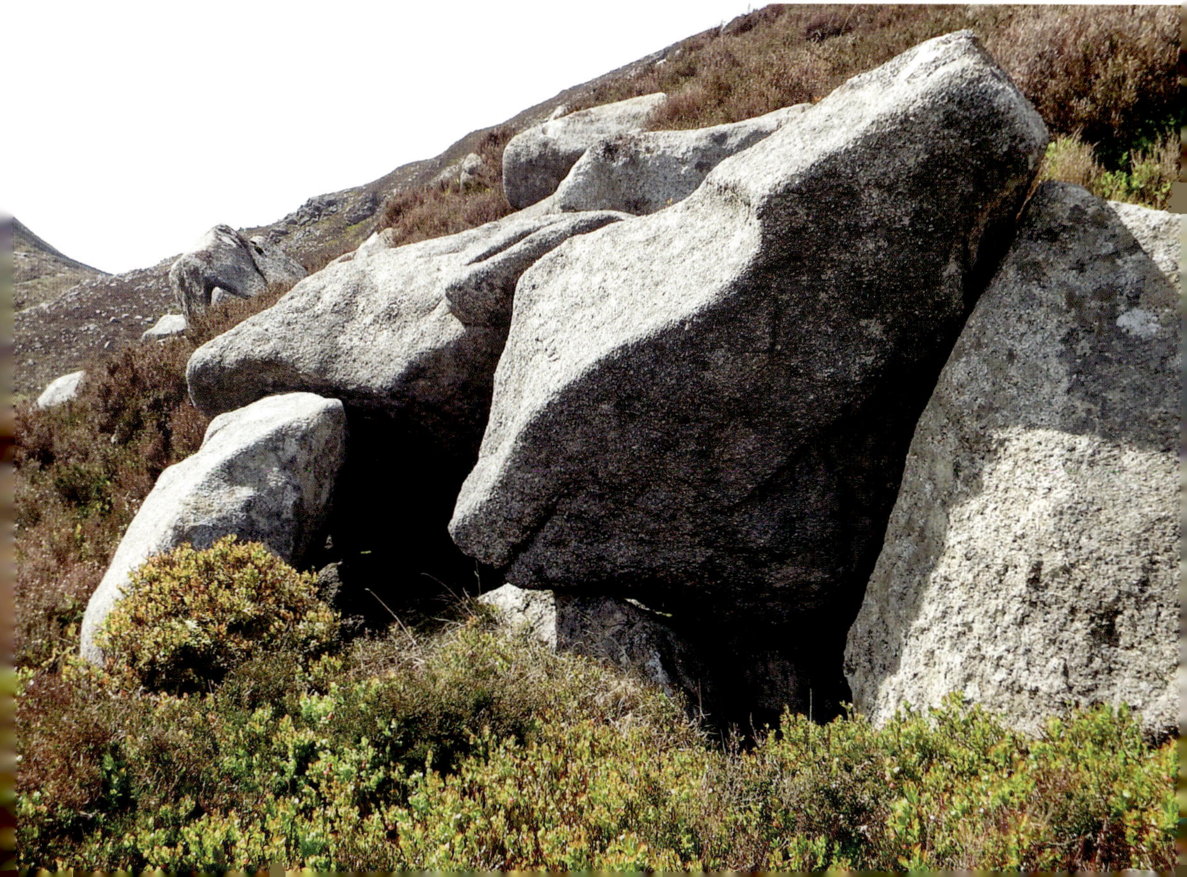

Above: The north side of Pollaphuca valley gives us such a profusion of womb stones. Indeed, directly behind is our next womb stone and, as we will see, another behind that again. This great block was named **An Cloch Fána**, 'The Tilted Stone'. Being propped up at the side a cavity is created underneath for summer solstice sun. The GPS is:

                N.   54º 11. 374'
                W. 005º 59. 646'   Elevation 491m.

Top opposite: This is the great granite capstone seen in the background of the previous megalith. It measures a substantial 3.5m along its length and is over 3m wide. Beneath is a great recess illumined at summer solstice dawn. There is much else to note here. The top of the sloping slab is concave and would funnel rainwater down almost to the lower point corner of the cap on which is a chopped vertical meatus groove. Such flowing water at a meatus groove was to symbolise ongoing fertility. This lower point corner is to winter solstice early sun appearance. Our next megalith, lower opposite, is in the background. The GPS is:

                N.   54º 11. 372'
                W. 005º 59. 664'   Elevation 467m.

Lower opposite: I remember being so impressed with this powerful construction in Pollaphuca valley that it was named 'Jewel of the Day'. The monstrous capstone was paced out at 5m. in length. Mightily raised up and supported by many boulders underneath, it makes for a great womb chamber for summer solstice dawn. The lower point on the capstone is directed to winter solstice sun appearance and the upper point is to summer solstice dawn. The womb under would be nearly 3m deep. The GPS is:

                N.   54º 11. 362'
                W. 005º 59. 672'   Elevation 478m.

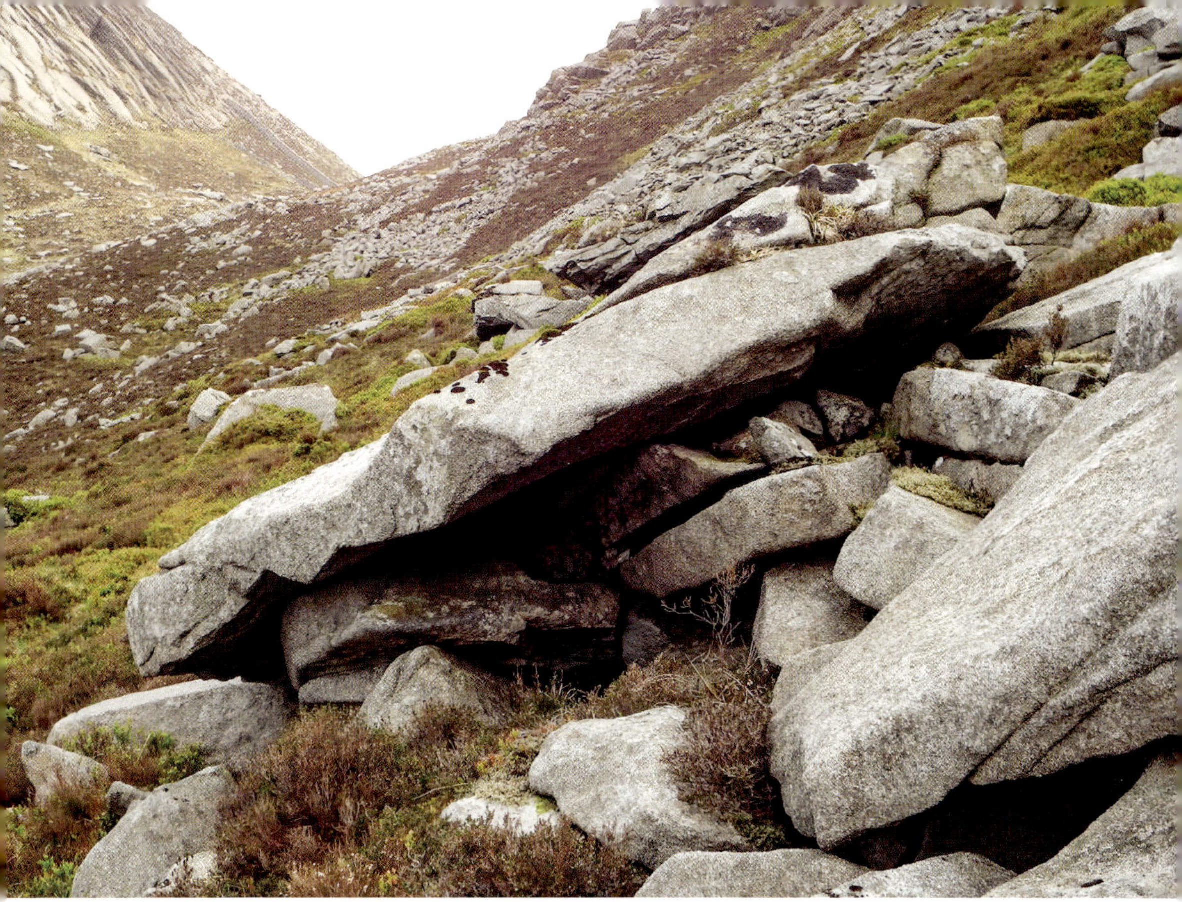

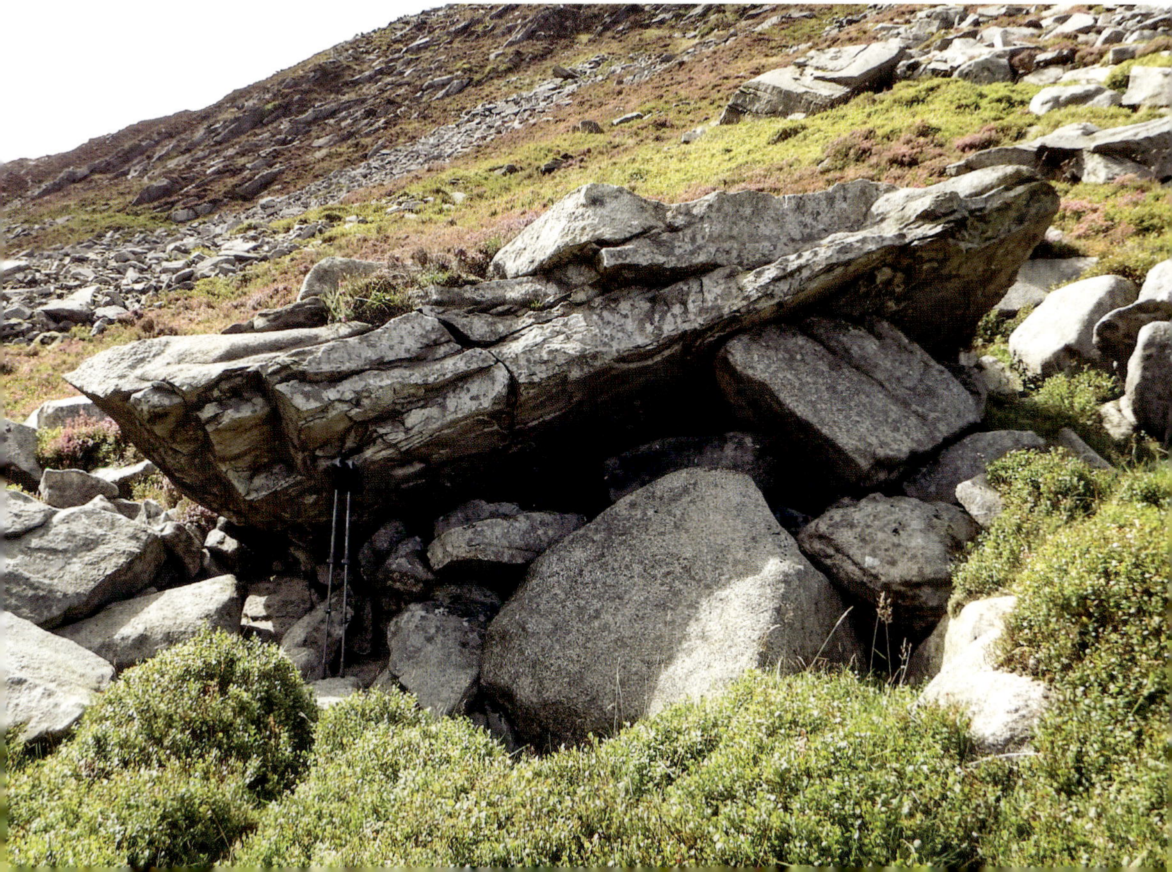

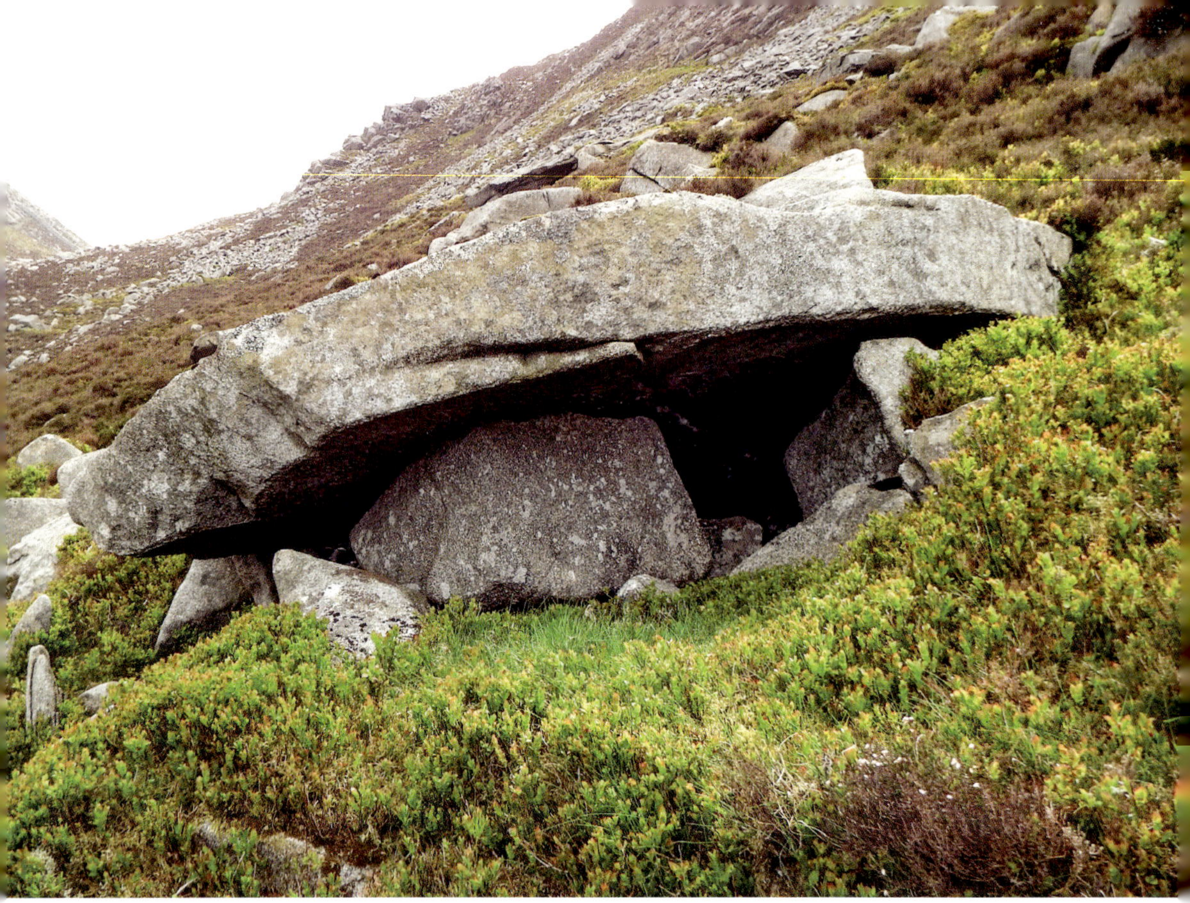

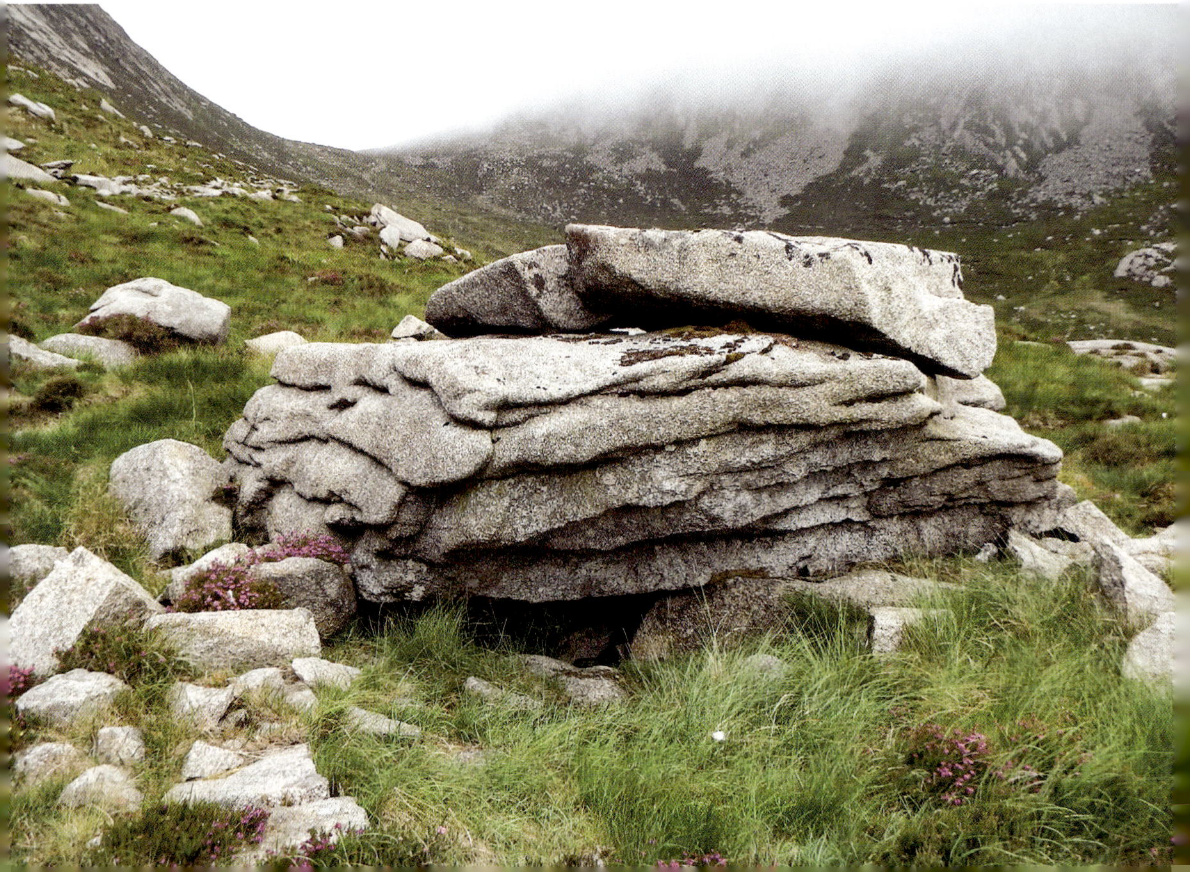

Top opposite: Such are the megalithic riches around Pollaphuca that, with a nod to the tombs of Egypt, the valley could worthily be called 'The Valley of the Queens'. This great monument has a 3m granite capstone. Support orthostats raise the slab to form a womb recess underneath and this, like others previous, is only open to summer solstice sun rising over at Shimial mountain. The GPS is:

      N. 54° 11. 367'
      W. 005° 59. 650'   Elevation 459m.

Lower opposite: This large chocked capstone is roughly 30m further up the valley from the Puca's hole capstone deliberately damaged by quarrymen. Low stone walls at front and back show that they also used this boulder for shelter. The slab is about 5.5m long and the small opening underneath at the bottom front was the entry point for summer solstice sunrise. The opening is minimal compared with its companion megalith a bit lower down the valley. The GPS is:

      N. 54° 11. 420'
      W. 005° 59. 228'   Elevation 434m.

Top of this page: Here is a carefully built-up recess, again in Pollaphuca valley. The womb opening at the back of the capstone is open to the first light of summer solstice sun. It sits on a series of support stones and displays a hooded frowning eye on the side. The top support stone projects sufficiently back that the notional fertilising shadow of its tip will be cast into the womb opening at solstice dawn. The GPS is:

      N. 54° 11. 506'
      W. 005° 59. 573'   Elevation 464m.

Above: Two colossal boulders on the northern flank of Chimney Rock above the quarry have been pushed together leaving a deep and dark womb opening for summer solstice sun. The location marks the solstice sun rising from the summit of Crossone mountain on the other side of the Bloody Bridge valley. It is as if Crossone was coming to a sexual climax and fertilising the womb.

Top opposite: Walking on treacherous scree slopes in not recommended but this great fertility slab on 'Dry Quarry' slope under Slieve Muck was just too impressive. It is called a 'fertility' slab as it is a union of shale and granite; shale on top and granite below. The slab is easily three metres across. The main feature of the propped megalith is the very large womb cavity below. The inset photograph shows the reason for placement, namely the sunlit tip of Chimney Rock as the 'penis in the vagina' between Lamagan and Bignian. This area of the slope was deemed soiled by the exudation of the landscape penis and thus had the Irish name of **Dríb Ceirbe**, 'filth of an excrescence', now 'Dry Quarry'. The GPS is:

N. 54º 09. 064'
W. 006º 02. 358'   Elevation 471m.

Lower opposite: A 2m by 1.5m granite slab under Slieve Lamagan acts as a capstone for a little womb cavity below that will be illuminated at dawn of winter solstice. The slab sits on a base of at least four other stones. The GPS is:

N. 54º 10. 016'
W. 005º 57. 496'   Elevation 491m.

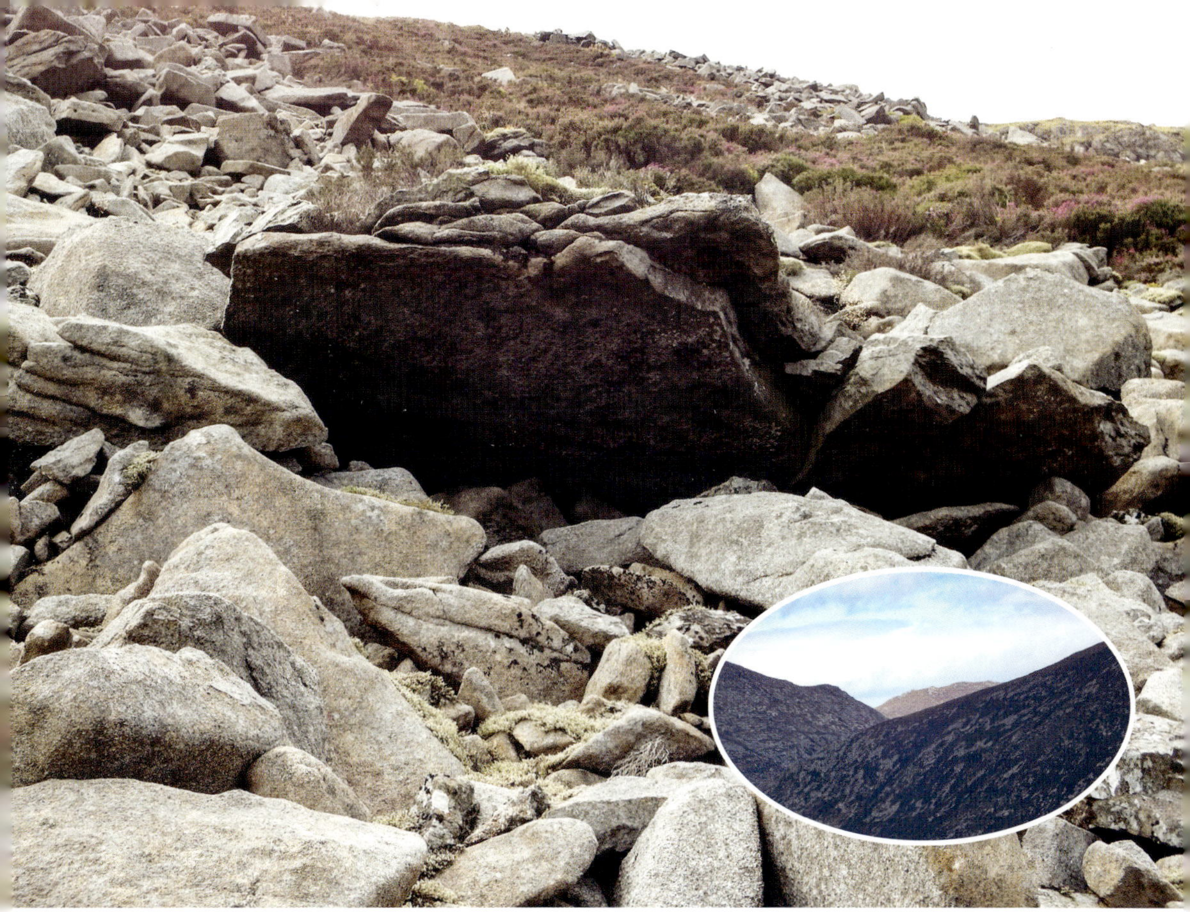

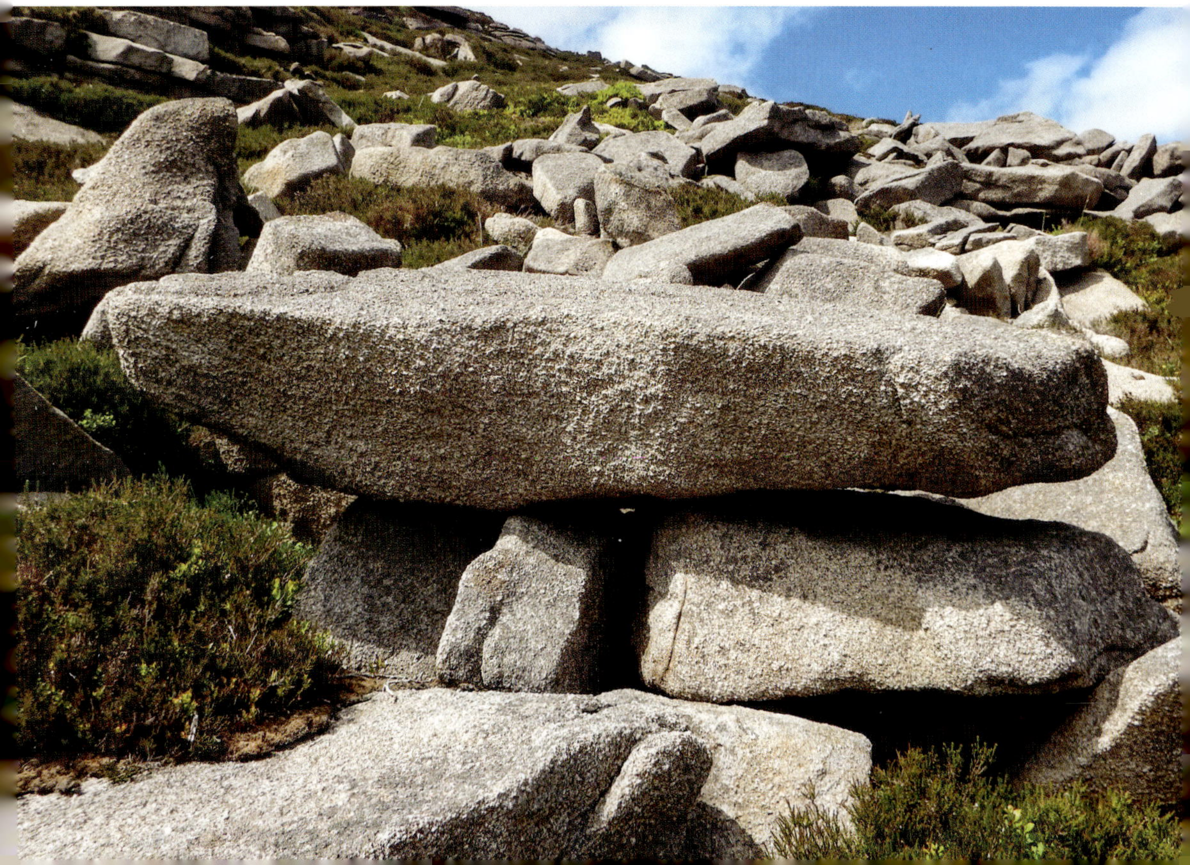

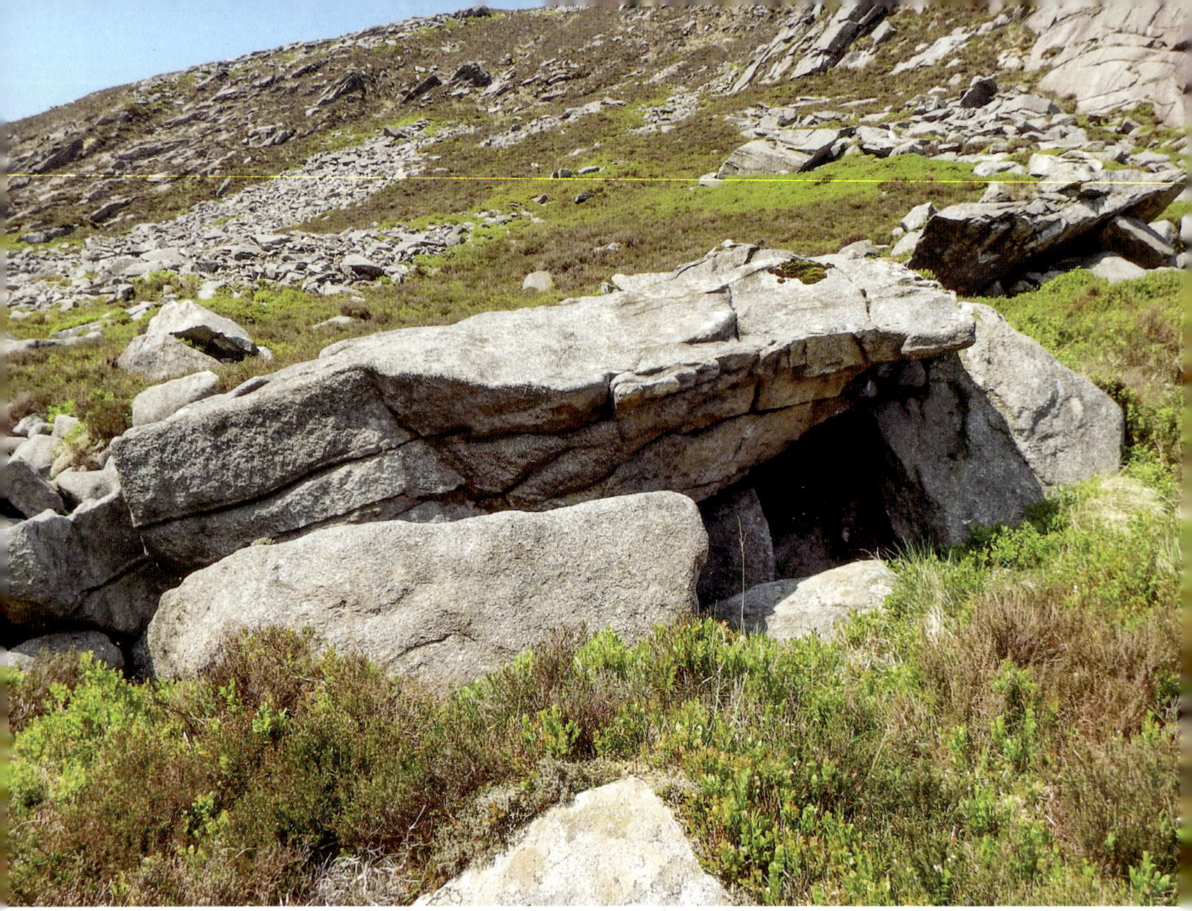

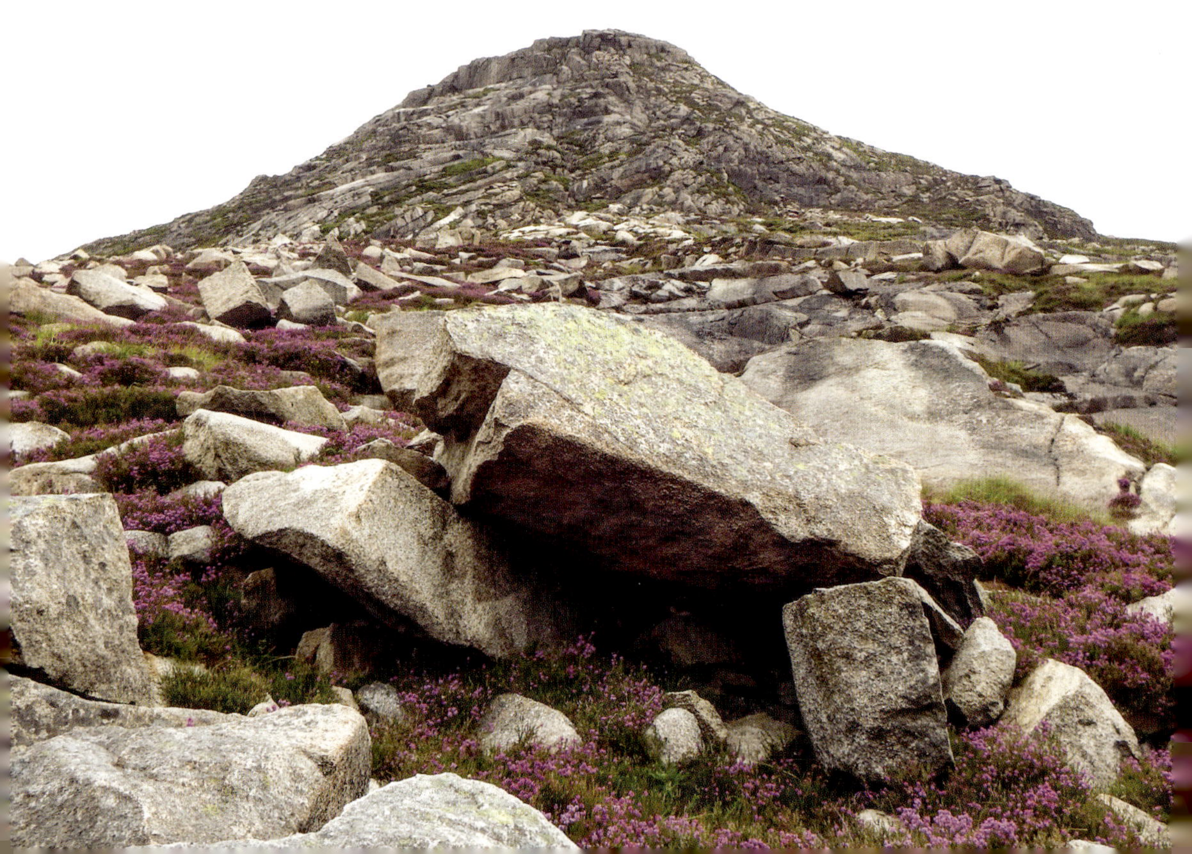

Top opposite: This mighty creation was given the tongue-in-cheek name of **An Céid-Bhean**, 'The Sweetheart' on account of its truly massive capstone. It is a monster slab measuring 6m from top to tail and 5m across the top. The capstone forms a great recess underneath for the womb that is illumined by summer solstice dawn. In the right background is yet another great womb construction, 'The Jewel of the Day'. The Sweetheart GPS is:

N. 54º 11. 362'
W. 005º 59. 659'   Elevation 464m.

Lower opposite: On the south-east slope of Slieve Lamagan sits this 2.5m boulder supported on two labial sides to make a large womb cavity for winter solstice dawn. The points on the capstone also point to the solstice. The GPS is:

N. 54º 09. 627'
W. 005º 57. 646'   Elevation 370m.

Top of this page: This impressive monument sits beside the quarry track on the way to Pigeon mountain. The massive granite capstone is 4.2m long by 2.5m high. The womb is the cavity between the support stones. The pile of blocks to the right are not added later to make a shelter but are an integral load-bearing part of the structure. The location marks the tip of Slievenamuck peeping up at the north end of the valley as shown in the circle inset. The area is locally known as 'Crook of the Wall' which derives from the Irish **Cruach a Baill**, meaning 'heap of the 'member' (where 'member' is a euphemism for a phallus). The name extends across the Moyad Road to the side of Slieve Muck where the same view of Slievenamuck can be seen. The GPS is:

N. 54º 08. 566'
W. 006º 03. 694'   Elevation 297m.

Above: Here on the upper southern slope of Meelmore is this womb recess facing the north tor of Slieve Bearnagh and ready to receive the light of winter solstice. The recess is surmounted by a capstone that is 1m across and about 1.2m from back to front. The recess is about 0.5m across and 1m high and nearly 1m deep. All around there are many other ancient constructions. The GPS is:

                N.   54º 11. 528'
                W. 005º 59. 844'   Elevation 631m.

Top opposite: High on the western slope of the Annalong valley a great 3.5m by 3.5m slab is propped up on two stones so as to present a womb cavity towards Rocky mountain from where winter solstice sun will finally emerge. The GPS is:

                N.   54º 09. 970'
                W. 005º 56. 978'   Elevation 362m.

Lower opposite: On the top front of Chimney Rock mountain great slabs are piled high. This construction has given us the local name of **Cnoc** (*Clocha*) **h-Úirín** 'Hill (of the stones) of the Cubby-hole' which is applied to Crock Horn Stream and to the parish church of Kilhorne at Annalong. The 'cubby-hole' is the womb opening aligned to dawn of summer solstice. The slab above the hole is a good 5m long. The GPS is:

                N.   54º 09. 963'
                W. 005º 54. 427'   Elevation 567m.

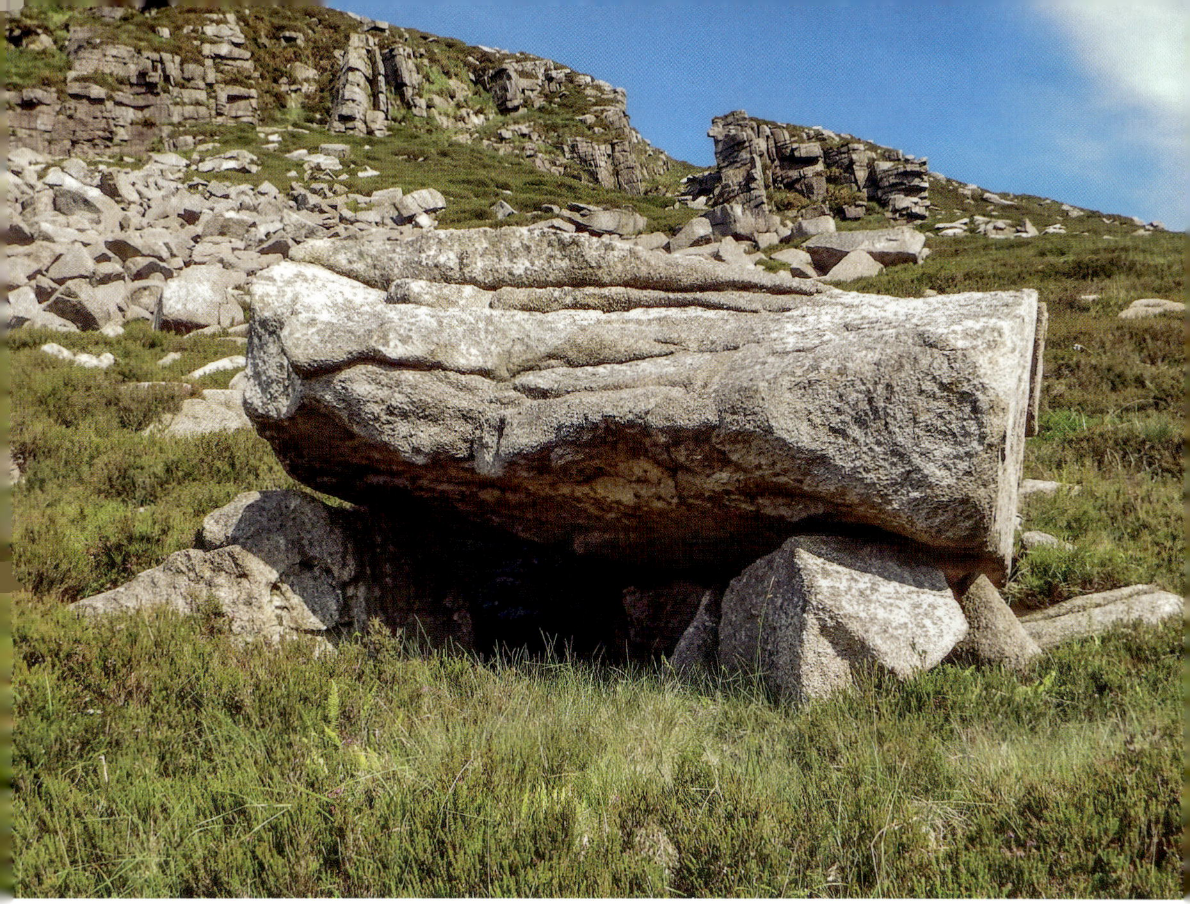

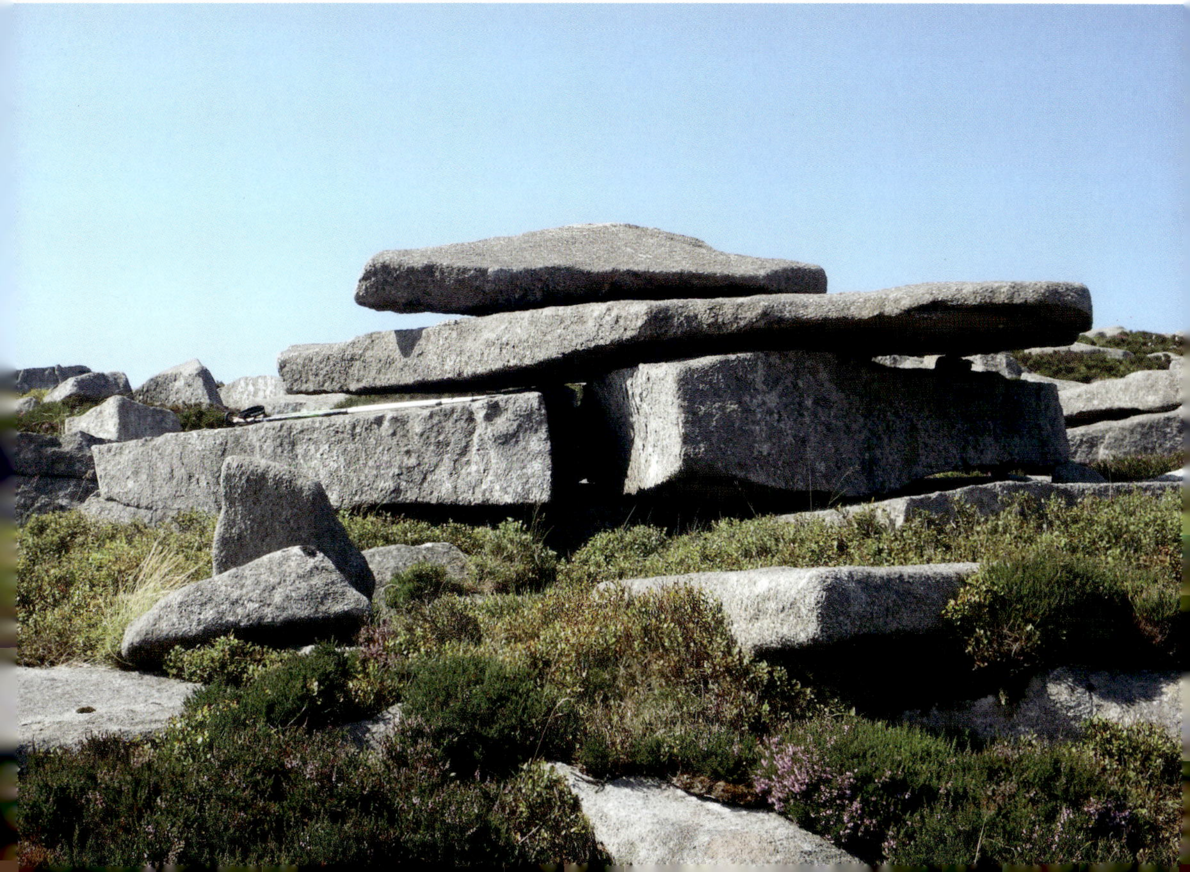

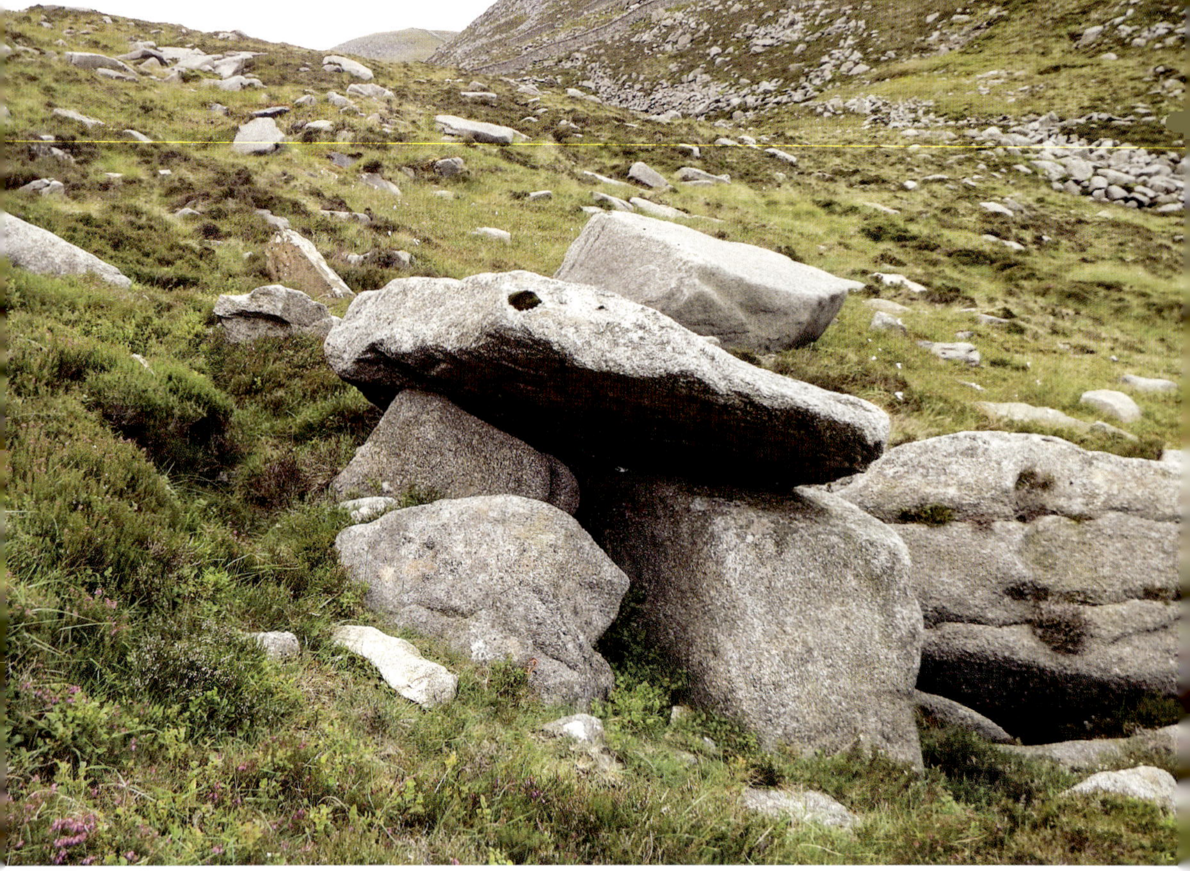

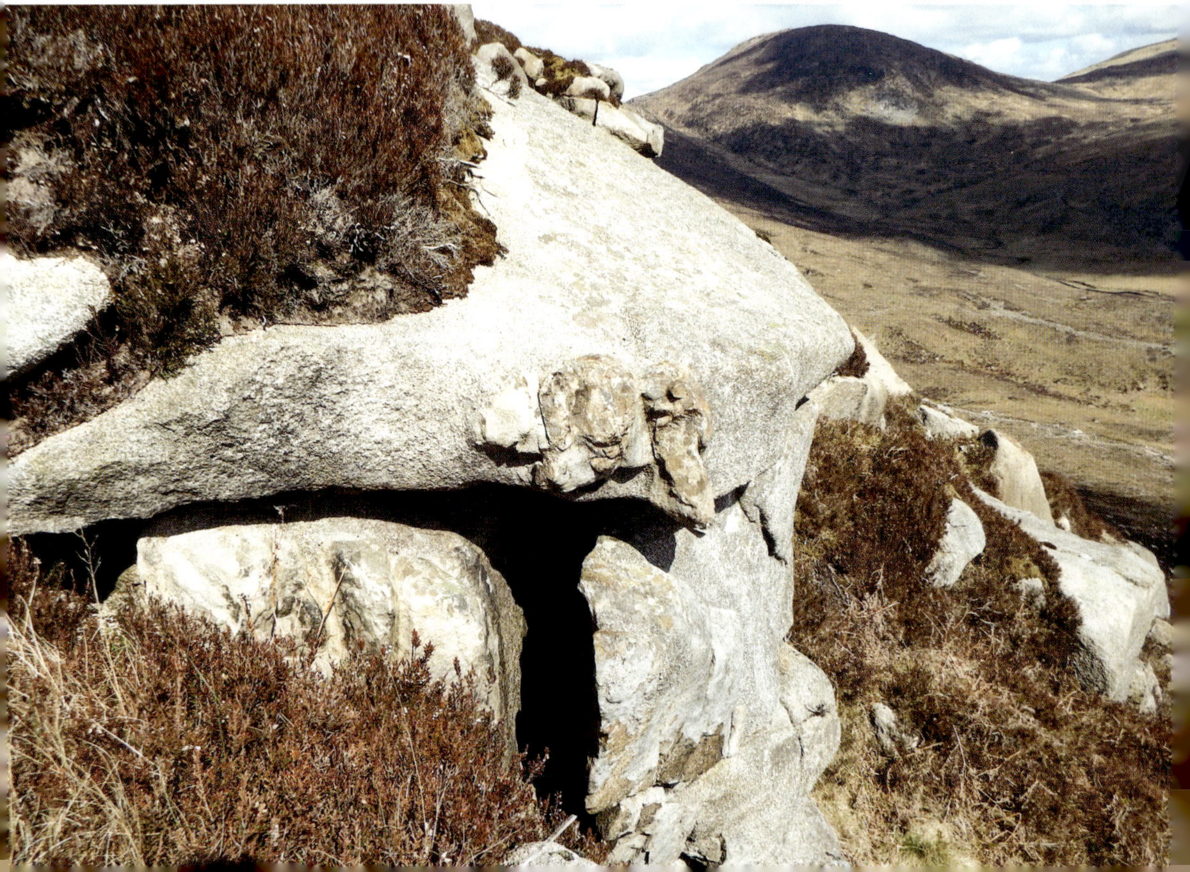

Top opposite: Approaching the stile at the head of Pollaphuca valley is this womb creation open to the light of summer solstice dawn. This is a fertility location and the construction marks the landscape 'penis in the vagina' motif of Meelbeg mountain in the notch in the background. The point on the low left-hand stone will cast its shadow into the recess behind it at solstice dawn to impart insemination. This is another instance of what is known in Irish as **Dúid lia Scáth**, 'Fertility stone shadow'.

Lower opposite: Overlooking the Windy Gap valley, a granite boulder uses an infusion in the rock to represent semen on the tip of the capstone raised over a .2m wide vaginal slit. The opening faces towards winter solstice dawn. The slit is about 1.5m high and goes back about the same depth into the rock. The GPS is:

        N.   54º 07. 697'
        W. 006º 04. 886'   Elevation 354m.

Top of this page: There is something mesmerising about this curved granite boulder sporting such a straight one centimetre infusion line along its length. Accordingly it was named **An Cloch Buin na Spéire**, 'The Stone of the Horizon'. It is to be found on the north side of Pollaphuca valley under the cliff. The curved belly of the stone forms a womb recess for the summer solstice sun and a little phallic spear stone has been propped up underneath to aid fertility. The GPS is:

        N.   54º 11. 364'
        W. 005º 59. 688'   Elevation 478m.

Above: The next few pages show a variation on womb structures; they are easily identified as 'See Throughs'. The principal of the solstice sun penetrating a hole, or erstwhile vagina, to bring fertility is still the same.

Our first example is on the north-west side of Luke's mountain. A slim slab has been propped against a larger stone forming a hole for the early winter solstice sun. These are two granite stones sitting on shale bedrock. The GPS is:

                   N.   54º 12. 585'
                   W. 005º 58. 083'   Elevation 304m.

Top opposite: Here on the northern slope of Slieve Bignian and a little more than a hundred metres from the great fissure of Buzzard's Roost, a number of great boulders have been pulled together to create a fertility hole for the light of summer solstice emerging from the side of Slieve Lamagan. The right hand boulder has a very distinctive face looking up towards the sky.

Lower opposite: A pleasing little window for the summer solstice sun has been made through a rock outcrop near to the seaward end of Slieve Bignian. The striated lines in the rock reminded people of piles of old pennies and so Bignian had its name from the Irish (*Sliabh na*) ***bPinginn***, '(mountain of the) money'.

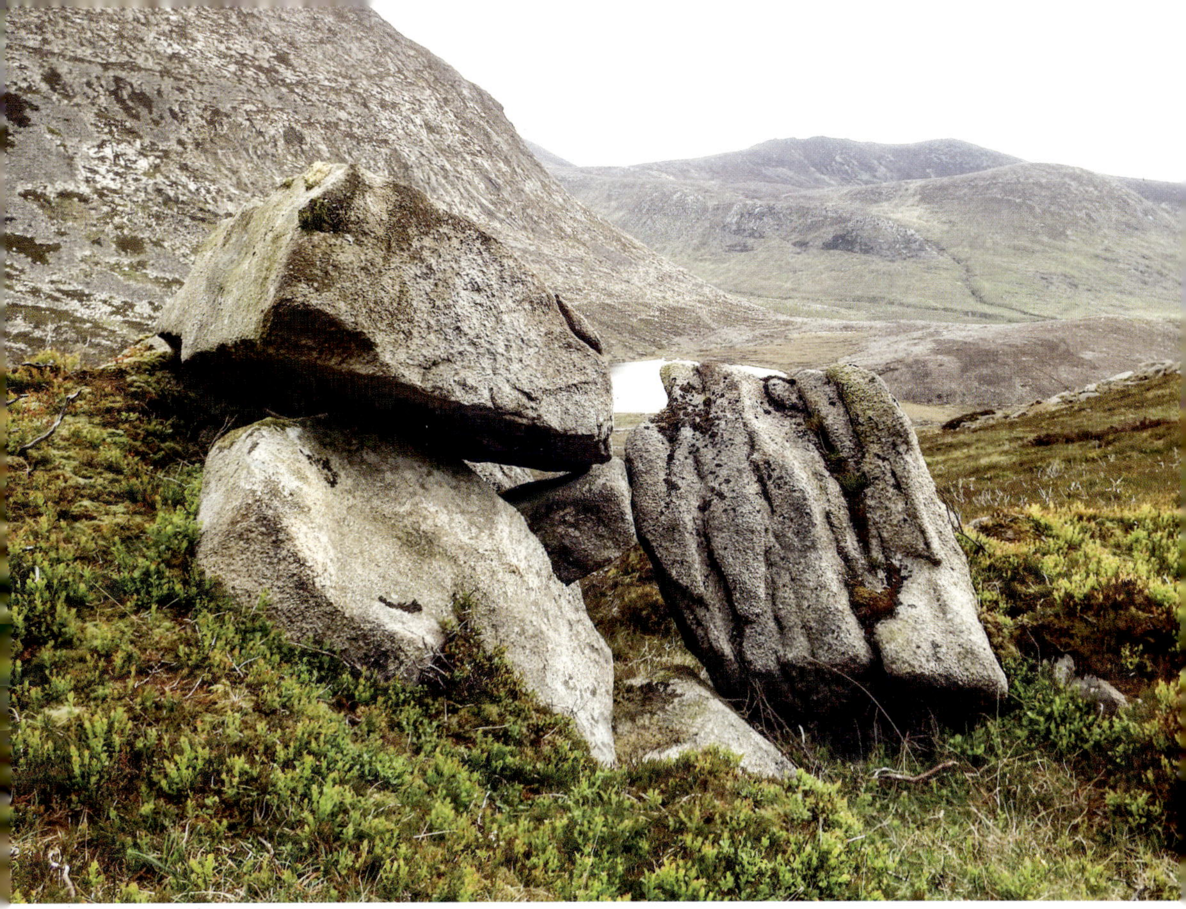

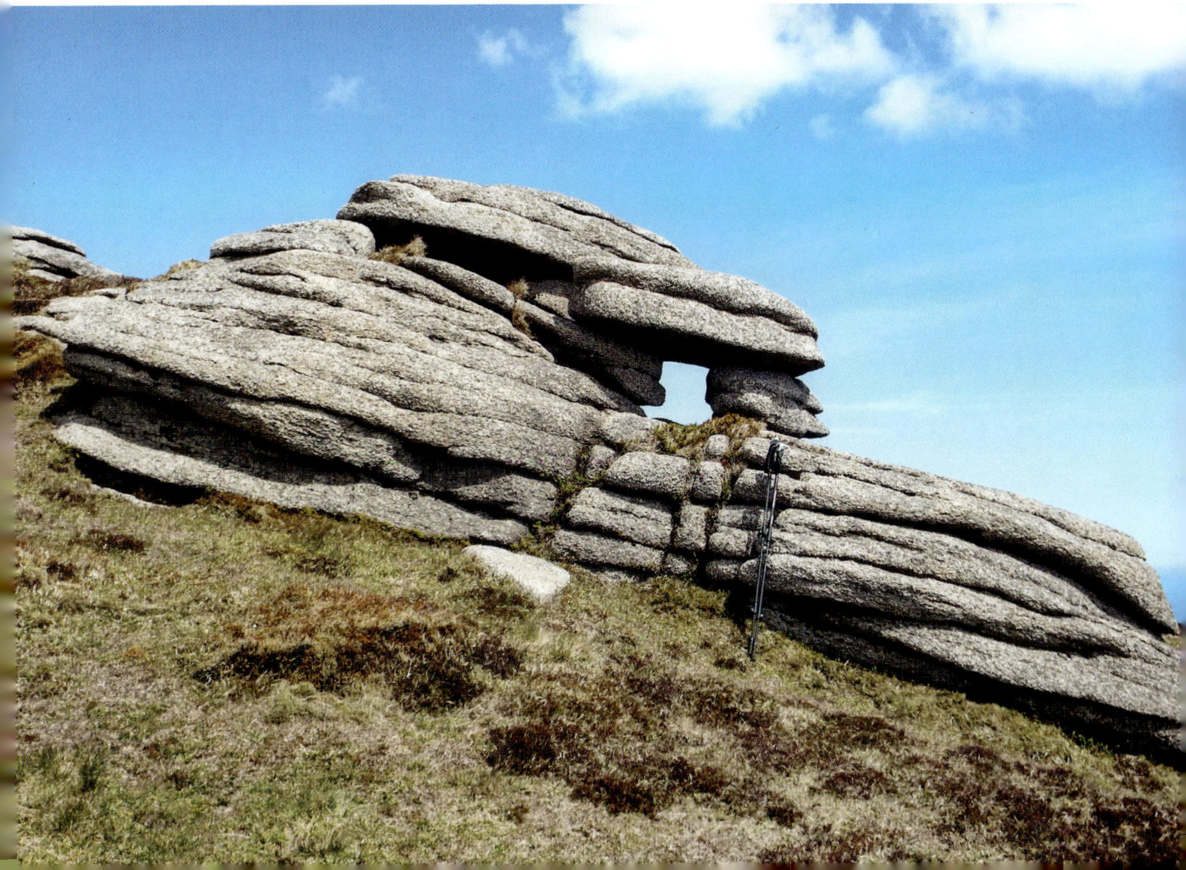

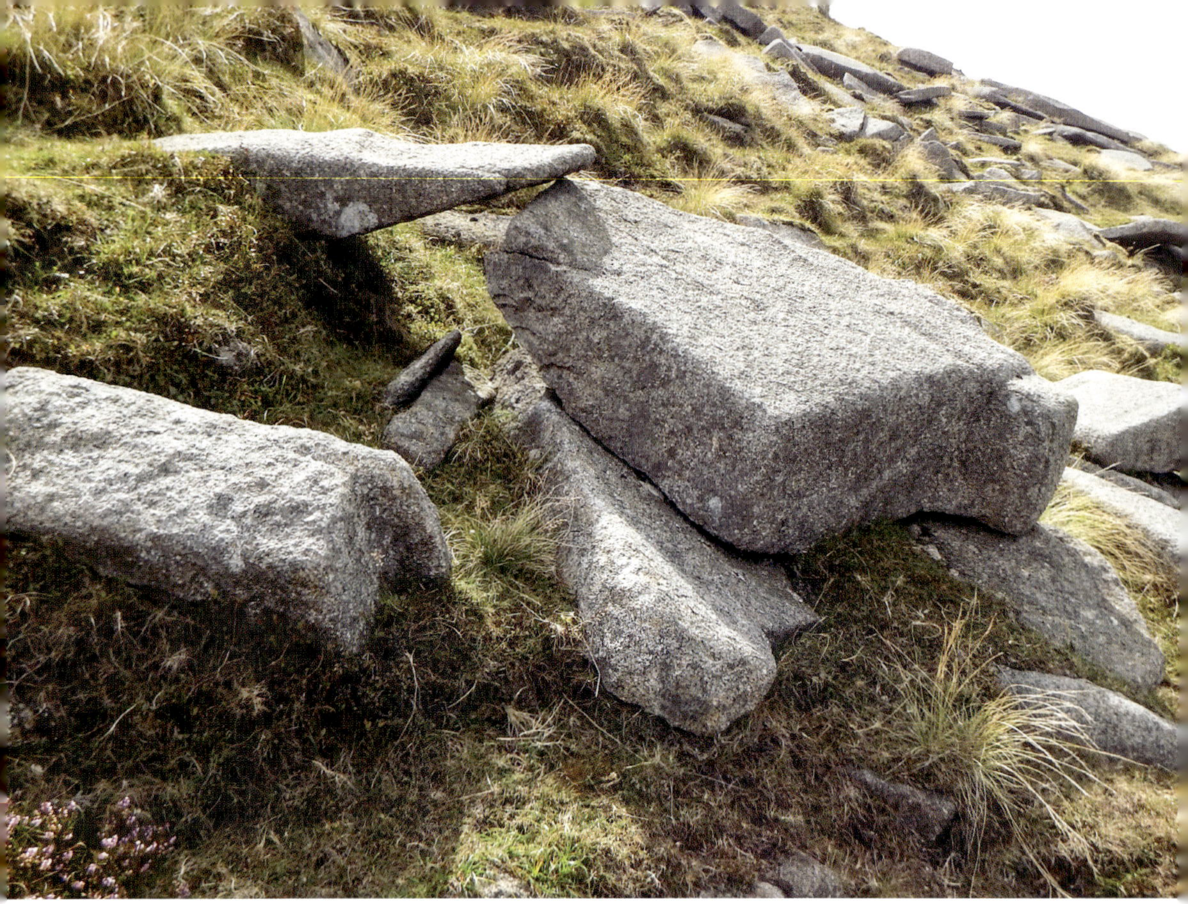
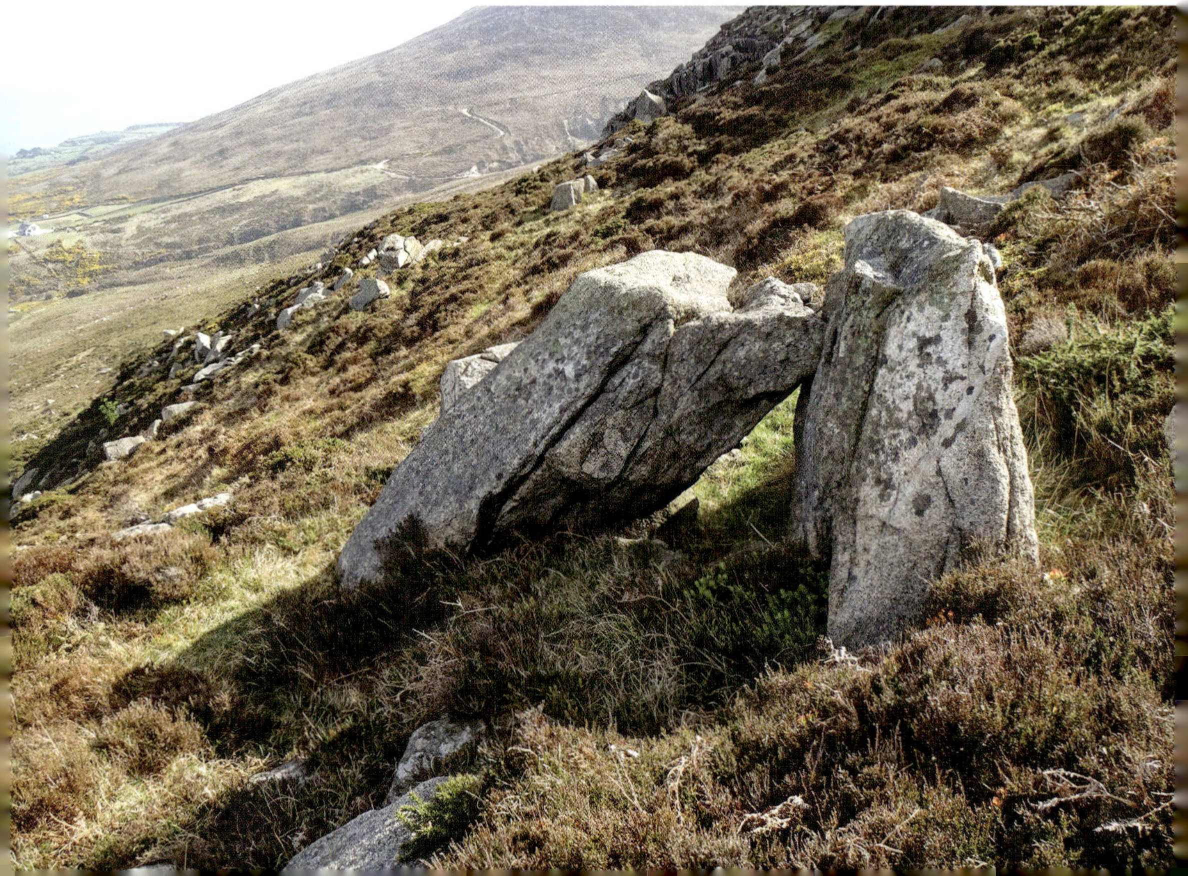

Top opposite: This breezy vaginal opening awaiting the light of summer solstice dawn is to be found on the top north-west side of Meelmore mountain. The GPS is:

        N.   54º 11. 630'
        W. 006º 00. 113'   Elevation 592m.

Lower opposite: On the east slope of Leganabruchan two attenuated granite boulders have been put together to make a vaginal opening for summer solstice dawn. The opening at the bottom is close to 1m wide but tapers up to where the seaward stone rests on the back labial. The GPS is:

        N.   54º 10. 830'
        W. 005º 53. 516'   Elevation 304m.

Top of this page: High on the south facing slope of Slieve Lamagan this long slab has been separated from the rock face by a small boulder acting as a penile insertion in a vaginal gap. The opening will be illuminated and pierced by dawn light of winter solstice. It is a beautiful arrangement.

    Many other see-through fertility creations await explorers of Mourne but exigencies of space preclude further illustrations.

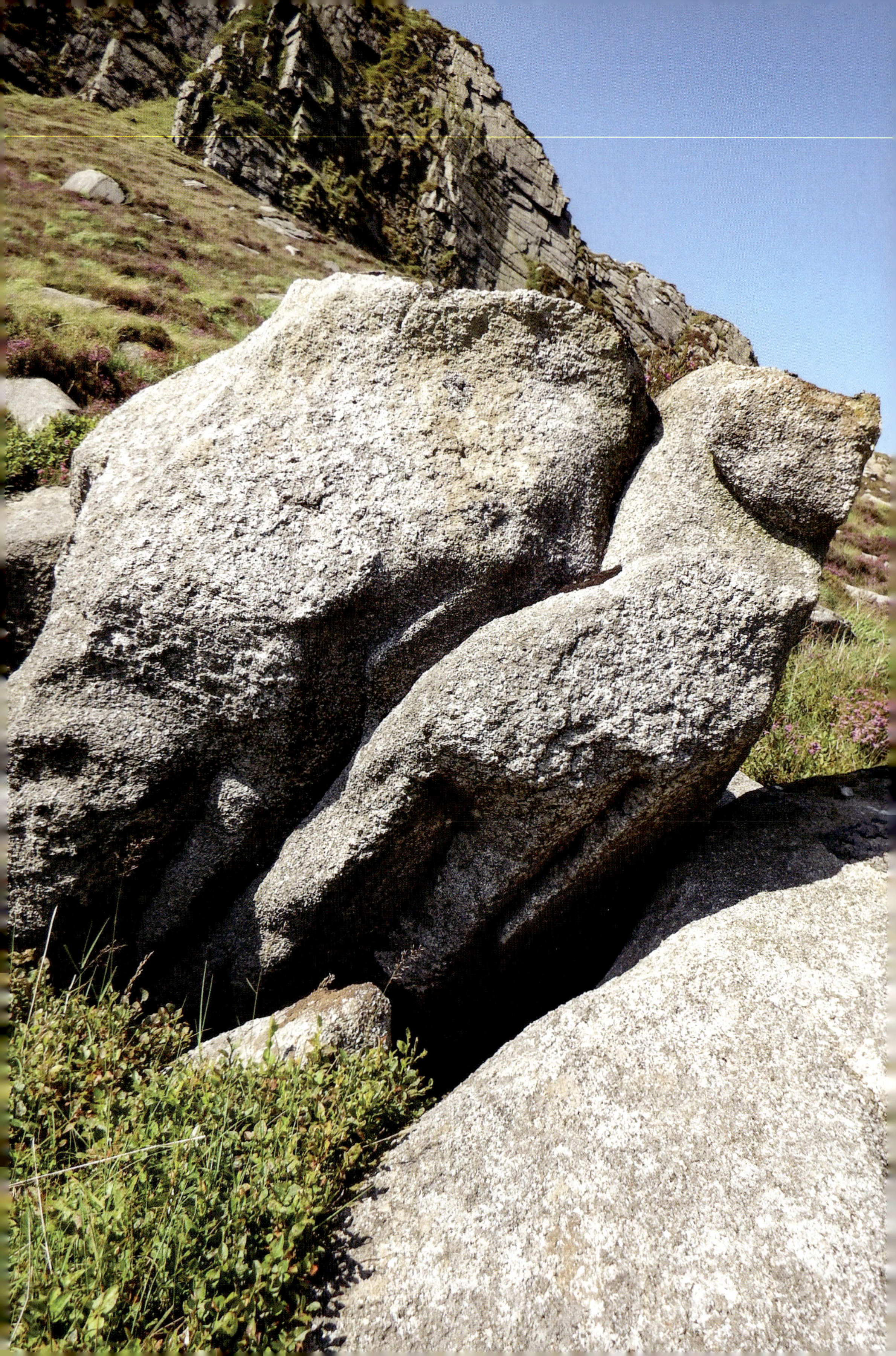

BEGETTING STONES

A favourite theme for the early fertility loving people of Mourne was, unsurprisingly, intercourse. Across the hills there are many megalithic displays of great stones being 'serviced'. These were known as *'gein'* stones after the Irish for the act of begetting, conception, or being born. The English 'giant' is a mnemonic of the genitive of *Gein*, namely *Geinte*, and there are certainly many legends about 'Giants' in Mourne. Michael Crawford, the raconteur of Legendary Stories of the Carlingford Lough District, (Newry, 1913), narrated the struggle between the mighty giant of summer, Finn Toirneach, 'Thunderclap' and Ruscire the giant of ice and winter. It was Toirneach, he said, who raised the enormous Cloghmore stone and hurled it across Carlingford Lough to crash onto the unlucky head of Ruscire and crushed him into the mountain. The giant of summer won.

There is frequently a grain of truth behind these legends even if scrambled over the millennia. The Cloghmore stone is indeed a victory for summer as the megalith marks the summer solstice sun rising from the top of Slieve Martin. Although the mountain has now been anglicised to a name the Irish would have been **Sliabh na mBáirr Teine**, 'mountain of the tip of fire'. Other place-names around Carlingford Lough mark where winter solstice shadows have been cast across the Lough from the Cooley mountains. Whatever mountain shadow reached across the Lough to 'Woodside', east of Rostrevor, the origin of the name lies with (*Tí na*) **Buid Sidhe**, (Place of the) Penis blast. The termination point of the erstwhile phallic shadow was believed to culminate in an ejaculation. One cannot help wonder if something similar lies behind the name of Warrenpoint. Think not in terms of English as if the place abounded in rabbits from a warren but rather look to the Irish **Bárr Áin Pointe**, 'Tip of pleasure point', perhaps the termination place of another phallic shadow. It is likely no accident that the coronation place of the Magennis Clan was up the old 'Bridal Lonan' above the town. [Bridal from the Irish **Brí Dála**, 'Hill of Meeting']. The Clan upheld the elder faith and the choice of meeting place was likely selected because the winter solstice marked it as an important place of fertility. *Dáil*, (gen.) **Dála**, means 'act of pouring out, conferring, meeting'. It combines the notion of assembly but also the fertility overtones of ejaculation in 'pouring out'.

Opposite: Under the cliff of Spellack a mighty male creature holds his companion by the neck for an act of copulation. The GPS is:
N. 54° 11. 856'
W. 005° 59. 285'   Elevation 328m.

Above: On the southern shoulder of Slieve Meelmore and overlooking the Pollaphuca valley, two spear stones have been placed in the act of copulation. The right-hand stone, the one receiving attention, was reckoned at 1.5m in length. The GPS is:

                        N.   54° 11. 635'
                        W. 005° 59. 653'   Elevation 554m.

Top opposite: Copulation takes place on the north side of Pollaphuca valley. The growth of grass and heather around these stones tends to mask the fact that these are two very substantial boulders. A smaller phallic stone has been deliberately placed on the right to address the vaginal cavity underneath.

Lower opposite: Begetting takes place on the top north-west side of Meelmore mountain. The great stone at the back is about 1.9m across and is more than just a hefty counterbalance. The 1.6m long granite stone that it services points to summer solstice sunset. The location has magnificent views. The GPS is:

                        N.   54° 11. 642'
                        W. 006° 00. 193'   Elevation 571m.

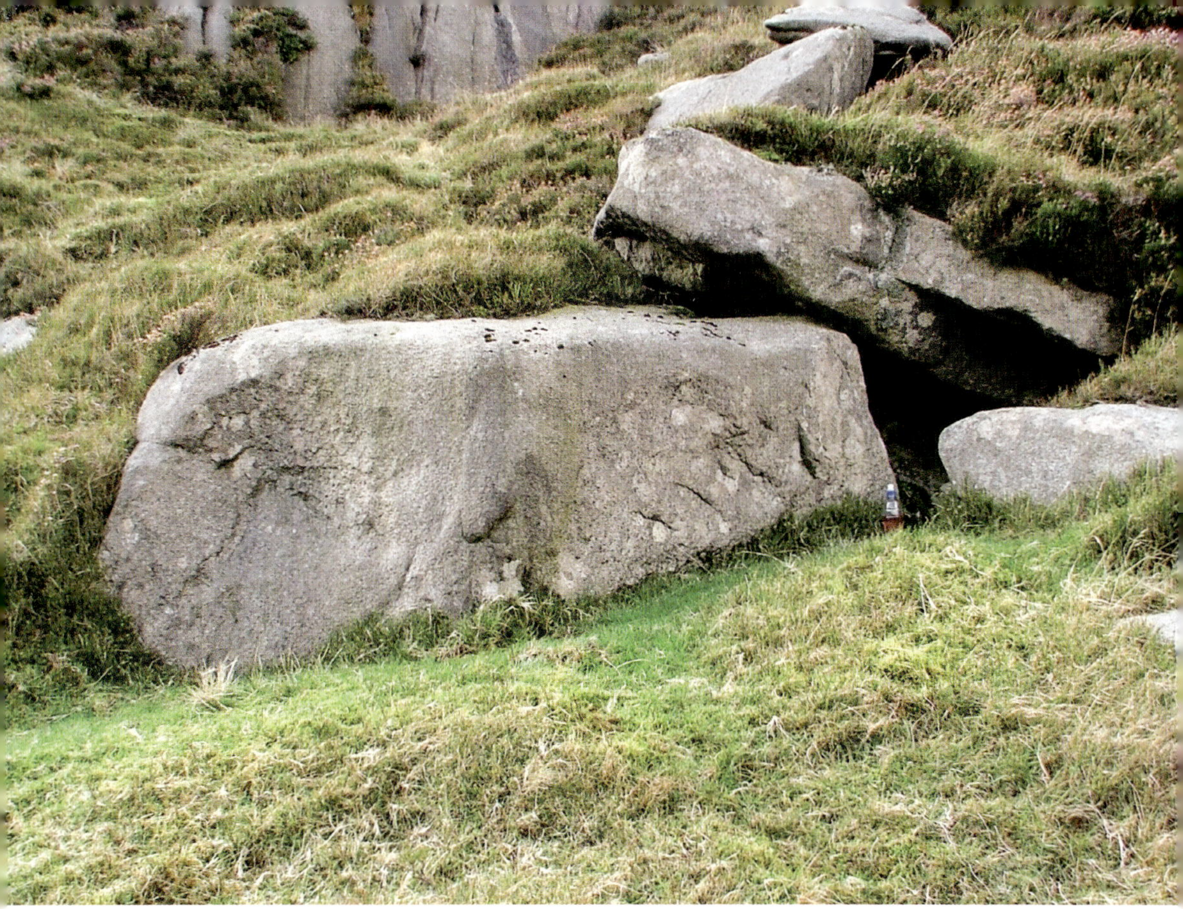

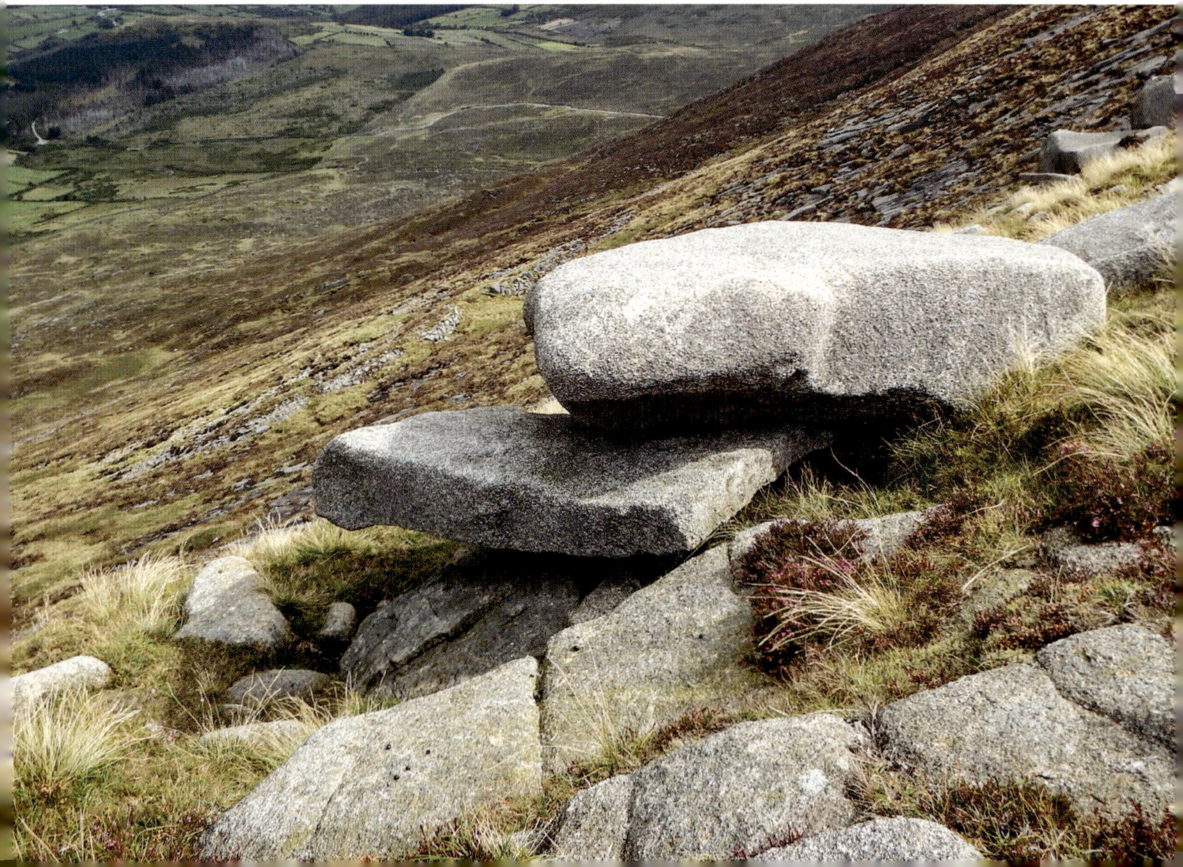

Above: High on the east slope of Slieve Bearnagh, about the 600m mark, is this enactment of intercourse. The lower stone is shown as crying out. Bearnagh is a rich hunting ground for monuments erected by the ancients.

Top opposite: These begetting stones are on the north-west side of Meelmore mountain commanding a great view over south Down. On the left of the photograph is a mountain marked on the OS map as Craigdoo. The pronunciation given to me by a local, however, was exactly as the Irish, namely **Créacht Duaigh**, 'gloomy ravine', a reference to a steep sided ravine behind the hill and out of sight from the Hilltown Road. The GPS of these begetting stones is:

                N.   54º 11. 620'
                W. 006º 00. 312'   Elevation 573m.

Lower opposite: A huge boulder indulges in copulation on the north flank of Shimial mountain. This part of Mourne, down to the former clachan of Clanawhillan, is still called by the shepherds, 'Horse's Meadow', from the Irish (*Tí na*) **h-Oiris Meadóg**, '(Place of the) landmark dagger'. The 'dagger' is a reference to Slieve Bearnagh as a phallic insert between Shimial and Meelmore.

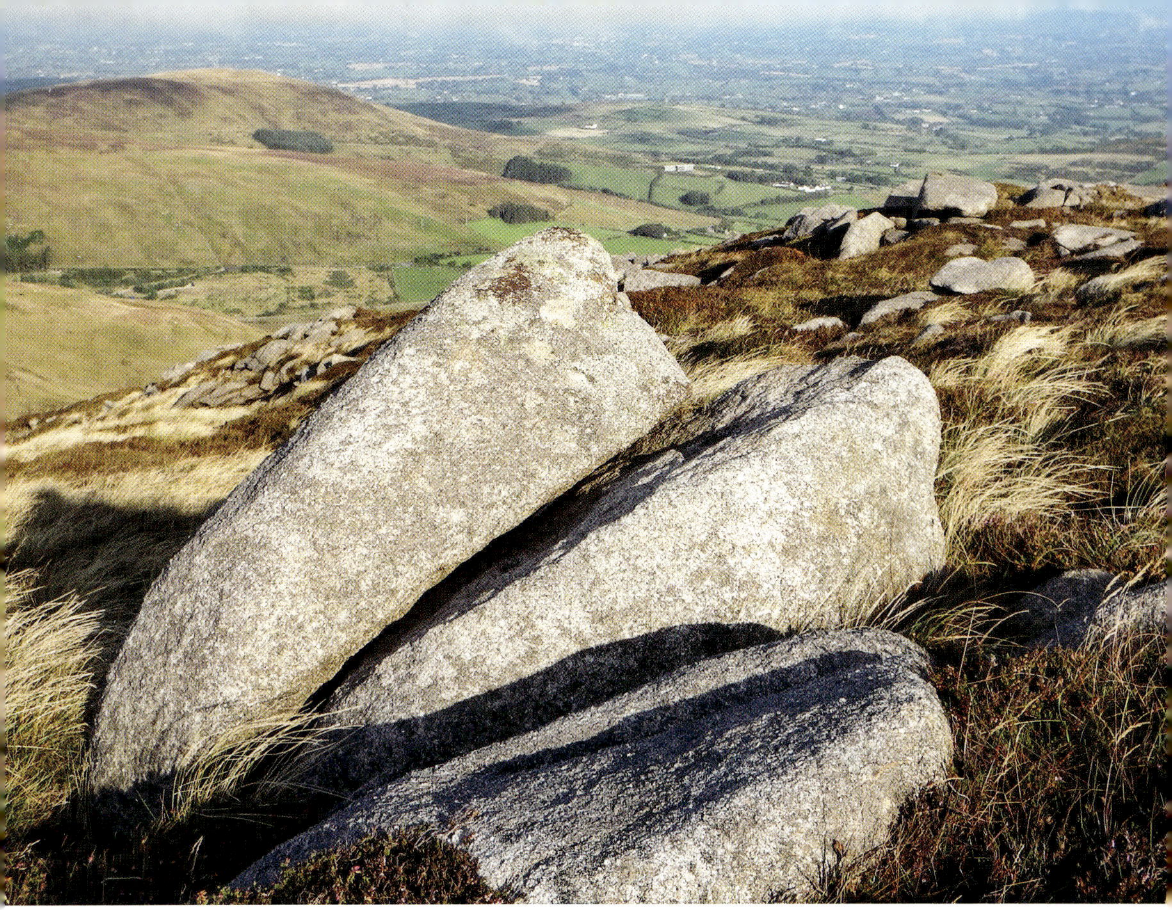

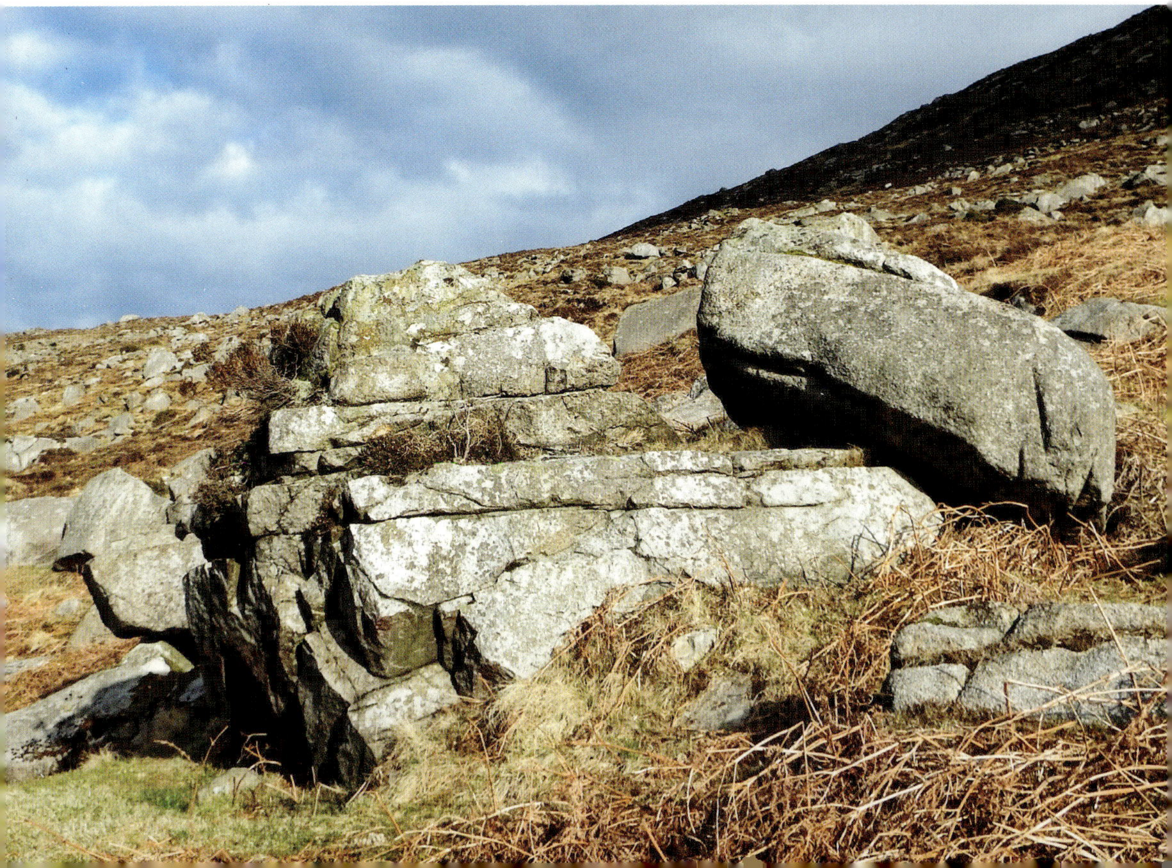

Above: We are looking at a monstrous granite boulder in the act of copulation on the west side of the Annalong valley under the cliff face. The stone is 4m across at the base, easily 3m up to the tip and about 1m thick. The size is a measure of the importance of this fertility location. The tip of the stone is directed to a 'vaginal cleft', or notch, on the cliff face above where the sun declines at summer solstice as if itself copulating with the earth. The GPS is:

                  N.   54° 09. 885'
                  W. 005° 56. 915'   Elevation 300m.

Top opposite: These substantial begetting slabs are found on the north side of Pollaphuca valley. The stone being serviced is a good 2.5m long. The GPS is:

                  N.   54° 11. 499'
                  W. 005° 59. 569'   Elevation 460m.

Lower opposite: This megalithic construction takes the word 'impressive' to a whole new level. It is found on the eastern side of Lamagan about level with the top of Lower Cove. Three slabs are presented in a great act of copulation. On approaching from below the smallest stone at the front is seen to be 'crying out'. The top stone is a mighty 5m long by 3m across by 1m thick and the orientation is to winter solstice sunrise beyond the south side of Rocky mountain. The GPS is:

                  N.   54° 09. 985'
                  W. 005° 57. 506'   Elevation 471m.

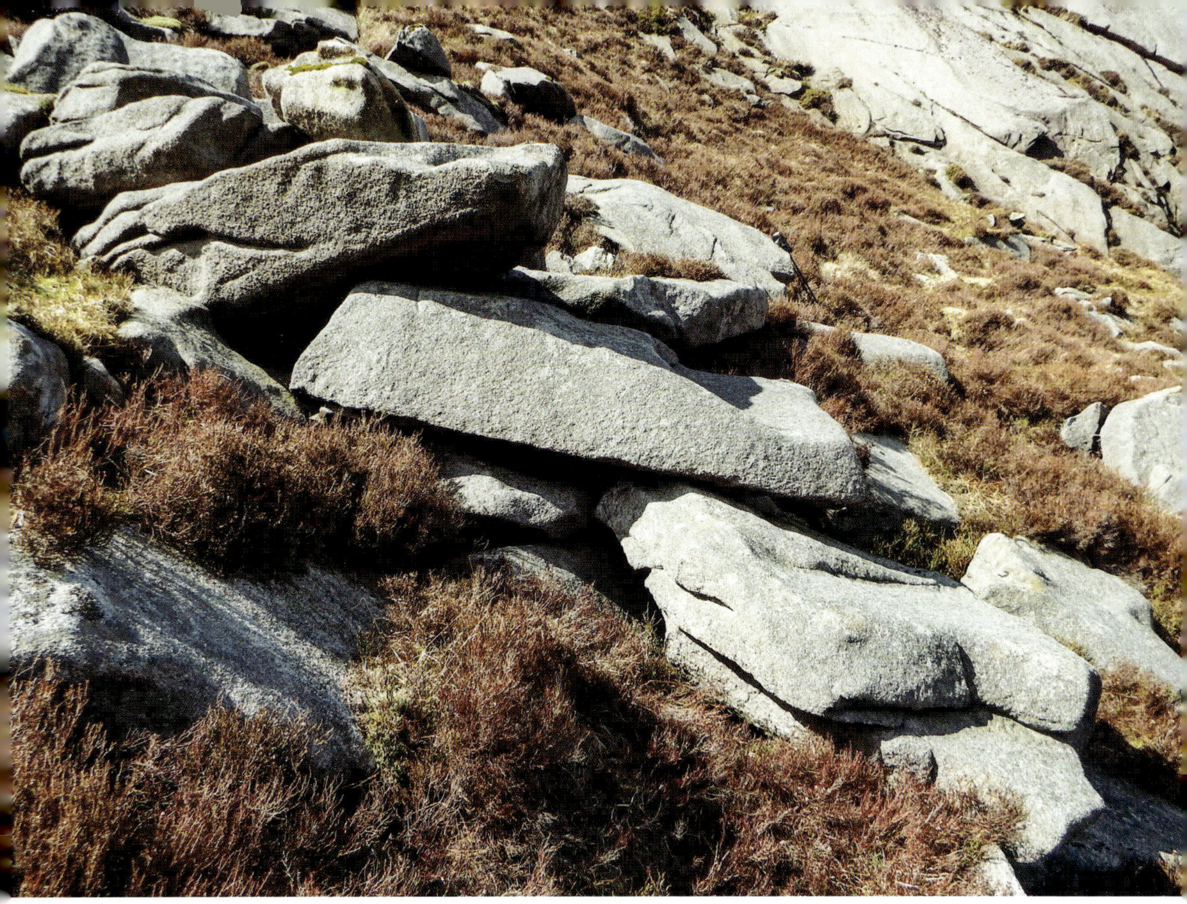
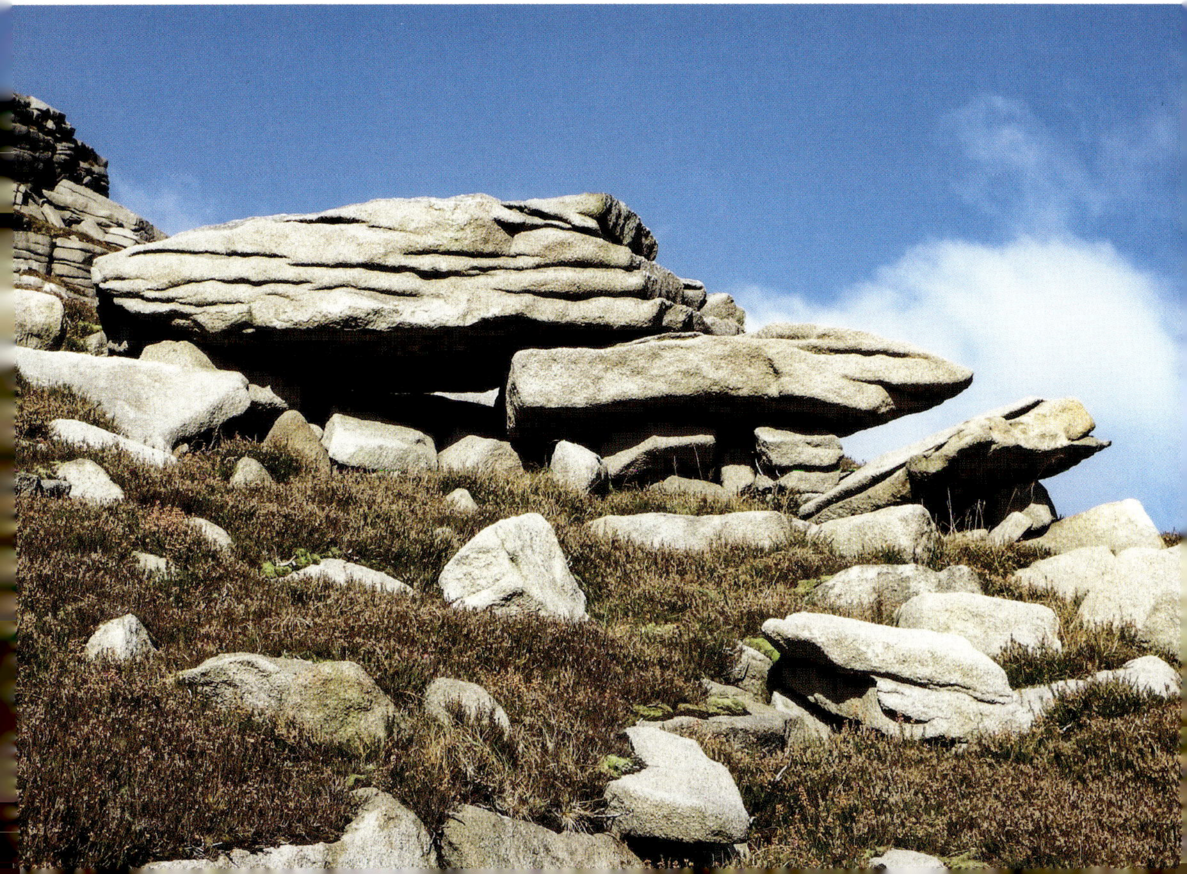

Above: A pleasing and low lying pair of copulating stones that could very easily be missed. They are on the plateau above Lower Cove.

Top opposite: This important monument of two stones in the act of begetting is on a little isolated mound at the mouth of the Drinneevar quarry. A corrupt version of the monument's name was recorded as a note by John O'Donovan of the ordnance survey when he visited the area in April 1834. The original Irish name is **Braighde a eibhir óg a Geinte**, 'Prisoners of the new granite of the act of begetting'. The lower of the fertility stones has been given the head of a turtle. Its head and body are of shale and its carapace is of granite. It is a simple yet very effective ancient sculpture. The GPS is:

N. 54° 11. 297'
W. 005° 53. 509'   Elevation 306m

Lower opposite: What a serious brute of a megalith. This construction is above the trail to Upper Cove on the seaward side of Lamagan. What cannot be fully gauged from the photograph is the truly intimidating size of the copulating monster. That top stone is nearly five meters across at the bottom back. The GPS is:

N. 54° 09. 999'
W. 005° 57. 482'   Elevation 467m.

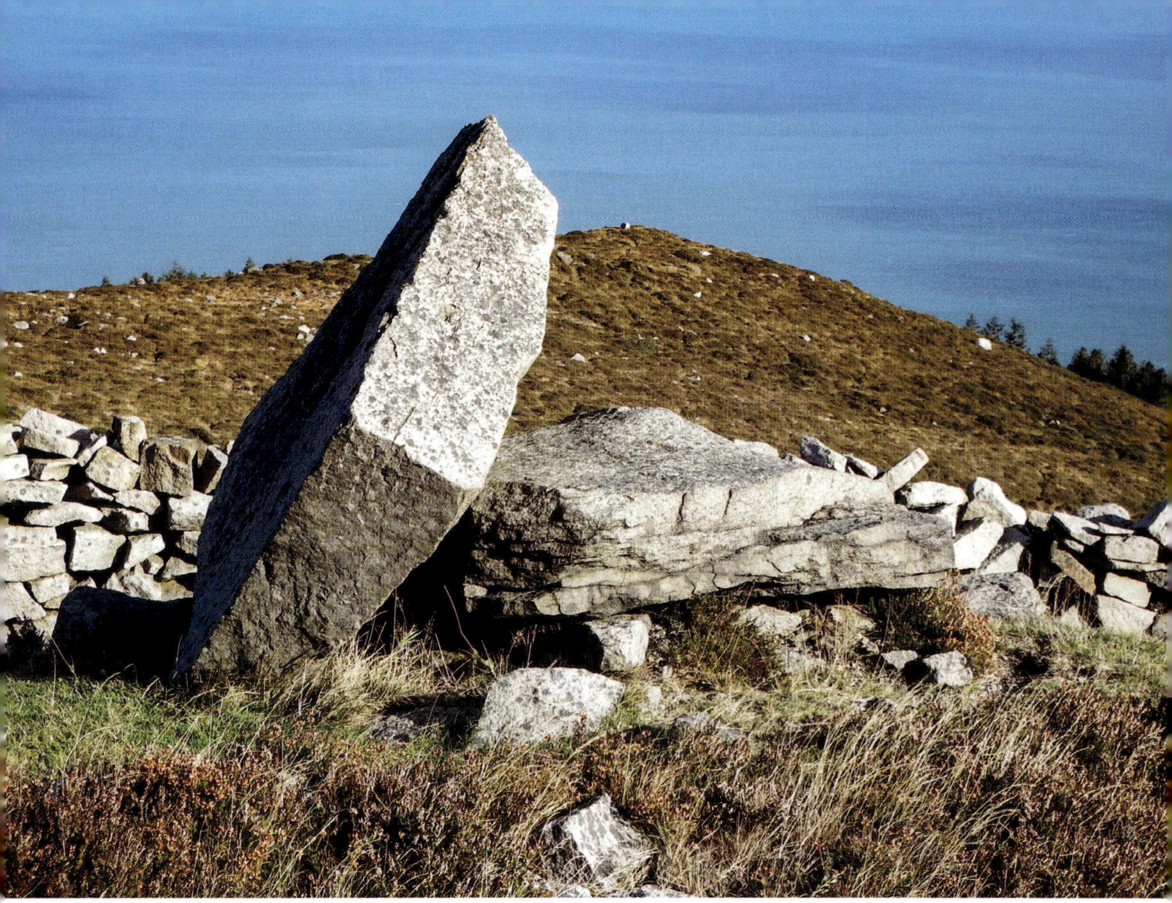

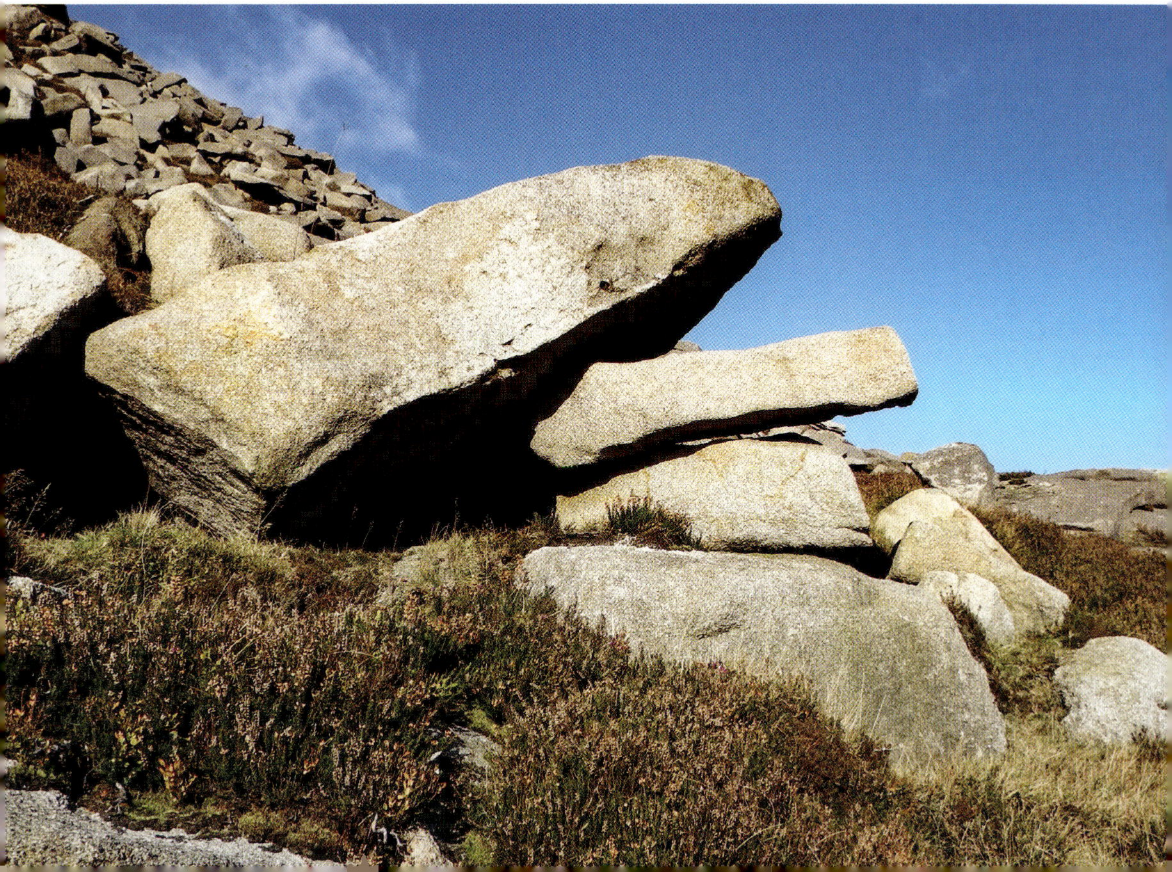

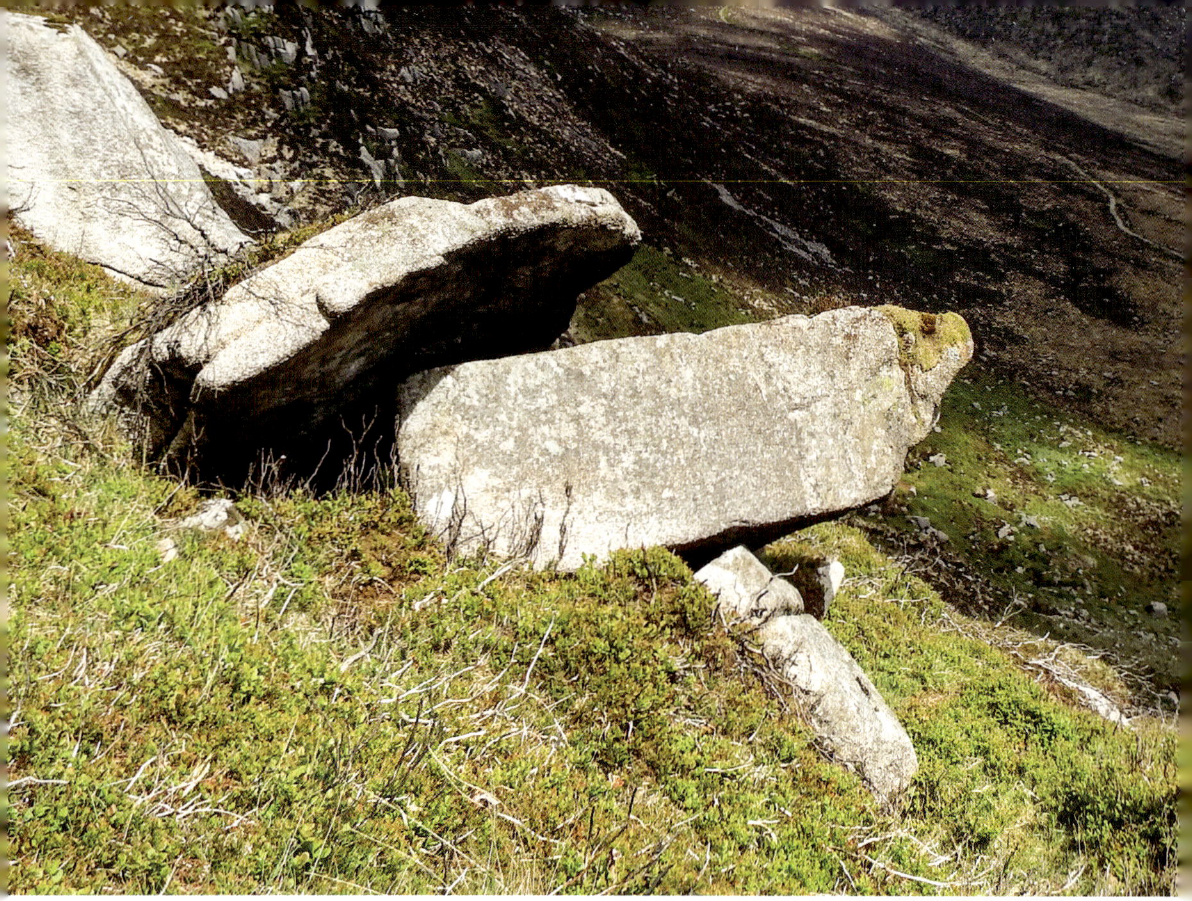

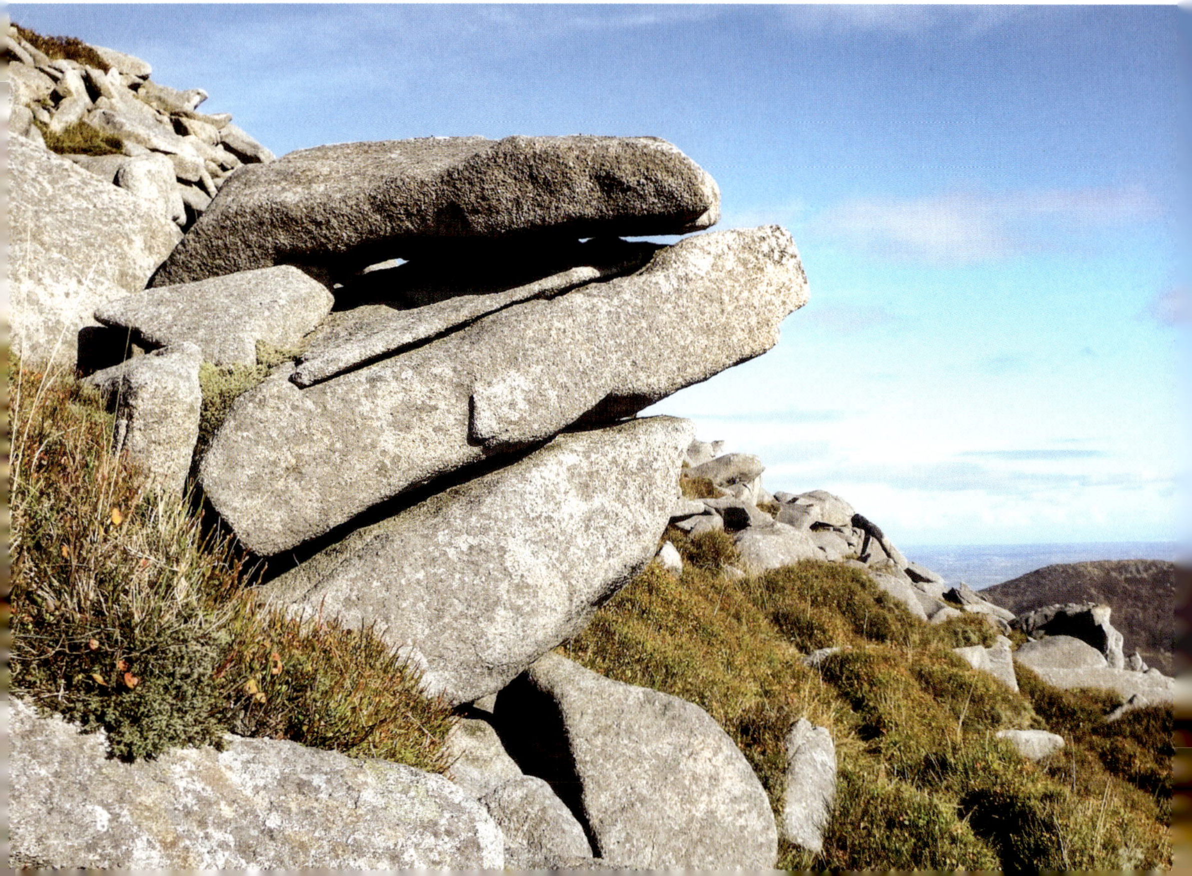

Top opposite: Two great stones are in the act of copulation. They are perched right on the edge of a precipitous slope overlooking the Windy Gap valley. Indeed, the lower stone could virtually be classified as a *Leachtán*, such is the projection out over a void.

Lower opposite: This compound megalith, featuring an act of begetting, is on the east side of Wee Slevanmore. It was named 'The Child's Seat'. Note how the middle stone has an 'open mouth' as if crying out at climax. Underneath this pyramid of spear stones, in a sheltered sunny spot, is the carefully constructed child size seat, no doubt for a *buachail*, 'a herd-boy'. The GPS is:

$$\text{N. } 54° \text{ 11. 166'}$$
$$\text{W. } 006° \text{ 00. 053'} \qquad \text{Elevation 621m.}$$

Top of this page: Truly one of the jewels of Mourne. It was a pleasure to name this fabulous compound megalith, **Ní'l a Leithéid Ann**, 'There is not another like him'. You will find it on the north side of Pollaphuca valley. Even when looked at from the opposite side of the valley, say from the Lecarry Loanin track, you can see how this gem is located on a particularly phallic looking rock outcrop. The mighty capstone is 3.2m by 2.2m across. There is a face on the top surface. This is a construction of many secrets. How, for instance, did they manoeuvre these stones in such an awkward position? The GPS is:

$$\text{N. } 54° \text{ 11. 438'}$$
$$\text{W. } 005° \text{ 59. 630'} \qquad \text{Elevation 479m.}$$

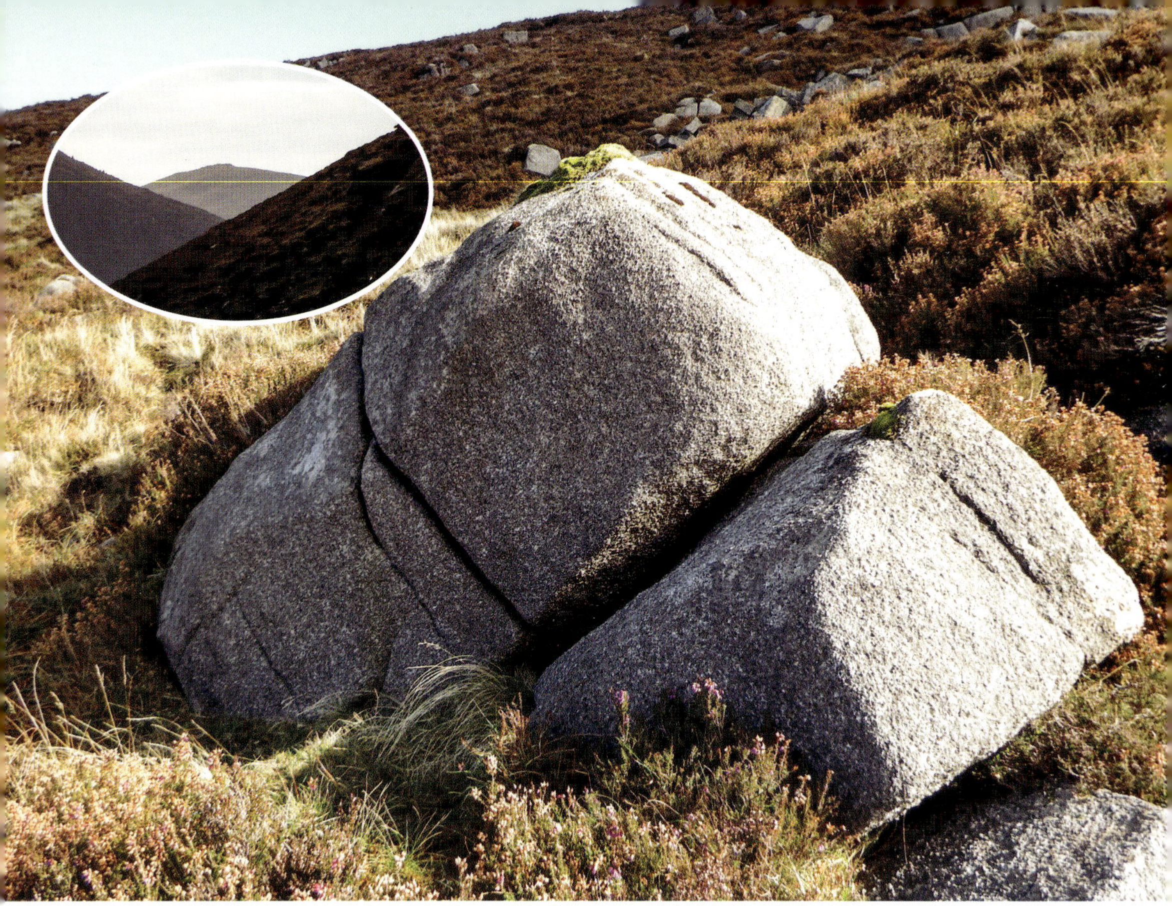

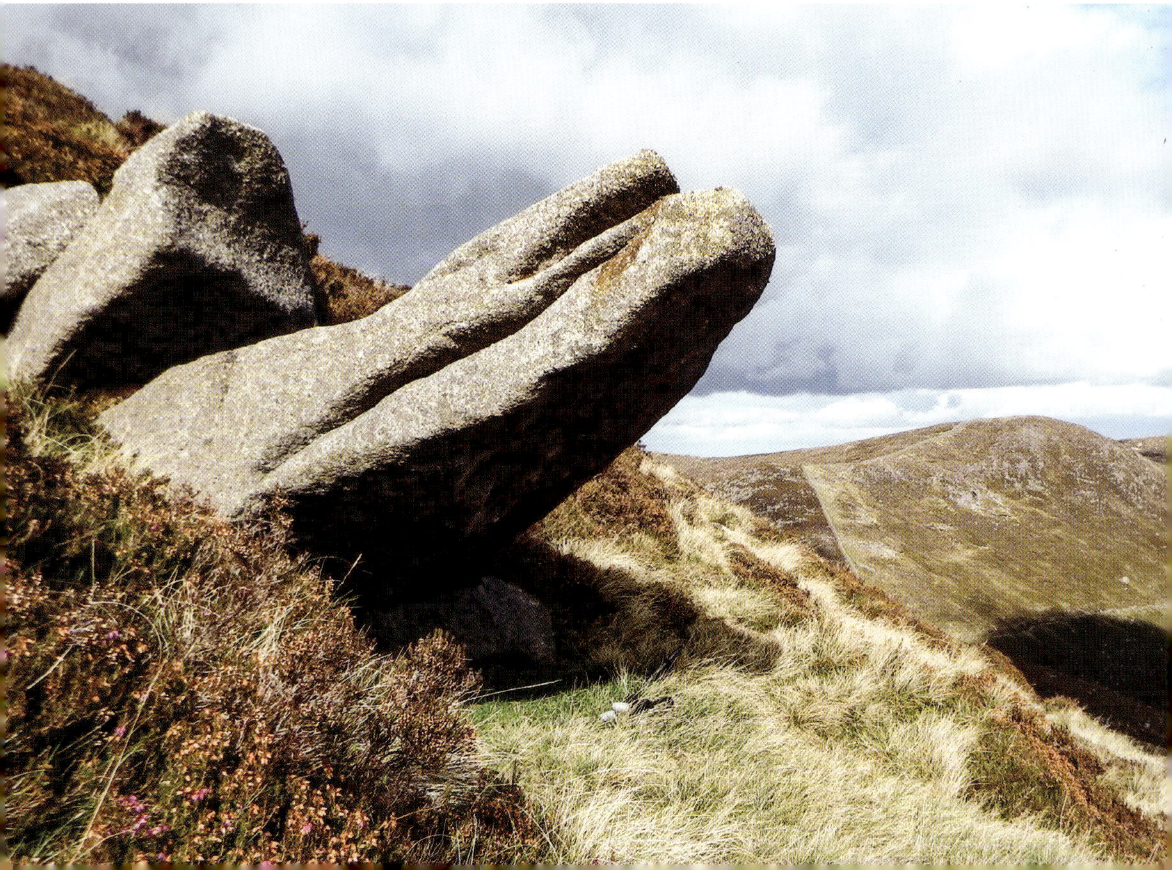

Top opposite: Overlooking the Trassey valley from the northern end of Slievenaglogh and below the eastern granite trail, will be found this large 2.5m priapic granite boulder raised up in the begetting position. The raison d'être behind the immense efforts in the stone's placement lie with the distant view of Slieve Bignian as seen through the Hares Gap. Our inset circle shows how the megalith marks the tip of Bignian as a 'penis in the vagina' in the landscape notch between Lamagan and Bearnagh. The GPS is:

N.   54° 11. 708'
W. 005° 58. 510'   Elevation 444m.

Lower opposite: The counter-balance stone in this fertility creation would seem to also service the stone below. The ensemble is found on the east slopes of Slieve Bearnagh. Slievenaglogh is in the background.

Top of this page: A great slab on the slope of Wee Slevanmore, perhaps 3m long by 2m wide, appears to cry out as it is serviced. The counter-balance has been given a smiling face as it goes about its work. The GPS is:

N.   54° 11. 115'
W. 006° 00. 099'   Elevation 572m.

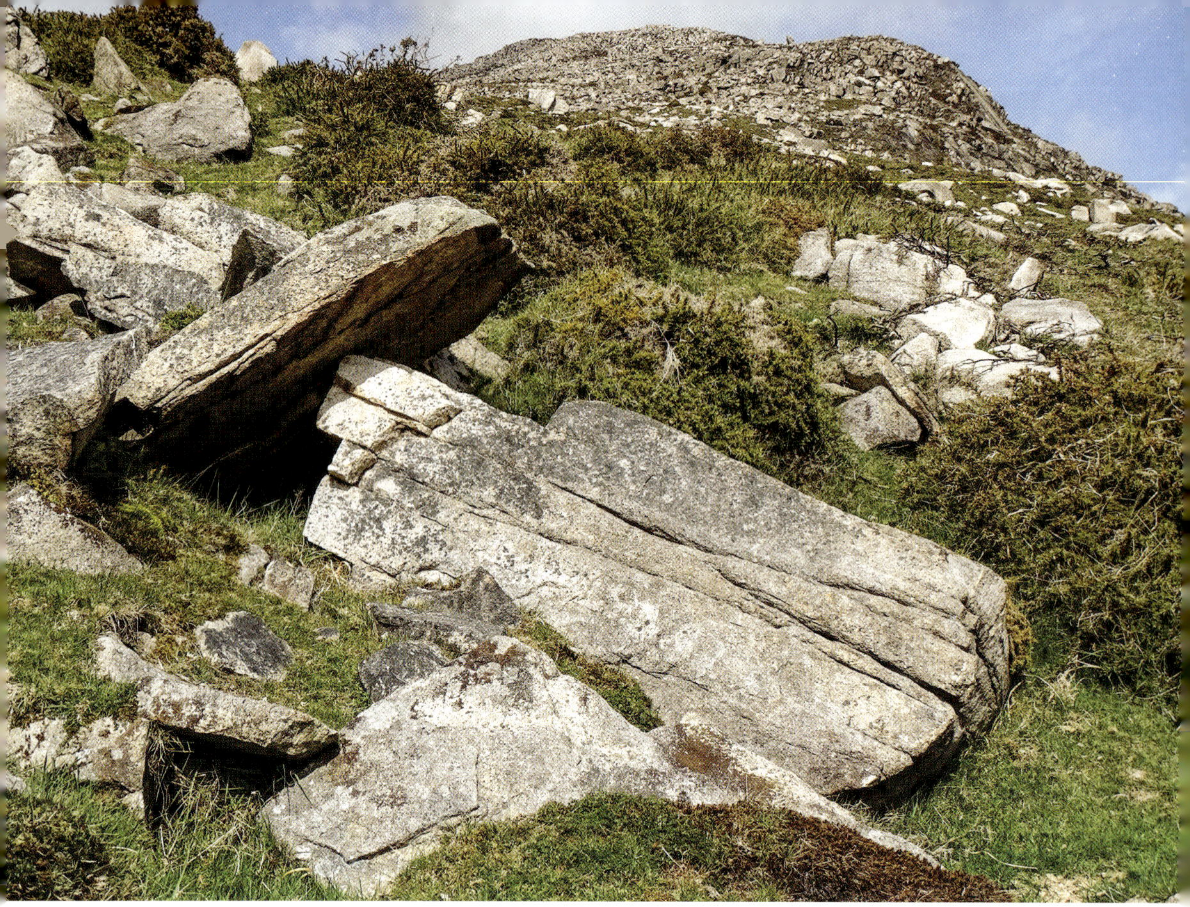

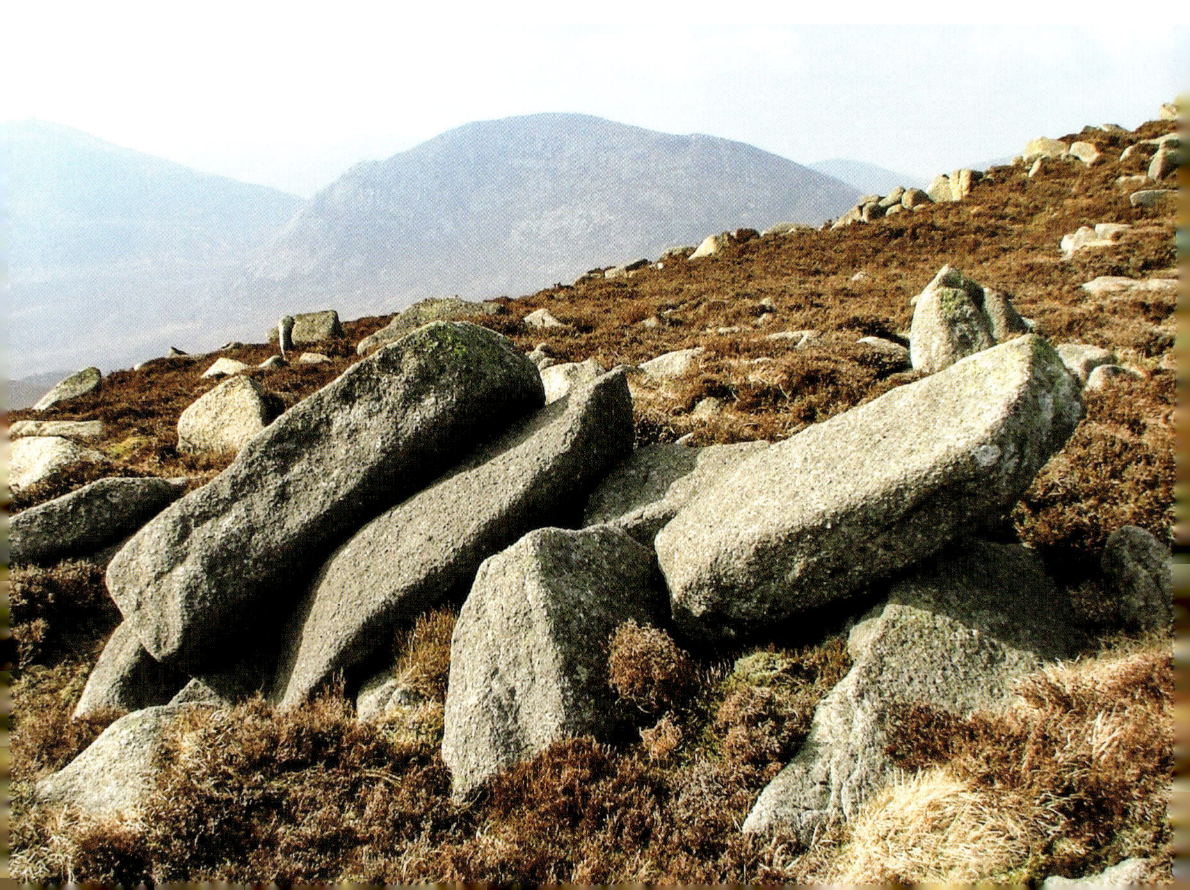

Top opposite: With lovely views out over Dundrum Bay, a comparatively small granite stone, of just over 1m length, indulges in copulation on the south-east slope of Leganabruchan. The GPS is:

                      N.   54º 10. 666'
                      W. 005º 53. 527'   Elevation 259m.

Lower opposite: Towards the eastern end of Chimney Rock is this unusual combination of stones. On the left two stones are placed in the act of begetting. On the right is a phallic stone raised erect, while behind it are two boulders to represent its testicles. The hazy bulk of Lamagan mountain is in the background.

Top of this page: Our photograph was taken on a summer solstice day on the south-east flank of Slieve Donard. It is a classic example of begetting. In fact it was named 'The Rear Shunt'. The tip of the upper slab has been directed at the end of the Isle of Man on the horizon (not shown). The GPS is:

                      N.   54º 10. 766'
                      W. 005º 54. 798'   Elevation 610m.

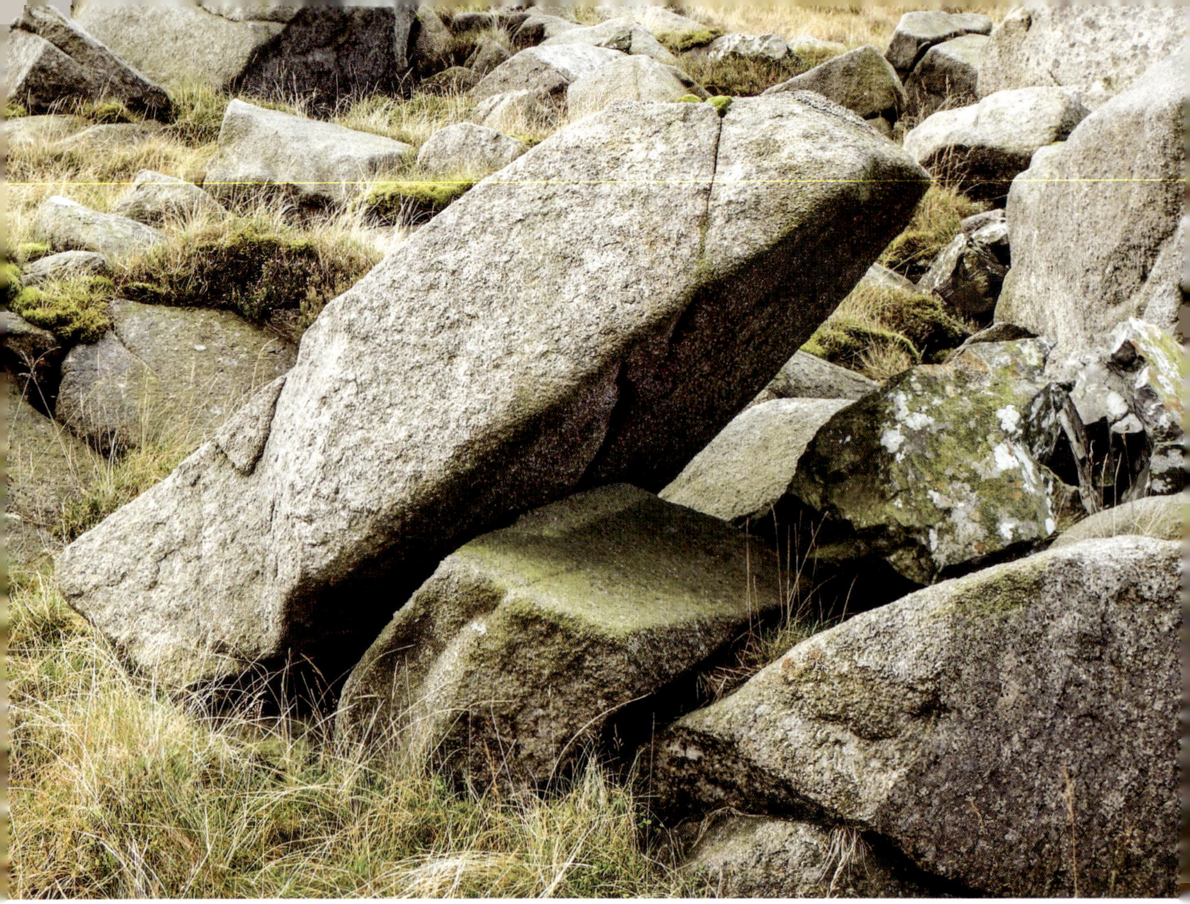

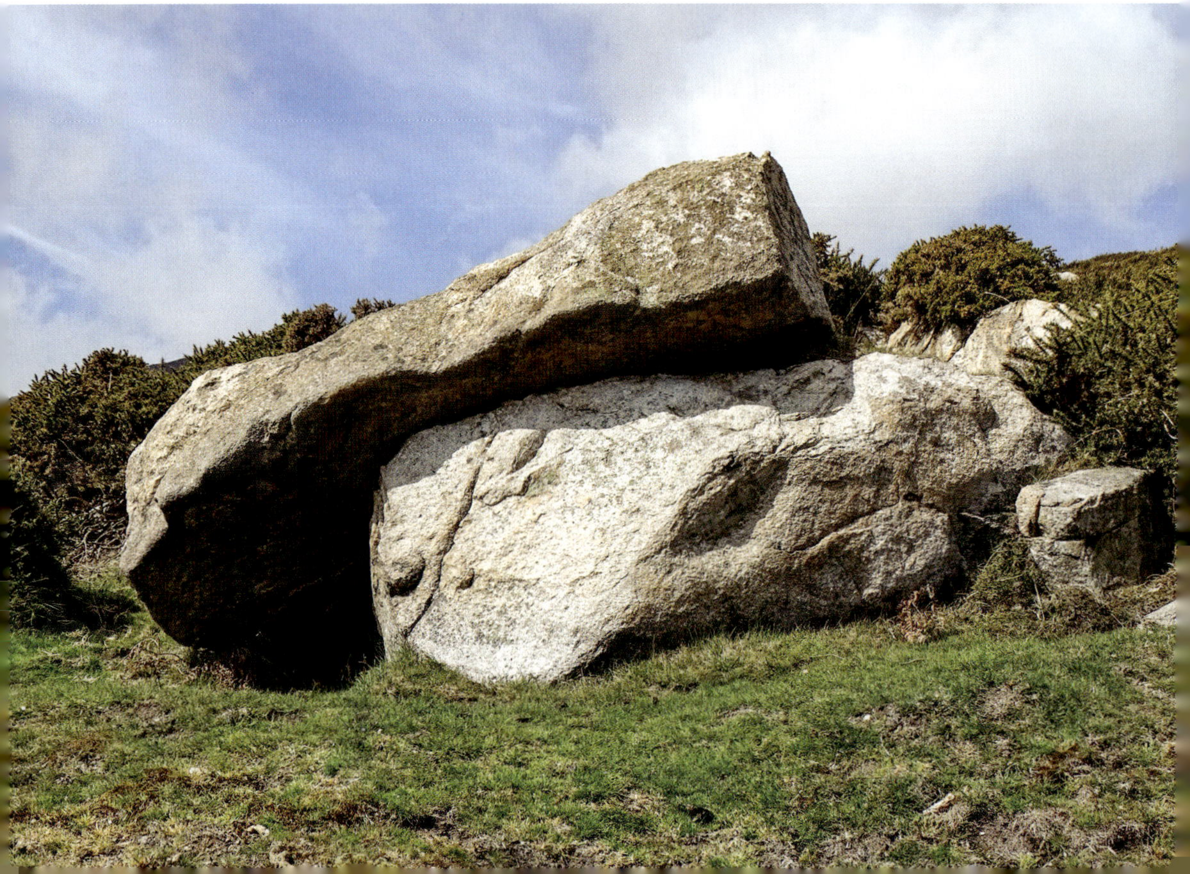

Top opposite: It was a misty morning along the south side of Happy Valley when this copulating phallic spear was photographed. The dull conditions could not detract from this wonderful megalith. The spear boulder is a sizeable 2.4m in length by 1m across. An interesting feature is the placing of a shale stone directly below the rearing tip which itself features a crack representing a coronal rim. The union, or proximity, of granite and shale is a frequently used metaphor for the union of man and woman. The GPS is
                    N.   54º 11. 422'
                    W. 006º 00. 848'   Elevation 429m.

Lower opposite: A mighty slab goes about its business of copulation on the south-east slope of Leganabruchan. The phallic spear point of the large upper megalith looks to the end of St. John's Point across Dundrum Bay. In the days of transition from Irish that projecting Point used to be referred to by fishermen as the 'Foreland'. This was a mnemonic of **Borr Lán**, 'a perfect lump', ie. an erect penis. Note the tiny little phallic knob at the tip of the upper stone. The GPS is:
                    N.   54º 10. 651'
                    W. 005º 53. 507'   Elevation 258m.

Top of this page: To be found above the quarry on Rocky Mountain. The large top stone is approximately 2m by 2m and these fertility stones have been left severely alone although the granite-men worked extensively all around. The location marks the fertility event of the summer solstice sun declining onto the summit of Rocky. The mountain was deemed to come to climax at the moment of joining of sun and earth. The GPS is:
                    N.   54º 09. 395'
                    W. 005º 55. 865'   Elevation 451m.

On the south-east side of Slieve Corragh, in a most beautiful location, is one of the more explicit portrayals of fellatio. The slim granite stone stands erect to over 2m. On the ground beside it is a large slab with a shadow eye and a big concave open mouth intent on fellatio. The GPS is:

N. 54º 11. 595'
W. 005º 57. 933'   Elevation 564m.

FELLATIO STONES

It was a different time, a different era and a totally different mind-set from what prevails today. Those were pagan times. The elder faith worshipped the sun and fertility and expressed itself in the erection of a multitude of megaliths of a sexual nature. Welcome or unwelcome, these megaliths are now part of our heritage. Portrayals of fellatio across the hills of Mourne are even more important by their very survival as so many monuments elsewhere were destroyed. The stones were preserved by their remoteness in the hills when others in the lowlands were often toppled and removed. The great naturalist, Robert Lloyd Praegar, told how he once went in search of a monument near Kilkeel only to find that the land owner had broken it up to sell the granite.*

The next few pages feature some of the more overt instances of the oral sex act portrayed in granite. It is much more common however to find examples of this artwork as subsidiary characteristics of a larger megalith. It is almost as if the ancients, having gone to a lot of effort to install some great stone, decided to 'get their money's worth' and chipped and chopped to convey the impression of multiple 'faces' and illustrations of sexually suggestive artwork.

Look again at the scenic view of the Pot of Legawherry on page v of the preliminaries. Notice the tiny 'open mouth' stone on the left-side of the rock in the pond. It doesn't take too much imagination to realise some Christian soul has turned it away from its little phallic object of interest on the right side. The humour of the ancients is all around us with their pagan depictions.

One last reflection before looking at fellatio stones concerns the phrase 'The Mystic Mournes' [p.154, 'Midst Mountainous Mourne' by M.G. Crawford, *Legendary Tales*, Newry, 1913]. On the face of it the term would seem quite innocuous and Crawford was using it in the sense of a place 'grand and majestic'. However, he placed the term in inverted commas which was often his code for Irish origins or a deeper meaning. Rather than implying something like the 'magical' Mournes in English, the term 'mystic' is a phonetic rendering of the Irish *Mí Stách*, 'evil stake or post' (ie. an erect phallus). Notions of fertility and procreation were never far away in Mourne.

---

* The 'Preservation' of Ancient Monuments by R. Lloyd Praeger.
 Pages 100-101, U.J.A., Vol 4, No: 2, January 1898.

Above: Near the top of Spellack two stones face each other. The lower stone with the 'open mouth' looks across the 1.2m gap with fellatio intent. If you get this far note that the spear point of the upper stone points to the distant sliver of Shan Slieve mountain in the landscape notch between Slievenaglogh and its shoulder, Shimial. This view is the fertility motif common in Mourne of the 'Penis in the Vagina'. The GPS is:

                     N.   54º 11. 788'
                     W. 005º 59. 439'   Elevation 482m.

Top opposite: High on a cliff face overlooking the Trassey Valley at the southern end of Spellack is this rock art; elevation would thus be a guess. The rock face has been given a deep shadow eye to compliment a fissure mouth on a large flat slab half way up the gully. The 'mouth' is pressed up against an upright phallic spear shape on the cliff suggesting immanent fellatio. Cliff-face rock art is quite common. The GPS is:

                     N.   54º 11. 810'
                     W. 005º 59. 331'

Lower opposite: Under Spellack's northern shoulder an impertinent granite boulder has a wide open 'mouth' for the little phallic stone below. Although it can hardly be seen in the photograph the location marks a sliver of Shan Slieve mountain peeping up in the distant landscape notch between Lukes Mountain on the left and Shimial on the centre right. The GPS is:

                     N.   54º 12. 037'
                     W. 005º 59. 660'   Elevation 291m.

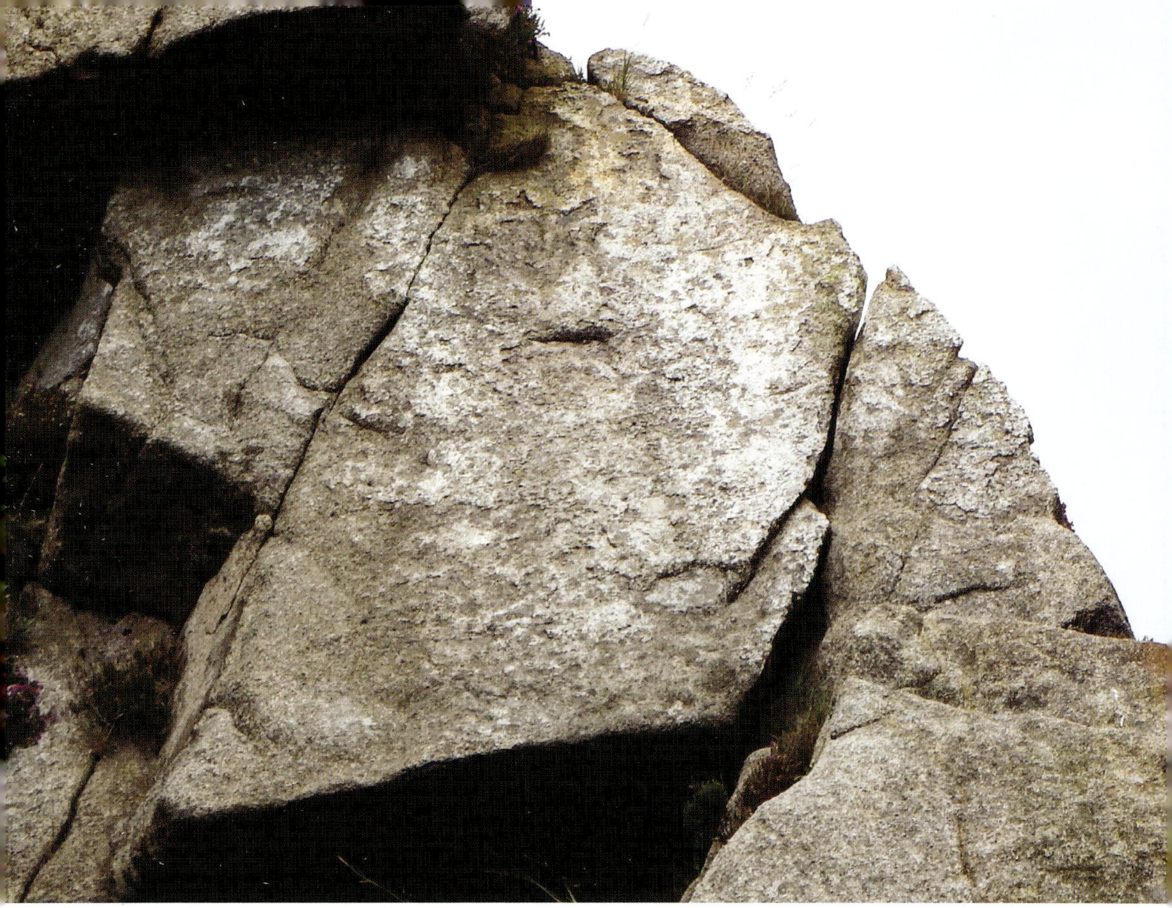

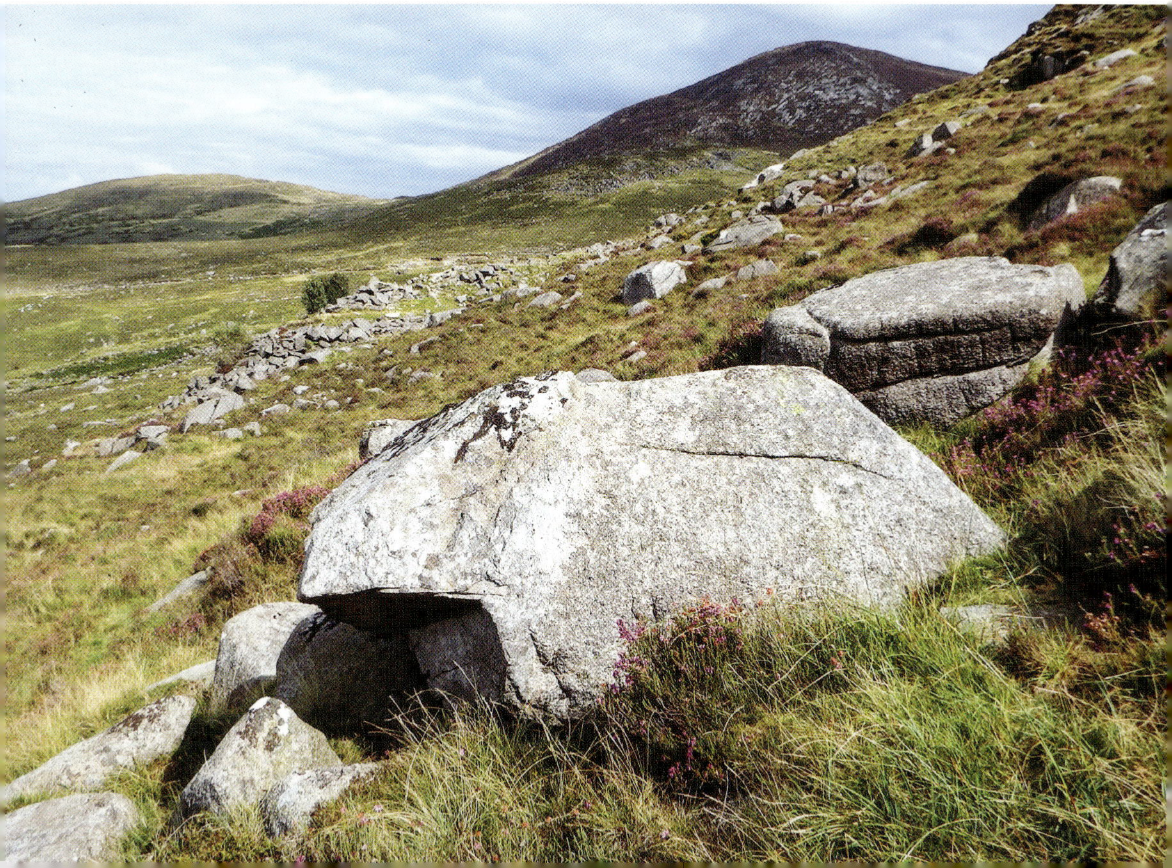

Above: Near Meelmore summit on the north west side of the mountain is **Blad**, 'open mouth', an upright curved granite slab that has been arranged so that the great curve becomes a 'mouth' intent on fellatio with a lower stone. There is a further instance of fellatio in the background. The GPS is:

                    N.   54° 11. 605'
                    W. 005° 59. 930'   Elevation 634m.

Top opposite: Along a rock outcrop on the flank of Wee Shimial hill will be found this scene of a stone with a great [L] shaped 'mouth' intent on fellatio with an adjacent companion. The GPS is:

                    N.   54° 12. 049'
                    W. 005° 59. 060'   Elevation 323m.

Lower opposite: There is nothing ambiguous about the intentions of this great slab on the eastern slopes of Slieve Bearnagh. It acts as a base support for the pointing phallic spear stone above and at the same time targets the tip of a second anchor stone beside it. A horizontal chopped line acts as a shadow eye for a face stone in the right background.

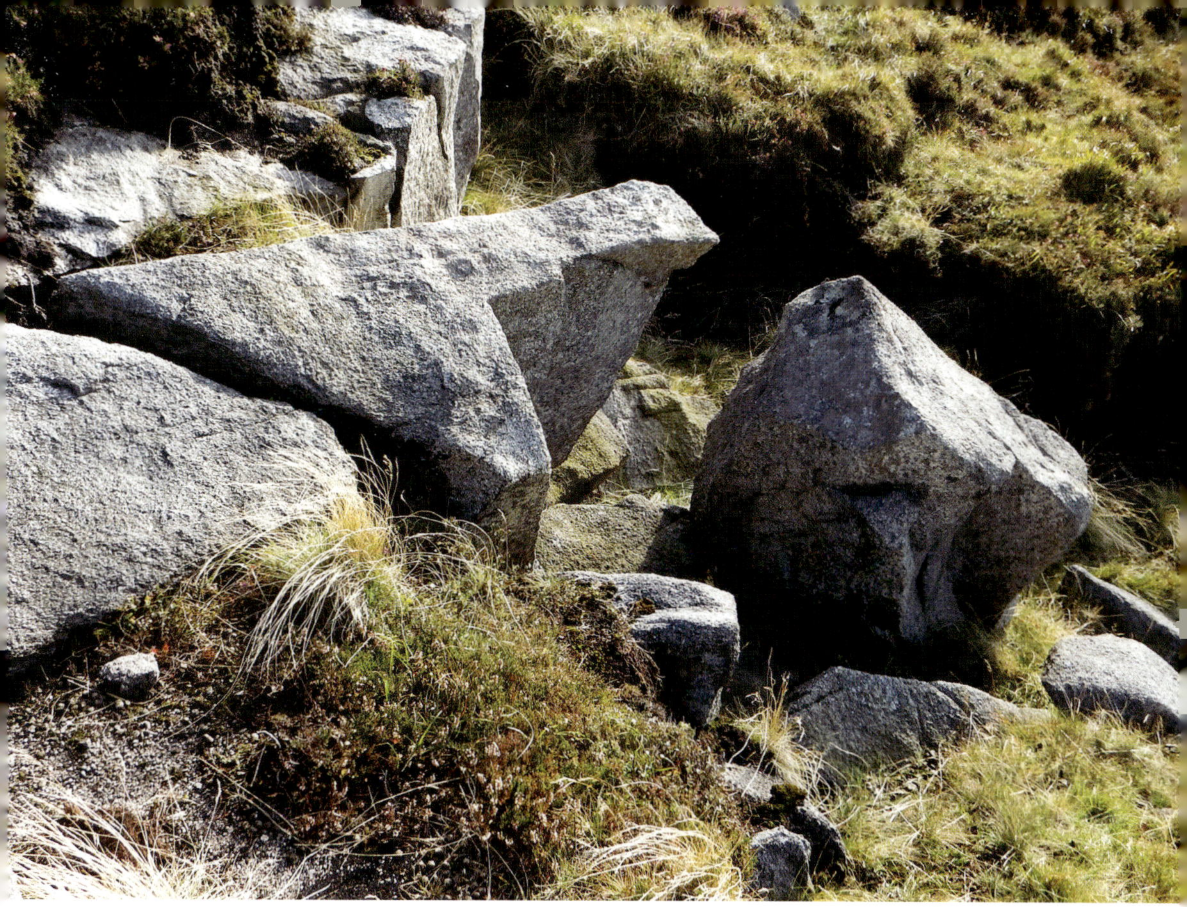

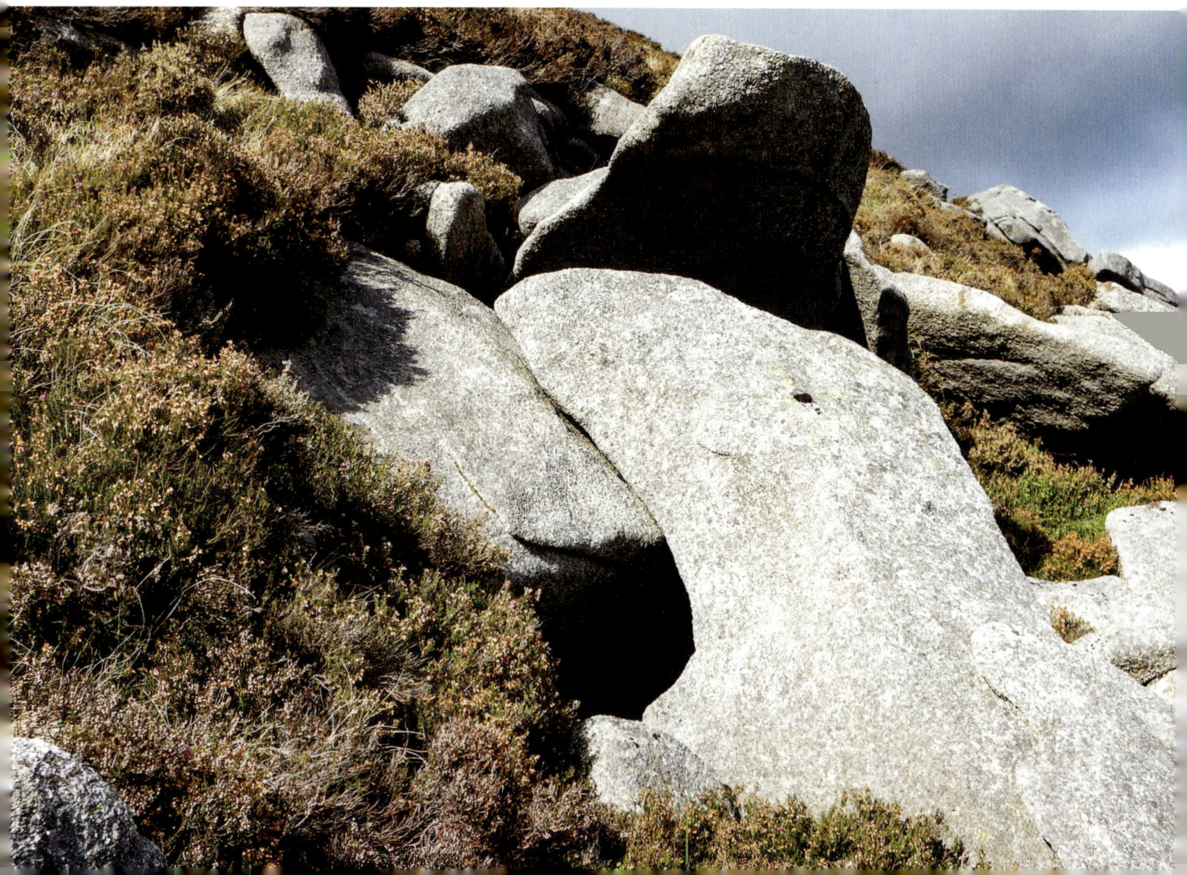

Above: When next you are here, take time to carefully examine the cliff face at Spellack's north corner. The ancients have exploited the natural lines on the cliff and, by the expedient of creating shadow eyes, have used the cliff as a giant canvas for their very fertile imagination to depict multiple instances of fellatio. Many may not be discerned now due to the small scale of the photograph but try a search to the left of the dark cavity on the left side to see a more obvious one. We should also remember the dangers undertaken by the artists in the making of so many eyes and faces on the cliff face as they dangled on ropes.

Top opposite: Under Spellack cliff the fine tapering point of a large diamond shaped spear stone becomes the object of desire for the open mouth stone beside it. Though it may not look it in the photograph, the spear stone is really large being over 3m long and 2m wide. The tip appears aligned to summer solstice dawn. The GPS is:

N. 54° 11. 966'
W. 005° 59. 430'   Elevation 348m.

Lower opposite: This little image is to be seen on a low outcrop in the upper reaches of the Aughnaleck river valley on Long mountain. While attention goes to the fellatio cartoon, the stone on the right has its own fertility symbolism. The two vertical lines on the rock are frequently used to represent a penis between two labial sides.

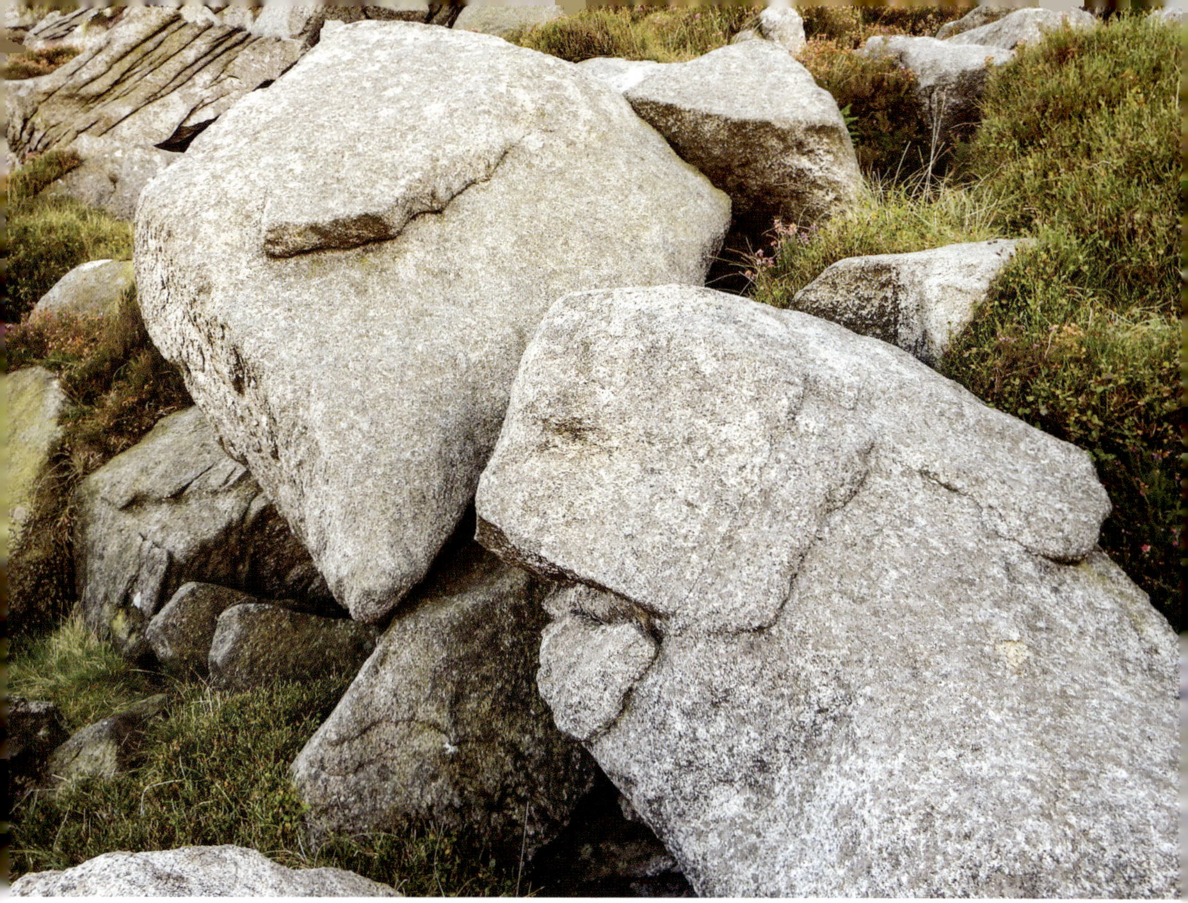

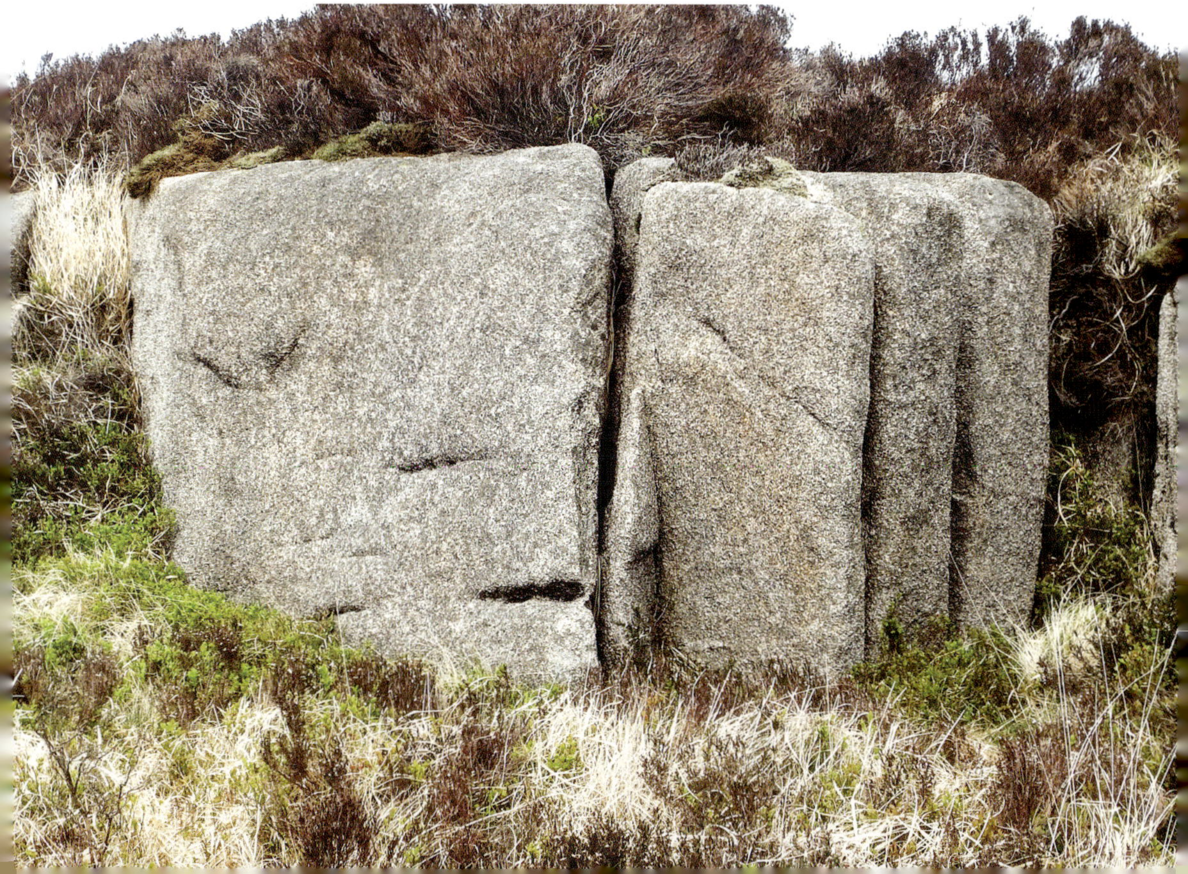

Above: A large granite boulder under the northern side of Spellack measures over 3m long by 2m wide. The big open mouth is about 1m across. It was named *Diúgálaim*, 'I suck'. The GPS is:

>> N. 54° 11. 970'
>> W. 005° 59. 432'   Elevation 346m.

Top opposite: On the north side of Pollaphuca valley and at the low end of a granite outcrop an ambitious little upright stone opens its mouth wide to attend to the phallic knob on the rock face beside it. The GPS is:

>> N. 54° 11. 409'
>> W. 005° 59. 551'   Elevation 433m.

Lower opposite: This powerful instance of fellatio is found on the west side of Wee Roosley. The area is generally off the beaten track but it is certainly rich in megaliths. Note, for instance, the phallic stone in the background.

Other large boulders have been placed along the hill-top, and some look to the summit of Slievemartin to the south-east as a phallic insertion on the distant skyline between two other hills. A sliver of what seems to be Finlieve is also visible elsewhere. Such fertility views were loved by the ancients. One of these tips was referred to as a 'reed', a euphemism for a phallus. In Irish the 'reed' was *Gáinne* which survives as the name for the present Ghann river. The bog below the megaliths was its source.

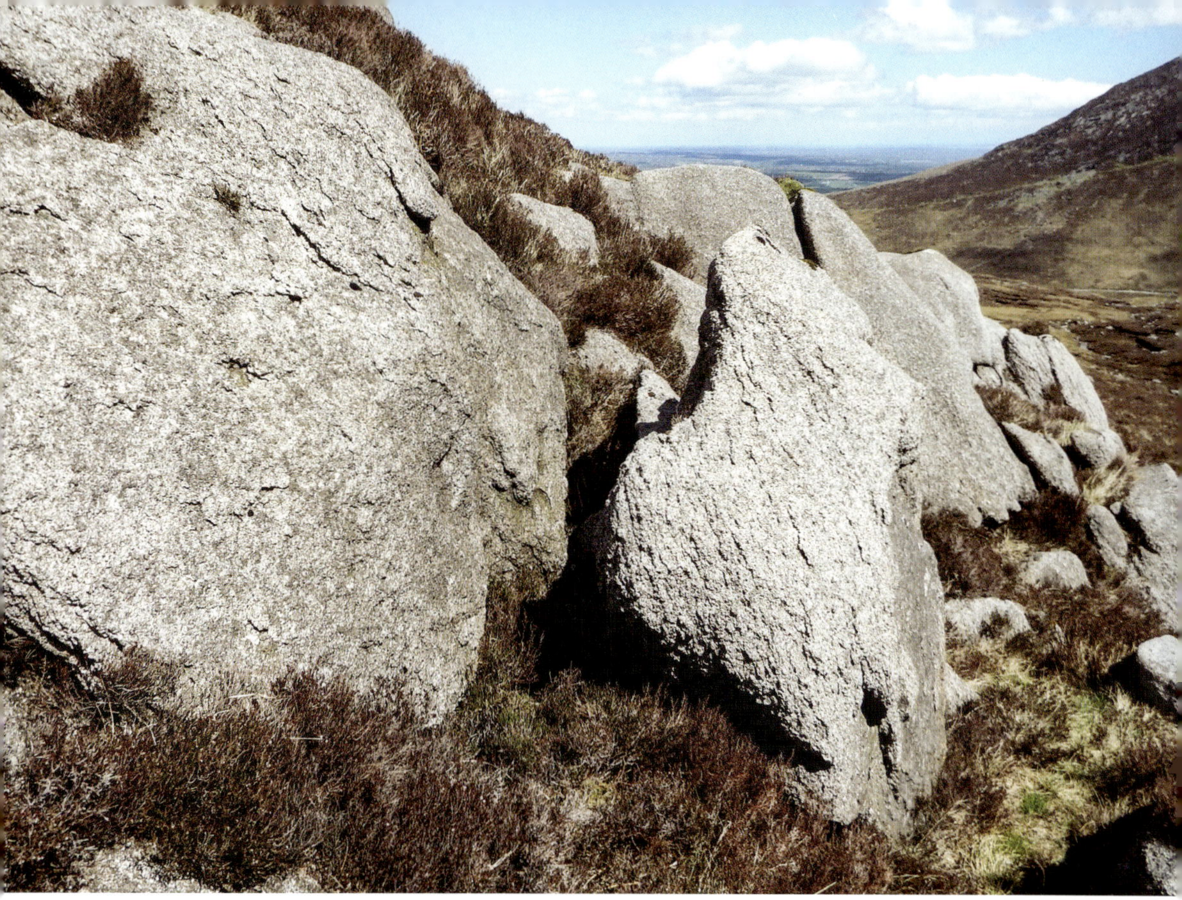

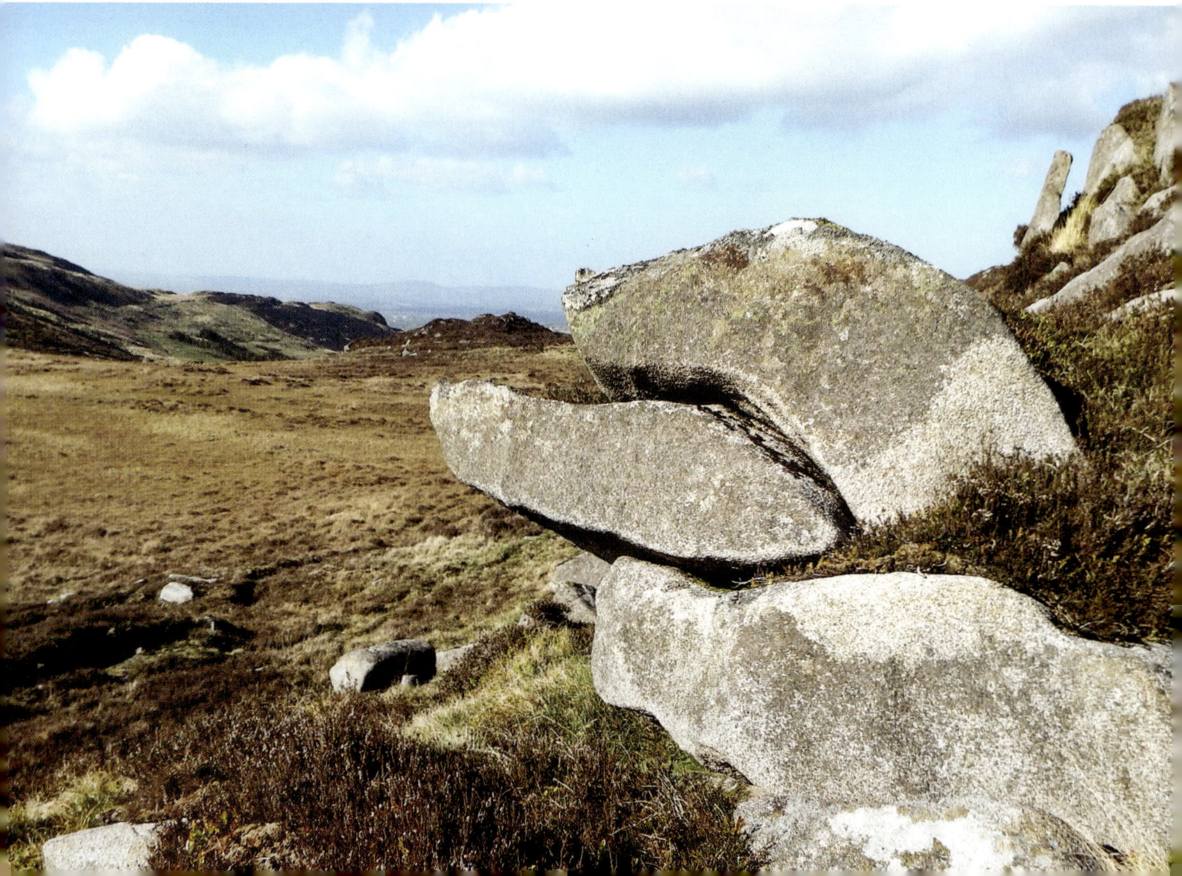

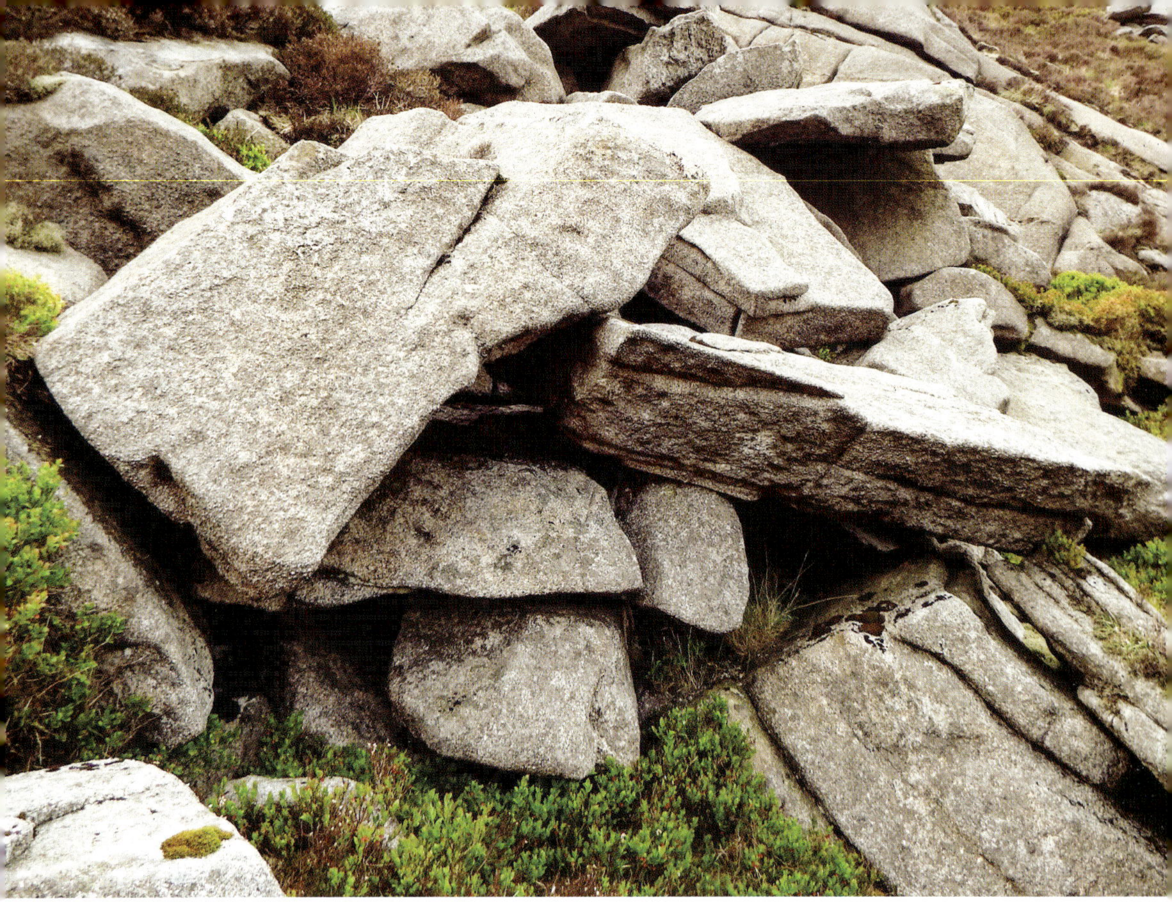

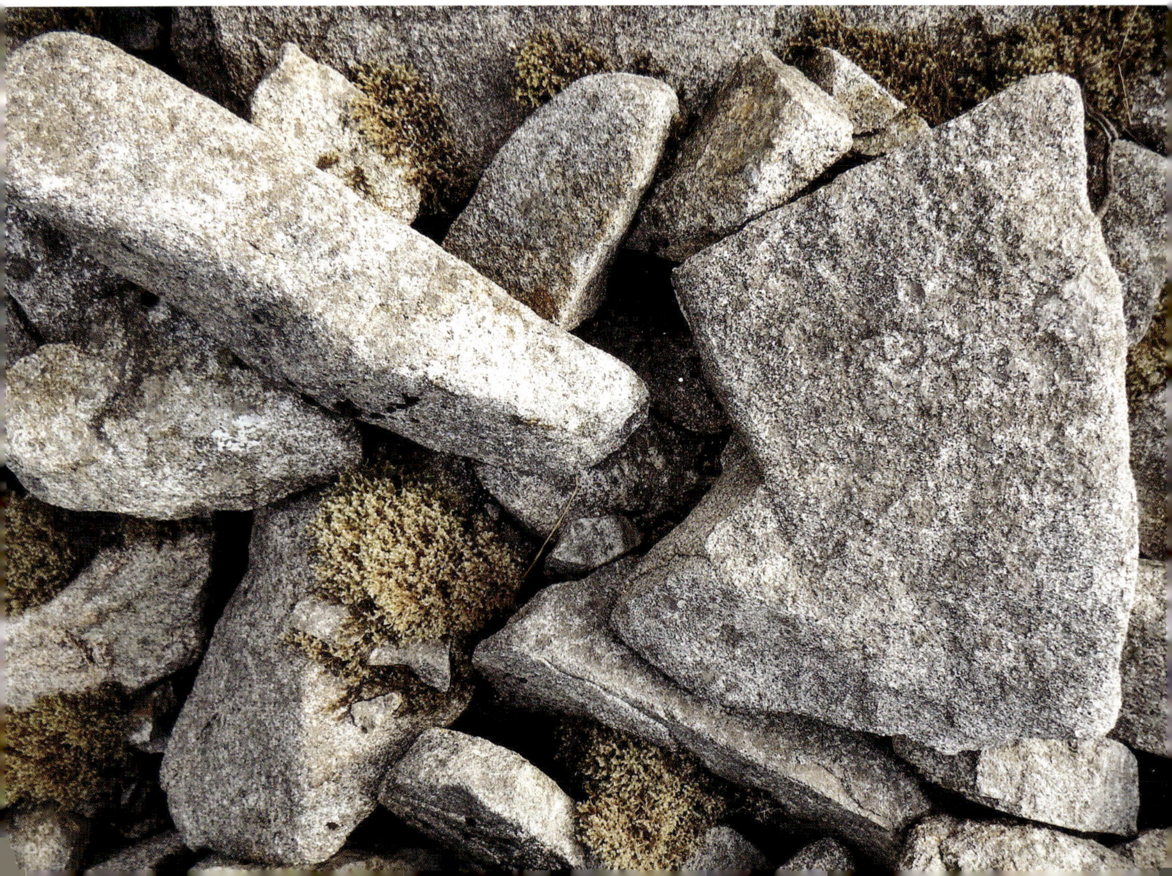

Top opposite: These stones showing fellatio are found in Pollaphuca valley under Meelmore. Notes from six years ago recorded, 'This area is so rich in megaliths I am just stepping from one to another'. The GPS is:

        N.   54º 11. 374'
        W. 005º 59. 653'   Elevation 467m.

Lower opposite: There is no denying the obvious intentions behind the deployment of these stones. They are located high on a scree slope on Pollaphuca's north side. The main attraction was a nearby mighty phallic projection with a womb cavity at the base for summer solstice dawn. The GPS is:

        N.   54º 11. 339'
        W. 005º 59. 721'   Elevation 525m.

Top of this page: A true delight and it's not a megalith. The little cartoon stone with only a chopped eye and an open mouth is about the size of an orange. It sits on top of a large megalith. The open mouth has pretensions on the 'phallic nose' of its neighbour. It is also a **Dúid lia Scáth** stone, meaning a 'Fertility stone shadow'. At dawn of summer solstice the little fellow's shadow will be cast into the hole below the larger companion. It is the smallest fellatio stone I have yet found. The GPS is:

        N.   54º 11. 296'
        W. 005º 59. 656'   Elevation 482m.

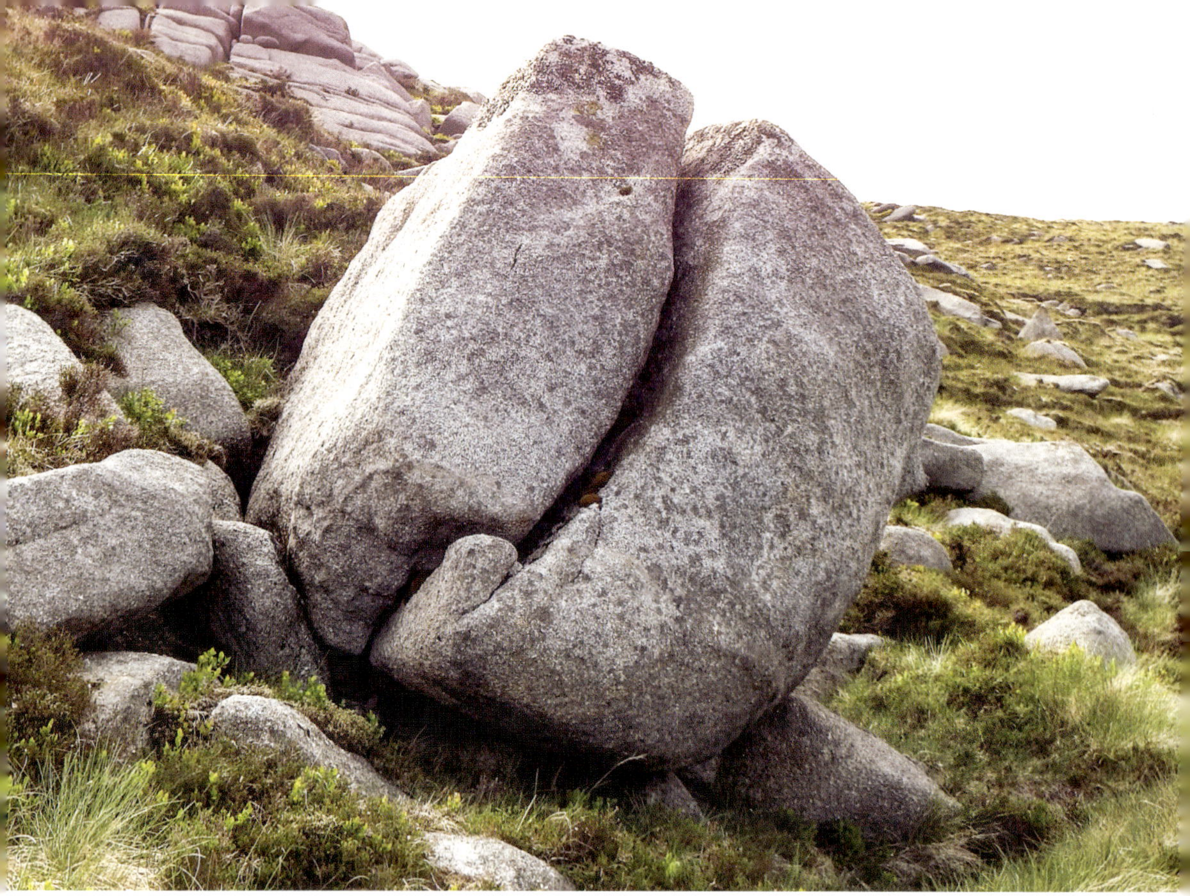

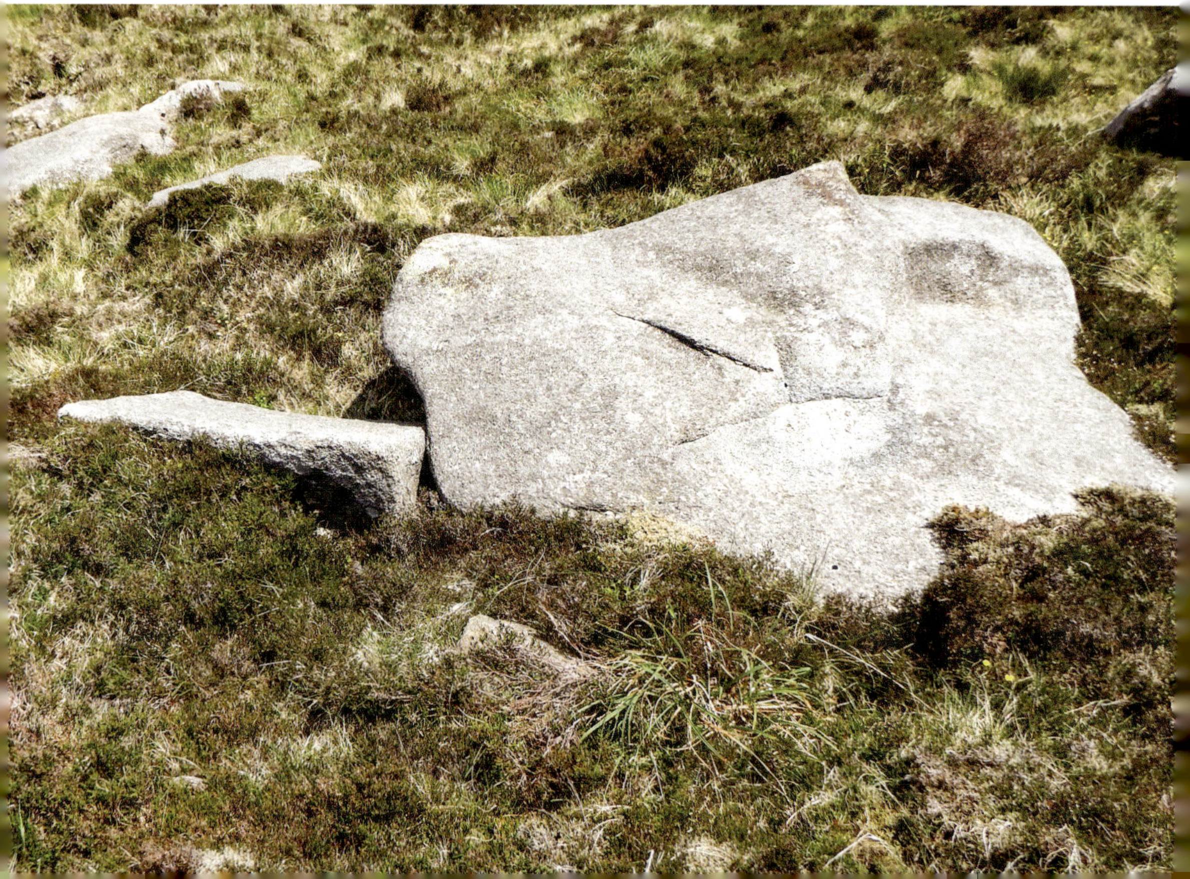

Top opposite: Two large granite slabs have been placed tight together in upper Happy Valley between the Mourne and Shepherd's walls. The knob on the bottom of the right-hand stone is at one time a lower jaw trying to swallow the other stone and at the same time the object of phallic interest for the left stone. The great monument 'Priest Smiths Well' (illustrated on page 360) is directly across the valley. The GPS is:

        N.   54º 11. 216
        W. 006º 00. 299   Elevation 576m.

Lower opposite: Here on the shoulder of Meelmore mountain above the Pollaphuca stile, a 2m slab with a 30cm chopped shadow eye is getting to grips with a straight phallic boulder provided for its attention. The big slab is not casually placed. The corner point at the top of the 'head' is directed to Doan mountain. The GPS is:

        N.   54º 11. 222'
        W. 005º 59. 945'   Elevation 598m.

Top of this page: This anchor slab on the shoulder of Meelmore in Happy Valley is a real piece of work. At its head it secures in place a beautiful arrow-head phallic stone. A chopped shadow eye on the top surface compliments the open mouth at the side, busy at fellatio with an insert. The GPS is:

        N.   54º 11. 194'
        W. 006º 00. 266'   Elevation 593m.

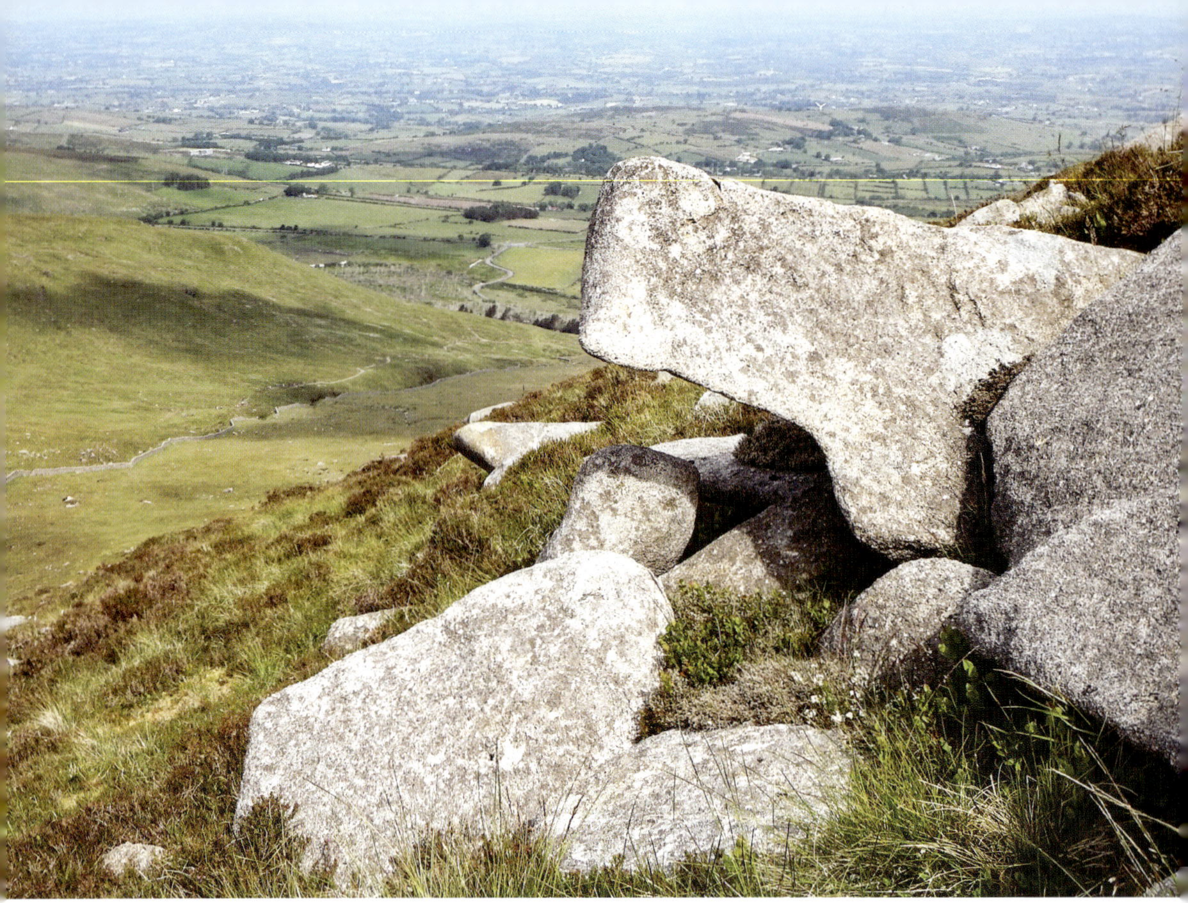

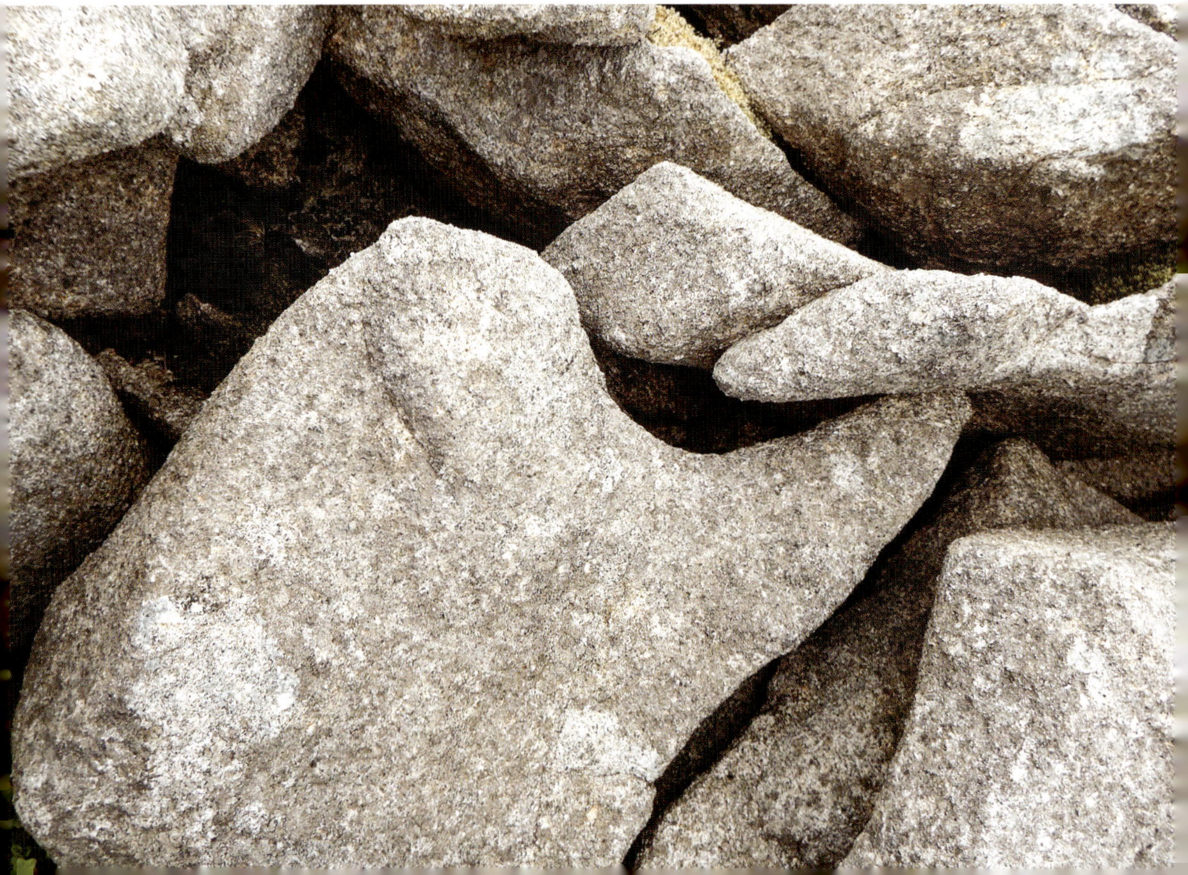

Top opposite: On the north side of Happy Valley, also known as Bug Hollow, and near the shepherd's wall, a 1m long granite stone is propped up in phallic mode. The distinctive feature of the stone is the wide open 'mouth' underneath intent on fellatio on the stones below. The GPS is:

      N. 54º 11. 294'
      W. 006º 00. 320'   Elevation 560m.

Lower opposite: The juxtaposition of stones to suggest fellatio is just too common across the hills. This example is on the south-east flank of Meelmore and a number of others were nearby. The GPS is:

      N. 54º 11. 435'
      W. 005º 59. 909'   Elevation 650m.

Top of this page: A 2m phallic stone on the east flank of Bearnagh's north tor finds itself as an object of desire. Below it, with its 'head' thrown back and its 'mouth' wide open, a companion stone appears resolved on fellatio. This is **An Cloch Súghacháin**, 'The Sucking Stone'. The GPS is:

      N. 54º 11. 195'
      W. 005º 58. 972'   Elevation 640m.

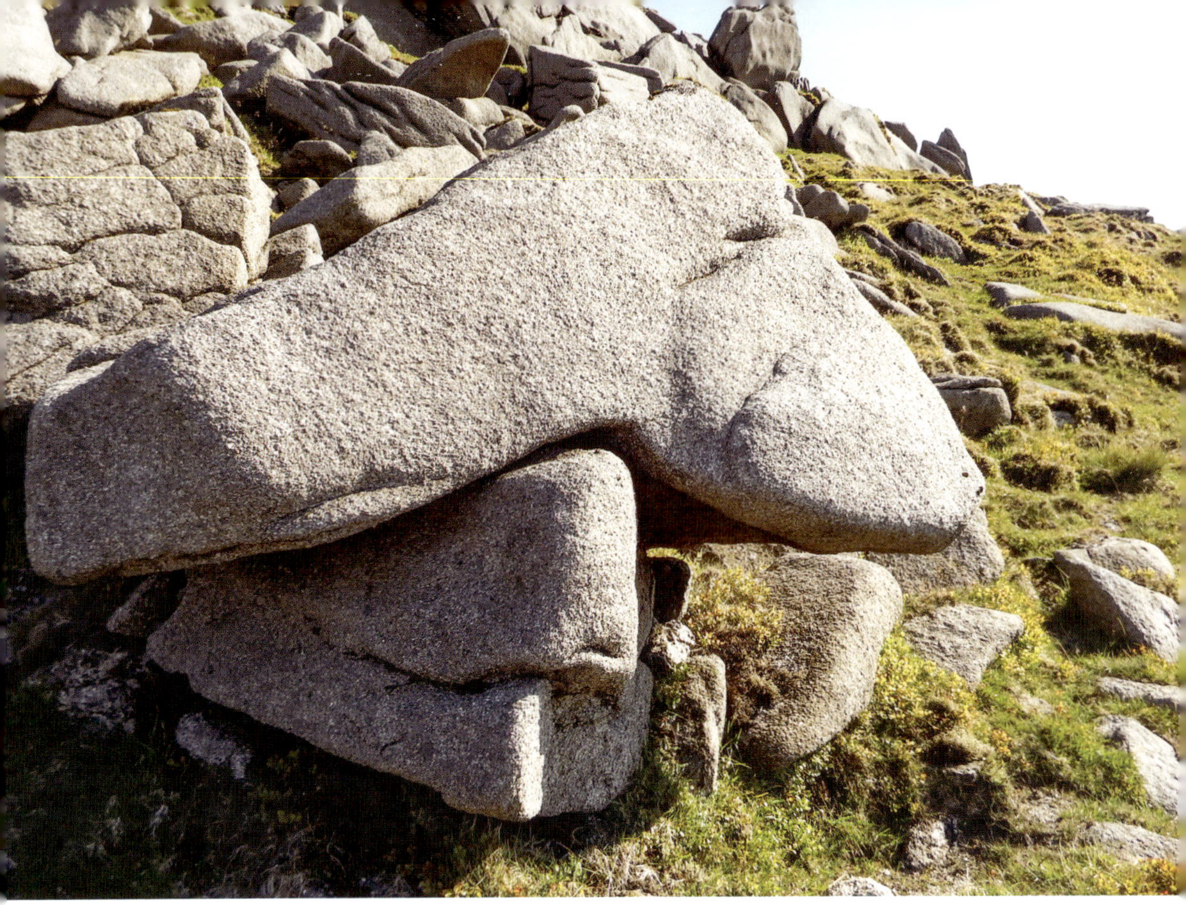

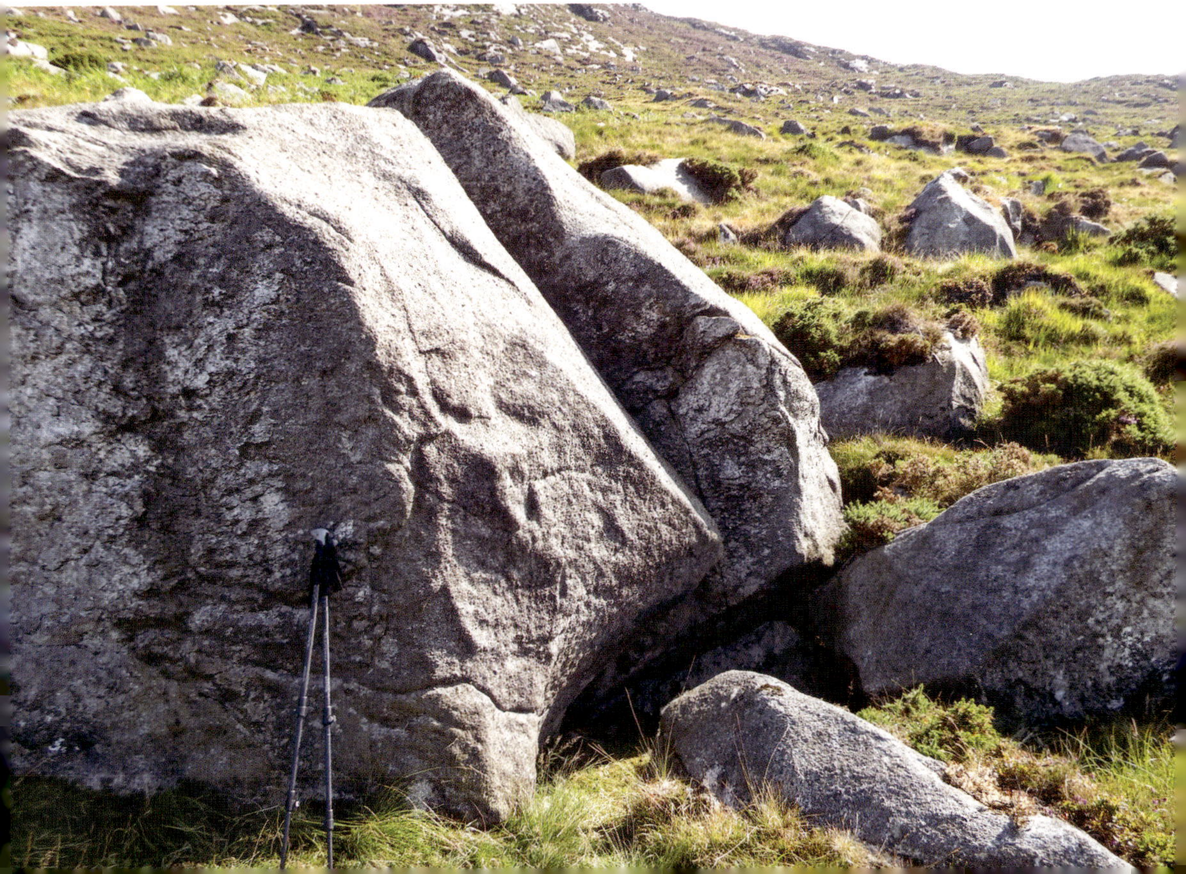

Top opposite: Given the name *Tómhaltóir*, 'A Great Eater', this megalith of fellatio is found near the top of Slieve Bearnagh's north tor overlooking Pollaphuca valley. This sculpture can only be seen from the slope underneath where you are out of sight of the north tor and the Mourne wall. The GPS is:

N. 54° 11. 210'
W. 005° 59. 220'   Elevation 680m.

Lower opposite: Under the northern shoulder of Shimial mountain two large granite boulders, both over 2m high, have been placed tightly together with a little flared vaginal opening facing towards winter solstice sun appearance. Accordingly the stones were named *Gág na Gréine*, 'Crack of the Sun'. The bottom of the front stone has been mauled to create a concave mouth. A long phallic stone lies in the grass underneath the mouth awaiting fellatio. The GPS is:

N. 54° 12. 174'
W. 005° 58. 507'   Elevation 292m.

Top of this page: These hefty stones are under Bignian's summit tor and not too far from the stile at the intersection of the Mourne and shepherd's walls. This is a particularly clever and careful arrangement. Yes, the fellatio is obvious but the real action is at winter solstice dawn when the rising sun casts the fertilising shadow of the 'lower jaw' of the right-hand stone into the erstwhile vaginal gap between the stones. This is an example of *Dúid lia Scáth*, a 'Fertility stone shadow'.

Above: This phallic stone is on the top of Bearnagh's most southerly tor. It was named *Áit iargcúlta*, 'A place hard to reach'. Somehow the ancients not only scaled the height but managed to manoeuvre the 2m high phallic stone on this pinnacle with so little room around it. A gleeful face on the rock surface behind contemplates fellatio. The approximate GPS is:

N. 54º 11. 011'
W. 005º 59. 341'   Elevation 715m.

Top opposite: Just one of a number of examples of fellatio on a rock outcrop on the east side of Slieve Corragh. You will find it easier to notice the great 4m raised slab engaged with a phallic looking knob. Look at the neat vaginal gap at the back of this great sliver illumined only at summer solstice dawn. The GPS for our photograph is:

N. 54º 11. 625'
W. 005º 57. 618'   Elevation 532m.

Lower opposite: Raised on an eminence and dominating the entrance trail up to the quarries, this 2m high granite block was known to the quarry-men as *Buinne Ceap*, 'Squirting forth block'. The huge boulder gave its Irish name to the Windy Gap valley but to make sense the English mnemonic version had to move to the col at the other end of the valley. Look carefully to see the art of a double mouth. The GPS is:

N. 54º 07. 588'
W. 006º 04. 331'   Elevation 185m.

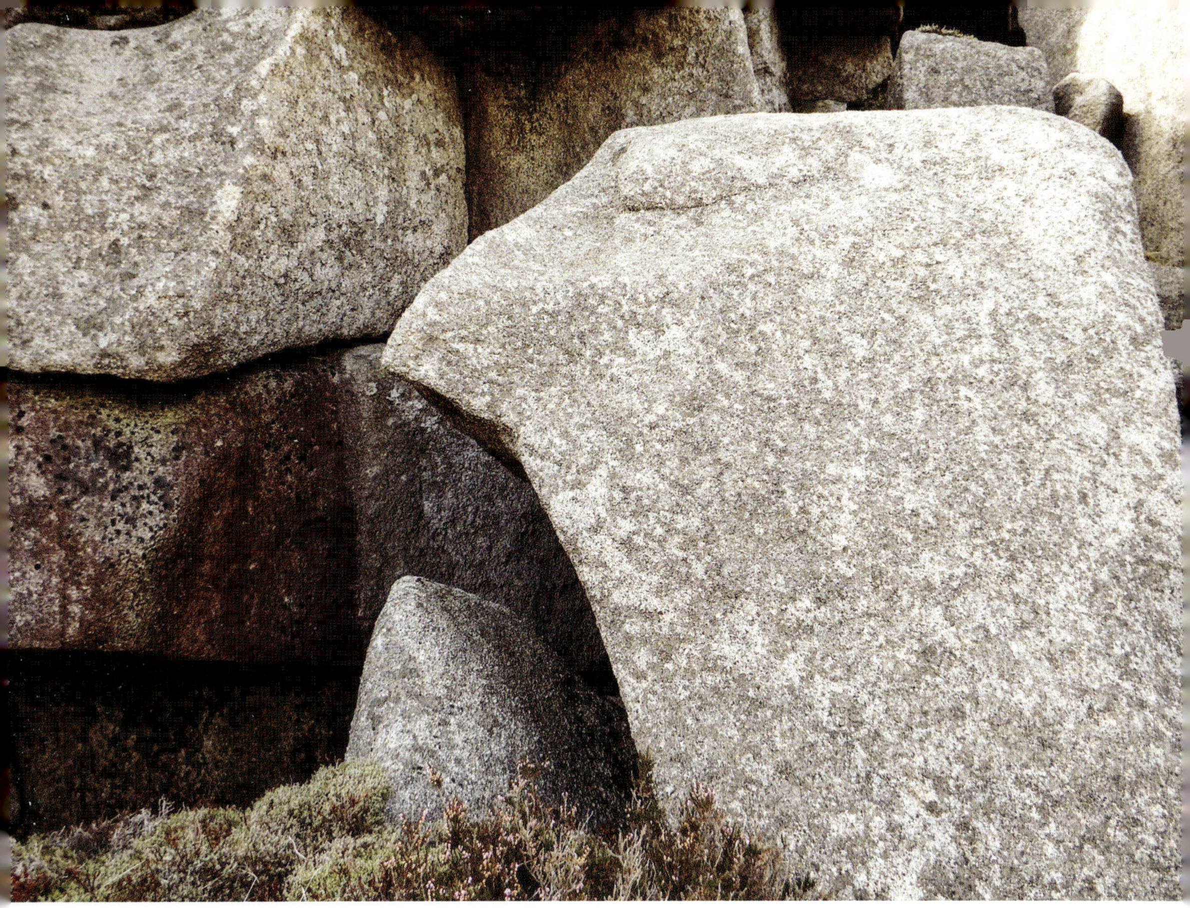

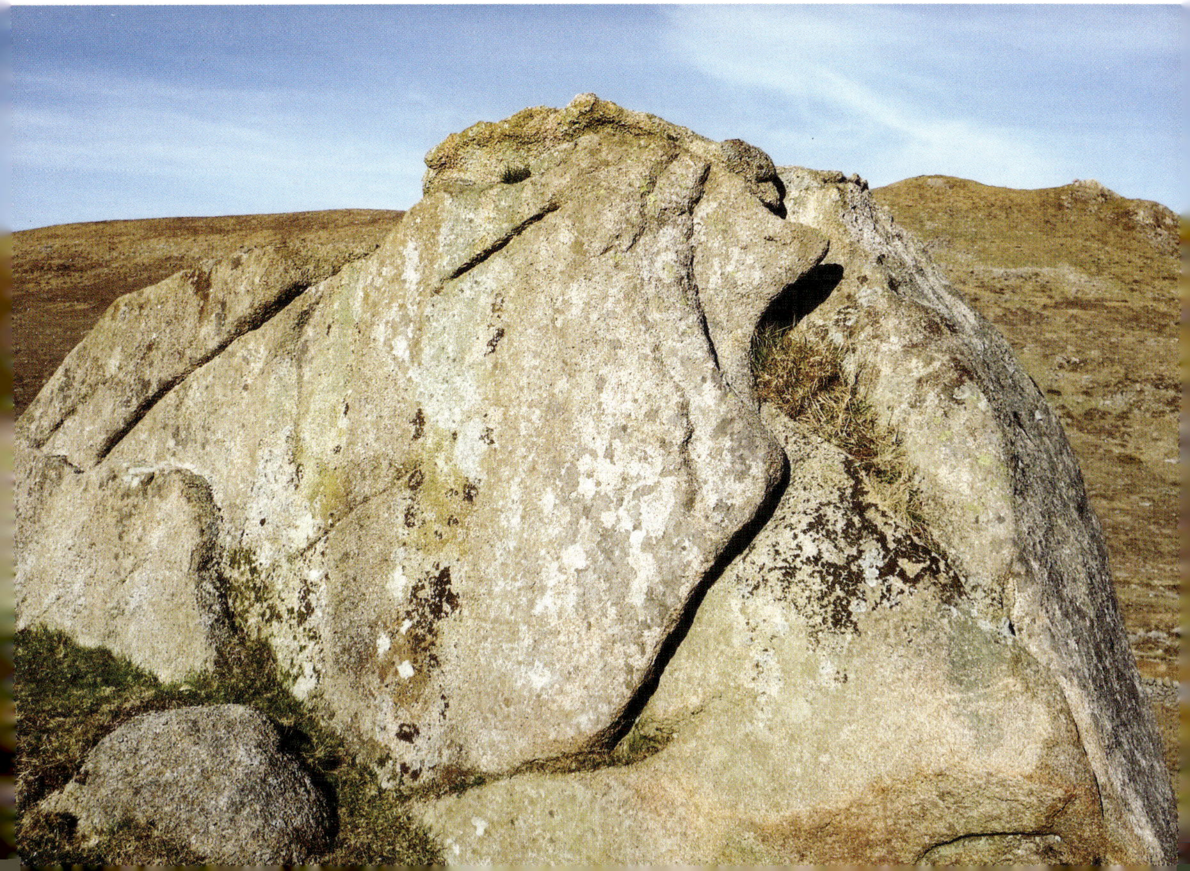

Above: In Happy Valley between the Mourne and Shepherd's walls, an upright granite stone, at least 2m long with an infusion crest and a great notch of a mouth, is set to devour the stubby phallic stone above it. This cartoon monument was named **Placaim**, 'I gobble up'. An adjacent 'semen tipped' stone that points to summer solstice sunset has already been illustrated on page 181. The GPS is:

      N. 54° 11. 214'
      W. 006° 00. 278'   Elevation 577m.

Opposite: Two photographs of the same megalith on the east side of Wee Slevanmore. The fellatio artwork along the 3m labial side, seen in the lower photograph, could not be shown without reference to the magnificent and sophisticated monument of which it is a part. The first photo shows the huge filled vaginal gap that has been given the name **Gailteann**, 'A fair lady'. In the centre is the great slab that is an inverted phallus. This is a monument of precision. At summer solstice sunrise the shadow of the tip of the phallus will be cast into the rather narrow gap behind it in a moment of notional fertilisation. This is another instance of **Dúid lia Scáth**, a 'Fertility stone shadow'. The GPS is:

      N. 54° 11. 167'
      W. 006° 00. 031'   Elevation 605m.

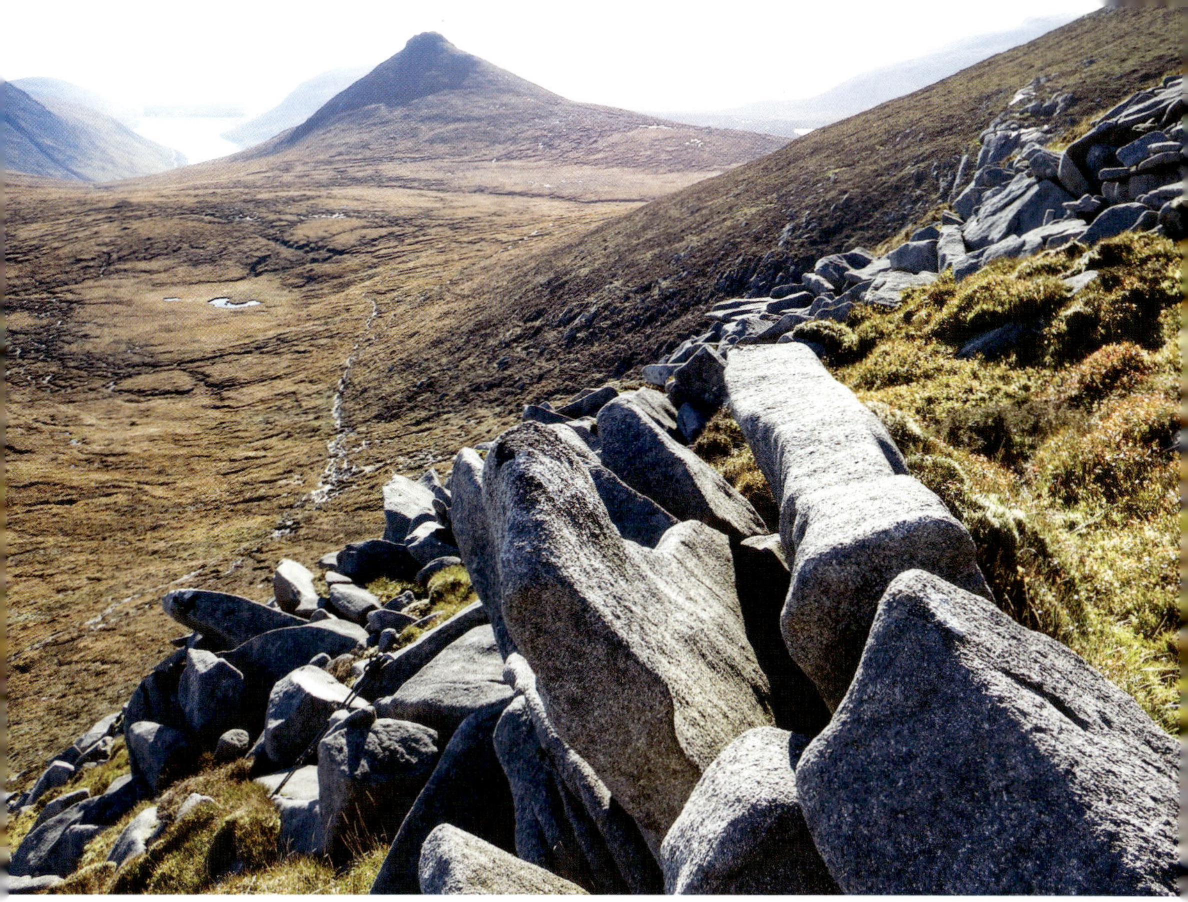

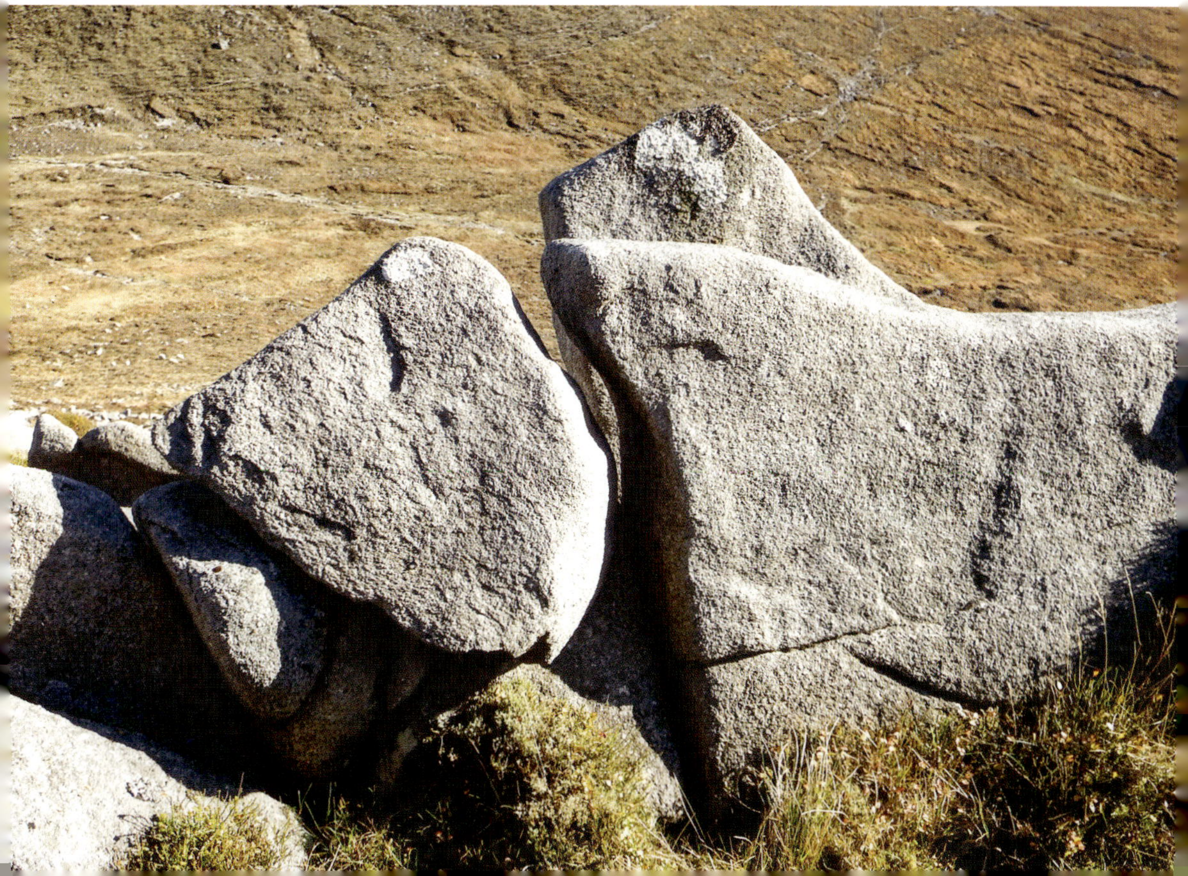

Above: A low 2m granite slab on the south-east flank of Meelmore mountain has an open mouth intent on fellatio. The GPS is:

      N. 54º 11. 439'
      W. 005º 59. 884'   Elevation 639m.

Top opposite: You will find this instance of fellatio at the top end of the Trassey valley beside the Brandy Pad [from (*Lorg na*) **bPránnaidhe Pead**, '(Trail of) the well packed ponies']. The GPS is:

      N. 54º 11. 413'
      W. 005º 58. 563'   Elevation 414m.

Lower opposite: True artistic genius lies behind the concept and marriage of these great stones at the south end of Slieve Bearnagh's summit tor. The mighty left-hand boulder is about 6m high; it has been reared up and its great curved open mouth positioned unmistakably for fellatio. The scene is so captivating that you could overlook a junior version limbering up below. The GPS is:

      N. 54º 11. 050'
      W. 005º 59. 371'   Elevation 714m.

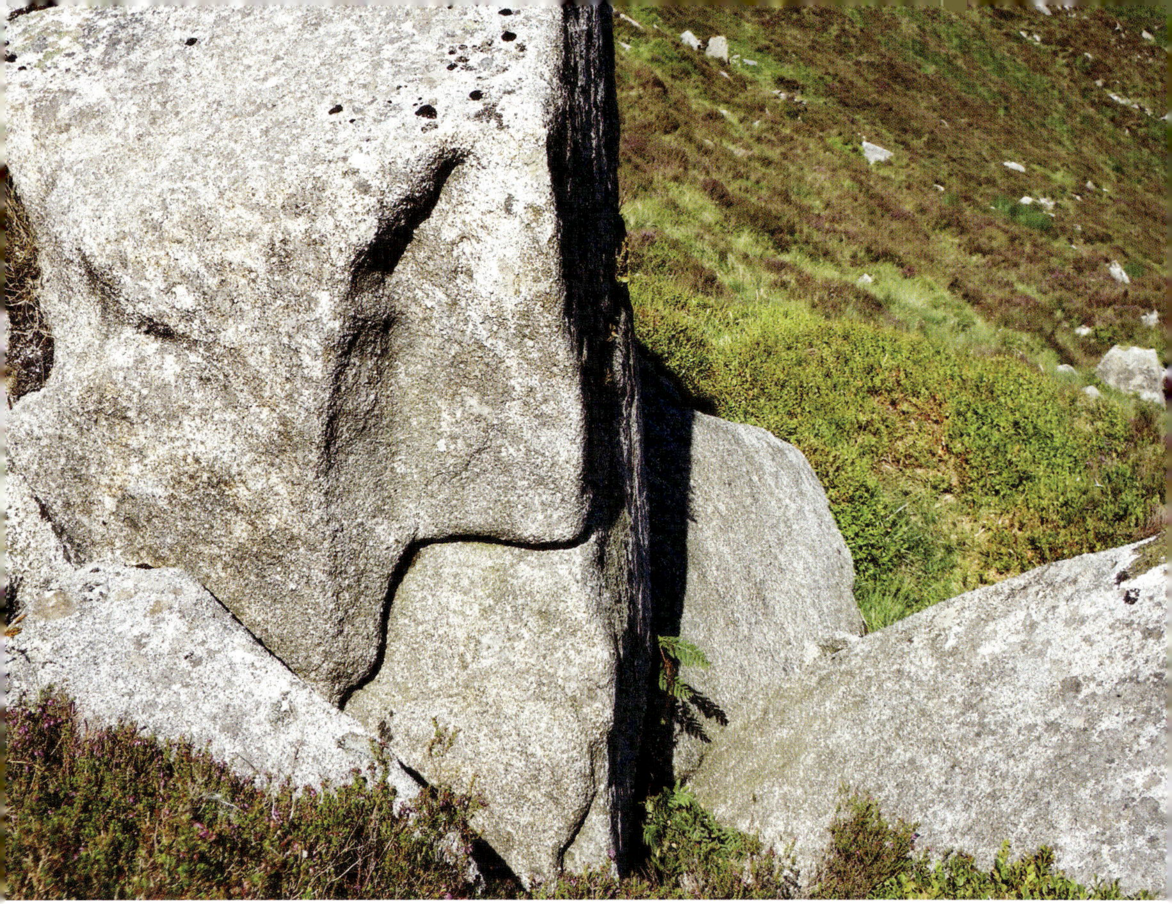

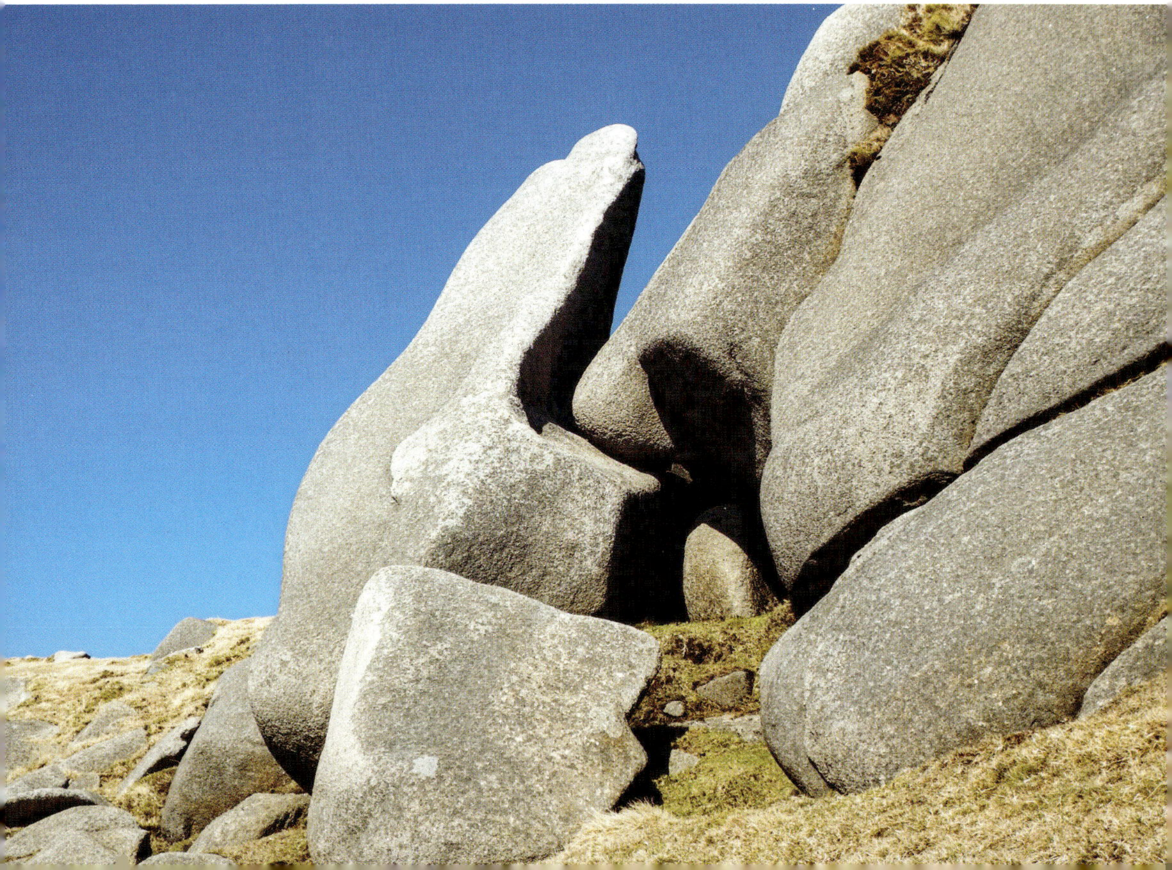

Above: On Wee Slevanmore a small granite stone has been propped up in phallic mode. The phallus has a most distinctive corona around the tip exploiting a fusion band. It also has a notch at the top giving the impression of an open mouth squealing out. Perhaps this is because of the fellatio attentions of the stone below. The GPS is:

      N. 54º 11. 108'
      W. 006º 00. 163'   Elevation 568m.

Top opposite: This large slab indulging in fellatio is on the south-east flank of Slieve Bearnagh. The slab in question is a good 3m long but it is only part of an even greater construction, not shown, prepared to receive the fertilising light of summer solstice sunrise. The GPS is:

      N. 54º 11. 245'
      W. 005º 58. 502'   Elevation 448m.

Lower opposite: These stones are to the north-east side of Bearnagh's summit tor. The big boulder puts out its tongue over a 1.7m gap to a nearby phallic tip.. This might also be construed as the moment a chameleon flicks out its tongue to catch its prey. The boulders are part of a line of colossal stones marking where summer solstice sun rises from the notch of Bearnagh's north tor. The GPS is:

      N. 54º 11. 098'
      W. 005º 59. 336'   Elevation 716m.

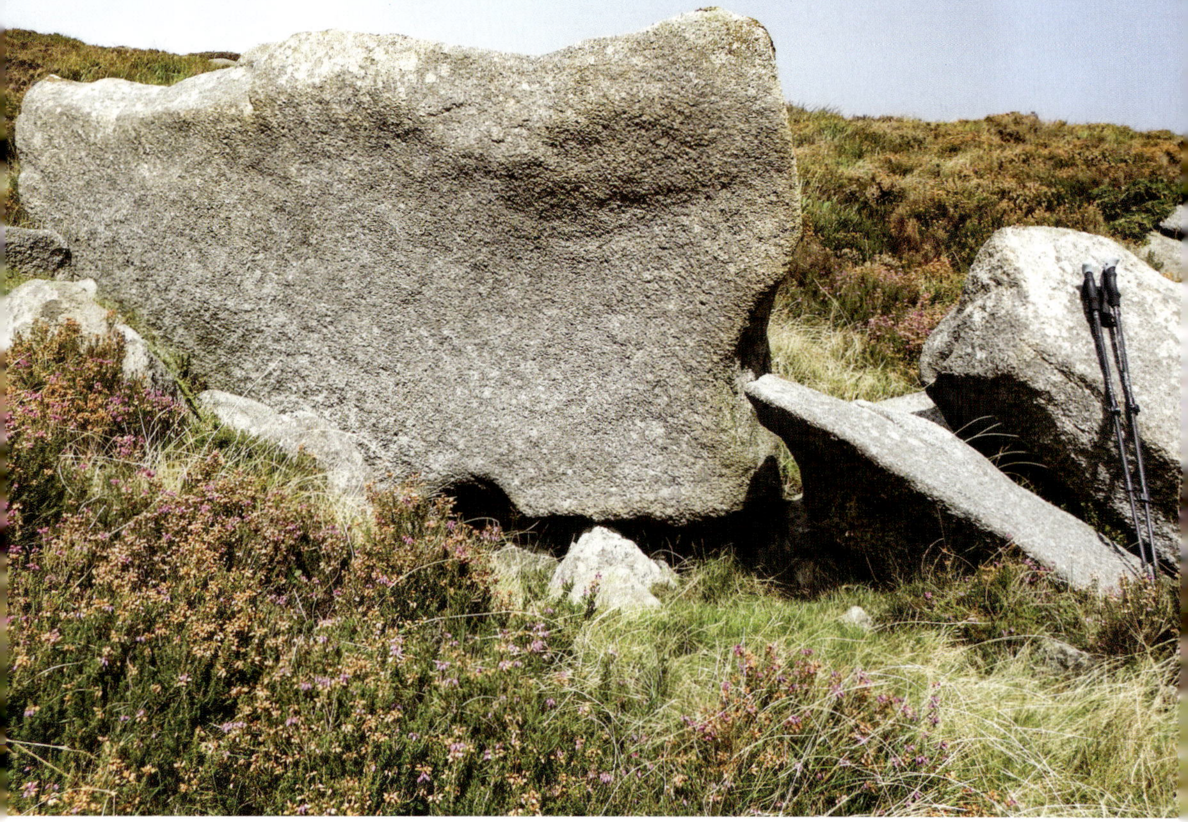

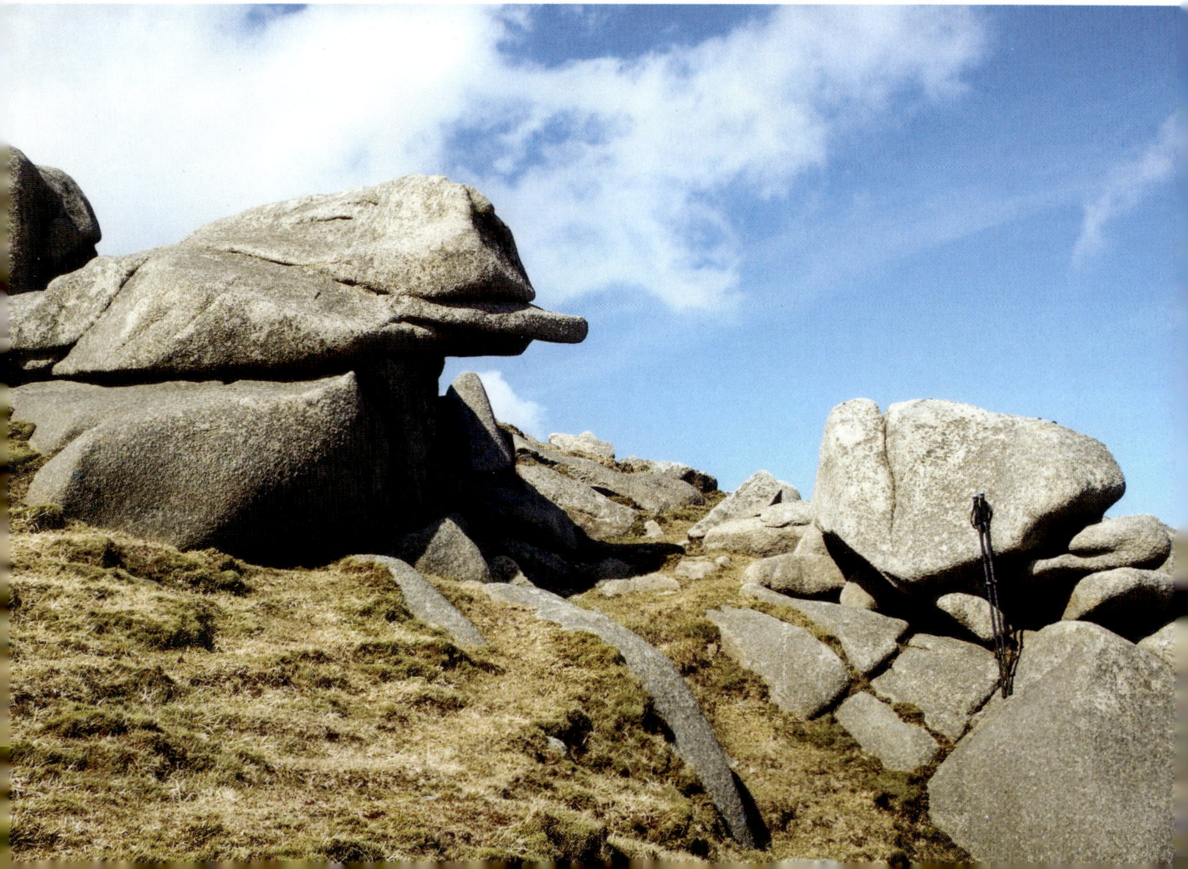

This magnificent construction is found on the crest of Long mountain. From its location at the top of a very steep slope it overlooks the Windy Gap valley and provides a panoramic vista of Mourne. The imposing capstone is circa .9m thick, 1.4m across and 2.5m long. The GPS is:

N. 54° 07. 729'
W. 006° 04. 957'   Elevation 360m

SOME MORE PLACE-NAMES AND MEGALITHS

If ever there was a reason for heeding and preserving the old names of Mourne then Moss Banks is up there with Craig Strucker and Hawk Rocks. Locals happily told me the two places in Mourne that enjoy the name of Moss Banks. One is found above Front Top on Slieve Muck and the other is across the valley on top of Pigeon Mountain. All names were once warnings of danger close to precipitous cliff edges. Craig Strucker on the top of Pigeon mountain is from the Irish **Creag Stríocatha**, 'Crag of Falling' and Hawk Rocks, on the western side of Pigeon, is from the Irish (*Tí na*) **h-Iachta**, 'Place of Shrieking'. These were previously illustrated on p.340 of *Place-names of Beanna Boirrche*, (2021). There is a second Hawk Rocks in Mourne at the north end of Knockchree hill in Mourne Wood.

The Hawk names are mnemonics of the Irish and are not derived from birds of prey in the English sense any more than Raven Rocks or Eagle Mountain. Indeed, the other 'avian' mountains, Cock and Hen, unworthily abbreviated on OS maps to just 'Hen' mountain, together with nearby Cock mountain and Pigeon mountain are also all mnemonics of the Irish. Cock and Hen mountain (J 2427), not far from Clonduff ruined chapel near Hilltown, has its name from **Cíocha h-Áine**, 'breasts of pleasure' while Cock mountain (J 2526) enjoyed the Irish name of (*Sliabh na*) **Cíocha**, 'mountain of the breasts'. There was nothing particularly prominent about the mountain's two petite crests and, as we will see, their rather diminutive size lies behind the name of Canavan's Bucht located on the north-west flank of Slieve Muck.

Moss Banks, that important cautionary old name of Mourne, has, in its present English skin, lost all sense of forewarning. The dangers inherent in the landscape can be best appreciated from the Moyad car-park under the Pot Hollow cliff of Pigeon. On the other side of the road rears the bulk of Slieve Muck's Far Top with its ominous circlet of rock faces and cliffs. Moss Banks is an eclipsed remnant of the Irish (*Tí na*) **mBáis Bannc**, '(Place of) Death Bank' where the operative word is **Bás**, (gen.) **Báis**, meaning 'death'. The use of the definite article '*na*', before the word *Bás* eclipsed it with [m]; that means the sound of [B] has been replaced by [M]. All that is heard nowadays is **m_ás**, or rather an approximate English sound 'Moss'. The 'Moss Bank' slopes above these cliffs on Pigeon and Muck would have been extremely hazardous places in the event of a shower of rain wetting the grass or a disorientating fog suddenly blowing in off the sea.

Above: Above: The two lower circles on this photo of Front Top on Slieve Muck show features that gave us the name *Piobar Tí*, '(sexual) excitement place'. The circle on the left shows the monstrous phallic megalith, shown in close-up on top opposite, while the circle on the right highlights the great vertical slit that was looked on as a vagina. The Irish *Piobar Tí* later morphed into the English mnemonic 'poverty'. Letters spelling out 'POV' can indeed be discerned elsewhere along the ridge but the Slieve Muck name of 'Poverty' derives from Irish and not from any English sense of penury.

Top opposite: This is a close-up of a great spear point megalith laid into a fissure on the side of Slieve Muck, as if it was a penis addressing a vagina. From the bottom of the megalith on summer solstice the declining sun passes behind the hill and spear tip above to give the impression of the phallic megalith coming to climax with a solar ejaculation. The dangerous cliffs above are self-explanatory for the Irish name (*Tí na*) *mBáis Bannc*, '(Place of) Death Bank', now known as Moss Banks.

Lower opposite: This is the great cauldron on the side of Pigeon Mountain known at Pot Hollow. The ground all along the top was known as 'Moss Banks' for the same reason as Moss Banks on Slieve Muck. One possible explanation for the name of Pot Hollow is the Irish *Pota h-uilc*, 'Pot of Evil'. The evil could refer to the real danger of falling over the top of the cliff if a fog came in off the sea.

←— Moss Banks —→

Above: Slieve Muck as seen from the summit of Slievenamiskan. Old place-names still used by local shepherds are marked. These have their origins in Irish.

Top opposite: The triangulation pillar on the summit of Slieve Muck was known as McAvoy's Tower. The summit of Slieve Muck was known as McAvoy's Tower and the name was probably strongly influenced by the phallic profile of Bignian mountain in the background. The first triangulation of Ireland was completed by Major-General Thomas Colby in 1846 but the country had a more comprehensive survey in 1867. The triangulation pillar might even date to as late as 1952 when Irish was still around, although definitely waning. The name McAvoy's Tower is a mnemonic of the Irish **Mac a Buid tuir**, meaning 'son of a penis tower'. [*Bod*, (gen.) **Buid**, 'a penis']

Lower opposite: These remaining stones of an old sheep pen on the north-west slopes of Slieve Muck are near the source of the Bann river. They also mark the approximate centre of the area known to the shepherds as Canavan's Bucht. The name derives from the Irish **Cian a Bean Bocht**, 'Distant poor woman' and relates to the view of Cock Mountain on the far left side of the Spelga reservoir. Cock mountain is from **Sliabh an Cíocha**, 'mountain of the breasts'. However, the 'breasts' were regarded as less than fulsome and the 'woman' was thus described as 'poor'; the Irish is **Bocht**, gen: *Boichte*, 'poor, needy; thin, slight; pitiful'. The GPS of the sheep-pen is:

                N.   54° 09. 749'
                W. 006° 02. 827'   Elevation 446m.

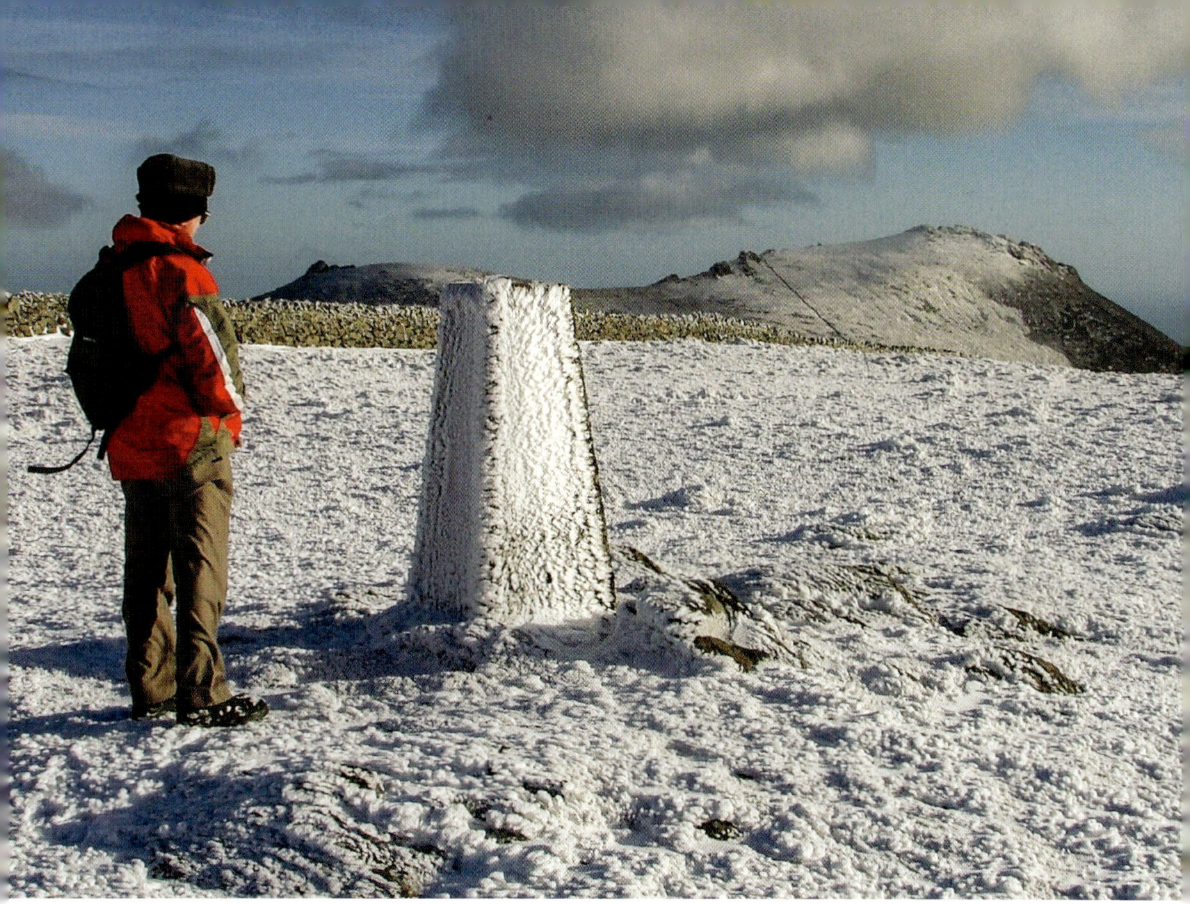

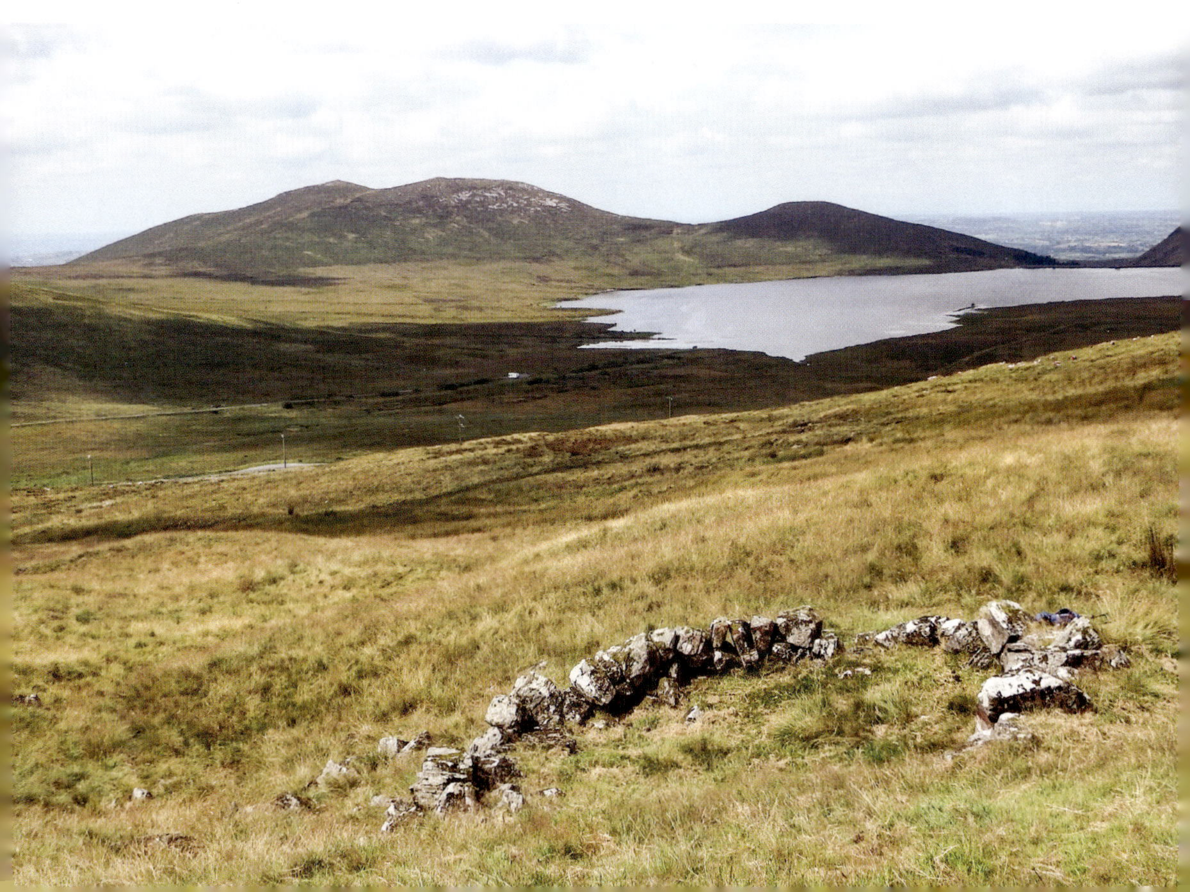

Above: This is the viewpoint that has given us the place-name 'Cat Nights'. The photo was taken from the top of Pigeon but it is the same view looking west as from the slopes of Slieve Muck. The name comes from the Irish **Cath Niata**, 'fierce temptation'; **Cath**, 'a battle, a war; a **temptation**' and the adjective *Niata*, 'fierce'. The 'temptation' lies in the gynaecomorphic interpretation of the landscape where the distant view of the tip of Pierce's Castle was regarded as a penis inserted into the landscape vaginal notch formed between Eagle mountain and Slimageen.

The same Irish word **Cath**, lies behind Kathleen's Castle a variant name for the phallic granite pillars at the Castles of Commedagh. 'Kathleen's Castle' is from **Cath Léin Cas Táile**, 'Temptation of the loin pouring forth'. From *Léan*, (gen.) *Léin*, 'Loin'.

Top opposite: This megalith on the ridge of Pigeon mountain marks the fertility viewpoint of Cat Nights. No confirmation could be found that this was 'The Castle' although it would answer to the landscape view and the Irish *Caise Tál*, 'pouring forth of love'. Some locals recalled their fathers using the name but no longer remembered where the place was. Note the deliberate upright placement of the striations in the rock to convey phallic symbolism. The GPS of this megalith is:

        N.   54° 08. 530'
        W. 006° 04. 081'   Elevation 455m.

Lower opposite: A great megalith on the shoulder of Slievemageogh marks the fertility view of distant Slievenamuck (arrowed) as a penis in the vagina between Pigeon on the left and Slieve Muck on the right. This is the area known as 'Crook of the Wall' from the Irish **Cruach a Baill,** meaning 'heap of the member(s)' ('member' being a euphemism for a phallus). The name was already mentioned on page 289 and applies to either side of the Moyal road valley where-ever the projection of Slievenamuck can be seen. The stone marks more than one fertility viewpoint and the Irish could be understood in the plural. The GPS of the great megalith is:

        N.   54° 08. 228'
        W. 006° 03. 652'   Elevation 296m.

Cat Nights

These pages: Many magnificent megaliths have been raised on the steep north-east flank of Commedagh to mark the passing of Slieve Donard's great phallic shadow at dawn of winter solstice.

The present name of Commedagh is from the Irish **Sliabh Coimeádaidhe**, 'mountain of the watcher'. The tiered megalith in the middle of Donard col, with its deep watching shadow eye, has already been illustrated on page 84. A case can be made however that *Sliabh Coimeádaidhe* is a 'softening' of an earlier blatantly pagan name consisting of three Irish words. The earlier version, and there are no written records to attest to it, was the closely similar **Sliabh Coime Mí Daibhleach**, 'mountain of the covering of evil flooding forth'. The Irish is *Coim*, (gen.), **Coime**, 'a cloak, a skirt, a covering', **Mí** with negative connotations meaning 'evil or wicked' and **Daibhleach**, 'act of pouring profusely'. The megaliths featured in our photographs mark the passing of Donard's great phallic shadow across the slopes of Commedagh at dawn of winter solstice. It was as if Slieve Donard was coming to climax and generously sending forth prolific seed 'covering' the slopes of Commedagh. There may be no written versions of **Sliabh Coime Mí Daibhleach**, but Commedagh also had the earlier name of 'Meadow Mountain'. In Irish the great phallic shadow was known as **Meadóg**, 'a dagger'. This fertility spectacle was the inspiration for the herculean labours to erect so many megaliths on this dangerously steep slope.

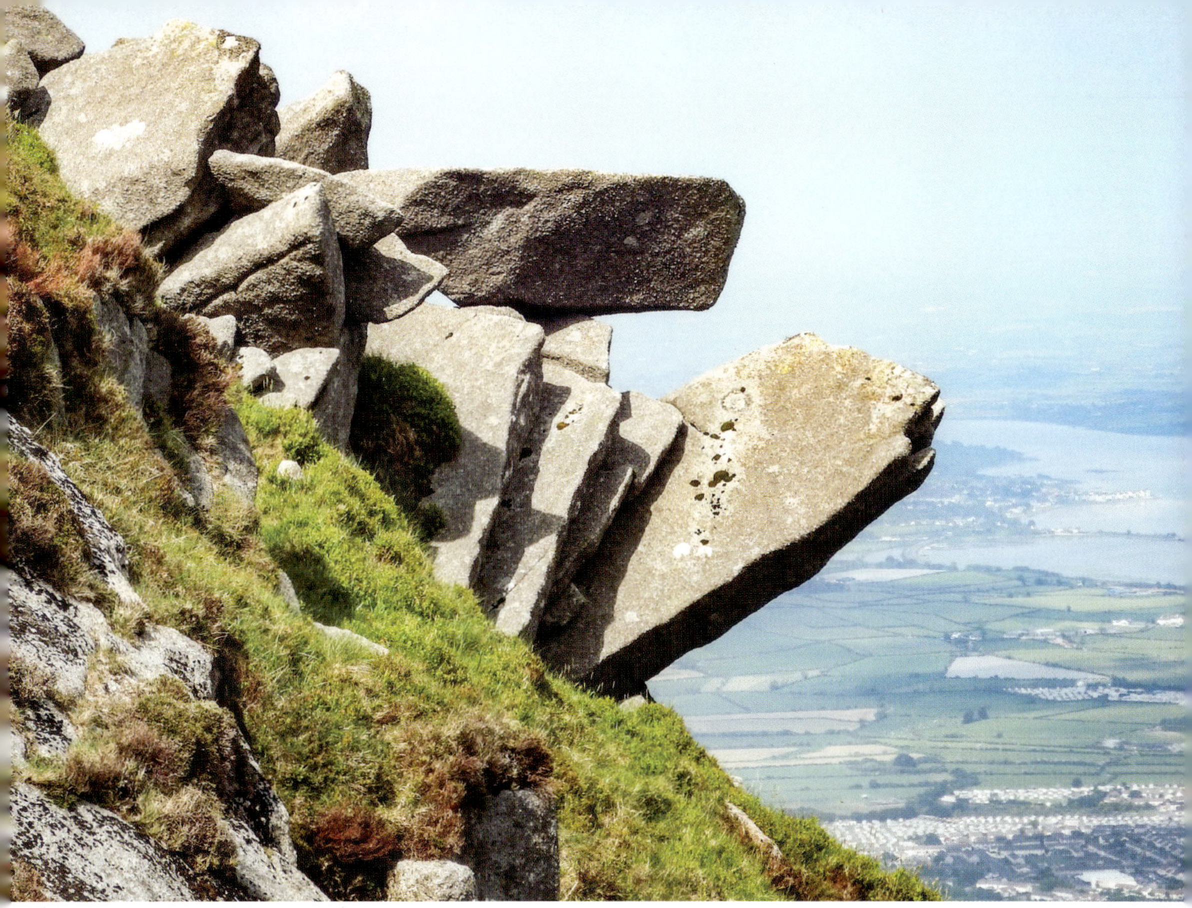

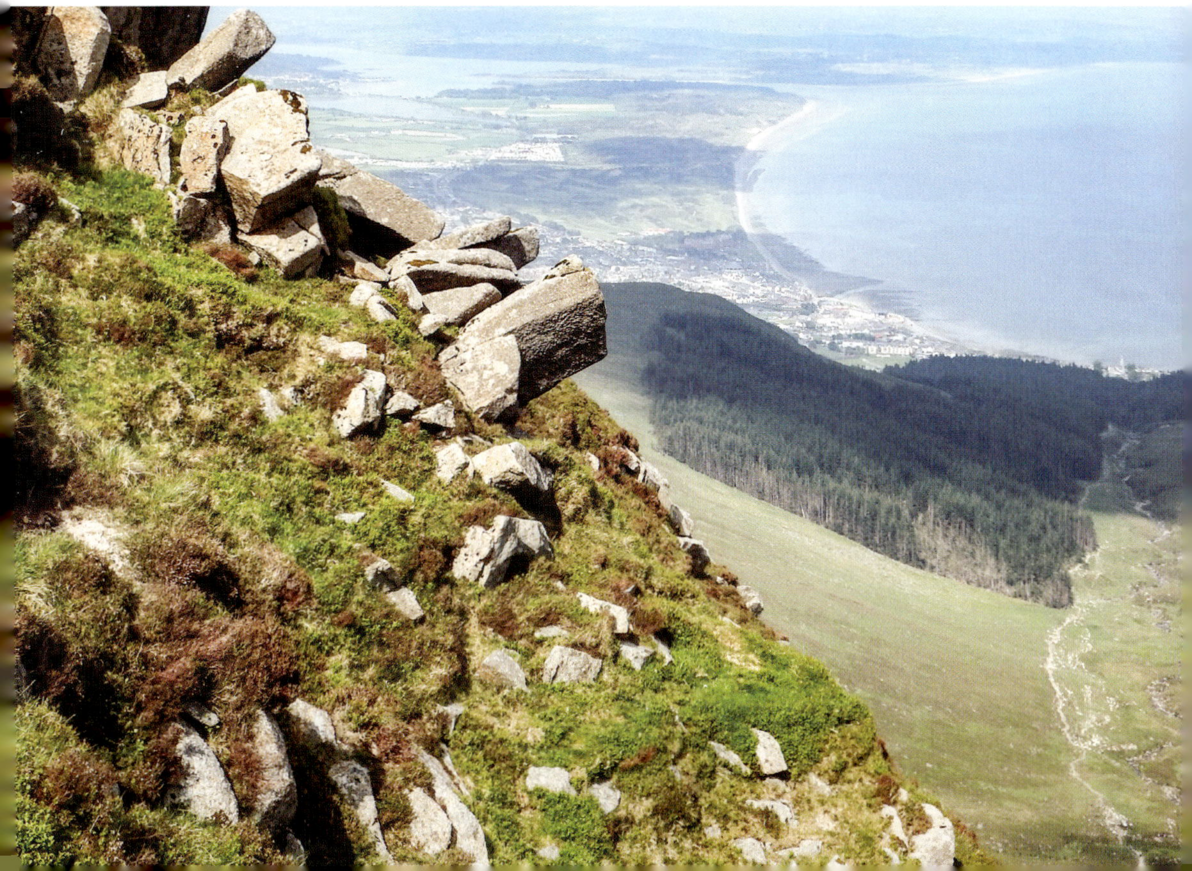

Above: The dogs were running and the sheep were going their own way in the Annalong valley yet the busy shepherd stopped to answer my question for place-names that were not on the Ordnance Survey maps. 'That is Scotch Rock', he said, pointing to the declivity and stream coming down from Bignian above. The Back Castles are on the skyline. It is only when you are nearly half-way down that pathway that you can see the tip of Slieve Bearnagh framed between Bignian and Lamagan (see insert) making the classic penis in the vagina motif. Scotch Rock is a mnemonic of the Irish **Scoth Ruic**, 'Top (in or) of the declivity'. The Irish is **Scoth**, meaning 'a tip, top, projection or point'; and Roc, (gen.) **Ruic**, 'a groove, hollow, declivity'.

Opposite: Almost like a mini saguaro cactus with three fingers up to the sky, this upright bit of mischief on the south slope of Slieve Donard measures .85m in height. This is a fertility stone as the three 'fingers' represent a penis between two labial sides. If you find this little megalith then look way to the south-west beyond the summit of Lamagan, seen here on the left, to see a distinct phallic mountain profile. The GPS of the stone is:

N. 54° 10. 646'
W. 005° 55. 336'   Elevation 773m.

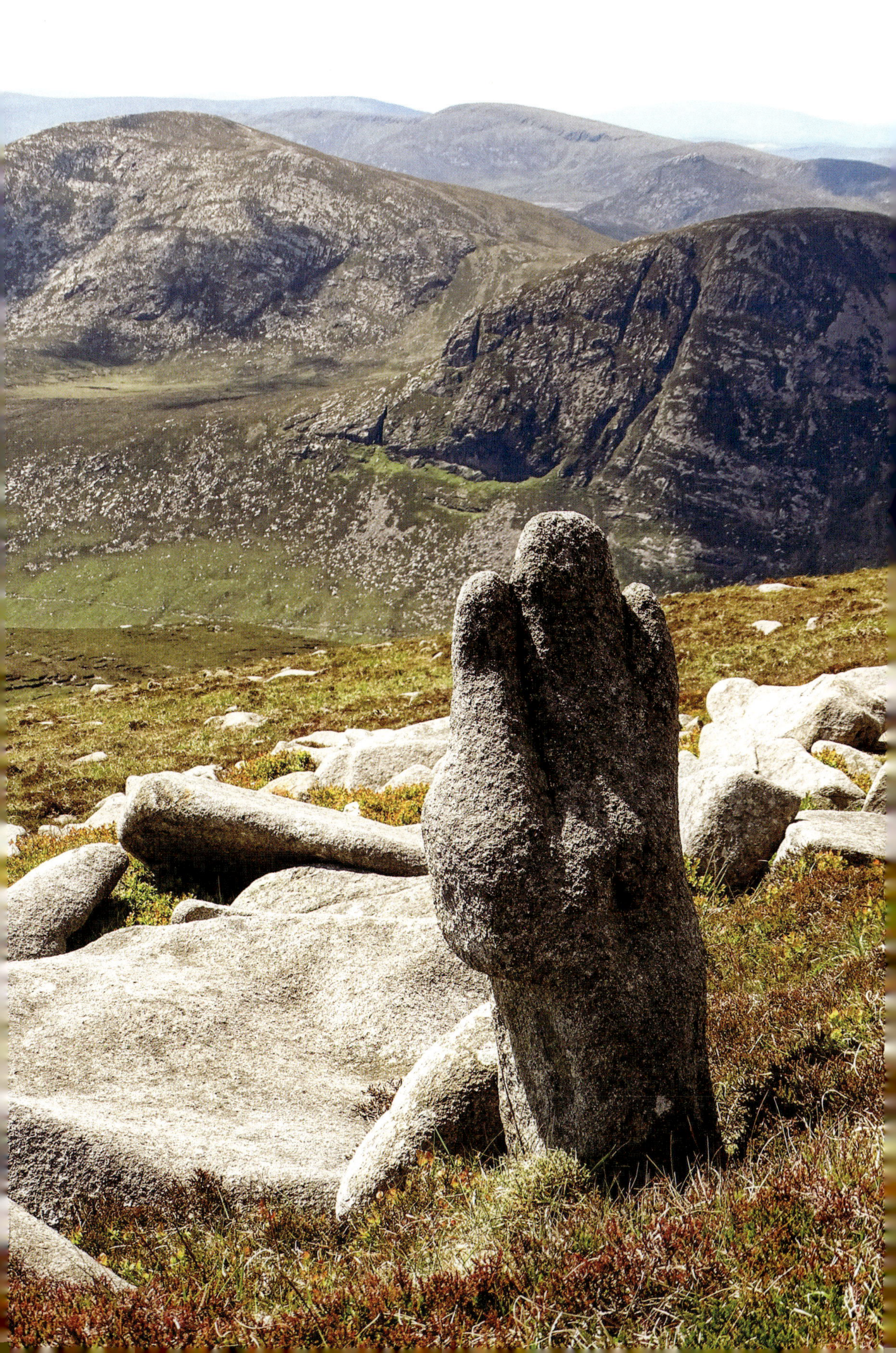

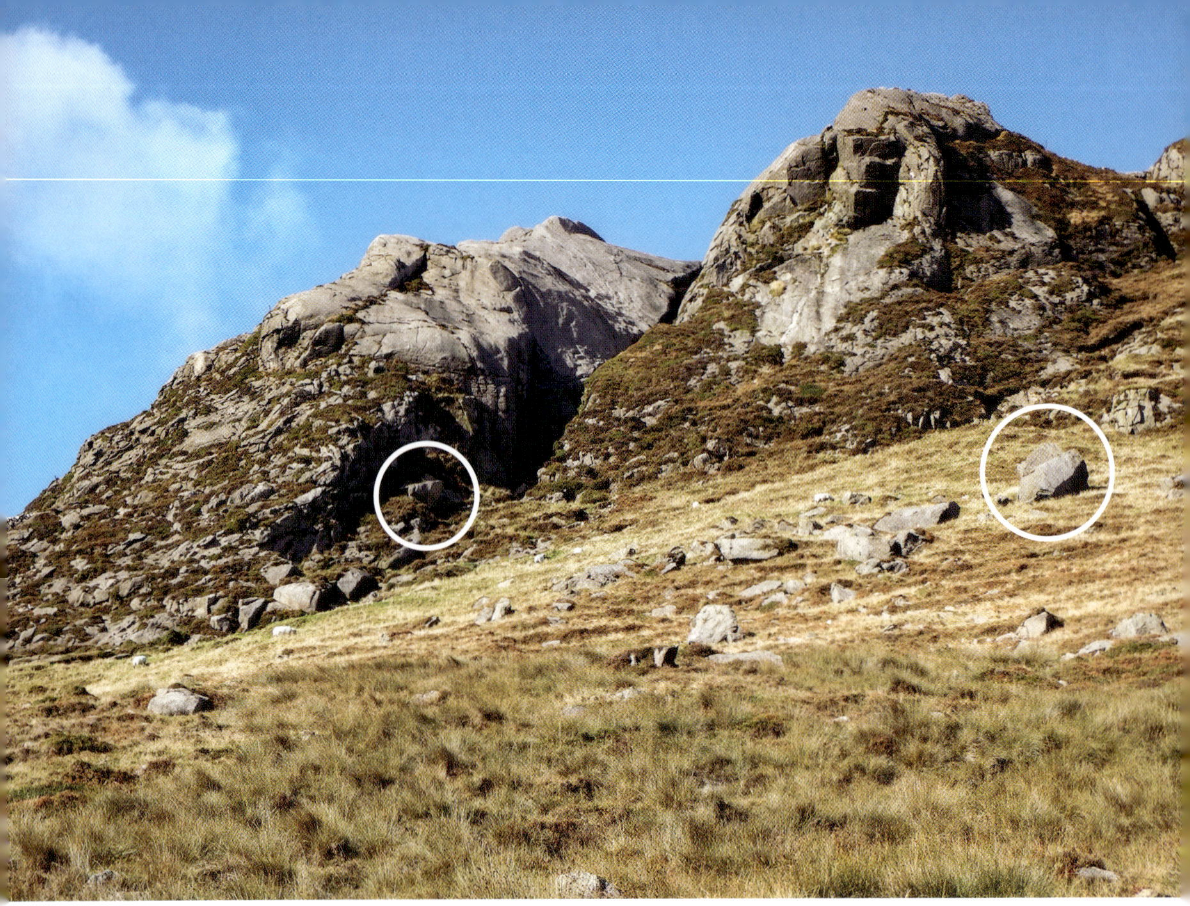

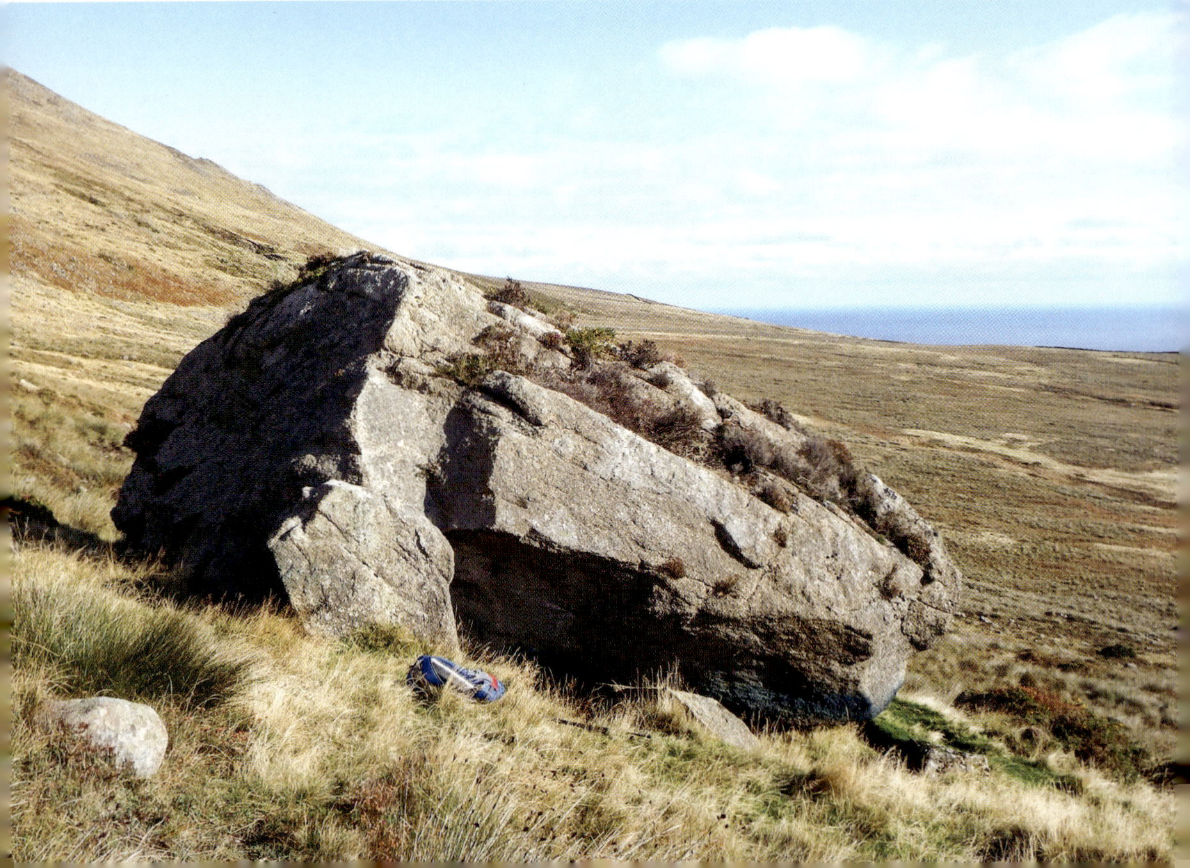

Here on the slopes under Wee Bignian is a really gigantic megalith (circled on the right) the name of which was believed to be *Carraig(e) a Cúinne h-áine*, 'rock(s) of the nook of pleasure'. The stone (right-hand circle opposite, with close-up below) was paced out at 7m in length, 5.5m across the back and is easily 2m high. The great stone had its Irish name from the view due south where a dip in the landscape formed between Moolieve and Wee Bignian featured a phallic profile formed from part of the Cooley hills (shown above). This was the 'nook of pleasure'. Well, almost. The problem is that there is another megalith that would answer to exactly the same name. This is the big stone circled on the left at the bottom of the fissure on the front of Wee Bignian. This stone is thought to mark the summer solstice sun passing over and seemingly touching the top of the fissure as if entering and fertilizing it. Such indeed would be a second 'nook of pleasure'. The dilemma between the stones would disappear if a plural was intended all along; this would be *Carraige*, with the -e ending, meaning 'rocks'.

References like these names to the past pagan interpretation of the landscape have become rare, corrupted or forgotten. Very fortunately there is a house on the Head Road that seems to preserve a remnant of this heritage. The name preserved is *Carraig a Choínín*, meaning 'Rock of the rabbit/coney'. If indeed there is a link between the two titles then the meaning has completely changed but the sounds of both names still have an uncanny closeness. Such is the ongoing evolution of tastes and language. The GPS of *Carraig a Cúinne h-áine* is:

N. 54° 08. 023'
W. 005° 59. 078'   Elevation 332m.

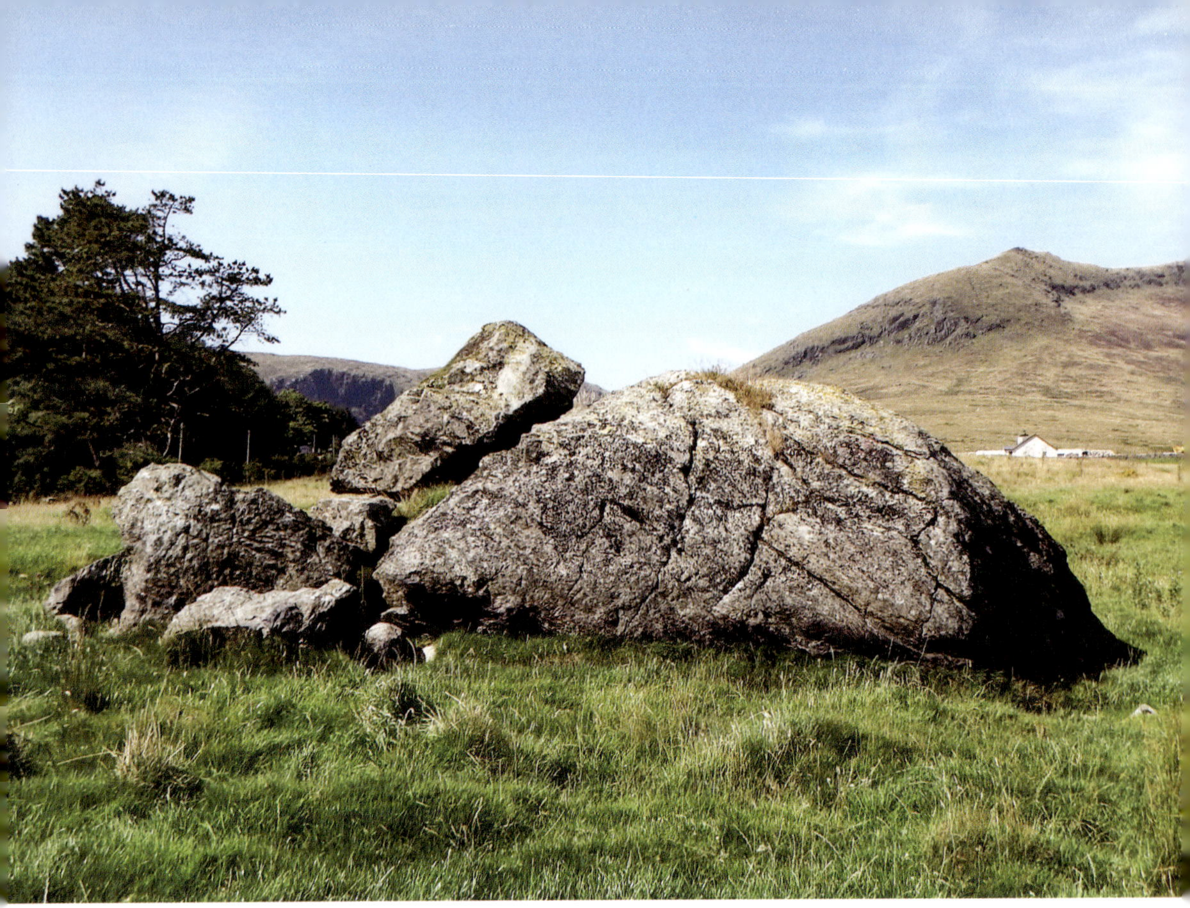

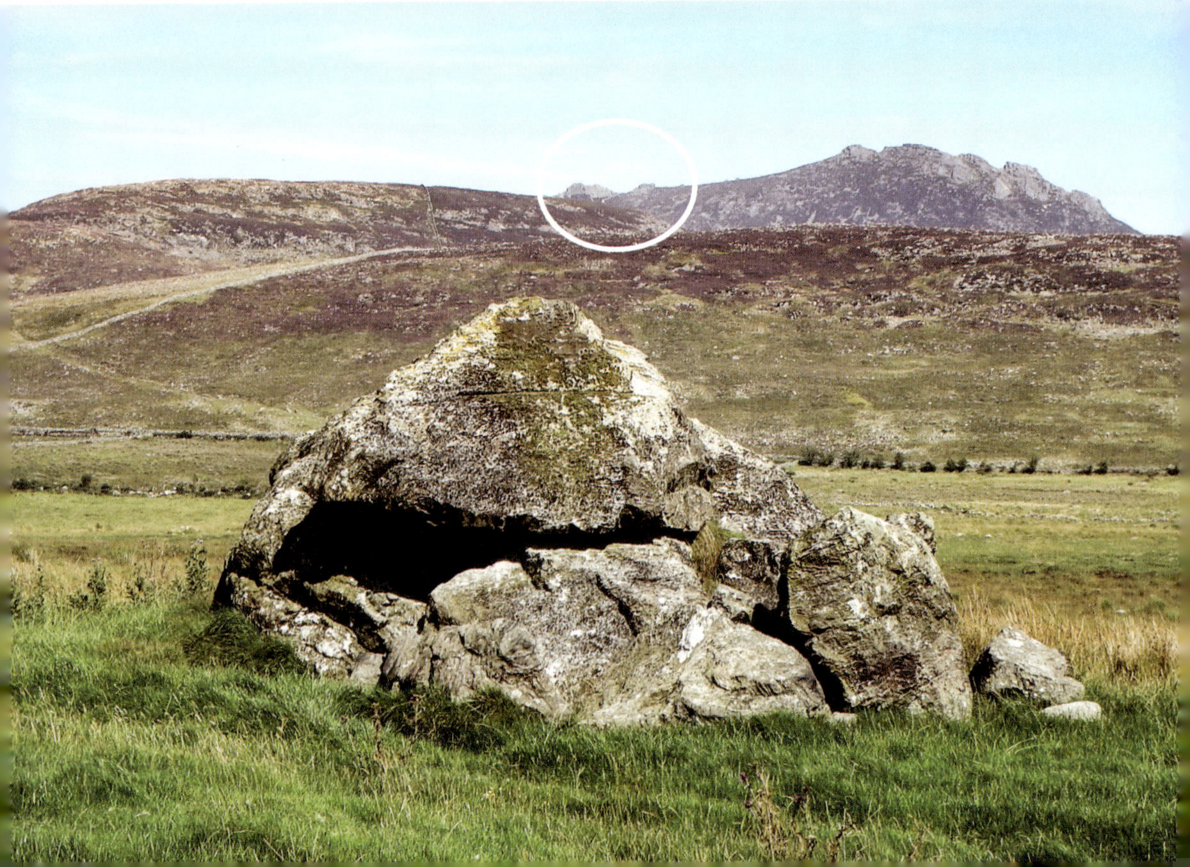

Opposite: Two views of the compound megalith along the Moyad Road known to the locals as 'Grey Stone Plan'. The mnemonic name derives from the Irish **Gríos-Stán Plannda**, meaning 'Torrid Stiffness of the offspring', a reference to the distant tors (circled) projecting from the vaginal dip along the crest of Slieve Bignian.

Above: This seriously big boulder in the valley below Buzzard's Roost is not just a random fall from above but is deliberately placed to mark the skyline phallic profile of Meelmore and its lower shoulder. The considerable size of the stone (it is 4m by 4m by maybe 3m high) is testament to the importance given to this fertility location by the ancients. The GPS of the megalith and the phallic viewpoint is:

                N.   54° 09. 494'
                W. 005° 58. 465'   Elevation 364m.

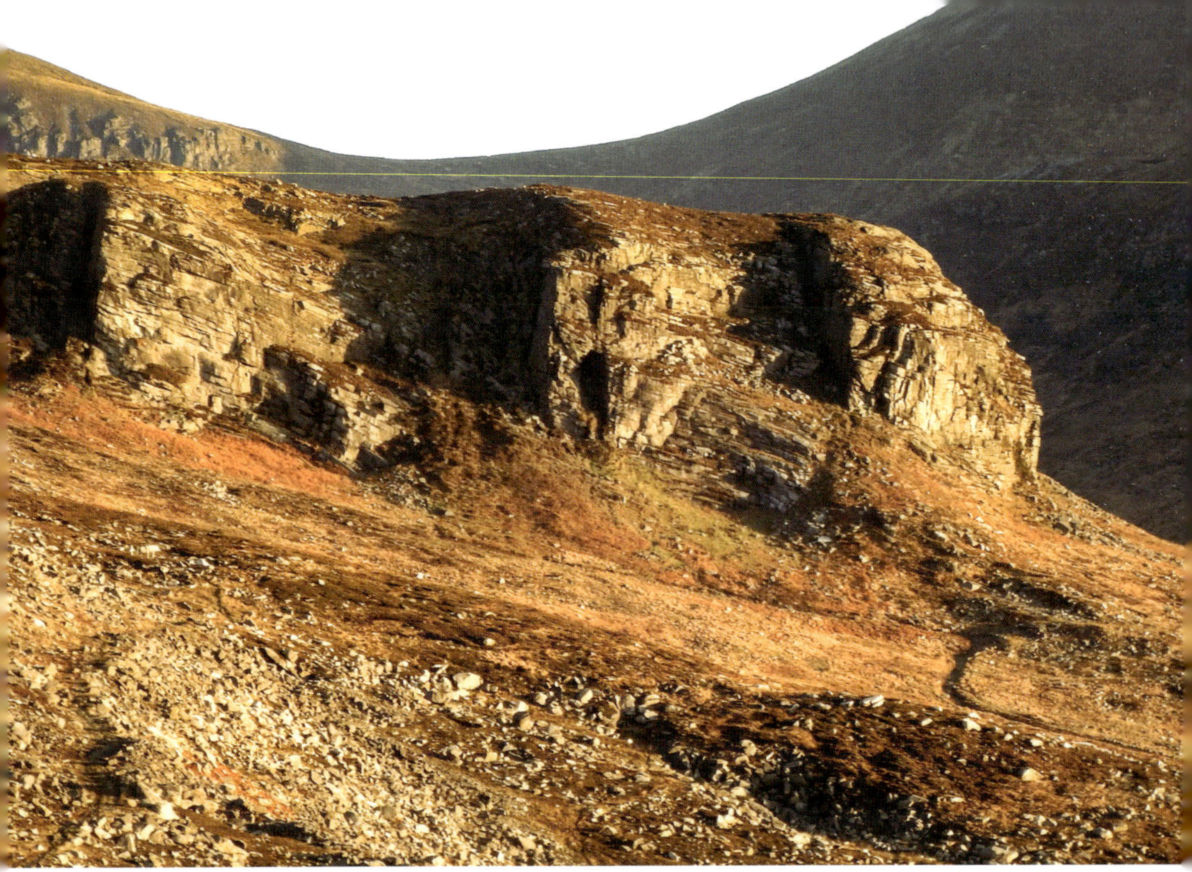

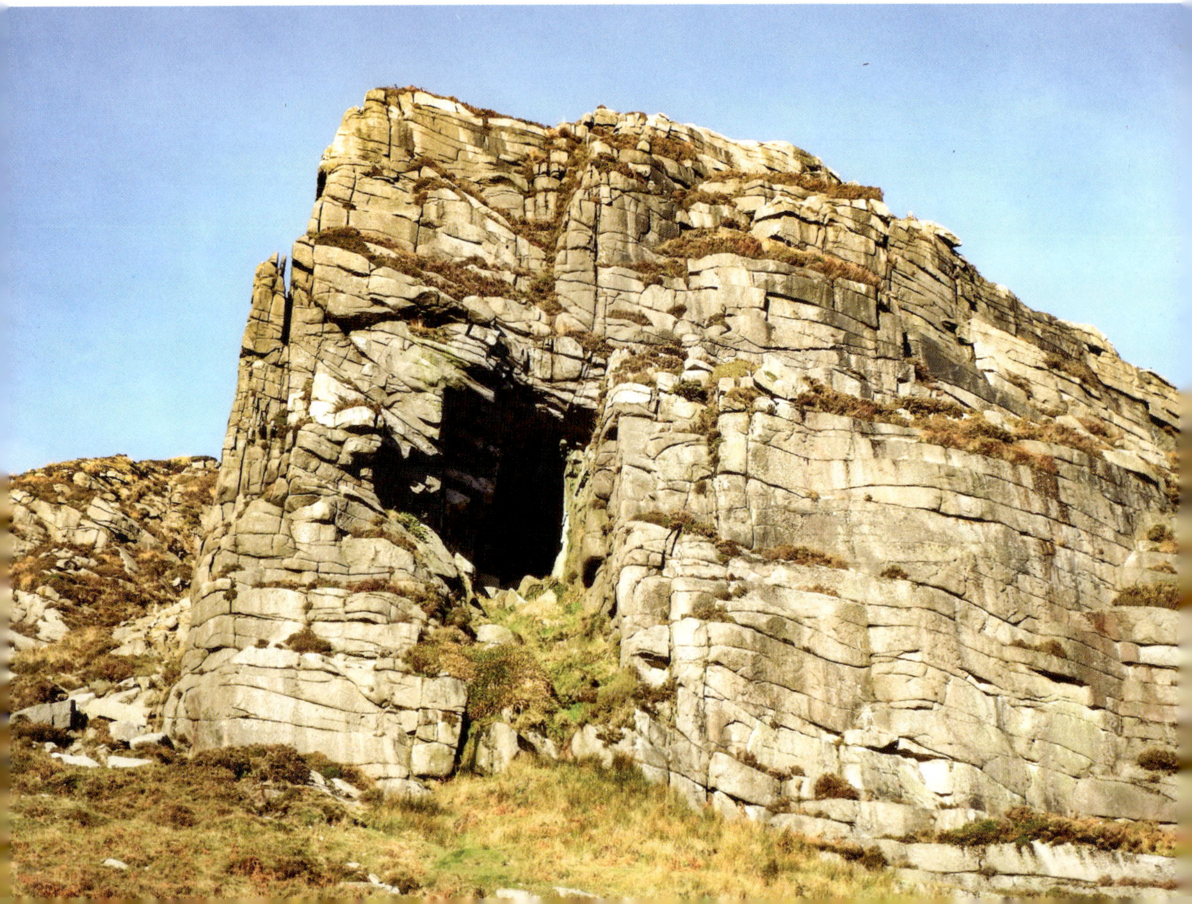

Top opposite: A winter morning view of three of the four buttresses that are marked on the ordnance survey as 'Lower Cove'. The OS English has played fast and loose with the Irish names in this part of Mourne. 'Lower Cove' is from the Irish **Leor-Cabhna**, 'a sufficiency of caves' and refers to three fissures on the seaward side of Slieve Lamagan at:	N. 54° 10. 006'
W. 005° 57. 530'	Elevation 503m.

Lower opposite: 'Upper Cove', otherwise the Chair of Enchantment, is explained and illustrated on page 380. The shepherds still refer to this cliff as 'Green Cove' which comes from **Grian Cabha**, 'Sun Cave'. This important name strongly suggests that an original fissure has been enhanced and widened to the present cave, shown opposite. The cave with its 'plucked' walls and flat floor, suggestive of the hand of man, was created to receive the declining sun from over at Bignian at winter solstice. Inside, towards the back, is a great upright spear stone megalith pointing to an erstwhile vaginal crack in the ceiling.

Above: The OS names of these mountains are, from the left, Slievemoughanmore, Wee Slievemoughan, Eagle mountain and Shanlieve. From the other side locals prefer to use the name Slimageen for Slievemoughanmore. From this side local shepherds still use the name 'Sheugmuggan' and 'Wee Sheugmuggan'. These Mourne names derive from the Irish **Súmachán**, 'a dilatory person' and refer to the late arrival of the winter solstice sun. In this respect it is similar to 'Green Rigs' (**Grian Righneálaidhe**, 'sun dawdler') on the north side of Meelmore. The name 'The Moors' will sometimes be heard in this vicinity. While some may now apply it to the heather and bog, the name originally comes from the Irish **Múr**, 'a wall'. This wall was built by Narcissus Batt, probably during the famine, to enclose the Leitrim estate which he had bought in 1834.

Above: This is a truly monstrous construction. I am grateful to the Grant family of Moyad Road for giving me the name 'Priest Smiths Well'. The mnemonic name has preserved the Irish **Próiste Smíste Béil**, 'the big strong 'skewer' of the col'. The location, near the top SW end of Happy Valley marks the fertility appearance of the phallic tors of Slieve Bearnagh filling the notch between Meelmore and Meelbeg. The GPS is:

      N. 54° 11. 189'
      W. 006° 00. 462'   Elevation 580m.

Top opposite: There must be fifteen or more stones used in this incredible construction on the very steep north side of Pollaphuca valley. The great labours here mark Slieve Donard appearing phallic-like in the [V] shaped landscape notch between Slieve Commedagh and the shoulder of Bearnagh. The ensemble was named **Ag Screadaigh le Pléisiúr**, 'Yelling with Pleasure' after a 'rictus face' on the top surface of the uppermost slab. I left two coins to mark my passing, a shilling and a 2p. The GPS is:

      N. 54° 11. 497'
      W. 005° 59. 605'   Elevation 490m.

Lower opposite: There are 'whopper' constructions and then there is this similarly named **Pleibidheach**, under Slievenaglogh's north flank. Multiple massive stones have been arranged like a stack of pancakes at the top of a steep slope. The 4m phallic spear stone at the top points to a tight gully on the cliff face of Bearnagh's shoulder on the far side of the Trassey valley. There is even a low deep dry cave at the bottom but it is only good enough to crawl into. The GPS is:

      N. 54° 11. 634'
      W. 005° 58. 474'   Elevation 458m.

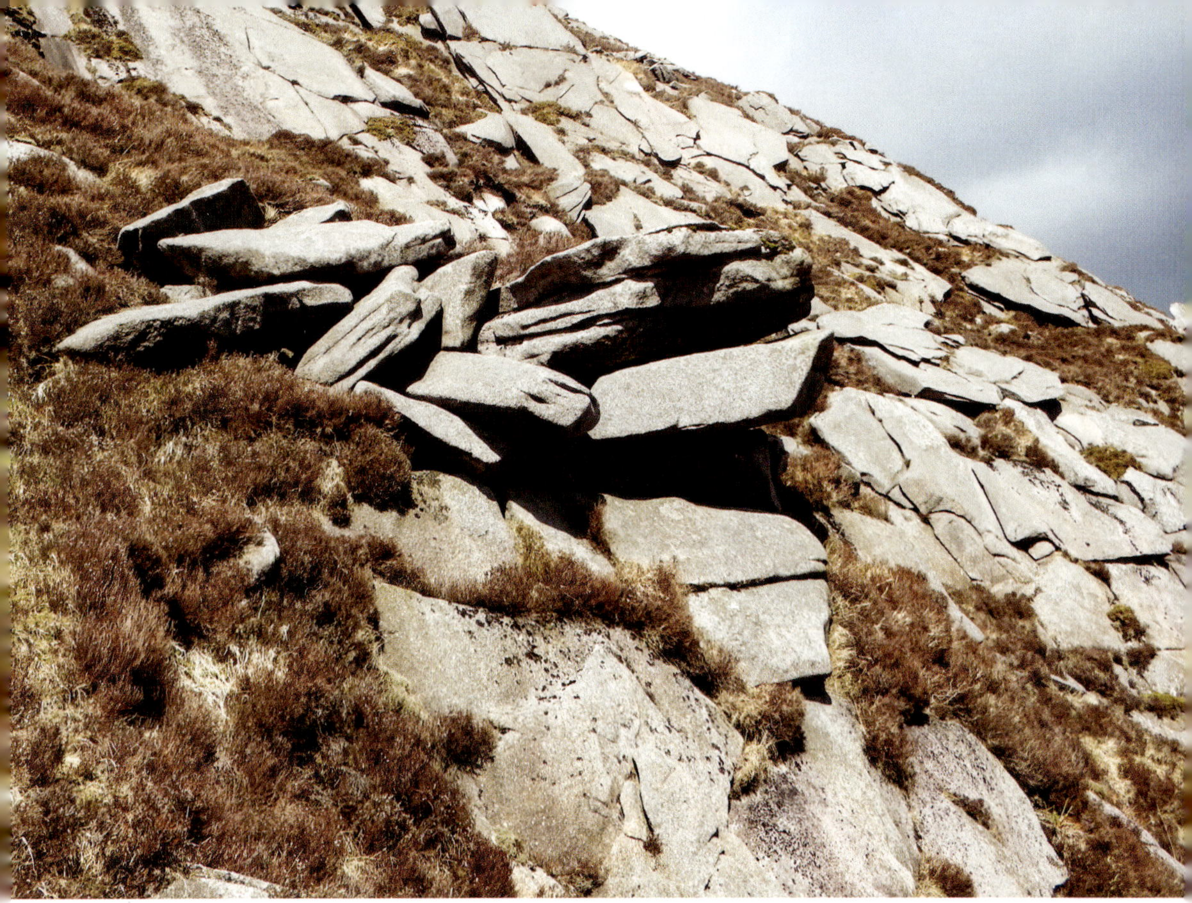

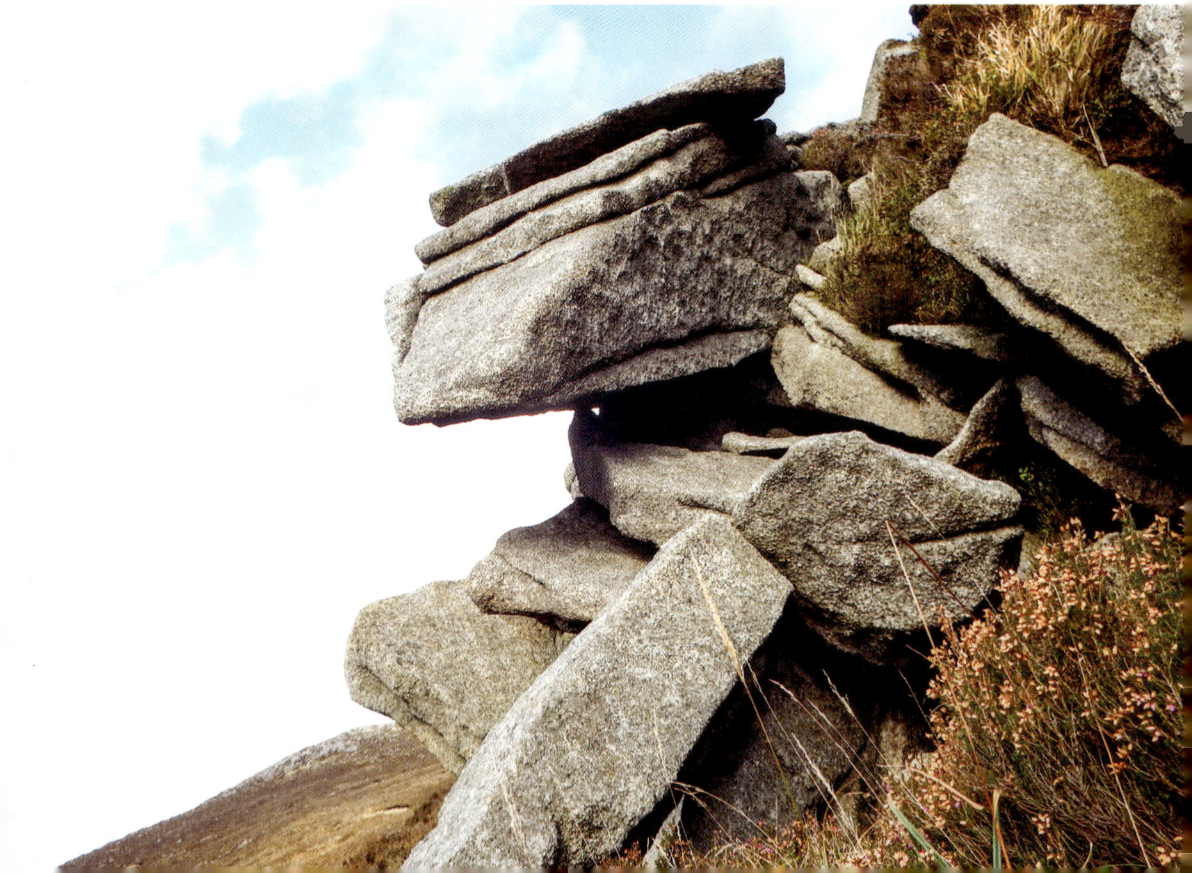

These two photographs are of **Salmon Leap**, a name local to the upper reaches of the Red Moss River in the Windy Gap valley. This name had been given to me by more than one shepherd. As expected, the term is a mnemonic of the Irish and has nothing to do with leaping fish or salmon. The name belongs to a huge vaginal gap construction about 150m northwest of the Red Moss River and very near the crest of the ridge as seen from the valley below. The GPS of the monument is:

        N.   54° 06. 879'
        W. 006° 05. 063'   Elevation 355m.

'Salmon Leap' is from the Irish *Sámh Áin Leachta*, 'Twin pleasures of the monument'. The Irish is:

Sámh, (gen.) *Sáimhe*, 'a yoke, a pair or couple, twins';
Áin, (gen.) *Áine*, 'pleasure, desire'; and
Leacht, (gen.) *Leachta*, 'a grave, cairn, any monument'.

The first pleasure is the vaginal opening itself. This is aligned to where winter solstice sun sets on the cliff behind it. The gap between the stones is 1.5m wide at the entrance, widening to 2.8m at the back. A 1m long penile stone in inserted at the rear and this would cast its shadow into the gap at solstice sunset. Such a shadow is a further instance of *Dúid lia Scáth*, 'Fertility stone shadow', which is explained and illustrated in the appendix.

    The lower labial side is truly a huge block which must have taken incredible effort to drag to this location. The stone was paced out at 8 metres in length and 2m wide. If you look to the lower right in the photograph above opposite you can see that a crack in the stone has been exploited to create the semblance of a smiling face.

    The second pleasure is to be seen on the triangular top of the higher or left-hand labial stone in the upper picture. The spear shaped top features a shadow slit of an eye on its right, while below its pointy nose the rock shows a long tongue doubtlessly extruded for the purposes of pleasure.

    A further feature that was checked by compass is that the top right corner of the rock triangle points across the Windy Gap valley to the landscape vaginal notch between Slimageen and Pigeon mountain where the summer solstice sun declines.

    There is a strong likelihood that the location for the monument was influenced by instances of the 'penis in the vagina' motif seen in the surrounding landscape. From the monument's position Eagle Mountain projects from a landscape dip as does distant Slieve Bearnagh.

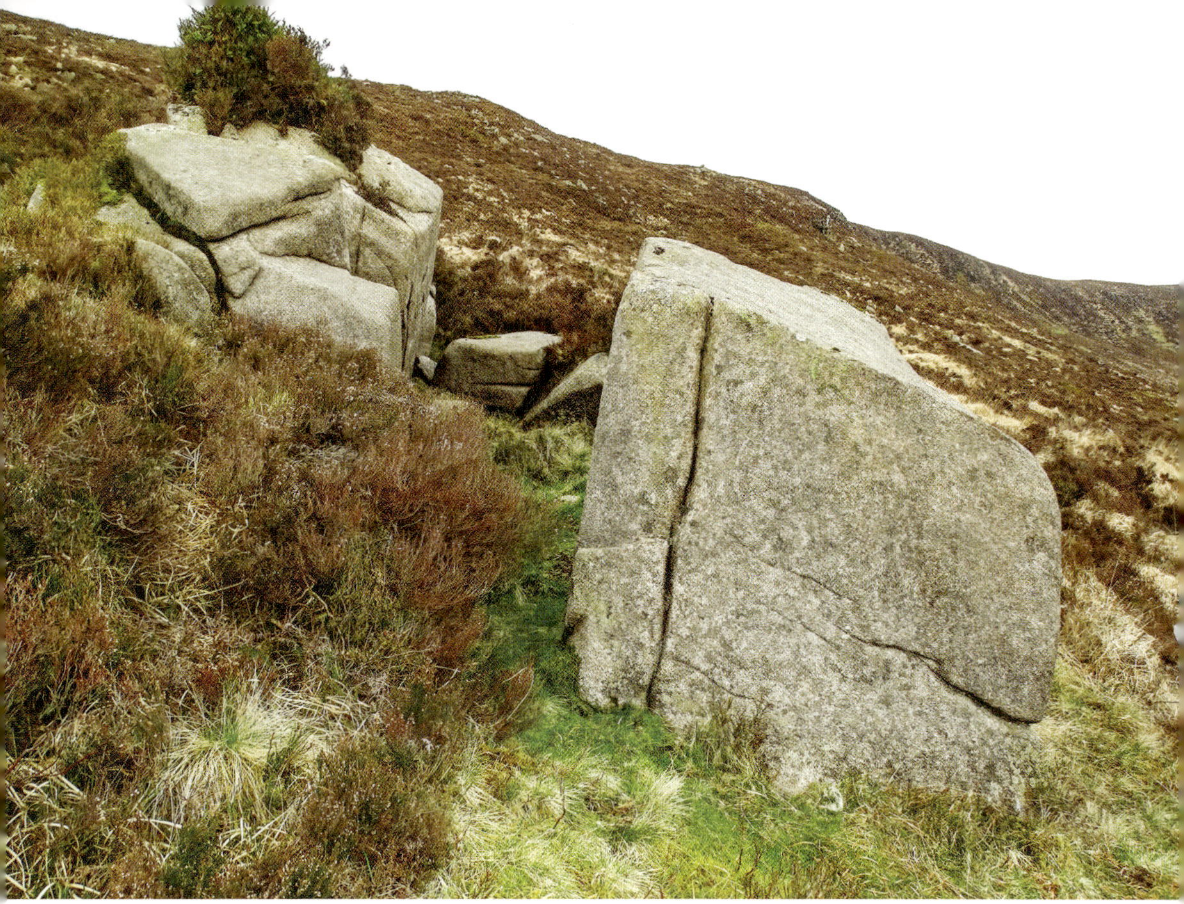
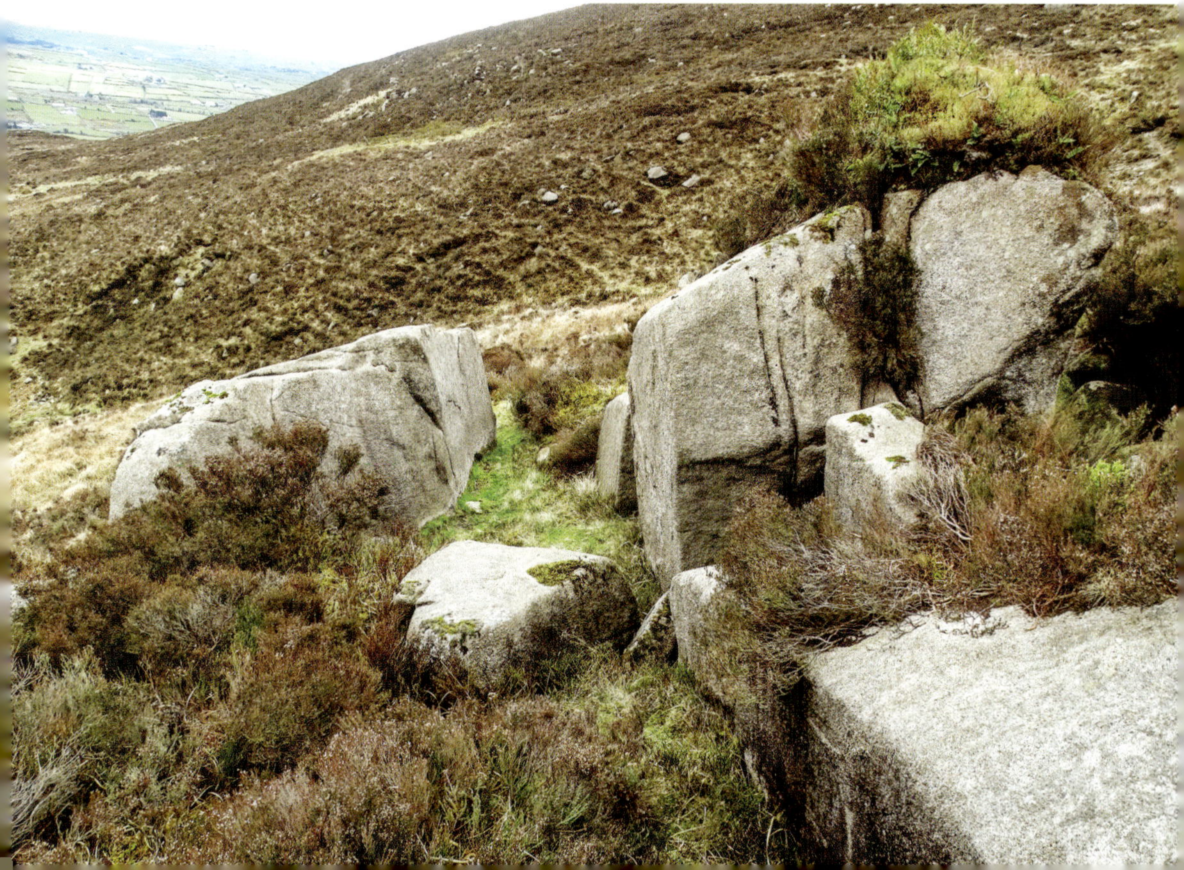

The great Hand of Ulster in the Annalong Valley as seen in sunshine at 8.53am on 22nd June. The Hand only shows 'red' when it is illuminated by dawn light a few days either side of winter solstice.

THE RED HAND OF ULSTER

The Red Hand of Ulster is not a myth. It is real and is to be found on a cliff face at Lower Cove on the western side of the Annalong valley in the heart of Mourne. It was first mentioned and illustrated in *Prehistoric Mourne* in 2015. Subsequently it was further illustrated and a GPS provided for it in *Place-names of Beanna Boirrche*, 2021. We return again to this great emblem of Ulster to add clarification to names used of the locality nearly three hundred years ago by Walter Harris in his work *The Ancient and present state of the county of Down*, (1744). This area was once rich in many Irish names. Indeed, writing about the Mournes, the collector of names for the ordnance survey, John O'Donovan, stated: 'The names of the Mourne Mountains are very curious… but I find that every *shoulder* on them bears a distinct appellation.'[*] This little part of Mourne has had at least three names and it is necessary to clear up some confusion around a fourth, 'Creeping Mountain', mentioned by Walter Harris. But first a résumé of the three surviving names.

Sliabh Snaib Báine, 'mountain of the white end' (OS reference: J 338259)
Gedic: (Sliabh) Geadaighe, '(mountain of the) white blaze on the forehead (like a horse)'
Láimh-Dhearg, 'The Red Hand'.

Slieve Snavan: Walter Harris did us a favour by preserving the important name of Snavan in his work *The Ancient and present state of the county of Down*, (1744) but then spoiled it by offering a translation of 'creeping mountain'. The name Snavan applies to the lighter colour area on the cliff face at Lower Cove in the Annalong valley. Snavan is from the Irish *Snab*, (gen.), ***Snaib***, which has the meaning of 'an end or fragment; a candle-end', together with the Irish for 'white', *Bán*, (gen.) ***Báine***.

Gedic: The cliff had yet another name, Gedic. This was mentioned by Canon Henry Lett, MRIA, in his article in UJA, 1902, entitled *Maps of the Mountains of Mourne*. He did not identify exactly where is was beyond stating 'Due west of (Knockgoran) is 'Gedic'. Knockgoran incidentally is 'the height of the pimple' and refers to a boulder megalith sky-lined on the eastern ridge of the Annalong valley. It has been illustrated on page 195.

Gedic, the alternative name for Slieve Snavan, is from the Irish *Geadach* (genitive: ***Geadaighe***) meaning 'having a white star on the forehead (as a horse)'.

---

[*] John O'Donovan's letter of 12th May 1834 to Thomas A. Larcom, Dublin. Page 68, *Ordnance Survey Letters Down*, by Michael Herity, Four Masters Press, Dublin, 2001.

Láimh-Dhearg:
The Red Hand of Ulster is to be found at ordnance survey reference J 338259 or GPS reference:

N. 54° 09. 912'
W. 005° 57. 072'   Elevation 355 m.

The GPS coordinates are actually about fifteen metres or so away from the cliff face as this provides a better overall view of the Hand.

Early Evidence: The existence of the Red Hand may indeed have been mislaid for a while but the great emblem of Ulster was never truly lost. The presence of the Hand in Mourne is attested to in early writings.

When the Place-names project of Northern Ireland was gathering the names of Mourne, one name of particular interest was recorded. It was ***Beannaibh Boirche, láimh re***, a name from circa 1600AD found in the work of Geoffrey Keating, vol 2, p.224.

[The literary work was *Foras Feasa ar Éirinn: The History of Ireland by Seathrún Céitinn*, edited by Rev. Patrick S. Dinneen, 4 volumes, Irish Texts Society iv, viii, ix & xv, London 1902-1914; The important reference of ***Beannaibh Boirche, láimh re*** was gathered by the Institute of Irish Studies in *The Mournes*, and features as no. 20, on p.119, Vol 3. County Down; *Place-Names of Northern Ireland*, QUB, 1993].

No comment was passed on this name back in 1993 possibly because its significance was not then appreciated. ***Beannaibh Boirche, láimh re*** can be translated as the 'peaks of swellings of the hand period'. The word *ré* in Irish usually means 'moon' but it also has the meaning of 'a time, a period, an interval, a duration'. In this respect the Red Hand is very like the great world heritage site of Newgrange where for a few days on either side of the winter solstice the rising sun would penetrate into the depths of the passage tomb. The spectacle of the Hand in its red livery can only be seen, weather permitting, for a period on either side of the winter solstice.

The Gaelic Lords of Mourne were the Magennis Clan and it is no surprise the Red Hand featured on their coat of arms especially as it was such an important part of their patrimony. The coat of arms can be seen on the grave of one of the last of the clan, Arthur Magennis who died in 1737 and was buried in the shelter of the gable of Clonduff chapel. The Red Hand can be seen in the upper right-hand quadrant of the shield. Sandstone is not local to the Clonduff area and the use of this material for the headstone not only enhances the Red Hand but could convey the subtle message of respect for, if not, adherence to, the old religion of sun worship.

The Red Hand on the grave of Arthur Magennis at Clonduff old chapel, Hilltown.

Not a Bloody Hand: The description of the Hand as Red has nothing to do with blood, rather it is the colour imparted to the granite cliff face of Cove by the rising sun. The often heard legend of the cutting off of the hand and casting it ashore to win a race and a kingdom was given short shift a century ago by one of the greatest authorities on heraldry in Ulster, John Vinycomb, M.R.I.A., who dismissed the story as 'not of any account'. At dawn, sunlight has to pass through more of the earth's atmosphere and meets more air molecules that scatter away the blue light; what is left is mostly the red component and this makes the rising sun seem red. Perhaps four or five thousand years ago there may also have been more volcanic dust in the atmosphere that would have intensified the red dawn colour because presently the colour of the Hand at early winter solstice would more accurately be described as light orange. As dawn progresses the sun would rise higher and the light would become brighter and colours changed. In the normal light of day the fresh granite appears so much cleaner, vivid and intensely white by comparison with the nearby grey weathered granite. This daylight change of colour brought the new name of *Snab Bán*, 'the white fragment' for the cliff face. This is the Slieve Snavan mentioned by Walter Harris in 1744, but mistakenly referred to by him as

*The profile of 'Creeping' Mountain as seen from the foot of the Red Hand. This is Chimney Rock mountain which had every appearance of a great phallus that would be painful to insert. It was known in Irish as **Crí Péine**, 'Shape of Suffering'.*

the 'creeping' mountain, leading to much confusion in subsequent years. The Irish for 'creeping, or crawling' is *Snáigheach*.

We have mentioned before that 'every piece of legend, every piece of folklore is based on some fact, however garbled'. This applies to the name 'Creeping Mountain'. Harris may have been quoting a name heard from his guide but the answer to the confusion is that 'Creeping' mountain is the sound of Irish, not English. The Irish refers to a viewpoint eastwards across the Annalong valley as seen from the bottom of the Red Hand cliff-face. The name of 'Creeping' is from the Irish **Crí Péine**, 'Shape of Suffering' and refers to the profile of Chimney Rock mountain on the other side of the valley which had every appearance of a huge phallus that would make a most painful insertion. The 'Creeping' mountain does not refer to Slieve Lamagan.

Appearing of the Red Hand at Solstice Dawn: At Mourne the azimuth for the appearance of winter solstice sun is 136° from North, and for summer solstice dawn 50° (both uncorrected, ie just as the compass reads). Sunsets, viewed on level terrain or where the horizon can be seen, are at 230° from North for winter solstice sunset and 316° from North for summer solstice sunset. If weather permits a clear dawn and no passing clouds mar the moment, the spectacle of the Red Hand should be visible for about ten days on either side of the winter solstice, from around 12th December to the 31st December. Thereafter the sun retreats from its southerly journey and then Rocky mountain and the far side of the Annalong valley intervene to block the early light shining on the end of Cove during the critical time when the sun is sufficiently low on the horizon to cast a ruddy glow. Due to the axis of the earth's rotation, and that the earth's speed varies in its elliptical orbit, there are eight minutes difference between sunrise on 12th December and the end of the month. A good place to check is the website www. timeanddate.com.

The Red Hand was first seen from the Carrick Little track at the end of December 2014. It was to be another two years before the weather was good enough to see the Red Hand close-up. That day was 17th December 2016. It took a gentle one hour forty minutes to get from the Head Road to within a quarter mile of Cove cliff in time for dawn at 08.39am. This distance was close enough for a zoom lens to give detail but still quite far enough back to give a good over-all sight of the movement of light on Lower Cove. When dawn comes, it takes a little while for the light to strengthen sufficiently to cast shadows but at 8.45am Slieve Bignian and Lamagan enjoyed the full warmth of the illuminating sun. A minute later and sunlight was shining on three buttresses of Lower Cove and starting to gild the top of the fourth. At 8.51am the top and side of the fourth buttress of Cove was in good warm light but the Red Hand was still in shade. However, at 8.54am golden light was touching the top of the fingers and a further two minutes

The first ever photograph of the Red Hand. It was taken at 8.49am on 17th December.

saw the thumb and the upper half of the Hand enjoying the special light it had missed for so long. At 8.59am as the sun finally emerged from behind Rocky mountain across the valley, the bottom of the cliff with the Hand was fully resplendent in its orange glow. The magnificent sight lasted for nearly ten minutes until a small cloud intervened to end the spectacle at 9.08am. The valley was quiet apart from a raven occasionally cawing and the sound of a little gurgle of water somewhere nearby. The air was crisp. There was no wind. All was calm and there wasn't another soul around. It was truly a beautiful day to behold what The O'Neill in Lisbon had called 'that terrible cognizance'.

Description: The Hand is at the end of the cliff face on the west side of the Annalong valley. At best reckoning the Hand might be about 15 metres high by about 12 metres from the thumb to the end of the cliff. The rock surface of the hand is rough and relatively unweathered; it is bright and clean as if freshly exposed which is quite a contrast to the dull grey smooth surface of the rock further along the cliff face. The rock face is slightly concave; water dripping from the top of the cliff falls nearly two metres away from the bottom of the cliff. This absence of water running down the cliff face has largely preserved the bright colour of the rock surface from staining to the darker grey colour.

The question will be asked whether the Hand is a purely natural feature or man made. The answer will await a close-up inspection but this observer's impression is that it is a bit of both. Looking at the cliff from below it would seem that most of the bright rock is original and similar to other light patches on the cliff face further along. That said, one rather suspects that the ancients, with ropes and a bit of imagination, sought to enhance the natural patches by creating a great Hand with the judicious removal of a bit more granite, specifically at the top of the thumb and the third finger. From evidence around the mountains the ancients certainly used ropes to access difficult places as, for instance, on the cliff of Spellack illustrated on page 322. Such is likely to have been the case here. The compound megalith, illustrated on page 155, half-way down the sheer cliff of Cove, and pointing to winter solstice sunrise, could only have been accessed by rope. There is the further evidence of the carving of an eagle's head below the first and second fingers. This was featured as a double page at 114/115.

There is no rock fall at the bottom of the Red Hand cliff to indicate any natural process of pealing foliation. The projecting outcrop at the bottom of the cliff, with its darker stain, suggests this may have been the original cliff face. The diagonal nature of the outcrop appears to have been left to represent a 'wisdom line' on the hand.

This treasure of Ulster and indeed of all Ireland, this symbol of our ancient ancestors and emblem of royalty is a worthy reward for undertaking a walk into the Mournes. There are no steep hill climbs involved to approach it, presuming of course that your approach is up the Annalong valley either via Carrick Little track or the Water Commissioners road. When you arrive, may good luck attend you and you are allowed a little war-cry of triumph, perhaps *Lámbh dearg a buaidh*, 'The Red Hand to victory'. And should a walk into the Mournes perhaps be a little too much for you then you could give your little war-cry from the comfort of a car for the spectacle of the Red Hand can be seen with binoculars on a sunny dawn around solstice from the northern end of the Longstone Road. As you enjoy the spectacle of the great emblem you could also breath a prayer of thanks for its preservation. In the search for water for Belfast over a century ago, the Annalong Valley had been chosen for the construction of a dam to augment that at Silent Valley with the result that the Red Hand would have been destroyed.

A view of the Annalong Valley which over a century ago was proposed as the site for a dam.

ПАОТ
РДОГА 13

ST PATRICK DRIVES OUT THE 'SNAKES'

'Aitcheam ort, a ógánaigh naomhta,
teacht chughainn is siubhal fós I n-ar measc.'
'A begging on you, oh holy youth, to come and
walk further among us.' (Confessions: 23)

Even in 1927 when Fr Patrick Dinneen produced the second edition of his great Irish Dictionary, *Foclóir Gaedhilge agus Béarla*, there was a very telling remark at the end of the entry on *Ulaidh*, 'Ulster'. 'The Province is', he said, 'associated with witchcraft in the folk imagination'. It was also at this time, 1925, that local poet, Richard Rowley, otherwise Richard Valentine Williams of Brook Cottage, Bryansford Road, Newcastle, wrote the poem *At the Ballagh* recording a story of encounter with evil.

St Mary's chapel at the Ballagh is as good a place as any to hear this story of evil. It is worth asking the question, why did they build a church in this remote location all those centuries ago? Even yet the place is rather isolated, secluded and detached from the nearest population centre. The truth is the chapel was not built at the entrance to the Bloody Bridge valley to attract a congregation of worshipers but to claim a pagan location for Christianity. St Mary's was a site of particular pagan importance as it was from here about 8.10pm on the summer solstice that the sun could be seen setting on the top of Slieve Donard. The pagans interpreted this spectacle as analogous to the sun copulating with a huge vulva of mother earth and thus ensuring fertility for another year.

We might further mention that across Dundrum Bay the winter solstice sun can be seen setting on the summit of Slieve Donard from the present Ballykinlar chapel. This is how Ballykinlar has its name. It is from the Irish **Baile Cinn Láir**, 'place of the centre of the head'. The previous earlier chapel at Ballykinlar was built down in the hollow across the road where it was out of sight and untainted by the pagan spectacle. Ballykinlar chapel was also claiming a pagan site for Christianity as were the other chapels around the edge of the Bay, namely St John's, Rossglass, Rathmullan, Tyrella, Killyglinnie, Lismohan and Drumcaw.

Also after millennia of human sacrifice in the Mournes, we can be sure that enormous superstition prevailed.[1] Travellers along the Ballagh coast

---

1 For Human sacrifice at Mourne, see page 225 of *Bethu Phátraic*, from *The Tripartite Life of Patrick, with other documents relating to that Saint*. Edited by Whitley Stokes, Eyre & Spottiswoode, London, 1887.

The sun setting on the summit of Slieve Donard at winter solstice as seen from the steps of Ballykinlar chapel. From a pagan viewpoint it was as if the mountain was coming to a sexual climax. This very potent fertility spectacle was one of the reasons Lecale had its Irish name of **Leath Caoile**, 'District of the Loins'.

road in earlier centuries would have had to deal with fear and a very real dread of evil spirits on passing the entrance to the Bloody Bridge valley. The nearby chasm of Armour's Hole, so called from the Irish **Ár Mór Olc**, 'great evil slaughter', was also a location provoking dread. We should not underestimate the comfort and courage conferred to travellers by the presence of the chapel.

This was the setting for Rowley's poem *At the Ballagh* that captured the menace and fears of the powers of hell. In the poem a dying shepherd spoke of the day he saw the very face of evil when he harboured angry thoughts in his mind against someone who was going to take a field he had long rented away from him.

> This was the story that oul' Davy told
> Lying upon his death-bed…

He couldn't work or rest and the anger burned fierce in his heart until he gripped his ash-plant and left the mountain eager to meet his enemy, 'murder in my heart an' blasphemy on my lips'. While on his way something far out at sea caught his eye. It was the shape of swirling fog but black and dark, rushing across the water straight for the land until it hung all trembling in the air above him.

> I looked an' saw
> Its misty curtains open. From its heart
> Black as if hewed from ebony a face
> Glowered upon me, leanin' out to peer
> Into my face. Twin branching horns o' jet
> Sprang from its head, an' in its taloned hand
> Was clutched a spear o' steel hideously pronged
> Wi' triple white-hot points. But oh! Its eyes,
> Its eyes were terrible. They glowed an' blazed
> Red-hot like fire or white like molten lead,
> Through me they looked into my very soul,
> And saw the evil thoughts deep in my heart,
> And when they saw, the sharp-fanged lips outstretched
> Into a grin o' malice an' wicked glee.
> A wind sprang up, the cloud was whirled away
> And as it passed I heard a fiend-like screech
> Of horrible laughter. When I dared look up
> O'er Donard's peak I saw a huge dark cloud
> Suddenly burst in flame an' disappear.[2]

Davy would safely lose his anger when a ray of sun shone out yet he never forgot the evil he encountered. It is significant that this tale was located at the Ballagh. The poem is didactic, telling of the dangers of giving way to anger. We cannot know whether such a death-bed story was ever really told but given Rowley's propensity for writing and basing his stories on what he had heard from local characters, there is a strong likelihood of truth behind this tale. Allowing even for a generous dose of poetic licence, there is a stronger likelihood that even so recent as a century ago, when these lines were penned, Rowley was encountering widespread and firm beliefs in fairies, banshees and evil spirits of the night. The deep seated and latent fears of the ancient gods lingered long in Mourne; such fears elicited words of wisdom that Rowley put into the mouth of a *Seanchaidhe* or one versed in folk-lore, stories and the wisdom of the ages about the dangers of dabbling with the ways of the spirits or wee folk.

> Crouched over the ashes,
> The Shanachie spoke,
> 'Tis ill to take gifts
> From the Hidden Folk;

---

2 *At the Ballagh*: Richard Rowley's poem of the shepherd's death bed tale is found on pages 51-59, in *The Old Gods and other poems*, printed by Gerald Duckworth, London, 1925.

> Drink not their drink,
> Eat not their bread,
> Share not their shelter
> The Shanachie said.[3]

'Thinking Long' and the Invocation of Malign Powers in Mourne

The expression 'thinking long' seems to be quite local to Mourne; an aunt of mine who had taught in Kilcoo was well familiar with it but the saying meant nothing to her husband who was from another county. It was a phrase that was familiar to the local poet Richard Rowley. He even wrote a poem *Thinkin' Long* the first verse of which sees an old man reflecting beside his fire.

> 'It's time the lamp was lit,
> A sit my lone,
> Watchin' the firelight play
> On the cracked hearth-stone.

3 From *'The Shanachie'*, in Richard Rowley's The Piper of Mourne, McCord, Belfast, 1944.

When seen from above, the floor of the ritual platform on Slieve Donard's south flank features a particularly evil and malevolent face. It overlooks the Bloody Bridge valley and the ruins of St Mary's chapel much further down. This platform is known as 'Bishop's Seat' so called from the Irish **bPis Óibhéala Seata**, 'wide open vulva of the harlot' a reference to the sexual imagery of the cliff face behind. The GPS is:

N.   54° 10. 510'
W. 005° 55. 393'   Elevation 668m.

Oul' dreams go through my head,
Like words o' a song.
A'm sittin' here my lone,
An A'm thinkin' long.'[4]

The expression 'Thinking Long' now has the meaning of taking one's time over something, being slow and deliberate or giving something careful consideration. The saying is a mnemonic that has preserved for us the Irish **Tincheadal Luain** meaning, 'Incantation of light' and harks back to the ancient chants and mantras that went on interminably in pagan times during the vigil for the rising of the solstice sun. It was this creed of sun worship and attendant fertility rituals that St Patrick had to contend with when he returned to Ireland to spread the Christian faith.

Besides the ritual platform on the south flank of Slieve Donard, there are at least two other Mourne locations likely identified with the *Tincheadal Luain* of winter solstice dawn. These are the great split at the north tor of Bignian and secondly the top of Lower Cove cliff which is the proper location for the OS name of Upper Cove.

The deep cleft in Bignian's north tor, evoking resemblance to a vaginal notch, is penetrated by first light of winter solstice and this made it a natural setting for the prayers, petitions and chants preceding the sun's appearance. The stone chair at the place of ritual can still be seen high on a rock platform at the back of the cleft. The name of North Tor is only a mnemonic of the Irish (*Sliabh na*) **n-Ortha**, meaning '(mountain of) prayers/incantations'.[5]

A second place that place-names would associate with the invocation of malign powers is what might be referred to as the 'Chair of Enchantment' on Lower Cove. A flat-topped granite block, at the perfect height for sitting on, has been placed on a level platform on the top of Lower Cove. This ledge gets the first dawn light of winter solstice. It also happens to be just round the corner from Ulster's great cliff-face emblem, the Red Hand, a fact attested to in Keating's *History of Ireland* (see under Slieve Snavan, pages 317f, *Place-names of Beanna Boirrche*, 2021). This is where Upper Cove gets its name. The terms 'Upper' and 'Lower' as used in English and on the present ordnance survey maps are really a later day distraction. 'Upper' Cove derives from the Irish **Upa, (gen.), Uptha**, meaning 'charms, sorcery, enchantment'. Time has obliterated what may have happened here. Nobody

---

4 *Thinkin' Long*: Page 68 of Richard Rowley's collection of poems, *City Songs and Others*, published by Maunsel & Co, Dublin & London, 1918.
5 **Ortha**: This Irish word for 'charm, curse, prayer or incantation' had so many uses in past times. Then, you had the like of **Ortha an leonta**, 'the sprain-cure', **Ortha na fiacaile**, 'the toothache charm', or **Ortha an dídin**, the protection-prayer, said while going three times round the house.

The ritual chair and platform (arrowed) in the cleft of Bignian's 'little mountain' (Binnean) gave this place the name of 'North Tor', a mnemonic of the Irish (*Tí na*) **n-Ortha**, meaning '(place of) prayers/incantations'.

can know for sure what evils this location saw. An inference that it may have involved blood sacrifice, perhaps even human sacrifice, is taken from the two neighbouring artworks of scavengers. On the cliff-face below the chair of enchantment the rock formation has been used to depict an open winged vulture while down below at the bottom of the cliff is the megalith of a rat gnawing on what could be construed as a bone. The rat was illustrated on page 102. If you get to this ritual platform look at the floor on the cliff's edge to see artwork of a bird's head with a deep mauled eye. The beak seemingly points to where the solstice sun declines behind Bignian. And, does it need to be said? Cliff tops are dangerous places demanding alertness and caution.

St Patrick comes to Saul

When St Patrick returned to Ireland tradition tells us that he made landing at Saul, County Down. He had arrived at *Leath Caoile*, the 'District of the Loins'. Such has been the sustained effort over time to expunge the pagan past that many accept the present interpretation of Lecale as *Leath Cathail*, meaning 'Cathal's portion'; Cathal being deemed a prince of Uladh about 700AD. A similar linguistic purge was made on the name of Saul which was regarded as deriving from *Sabhal*, 'a barn', the story was that Patrick was given the barn by Dichu after he had been converted. The place-name of Saul comes from, not one but two, Irish words. The name also comes from a pagan and sexual interpretation of the landscape. The source of the name can still be seen today unlike any ephemeral barn of the ancient past. The great statue of St Patrick atop Saul hill faces west. It is the phallic profile of the Slieve Croob hills in the west that lies behind the name of Saul. The place-name comes from the two Irish words **Sab Áil** meaning 'rod of pleasure'. For all we know perhaps St Patrick deliberately chose to start his mission at this part of Ireland. It may have been the preponderance of pagan sites that drew a man anxious to get 'stuck in' with his vocation to bring the faith to his former land of captivity.

St Patrick and Mourne[6]

Close by Armour's Hole at the Ballagh, south of Newcastle, is the little stream of Srupatrick. Most visitors will only realise they are crossing Srupatrick when they see the 'Welcome to Mourne' sign at the side of the road. The tiny stream marks the boundary between Mourne and Iveagh

---

6 Parts of this chapter were previously recorded in *Prehistoric Mourne* but with so many copies of the book being destroyed in the 2021 floods that ravaged Newcastle it has been thought worthwhile to reproduce these parts again.

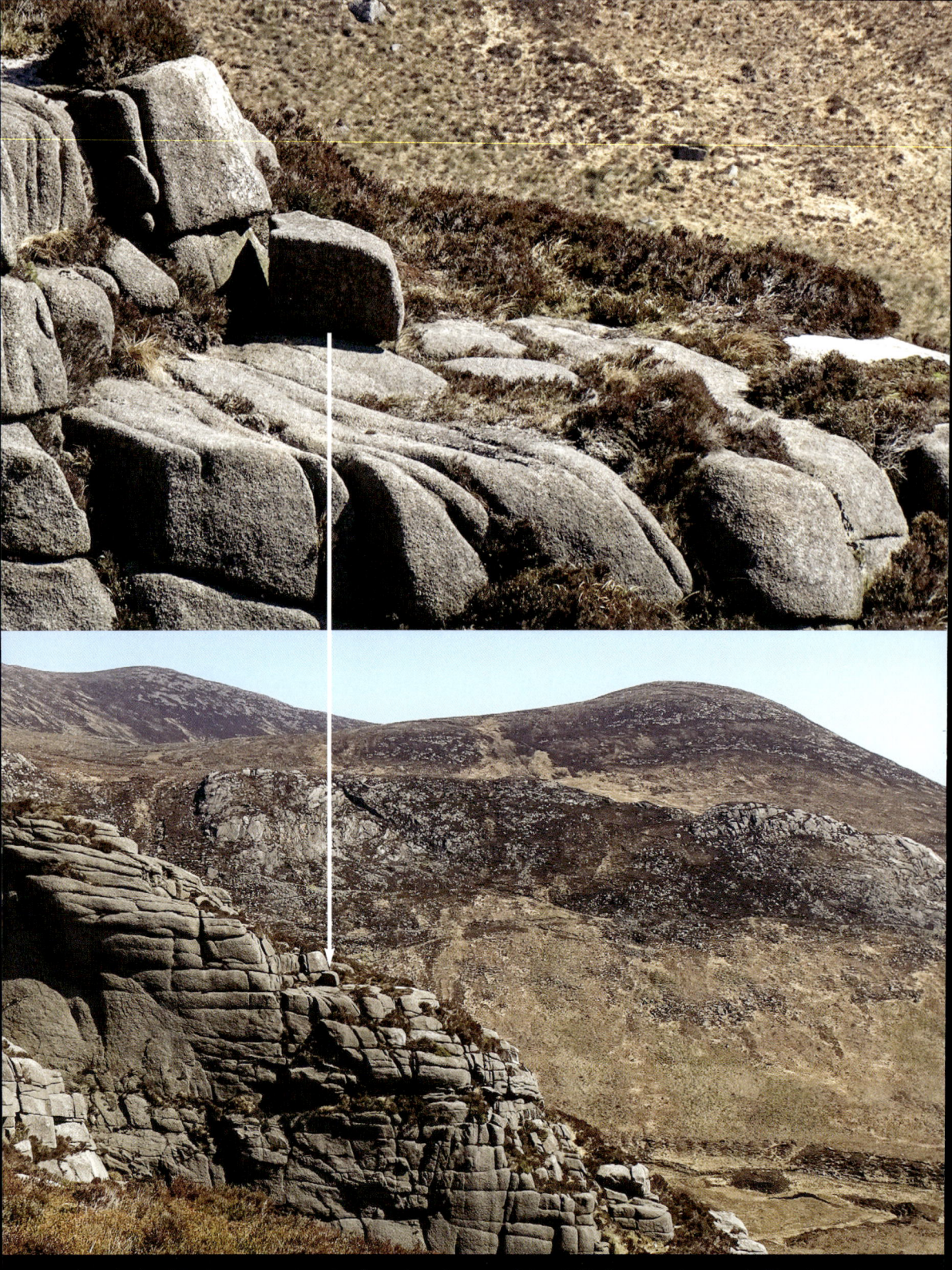

The Chair of Enchantment is to be found at the top of the cliff of Lower Cove. It is illuminated at dawn of winter solstice. This place of incantation gave us the name 'Upper' Cove, from the Irish *Uptha*, meaning 'charms, sorcery, enchantment'. The ominous artwork of 'The Vulture', illustrated on pages 116/117, is on the cliff-face below the chair. The GPS of the chair is:

N.　54° 09.　91'

*The phallic profile of the Croob hills as seen from Cathedral Hill, Downpatrick. It is the same view that would be seen from Saul only closer. The profile gave Saul its Irish name **Sab Áil** meaning 'rod of pleasure'.*

and until 1972 marked the administrative boundary for the town of Newcastle after it separated from the union of Kilkeel at the start of the twentieth century. Srupatrick, or Patrick's stream, was alleged to be as far as St Patrick came in his mission of converting this part of Ireland. The legend has been recorded for us by professor Evans in his seminal work, *Mourne Country*, and it is worth quoting the relevant part.

> 'The conversion of Mourne to Christianity was, it must be supposed, a slow process, for this isolated region, steeped in old custom, would have offered strong resistance to new ideas. There is a tradition that St Patrick founded a church somewhere in the Kingdom which has long since disappeared, but this runs counter to a stronger tradition that the Saint did not set foot beyond St Patrick's Stream, which was so named because it was the limit of his travels. The story goes that when he reached the little river that marks the northern boundary of Mourne he took off his sandal and threw it… As he threw it he uttered a prophecy: "The length of that there will never be blood spilled"… One cannot help feeling that St Patrick was not well received when he entered the mountain pass.'[7]

---

7 From the chapter 'Raths and Saints', p.99-100, in *Mourne Country* by Prof. E.E. Evans, Dundalgan Press, Dundalk, 1951.

The strange behaviour of St Patrick throwing his sandal in the vicinity of Srupatrick, taken in conjunction with the prophecy of ending bloodshed, can be reasonably interpreted as Christianity putting an end to killings at Armour's Hole. Some have thought to wonder how far St Patrick's sandal flew or its significance for wherever it landed but there really is no need to look further than Armour's Hole for when 'sandal' is transposed into Irish it gives us *An Scáine Dall* 'The Black Fissure'.

Returning to the remark by professor Evans that he felt 'St Patrick was not well received when he entered the mountain pass', this has a serious implication for the term 'Kingdom of Mourne' beloved by the local tourist industry. It is pleasing to think of tourists being welcomed here in kindly Kingdom of Mourne. They most certainly are; but unfortunately it is the legend of the poor reception given to St Patrick that endures in the kingdom title. The word 'kingdom' does not bespeak a region that was once a monarchical state; rather it is from the Irish *Cean Doim*, 'miserable welcome'. The Irish *cean* normally means 'affection, passion' but can be used about the reception given to a guest as in the phrase *Ní cean gus a dtig*, 'he was not welcome'.

St Patrick and the Shamrock

Customs must be changing. Near seventy years ago wearing shamrock on St Patrick's Day would have been *de rigueur*. Back then the best place to find it at Newcastle was among the rock ballast between the railway lines out past the station. Nowadays the custom of wearing a sprig seems to be declining but the shamrock is still one of the most identifiable emblems of Ireland.

There is no written evidence of St Patrick ever having used the shamrock as a teaching aid. We might note, for instance, that the shamrock does not feature in Dick's engraved illustration of the banishing of the snake. The long standing legend tells of St Patrick taking up a leaf of shamrock and pointing to three separate leaves on one stem to explain the mystery of the Blessed Trinity when early converts had difficulty grasping the concept that in One God there were three Divine Beings, really distinct and equal in all things. The emphasis in Ireland has always been with the three leaves of the shamrock; surprising there is no reference to the lovely little yellow flowers. Aer Lingus has the trefoil on its wings, bowls of shamrock are presented annually to the American president at the White House on St Patrick's Day and there will be advertisements galore featuring the leaves

Christianity symbolically takes pride of place on a pagan standing stone at Sandy Brae outside Attical in the Mournes.

but no-where will the flowers be found. The adoption of the shamrock by Christianity is a case of an erstwhile pagan symbol being taken over and 're-invented'. The attraction of the plant to the pagans was its little yellow petal flower that was a great symbol of the sun. On the shamrock it is the yellow flowers that turn into the seeds so the flower represented not only the sun but also the promise of fruitfulness. The sun was the great god of fertility and as such was often synonymous with the human source of fertility, the female vagina. It was the yellow flower of the shamrock, suggestive of the sun, that gave the plant its name. The present word in Irish for shamrock is *seamróg* (a Munster variation would be *Simearóg*) but the earliest derivation comes from a compound of *Sámhais Roc*. The aspirated version of *Sámhas* would have a sound similar to the beginning of our Newcastle river the Shimna, where the Irish for bulrushes, *Simhean*, has the [sh] sound, as in 'shawl, sheaf or ship'. It is easy to understand why the little flower of the shamrock needed to be overlaid with a Christian interpretation for in pagan times the original *Sámhais Roc* [*Shámhais*] had an explicit sexual meaning that would have been incompatible with the Christian message. *Sámhas Roc* means 'bodily pleasure hole'.

This engraving from *Lives of Irish Saints and Martyrs* is the work of Archibald L. Dick (c.1793-1856) of Brooklyn, New York. It is a classic rendering of St Patrick driving out the snakes from Ireland. The mountains of Mourne are featured on the bottom left. Might an Irish emigrant have informed the engraver of the enormity of Mourne's pagan past?

Patrick Drives out the 'Snakes'

Back in the twelfth century the Welshman Giraldus Cambrensis, after a visit to Ireland in 1185 as secretary to prince John, passed dismissive comment on the absence of snakes in Ireland.

> 'Of all sorts of reptiles, Ireland possesses those only which are harmless, and does not produce any that are venomous… Some indeed conjecture, with what seems a flattering fiction, that St. Patrick and the other saints of that country cleared the island of all pestiferous animals; but history asserts, with more probability, that from the earliest ages, and long before it was favoured with the light of revealed truth, this was one of the things which never existed here, from some natural deficiency in the produce of the island.'[8]

Indeed it is accepted by naturalists that snakes were unable to inhabit Ireland as the country had been early isolated after the ice age by rising sea-levels. The legend still endures throughout the world that St Patrick rid Ireland from snakes as the people were converted from paganism to Christianity during the fifth century. If there never were snakes to be banished in the first place how could the legend be so widespread and enduring. What happened?

The answer lies in a combination of Irish terms used in farming, particularly with an analogy involving the milking of animals and in understanding the greatness of the accomplishment of Patrick in ending the pagan fertility practises associated with sun worship. We should also remember that at a purely human level it would have been exceedingly embarrassing and distressingly uncomfortable for Christian converts to acknowledge that any of their ancestors engaged in pagan debauchery; a euphemism was called for to alleviate explicit mention of something that was humiliating to talk about. The nature of the ceremonies that took place at winter solstice dawn cannot be known; we may only guess. May we imagine that processions took place bringing up candidates to be initiated or victims to be sacrificed. The vigil fires would have been lit on the mountain tops and preparations for feasting attended to. Incantations, prayers and petitions would be offered up, perhaps involving long repetitious and trance inducing chanting, drumming, singing or dancing. The coming of the fertility light of the new sun was probably a signal for complete indulgence in sexual

---

8 Of reptiles and those which are not found in the island: Chapter 23 of *The Historical Works of Giraldus Cambrensis*, edited by Thomas Wright, published by H.G. Bohn, London, 1863.

The Cross on the height of Tievedockaragh marks a Penal Mass site.

licentiousness, the beginning of a sexual orgy. Rather than give graphic details of what went on at these ceremonies redress was had centuries ago to a farming analogy of milking the animals. The operative Irish word that conveyed the import of what went on without spelling out the dissipation was **Sniogaigh**, 'milking the very last drop, milking after the teat-flow ceases, draining completely'. The parallels with unrestrained hedonism that went beyond the ending of semen flow were obvious. It was this utterly dissolute behaviour that St Patrick ended by his preaching. By bringing the message of the gospel, of love, mercy, restraint, purity and no bloodshed, Patrick terminated the pagan fertility rituals. The sexual excesses represented by *Sniogaigh* were banished. 'Snakes' is both a metaphor and an English mnemonic for the Irish *Sniogaigh*. So indeed St Patrick did banish the 'snakes' from Ireland. Patrick ended the wanton sexual practices that had been followed for millennia but while the English speaking world from Giraldus Cambrensis to the present day have heard about the 'snakes', none seem to have known about the deeper meaning of *Sniogaigh*. Perhaps, for all we know, the stream that bears St Patrick's name at the Ballagh, namely Srupatrick, may have been used to baptise converts. Returning again to Patrick's action mentioned above, that St Patrick threw his sandal

It took twelve men fourteen days at the start of 1900 to move this great granite slab from Slievenalargy to the county road to mark St Patrick's grave.

and prophesied no more blood, there may yet possibly be another residual message. There is a closeness of sound between the English 'Patrick threw…' and the Irish *Aithrighe Truagh* but significantly *Aithrighe Truagh* means 'deep repentance'.

The sun worshipping days of Mourne's pagan past have gone so we need not be diffident about claiming the works of the ancients as part of our heritage. As we look on the many works of the ancients throughout Mourne, their achievements stand testimony to the mighty efforts and dignity of man. The more we look on their accomplishments, the more we can remind ourselves of how far we have come and how very fortunate we are for the faith brought to us by St Patrick. To him we leave the last word:

Mar adubhairt Sé féin tré bhéal a fháidhe: Athghoir orm lá do bhuaidheartha, agus bhéarad fuascailt duit, agus déanfair mórughadh orm.

'For he himself said through the prophet, Call upon me in the day of your trouble and I will deliver you, and you will glorify me.'
(St Patrick's Confession; section 5)

APPENDIX

Some American terms of Irish Origin

When the Irish emigrated in their droves to America centuries ago they brought their language with them. Being essentially a pastoral people their use of language could be described as 'earthy'. It was open, robust, direct, and frequently coarse. The language could convey great beauty, yet harking back to a distant pagan past the people could also openly talk about subjects which others preferred to avoid or felt ashamed about. We shouldn't think of the Irish speakers as being crude for the rich Celtic imagination certainly had a wealth of euphemisms that allowed erstwhile indelicate topics to be alluded to with understanding and humour.

The following terms were culled from the works of American authors. These words, while being understood back here in Ireland and the UK, would be looked on as 'Americanisms' and are seldom used this side of the pond. I expect that many readers will be taken aback by the blunt sexual origins of many of the words. The literal meaning may have been concealed over time but it is surprising how the intended sense has often remarkably prevailed.

A few things to note. Many of the words in this appendix begin with the letter [h]. This has helped disguise the Irish roots. For linguistic reasons the letter [h] is often interposed between two vowels as for example, *na h-Éireann,* (Ireland). There are only eighteen letters in the Irish alphabet; it does not contain (j, k, q, v, w, x, y, z), although they can be found in scientific terminology or words of foreign origin. This is something to remember when looking, for instance, at the words 's<u>q</u>uat' or '<u>v</u>armit'. The assimilation of the Irish has been going on since the earliest of times as may be seen from the first entry.

I haven't a <u>bean</u>
I'm destitute. I haven't any money. It harks back to the days of the trappers on the American frontier. It is from the Irish **Bian**, 'a pelt, fur' from the days when pelts such as beaver furs were a substitute for currency and used in barter.

Aw-Shucks
The original gross exaggeration is reduced now to almost the exact opposite; it has become a folksy interjection of self-depreciation as in 'Aw shucks, it was nothing'. From the Irish ***Abha Súgha***, 'a river of semen'.

Abha, 'a river, a stream'
Súgh, (gen. *Súgha*) means 'juice, essence, extract, sap, secretion'. Used here to denote 'semen'.

Aw Nuts
You could say this is a close 'cousin' of the phrase above.
'Aw nuts', was the initial response of Brig. General Anthony McAuliffe, acting commander of 101st Airborne Division, when asked to surrender Bastogne by the Germans during the battle of The Bulge. When McAuliffe consulted with his staff-officers, they liked his first remark and so the answer to the surrender request was the famously concise reply: 'To the German Commander, NUTS! The American Commander'.
It is no surprise that the Germans were mystified. General McAuliffe's Irish name gives the clue to the origin and explanation. 'Nuts!' in this instance has nothing to do with the English meaning of a hard shell enclosing an edible kernel. Rather it is the sound of Irish in an English skin. Mind you, it is a phrase that was long bandied around before it saw print, becoming rather corrupted in the process, but the expression still seems to retain the original coarse sense of derisory contempt and rejection and would probably earlier have seen use as a curse. The Irish behind 'Aw Nuts' is likely to have been, **Abha n'Ótaise (ort),** 'river of a slut (on you)', where the 'river', closely resembling the usage above previous, is understood as a stream of liquid from a woman's vulva.
In Irish the letter [n] is frequently inserted between two vowels. The shorthand version of the Irish, **N'Ótaise,** has thus become the English mnemonic 'Nuts'.
Four days later, on 26th December, 1944, the siege of Bastogne was lifted when Patton's 4th Armoured Division broke through the German lines.
   Abha, 'a river, a stream'
   Ótais, **(gen.)** *Ótaise,* a term of contempt for a woman; means 'a harlot', 'a slut'

Baloney
'Rubbish, nonsense, foolish talk'. The Irish is similar in vein to 'A load of Balls!'
The word comes from two Irish words **Ball Áine,** 'a limb of pleasure', i.e. a penis.
   Ball, (gen: *Baill*) 'a limb, a member'
   Áin, (gen. *Áine*), 'pleasure, desire'.

Bamboozle

To deceive by underhand methods, to dupe, fool or cheat someone, to confuse especially by trickery. Usage and quick pronunciation has seen the spelling of the Irish slightly modified [the double [nn] contracted to [m], and the three Irish words have been telescoped into one but the original sense is remarkably intact. The term derives from the shouts of ecstasy at climax of intercourse and whether such sounds are genuine, or a simulation or pretence to fool someone. Bamboozle is a phonetic rendering of ***Beann Búise Áil,*** 'peak of a shout of pleasure'.

Beann, (gen) *Beinne,* 'a point, a peak, top, a climax'
Búis, (gen.) ***Búise,*** 'a shout, cry, a roaring, a bellow'
Áil, 'pleasure, desire'

Boogie

Dancing enthusiastically and vigorously especially to rock music.

From the Irish ***Bogaigh,*** 'moving, shaking, rocking'. The dancing term 'Boogie Woogie' is from ***Bogaigh Uige,*** where a piece of light fabric was imagined being blown about and twisting vigorously in the wind.

Uige, 'web or tissue, material'; the word also has overtones of style as if the moving was a 'work of art' rather than a lumpy jerking around.

Boondoggle

Extravagantly wasteful and unnecessary.

This comes from three Irish words: ***Buinne Doige Áil,*** 'discharge of a spasm of pleasure', i.e. an ejaculation.

Buinne (gen id.), 'a discharge, a squirting forth; a flood, a wave, a torrent; passion, excitement'.

Doigh, (gen. ***Doighe***), (a word with various meanings) 'a pang, a sting, a spasm'

Áil, 'pleasure, desire'

A Broad

Maybe I've watched too many gangster movies. A rather demeaning, if not contemptible, term for a woman. As one dictionary put it, 'a word for a woman that is less respectable than lady but much more respectable than bitch'. From the Irish ***Bród,*** (gen.) *Bróid,* 'delight, joy'.

Bugaboo

An annoying person, especially one making unwanted sexual advances; an object of fear, anxiety or irritation'. The original Irish behind the term is

Buacaire Buid, 'squirt of a penis'.
   Buacaire, 'a tap, a spout, a squirt'
   Bod, (gen) *Buid,* 'a penis'
Troll: Nowadays the annoying or vexatious person is more likely to be called a 'troll'. This is the internet slang for a person who intentionally tries to instigate conflict, hostility or arguments online. From roots in Scandinavian folklore the idea of a nasty demon was probably brought to Ireland by the Vikings. The wrecking, burning and devastation wrought by the Vikings influenced the word's origins in Irish. Troll is a contraction of the Irish <u>**Trolluighthe**</u>**,** meaning 'I defile, taint, rot, profane, tire'.

Darn Tootin

Sure thing! Absolutely right! An exclamation of agreement.
   The origin lies in the Irish asseveration **Dar an Tuth Áine,** 'By the juice of pleasure'; i.e. swearing by an ejaculation.
   Dar (preposition) 'by', (in asseverations), e.g. *Dar Pádraig,* 'By Patrick!'
   Tuth, (gen.), *Tuithe,* 'juice or essence'; in this case 'semen'.
   Áin, (gen. *Áine*), 'pleasure, desire'
   Likewise, **Rootin-Tootin,** is an alliterated version of **Ruathar Tuithe Áine** 'a rush of the juice of pleasure'.
   Ruathar, 'a rush, charge, the rush of the tide or current'

Doggone It

An exclamation of exasperation, irritation or anger; equivalent to 'Damn it'.
   The original Irish was a curse though not really a vindictively serious one. It was a 'gentle' curse more along the lines of 'may your back itch in an unscratchable position'. From the Irish **Doigh Ionnat!** 'A curse (literally – a pang, stitch, dart of pain) on your bowels'.
   Doigh, (gen. *Doighe*), 'a pang, a stitch, a sting, spasm'
   Ionnat, (from *Ionathar*), 'bowels, entrails, intestines'.

Doozy

Something extraordinary, remarkable, excellent, or one of a kind. 'That's a real doozy.' From the Irish *Dó-Sidhe,* 'a tremendous blast', i.e. a great ejaculation.
   Dó, used as an intensive prefix.
   Sidhe, 'a blast, a rush' [to be distinguished from the Irish *Sídhe* that has an accent on the [i] and which means 'fairy, magic']

Dude
An informal term of address for a man. It no longer seems to have disrespectful or derogatory overtones which is a far cry from its original meaning.
Dúid, 'a cad; a penis'.

Hanky Panky
Usually illicit sexual relations; questionable, devious or underhand activity that would be thought of as improper, suspicious or inappropriate. From the Irish **(na) h-Anga Pianaighe**, 'of a painful insertion', as at intercourse.
Anga, (gen. id.), 'a notch; an insertion'
Pianach, (gen) *pianaighe,* (a.), 'painful, dreadful'

Hinky
Something is not right or is out of place; it is wrong, strange or weird. From the Irish **h-ionghar**, from *ionghar, -air,* meaning 'pus, matter'.

Hoity-Toity
Affecting airs and graces, being pompous and thinking oneself important; people with 'stuck up noses'; nowadays the popular term seems to be 'entitled'. From the Irish (*na*) **h-Oiteog Toite**, 'a puff of smoke'.
Oiteog, 'a puff'
Toit, (gen.) *Toite,* 'smoke, fume, vapour, agitated dust'

Hokey or Hoaky
It is phony, as if a hoax. Something noticeably contrived.
The origin lies with the exaggerated lamenting, weeping, wailing and keening by women at Irish funerals. From the Irish **(na) h-Ocheacha**, 'moans', the root being *Ochaim,* 'I sigh or sob'.

Honky-Tonk
A wild, rowdy and raucous place that sold alcohol to workers. Although now regarded as much loved places of dancing and live entertainment the earlier image was a rather disreputable one associated with drunkenness and prostitution. It was the less than respectable and frequently scandalous aspect of these distractions that gave them the bad reputation as tawdry places of sleaze and notoriety. From the Irish **(Tí na) h-Oingí Tónacála**, '(Place of) slowly shifting 'spouts'; i.e. a place for intercourse.
Oing, (plural) *Oingí,* 'spouts'; (a euphemism for penises)
Tónacáil, (gen.) *Tónacála,* 'moving uneasily while seated, shifting one's position slowly, shunting, sliding on one's back'…

Kibosh
As in, 'Put the Kibosh on Something'. The meaning is to put a stop to something, to frustrate it or bring it to an end. The Irish behind the phrase is **Caibe bós** (an older form of '*Fós*'), meaning 'resting the spade', i.e. stopping work, coming to a stand-still.

   Caibe, meaning 'a spade'

   Bós, an older form of *Fós* meaning 'act of stopping; resting, easement, inertia'

Hollywood (Hollywoodland)
There were certainly plenty of Irish in California in the early days. They did so well at the gold diggings that we still have the rather envious expression, 'The Luck of the Irish'. It seems they also left behind a place-name or two. Many northern Irish place-names were influenced by the elder faith; this put a sexual interpretation on the landscape. For instance, there are twenty-two Ballykeel townlands in the North of Ireland, fourteen of which are in County Down. Ballykeel is from the Irish *Baile Caoile*, 'townland of the loins'. Or again, we have Lecale in St Patrick's country; Lecale is from the Irish *Leath Caoile*, 'district of the loins'.

Whatever about the entry for Hollywood in Wikipedia the determination for the origin of the name can clearly be seen in vintage photographs. The name derives from the phallic profile of the top of the famous hill. Hollywood comes from the Irish (*Tí na*) **h-Olla Buid**, '(Place of the) Great Penis'. The earlier version of the sign was Hollywoodland. The word 'land' removed in 1932 was only a mnemonic of the Irish adjective *lán* meaning 'perfect'. The Irish named it first, the 'Perfect Great Penis'.

   Oll-, (**Olla-**), 'great, huge, chief, monstrous'

   Bod, (gen.) **Buid**, 'penis'.

   Lán, 'full, complete, satisfied, perfect'.

Rookie
This term is believed to have emerged during the American Civil War. It was applied to new recruits in a rather disparaging way because their inexperience and unreliable discipline made them a liability both to themselves and to the veterans. The term is now used of newcomers, apprentices, beginners, novices, trainees or learners in a trade, or organisation. On account of its source of origin it is no surprise that the term 'rookie' is still frequently used in the American army and police. The term 'Greenhorn' is likewise often used for a trainee at boot camp though it would probably be deemed more offensive and may have originated with the Irish (*Éirghe*) **Gréine h-Orainn**. This originally was literally a blessing

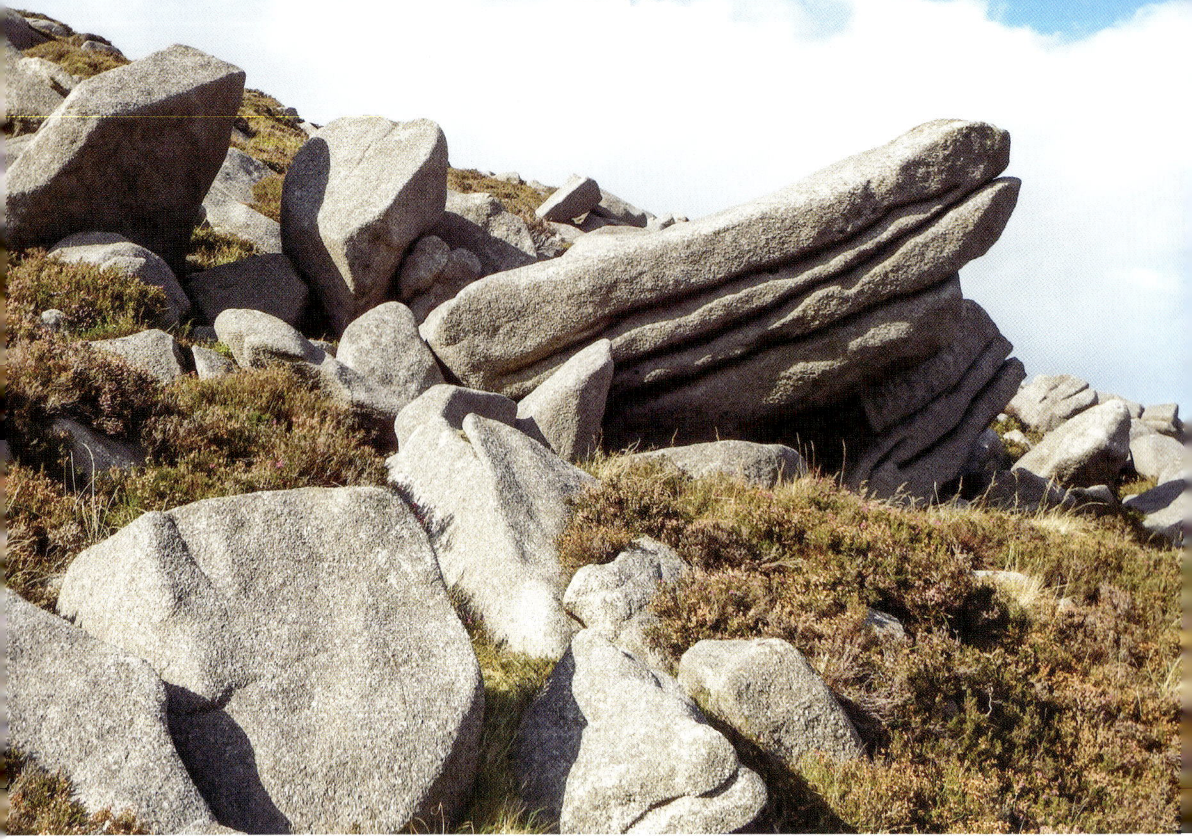

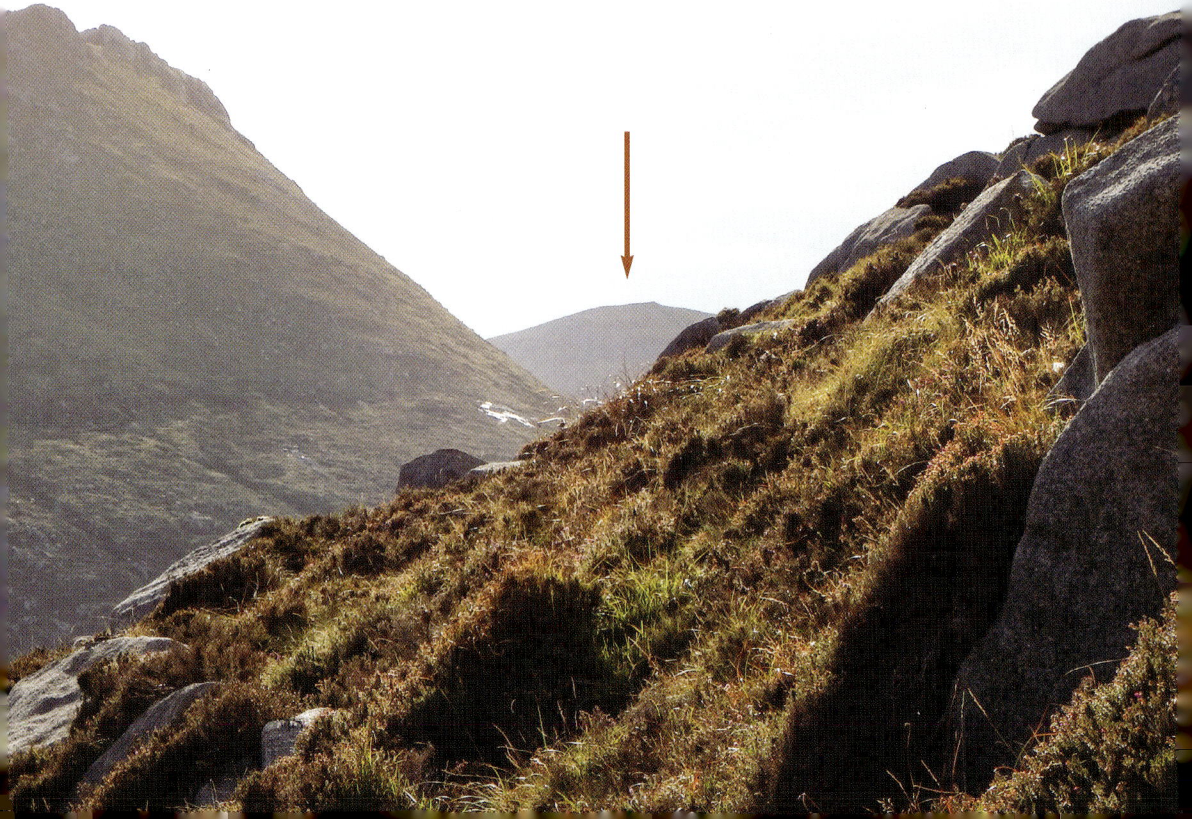

and meant '(Rise of the) Sun upon us', where the first light of the sun was regarded as something precious, but the term seems to have been used more ironically in the sense of 'God help us'. Apparently there wasn't much sympathy for new recruits.

The word Rookie is from the Irish **Rúcaigh**, 'a new arrival, blow-in, a summer visitor who doesn't know his way around'.

Diddly Squat
Something of little or no value. It is something that is a poor substitute for the real thing; something useless or virtually worthless. From the Irish ***Dúid lia Scáth***, 'Fertility stone shadow'. The fertility stone, invariably phallic, casts its solstice shadow into a hole, cavity or fissure that is representative of the female genital opening. We might regard the phallic shadow as symbolic and not accomplishing anything but I rather think that the ancient ones may have had other ideas and fully believed in the shadow's efficacy.

Dúid, 'a cad; a penis'

Lia, 'a great stone, especially a standing stone or megalithic stone'

Scáth, 'A shadow, shade'. Remember there is no letter Q in Irish.

Opposite we have a megalith on the south east slope of Slieve Corragh. The GPS location is:

N. 54° 11. 565'
W. 005° 57. 935'   Elevation 548m.

This mighty phallic monument has been named **Baraoid Mór,** 'Great Desire'. It is a very substantial megalith being just over three metres in length along the top surface and two metres across. The stone is approximately 1.4 metres thick making it a fertility monument of considerable size and importance. It is also a good example of *Dúid lia Scáth*.

The front tip of the stone points to where winter solstice sun rises over at Chimney Rock mountain. As the solstice sun appears the shadow of the phallic point will be cast backwards to enter the gap between the two stones behind it on the left, representative of the labial sides of a female opening and thus bestow fertility.

A further reason for the great exertions here is the fact that the location marks the fertility motif of 'the penis in the vagina'. The tip of Meelbeg mountain (arrowed) appears as the 'phallus' in the erstwhile 'vagina notch' formed between Slieve Bearnagh and the descending slope of Slieve Corragh. The steepness of the slope would have made the positioning of the stones one of great difficulty, a fact that only adds to the importance of the stones and significance given to such vistas by the ancients.

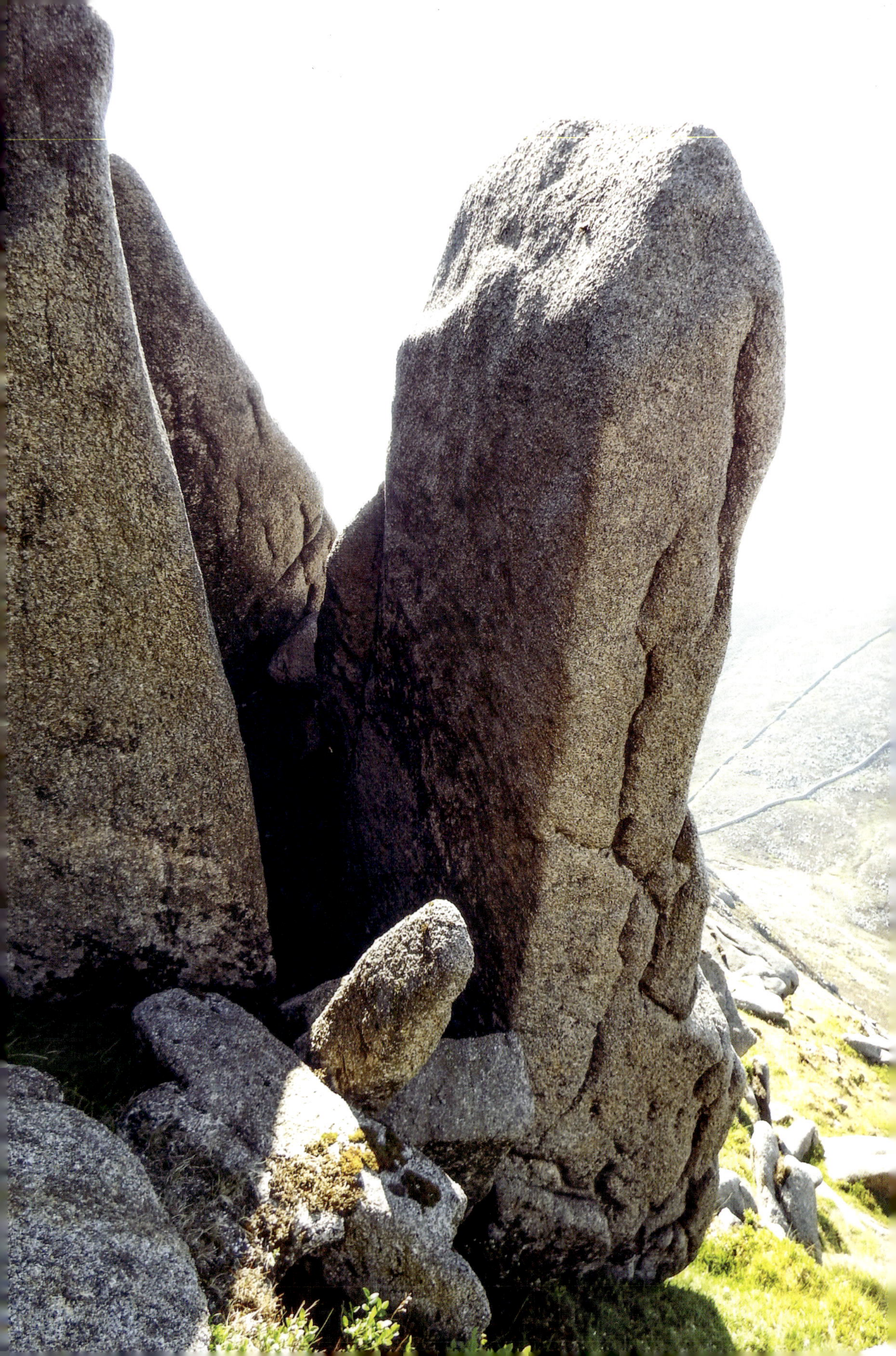

Opposite: Another instance of *Dúid lia Scáth*. This is **Grianán Doimhin** (A Deep Sunny Chamber). It is to be found on the top of the north tor of Slieve Bearnagh at GPS:

                    N.   54º 11. 203'
                    W. 005º 59. 212'   Elevation 682m.

The photo was taken around 4.30pm on a July afternoon so the large vaginal opening does not look particularly sunny. It is at summer solstice dawn that this great 'female cavity' is flooded with light and comes into its glory. It is then that the slim phallic stone, jammed at the front, casts its shadow into the back of the recess with fertility intent.

The left hand side of the opening is bedrock but the right hand labial side is a monumental block close to five metres in length. Trying to manipulate this monstrous stone on the exceedingly steep slope at the top of Bearnagh testifies to the seriousness of the fertility beliefs of the ancient ones. There are other large fertility constructions in this locality but such are the dangers of the steep slope it is certainly not a place to go lightly traipsing around.

Top of this page: Above the buttresses of Lower Cove this granite finger, or erstwhile phallus, projects out over the edge so as to cast its 'diddly squat' fertilising shadow into the 'vaginal' fissure. The GPS is:

                    N.   54° 09. 977'
                    W. 005° 57. 343'   Elevation 452m.

Hooker
A street walker, courtesan, a call girl or prostitute.
   From the Irish **h-Uachais,** 'an excavation, a fissure', i.e. a woman's vagina.

Hootchie Coochie
A sexually promiscuous woman. The term is associated with provocative belly dances of the mid to late 1800's, where enticing and seductive movement emphasised the vagina. From the Irish **h-Úthach Cuithe,** 'a great desire for a (female) 'pit'.
   Úthach, (gen.) **Úthaigh,** 'a devouring or overwhelming desire for drink or sex, a great thirst.
   Cuithe, 'A pit', (otherwise a euphemism for a vagina)

Humdinger
Something remarkable, extraordinary or outstanding; something impressive, exciting or enjoyable. From the Irish **(na) h-Uaim Dingeadh,** 'the joining of thrusting'.
   Uaim, (gen.) **Uama,** 'act of joining, sewing or riveting together; welding'
   Dingeadh, 'the act of thrusting, pushing'

Hunky-Dory
'All is well or satisfactory'. The Irish emigrants brought with them the farmer's relief and happiness at the spring sun and returning heat making the grass grow again to provide much needed grazing for cattle after the dreary days of winter. The saying Hunky Dory is a phonetic remnant of the Irish **(na) h-Uaineacht deoradh,** '(the) greenness of the wanderer'. The 'wanderer' was, of course, the sun and now that the days were lengthening the grass would grow, the milk would flow and all would be well again.
   Uaineacht, 'greenness, verdure'
   Deora (gen. **Deoradh**), 'a wanderer'

Hurly-Burly
'Disorder and confusion; turmoil, disarray, mess, muddle and bedlam'. The mnemonic term is found in Shakespeare and the term is common to the UK and America. It derives from the Irish description of long hair being blown across the face. Strands of hair blowing around, bundling up, tangling and plastering across the face and probably blinding the eyes in the process, was certainly a recipe for confusion. It is a contracted version of the Irish **(na) h-Urlaí Búrlála,** '(the) smothering tresses'.

Urla, lock of hair, any long hair, ***Urlaí, (pl.)*** tresses
Búrlála, the act of bundling up, muffling

Kook
This term now has the sense of 'an empty head, a spacer'. The urban dictionary gives meanings such as 'crackpot, crank, eccentric, fruitcake, head-case, nut, oddball, oddity'. Remember, there is no letter [K] in Irish. From the Irish ***Cuach,*** (gen.), ***Cuaich,*** 'a bowl, a basin; **a void or cavity**'.

Malarkey
This is a word enjoying a renaissance since being widely used in American politics. It has the meaning of 'nonsense, rubbish, absurdity, gibberish, drivel, hot air, bunk' and as such is still in accord with its withering sarcastic original meaning in Irish although not just as blunt or reproachful. Malarkey is derived from three Irish words, ***Mol Ára caibe*** meaning 'Your penis is sticking out!', literally 'sticking out of a loin spade'.

Mol, 'extremity or protuberant part of anything'.

Ára, 'the loin, kidney'

Caibe, 'a spade, the iron part of any delving instrument (and as such it was a frequent euphemism for a penis).

In the Mournes one of the old names for Slieve Commedagh was Kiviter. While it is a long time since I heard anyone using the name of Kiviter to refer to Commedagh, you could still find that name used in the 1959 guide to Tollymore Forest Park and professor E. Estyn Evans, in his 1950 work, *Mourne Country,* tells us on page 15 that Commedagh was 'known throughout Mourne as Kiviter'. The name originates from the great summer solstice shadow cast onto the side of Slieve Donard at sunset. The shadow was regarded as phallic. The Irish is ***Caibe eitire,*** 'spike or probe of vigour'. As mentioned, *Caibe* in Irish normally means 'spade' but here is enjoys its other meaning of 'the iron part of any delving instrument', a metaphor for an erect phallus. To this is added *eitir,* (gen.), *eitire,* vigour, strength'.

Slieve Commedagh, formerly Kiviter, as seen on the right, casts its phallic shadow (arrowed) onto the flank of Slieve Donard at summer solstice sunset.

Mickey Finn

This is a phrase that ostensibly originated in Chicago about the 1890's. It is associated with a bartender who slipped drugs into drinks prior to robbing or assaulting customers. The original Irish however, had sexual overtones. 'Mickey Finn' is from the Irish **Mí-Caibe Fionn,** (literally), 'wicked white spade', i.e. an erect phallus. However, the strong link with a spiked drink probably means the adjective 'white' had less to do with pale skin and more to do with semen and a penis come to climax through fellatio. This connection with fellatio is more obvious in the phrase 'slipping a mickey' for the original 'slipping' did not derive from the English sense of 'sliding' or 'falling' but rather from the Irish **Sliop Áin,** meaning 'a mouth of pleasure'.

Mí-, a negative prefix with the meaning of 'bad, wicked, evil'.

Caibe, (as mentioned before) 'a spade, the iron part of any delving instrument (and as such it was a frequent euphemism for an erect penis).

Fionn, 'white, pale, fair'; it also has a meaning of 'beautiful', and 'famous'.

Sliop, 'a lip, mouth' (in a vulgar sense)

Áin, 'pleasure, desire'

Mug Shot

This is an image or picture of a person's head, particularly a police photograph of a suspect's face or profile intended for identification purposes. The term was very much in the news last year when a mug shot of Donald Trump was taken at the Fulton County Jail in Atlanta, Georgia on 24th August 2023. The term is from the sound of the Irish **Múig Soith,** 'a wicked surly countenance'. The letter [S] in Irish often has the sound of 'sh', as in 'ship, shelter, shirt'. Although the local usage is now discontinued, Slievemoughanmore in the Mournes was formerly known as **Múig** because the cliff-face beside the Windy Gap trail had the look of an unfriendly, disagreeable face. The name featured as 'Mogh' in Mercator's map of Ulster 1595.

Múig, 'a surly countenance'

Soith, (for which see *Saith*), (adj.), 'bad, evil, vile, despicable'

Scam

An all too present danger on-line or in messages to phones. The present meaning is 'to trick, swindle, deceive or perpetrate a fraud.' Fraud is understood as a false representation of a matter of fact by making untrue or misleading allegations, or by concealing what should have been

Former Múig mountain, at the head of Windy Gap valley in the Mournes, earned its name from the cliff profile of a rather grim, nasty and inimical face.

disclosed. The word 'Scam' is directly from the Irish and its original meaning is close to the idea of 'concealing' but through detachment by a drape, curtain, or partition. Initially the meaning was more benign, as in <u>Scamh</u> na fuinneoige, 'a window screen'. The present 'screen' is duplicity, lies and deceit and many unprintable Irish curses could be found for such perpetrators.
    Scamh: 'a screen, a shield for the eye'.

Shindig
Understood as a rather boisterous and lively party'; a social gathering with dancing. The term is from the Irish **Sine Dóigh,** 'a promising nipple'.
    Sine, (gen. id.), 'a nipple, teat',
    Dóigh, -e, 'a likelihood, a promising place, person or thing'

All Correct (OK)
Mentioned here with a measure of trepidation. The abbreviation OK is now understood as 'all correct'. The term is believed to have come from among the Boston Irish in the 1830's but Irish origins have seemingly not been considered for its derivation. Present understanding of 'all being in order'

is determined by the mnemonic 'all correct' but the meaning of the original Irish was utterly and totally contrary to the English. This is one serious antonym. 'All Correct' is the mnemonic sound of **Óil Corbaighe,** 'of wicked drinking'. The Irish is: *Ól,* (gen.) *Óil,* 'act of drinking, absorbing'; and *Corbach,* (gen.) ***Corbaighe,*** 'wicked, lewd'. Because of the lecherous overtones of ***Corbaighe*** this adjective is not a reference to over indulgence in alcohol but to the act of fellatio.

Shee-Bang

Pure Irish in all but spelling. The original is **Sídhe Bang,** 'a fairy spell'. A few centuries back, in superstitious times, a fairy spell was considered a very serious matter. People believed in fairies, the little people, and the evil that could come from crossing them. They were referred to as **na daoine maithe,** 'the good people', for to call them otherwise was to court trouble. Ill health or sickness in livestock was often laid at their door. A spell was something critical, consequential and which could be fraught with danger. It was no laughing matter. The term is now often expressed as 'the whole Shee-bang' and in this sense is very similar to 'the whole nine yards'. It carries with it a sense of complete commitment as in 'the whole shooting match'. The 'nine yards' derives from the Second World War when machine gunners were armed with an ammunition belt which was twenty-seven feet long. To use the whole belt on the enemy was to go the whole nine yards. Now-a-days Americans might be more inclined to use an expression like 'the whole deal'.

Sídhe, 'fairies, the shee'

Bang, 'a spell, taboo

Spoof

This term has taken on a whole new lease of life in the computer age. It is usually understood as trying to trick or deceive, to hoax, bluff, or generally cheat, mislead or defraud someone. The original sense in Irish may have been closer to a sarcastic, derisive retort such as, 'Sure thing!', 'Nonsense', when confronted with a suave spiel of lies; the original Irish however was much blunter. Its sense and usage was probably closer to other terms from Irish such as 'Malarkey' or 'Baloney'.

Spoof is a contraction of two Irish words that has seen the elision of the [T] at the end of **Spút**. The Irish behind 'spoof' is **Spút Ibhe,** 'a spout of soaking', namely an ejaculating penis.

Spút, (gen.), *Spúit,* 'a spout' (a euphemism for a penis)

Ibhe, 'act of soaking, drinking'

Topsy Turvy

The sense now-a-days is one of 'confusion, things being upside down from what was expected, muddle and disorder'. This is still close to its origin in Irish where it was a reference to an ejaculation meeting the vagaries of a woman's menstrual cycle. The term comes directly from the sound of the four Irish words, *Tiop sidhe, tur bé*, meaning 'a gushing blast, a dry woman'.

Tiop, 'a tap, a gush'
Sidhe, 'a blast, a puff, a rush'
Tur, 'dry, sapless, plain'
Bé, 'a maid, a woman'

Varmit

An American colloquial term for a predatory wild animal that is considered a pest, undesirable and good for nothing. It is usually a predator that can kill domestic animals and includes hunters such as coyote, foxes, mink, snakes, raccoons, weasels, badgers, bobcats, or wolverines. From the Irish *Bárr Meath,* 'flaccid penis', that is 'useless and good for nothing'.

Bárr, 'top, tip; **a branch**' (a euphemism for a penis)
Meath, 'weak, pliable, slight, flaccid'

Yankee

This is a term that saw its origins in the American Revolutionary War of 1775-1783 otherwise known as the War of Independence. The name began as a term of contempt for the New English settlers coming from Irish soldiers in the British ranks (of which there were many). Essentially the settlers were being crudely dismissed as 'women'; they were looked on as weak and inferior. Chauvinism was certainly alive and well in those days.

In the American civil war the name 'Yankee' was applied derisively by Confederate soldiers to refer to all Northerners. In the Second World War, however, the derogatory meaning was lost, 'Yankee' was abbreviated to 'Yank' and it was now simply used for all Americans.

The original word 'Yankee' crudely referred to the New English settlers in terms of female genitalia. The word comes from the Irish *Eangaí,* 'slits or notches'; nowadays the equivalent contemptuous word would be c**ts.

The revolutionary settlers took the name as a badge of honour and in the end George Washington defeated the British and secured the independence of the United States.

May the road rise up to meet you.
May the wind be always at your back.
May the sun shine warm upon your face;
the rains fall soft upon your fields
and until we meet again,
may God hold you in the palm of His hand.

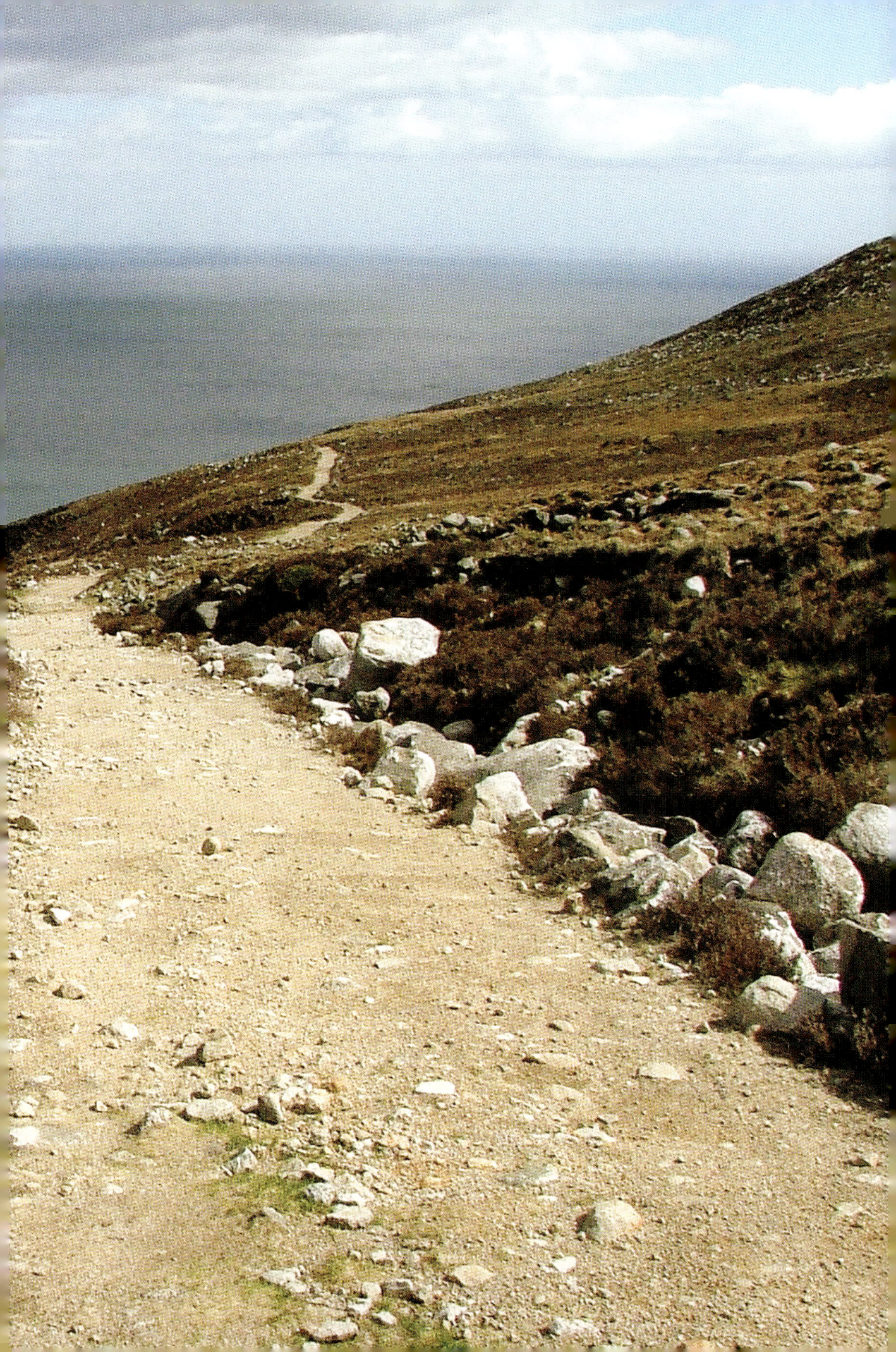

Also by the same author

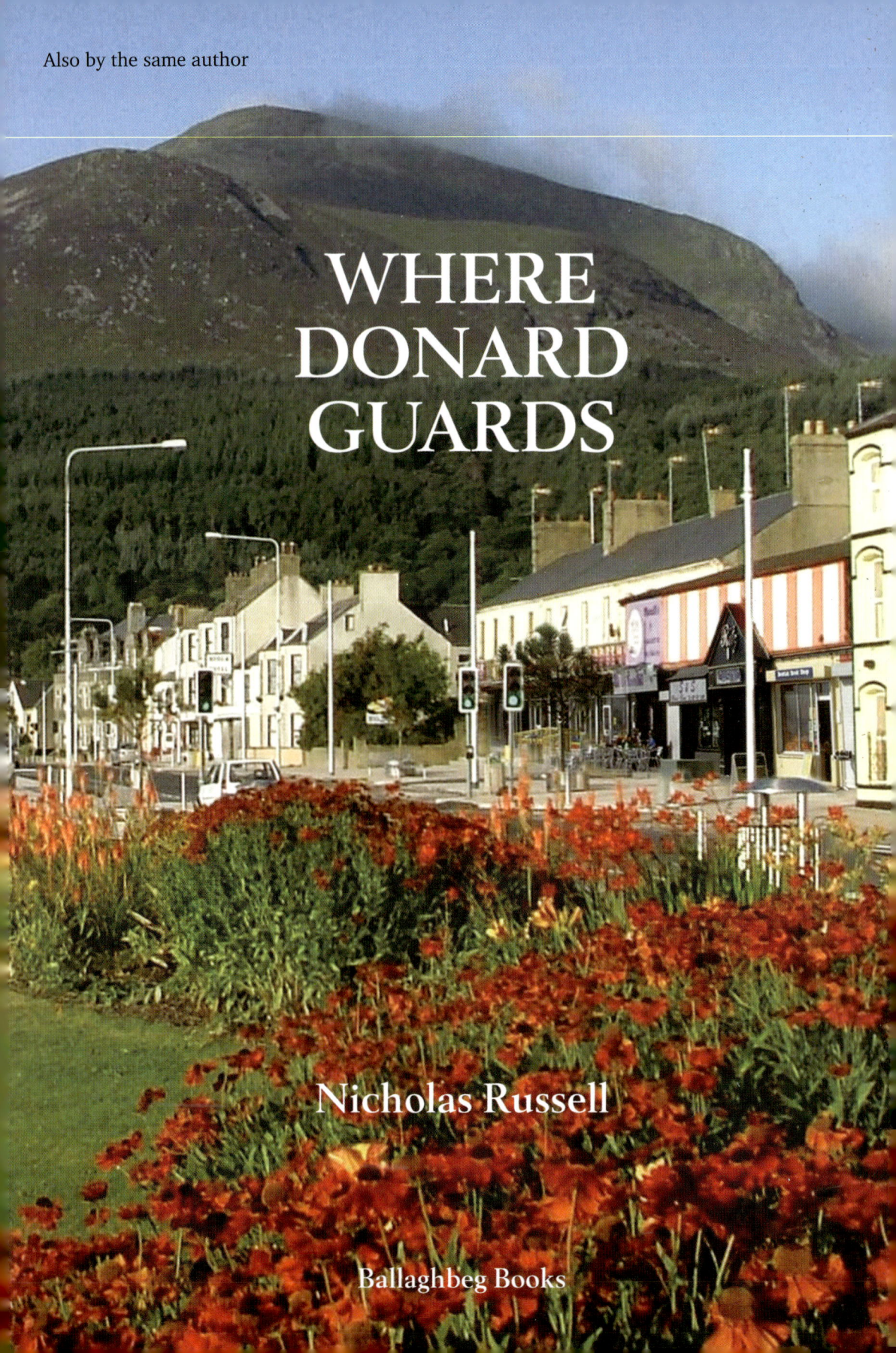

WHERE DONARD GUARDS

Nicholas Russell

Ballaghbeg Books

SLIEVE DONARD'S DOMAIN

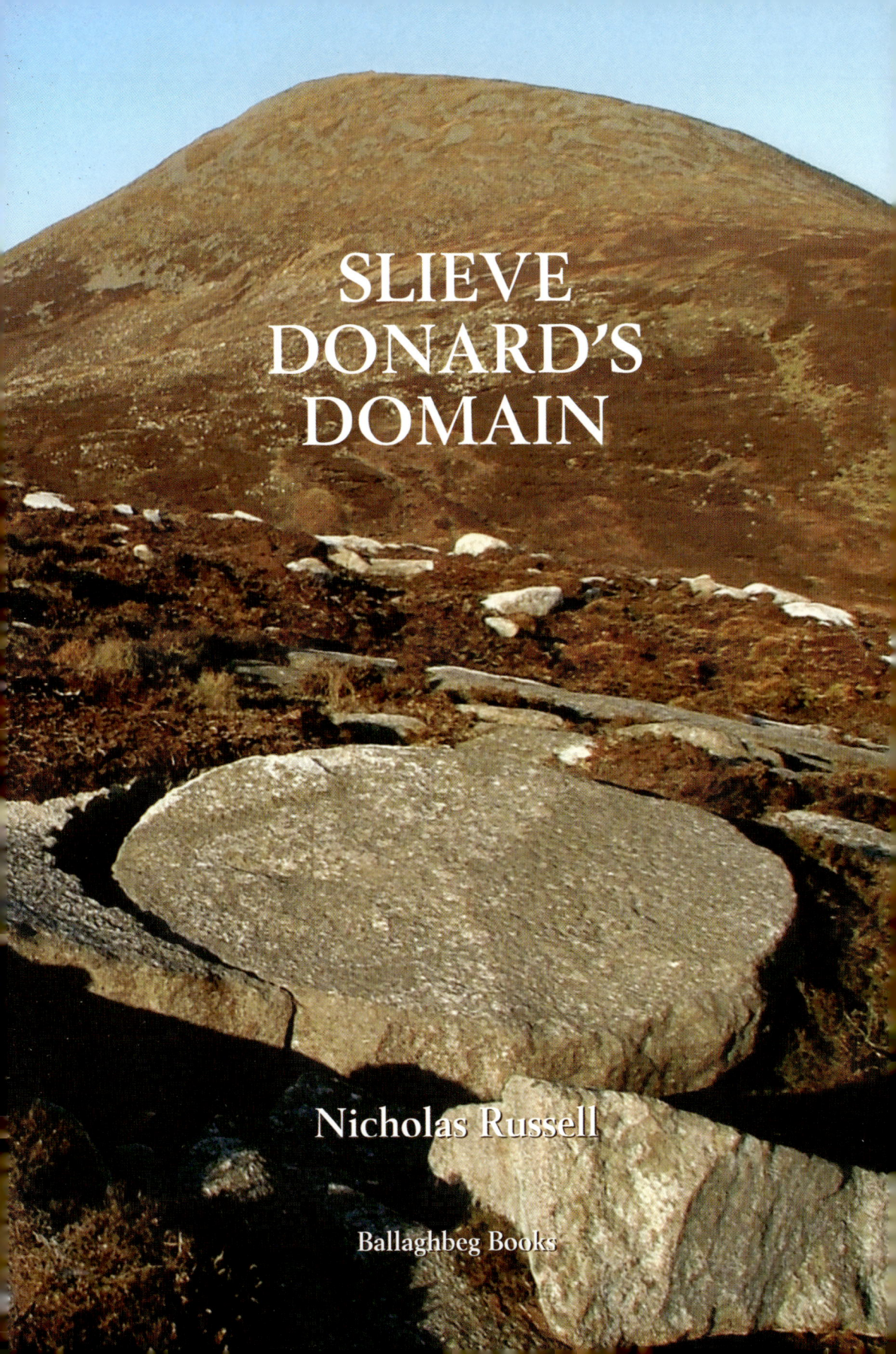

Nicholas Russell

Ballaghbeg Books

PREHISTORIC MOURNE

Inspiration for Newgrange

Nicholas Russell

Ballaghbeg Books

PLACE-NAMES OF BEANNA BOIRRCHE

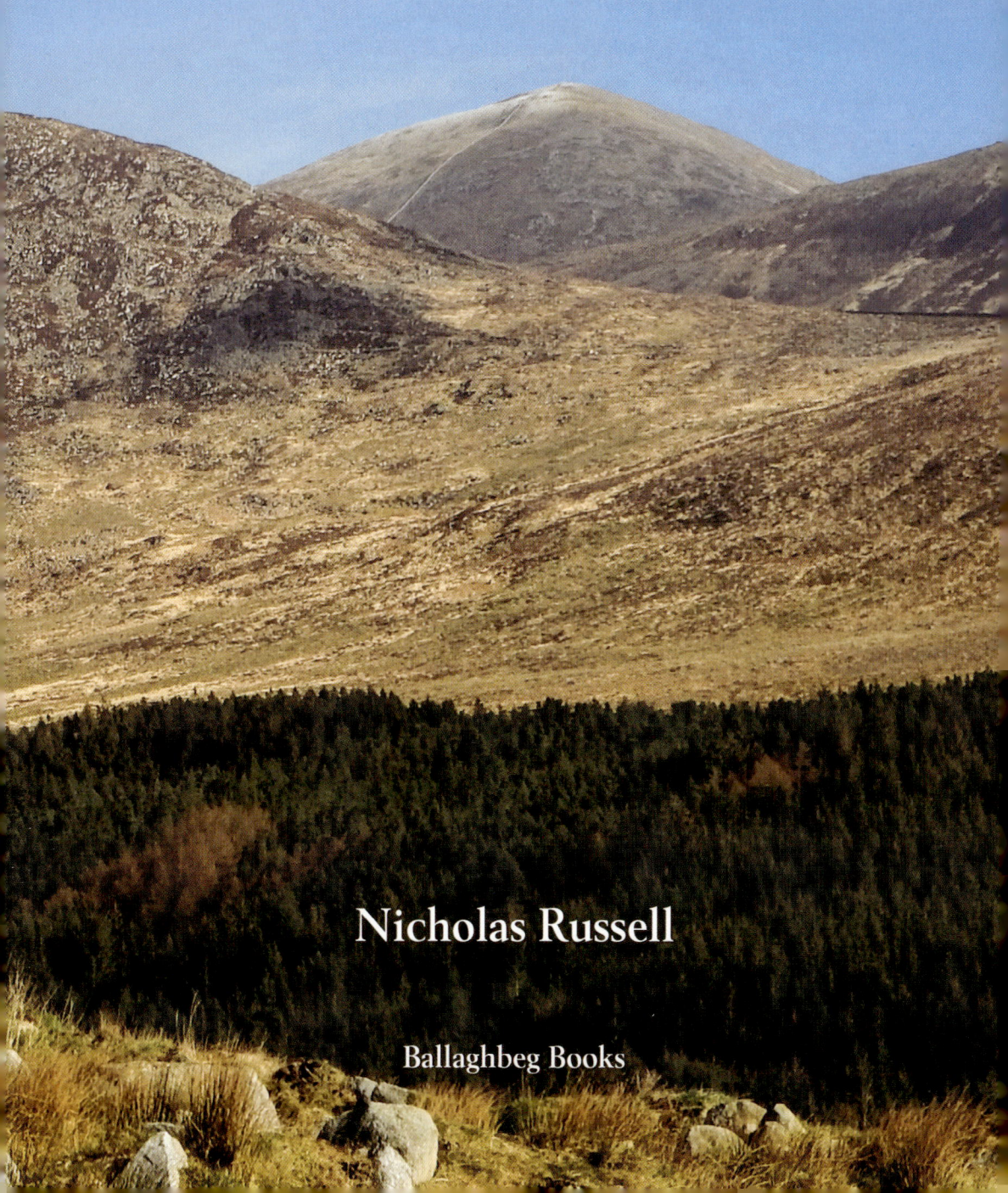

Nicholas Russell

Ballaghbeg Books

A Dhé Dhil, an Peacach scaoil it dhún